Miracle and Machine

John D. Caputo, *series editor*

PERSPECTIVES IN
CONTINENTAL
PHILOSOPHY

MICHAEL NAAS

Miracle and Machine

Jacques Derrida and the Two Sources of Religion, Science, and the Media

FORDHAM UNIVERSITY PRESS
New York ■ 2012

Library of Congress Cataloging-in-Publication Data

Naas, Michael.
    Miracle and machine : Jacques Derrida and the two sources of religion, science, and the media / Michael Naas. — First edition.
        pages cm.— (Perspectives in Continental philosophy)
    Includes bibliographical references and index.
    ISBN 978-0-8232-3997-9 (cloth : alk. paper)
    ISBN 978-0-8232-3998-6 (pbk. : alk. paper)
    1. Derrida, Jacques—Religion.   2. Derrida, Jacques. Foi et savoir.   3. Philosophy and religion.   I. Title.
B2430.D484N325   2012
194—dc23

                                                                2011046658

Printed in the United States of America
14 13 12   5 4 3 2 1
First edition

Contents

Acknowledgments

This work grew out a series of three lectures delivered at the Collegium Phaenomenologicum in Città di Castello, Italy, during the summer of 2008. Invited by my friend and former colleague at DePaul University Paul Davies, now at the University of Sussex, to speak on the subject "Belief after Reason," I could think of no better way to approach the topic than through a reading of Jacques Derrida's 1994–95 essay "Faith and Knowledge: The Two Sources of 'Religion' at the Limits of Reason Alone." What thus began as an attempt to provide an exegesis of this crucial but difficult text in three ninety-minute sessions quickly developed into something much longer and, as the reader will see, quite a bit different. A graduate seminar at DePaul University devoted to the same topic in the fall of 2008 allowed me to continue these reflections and expand them in other directions. I would like to express my heartfelt thanks, first, to Paul Davies, for his generous invitation, and then to the students and faculty at the Collegium Phaenomenologicum, and particularly Robert Bernasconi, for their many helpful comments and suggestions.

An earlier version of part of this work was presented at the Chicago Theological Seminary in December 2008, thanks to an invitation from Ted Jennings and Kunitoshi (Kuni) Sato. I am grateful to them and their colleagues at CTS for their warm hospitality and insightful questions. An early version of Chapter 5 was presented at Missouri State University, at the invitation of Ralph Shain and Andrew Baird, and then again at Columbia College in Chicago, at the invitation of Ann Gunkel. A skeletal version of three chapters was presented at the University of Alberta in Edmonton, thanks to a very generous invitation from Michael O'Driscoll. I am indebted to all these friends and their colleagues for the many helpful remarks that went to improving this work. An early version of Chapter 4 was published under the title "Miracle and Machine: The Two Sources of Religion and Science in Derrida's 'Faith and Knowledge'" in *Research in Phenomenology* 39 (2009) 184–203. I would like to thank the journal's editor, John Sallis, for allowing me to publish a revised version of that chapter here.

Once again I wish to thank my students and colleagues at DePaul University for their friendship and for the many hours of conversation that helped refine this work. My thanks in particular to Peg Birmingham, Avery Goldman, Sean Kirkland, David Krell, Rick Lee, Bill Martin, Will McNeill, Mollie Painter-Morland, David Pellauer, Elizabeth Rottenberg, H. Peter Steeves, and Kevin Thompson, as well as to Eileen Daily at Loyola University, Rodolphe Gasché and Henry Sussman at SUNY Buffalo, Martin Hägglund at Harvard University, Elissa Marder at Emory University, Ginette Michaud at the University of Montreal, Jeffrey Nealon at Pennsylvania State University, Nicholas Royle at Sussex University, and Alan Schrift at Grinnell College. All of them will be able to discern here the traces of their comments, questions, and suggestions. This work has also benefited from conversations with fellow members of the "Derrida Seminar Translation Project," Geoffrey Bennington, Peggy Kamuf, David Wills, Elizabeth Rottenberg, and, once again and first and foremost, Pascale-Anne Brault. I would also like to thank the University Research Council at DePaul University for its generous support of this work, as well as DePaul's College of Liberal Arts and Social Sciences, and especially Dean Chuck Suchar, for a 2009 Summer Research Grant that helped me bring this project to completion.

Abbreviations of Works by Jacques Derrida

The abbreviation *U* will be used for Don DeLillo, *Underworld* (New York: Simon & Schuster, Inc., 1997). All other abbreviations refer to works by Jacques Derrida and appear below.

AA   *Au-delà des apparences.* An interview with Antoine Spire. Latresne: Éditions le bord de l'eau, 2002.

"AANJ"   "Above All, No Journalists!" Trans. Samuel Weber. In *Religion and Media*, ed. Hent de Vries and Samuel Weber, 56–93. Stanford, Calif.: Stanford University Press, 2001. (In *Cahier de l'Herne: Derrida*, ed. Marie-Louise Mallet and Ginette Michaud, 35–49. Paris: Éditions de l'Herne, 2004; rpt. as *Surtout pas de journalistes!* Paris: Éditions de L'Herne, 2005.)

AD   *Arguing with Derrida.* Ed. S. Glendinning. Oxford: Blackwell, 2001.

AEL   *Adieu to Emmanuel Levinas.* Trans. Pascale-Anne Brault and Michael Naas. Stanford, Calif.: Stanford University Press, 1999. (*Adieu à Emmanuel Lévinas.* Paris: Éditions Galilée, 1997.)

AF   *Archive Fever.* Trans. Eric Prenowitz. Chicago: University of Chicago Press, 1996. (*Mal d'archive.* Paris: Éditions Galilée, 1995.)

"AI"   "Autoimmunity: Real and Symbolic Suicides—a Conversation with Jacques Derrida." Trans. Pascale-Anne Brault and

Michael Naas. In *Philosophy in a Time of Terror*, ed. Giovanna Borradori, 85–136. Chicago: University of Chicago Press, 2003. ("Auto-immunités, suicides réels et symboliques," in *Le "concept" du 11 septembre*, 133–96. Paris: Éditions Galilée, 2003.)

"AID" "As *If* I Were Dead: An Interview with Jacques Derrida." In *Applying: To Derrida*, ed. John Brannigan, Ruth Robbins, and Julian Wolfreys, 212–26. New York: St Martin's Press, 1996.

AM *Artaud le Moma: Interjections d'appel.* Paris: Éditions Galilée, 2002.

"AO" "Abraham, the Other." Trans. Gil Anidjar. In *Judeities: Questions for Jacques Derrida*, ed. Bettina Bergo, Joseph Cohen, and Raphael Zagury-Orly, 1–35. New York: Fordham University Press, 2007. ("Abraham, l'autre," in *Judéités: Questions pour Jacques Derrida*. Ed. Joseph Cohen and Raphael Zagury-Orly, 13–42. Paris: Éditions Galilée, 2003.)

AP *Aporias.* Trans. Thomas Dutoit. Stanford, Calif.: Stanford University Press, 1993. (*Apories.* Paris: Éditions Galilée, 1996.)

AR *Acts of Religion.* Ed. and introd. Gil Anidjar. New York: Routledge, 2002.

"AR" "Artaud, oui . . . Entretien avec Évelyne Grossman." *Europe*, "Antonin Artaud," no. 873–74 (January-February 2002): 23–38.

ASR *Athens, Still Remains.* Trans. Pascale-Anne Brault and Michael Naas. New York: Fordham University Press, 2010. (*Demeure, Athènes: Photographies de Jean-François Bonhomme.* Paris: Galilée, 2009.)

ATT *The Animal That Therefore I Am.* Trans. David Wills. New York: Fordham University Press, 2008. (*L'animal que donc je suis.* Ed. Marie Louise Mallet. Paris: Éditions Galilée, 2006.)

"AV" "Avances." Preface to *Le tombeau du dieu artisan*, by Serge Margel. Paris: Éditions de Minuit, 1995, 7–43.

BS 1 *The Beast and the Sovereign.* Vol. 1, *Seminar of 2001–2002.* Trans. Geoffrey Bennington. Chicago: University of Chicago Press, 2009. (*La bête et le souverain.* Vol. 1, *2001–2002.* Ed. Michel Lisse, Marie-Louise Mallet, and Ginette Michaud. Paris: Éditions Galilée, 2008.)

BS 2 *The Beast and the Sovereign.* Vol. 2, *Seminar of 2002–2003.* Trans. Geoffrey Bennington. Chicago: University of Chicago Press, 2010. (*La bête et le souverain.* Vol. 2, *2002–2003.* Ed.

Michel Lisse, Marie-Louise Mallet, and Ginette Michaud. Paris: Éditions Galilée, 2009.)

"C" "Circumfession." In *JD*, 3–315. ("Circonfession." In *JD*, 5–291.)

CAS *Copy, Archive, Signature: A Conversation on Photography*. Interview with Hubertus von Amelunxen and Michael Wetzel. Ed. and introd. Gerhard Richter. Trans. Jeff Fort. Stanford, Calif.: Stanford University Press, 2010.

"CF" "Le cinéma et ses fantômes." Interview with Antoine de Baecque and Thierry Jousse. In *Les cahiers du cinéma*, no. 556 (April 2001): 74–85.

CFU *Chaque fois unique, la fin du monde*. Ed. Pascale-Anne Brault and Michael Naas. Paris: Éditions Galilée, 2003. See *WM*.

"CIA" "Comme il avait raison! Mon cicérone Hans-George Gadamer." Trans. G. Leroux, C. Lévesque, and G. Michaud. In *"Il y aura ce jour . . ." À la mémoire de Jacques Derrida*, 53–56. Montréal: À l'impossible, 2005. (*Frankfurter Allgemeine Zeitung*, 23 March 2002.)

CP *Counterpath: Traveling with Jacques Derrida*. With Catherine Malabou. Trans. David Wills. Stanford, Calif.: Stanford University Press, 2004. (*La contre-allée*. Paris: Quinzaine Littéraire-Louis Vuitton, 1999.)

"CS" "Countersignature." Trans. Mairéad Hanrahan. In *Paragraph*, Special Issue Genet, vol. 27, no. 2 (2004): 7–42. ("Contresignature." In *Poétiques de Jean Genet: La traversée des genres*. Actes du Colloque Cérisy-la-Salle 2000. Ed. Albert Dichy et Patrick Bougon. Paris: IMEC, 2004.)

"D" "Différance." In *MP*, 1–27. ("La différance." In *Marges*, 1–29.)

"*D*" "*Demeure*: Fiction and Testimony," in *The Instant of My Death / Demeure: Fiction and Testimony*, Maurice Blanchot / Jacques Derrida, trans. Elizabeth Rottenberg, 15–103. Stanford, Calif.: Stanford University Press, 2000. (*Demeure: Maurice Blanchot*. Paris: Éditions Galilée, 1998.)

"DA" "Deconstruction in America: An Interview with Jacques Derrida." With James Creech, Peggy Kamuf, and Jane Todd. *Critical Exchange* no. 17 (Winter 1985): 1–33.

DIS *Dissemination*. Trans. and introd. Barbara Johnson. Chicago: University of Chicago Press, 1981. (*La dissémination*. Paris: Éditions du Seuil, 1972.)

"DMR"   " 'Dead Man Running': Salut, Salut: Notes for a Letter to 'Les Temps Modernes.' " Trans. Elizabeth Rottenberg. In *N*, 257–92. ("Il courait mort: Salut, salut." *Notes pour un courrier aux Temps Modernes*," in *PM*, 167–213.)

DN   *Deconstruction in a Nutshell: A Conversation with Jacques Derrida*. John D. Caputo and Jacques Derrida. Ed. and with a Commentary by John D. Caputo. New York: Fordham University Press, 1997.

"DOI"   "Declarations of Independence." Trans. Tom Keenan and Tom Pepper. In *N*, 46–54. ("Déclarations d'Indépendance," in *Otobiographies: L'enseignement de Nietzsche et la politique du nom propre*, 13–32. Paris: Galilée, 1984.)

DP   *Déplier Ponge: Entretien avec Gérard Farasse*. Villeneuve d'Ascq: Presses Universitaires du Septentrion, 2005.

"EF"   "Epochē and Faith: An Interview with Jacques Derrida." An interview with John D. Caputo, Kevin Hart, and Yvonne Sherwood. In *Derrida and Religion: Other Testaments*, ed. Yvonne Sherwood and Kevin Hart, 27–50. New York: Routledge, 2005.

EIRP   *Ethics, Institutions, and the Right to Philosophy*. Trans. Peter Pericles Trifonas. Lanham, Md.: Rowman & Littlefield Publishers, 2002.

"EL"   "The Eyes of Language: The Abyss and the Volcano." Trans. Gil Anidjar. In *AR*, 189–227. (*Les yeux de la langue*. Paris: Éditions de L'Herne, 2005.)

ET   *Echographies of Television*. With Bernard Stiegler. Trans. Jennifer Bajorek. Cambridge: Polity Press, 2002. (*Échographies de la télévision: Entretiens filmés*. Paris: Éditions Galilée/Institut national de l'audiovisuel, 1996.)

"EW"   " 'Eating Well,' or the Calculation of the Subject." An interview with Jean-Luc Nancy. Trans. Peter Connor and Avital Ronell. In *P*, 255–87. (" 'Il faut bien manger,' ou le calcul du sujet." In *Cahiers Confrontation* 20 [Winter 1989]: 91–114.)

"FI"   "*Fichus*: Frankfurt Address." In *PM*, 164–81. (*Fichus: Discours de Francfort*. Paris: Éditions Galilée, 2002.)

"FK"   "Faith and Knowledge: The Two Sources of 'Religion' at the Limits of Reason Alone." Trans. Samuel Weber. In *Religion*, ed. Jacques Derrida and Gianni Vattimo, 1–78. Stanford, Calif.: Stanford University Press, 1998; also published in *AR*, 40–101; the final fifteen sections of this essay were published separately in the translation of Samuel Weber as "and pomegranates," in *Violence, Identity, and Self-Determination*, ed. Hent de Vries and Samuel Weber (Stanford, Calif.: Stanford University Press, 1997), 326–46. ("Foi et savoir." In *La religion*, ed. Jacques Derrida et Gianni Vattimo, 9–86. Paris: Éditions du Seuil, 1996. Rpt. in *Foi et Savoir*, together with *Le siècle et le pardon*, 7–100. Paris: Éditions du Seuil, 2001.) All references are to section (§) numbers.

"FL"   "Force of Law: The 'Mystical Foundation of Authority.'" Trans. Mary Quaintance. In *AR*, 230–98. (*Force de loi*. Paris: Éditions Galilée, 1994.)

"FS"   "Force and Signification." In *WD*, 3–30. ("Force et signification." In *L'écriture et la différence*, 9–49.)

"FSW"   "Freud and the Scene of Writing." In *WD*, 196–231. ("Freud et la scène de l'écriture," in *L'écriture et la différence*, 293–340.)

"FTA"   "Fifty-two Aphorisms for a Foreword." Trans. Andrew Benjamin. In *PSY 2*, 117–26. ("Cinquante-deux aphorismes pour un avant-propos." In *Psyché 2*, 121–30.)

"FW"   "Final Words." Trans. Gila Walker. In *The Late Derrida*, ed. W. J. T. Mitchell and Arnold I. Davidson. Chicago: University of Chicago Press, 2007, 244.

FWT   *For What Tomorrow . . . : A Dialogue*. With Elisabeth Roudinesco. Trans. Jeff Fort. Stanford, Calif.: Stanford University Press, 2004. (*De quoi demain . . .: Dialogue*. With Elisabeth Roudinesco. Paris: Libraire Arthème Fayard et Éditions Galilée, 2001.)

GD 2   *The Gift of Death*, 2d ed., and *Literature in Secret*. Trans. David Wills. Chicago: University of Chicago Press, 2008. (*Donner la mort*. Paris: Éditions Galilée, 1999.)

GGP   *God, the Gift, and Postmodernism*. Ed. John D. Caputo and Michael J. Scanlon. Bloomington: Indiana University Press, 1999. Includes "On the Gift: A Discussion between Jacques Derrida and Jean-Luc Marion, Moderated by Richard Kearney," 54–78.

GL   *Glas*. Trans. John P. Leavey, Jr., and Richard Rand. Lincoln: University of Nebraska Press, 1986. (*Glas*. Paris: Éditions Galilée, 1974.)

"HAS"   "How to Avoid Speaking: Denials." Trans. Ken Frieden and Elizabeth Rottenberg. In *PSY 2*, 143–95. ("Comment ne pas parler: *Dénegations*." In *Psyché 2*, 145–200.)

IW	*Islam & the West: A Conversation with Jacques Derrida.* Mustapha Chérif. Trans. Teresa Lavender Fagan. Chicago: University of Chicago Press, 2008. ("L'Islam et l'Occident: Rencontre avec Jacques Derrida." Mustapha Chérif Paris: Odile Jacob, 2006.)
"IW"	"Interpretations at War: Kant, the Jew, the German." Trans. Moshe Ron. In *AR*, 135–88. ("*Interpretations at war:* Kant, le Juif, l'Allemand," in *Psyché 2*, 249–305.)
JD	*Jacques Derrida.* With Geoffrey Bennington. Chicago: University of Chicago Press, 1993. (*Jacques Derrida.* With Geoffrey Bennington. Paris: Éditions du Seuil, 1991.)
"K"	"*Khōra.*" Trans. Ian McLeod. In *ON*, 87–127. (*Khōra.* Paris: Éditions Galilée, 1993.)
LLF	*Learning to Live Finally: The Last Interview.* Trans. Pascale-Anne Brault and Michael Naas. Hoboken, N.J.: Melville House Publishing, 2007. (*Apprendre à vivre enfin: Entretien avec Jean Birnbaum.* Paris: Éditions Galilée/Le Monde, 2005.)
"LO"	"Living On: Border Lines." Trans. James Hulbert. In *Deconstruction and Criticism*. New York: The Seabury Press/Continuum Press, 1979, 62–142. ("Survivre." In *PAR*, 117–218.)
"LPS"	"La parole soufflée." In *WD*, 169–95. ("La parole soufflée." In *L'écriture et la différence*, 253–92.)
MAR	*Moscou aller-retour.* La Tour d'Aigues: Éditions de l'aube, 1995.
MB	*Memoirs of the Blind: The Self-Portrait and Other Ruins.* Trans. Pascale-Anne Brault and Michael Naas. Chicago: University of Chicago Press, 1993. (*Mémoires d'aveugle: L'autoportrait et autres ruines.* Paris: Éditions de la Réunion des musées nationaux, 1990.)
MO	*Monolingualism of the Other; or, The Prosthesis of Origin.* Trans. Patrick Mensah. Stanford, Calif.: Stanford University Press, 1998. (*Le monolinguisme de l'autre; ou, la prothèse d'origine.* Paris: Éditions Galilée, 1996.)
MP	*Margins of Philosophy.* Trans. Alan Bass. Chicago: University of Chicago Press, 1982. (*Marges de la philosophie.* Paris: Éditions de Minuit, 1972.)
"MS"	"Marx & Sons." Trans. G. M. Goshgarian. In *Ghostly Demarcations: A Symposium on Jacques Derrida's Specters of Marx*, ed. Michael Sprinker, 213–62. London: Verso Press, 1999. (*Marx & Sons.* Paris: Presses Universitaires de France/Galilée, 2002.)

N   *Negotiations: Interventions and Interviews, 1971–2001.* Ed.,
           trans., and introd. Elizabeth Rottenberg. Stanford, Calif.:
           Stanford University Press, 2002.

"NA"   "No Apocalypse, Not Now: Full Speed Ahead, Seven Missiles,
           Seven Missives." Trans. Catherine Porter and Philip Lewis. In
           PSY 1, 387–409. ("No apocalypse, not now (à toute vitesse,
           sept missiles, sept missives," in *Psyché 1*, 395–418.)

"NAAT"   "On a Newly Arisen Apocalyptic Tone in Philosophy." Trans.
           John P. Leavey, Jr. In *Raising the Tone of Philosophy*, ed. Peter
           Fenves, 117–71. Baltimore: Johns Hopkins University Press,
           1993. (*D'un ton apocalyptique adopté naguère en philosophie.*
           Paris: Éditions Galilée, 1983.)

"NM"   "Nietzsche and the Machine." Trans. Richard Beardsworth. In
           N, 215–56.

"NW"   "The Night Watch." Trans. Pascale-Anne Brault and Michael
           Naas. In *Joyce and Derrida: Between Philosophy and Literature*,
           ed. Andrew J. Mitchell and Sam Slote. Stanford, Calif.: Stan-
           ford University Press, forthcoming. ("*La veilleuse.*" Preface to
           Jacques Trilling's *James Joyce ou l'écriture matricide*, 7–32. Bel-
           fort, France: Éditions Circé, 2001.)

OG   *Of Grammatology.* Trans. with a preface by Gayatri Chakra-
           vorty Spivak. Baltimore: Johns Hopkins University Press,
           1976. (*De la grammatologie.* Paris: Éditions de Minuit, 1967.)

OFH   *Of Hospitality.* With Anne Dufourmantelle. Trans. Rachel
           Bowlby. Stanford, Calif.: Stanford University Press, 2000. (*De
           l'hospitalité.* Paris: Calmann-Lévy, 1997.)

OH   *The Other Heading: Reflections on Today's Europe.* Trans.
           Pascale-Anne Brault and Michael Naas. Bloomington: Indiana
           University Press, 1992. (*L'autre cap.* Paris: Éditions de Minuit,
           1991.)

ON   *On the Name.* Ed. Thomas Dutoit. Stanford, Calif.: Stanford
           University Press, 1993; includes "Passions: 'An Oblique Of-
           fering,'" 3–31 ("P"); *Sauf le nom (Post-Scriptum)*, 35–85
           ("*SN*"); *Khōra* ("*K*"), 87–127. (*Passions.* Paris: Éditions Gali-
           lée, 1993; *Sauf le nom [Post-Scriptum].* Paris: Éditions Galilée,
           1993; *Khōra.* Paris: Éditions Galilée, 1993.)

OS   *Of Spirit: Heidegger and the Question.* Trans. Geoffrey Benning-
           ton and Rachel Bowlby. Chicago: University of Chicago Press,
           1991. (*De l'esprit: Heidegger et la question.* Paris: Éditions Gali-
           lée, 1987.)

OT   *On Touching—Jean-Luc Nancy*. Trans. Christine Irizarry. Stanford, Calif.: Stanford University Press, 2005. (*Le toucher, Jean-Luc Nancy*. Paris: Éditions Galilée, 2000.)

"P"   "Passions: 'An Oblique Offering.'" Trans. David Wood. In *ON*, 3–31. (*Passions*. Paris: Éditions Galilée, 1993.)

PAR   *Parages*. Ed. John P. Leavey, Jr. Trans. Tom Conley, James Hulbert, John P. Leavey, and Avital Ronell. Stanford, Calif.: Stanford University Press, 2010. (*Parages*. Revised and augmented. Paris: Éditions Galilée, 2003.)

PC   *The Post Card: From Socrates to Freud and Beyond*. Trans. Alan Bass. Chicago: University of Chicago Press, 1987. (*La carte postale: De Socrate à Freud et au delà*. Paris: Flammarion, 1980.)

"PCQ"   "Penser ce qui vient." In *Derrida pour les temps à venir*, ed. René Major, 17–62. Paris: Éditions Stock, 2007.

PF   *Politics of Friendship*. Trans. George Collins. New York: Verso, 1997. (*Politiques de l'amitié*. Paris: Éditions Galilée, 1994.)

PM   *Paper Machine*. Trans. Rachel Bowlby. Stanford, Calif.: Stanford University Press, 2005. (*Papier machine: Le ruban de machine à écrire et autres réponses*. Paris: Éditions Galilée, 2001.)

POS   *Positions*. Trans. Alan Bass. Chicago: University of Chicago Press, 1981. (*Positions*. Paris: Éditions de Minuit, 1972.)

"PP"   "Plato's Pharmacy." In *DIS*, 61–171. ("La pharmacie de Platon." In *Dissémination*, 69–197.)

"PPW" "Poetics and Politics of Witnessing." Trans. Outi Pasanen. In *SQ*, 65–96. ("Poétique et politique du témoignage." In *Cahiers de l'Herne: Derrida*, 521–39. Paris: Éditions de l'Herne, 2004.)

"PSI"   "The Pocket-Size Interview." Trans. Tupac Cruz. *The Late Derrida*, ed. W. J. T. Mitchell and Arnold I. Davidson, 144–70. Chicago: University of Chicago Press, 2007.

"PSS"   "Psychoanalysis Searches the States of Its Soul: The Impossible Beyond of a Sovereign Cruelty." Trans. Peggy Kamuf. In *WA*, 238–80. (*États d'âme de la psychanalyse: L'impossible au-delà d'une souveraine cruauté*. Paris: Éditions Galilée, 2000.)

PSY 1   *Psyche 1: Inventions of the Other*. Ed. Peggy Kamuf and Elizabeth Rottenberg. Stanford, Calif.: Stanford University Press, 2007. (*Psyché: Inventions de l'autre*. Vol. 1. Paris: Éditions Galilée, 1987, 1998.)

PSY 2   *Psyche 2: Inventions of the Other*. Ed. Peggy Kamuf and Elizabeth Rottenberg. Stanford, Calif.: Stanford University Press,

2008. (*Psyché: Inventions de l'autre.* Vol. 2, Paris: Éditions Galilée, 1987, 2003.)

R   *Rogues: Two Essays on Reason.* Trans. Pascale-Anne Brault and Michael Naas. Stanford, Calif.: Stanford University Press, 2005. (*Voyous.* Paris: Éditions Galilée, 2003.)

RES   *Resistances of Psychoanalysis.* Trans. Peggy Kamuf, Pascale-Anne Brault, and Michael Naas. Stanford, Calif.: Stanford University Press, 1996. (*Résistances de la psychanalyse.* Paris: Éditions Galilée, 1996.)

"S"   "Le sacrifice." First published in *La métaphore.* Éditions de la Différence, no. 1 (Spring 1993); rpt. as the post-face to Daniel Mesguich, *L'éternel éphémère*, 141–54. Lagrasse: Verdier, 2006.

"SEC"   "Signature Event Context." In *MP*, 307–30. Also in *Limited Inc* (Evanston, Ill.: Northwestern University Press, 1988), 1–24. ("Signature événement contexte," in *Marges*, 365–93.)

"SH"   "Shibboleth: For Paul Celan." Trans. Joshua Wilner; rev. Thomas Dutoit. In *SQ*, 1–64. (*Schibboleth: Pour Paul Celan.* Paris: Éditions Galilée, 1986.)

SM   *Specters of Marx: The State of the Debt, the Work of Mourning, and the New International.* Trans. Peggy Kamuf. New York: Routledge, 1994. (*Spectres de Marx.* Paris: Éditions Galilée, 1993.)

"SN"   *"Sauf le nom (Post-Scriptum)."* Trans. John P. Leavey, Jr. In *ON*, 33–85. First published under the title *Post-Scriptum (Aporias, Ways, and Voices)* in *Derrida and Negative Theology*, ed. Harold Coward and Toby Foshay, 283–323. Albany: State University of New York Press, 1992. (*Sauf le nom [Post-Scriptum]*, Paris: Éditions Galilée, 1993.)

SP   *Speech and Phenomena: And Other Essays on Husserl's Theory of Signs.* Trans. and introd. David B. Allison. Preface by Newton Garver. Evanston, Ill: Northwestern University Press, 1973. (*La voix et le phénomène: Introduction au problème du signe dans la phénoménologie de Husserl.* Paris: Presses Universitaires de France, 1967.)

SQ   *Sovereignties in Question: The Poetics of Paul Celan.* Ed. Thomas Dutoit and Outi Pasanen. New York: Fordham University Press, 2005.

"SSS"   "Le survivant, le sursis, le sursaut." In *La Quinzaine littéraire*, no. 882, 1–31 (August 2004): 15–16.

"SW"   "A Silkworm of One's Own: (Points of View Stitched on the Other Veil)." Trans. Geoffrey Bennington. In *Veils*, with Hélène Cixous (Stanford, Calif.: Stanford University Press, 2001), 23–85; rpt. in *AR*, 309–55. ("Un ver à soie: Points de vue piqués sur l'autre voile." In *Voiles*, with Hélène Cixous, 23–85. Paris: Éditions Galilée, 1998.)

"TA"   "Trace et archive, image et art: Dialogue." Transcription of a talk given on 25 June 2002; available at http:// www.ina.fr/ inatheque/activites/college/pdf/2002.

"TB"   *"Des tours de Babel."* Trans. Joseph F. Graham. In *AR*, 102–34. First published in *Difference in Translation*. Bilingual edition. Cornell University Press, 1985; also in *PSY 1*, 191–225. ("Des tours de Babel." In *Psyché*, vol. 1, 203–36.)

"TG"   "A Testimony Given. . . ." In Elisabeth Weber, *Questioning Judaism: Interviews by Elisabeth Weber*, trans. Rachel Bowlby, 39–58. Stanford, Calif.: Stanford University Press, 2004. ("Un témoignage donné . . .," an interview with Elisabeth Weber, in *Questions au judaïsme*, 73–104. Paris: Desclée de Brouwer, 1996.)

TP   *The Truth in Painting*. Trans. Geoff Bennington and Ian McLeod. Chicago: University of Chicago Press, 1987. (*La vérité en peinture*. Paris: Flammarion, 1978.)

TS   *A Taste for the Secret*. With Maurizio Ferraris. Trans. Giacomo Donis. Ed. Giacomo Donis and David Webb. Cambridge: Polity Press, 2001.

"TSA"   "Taking a Stand for Algeria." Trans. Boris Belay. In *AR*, 299–308; also translated by Elizabeth Rottenberg as "Taking Sides for Algeria," in *N*, 117–24. ("Parti pris pour l'Algérie." In *PM*, 219–27.)

"TYM"   "Tympan." In *MP*, ix–xxix ("Tympan." In *Marges*, i–xxv.)

"UG"   "Ulysses Gramophone: Hear Say Yes in Joyce." Trans. Tina Kendall, rev. Shari Benstock. In *Acts of Literature*, ed. Derek Attridge, 253–309. London: Routledge, 1992. ("Ulysse gramophone: Ouï-dire de Joyce." In *Ulysse gramophone: Deux mots pour Joyce*, 55–143. Paris: Éditions Galilée, 1987.)

"US"   "Unconditionality or Sovereignty: The University at the Frontiers of Europe." Trans. Peggy Kamuf. *Oxford Literary Review* 31 (December 2009): 115–31. (*Inconditonnalité ou souveraineté: L'université aux frontières de l'Europe*. Athens: Editions Patakis, 2002.)

"VA"   "Les voix d'Artaud (la force, la forme, la forge)." Interview with Évelyne Grossman. In *Magazine littéraire*, no. 434 (September 2004): 34–36.

"VM"   "Violence and Metaphysics: An Essay on the Thought of Emmanuel Levinas." In *WD*, 79–153. ("Violence et métaphysique: Essai sur la pensée d'Emmanuel Levinas." In *L'écriture et la différence*, 117–228.)

WA   *Without Alibi*. Ed., trans., and introd. Peggy Kamuf. Stanford, Calif.: Stanford University Press, 2002.

WD   *Writing and Difference*. Trans. and introd. Alan Bass. Chicago: University of Chicago Press, 1978. (*L'écriture et la différence*. Paris: Éditions du Seuil, 1967.)

WM   *The Work of Mourning*. Ed. Pascale-Anne Brault and Michael Naas. Chicago: University of Chicago Press, 2001. (For the French version, see *CFU*.)

"WOG"   "We Other Greeks." Trans. Pascale-Anne Brault and Michael Naas. In *Derrida and the Greeks*, ed. Miriam Leonard, 17–39. Oxford: Oxford University Press, 2009. ("'Nous autres Grecs.'" In *Nos Grec et leurs modernes*, ed. Barbara Cassin, 251–76. Paris: Éditions du Seuil, 1992.)

Miracle and Machine

Introduction

Miraculum ex Machina

In February 1994, Jacques Derrida participated in a small conference on the island of Capri devoted to the question of the nature and role of religion in the world today. Derrida's essay "Faith and Knowledge: The Two Sources of 'Religion' at the Limits of Reason Alone," first published in French in 1996 and then in English translation in 1998, is a revised and expanded version of the reflections Derrida offered on that occasion.[1] It is a dense and difficult, highly synthetic and sometimes elliptical essay, in which Derrida gives us his most sustained engagement with the question of the nature of religion in general, the two "sources" of religion, as his subtitle puts it, as well as his most provocative and speculative interrogation of the forms religion is taking today. It thus includes themes we would expect to find in a work on religion (e.g., the nature of revelation, faith, prayer, sacrifice, testimony, messianicity, secularism, and so on) as well as themes that are a little more surprising and that Derrida will have treated elsewhere (e.g., teletechnology, telecommunications, globalization, media, sexual difference, sovereignty, democracy, literature, specters, and so on). What began, then, as an informal discussion with a small group of scholars, including Gianni Vattimo, Hans-Georg Gadamer, and Maurizio Ferraris, would thus become a seventy-eight-page essay that condenses a great deal of Derrida's prior work and anticipates much of his work in the decade to follow.[2] In other words, what began as a series of more or less improvised remarks on religion would become, as I will try to demonstrate in what follows, an absolutely crucial essay, a text *charnière*, as one says in French, for understanding not just Derrida's work on religion but his work as a whole.[3]

Miracle and Machine is, in a first moment, an attempt to explicate and elucidate this seemingly improvised and yet, as we will see, rigorously structured, highly articulated, and tightly argued essay on the topic of religion. It is intended, on one level, as a kind of "reader's guide" to Derrida's text, providing essential background to "Faith and Knowledge," explaining its premises, justifying its unique formatting and argumentative style, commenting on its texts, figures, and themes, making "suggestions for further reading," and, of course, analyzing the claims and arguments Derrida makes throughout on the relationship between religion, science, and the media.[4]

But *Miracle and Machine* is intended to be more than just a commentary on a single text. It also aims to be something of an introduction to Derrida's work in general through a close reading of this one essay. I thus refer throughout to many other Derrida texts, both to illuminate key points in "Faith and Knowledge" and to show how this one essay is exemplary of themes, motifs, arguments, and argumentative strategies that can be found in Derrida's work from the beginning right up until the end. My belief is that by reading an exemplary text such as this one as closely, critically, and patiently as possible, in its spirit and in its letter, one will be much better prepared to read Derrida elsewhere on other themes and in other contexts.

If readers have generally acknowledged the importance of "Faith and Knowledge" in Derrida's corpus, the telegraphic and sometimes even cryptic style of the essay has made it difficult to give a coherent reading of the essay as a whole. Though "Faith and Knowledge" has thus already provoked a great deal of discussion about, for instance, the precise relationship between a general structure of religiosity and various determinate, revealed religions, or else the role played by the Greek *khōra* in a text that is ostensibly about the three Abrahamic monotheisms, or the relationship between Derrida's and Kant's respective views on religion, little attempt has been made to spell out the general argument about religion in this essay and the way in which Derrida's writing and style contribute to and exemplify that argument. To carry out such a reading, one must do something more than just distill Derrida's *positions* on religion in this work. While I will indeed develop what I believe to be a series of philosophical claims or theses regarding the relationship between religion, science, and the media, I will get there by looking at the *letter* of Derrida's text, at its structure and form, at its mise-en-scène—aspects of the text that are often ignored in philosophy as we attempt to strip away these mere "supplements" or *parerga* in order to get to the work itself, to Derrida's position, for example, on whether revelation is more originary than revealability, or to his claim about the role played by the media in the dissemination or perhaps determination of the religious message. In short, my goal is to give to Derrida's text the kind of close textual attention that Derrida always gave to the texts of others, in the belief that another, more interesting and more powerful textual logic will emerge.

I thus try to move throughout this work from the greatest levels of generality regarding Derrida's understanding of religion, science, and the media to the smallest details that reflect or exemplify that understanding. I consider everything from the three principal theses that, on my reading, run beneath the entirety of "Faith and Knowledge" to a consideration of the structure of the essay (the reason why, for example, it is divided into fifty-two sections), to a line-by-line, indeed word-by-word analysis, in both English and French, of a single, brief passage near the middle of the essay where Derrida recounts the genesis of "Faith and Knowledge" and where, I will argue, this genesis reflects and illuminates the overall structure of the essay and its three theses. As we will see in an exemplary fashion through this reading of "Faith and Knowledge," Derrida's most general ideas and far-reaching claims are often developed through or reflected in his most rigorous attention to the details of language and of writing. If that is always true of Derrida's work, it is especially so in a text that concerns the irreducible relationship in religion between the meaning of the religious message and its expression, manifestation, or, indeed, revelation in a particular language or medium.

The questions at the center of this work regarding the relationship between faith and knowledge, belief and reason, religion and science, are, obviously, hardly new. They have been with us in this form and posed in these terms since at least the beginning of modernity, and there seems to be no sign of their losing any of their relevance. From debates about teaching creationism or intelligent design to controversies over stem-cell technology or the publication of what are taken to be offensive representations of religious figures, there has been no shortage of public discussion or scholarly research about the relationship between religion, science, and the media.[5] Few of these contemporary issues are broached directly in "Faith and Knowledge," but almost all of them call out to be rethought in light of the provocative analyses and arguments Derrida offers there concerning the relationship between religion and contemporary tele-technoscience and the processes of globalization that are facilitated by it. Central to these analyses will be what Derrida understands to be the paradoxical (what he will call *autoimmune*) relationship between religion and science, and in particular the rejection of technoscientific modernity by many so-called extremist or fundamentalist religious groups through a hyper-sophisticated appropriation and manipulation of this very same technoscience. Derrida attempts in this important essay to explain at once the logic behind religion's simultaneous rejection and appropriation of science and the global stakes of this paradoxical relationship. Part of this explanation will involve the claim that an originary or elementary (though nondogmatic) faith is at the origin of both religion and science, a claim that can shed much light on all kinds of contemporary issues regarding the role of religion in civil society or education, the desirability or possibility of a truly secular state, or, indeed, the very possibility of clearly distinguishing today between religion and science.

While all these issues and questions can benefit from thoughtful reflection on Derrida's "Faith and Knowledge" and other texts, this work does not pretend to take on any of these questions directly, let alone the enormous question of "religion itself" or "religion today." It does not even pretend to treat in a comprehensive manner Derrida's many works on religion. Others have already carried out this task much better than I ever could.[6] But because "Faith and Knowledge" was hardly the first time Derrida treated questions of religion, faith, belief, testimony, sacrifice, and so on, it will be important to cast an eye back on some of Derrida's other important texts on religion, from, to give just a few examples, *Glas* (1974) and "How to Avoid Speaking: Denials" (1986) to "Circumfession" (1991) and *The Gift of Death* (1992). For reasons that should become clear in the course of this work, however, a certain priority has been granted to those texts written within just a year or two of "Faith and Knowledge," from "*Sauf le nom (Post-Scriptum)*" and *Archive Fever* to "*Demeure*" and "A Silkworm of One's Own."

My intention here is thus to demonstrate the richness and complexity of Derrida's thought and writing, as well as the coherence and unity of his corpus, by means of a single text on the topic of religion and its relationship to science and the media.[7] For if "Faith and Knowledge" is, as I will argue, an absolutely unique text in Derrida's corpus, uniquely structured and argued, if it takes on more directly than any other the question of religion today, there is little in it that is not anticipated or announced in earlier works, and there is, as I have already suggested, much in it that can help us understand Derrida's "project" more generally. If the focus of this work is thus a single essay of Derrida and the issues raised in it, reference will be made throughout, both in the text and the notes, not only to other Derrida texts, both early and late, but to the texts in the history of philosophy that are being referred to. As I will argue in the opening chapter of this work, in order to understand the unique *signature* of "Faith and Knowledge," in order to understand its *event*, one must first understand its *context*. Though the context never completely determines the event, and the signature always breaks with the context it signs, a signature can never be read without its context. Because Derrida is working within a Western philosophical tradition with well-known arguments and a well-established vocabulary with regard to religion, I have supplemented my reading of Derrida with multiple references to, and then four supplementary "observations" on, the figures Derrida refers to most throughout "Faith and Knowledge"—Immanuel Kant (and particularly his *Religion Within the Limits of Reason Alone*), G. W. F. Hegel (especially *Faith and Knowledge*), Henri Bergson (especially *The Two Sources of Religion and Morality*), and Martin Heidegger. My intention here is thus to read "Faith and Knowledge: The Two Sources of 'Religion' at the Limits of Reason Alone" as my "original source," and then to see how that single source is immediately compromised and multiplied, automatically divided, so as to engulf or inscribe other texts, beginning first with the historical sources of the essay but moving then to Derrida's own works, to all those written around the time of "Faith and Knowledge" and to some written by Derrida near the very beginning of his career and some written right near the end.

In addition to earlier and later texts of Derrida, I also put some emphasis on a few lengthy and, in my view, very telling interviews given around the same time as "Faith and Knowledge." *A Taste for the Secret*, for example, is a series of six interviews with Maurizio Ferraris, the organizer of the Capri conference, which date from July 1993 to January 1995, that is, from just months before the Capri conference to almost a year after, as Derrida was no doubt completing his written text. A long interview with Bernard Stiegler on questions of technology and the media that dates from December 1993, just weeks before the Capri conference, also anticipates much of what will be said in "Faith and Knowledge." In order to understand some of Derrida's most difficult remarks about the autoimmunity of religion in its appropriation of the media and teletechnologies, I will turn at several junctures to these interviews, as well as to some improvised remarks from December 1997, where Derrida, at a conference in Paris on religion in the media, develops even more fully and provocatively much of what is only suggested in "Faith and Knowledge."[8] By reading widely around "Faith and Knowledge" in this way, we should be able to see how Derrida's views on religion and faith are inextricably related to a whole host of other concerns in his work, from questions of language, media, community, politics, sovereignty, technology, sacrifice, and so on, to the entire "project" of deconstruction.

"Faith and Knowledge" is, we will see, a major philosophical text on the great question of the relationship between faith and knowledge, or revelation and reason, or religion and science or technology. But it is also, precisely, a text, one that operates on many levels, some in continuity with the great philosophical tradition on this question and some that break with that tradition. In *Miracle and Machine* I am interested in showing just how well Derrida's essay works, just how well it succeeds in explaining the relationship between science and religion by means of a philosophical text that exemplifies and puts that relationship to the test. Only when we see how this text functions, how it puts to work everything from the lifted title to the doubled subtitle to the untranslatable subtitle "*et grenades*," will we really be able to understand the theses of this major work. To invoke the name of one of Derrida's own pedagogical influences, a name that is rarely cited and easily forgotten alongside those of Althusser, Foucault, or Levinas, I would like to give here a reading of Derrida that will be, in certain ways, *à la Guéroult*, that is, in the manner of Martial Guéroult, specialist at the Collège de France in seventeenth-century philosophy.[9] In *A Taste for the Secret* Derrida describes Guéroult as offering a "type of reading that reconstructed the internal concatenation of a system, step by step and with the maximum care for detail," with "a respect for the way the text works, for the logic of the philosophemes." As Derrida goes on to argue: "It was not a question of subscribing or not subscribing to a thesis or of philosophizing for its own sake, but of seeing how things *worked*—a sort of philosophical technology. At the same time, there was an attention to the letter, to literality: not to the breath that breathes through a text, to what it *means*, but to its literal working, its functioning" (*TS* 45).

It will indeed be the working or functioning of "Faith and Knowledge" that will interest me most here, though this will often require, perhaps contra Guéroult, taking the author or at least a certain signature effect into account and, if not the text's animating breath, at least the theme of the breath as it is inscribed, as we will see, at the very origin of this great text on religion. My task is thus not to try to explain Derrida's text as he himself might have done; it is not to reanimate some animating breath of the text or return to Derrida's original intentions. It is, rather, to clarify and to analyze both the theses of this essay and its unique mise-en-scène, to explicate not only the main storyline but the background and the back story, the actors and the voices (even the prompters or *souffleurs*), the staging and the setting, even the props and the lighting. If this will involve a certain ventriloquy on my part, if it will resemble here and there a kind of marionette theater, it will all be in the service of trying to demonstrate that philosophical ideas and argumentation never come without such a mise-en-scène and that any claim to have done away with such theatrics is always the most theatrical and naïve of all. In a 2001 interview on Artaud, Derrida seems to invite just this kind of reading when he says:

> I have never written for the theater, but my feeling is that, when I write something, even the most classical of philosophical texts, what is most important to me is not the content, the doctrinal body, but the mise-en-scène, its spatial arrangement [*la mise en espace*]. I have the impression that someone is reading me well when he or she reads the most university-like and most academic of my texts by taking an interest in the spatial arrangement, in the mise-en-scène. Such readings are rather rare, but, believe me, that's what interests me and is most important to me. ("AR" 38)

I hope to persuade the reader of *Miracle and Machine* that, if "Faith and Knowledge" invites the kind of reading I am attempting here, a reading at once macro- and micro-scopic, one that attempts both to survey the whole and zoom in on certain key arguments, passages, lines, even words, this essay is hardly unique in Derrida's corpus. Indeed I wish to suggest that, despite the hundreds of books and thousands of articles on Derrida, we still find ourselves, several years after his death, only on the threshold of the serious, rigorous, detailed, and, yes, sometimes playful reading his work deserves. A reading worthy of the name, that is, worthy of the name *reading* but also worthy of the name *Jacques Derrida*—that is what I would like to try, at least, to begin here.[10]

Miracle and Machine—a title that attempts to translate in its own way a certain *deus ex machina* or, indeed, "Faith and Knowledge" itself— begins by reading Derrida's 1994 essay as a philosophical essay, to be sure, but as one that cannot be understood without thoughtful consideration of how it works as a discursive machine. As we will see in what follows, the unexpected and the unforeseeable—even the miraculous, as I will come to understand it through Derrida—can come about only within or by means of a certain machine, the singular event only thanks to a kind of repetition, only from within a setting or a scene that has already been well rehearsed. If this work thus resembles in places "this very French model of philosophy à la Guéroult" (*TS* 45), if it takes an interest not only in "the content, the doctrinal body, but [in] the mise-en-scène, its spatial arrangement," it will also try to remain open and attentive to a certain displacement and relocation. For deconstruction can continue to work today only by being repeated, reread in its letter, *and* transplanted elsewhere, uprooted and translated into other idioms, grafted onto other contexts, reformatted according to other protocols, taken out of its original context and, sometimes, brought closer to "home."[11] For me here, that means bringing it closer to America—a "privileged" reference for Derrida in "Faith and Knowledge" and elsewhere, particularly with regard to the relationship between religion, globalization, global media, and the hegemony of the Anglo-American idiom. But instead of supplementing "Faith and Knowledge" with contemporary scholarship on the question of religion in America, I have opted instead to turn to a great twentieth-century American novel that depicts in an exemplary and perhaps prophetic fashion the relationship between faith and knowledge, religion and science, in late-twentieth-century America, though also the relationship between religion and the weapons industry, religion and waste, religion and the World Wide Web, and religion and—no kidding—baseball, American's national pastime: Don DeLillo's 1997 *Underworld*. My analysis of Derrida's "Faith and Knowledge" is thus framed by a prologue, an epilogue, and two brief interludes on DeLillo's extraordinary novel, which not only treats many of the same themes as Derrida's "Faith and Knowledge" but has the additional merit of being written at almost exactly the same time. As we will see, the lines connecting these two texts are innumerable, and, while some are rather clear, right on the surface of the text, some are far below, in the underworld, precisely, in a place where phantoms roam, haunting our history and our unconsciousness. If this frame and these brief interruptions from DeLillo appear at the outset to be a rather unlikely supplement to Derrida's essay, a bit out of left field, I hope to demonstrate by the end of this work, if not their necessity, at least their strategic utility and interest.[12] For "Faith and Knowledge"—or "Faith and Knowledge in America"—could well have been the subtitle of DeLillo's great American novel, which traces the place of religion in American culture from a "miraculous" event on a baseball field in 1951 to an "apocalyptic" apparition on a billboard in the Bronx some four decades later. As for the theme of the underworld itself, we will see that, while Derrida explores everything from the role of cyberspace and telecommunications satellites in making religion a truly global phenomenon to the relationship between religion and certain Enlightenment values of publicity and universality, "Faith and Knowledge" also has its subtexts, its phantoms and its specters, in short, its own underworld, a place where the ghosts in the machine can lead not only to the miracle of an unrepeatable event but to mass delusions or unimaginable mass destruction. As both Derrida and DeLillo seem to believe, we always begin late in the game, with men on base, behind in the count, and it really could swing either way.

Miracle and Machine is divided into three main parts—I: The Island and the Starry Skies Above, II: The Religion(s) of the World, and III: Afterlives and Underworlds—corresponding roughly to Heaven, Purgatory, and the Underworld, a Divine Comedy in reverse that leads from general questions of context and history to questions about what is happening to religion in the world today to, finally, a consideration of what is "repressed" in certain religions or religious discourses, confined to some unspoken and unseen underworld, only to resurface to haunt our discourses and our history. Though I will offer only a very poor imitation of Virgil as I try to guide the reader through Derrida's text, the reader should not be surprised to see shades of all kinds—if not Beatrice, at least a certain Esmeralda—emerge from out of the shadows to accompany us through the final stages of this work.

Miracle and Machine thus begins with something of an aerial, Google-eye view of "Faith and Knowledge," before going down beneath the surface. The three chapters of Part I all look at various conditions and contexts for understanding and interpreting "Faith and Knowledge." In Chapter 1, "Content Event Signature," I look in some detail at the context of the Capri conference, the place and the participants, along with their languages, nationalities, and religions, since these are all essential to understanding Derrida's presentation at that conference and the essay "Faith and Knowledge" that resulted from it. In the next chapter, "Duplicity, Definition, Deracination," I turn to the structure and organization of "Faith and Knowledge" and Derrida's initial attempts to "define" the nature of religion or the role religion is playing in the world today. This chapter demonstrates how the first two sections of the essay adumbrate almost everything that follows, from the sources, terms, and themes of the essay to the significance of *khōra*. I also turn in this chapter to the question of language, which is never just one question among others for Derrida, and particularly not for the theme of religion, where the Latin origins of the word and concept *religion* are related to the way in which religion is spreading across the globe through a process Derrida calls *Globalatinization*. Finally, in the third and concluding chapter of this section, "Three Theses on the Two Sources and Their One Common Element," I attempt to develop the three principal theses I see running throughout "Faith and Knowledge." While Derrida does not himself identify these three theses as such, I try to show the extent to which they structure the entirety of his essay. It is in this chapter that I address Derrida's claims regarding the autoimmune relationship between religion and science, and particularly the techno-science of the media.

In Part II, I turn to larger questions regarding the relationship between religion and technology as it is developed in "Faith and Knowledge." Chapter 4, "*La religion soufflée*: The Genesis of 'Faith and Knowledge,'" begins by looking at a single, very brief passage in the essay where Derrida recounts the origin of the Capri conference and its theme of religion. It then goes on to demonstrate how Derrida's approach to the question of religion echoes—or doubles—his approach to other questions, such as the relationship between speech and writing, or breath and the machine, in a couple of important early texts. We also see in this chapter how, as I noted above, Derrida's thought always develops through a mise-en-scène of other texts and other voices, in this case, the two versions of the creation of mankind in Genesis. It is also here that I attempt to give a succinct definition of the first key word of my title—*miracle*—with the definition of the second, *machine*, being reserved for the following chapter. In Chapter 5, then, "The Telegenic Voice: The Religion of the Media," I look at the distinctions Derrida makes in several places *between* religions on the basis of their use of and/or reaction to the teletechnological machine and the media. I thus consider here why Derrida suggests that perhaps only Christianity should go by the name *religion* and why globalization is perhaps first and foremost a Christian phenomenon. Chapter 6, "'Jewgreek is greekjew': Messianicity—*Khōra*—Democracy," returns much more closely to "Faith and Knowledge" in order to explain two "'historical' names," messianicity and *khōra*, for the opening or the promise that, on my reading, is one of the two sources of religion as well as science. I thus ask in this chapter why Derrida sees the need to supplement a Judeo-Christian notion of messianicity with a thinking of the Greek *khōra* from Plato's *Timaeus*, a text he once called, no doubt weighing his words, a "Bible avant la lettre" ("Av" 12). Finally, I try to explain here a few of Derrida's more elliptical comments in "Faith and Knowledge" on democracy and literature as the right to say everything in light of other texts from around the same time on these same subjects. As we will see, such themes are hardly extrinsic to the principal theses of Derrida's essay, since they require a rethinking of what Derrida believes to be the Judeo-Christian origins not only of the concept of religion but of literature, democracy, tolerance, even secularism.

As I suggested a moment ago, Part III is the place where *Miracle and Machine* goes underground, into the underworlds of "Faith and Knowledge," in order to explore, sometimes with Derrida and sometimes well beyond his explicit arguments and themes, the hidden sources that will have motivated his text and that can be seen to be lurking just below the surface. In Chapter 7, "Mary and the Marionettes: Life, Sacrifice, and the Sexual Thing," I look at Derrida's contention that religion's attempt to indemnify a relationship to the holy or the sacrosanct takes the form of an absolute respect for life that sometimes requires a sacrifice of the living in the name of a life more valuable than life itself. This then leads to the question of sexual difference and sexual violence in religion, to all the attempts to indemnify the living body—and often the female body—by protecting or safeguarding it or else, for this is the other side of the same logic, scarifying or sacrificing it. According to the autoimmune logic we will have seen developed throughout, religion often attacks the very things it wants to safeguard and protect. What Derrida calls "the sexual thing" will thus not be just one place among others to see this logic at work. It is for this reason, I will argue, that Derrida constantly reminds us in "Faith and Knowledge" that in today's "wars of religion" women are often the principal victims of violence, often by sexual assault or mutilation. Awaiting us here will thus be not the divine and radiant Beatrice of Dante's *Paradiso* but Persephone and Freud's Gradiva, the first an important symbol in Western mythology of sexual aggression and the underworld and the second an emblem of repressed sexual desire and the phantasms that are likely to result from it.

If the opening chapters of *Miracle and Machine* look in some detail at the opening sections of "Faith and Knowledge" before going on to read the essay as a whole, the final chapters focus on elements from the final three sections (§§50–52) and the unnumbered paragraph that concludes the essay. These sections, all very brief, bring together a series of images and themes that at once reflect back on the essay and lead it in other directions, from the image of an opened pomegranate or of scattered ashes to the references to calculation, violence, the Spanish Marrano, and a cryptic recollection at the very end of Jean Genet. In Chapter 8, I explore some of these images and issues and try to think them in relationship to the themes of calculability and incalculability, the limits imposed by the machine and the possibility for something unforeseen to arrive in the remaining "space available." In the final chapter, "The Passion of Literature: Genet in Laguna, Gide in Algiers," I look at two important figures for Derrida: Jean Genet, who emerges right at the end of "Faith and Knowledge," and André Gide, who is not explicitly referred to in the essay but who must nonetheless be included in any account of Derrida on religion because of Derrida's repeated claim that Gide's *Fruits of the Earth* was—as he put it at once playfully and, I believe, in all seriousness—"the Bible of my adolescence." Through a reading of Genet, we will see why

Derrida draws attention in "Faith and Knowledge" to the striking absence not only of women at the Capri conference but of representatives of the Muslim faith, along with all those who have been displaced by today's wars of religion, refugees of all sorts, and perhaps the Palestinians first and foremost. Through a reading of Gide we will be able to ask not only about the origins of Derrida's affirmation of life but whether or not—for how could this question be avoided in a book on religion?—Derrida believed in any kind of personal immortality or any kind of an afterlife.

While *Miracle and Machine* does not work through "Faith and Knowledge" section by section, preferring instead to find other groupings by motif, theme, or figure, it nonetheless moves roughly from the beginning of the essay to the end. Part I treats the overall structure and form of the text, as well as some of its opening sections; Part II looks at a few crucial middle sections on technology, media, democracy, and so on; and Part III focuses primarily on the final sections, where the ghosts of religious discourse and of Derrida on religion emerge and are given space to roam. The trajectory I suggested earlier of moving from the heavens to the earth to the underworld is thus not mine, in the end, but Derrida's, and it will tell us a great deal about what Derrida believed any serious analysis of religion or of the relationship today between religion, science, and the media should attempt to understand.

If "Faith and Knowledge" was hardly the beginning of Derrida's thinking on religion, it nonetheless feels like something of a new beginning for him on the subject, complete with its own genesis story and its own messianic visions. Whether read as an expression of Derrida's most visionary and poignant revelations about the nature of religion or, as will be my inclination, as an extraordinarily intricate discursive machine that makes the truth around which it then turns, "Faith and Knowledge" is a text that makes serious demands upon us. It demands to be read and reread, interpreted and studied, as the unique, unforeseeable, and unrepeatable event that it is, though also, and especially, to be taken apart and broken down, analyzed and reassembled, "deconstructed," if you will, so that we might understand the machinery behind the event, the machine at the origin of the miracle, and the miracle that will have always primed the machine.

Prologue

Miracle and Mass Destruction (Underworld I)

> "You believe in God?" he said.
> "Yes, I think so."
> "We'll go to a ball game sometime."
> **—Don DeLillo, *Underworld***

Because there is—as I believe—no proper place to begin reading Derrida on religion or anything else, because all one can do is prepare, calculate, strategize, and then give it a shot, I would like to begin with a religious tale that is rather far away from Derrida's interests, idiom, and culture, an American prophesy followed up by an American tale of faith and knowledge, testimony and technology, the miracle and the machine. The prophecy I am alluding to is not to be found, however, in what would generally be recognized to be a religious text. Worse, it is not exactly a prophecy about the future, about some future event that has not yet taken place but is promised one day to come to pass, on December 21, 2012, for example, to cite just the latest in a long line of Doomsday predictions. No, the prophecy I am alluding to has in some sense already happened, even if, as we shall see, it has never been taken fully into account and so has never fully arrived, like a trauma that has been registered in our collective conscience but has yet to be revealed and understood. And while it has left traces and will continue to leave traces in our history, the prophecy I am alluding to was first and most clearly pronounced in literature, in a couple of works of American fiction, which does little, in my view, to annul its prophetic power. For inasmuch as prophecy—and particularly prophecies of apocalypse and a final judgment—can be uttered and heard only in a time before the end of time, fiction has perhaps always been their proper place.

The first attempt to voice this prophecy in American fiction is to be found in Carson McCullers's 1940 novel *The Heart Is a Lonely Hunter*, where an African-American street preacher proclaims the Day of Judgment to be near and even takes the risk of giving it a precise date. Speaking in 1939, the time in which the novel is set, the preacher in McCullers's novel stands on a soapbox with Bible in hand and preaches to the crowd that has gathered around him that the apocalypse will not be long in coming. "He talked of the second coming of Christ. He said that the Day of Judgment would be October 2, 1951."[1] Now while it is tempting to read this passage today with a smile as yet another example of a mistaken or false prophecy, as one that simply never came to pass as predicted, I would like to suggest that we not be so quick to dismiss it in this way. If prophecy must always be thought in relation to fiction, and fiction can never simply be measured against history, then it might be said that the prophecy has either not yet happened, that it remains imminent, or that it has *already* happened, that the end has already come, and that our historical knowledge is simply trying to catch up to what has always been known or registered by our fiction.

Entertaining this last hypothesis, one might speculate that McCullers's street preacher was perhaps not as mistaken as all that but was simply off by a single day, that the Day of Judgment actually came not on October 2 but on October 3, 1951. This would have been the day of a true apocalypse, one that, again, will have left traces in history but will have been registered most profoundly in literature, in fiction, where a certain revelation and a certain end of the world are foretold and where what comes to pass is an event, a miracle, that so shocked those who witnessed it that they could express little more than their disbelief, a sign of their belief after reason, their faith in the wake of knowledge. As the announcer of the event would say in words that live on today as a testament to the miracle, words recorded but first pronounced "live" over the radio, as if radio waves were the proper element for this miracle: "I don't believe it. I don't believe it. I do *not* believe it. Bobby Thompson hit a line drive into the lower deck of the left-field stands and the place is going crazy" (*U* 44–45). In case some of you have not yet heard the good news, the evangelist in question here is Russ Hodges, a baseball radio announcer, and the line drive home run he is speaking of is Bobby Thompson's ninth-inning home run off Ralph Branca that gave the New York Giants a victory over their cross-city rivals the Brooklyn Dodgers to win the 1951 National League baseball pennant. Thompson's home run, which came to be known as the "shot heard 'round the world," so tested the limits of belief that it would be compared to a miracle and so shattered the horizon of everyday expectations and events (the Dodgers had been leading the Giants by thirteen games just six weeks earlier) that it would be compared to the Final Judgment. Though life would go on after the miracle, and time would continue on after the Final Judgment of that day in October 1951, the Polo Grounds in New York City would forever be remembered as the place of a singular—I would even risk calling it a religious— experience.[2]

That's the event, the miraculous event, that was recorded and handed down to posterity through the marvels of a tape recording of the announcer's voice as it was broadcast "live" on the radio on October 3, 1951. If there are thus fewer and fewer of the original eyewitnesses to bear testimony to the event, fewer and fewer of the original disciples on the field or in the stands, there is still the recorded voice of the announcer, Russ Hodges, the first evangelist, as I would like to call him, and then there is *Underworld*—another American fiction, another American prophecy— Don DeLillo's 1997 novel, which begins with this singular event and unfolds its implications and its consequences as a way of exploring and encapsulating the entire latter half of the twentieth century in America. DeLillo's novel begins with this so-called "shot heard 'round the world," this single moment of revelation, this single stroke of the bat, this single instant of impact, in order to show how a singular event can ripple outward to touch an entire half century and beyond. I know it may seem heterodox or heretical, but I would like to argue that DeLillo's *Underworld*, one of the great works of literature about religion and faith in America, about the relationship between religion, science, and the media, calls out to be read alongside Derrida's work on religion, and particularly "Faith and Knowledge," an essay written in 1994–1995 and published in 1996, just a year before the publication of DeLillo's novel.

Underworld is a major American novel about quintessentially American things, like baseball, conspicuous consumption, shameless waste, and weapons of mass destruction. But it is also—and precisely through these very things—a great work of fiction about American exceptionalism and exceptional revelations, about both miracles and a day of reckoning that may be looming over us all in the form of a global catastrophe of human origin. The language of religion and miracles runs through *Underworld* from beginning to end, with one of the characters in the opening pages saying as he watches the game in the Polo Grounds, "This is the miracle year. Nobody has a vocabulary for what happened this year" (*U* 18). Or as another puts it, "What could not happen actually happened" (*U* 57–58). Though it may seem sacrilegious or quite simply banal, we must, I believe, consider taking such pronouncements seriously, for whenever the impossible happens, and even in the most seemingly secular of places, we are somewhere in the ballpark of a miracle. If there were, quite unexpectedly, some twenty thousand empty seats at the Polo Grounds that miraculous day in October 1951, it was perhaps because "people had a premonition that this game was related to something much bigger" (*U* 172), because there is an "underground," a "consciousness" of baseball (*U* 179) that links this national sport to a national spirit and perhaps a national religion. One might be tempted to hear nothing more than ironic detachment or postmodern cool in these references to faith and religion in *Underworld*—after all, revelations take place in the desert or on deserted islands, in the depths of some religious experience, and not during a ballgame at the Polo Grounds—but, again, I would not be so quick to write off the miraculous nature of these everyday things or to assume that a baseball diamond in New York City could not be the place of a revelation or a miraculous apparition.

As for the Final Judgment, it plays just as important a part as the miracle in DeLillo's epic novel, in this American Odyssey or Aeneid called *Underworld*. The prologue to the novel, entitled "The Triumph of Death," recounts the miraculous win by the New York Giants over the Brooklyn Dodgers from the home run of Bobby Thompson by cutting back and forth, in vintage DeLillo fashion, from the voice of Russ Hodges in the announcer's booth doing the play by play to the action on the field to the reactions of the spectators in the crowd, with each out, each pitch, being drawn out as in the game of baseball itself to heighten the narrative tension. From the game to the announcer to the crowd, that is, from the miracle on the field to its announcement and its reception, DeLillo jump cuts between these three moments or locations as if to demonstrate that the event itself really depends upon—or, really, *is*—all three at once. It is thus only in the crowd that the miraculous begins to merge with the apocalyptic, the announcement of the miracle with forebodings of imminent doom, the celebration on the baseball field with the fears of killing fields and mass destruction. For among those in the crowd watching the game are four celebrities, four almost mythic, iconic American figures, sitting together like the four horsemen of the apocalypse, four legendary personalities drinking beer, eating hot dogs, and yucking it up on an early autumn afternoon: the comedian Jackie Gleason, restaurateur Toots Shor, singer and actor Frank Sinatra, and, finally, FBI Director J. Edgar Hoover—four kings, we might say, the King of Clubs or King of Comedy (Gleason), the King of Diamonds (Shor), the King of Hearts (Sinatra), and, finally, the King of Spades or the King of Death (Hoover)—the one who will see death coming before anyone else, who will see in this miraculous event at the Polo Grounds the signs of the coming Apocalypse.[3] For just as Bobby Thompson is set to hit his game-winning home run, J. Edgar Hoover is informed by one of his G-men that FBI intelligence sources have learned that the Russians have detonated an atomic test bomb somewhere in the Soviet Union (*U* 23), a bomb with a radioactive core, as we will later learn, about the size of the baseball about to be hit into the stands by Thompson, a "five-ounce sphere of cork, rubber, yarn, horsehide and spiral stitching" (*U* 26, 176), a baseball, a simple baseball, that begins already to look a lot more ominous in the radioactive light of its plutonium double.

The miraculous event on the field, the singular stroke of Bobby Thompson's bat, is thus immediately divided in two—like an event in fission; it is immediately opposed to its other and confounded with it, immediately linked to an atomic blast in the Soviet Union that portends the apocalyptic underside or underworld of the Giants' victory. As the crowd celebrates the Giants' win by throwing everything they can get their hands on onto the field—ticket stubs, napkins, newspapers, torn magazines—a picture from a recent issue of *Life* magazine reproducing a sixteenth-century painting comes floating down from the upper deck and lands auspiciously in J. Edgar's hands. The painting is Pieter Bruegel's *Triumph of Death*, a gruesome scene of death and destruction that mesmerizes Hoover and introduces the apocalypse into the miracle celebration on the Polo Grounds (*U* 41, 50). When Thompson thus hits his "shot heard 'round the world," J. Edgar Hoover—and, by extension, the reader of DeLillo's novel—hears this shot in two different ways, as a phrase with two different origins, two different sources, to anticipate Derrida, one related to America's favorite pastime and one to the Soviet war machine, one to faith, we might say, and one to knowledge, one to life and one to death, one to a miracle made in America and one to the machine, it too American, that might well be the engine of the apocalypse. It is as if a single stroke, a single source, had spontaneously or automatically split in two, so that perhaps, just perhaps, a fuller understanding or appreciation of *Underworld* might not only benefit from but might actually require an analysis of the relationship between faith and knowledge at the core of an essay with the subtitle "The Two Sources of 'Religion' at the Limits of Reason Alone." It is as if, in short, this great novel by the

American DeLillo called for the supplement of a text by Derrida first written for a conference in Italy but then completed and signed in Southern California.[4]

Since DeLillo (to whom we will return throughout this work) sees in baseball a series of mystical trinities defining the game itself—three strikes, three outs, nine innings, nine players, and so on—and since, as he writes in *Underworld*, "the repeated three-beat has the force of some abject faith, a desperate kind of will toward magic and accident" (*U* 36), I have divided my reading of Derrida's "Faith and Knowledge," as I explained in the introduction, into three parts, each of these with three chapters, giving me nine different chances, nine new beginnings, nine shots at convincing you that this essay is indispensable to understanding today both Derrida and the relationship between religion and science, the miracle and the machine, though also between the ordinary and the extraordinary, the playful and the apocalyptic, a simple horsehide baseball and the plutonium core of a nuclear weapon.

The Island and the Starry Skies Above

Voir Capri et mourir.

—French proverb

This is what I want to show by deporting you as swiftly as possible to the limits of a basin, a sea, where there arrive for an interminable war the Greek, the Jew, the Arab, the Hispano-Moor. Which I am also (following), by the trace [*Que je suis aussi, à la trace*].

—*Glas* 37b

Context Event Signature

If "Faith and Knowledge" is Derrida's most direct and ambitious attempt to answer the question of the nature of religion in general and its relationship with science and the media, it is hardly the first text in which Derrida treats themes and topics related directly to religion or religious discourse. Already in 1974 in *Glas* the question of religion is front and center in Derrida's reading of Hegel's early writings on religion and Genet's novels and plays. One can then trace Derrida's continuing engagement with the question of religion in his many references to negative theology throughout the 1980s and 1990s, particularly in "How to Avoid Speaking: Denials" (1986) and "*Sauf le nom (Post-Scriptum)*" (1993), and in a series of works that take up religious texts or themes in order to rethink, for example, the question of translation in sacred texts (in "*Des tours de Babel*," first published in 1985), or else the questions of confession, faith, and mourning (in "Circumfession" in 1991 or in "*Sauf le nom [Post-Scriptum]*"), or the relationship between justice and divine violence (in "Force of Law" in 1990), or prayer (in "A Silkworm of One's Own" in 1996), or hospitality (in *Of Hospitality* in 1997 and *Acts of Religion* from 2002), or else forgiveness, the gift, apocalypse, or messianicity, in too many texts to mention.

In many of these texts, moreover, from "Circumfession" to "*Sauf le nom (Post-Scriptum)*" to *Memoirs of the Blind*, Derrida not only evokes religious themes but actually engages in or with religious genres of discourse, from apophatic discourse to confessional writing and conversion narrative.[1] We must thus resist the simple narrative according to which Derrida's work somehow took that now infamous "theological turn" in French phenomenology during the 1980s and 1990s, under the influence, so speculation often runs, of Emmanuel Levinas. Derrida was from the very beginning engaged by questions of religion, though always, as we shall see, in his own way, and he was writing on Levinas—and never without some degree of critique—as early as 1963.[2] "Faith and Knowledge" is thus hardly a radical turn in Derrida's earlier work, even though it addresses even more directly than these early works the question of religion in general and the unique forms it is taking today. Though I will try in the next couple of chapters to read the essay more or less on its own terms, beginning with its context, with the event for which it was prepared, and with its signature, we must constantly bear in mind these earlier texts in which Derrida approached similar questions and themes related to religion.

How, then, should one begin to read "Faith and Knowledge"? When French high school or university students are given a text to read and study, it is common for them to speak of trying to *décortiquer* it, that is, to translate this French verb in this context, to try to peel off its outside layers, to husk it, shell it, or debark it, so as to get inside, "dissect," and analyze it. If decortication—a word that exists in English as well as French—is not the same thing as deconstruction, it is often a very good place to begin, starting with a decortication of the décor or the setting.[3] To read a text of Derrida it is often necessary to begin by considering the context and the occasion for which it was written, the time and place it was first read or published, the anticipated audience, the expectations Derrida would have had of his audience, and the expectations he would have expected his audience to have of him. Since, as Derrida often remarked, almost all if not all his texts were *occasioned* or *occasional*, that is, since his texts were always responses to requests for a talk, paper, or publication, the context for these works inevitably becomes part of the works themselves, as if to mark the historical and contingent nature of all speech acts. "Each time I write a text," he says in a conversation with Maurizio Ferraris in May 1994—the very person, as we will later see, who organized the Capri conference—"it is 'on occasion,' occasional, for some occasion. I have never planned to write a text; everything I've done, even the most composite of my books, were 'occasioned' by a question. My concern with the date and the signature confirms it" (*TS* 62). This is particularly true of "Faith and Knowledge," an essay first conceived as an improvised talk on a subject Derrida himself had a hand in "determining," even if, as we will see in Chapter 4, he himself did not exactly "choose" it.

In a couple of early sections of "Faith and Knowledge," Derrida points to the context and pragmatic conditions of the essay, as if these programmed to some extent the content of the essay itself. I will thus spend the majority of this chapter looking at some of these circumstances or conditions, since they are absolutely critical, as we will see, to understanding the themes and claims of the essay. Before looking, then, in the following chapter, at the machinery of this text, at the way the various parts work together, I propose looking at the circumstances or conditions of time, place, setting, audience, subject, language, and, of course, source in Derrida's "Faith and Knowledge."

First, then, *time*. In §3, Derrida himself provides the date for the original meeting for which this text was written or first prepared. "Faith and Knowledge" began as an improvised discussion, Derrida tells us, that took place on 28 February 1994, a discussion that was subsequently written up and dated in the final paragraph of the text, a brief sequence in parentheses and italics that bears the date 26 April 1995. There are, then, notice, two dates, separated by about fourteen months, two origins, we might already speculate, of this text that will speak about the two origins or sources of religion.

As for the *place*, it too is doubled—at the very least—and Derrida explicitly marks this doubling as well. In addition to recalling in that final paragraph the date on which the essay was completed, Derrida marks the place, "Laguna"—that is, Laguna Beach in California, just a few miles south of Los Angeles.[4] But this is, of course, the second place-name of the text, the secondary source or origin, the second seaside setting. In §3, Derrida recalls that the setting for the original conversation about religion was the Italian island of Capri, just south of the bay of Naples. A place of isolation, contemplation, even revelation, in the West, the island is the place where religious communities throughout the world, and particularly in the Mediterranean, have traditionally retreated from the world as if into a kind of desert. Derrida thus compares the participants in the Capri conference to a group of monks or hermits, to *anchorites*, a word that comes from the Greek *anakhōreō*, meaning to "withdraw," "retire," or "seclude oneself."[5] "Faith and Knowledge" began, then, as a conversation among a few friends or colleagues who had secluded themselves on an island to talk about the nature of religion.

An island is thus surely not just any setting for a discussion about religion, and Capri is not just any island. A tourist destination during the spring and summer months, Capri would have been relatively deserted in February, making it an appropriate setting for the conference participants to seclude themselves so as to consider what Derrida will label this "abstraction" called "religion."[6] On this island or in this desert, they would withdraw from the world or withdraw from history in order to tell themselves, says Derrida, a story of the sort: " *'Once upon a time,' just once,* one day, *on an island or in the desert, imagine, in order to 'talk religion,' several* men, *philosophers, professors, hermeneuticians, hermits or anchorites, took the time to mimic a small, esoteric and egalitarian, friendly and fraternal community"* (§3).

Though isolated and cut off from the mainland, the desert island of Capri is nonetheless not too far from Rome, one of the four places, says Derrida in §5, in the holy quartet *Athens—Jerusalem—Rome—Byzantium,* names that right up to today evoke terrible wars of religion, in the question, for example, of the division and control of Jerusalem and its holy sites. But if Capri is not too far from Rome, it is even closer to Pompeii, which is in fact visible from the island, Pompeii being not only the site of the famous eruption of Mount Vesuvius in 79 A.D. but the setting for Wilhelm Jensen's novella *Gradiva,* which Freud will analyze in *Delusion and Dream* and which Derrida will allude to more than once in "Faith and Knowledge." We will return to this theme later, or rather, this theme will later return to us, it will resurface; for the moment, let us simply note that within eyeshot of Capri there is the scene of one of the most famous disasters in history—a truly apocalyptic event—and the setting of the story of the return of the dead, and particularly a dead woman, Gradiva, she of the "graceful walk."

Gathered on the island of Capri in February 1994, isolated in order to talk about this abstraction called "religion," the setting resembles, says Derrida, a sort of retreat, a place for religious exercises, a kind of monastery for a little religious community or, indeed, fraternal order that would exclude—and I think we are to hear in Derrida's comments that this was not his choice or decision—women. As Derrida will remark (in §5) as he gazes, we might imagine, around the conference table during their gathering: *"Not a single woman!"* to discuss a subject as important as religion, a subject that, obviously, not only concerns women but in many respects—and particularly with regard to the theme of respect—should place the question of women at its center.[7]

As for religious affiliation or the religious culture of the participants in the Capri conference, this too was rather limited or insular. Once again, Derrida seems to look around the conference table before commenting: *"We represent and speak four different languages, but our common 'culture,' let's be frank, is more manifestly Christian, barely even Judeo-Christian. No Muslim is among us, alas, even for this preliminary discussion"* (§5). Present at the gathering, at the retreat, were, therefore, only men, and, Derrida remarks, only European men—**"we Europeans"** (§§32–33), as Derrida will say, echoing Nietzsche's "we good Europeans" from *Beyond Good and Evil*—indeed only European men with a Judeo-Christian background, whether Jewish (Derrida), or Catholic (Gianni Vattimo), or Protestant (Hans-Georg Gadamer).[8] No women, therefore, and no Muslims or representatives of other cults in attendance to discuss a topic such as religion or the state of religion in 1994, no Muslims to speak of or to represent Islam, which is clearly not just one religion among others in the current debates about the fate or place of religion in the contemporary world. And so Derrida says they must speak *for* these silent witnesses without speaking in their place, speak for them without claiming to speak *as* them. Women, Islam, women in Islam—all these important figures and themes that had been excluded at Capri will return, as we will see, by the end of "Faith and Knowledge." They will return, both for Derrida and for us, from the underworld into which they might have seemed to be confined.

There are thus two times and two places, 26 April 1995 in California, an American place—as if the supplement of "deconstruction in America" were essential to thinking religion today—and 28 February 1994 on the island of Capri, a European, indeed an Italian place, where Italian would have been the language spoken around them, not just any language, to be sure, when it comes to religion. Another important condition or context for this more or less improvised discussion of religion was thus *language*, the fact that, as we saw Derrida affirm in the passage cited above, four languages were spoken in Capri, all of them European, namely, Italian, French, Spanish, and German.[9] In "Faith and Knowledge," Derrida will speak a great deal about language, and especially about the relationship between religion, the nation state, and language or the national idiom. As he will remark early on (in §4), these questions are unavoidable insofar as language or writing is the element of all revelation and belief and insofar as language or the idiom is always linked to a social, familial, or ethnic place—to a particular nation, people, or land. In thinking about religion, therefore, in *speaking* about religion, one must always ask about the relationship between the national idiom and all claims to autochthony, blood, earth, land, place, citizenship, the nation state, and so on, about the possibility of a sacred language related to a people if not a place—themes treated by Derrida in several texts from *"Des Tours de Babel"* to "The Eyes of Language," to name just two. It is, moreover, in "Faith and

Knowledge" that Derrida will introduce the neologism *mondialatinisation*, or globalatinization, to remind us that it was through Latin that the contemporary notion of religion was defined and disseminated, a thesis that will lead him to claim, as we will see more clearly in Chapters 2 and 5, that perhaps only Christianity merits being called a "religion."

If all these conditions or contexts for speaking about religion—time, place, setting, religious affiliation, and language—already from the outset exclude certain perspectives (women, Muslims, non-Europeans, non-European languages, and so on), they would at least seem to assure that their discussion can take place within a certain shared tradition or *"common 'culture'"* (§5), in short, a Judeo-Christian culture, and by means of what Derrida calls a certain *"pre-understanding"* of their subject matter (§3). Though they have as yet no assurance that they understand what religion is, what the name *religion* means—after all, that's what they have gathered to discuss—there is nonetheless a kind of faith, says Derrida, in what might be called a "preunderstanding" of what it means, a kind of minimal "trustworthiness" or "reliability," as he will call it, in this word *religion*. They don't know exactly what it means, but they would seem at least to share a kind of faith in what might be called the horizon of the question of religion: *"We believe we can pretend to believe—fiduciary act—that we share in some pre-understanding. We act as though we had some common sense of what 'religion' means through the languages that we believe (how much belief already, to this moment, to this very day!) we know how to speak"* (§3).

One can already hear hesitation if not skepticism in Derrida's language (we *believe* we can *pretend* to believe, we *act* as though . . .). Derrida thus goes on to link this belief to the kind of preunderstanding Heidegger speaks of in *Being and Time* with regard to our—or Dasein's—preunderstanding of Being: *"We believe in the minimal trustworthiness* [fiabilité minimale] *of this word. Like Heidegger, concerning what he calls the* Faktum *of the vocabulary of being (at the beginning of* Sein und Zeit*), we believe (or believe it is obligatory that) we pre-understand the meaning of this word, if only to be able to question and in order to interrogate ourselves on this subject"* (§3). But, Derrida continues, *"nothing is less pre-assured than such a Faktum (in both of these cases, precisely) and the entire question of religion comes down, perhaps, to this lack of assurance"* (§3). As we will see, it will be not so much hesitation, uncertainty, or skepticism but the very notion of faith itself that will puncture this supposed preunderstanding and call into question all assurances with regard to religion. Faith beyond assurance, beyond a common culture and beyond a shared horizon, will be what makes religion possible and impossible. Though an originary or elementary faith will be, as we will see, the very element of religion, it will be anything but a horizon or a shared preunderstanding.

These references to a shared horizon and preunderstanding recall yet another condition, another shared point of reference. Though the participants in the Capri conference speak four different languages, come from four different nation states, and have somewhat different religious backgrounds, all of them have been formed by European philosophy, and all of them have been attracted, says Derrida (in §10), by a certain *phenomenology*, that is, by a certain philosophy of *light* that took its inspiration from Husserl but that also ended up taking its distance from him. Moreover, all of them had been drawn at various moments in their intellectual itineraries toward a hermeneutics and exegesis of religious texts. Their common horizon is thus, among other things, the phenomenological notion of horizon, and their common preunderstanding that of a certain hermeneutic conception of preunderstanding.

Politically, says Derrida, the members of this little quasi-religious community or fraternity share a common rejection of the intervention of religion in the public sphere and all of them have "*an unreserved taste, if not an unconditional preference, for what, in politics, is called republican democracy as a universalizable model*" (§11). Hence all of them are interested in a kind of thinking that links philosophy to publicity and light, to a public space freed from external powers and, especially, from all religious authority. And yet, while all of them are against the imposition of religious dogma or doctrine upon the public realm, none of them can be considered sworn enemies of religion or preachers of secularism—a notion, as we will see in Chapter 6, that will elicit serious reservations on Derrida's part. Derrida thus recalls that, whatever their respective religious affiliations, none of them are "*priests bound by a ministry*" or "*theologians*" or "*qualified, competent representatives of religion*," and none of them are "*enemies of religion as such, in the sense that certain so-called Enlightenment philosophers are thought to have been*" (§11). While they would all like to see public space freed of religious dogma and authority, none of them would disavow faith entirely, and all of them, including Derrida, would staunchly defend religious freedom. Indeed just three weeks before the Capri meeting, that is, on 7 February 1994, Derrida spoke in Paris on the occasion of a public meeting organized by the International Committee in Support of Algerian Intellectuals in order to call for "the effective dissociation of the political and the theological" in Algeria as the best way of "protect[ing] the practices of faith and . . . the freedom of discussion and interpretation within each religion" (*AR* 306). Derrida thus called for the dissociation or separation of the theological and the political, in short, the separation of church and state, not in order to reject religion or religious faith or relegate it to the margins of the state but in order to guarantee the freedom of religious practice and expression *within* the state.

Thus far we have considered—and, notice, Derrida has himself explicitly marked—the time and setting of the meeting from which "Faith and Knowledge" arose, the language or languages in which the meeting was held, the gender, nationality, and the religious and philosophical backgrounds of the participants. Derrida draws our attention to these conditions and these contexts and points out the necessity of taking into account everything that contributed to making the Capri conference *"an effective and unique situation"* (§4). If Derrida is always interested, as I suggested in the introduction, in the mise-en-scène of a text, that is because he believes that a discourse must always be *situated* in order to be understood, its specific context clarified in order to understand its unique event. What Derrida thus demonstrates here, as he has done elsewhere, indeed everywhere, is the "the necessity of dating, that is, of signing a finite meeting in its time and in its space" (§36). In order to address the question of religion today, everything about the day must be taken into account:

> *Perhaps it would be necessary in addition to* situate *such arguments, limit them in time and space, speak of the place and the setting, the moment past,* one day, *date the fugitive and the ephemeral, singularize, act as though one were keeping a diary out of which one were going to tear a few pages. Law of the genre: the ephemeris (and already you are speaking inexhaustibly of the day). Date: 28 February 1994. Place: an island, the isle of Capri. A hotel, a table around which we speak among friends, almost without any order, without* agenda, *without order of the day, no watchword* [mot d'ordre] *save for a single word, the clearest and most obscure:* religion. (§3)

These are the most obvious and immediate internal conditions and contexts for the discussion of religion that forms the basis of Derrida's "Faith and Knowledge." There were also, however, countless external conditions for this meeting, just a couple of which should be mentioned here. In the political or geopolitical arena, relations in the Middle East between Israel and the Palestinians were tense and on the verge of breaking out into armed conflict, the phenomenon of Christian fundamentalism in America or Islamic extremism in the Middle East and elsewhere was being widely discussed, and the term *ethnic cleansing* had become a staple of the media to describe what was happening in the Yugoslav wars, with an emphasis on the violence—and often the sexual violence—

perpetrated against women.[10] Finally, as might be inferred by that February 1994 meeting of the International Committee in Support of Algerian Intellectuals, death threats were being issued against intellectuals by fundamentalist Islamic groups in Derrida's native Algeria and violence was threatening the fragile democratic institutions of that former French colony and, especially, the place or role of women in politics and Algerian society more generally. As we will see, all these things that form the backdrop or the larger context of "Faith and Knowledge" will inevitably make their appearance in one shape or another in the text—either on its surface or deep down within it, in its underworld.

As for the choice of the theme of religion, Derrida recalls that it was he himself, when asked by Maurizio Ferraris in the Hotel Lutétia in Paris, who came up automatically, mechanically, almost without reflection, with the topic. Derrida recounts their discussion this way:

> **In the beginning,** Maurizio Ferraris at the Hotel Lutétia. "I need," he tells me, "we need a theme for this meeting in Capri." In a whisper, yet without whispering, almost without hesitating, machinelike, I respond, "Religion." Why? From where did this come to me, and yes, mechanically? Once the theme was agreed upon, discussions were improvised—between two walks at night towards Faraglione, which can be seen in the distance, between Vesuvius and Capri. (Jensen refers to it, Faraglione, and Gradiva returns perhaps . . .) (§35)

This automatic or machinelike response gives us our first indication of what, for Derrida, will be at the origin of religion, namely, an automatic or machinelike splitting of every source in two, every single source into two sources, an origin, then, an origin of religion, that in its automatic duplicity will also be, as we will see, the common source of religion and science. We will have occasion to return repeatedly to these themes and, in Chapter 4, we will look in much greater detail at this scene from §35, where the genesis of the Capri meeting is recounted.

But, one might ask, why religion? One of the reasons for Derrida's quasi-automatic or mechanical response to the question of what they should discuss in Capri no doubt had to do with the fact that in the mid-1990s it was common to talk about a seemingly unexpected and spontaneous "return to religion" or a "return of the religious," a surprising resurgence or revival in religious interests, church attendance, and so on (see §6).[11] Derrida will, however, question throughout "Faith and Knowledge" whether such a so-called return to religion really is as surprising as so many commentators have thought and whether it really can be characterized as a *return*. He will question the assumption that religion is today or really ever has been on the one side while reason, the Enlightenment, science, and critique are on the other. In other words, he will argue that those who have assumed that secular society eschews religion and that science or technology simply excludes faith overlook or misread the fundamental relationship between science and religion or science and faith.

It was also no doubt in part because of the growing interest in the topic of religion that publishers agreed right from the start to publish in book form the texts of the Capri conference. This meant, of course, that yet further restrictions—yet another aspect of the context—would come to limit what could and could not be said, an "economy dictated by publishing exigencies" (§35). However improvised, speculative, or informal their initial discussion might have been, the participants of the Capri conference knew from the very start that their discussion was destined for an "*international publication*" that would be "*first of all 'Western,' and then confided, which is also to say confined, to several European languages . . .: German, Spanish, French, Italian*" (§4).[12] Nothing more ordinary, it might be said, for a group of internationally known philosophers to be "asked, in the collective name of several *European* publishers, to state a position in a few pages on religion," even if such a proposal, as Derrida says, might well "appear monstrous today, when a serious treatise on religion would demand the construction of new Libraries of France and of the universe" (§35).

"Faith and Knowledge" thus cannot be read without consideration of the discourse of the 1990s surrounding the so-called "return" to religion. One of the principal objectives of "Faith and Knowledge" will thus be, as we will see more clearly in Chapter 3, to show that we misunderstand the nature of this so-called return so long as we continue to think faith apart from knowledge, or religion apart from science. Derrida will argue throughout the essay that today's "return to religion" cannot simply be reduced to, and so written off as, "extremism," "fanaticism," or "fundamentalism." If certain forms of Christian fundamentalism or Islamic extremism occupy a privileged but hardly unique position in this so-called return to religion, we will have to ask about the precise relationship between such extremisms and the science they appropriate and manipulate in particularly sophisticated ways. It was no doubt in large part to explore this relationship between religion and science or faith and so-called secular society that Derrida suggested that the Capri conference address the question of religion and the putative "return to religion" in contemporary society.

In an interview conducted in 1999 and subsequently published in *Paper Machine*, Derrida does us the enormous favor of summarizing much of what he argues at length and more cryptically in "Faith and Knowledge" and, indeed, much of what he will develop in subsequent works such as *Rogues*. Asked by the interviewer, "What is your explanation for the return to religion that is occurring in so many parts of the world, but not in Europe?" Derrida responds: "In Europe too! Is it a return? Church attendance isn't the only way of measuring religion" (*PM* 116). This response is vintage Derrida. He begins by questioning first the fact assumed by the interviewer's question and then the principle or premise upon which the supposed fact relies.[13] Asked to explain the return to religion that was occurring in many parts of the world—the interviewer no doubt had in mind the Middle East and the United States—but not Europe, Derrida first suggests that the return is happening in Europe as well, "In Europe too!" he says, since one cannot simply measure such a return by citing church attendance figures. But Derrida then goes on to question whether this really is a *return*, as the interviewer seems to assume, and whether such a so-called return does not invite other kinds of interpretation. He continues:

> What gets called for short a "return," and is not confined to Islam, far from it, is marked above all by the appearance of "fundamentalisms" or "integration movements" that are aggressively "political." They seek either to contest the authority of the political or the state or else quite simply to subject democracy to theocracy. The thing needs to be analyzed in many dimensions. For instance, it would be difficult to explain the force of these movements if the concepts of the "political," the state, and sovereignty especially, weren't themselves concepts that are theological in origin. And hardly secularized at all. (*PM* 116)

Derrida here introduces a theme that is at the center of much of his work from at least the 1990s through 2004, and most prominently in works such as *Rogues*: the theological or ontotheological origins of political concepts such as sovereignty, and not only as it is embodied in monarchies but as it is identified with the nation or the people, notions that are often considered—and quite wrongly so, according to Derrida—to be completely secular. For Derrida, even our most seemingly secular notions of modernity, from the sovereignty of the people to religious tolerance to human rights and the institution of literature, contain an irreducible theologico-political remainder.[14] From this perspective, then, the *return* to religion is hardly a return at all, insofar as religion—in the form of theological concepts—continues to operate even in Western political concepts that are mistakenly understood to be purely secular. We will return to this argument in much greater detail in subsequent chapters.

After relating religion or the theological to the political, Derrida goes on in the interview to relate religion to science, a theme that is really at the center of "Faith and Knowledge": "On the other hand, contrary to what is often thought, these 'fundamentalisms' fit very well with the advances in technology and science. Iran is just one example. So it is a matter of actively opposing the modern technologies that result in delocalization, uprooting, and deterritorialization—and, simultaneously, of reappropriating them" (*PM* 116). Derrida here begins articulating the paradoxical—or, really, the autoimmune—relationship between religion and science or religion and technology (a distinction we will make in Chapter 3) that will be at the "epicenter" (an epicenter, we can already imagine, that is always in a state of dehiscence) of "Faith and Knowledge." If religion reacts against science and technology in order to return to what is assumed to be a prescientific, nontechnological order, it does so only by appropriating the very technology and science it eschews. I will treat this theme in much greater depth later, but by way of introduction let me simply read the rest of Derrida's response to the question of religion in the interview published in *Paper Machine*:

> The so-called return of religion tries to go back to the literality of idiom, the proximity of home, the nation, the earth, blood, filiation, and so on. In order to spirit away the threat, you therefore incorporate it in yourself, by appropriating technology, telecommunications, internet access, the effects of globalization, and so on. A process of self [or auto]-immunization. It destroys the organism that it thereby seeks to protect, and that is why, in the end, I do not believe in the future of these "fundamentalisms" as such, at any rate not in their political expression. But what is interesting to observe is this sometimes refined marriage of rationalism, even scientism, and obscurantism. But in the same way as I make a distinction between justice and law, I think you have to distinguish between faith and religion. (*PM* 116–17)

In this one tight little paragraph, Derrida introduces many of the themes we will encounter in "Faith and Knowledge": the relationship between religion and technology or religion and science, faith and knowledge, the questions of democracy, globalization, and autoimmunity, and, finally, a crucial distinction between religion and faith, which might be thought, Derrida suggests in a quasi-analogy, along the lines of the difference developed in "Force of Law" and elsewhere between the law and justice. According to this analogy—which we will pursue in more detail in Chapter 6—faith has to be thought in relation to religion or in relation to determinate religious beliefs in the same way that justice has to be thought in relation to law. Hence Derrida will argue that "*faith has not always been and will not always be identifiable with religion, nor . . . with theology*" (§13). If the theme of faith will have thus been of interest to Derrida from the very beginning, it will have never been reducible to religion. To understand Derrida's skepticism with regard to the so-called return *to* religion or return *of* religion in 1990s, we will have to bear this crucial distinction in mind.

Now, if religion was undergoing in the 1990s something like a resurgence or a reemergence on the public stage but not exactly a "return," "Faith and Knowledge" and other texts written around the same time would seem to represent a similar resurgence—though, again, not exactly a "return"—in the "life" of Jacques Derrida. This will be the last of the conditions or contexts we will look at here, the place of religion not in Derrida's work but in his life, and particularly his childhood, Derrida's own "acts of religion," to borrow the title of an anthology edited by Gil Anidjar that brings together many of Derrida's most important writings on religion, including "Faith and Knowledge."[15] Though I cannot treat the topic in any detail here, a few words seem necessary to put the discussion of religion in "Faith and Knowledge" into the context of the author's early relationship to religion, just a few things about Derrida's own background, and particularly his "religious background," to help situate our reading.[16]

While it would be imprudent to want to explain Derrida's longstanding interest in margins, borders, borderlines and, here, *limits* solely in terms of his unique personal history, it would be just as imprudent to claim that this history played no role in the formation of this interest. For in terms of nationality or national affiliation, language and ethnic identity, and, of course, religion, Derrida's position was in each case marginal to the dominant culture in which he lived. Born on 15 July 1930 in El-Biar, a suburb of Algiers, in what was then the French colony of Algeria, Derrida grew up, one might say, in the margins of France, in France but not exactly, a French citizen but not like the others. Growing up in a French-speaking family in a predominantly Arabic-speaking neighborhood, Derrida would thus have cultivated from within this marginal place of a French colony the language of France, the colonizer, but he would have been at the same time more or less isolated from the language spoken around him. From this marginal position Derrida would develop a desire to master this French language or, better, a desire to cultivate and adore it, to speak it better and respect it more than those born in metropolitan France.[17]

Born into a Jewish family living in a mostly Muslim community within the colony of a predominantly Catholic nation, he would have experienced firsthand not just the discomfort of being in the minority but the pains of exclusion, marginalization, even persecution. Derrida recalls in several places, including *Monolingualism of the Other; or, The Prosthesis of Origin*, being subject to individual acts of anti-Semitism as well as to institutional and governmental anti-Semitism in 1942, when he was prohibited by the French authorities from attending public schools and his French citizenship, which had been granted to the Jews of Algeria by the Crémieux decree of 1870, was revoked. Though his citizenship would eventually be reinstated, Derrida says he experienced this event as nothing less than "a fracture or a trauma" (*TS* 37), an event, as he put it in 2000, that "no doubt killed in me an elementary confidence in any community, in any fusional gregariousness" and that "cautioned me against community and communitarianism in general" ("AO" 15). In the face of this "fracture" or this "trauma," Derrida did not seek to identify with or seek refuge in the Jewish community or his own Jewish identity. He began instead to view with suspicion any kind of community bond, especially one that would be based on religion. In an interview from January 1994, just weeks before the Capri conference, he says: "My spontaneous or infantile reaction to anti-Semitic violence consisted in saying 'no, I am part neither of this nor of that,' neither of this anti-Semitism nor of its victims—a haughty and affected gesture, without sympathy for the self-protecting attitude of the Jewish community, which tended to close ranks when endangered" (*TS* 39).

If Derrida's attitude toward this violence would become less spontaneous and infantile over the years and would in fact play a large role in his seminars of the 1980s that went under the title "Philosophical Nationality and Nationalism," he would continue to resist identifying in full with any particular group. Though he would leave Algeria for France in 1949 and would not return for any extended period of time apart from his years of military service from 1957 to 1959, it is hard not to think that these early years of living in a Jewish family within a largely Muslim community and speaking French in a predominantly Arabic-speaking culture did not leave traces in the life—and thus the work—of Derrida. If, as Gil Anidjar argues in his excellent introduction to *Acts of Religion*, Derrida would live most of his life in Judeo-Christian France, if he would refer to himself as "the last of the Jews," he would also describe himself as "a little black and very Arab Jew" or, elsewhere, as "a *kind* of African" (cited in *AR* 33; see also *MO* 14).[18] Arab, Jewish, Judeo-Christian, African, Maghrebin, Franco-Maghrebin . . . Jacques Derrida was all of these and yet none of them completely, just as, in *The Other Heading*, he would say that he was European without being "European *in every part*, that is, European through and through" (*OH* 82).

In terms of religion, then, Derrida grew up Jewish in a predominantly Muslim colony of France, and he lived almost all of his adult life in the Christian, indeed, Catholic country of France. But in addition to inheriting, as we will see in the chapters that follow, various aspects of all three of these Abrahamic religions, Derrida also—or nonetheless—cultivated a certain atheism by means of or even through the various communities of which he both was and was not a part. As he writes to Catherine Malabou in *Counterpath*, "My atheism develops in the churches, all the churches" (*CP* 95).[19] It is this belonging without belonging, or this atheism within religious tradition, that makes deconstruction in general and Derrida's work in particular resemble, as we will explore in Chapter 6, a certain "negative theology."[20]

With regard to citizenship, Derrida would thus be French and yet not quite French, French but because Jewish not French for a time, French but because Algerian never really French enough. In terms of language, he would speak French both at home and at school, putting him at a remove from "the language of the neighborhood," which was Arabic, as well as from the language of the synagogue, of which he would admit to having only a passing knowledge.[21] About Arabic, which was spoken around him but which he never really learned to speak, especially since it was offered in school in Algeria only as "an optional foreign language," Derrida says in a public discussion about a year and a half before his death, "sometimes I wonder whether this language, unknown for me, is not my favorite language" (*IW* 33–34).

With regard to culture, Derrida's schooling would have focused essentially on the history and culture of France—and not Algeria.[22] All eyes would have thus been oriented from the start toward France—the *métropole*—and particularly Paris, the capital of the colonial power and the place from which the culture most valued would have emanated.[23] As Derrida would say in *The Monolingualism of the Other* and perhaps even more poignantly in a public conversation with the Algerian intellectual Mustapha Chérif in the spring of 2003, the community to which he belonged was so isolated in terms of language, culture, history, religion, and so on that he would come to question throughout his work the very nature of community and the very notion of "belonging":

> The community to which I belonged was cut off in three ways: it was cut off first both from the Arab and the Berber, actually the Maghrebin language and culture; it was also cut off from the French, indeed European, language and culture, which were viewed as distant poles, unrelated to its history; and finally, or to begin with, it was cut off from the Jewish memory, from that history and that language that one must assume to be one's own, but which at a given moment no longer were—at least in a special way, for most of its members in a sufficiently living and internal way. (*IW* 34–35)

Much more could obviously be said here about the "influence" of this rather unique historical, cultural, and linguistic background on the thought of Jacques Derrida, and particularly with regard to religion. It would be very unwise, as I said, to reduce everything here to biography, but it is hard to deny that Derrida's interest in margins and limits, in a certain "outside" or "elsewhere," his suspicion of all communities based on race, territory, language, culture, or religion, can be traced back to some extent—even if this alone will not get us very far—to these early years in Algeria where Derrida occupied an ambiguous and marginal place with regard to all these categories.[24] As Hélène Cixous has written somewhere, "There is only one Jacques Derrida. He's a thousand different things." Or as Derrida says of himself in *The Post Card*, in a memorable phrase that my friend and colleague David Farrell Krell adopted as the title of an important work on Derrida, he was "the purest of bastards" (see *PC* 84).[25]

Much more could also obviously be said about Derrida's education and upbringing in Algeria, as well as his attachment to the Jewish religion, everything from his refusal to circumcise his two sons to his calling himself a Marrano. Let me simply conclude these very brief remarks by citing Derrida again from his conversation with Mustapha Chérif in the spring of 2003. The conversation took place, Chérif informs us in the introduction to the book in which these remarks are published, just hours after Derrida had received confirmation of the diagnosis of the pancreatic cancer that would lead to his death less than a year and a half later, on 9 October 2004. Speaking in Paris at the Institute of the Arab World, at a conference of French and Algerian intellectuals organized by Chérif under the title "The Future of Civilizations," Derrida begins: "I want to speak here, today, as an Algerian, as an Algerian who became French at a given moment, lost his French citizenship, then recovered it. Of all the cultural wealth I have received, that I have inherited, my Algerian culture has sustained me the most" (*IW* 30). For someone who would go on to spend fifty years of his life writing and teaching a decidedly *European* philosophical tradition, this is perhaps a rather surprising admission. He continues:

> The cultural heritage I received from Algeria is something that probably inspired my philosophical work. All the work I have pursued, with regard to European, Western, so-called Greco-European philosophical thought, the questions I have been led to ask from some distance, a certain exteriority, would certainly not have been possible if, in my personal history, I had not been a sort of child in the margins of Europe, a child of the Mediterranean, who was not simply French nor simply African, and who had passed his time traveling between one culture and the other. . . . Everything that has interested me for a long time, regarding writing, the trace, the deconstruction of Western metaphysics . . . all of that had to have come out of a reference to an *elsewhere* whose place and language were unknown or forbidden to me. (*IW* 31–32; my emphasis)

I would like to think that Derrida's attention to this *elsewhere*, his allergy to community, had something to do with his interest in a kind of originary or elementary faith that would be at the source of but also in excess of all dogmatic or revealed religions, an elementary faith that would be at the origin of every social bond but could never be reduced to any particular community or communitarian vision.

When reading "Faith and Knowledge" we must not lose sight of these "autobiographical" details, not only because they form the background or context for Derrida's discussion of religion but because they are commented on in several places in Derrida's own work. Indeed few philosophers have integrated autobiographical elements into their philosophical works to the extent Derrida has, from "Circumfession," where Derrida combines a reading of the *Confessions* of Augustine (who was also born, of course, in northern Africa) with reflections concerning his mother's own impending death, to *Memoirs of the Blind, Monolingualism of the Other,* and, of course, *The Post Card*.[26] In an interview from January 1994, just weeks before the Capri conference, Derrida says that "in literature what always interests me is essentially the autobiographical—not what is called the 'autobiographical genre,' but rather the autobiographicity that greatly overflows the 'genre' of autobiography." He then goes on to speak of the place of autobiography in philosophy, of "the wild desire to preserve everything, to gather everything together in its idiom. To gather together even that which disseminates and, by its very essence, defies all gathering."

"Philosophy, or academic philosophy at any rate," he goes on to say, "for me has always been at the service of this autobiographical design of memory" (*TS* 41).[27] We will want to recall this emphasis on the autobiographical as we begin reading "Faith and Knowledge" in light of the circumstances for and in which it was written and as we try to interpret, much later, what looks like an autobiographical detail—the memory of an opened pomegranate at the end of the next to the last of the fifty-two numbered sections of the essay.

2

Duplicity, Definition, Deracination

All of the conditions we have looked at thus far form the context for Derrida's choice of theme and for his treatment of it in "Faith and Knowledge." These conditions must be constantly borne in mind as we see how Derrida on *this* day, in *this* place, with *this* background, for *this* audience, and in *his* language, approaches the question of religion. If an analysis of such conditions is always essential, as I argued earlier, to understanding the form of Derrida's arguments, it is even more so for "Faith and Knowledge," insofar as Derrida will not simply refer to or take account of these conditioning factors in his approach to the subject but will transform each one of them into a theme within his text: hence the place, the island as a place of desertion and abandonment, will become a thinking of the space of revelation, of *khōra*, and so on; the time will become a thinking of history and the historicity of religion, a thinking of the state of religion today; the languages spoken at the conference will become a thinking of the Latin origins of our discourse on religion; the absence of women will become a discreet though unmistakable inscription of women's voices throughout the essay; and the absence of Muslims will become a series of reminders about the role Islam must play in any serious thinking about religion today.

After having laid out some of the conditions, both internal and external, personal and political, national and international, for "Faith and Knowledge," we should be better prepared to enter even further into the core, so to speak, of this essay, even if, as I have already suggested, this core is always in a constant state of fission. If "Faith and Knowledge" was originally presented orally and in an improvised fashion on the island of Capri in February 1994, we must now consider the fact that what we now have before us is a written text. Let us begin again, then, by reading this text, beginning with its title—or its titles—but then also by looking at its form and its fonts, its numbers and numerology, all of which, we might already suspect, will say something essential about the fundamental duplicity at the heart of the relationship between religion and science.

The principal title, "Faith and Knowledge"—"Foi et Savoir"—brings together two nouns, or, in French, a noun and a substantivized verb, into what appears to be a fairly straightforward conjunction. But this conjunction already suggests a kind of originary duplicity or conflict, perhaps even an antinomy, between what are commonly believed to be two very different and perhaps even irreconcilable realms or domains: faith or religion, on the one hand, everything that would come before or after reason; and knowledge, science, and the reason or rationality on which these are founded, on the other. But talk about duplicity—Derrida's title is not simply a play on but more or less a repetition of Hegel's *Glauben und Wissen*, from 1802–3, a work Derrida refers to briefly (in §18) under its French title *Foi et Savoir* and whose final paragraph he more or less paraphrases, having cited it in its entirety some twenty years earlier in *Glas*. This is the famous passage, which I will look at in more detail in Observation 2, in which Hegel speaks of the death of God and of the need to reestablish "for philosophy the Idea of absolute freedom and along with it the absolute Passion, the speculative Good Friday in place of the historic Good Friday."[1] If the title of the essay already evokes Hegel, and thus Derrida's reading of Hegel in the left-hand column of *Glas*, it may not be insignificant that the essay concludes some seventy-eight pages later with a reference to Jean Genet, the central figure of the right-hand column. It is as if "Faith and Knowledge" were at once a nod toward that monumental work of 1974 and a development or displacement of it, a development in the direction of not only Hegel but Kant and Bergson, and a displacement into concerns of Genet that emerged well after the appearance of *Glas*.

Derrida's title is thus not simply a play on Hegel's but a repetition of it or, more pointedly, a rip-off or plagiarism of it; as one says in French, it is a title that has been—and we will look at this term in more detail in Chapter 4—*soufflé*, that is, whispered to him from a distance but also lifted, stolen. And yet Derrida's essay has in fact not just one title but two, one that just conjoins two words, "Faith and Knowledge," and then another, a subtitle, that speaks of two sources, "The Two Sources of 'Religion' at the Limits of Reason Alone." But this subtitle is itself little more than a condensation or elision of the titles of two classic works on religion, Kant's 1793 *Religion Within the Limits of Reason Alone* and Henri Bergson's 1932 *The Two Sources of Morality and Religion* (§36).[2] Hence Derrida's title, like the layout of his text itself, as we will see shortly, is double, and the second of the titles, the subtitle, is itself doubled, as if Derrida were crossing these two canonical secondary sources on the nature of religion in order to say something different about the nature of religion today. Though "Faith and Knowledge" is not anything like a reading of Kant or Bergson (as *Speech and Phenomena*, for example, is a reading of Husserl, or "Plato's Pharmacy" is a reading of Plato), any truly responsible reading of Derrida's essay must take these two canonical works into account, since they provide the terms and premises of Derrida's discussion.[3]

But here is already a first hint of how to understand deconstruction, as opposed to other kinds of textual analysis, such as the one I referred to earlier as decortication. While a good deconstructive reading will always want to determine first what Bergson or Kant or Heidegger meant to say about a particular topic, what they themselves would have said they meant, that is, what they themselves wished to bring to light or reveal about the topic of, say, religion, Derrida will want to ask about the nocturnal source of this revelation or this critical light, the source of this Enlightenment impulse to bring the source of religion to light. Deconstruction will thus attempt to "bring to light" or "develop" what Derrida will risk calling here the "negative" of the text or of what is brought to light in the text, something that might be *like* the unconscious, or *like* some kind of latent meaning below the manifest or phenomenal meaning of the text—analogies that must be treated with some caution but that will perhaps prove useful later on in our analysis when themes from the underworld well up to visit us from some invisible or unconscious source. To approach the question of religion, then, Derrida begins with traditional philosophical approaches to the topic of religion (Kant, Hegel, Bergson, and, as we will see, Heidegger) in order to uncover not simply some hidden assumption or presupposition but the source—the nocturnal source—of their reflections on religion, a source that, as we will see, could go by many names, since it has no proper name: one could call it an elementary faith that would itself be blind, a source of revelation or light that would itself be nocturnal, or *khōra* as that which gives rise to everything that might appear in the light.

There are thus two titles, identifying two sources, Kant and Bergson, each of whom will identify or isolate two realms for religion: for Kant, dogmatic religion that goes beyond the limits of reason alone and true religion or true morality that stays within those limits; and, for Bergson, a closed morality and static religion, on the one hand, and an open morality and dynamic religion, on the other. In order to think not just the essence of religion as such but, more importantly, what is happening to religion today, Derrida seems to be suggesting that we return to Kant's great book about, among other things, "radical evil," and to a book by Bergson—this "great Judeo-Christian," as Derrida calls him—who wrote about religion after the First World War and on the eve of the Second World War and thus on the eve of events that, as Derrida puts it, "one knows that one does not yet know how to think" (§36). Derrida does not name those events in this passage, but it is not difficult to imagine what he has in mind: the horrors of the Holocaust, first and foremost, though perhaps also advances in weapons technology that would lead to the development of the atomic bomb and, eventually, the Cold War, events that still haunt us today and perhaps portend the unimaginable in the form of a truly global apocalypse.

As for the form of the text, "Faith and Knowledge" is divided into fifty-two numbered sequences or sections, which vary in length from just a few lines to a few pages. In the second of these sections, Derrida makes clear that this numbering bears some relation to what he will hypothesize to be an ineluctable relationship between religion and science, and thus between religion and the question of calculation, technology, and the machine. Hence Derrida—already crossing the idioms of Bergson (who famously concludes *The Two Sources* with a reference to the universe as "a machine for the making of gods") and Kant (who wishes to think religion within the "limits" of reason alone)—speaks of his own essay as a little "*discursive machine*" (§§ 2, 33), whose task is to say something about religion today "*within the limits assigned us*" (§2).[4]

In addition to this reference to the machine, which reflects the elliptical, telegraphic, and calculated nature of this essay and is indicative of the way religion is today being transformed by technology, Derrida's use of the term *limits* is telling. By analyzing the contexts and conditions with which Derrida had to work in "Faith and Knowledge," I have in effect been looking at the limits Derrida found imposed upon him or that he imposed upon himself. In addition to asking, then, what it means for Kant to want to think religion "within the *limits* of reason alone," Derrida asks what such a Kantian project might mean for us today, especially when, as we will see, Derrida will want to think reason in relation to faith.

In addition, then, to the numerous references to limits in the passages explicitly treating Kant (§§11–12, 14–16, 36, 41), there are, first, the limits of time, space, and format for treating such a serious question as religion within a certain number of pages, the necessity of producing on the topic of religion *"a short treatise"* (§2) within *"the merciless limits of time and space* (§4; see §§3, 9, and 33).[5] These limits of time and space are not just the Kantian conditions of experience but a matter of "economy," the necessity of treating the question of religion "in a limited number of words" because of the constraints of time, space, and, yes, publishers (§35).

As for the exact nature of these limits, Derrida tells us much later when he recounts the genesis of the conference and thus the genesis of "Faith and Knowledge" that it had been agreed that everyone at the conference would contribute an essay of about twenty-five pages, a "page limit" that would inform the very layout of Derrida's essay and inspire him to select

> a quasi-aphoristic form as one chooses a machine, the least perni-cious machine to treat of *religion* in a certain number of pages: 25 or a few more, we were given; and, let us say, arbitrarily, to de-cipher or anagrammatize the 25, 52 very unequal sequences, as many *crypts* dispersed in a non-identified field, a field that is nonetheless already approaching, like a desert about which one isn't sure if it is sterile or not, or like a field of ruins and of mines and of wells and of caves and of cenotaphs and of scattered seedings. (§35)[6]

Faced with a limited number of pages, with limited ink for a theme as large and important as religion, Derrida will mark the necessarily incomplete and elliptical nature of his contribution by writing not a complete or completed essay but, simply, a series of fifty-two aphorisms, sequences, or crypts, or else, as we will see, fifty-two pomegranate seeds or pieces of shrapnel, depending upon whether you choose your metaphor from nature or culture, from a cult of life or the cultivation of death.

But if this explains why Derrida writes in aphorisms or abbreviated sections, what justifies numbering them in this way? First, because the question of numbers and of calculation, of the calculable and the incalculable, will return throughout this essay as it explores the relationship between faith or a certain incalculability and a knowledge that makes possible various forms of calculation. This numbering of paragraphs or sections is also, of course, reminiscent of the papal encyclical, a form of religious or Catholic publication that Derrida himself explicitly evokes in "Faith and Knowledge" (Derrida speaks in §27n17 of *Evangelium vitae*)—an essay, let me again recall, that was first presented in a conference not far from Rome. Even the title "Faith and Knowledge" sounds a bit like the title of a papal encyclical, and, in fact, in 1998, just a couple of years after the French publication of Derrida's essay, Pope John Paul II would issue an encyclical entitled, precisely, "Fides et ratio"—"Faith and Reason." If the publication of an encyclical by this name is, to be sure, little more than a happy coincidence, the encyclical laments—without ever mentioning, of course, Derrida—the advent of "postmodernity" and "nihilism" in philosophy, things often (though wrongly) associated with Derrida and deconstruction. Moreover, the thesis of the encyclical is, not completely unlike that of "Faith and Knowledge," that faith and reason must be thought together and reason must rediscover its foundation in faith. Though the understanding of faith and reason—not to mention foundation—will be quite different in these two texts, there is, it could be shown, more than a superficial similarity between them.[7]

Now, I say that this encyclical does not "of course" mention Derrida, but it is perhaps worth noting that in 2004 the eventual successor to John Paul II, Pope Benedict XVI, then Cardinal Ratzinger, actually did mention Derrida by name in a not unrelated way in a German newspaper article entitled "In Search of Freedom: Against Reason Fallen Ill and Religion Abused," in which he argued that, in a world where reason has become detached from God, that is, in a word, where reason has become divorced from faith, "all that remains is reason's dissolution, its deconstruction, as, for example, Jacques Derrida has set it out for us."[8] Ratzinger thus attributes to Derrida a distinction between faith and reason or faith and knowledge that Derrida himself will spend a good bit of "Faith and Knowledge" trying to question. Derrida and Ratzinger will have very different conceptions of both faith and reason and of the relationship between them, but Derrida surely will not want, as Ratzinger suggests, to divorce faith from reason, indeed quite the opposite, and his deconstruction of a certain kind of reason (the Greek *logos*, for example, which Ratzinger goes on in the article to discuss) is not at all aimed at "reason's dissolution."

Like a papal encyclical, then, first written on retreat on the Italian island of Capri, "Faith and Knowledge" is broken up into fifty-two numbered sections. But why fifty-two? There are no doubt several reasons for this choice, fifty-two being, of course, a number of chance as the number of cards in a deck,[9] as well as a number of nature or necessity as the number of weeks in a year,[10] each week made up of 5 + 2 or 7 days—7 being yet another number that is dear to J-a-c-q-u-e-s D-e-r-r-i-d-a (two names with seven letters), that is, dear to someone who will have received yet another name, a secret name, on the seventh day of his life during the ceremony of circumcision.[11] "Faith and Knowledge" will not have been the first time, moreover, that Derrida used the number fifty-two, or divided a work into fifty-two numbered parts. Seven years before "Faith and Knowledge," in 1987, Derrida published a short text on architecture entitled "Fifty-two Aphorisms for a Foreword," a text that begins: "1. The aphorism decides, but as much by its substance as by its form, it determines by a play of words" (*PSY 2*, 117).

But the number fifty-two is most reminiscent in Derrida's work of the blank spaces of *The Post Card*, blank spaces—each time exactly fifty-two—that are like the very respiration of the text, the attention or breath of a prayer, or, as he says in the preface to *The Post Card*, the trace of an incineration, something (whether a proper name or just a letter or punctuation mark) that has been left out of the text and risks being forgotten, perhaps even by its author.

> Whatever their original length, the passages that have disappeared are indicated, at the very place of their incineration, by a blank of 52 signs   and a contract insists that this stretch of destroyed surface remain forever indeterminable. . . . As for the 52 signs, the 52 mute spaces, in question is a cipher that I had wanted to be symbolic and secret—in a word a clever cryptogram, that is, a very naïve one, that had cost me long calculations. If I state now, and this is the truth, I swear, that I have totally forgotten the rule as well as the elements of such a calculation, as if I had thrown them into the fire, I know in advance all the types of reaction that this will not fail to induce all around. (*PC* 4–5)[12]

In addition to the fifty-two numbered sections, there is a particularly baroque typographical structure that involves not only a couple of internal divisions within the fifty-two sections but certain passages in italics and words in bold. The fifty-two sections are thus divided evenly into two sets of twenty-six, two times, then, the number of letters in the French or English alphabet, with the first set not only printed in italics but actually entitled (though the title is not in italics) "Italics," that is, named after a style of script first used in the Aldine press edition of Virgil published in Venice in 1501 and dedicated to Italy.[13] These italics might thus, writes Derrida, "*potentially symboliz[e] everything that can incline—at a certain remove from the Roman in general*" (§5), everything that, from another source, another font, would introduce a certain difference or distance from Rome or from Latin.

Hence there are two times of writing—at least two[14]—and at least two different kinds of "writing," one spoken and one written. The first twenty-six sections would correspond, it seems, to Derrida's *spoken* remarks at Capri: *"At the beginning of a preliminary exchange, around the table, Gianni Vattimo proposes that I improvise a few suggestions"*: these first twenty-six sections would thus be *"a sort of schematic and telegraphic preface"* that summarizes the improvised words presented by Derrida at Capri (§4). The second twenty-six sections, which run more than twice as long as the first twenty-six, would correspond to Derrida's written reflections after the conference. Derrida says—writes: *"Other propositions, doubtless, emerged in a text of different character that I wrote afterwards, cramped by the merciless limits of time and space. An utterly different story, perhaps, but, from near or afar, the memory of words risked in the beginning, that day, will continue to dictate what I write"* (§4). "Written after" the Capri conference and added on ex post facto to the earlier italic script, this second set of twenty-six sections is appropriately entitled "Post-scriptum."[15] "Faith and Knowledge" would thus be an essay made up of *"a sort of . . . preface"* and a "Post-scriptum," with nothing else, nothing "proper" to the essay, between them.

As if this division or duplicity were not enough, the twenty-six sections of the "Post-Scriptum" are themselves divided into one group of eleven sections labeled "Crypts . . ." and a group of fifteen that are entitled or are at least preceded by the title—let me leave it in French for the moment—". . . et grenades," the ellipsis here suggesting that it is the second half of the fragmented title "Crypts . . . et grenades." There are thus two sets of twenty-six sections, distinguished by two different typescripts, italics and, let's say for the sake of argument, Times New Roman, two different type faces, two different, as we say, *fonts* (a word that means, of course, sources), and then a further division within the second set, which is divided not down the middle into two sets of thirteen but—and this could hardly be random—into eleven and fifteen.

As if this duplicity were not enough, Derrida introduces in §27, in the first of the nonitalicized sections in his long "Post-scriptum," that is, in the first of the eleven "crypts," yet another graphic peculiarity. Beginning in this section, Derrida puts two different words or phrases in bold in each section, the first of these being a repetition of the second word or phrase in bold in the preceding section and the second becoming the word or phrase that will be repeated in bold in the subsequent section. We thus get a kind of braiding or interweaving of words and phrases, a kind of textual DNA that adds yet another level of complexity to this already dizzying proliferation of divisions and doublings, beginning with the one named in the subtitle "the two sources of religion."

Now, all these divisions (into fifty-two sections, into two sets of twenty-six, into eleven and fifteen) are not arbitrarily or randomly inserted interruptions of what would otherwise be a continuous or uninterrupted argument. The sections are, as Derrida puts it, aphoristic and much more "improvised" than this, with themes being introduced early on and then returned to later in the essay, broken off and then picked up again later, a bit like the textual braiding we just recalled. Rather than developing in a logical and linear manner from beginning to end, Derrida's argument is instead distributed or indeed scattered throughout— like a good game of fifty-two-card pickup, perhaps, where the cards have been gathered together in a particular order but where other groupings or configurations are not only possible but necessary. Despite this constant doubling back on themes and motif, there is nevertheless, as I have suggested, a kind of movement or progression to the essay. We see this most clearly in the opening sections of the "Italics" and the "Post-scriptum," where Derrida is anticipating or adumbrating in a kind of summary or abstract the themes and theses to follow.

Let us begin again, then, by looking at the way Derrida begins, that is, at the first two, relatively brief sections of the essay. In these sections Derrida introduces a whole series of themes that will cross and mingle throughout the essay, and he adumbrates in an economical and allusive way the three theses that run through the essay. Here is the first paragraph of the first section:

> How 'to talk religion'? Of religion? Singularly of religion, today? How dare we speak of it in the singular without fear and trembling, this very day? And so briefly and so quickly? Who would be so imprudent as to claim that the issue here is both identifiable and new? Who would be so presumptuous as to rely on a few aphorisms? To give oneself the necessary courage, arrogance or serenity, therefore, perhaps one must pretend for an instant to abstract, to abstract from everything or almost everything, in a certain way. Perhaps one must take one's chances in resorting to the most concrete and most accessible, but also the most barren and desert-like, of all abstractions. (§1)

Derrida thus begins by evoking the difficulty of speaking of religion today, of talking of religion, or, really, for here's the problem, of "talking religion"—as if religion were the direct object of the talking or, better, the form or manner of the talking itself. The question is thus not only how to talk of religion without generalization or perhaps even profanation but how not to talk religion when the language we use is perhaps already and from the very beginning a language *of* religion, that is, as we will see more clearly later, a Latin language that will have informed so many of our words and our concepts, beginning with the word or concept *religion* itself. To ask the question of what religion *is* by using the term *religion* is thus perhaps already to have provided a kind of response.

Derrida goes on to ask how we can talk of religion in the singular—that is, religion as a whole, religion as one monolithic entity, monolithic and no doubt monotheistic, as if there were no essential differences between the three great monotheisms of the West, not to mention the other "religions" of the world. Expressing what has to be a genuine respect or reticence before such a subject, a fear and trembling before it, says Derrida, citing Philippians 2:12 but also already evoking Kierkegaard,[16] he introduces the notion of abstraction, which can be understood here in a couple of different ways. Derrida is first asking whether we must abstract from or bracket everything else in order to consider religion alone and by itself, religion apart from everything else, and perhaps first and foremost from reason or from science. But Derrida is also asking whether it is possible to discover a single essence of religion by abstracting from the multiplicity of religions, by abstracting or distilling the element that is common to all religions. Both senses of abstraction already beg the question of what religion *is*, however, and already assume to some degree what they are looking for—a notion of religion that, it is assumed, can be abstracted or separated from what is assumed to be foreign to it, a common essence of "religion" that all religions would share even when, as we will see, the essence is perhaps defined by one religion and one alone.

The first thing to note, then, is that Derrida appears to be approaching the question of religion as a philosopher or at least from the perspective of philosophy. He begins in a sense by reminding us not only, as we will see shortly, of the Hegelian notion of abstraction but of the very origins of philosophy itself in the Platonic *ti esti* or "What is?" question, which is called in *Of Grammatology* the "instituting question of philosophy" (*OG* 19). While Plato thus asks "What is justice?" in the *Republic* or "What is piety (or holiness)?" in the *Euthyphro*, Derrida would in essence be asking "What is religion?" which is to say, religion in general, religion in the abstract, religion as a concept, idea, essence, or form abstracted from all particular or determined religions. What is it, he might seem to be asking in good Platonic fashion, that makes all religions religions, what essential characteristic or form is it that religions share that warrants our giving them all the name *religion*? But because Derrida is always circumspect with regard to the "What is?" question, other questions quickly intervene—and particularly when it comes to religion. Can we really ask the question of the concept of religion without asking about the word *religion* itself? Is it really possible to think religion itself or a general religiosity apart from particular or determinate religions? Which comes first, revelation or revealability? Can one really abstract from the particulars to the general, from the many religions to a definition of religion in the abstract, or else from particular religions to a general structure of religiosity? And, finally, is questioning the proper mode for considering such a thing?[17]

At the very end of this first paragraph, Derrida seems to evoke yet another kind of abstraction, saying in a rather elliptical fashion that he would wager on the most concrete and accessible, the most "desert"-like, of abstractions. In addition to the possibilities of abstraction we have already seen, possibilities instituted in Western philosophy along with the very idea of idea, essence, or concept, Derrida seems to be alluding here to the one thing that, on his reading, most explicitly resists or eludes the "What is?" question in Plato, the one thing that cannot be considered an idea, essence, or abstraction, that most barren and desertlike of "abstractions" called *khōra*, one of the fundamental quasi-concepts Derrida will turn to in "Faith and Knowledge" in order to think what has always resisted philosophy—and thus the movement of that first abstraction—from within. We will return to this notion of *khōra* in much greater detail in Chapter 6, but for the moment it is important to underscore that abstraction is being thought here not only in relation to the idea of idea, essence, or form, to what Plato in *Timaeus* will call the "intelligible form" or "intelligible paradigm" (48a), but to what resists such intelligibility from within by being itself completely barren of attributes while providing the "space" within which the form or paradigm might be stamped, imprinted, or copied in the sensible world (50a-c). *Khōra*, it seems, would be a form of abstraction that is already at a certain remove—that already abstracts from—the philosophical abstraction of ideas or concepts.

There are thus, in this first paragraph, two abstractions or two concepts of abstraction, one corresponding to the concept and one not, and "Faith and Knowledge" will attempt to articulate the relationship between these. One form of abstraction would thus be located squarely within philosophy while the other (*khōra*) would resist philosophy from "within." Related, then, to these two forms of abstraction, are two figures of the desert, the one religious, Judeo-Christian, a place of temptation and revelation, and the other philosophical, Greek, a figure that—as Derrida will underscore later when he contrasts a thinking of *khōra* with the discourse of negative theology—has resisted all Judeo-Christian appropriation.

In the second paragraph of the first section of "Faith and Knowledge," Derrida relates this question of abstraction to Hegel and then—via a line from Hegel's 1807 "Wer denkt abstrakt?"—to the question of salvation: *"Should one save oneself by abstraction or save oneself from abstraction? Where is salvation, safety [Où est le salut]? (In 1807, Hegel writes: 'Who thinks abstractly?': 'Thinking? Abstract? –Sauve qui peut!' he begins by saying, and precisely in French, in order to translate the cry—'Rette sich, wer kann!'—of that traitor who would flee, in a single movement, thought and abstraction and metaphysics: like the 'plague.')"*[18]

As in *"Fichus,"* a text ostensibly on Adorno that revolves around a line written by Walter Benjamin in French in a letter that is otherwise in German, Derrida cites Hegel in a place where he uses a French phrase in an otherwise German text (*PM* 164–81). He does this, it would appear, in order to draw attention to the irreplaceability of the French idiom used by Hegel and to introduce a theme that will be central to Derrida's essay—the notion of saving or being saved, of gaining or granting salvation. Having spoken of religion as abstraction, Derrida asks whether abstraction *saves* us or whether we should save ourselves from it, whether we should thus save abstraction or save everything save it.

In this very first section of "Faith and Knowledge" Derrida thus raises the crucial question of salvation, or, more generally, of *salut* as salvation or as safety—the English translation by Samuel Weber quite rightly doubling the single French word *salut* with two possible translations. Bringing together, then, in a very suggestive and telescopic but not yet developed way the notions of religion, abstraction, and salvation, Derrida begins §2: "Save, be saved, save oneself. *Pretext for a first question: can a discourse on religion be dissociated from a discourse on salvation: which is to say, on the holy, the sacred, the safe and sound, the unscathed [indemne], the immune (sacer, sanctus, heilig, holy, and their alleged equivalents in so many languages)?"* (§2). Derrida is here asking, in effect, whether one can speak of religion without speaking of *salut*, that is, of *salut* as salvation or redemption in the wake of evil or sin,[19] or else as safety, the safe and sound, the sacred, the holy, the indemnified, or the immune. Derrida will not tire throughout this essay of invoking this long semantic series every time the word *salut* comes up. He does this, it seems, because the word *salut* cannot be translated into another language, or even parsed in French, with a single word, since it carries within it so many different meanings or gradations of meaning that qualify, support, and, as we are about to see, are sometimes in real tension with one another. For Derrida wishes to draw our attention not just to two but to three different meanings or sets of meaning of the word *salut*, two of which will be set over against the third: on the one hand, *salut* as redemption and salvation, though also as health and safety, indemnity and immunity, and, on the other—and this would be a third distinct set of meanings—*salut* as the "greeting" or "welcoming" of the other or else the "farewell" to him.[20] Like the word *adieu*, which Derrida works with throughout *Adieu to Emmanuel Levinas*, *salut* is a word spoken on the threshold, at the very beginning or the end of an encounter or a relationship.[21] To put it in terms developed in more detail in *Rogues* (see xv, 112–14), Derrida distinguishes a *salut* of sovereignty and ipseity, a *salut* that affirms and sustains identity, that protects or indemnifies identity, that is, a *salut* that offers either salvation or health, redemption or indemnity, from the *salut* of an unconditional welcoming that, as we will see, compromises every identity and opens it up in an autoimmune fashion to what is beyond or outside it. Derrida sets up this distinction in §2 by asking, *"And salvation* [le salut], *is it necessarily redemption, before or after evil, fault or sin?"*

There are then, we might say, two sources of *salut*, one seemingly within the power or capacity of a subject or perhaps of religion to grant safety or salvation, and one utterly dependent on the coming or visitation of the other, a welcome without power or capacity, indeed a welcome that just may compromise the power, capacity, and even the identity of a subject who believes him or herself capable of offering safety or salvation in the first place, or, as we will see, the integrity of a religion that tries to indemnify itself or protect itself from contamination. There are two sources and, notice, two regimes of language, *salut* as a substantive in a phrase, something to be mentioned or invoked, the safety or salvation, say, of a people, the redemption offered by a religion, and *"salut!"* as a performative, as an address or greeting that is used and not just mentioned, an originary or elementary faith that is performed before or on the threshold of any determinate or dogmatic religion. These two sources or two strains of *salut*, salvation or health, on the one hand, and unconditional welcoming of the other, on the other, might thus be other names for the two sources of religion that Derrida alludes to in his subtitle and that he will attempt to unfold and analyze in "Faith and Knowledge."

If Derrida thus discreetly introduces what I will identify as the first of his three principal theses in these first two sections—namely, that there are two sources of religion—he will go on in the second to suggest without fully explaining the other two.

Where is evil today, at present? Suppose that there was an exemplary and unprecedented figure of evil, even of that radical evil which seems to mark our time as no other. Is it by identifying this evil that one will accede to what might be the figure or promise of salvation for our time, and thus the singularity of the religious whose return is proclaimed in every newspaper?

Eventually, we would therefore like to link the question of religion to that of the evil of abstraction. To radical abstraction. Not to the abstract figure of death, of evil or of the sickness of death, but to the forms of evil that are traditionally tied to radical extirpation *and therefore to the deracination of abstraction, passing by way—but only much later—of those sites* of abstraction *that are the machine, technics, technoscience and above all the transcendence of tele-technology.* (§2)

As a way of introducing the themes he will treat in the rest of the essay, Derrida here raises a question often related to salvation, namely, evil, and particularly radical evil. Working within a Kantian idiom but, clearly, up-rooting it from its original context and rerooting it in the technoscience of today, Derrida is suggesting that, in order to get to the root of the problem of radical evil, we need to look at the root of the term *radical* evil, which is, of course, the Latin *radix*, or "root." Radical evil will not be, as it is in Kant, the ineradicable impulse to act on motives other than that of the moral law but the *evil*—the putative evil—of radical abstraction, of de-racination, of the uprooting and delocalizing movement brought about by the machines of today's teletechnology and the virtuality of today's telecommunications. As we will see, religious discourse will react against this deracination by appropriating, through what Derrida will call an autoimmune process, the very technological resources it rebels against. We thus already have a hint here of the relationship between *salut* and radical evil: though radical evil may indeed be a deracinating, delocalizing movement, religion will seek its *salut*, its health and/or salvation, by appropriating in an autoimmune fashion these very same deracinating and delocalizing teletechnologies. Religion will thus appropriate the essentially unappropriable resources of teletechnology in order to try to return to and preserve "the literality of idiom, the proximity of home, the nation, the earth, blood, filiation," and so on, to cite again the interview from 1999 published in *Paper Machine*—a title that by itself, it is worth noting now, brings together two seemingly conflicting sources, the supposed unique-ness and irreplaceability of paper, the organic, material support of the sig-nifier, of this piece of paper right here now, signed by me and not another in my own hand, and the inherent anonymity, iterability, and reproduc-ibility of the machine. "Paper Machine"—like "Faith and Knowledge"—would thus bring together two seemingly distinct sources, one apparently immediate and the other mediated, one related to presence and the other to absence, one to the values of proximity that would appear to favor reli-gion and the other to the values of distance, abstraction, and dislocation that would seem to be so central to science.

This brings Derrida to what I will identify in the following chapter as the second thesis of "Faith and Knowledge," the central thesis of the essay, namely, the ineluctable and autoimmune relationship between religion and science: "*In order to think religion today* abstractly, *we will take these powers of abstraction as our point of departure, in order to risk, eventually, the following hypothesis: with respect to all these forces of abstraction and of dissociation (deracination, delocalization, disincarnation, formalization, universalizing schematization, objectification, telecommunication etc.),* 'religion' is at the same time *involved in reacting antagonistically and reaffirmatively outbidding itself*" (§2). It is the relationship between *salut* as salvation and health and radical evil as abstraction that leads Derrida in this second section of the essay to identify the second and perhaps central hypothesis in "Faith and Knowledge." Stated in as succinct and straightforward a way as possible, Derrida's hypothesis is that, when confronted with all these forces of abstraction (disincarnation, deracination, delocalization, universalizing schematization, telecommunication, and so on) "religion" is at once in "reactive antagonism" to these forces and in constant reaffirmation of them, not simply appropriating them in a minimal way but actually upping the ante of them through what Derrida calls a *surenchère réaffirmatrice*. In other words, religion reacts against the movements of abstraction, deracination, delocalization, and universalization as they are deployed in teletechnoscience and telecommunication by appropriating these same movements so as to return to all those things threatened by them, namely, the "literality of idiom, the proximity of home, the nation, the earth, blood, filiation, and so on." As Derrida will declare in the penultimate section of "Faith and Knowledge" (§51)—the one that corresponds in many ways to the second as its quasi-mirror image—"the possibility of **radical evil** both destroys and institutes the religious." Radical evil institutes the religious by identifying the evil as the deracination that takes us away from a relationship to the sacrosanct, to the indemnified and the safe and sound, and it destroys religion by appropriating technological means for protecting this safe and sound. While *all* religions react against technology in this way, some, as we will see in Chapter 5, do so more forcefully and more successfully, or more forcefully and so less successfully, than others.

The forces of abstraction, technoscience, telecommunication, universalization, and so on are thus always at once bound to and in open antagonism against certain values of religion. This will be the central relationship Derrida will interrogate throughout "Faith and Knowledge." To ask about "religion" itself, religion alone, religion in the abstract, Derrida seems to be suggesting that we must consider things that would appear to be extrinsic to religion or outside religion properly speaking, namely, science, technology, and, especially, the teletechnologies of communication and language. That, it seems, is the ultimate reason for all the doublings and duplicities we have been following here.

After this first thesis about the essential duplicity of religion, a second thesis would claim that religion must be from the very beginning open to science, abstraction, and deracination, its essence from the very start compromised, opened up, in a word that we will have occasion to turn to again later and that has no precise English equivalent, *entamé*. But then, right after this second thesis, Derrida adds what appears to be the third major thesis of "Faith and Knowledge," right at the very end of §2: "In this very place, *knowledge and faith, technoscience ('capitalist' and fiduciary)* and *belief, credit, trustworthiness* [la fiabilité], *the act of faith will always have made common cause, bound* [eu partie liée] *to one another by the band* [au noeud d'alliance] *of their opposition. Whence the aporia—a certain absence of way, path, issue, salvation—and the two sources*" (§2). We saw just a moment ago that religion is opposed to science, in open antagonism against it, at the same time as it appropriates the means of science in order to seek salvation or restore its health. But now Derrida adds that faith and knowledge are not only in an autoimmune relationship with one another, in a relation of attraction and repulsion, but that knowledge is always linked to faith, that technoscience is always linked to—in an alliance with—belief, credit, reliability, acts of faith, and so on. That is why Derrida will say directly later in the essay that "one would blind oneself to the phenomenon called 'of religion' or of the 'return of the religious' *today* if one continued to oppose so naïvely Reason *and* Religion, Critique or Science *and* Religion, technoscientific Modernity *and* Religion" (§29).

Because—as we will see more fully in the next chapter—the performativity of the machine, of science and technology in general, also depends upon a performative, the machine cannot be thought without the miracle, as knowledge "makes common cause" with faith. That would be the third major thesis of "Faith and Knowledge." After the thesis that there are two sources of religion, the one an experience of the holy or the sacrosanct that has to be safeguarded and indemnified and the other an affirmation of or elementary faith in an alterity *before* any such experience, and after the thesis that religion must enlist and cooperate with the powers of teletechnology in order to indemnify the first of these two sources, there is the thesis that science too relies upon an original performative or an elementary faith and that religion and science thus share a single source. This originary source of both religion and science, this origin of the difference between faith and knowledge, religion and science, the miracle and the machine, would thus be at the root of all those doublings and duplicities in Derrida's text, from the title to the subtitle to the fonts and the sources.

Before developing in greater detail what is only adumbrated in these opening two sections concerning the relationship between science and religion, it is essential to turn briefly to the question of language. For if Derrida begins "Faith and Knowledge" by introducing or announcing many of the themes to follow, for example, abstraction, the desert with the desert, salvation, the relation between faith and knowledge, and so on, implicit in all of this is the question of language, the relation between the rootedness of the idiom and the deracinating function of a language that tends toward universalization, along with the question of the sources if not the etymological roots of *religion* spoken of in the subtitle.

> *Now if, today, the "question of religion" actually appears in a new and different light, if there is an unprecedented resurgence, both global and planetary, of this ageless thing, then what is at stake is language, certainly—and more precisely the idiom, literality, writing, that forms the element of all revelation and of all belief, an element that ultimately is irreducible and untranslatable—but an idiom that above all is inseparable from the social nexus, from the political, familial, ethnic, communitarian nexus, from the nation and from the people: from autochthony, blood and soil, and from the ever more problematic relation to citizenship and to the state. In these times, language and nation form the historical body of all religious passion. (§4)*

This emphasis on the supposed fixity or irreducibility of the idiom and its relationship to the nation and the people is but the most glaring face of the question of language and religion today. From questions concerning the name or names of God to the question of translating a sacred language, from the question of the iterability of language in general and of telecommunications in particular to the question of the performative aspect of language in prayer, Derrida will return repeatedly throughout "Faith and Knowledge" to the theme of language.

> *Here we are confronted by the overwhelming questions of the name and of everything "done in the name of": questions of the name or noun "religion," of the names of God, of whether the proper name belongs to the system of language or not, hence, of its untranslatability but also of its iterability (which is to say, of that which makes it a site of repeatability, of idealization and therefore, already, of* technē, *of technoscience, of tele-technoscience in calling at a distance), of its link to the performativity of calling in prayer (which, as Aristotle says, is neither true nor false),*

of its bond to that which, in all performativity, as in all address and attestation, appeals to the faith of the other and deploys itself therefore in a pledge of faith. (§7)[22]

So let's begin again—this time, once again, with the question of language. Derrida begins "Faith and Knowledge," recall, by asking us or asking himself, *"How 'to talk religion'? Of religion? Singularly of religion, today?"* (§1). Earlier, we underscored the apparently deracinating, abstracting function of such questions as they call out for translation and universalization in the search for a definition for religion itself, religion in general, religion in the abstract. But instead of looking at the aim or object of these questions, let us consider the language in which they are posed, the way in which the name *religion* is used in today's new "wars of religion." Derrida speaks throughout "Faith and Knowledge"—and particularly in §27, which, as the first section of the "Post-scriptum" seems to develop the themes of §1—of what it means to speak "in the name" of religion, that is, to speak from out of or to speak for a particular religious belief, perhaps even to be an apologist for it, or else to act in its name, to give oneself legitimacy by using its name or speaking in its name. Derrida argues that we must take account not only of "what religion at present might *be*" but "what is *said* and *done*, what *is happening* at this very moment, in the world, in history, *in its name*" (§27). This would be true for everything that is said and done in the name of *religion* in general but also, of course, for everything said and done in the name of a particular religion. Derrida recognizes here a certain "prerogative" of Islam on the global stage today, though he hastens to warn us that we *"not make use of this name too quickly,"* for *"Islam is not Islamism"* even if *"the latter operates* in the name of *the former"* (§6). On the one hand, then, an account must be given of everything that might be said and done *in the name of* religion as an alibi for other interests, whether political or economic. On the other hand, we must ask whether the political and economic discourses that seem the furthest removed from religion, those that dare not even speak its name, might not actually harbor within them religious interests and motivations. According to this latter hypothesis, today's "wars of religion" might be waged in places and through discourses that bracket all talk of religion but that, in the end, are about nothing other than it. Derrida asks:

> Wars or military "interventions," led by the Judeo-Christian West in the name of the best causes (of international law, democracy, the sovereignty of peoples, of nations or of states, even of humanitarian imperatives), are they not also, from a certain side, wars of religion?

The hypothesis would not necessarily be defamatory, nor even very original, except in the eyes of those who hasten to believe that all these just causes are not only secular but *pure* of all religiosity. (§28)[23]

This hypothesis would be even more compelling insofar as even our most seemingly secular concepts, such as democracy, international law, popular sovereignty, and so on, are, according to Derrida, marked by a certain religious language and theological tradition.

For Derrida, then, a "war of religion" might be waged under this or any number of other names. Insofar as the language of international law, for example, is an essentially Latin or Latinate language, it is itself already religious. One would thus be "speaking religion," to return to the opening phrase of the essay, even when one is speaking of other things. And the possibility of escaping this idiom would be even more remote, it seems, when explicitly addressing the question of "religion" itself. As Derrida argues (in §30), as soon as one begins to speak of religion one is already speaking the language of a certain empire and a certain *universalization* and, thus, a certain religious idiom. As he puts it in bold in §29 and §30 "**we**"—by which he means "**we 'Europeans'**" (§33)—"**we are already speaking Latin**" inasmuch as he and the others are approaching from within their various Latin idioms (Italian, French, and Spanish), and from within a philosophical thinking informed by these idioms, the question of "religion," something that in this form and, especially, under this name achieved a kind of worldwide preeminence through Latin. The fact that Latin is today, as we say, a "dead language," means not that it is no longer spoken but that it speaks today through the new lingua franca of the world, namely, English, or rather Anglo-American, which is attempting to spread its empire—in the wake of America's loss of economic and military power—across the globe: "the world today speaks Latin (most often via Anglo-American) when it authorizes itself in the *name* of *religion*" (§29). This is a theme that returns in many of Derrida's writings from the 1980s up through 2004, the hegemony of the Anglo-American idiom in international law and politics and in the religious language and discourse that informs them.

For everything that touches religion in particular, for everything that speaks "religion," for whoever speaks religiously or about religion, Anglo-American remains Latin. *Religion* circulates in the world, one might say, like an *English word* [*comme un* mot anglais] that has been to Rome and taken a detour to the United States. Well beyond its strictly capitalist or politico-military figures, a hyper-imperialist appropriation has been underway now for centuries. It imposes itself in a particularly palpable manner within the conceptual apparatus of international law and of global political rhetoric. Wherever this apparatus dominates, it articulates itself through a discourse on religion. (§30)

Combine this theme of an Anglo-American hegemony that remains nonetheless Latin with Derrida's constant emphasis throughout this period on the ontotheological origins of so many of our seemingly nontheological and even secular concepts, from sovereignty to tolerance to, finally, the very notion of the world, and we can better understand Derrida's tongue-twisting neologism *mondialatinisation*. Fortunately we don't have to conjugate or decline it, just explain it, or, as suggested in the previous chapter, decorticate it. Taking the *latin* out of the word we are left with *mondialisation*—at the root of which is the French word *monde*, "world." *Mondialisation* is the term Derrida and other French thinkers prefer to use in place of the English word *globalization* and its French counterpart *globalisation*. Because the idea of a world is precisely not that of a globe, because we live or "dwell" in a world rather than simply in or on a globe, because our being is, as Heidegger puts it, a being-in-the world and not simply a living on the earth, because, for Kant, it is the world and not the globe that functions as a regulative idea, Derrida and others prefer to speak of *mondialisation* rather than *globalisation*.[24] *Mondialisation* might thus be translated more accurately but also more awkwardly into English as "worldwidization," or as the process of "becoming-world-wide." *Mondia-latin-isation*, then, would draw attention to the way in which this worldwidization or this process of becoming-world-wide is inextricably linked both to religion, to Christianity, and to the language in which Christianity spread, namely, Latin, or, today, Anglo-American. As Samuel Weber, the translator of "Faith and Knowledge," notes, the fact that *mondialatinisation* has been translated throughout as *globalatinization* has stakes that go far beyond those of translation: "For if, as Derrida argues in this chapter, the major idiom and vehicle of the process of *mondialatinisation* today is precisely Anglo-American, then the very fact that the notion of 'globality' comes to supplant that of 'world' in the most common usage of this language must itself be highly significant" (§15; translators note 7).[25] By means of the neologism *mondialatinisation* Derrida draws attention to the very specific and determinate origins of a concept that would pass itself off as, precisely, global, transnational, worldwide. *Mondialatinisation* or globalatinization, despite its rhetoric of universality, would thus be, for Derrida, "European-Anglo-*American* in its idiom" (§37).

Now, Derrida is not arguing that we could or even should try to speak completely outside or beyond this version of universality called *mondialatinisation*. What is essential is to recognize the particularities of this language and to acknowledge that those things that present themselves as universal or worldwide always rely upon a particular history, culture, and language. For globalization, or *mondialisation*, might be precisely not as worldwide and universalizing as it claims to be. Or, rather, its version of universalization or globalization might be less universal and global—more culturally specific—than it imagines. If certain aspects of globalization have thus succeeded in extending such notions as citizenship and human rights to those who were previously deprived of them, it must be acknowledged that this same globalization has also led to unprecedented concentrations of wealth in certain parts of the world and not others, that it has marginalized if not effectively silenced certain idioms and languages in favor of just a couple dominant ones, and that what has been globalized has been certain notions of law and justice, of democracy and human rights, of economic fairness and progress, and not others. As Derrida put it rather baldly some years later during a public discussion, "I believe that, paradoxically, globalization hasn't occurred. It is a false concept, often an alibi; never has the world been so unequal and so marginally shareable or shared" (*IW* 62). The worldwide domination of the word *globalization* would be but a single, striking symptom of the glaring fact that this worldwide movement is marked by particular nation states, ideologies, languages, and not others. Globalization or "*Globalatinization* (essentially Christian, to be sure)" (§30) is thus not the same thing as universality, even though the former may present itself as being coextensive with the latter.

If "*to think 'religion' is to think the 'Roman,'*" and if the very concept of religion is "*European*" and "*first of all Latin*" (§5), then one must ask about the language in which this concept was first formulated and whether it can be translated into other languages. When Derrida asks, near the end of §30 and the beginning of §31, "**And what if *religio* remained untranslatable?**" he is in effect reminding us that the word *religio* brings along with it a unique history that cannot simply be bracketed or abstracted from in order to get at an essence of *religio* or religion that might then be translated into all the languages of the world. In other words, *religio* may remain untranslatable inasmuch as it is always rooted in particular historical conditions and in a particular language. It is no doubt for this reason that Derrida puts the word *religion* in the subtitle of his essay between quotation marks. On the one hand, this word—like any word—calls out for translation; it invites other idioms or the idiom of the other in order to be read or even understood; on the other hand, the word is untranslatable insofar as it is a unique Latin event, related to a particular history and language and particular discursive practices.

Globalatinization is thus a process of universalization and translation born out of a specific language and religious culture. As powerful as it has been and continues to be, its birth suggests that it is finite and that it will one day come to an end. *Globalatinization—"this strange alliance of Christianity, as the experience of the death of God, and tele-technoscientific capitalism"*—is thus, argues Derrida, *"at the same time hegemonic and finite, ultra-powerful and in the process of exhausting itself* [en voie d'épuisement]" (§15). Though "we no longer perceive its limits, we know that such globalization is finite and only projected" and that it appears today to be "running out of breath [*essoufflée*], however irresistible and imperial it still may be" (§30). We must thus try to think and take what is best from this *mondialatinisation*, including certain standards of international law and human rights, a *certain* universality, *at the same time* as we recognize and question the contemporary Anglo-American hegemony of such notions *and* the Latin roots and origins of so many of them. That is, we must take from this *mondialatinisation* certain notions of universality and critique in order to call into question the very roots and origins of this *mondialatinisation* and, thus, of all the concepts related to it.

Beginning, for example, with religion, that is, with the concept or abstraction "religion," but also, and at the same time, the word "religion." We must at once think this abstraction by attempting to understand religion as such, religiosity as such, as a concept, *and* see the roots of this abstraction in a particular language and history. That is, we must come to understand that the very language of abstraction, of concept formation, has a particular origin, a philosophical origin, a Greek origin, and that the concept of religion, related inextricably to the word *religion*, has an origin, a Latin origin, from which we cannot so easily abstract ourselves. If this remains true for *all* concepts, if *all* concepts are in some sense tied to the language in which they are articulated, this is all the more true for "religion," since it is not only every discussion of religion that takes place in a particular language but every revelation in every religion and every bearing witness to that revelation.

If the question of language is thus important for the question of religion in general, it is absolutely essential for thinking the way in which religion is being transformed and so must be reconsidered today. Derrida identifies in §33 three different kinds of resources or what he calls "discursive practices" for understanding "religion" today: (1) etymologies (investigations into the provenance or origin of words related to religion—beginning with the word "religion" itself); (2) "historico-semantical **filiations** or **genealogies**" (an investigation into the way words and discourses are transformed historically or by institutional structures, "in the style of Nietzsche, for example, as well as in that of Benveniste when he holds 'Indo-European institutions' as 'witnesses' to the history of meaning or of an etymology") and, finally, (3) analyses with "**pragmatic** and functional effects, more structural and also more political," analyses that would look at the ways in which the lexicon of religious language is being used today, at the ways in which discourse "liberates words and meaning from all archaic memory and from all supposed origins."[26]

Derrida goes on to argue that since the Capri conference would be devoted especially to the question of what is happening to religion today the participants should privilege the third of these discursive practices and look at the ways certain discourses are today using the language of religion, at once reinscribing and reinventing it. They should thus "privilege the signs of what in the world, *today*, singularizes the use of the word 'religion' as well as experience of 'religion' associated with the word, there where no memory and no history could suffice to announce or gather it, at least not at first sight" (§33). Hence Derrida will speak at great length of the ways in which technology and telecommunications are today changing and reinventing religion and religious practices and of the ways in which the word *religion*—in the "return to religion," for example—is being used today. But in order to do this effectively, Derrida will often employ the first two of these three resources, and particularly the first, insofar as etymology is precisely an investigation into the putative source or sources of a given word. While etymology never reveals some truer or more authentic understanding of a word, while it never, as Derrida puts it, "provides a law and only provides material for thinking on the condition that it allows itself to be thought as well" (§33), it can often help us think what is unthought in a word or concept. That is perhaps why Derrida so often turns—though never uncritically and sometimes in fact very critically (see §31)—to Emile Benveniste's important work *Indo-European Language and Society*.[27]

Derrida cites Benveniste in "Faith and Knowledge" on several occasions, noting, for example, in §8 that the word for god in French, *dieu*, apparently comes from a word meaning light or celestial—an interesting connection, clearly, for Derrida, who is trying to find, as he puts it, the "undeveloped" or "negative" or "nocturnal source" of religion as it is related to light and revelation.[28] He will later cite Benveniste on the etymological origins of the words *sovereignty* (*kurios* in Greek; §39n30) and *responsibility* (§30), among others. But in §33 Derrida brings this interest to bear on the word *religion* itself in order to note that, as if by a happy accident that helps reinforce the duplicity he has been following throughout, there are not one but "*two possible etymological sources of the word religio*," two sources or two *theories* regarding the origin of *religio*. According to etymologists, who are appropriately divided on the question, the word *religio* would come either from the Latin *relegere, legere*, meaning to harvest, collect, or gather, or from the Latin *religare, ligare*, meaning to link or to bind. These two sources or two theories of the etymology of religion lead to two very different lines of thought regarding the nature of religion. On the one hand, religion would be related to gathering and recollection, to "scrupulous attention, respect, patience, even modesty, shame or piety," and, on the other, by means of an "etymology 'invented by Christians,' as Benveniste says," it would be linked to "the *link*, precisely, to obligation, ligament, and hence to obligation, to debt, etc., between men or between man and God" (§34). One of these etymological sources would thus be related more to the attention, practices, and piety of a religious subject and one more to the link or bond *between* religious subjects or between a religious community and God.

As I read him, Derrida will not come down on one side or the other of this etymological question. He will instead reiterate his limited reliance on etymology and then try to find an element common to both etymological theories. After stating that "such a divergence is for us limited in scope" since "nothing gets decided at the source"—indeed, as we have seen, everything is always already doubled at the source—Derrida suggests that these two competing etymologies "can be retraced to the same, and in a certain manner to the possibility of repetition" (§34). In other words, as Derrida had suggested in the previous section, these "two semantic sources perhaps overlap" (§33), and the sign of this overlap or repetition would be nothing other than the *re-* that is found in both theories or etymologies. Whether we are talking about *re-legere* or *re-ligare*, "what is at issue is indeed a reunion [*rassemblement*], a re-assembling, a re-collecting" and "a resistance or a reaction to dis-junction," that is, a resistance or a reaction "to ab-solute alterity" (§34). This critique of *rassemblement* as gathering is a familiar one in Derrida, particularly in his readings of Heidegger, where a certain thought of disjunction or dissemination is always opposed to this gathering or gathering together into a self or into a community.[29] What Derrida finds in both etymologies is thus a *reaction* to radical alterity in the name of gathering, recollection, sameness, and so on—notions that all need to be thought in relation to the so-called *re-*turn of religion, the theme with which Derrida begins and to which he will return throughout "Faith and Knowledge."

Derrida thus uses etymology to lay out the semantic field in which the word *religion* might be thought, but he then goes on to oppose both etymologies to another thinking of religion. The *re-* of the two etymologies of re-ligion will have already hinted at this third possibility: religion must be thought in relationship not only to recollection, reflection, regathering, rebinding, repayment, and so on, but to *re*-sponse and *re*-sponsibility, a response and responsibility, as we will see in what follows, that precedes any recollection of an origin or any rebinding into a religious community, a responsibility that will be related to an originary response to the other or faith in the other.[30]

Derrida seems to be suggesting that, in order to think either religion in its origins or what is happening to religion today, we just may have to think a faith that comes before or after religion. The work of Benveniste will have helped sketch out this possibility, as well. For if Benveniste "recalls that there is no 'common' Indo-European term for what we call 'religion,'" then we just might want to conclude, contra Benveniste, who believes that despite this lack of a common word there is nonetheless— and these are his words—an "omnipresent reality that is religion," that *religion*—like *globalatinization*—is marked by a history, a culture, and a language and so has not always been and perhaps will not always be present as such or under this name. Derrida concludes this reading of Benveniste: "There has not always been, therefore, nor is there always and everywhere, nor will there always and everywhere ('with humans' or elsewhere) be *something*, a thing that is *one and identifiable*, identical with itself, which, whether religious or irreligious, all agree to call 'religion'" (§34). There was not, according to Benveniste, and there perhaps *will not be again some day*, suggests Derrida, a common term, Indo-European or global, for the term *religion*, or a common "reality" that would correspond to it. This would suggest not only that there are determinate religions conditioned by history but that *religion itself* may be a determinate moment of faith, a determinate epoch, perhaps, of the elementary faith that opens the possibility of religion but cannot be reduced to it. The very turn to the etymologies of *religion* may thus itself be more than a scholarly or philological exercise but already a response to the exigencies of today, a response to the demands of a deconstruction of the theologico-political— that is, Judeo-Christian—origins of so many of our concepts, beginning with the notion of religion. "Henceforth, despite the ethical and political urgencies that do not permit **the response** to be put off, reflection upon the Latin noun 'religion' will no longer be held for an academic exercise, a philological embellishment or an etymological luxury" (§28).

Derrida thus appears to have done with the noun or name *religion* what he did in the opening sections of "Faith and Knowledge" and will do in later texts such as *Rogues* with the word *salut*. As we saw earlier, he opposes two meanings of *salut* to a third; he opposes *salut* as either salvation or safety, redemption or health, two meanings related to one of the two sources of religion, to *salut* as welcoming or reception, the other of religion's two sources. Here, he opposes the two traditional etymologies of the name or noun *religion* to a notion of response and responsibility, to the performativity of the prayer and the promise, that would first open the domain of religion without being reduced to it. But in order to understand how this promise, this second source of religion, is related to the first, we need to develop more fully the three theses of "Faith and Knowledge," that is, the three theses on the two sources of religion and the one element that is common to both science and religion.[31]

Three Theses on the Two Sources and Their One Common Element

In the previous two chapters I have tried to describe and analyze the various conditions of the essay "Faith and Knowledge" and of the Capri conference where a first version of the essay was presented. We saw how Derrida approaches the question of religion today by means of the essential duplicity of origins, and how that duplicity is inscribed into not only the content but the form of his essay: we saw this in the two words of the title, in the two titles, one of which names two sources of "religion," in the two forms or fonts of type, and in the division of the essay's fifty-two sections in two and then of the second half in two again. All this, I speculated, was indicative of the fact that there are two sources of religion and that religion and science are somehow related. But what exactly is the relationship between them? Is their relation one of simple opposition or exclusion or is it more complex than that?

Though Derrida seems to make a point *not* to develop his argument in "Faith and Knowledge" in any kind of a straightforward or linear fashion, preferring instead to scatter or disseminate his claims throughout the fifty-two sections like seed or shrapnel, as we have said, I would like to argue in this chapter that there are essentially three main theses underlying the essay and that these can and should be ordered in a particular way.[1] These three theses express the fundamental duplicity of religion, the fundamental conflict or antagonism between religion and science, and, finally, the fundamental complicity of religion and science.

First thesis, then, first thesis of duplicity—religion has not one but two sources. On the one hand, argues Derrida, religion has its source in an experience of sacrality or holiness, the indemnified or the unscathed, the safe and sound, in short, an experience of *salut* as health or restoration, salvation or redemption. Derrida asks, we recall, right at the outset of the essay: *"can a discourse on religion be dissociated from a discourse on salvation: which is to say, on the holy, the sacred, the safe and sound, the unscathed* [indemne], *the immune* (sacer, sanctus, heilig, *holy, and their alleged equivalents in so many languages)?"* (§2) In the beginning of the "Post-scriptum" the very same language is used. After an ellipsis that is presumably used to indicate the time that has lapsed between the "Italics" and the "Post-scriptum,"[2] that is, between Capri and Laguna, Derrida begins: "(27) [. . .] **Religion?**" And then a few lines later: "Unscathed in the experience of the unscathed that it will have wanted to be. Is not the unscathed [*indemne*] the very matter—the thing itself—of religion?" (§27) It is right at this point that Derrida appends a footnote on this notion of the unscathed (*indemnis*), the intact, the uncompromised or the unspoiled, on everything this is, in French, *indemne*. In that note Derrida explains that in speaking of *indemni-fication* he wishes to suggest "both the process of compensation and the restitution, sometimes sacrificial, that *re*constitutes purity intact, renders integrity safe and sound, restores cleanliness [*propreté*] and property unimpaired. This is indeed what the word "unscathed" [*indemne*] says: the pure, non-contaminated, untouched, the sacred and holy before all profanation, all wound, all offence, all lesion" (§27n16).

Indemnification is thus used to designate both the protection of what is assumed to be unspoiled or intact and the restoration of a supposedly original or uncompromised state. It is difficult to imagine a religion, claims Derrida, that does not promote or promise in some fashion a restoration of health, some redemption or indemnification of the self or the community through various kinds of ritual, sacrifice, or prayer. There is no religion without some promise either to heal and make whole the self or the community or else to keep it safe and sound, protected from all corruption, contamination, or desecration. Referring to Benveniste on the term *heilig*, Derrida speaks of "the necessity for every religion . . . to involve healing—*heilen*—health, hail or promise of a cure—*cura, Sorge*—horizon of redemption, of the restoration of the unscathed, of indemnification" (§39n30). In *The Animal That Therefore I Am*, Derrida uses very similar terms in his analysis of the philosophical claim that only the human animal can feel shame: "This movement of shame, this reticence, this inhibition, this retreat, this reversal is, no doubt, like the immunizing drive, the protection of the immune, of the sacred (*heilig*), of the holy, of the separate (*kadosh*) that is the very origin of the religious, of religious scruple" (*ATT* 47). Indemnification is thus a process—or a drive—of immunization that promises to protect what is thought to be sacred or holy by immunizing the self or the community against what is considered unclean, unhealthy, or unholy.

But these references to the promise already suggest another source for religion, one related not to the object of that promise (indemnification, sacralization, health, or redemption) but to the act of the promise itself. For there is also, writes Derrida, "no religion without the promise of keeping one's promise to tell the truth—and to have already told it!—in the very act of promising" (§30). Religion's other source, its second source, would thus be located not in the prospect of health, redemption, or salvation, but in the promise that would precede, exceed, and condition such a prospect in the form of an originary gage or engagement to the other, an experience of faith that has to do not with the indemnified community but with credit, confidence, and the good faith of witnessing, in a word, with a kind of elementary faith, reliability, or trustworthiness *before* any particular religion or any attempt at indemnification. These are, in short, the two sources of religion: "the sacrosanct, the safe and sound on the one side, *and* faith, trustworthiness [*fiabilité*] or credit on the other" (§27). While the first source is thus an appeal to a certain presence that must remain unscathed, intact, indemnified, the second source is an appeal to a certain blindness or absence beyond all presence, "the fiduciary or the trustworthy in the act of faith, fidelity, the appeal to blind confidence, the testimonial that is always beyond proof, demonstrative reason, intuition" (§32). The second source is thus related to the experience of faith in the testimony or witnessing of the other, that is, in an other who is *totally other*, absolutely other as an *absolute source*, a source to come or a source of the to-come, a source of the future or of what opens up the future. As Derrida put it in *The Gift of Death*, among other places, "*tout autre est tout autre*," every other is absolutely other, every bit other. While the first source, the experience of the unscathed, may appear to be "the very matter—the thing itself—of religion" (§27), this second source, "the fiduciary credit of an elementary faith," appears to be "the elementary condition, the milieu of the religious if not religion itself" (§37).

In §34 Derrida reiterates this distinction between the two sources. He begins by suggesting that among the many distinctions that would need to be made today in order to address the question of religion—distinctions between religion and faith or piety or cult or theology or ontotheology, or between belief and faith, and so on—one of these must be granted a "quasi-transcendental privilege," since it can provide us with what can be identified as the two sources of religion: on the one hand, "the experience of sacredness, even of holiness, of the unscathed that is safe and sound (*heilig*, holy)," and, on the other, "the experience of belief (trust, trustworthiness, confidence, faith, the credit accorded the *good faith of the utterly other* in the experience of witnessing)" (§34). One might recall our earlier claim that Derrida distinguishes three different meanings of *salut*, opposing two of them to a third. The first of these two sources of religion, the experience of sacrality, holiness, the indemnified, and so on, would thus be identified with *salut* as either salvation or health, with salvation through health or with health as a kind of restoration or salvation, while the other source of religion, namely, faith or trustworthiness, credit or confidence, would be related to *salut* as the welcoming or greeting of the other, as a promise to the other or a faith in the coming of the other. This second source must thus be thought *before* any particular promise of health or redemption as an originary greeting or an originary turn toward or address to the other before any attempt even to recognize the other and affirm them within a community. It would thus correspond to that third meaning of the French word *salut*: no longer understood as health or salvation, no longer a noun to be referred to, invoked, or promised, the second source of religion would have to be thought in relationship to the *salut!* as an originary performative greeting of the other, a threshold greeting that would precede and condition the constitution of any religious community or any community in general. There would be, then, no religion without a promise of health or salvation, but also no religion without a promise to the other for such health or salvation.

On the one hand, then, religion would have its source in an experience of something that must remain intact or that must be restored, protected, safeguarded, indemnified or, let me underscore the term, *restituted*, while on the other it has its source in a kind of faith, promise, or, let me again underscore the word, *engagement* with an other who offers no assurances, no intact presence, and so requires a sort of credit or trustworthiness, a kind of—we saw this word earlier—*fiabilité*. While one source would thus be turned toward a presence that must be restored or restituted, toward a protection or indemnification of the self or the community, toward an immunization of these from outside aggression or contamination, the other would be turned precisely *toward* this outside, or toward this outside within, toward all the resources that, as we will see, threaten the self or the community but also make these possible in the first place.

Before going on to demonstrate the relationship, the dynamic, the mechanism that links these two sources, I would like to look very briefly at the two words I have just emphasized in my recapitulation of the two sources, *restitution* and *engagement*, in order to suggest that Derrida had attempted to think in many other places prior to "Faith and Knowledge" these two sources of religion, whether under these or other names. One such place is *The Truth in Painting*, where Derrida attempts, through a reading of Heidegger, to think a kind of immunization or indemnification drive along with a sort of trustworthiness or faith that would first open up the relationship to the object to be indemnified or protected. Let me turn then briefly to this earlier reading of Heidegger. The detour is justified not only by Derrida's long engagement with Heidegger throughout his work but by the fact that the second half of "Faith and Knowledge" refers to Heidegger much more than to any other thinker. If the title of the essay is borrowed from Hegel, and the subtitle is a conflation of titles of Kant and Bergson, these figures more or less fade away in the second half of the essay, while Heidegger (as we will see in more detail in Observation 4) comes to play a more and more central role. For the moment, let us look at a passage in Derrida's essay "Restitutions" in *The Truth and Painting* where the notions of restitution and gage or engagement are put into relationship with this notion of *fiabilité*, which is used throughout "Faith and Knowledge," and almost from the very beginning. Recall Derrida's first attempt in §2 to sketch out the relationship between knowledge and faith, science and religion: "In this very place, *knowledge and faith, technoscience ("capitalist" and fiduciary) and belief, credit, trustworthiness* [la fiabilité], *the act of faith will always have made common cause, bound* [eu partie liée] *to one another by the band* [au noeud d'alliance] *of their opposition. Whence the aporia—a certain absence of way, path, issue, salvation— and the two sources*" (§2).

Derrida is suggesting here that there is a certain relationship or *alliance* between faith and knowledge, between these two commonly opposed notions that he, following Hegel, links with a simple *and* in his title. To indicate the nature of this *alliance*, however, Derrida ties together several related words in a particularly dense and condensed passage. Let's look closely here at the letter of Derrida's text, since it requires more than a little unraveling. What is translated quite elegantly by Samuel Weber as "will always have made common cause, bound to one another by the band of their opposition," is *auront toujours eu partie liée*, dans le lieu même, *au noeud d'alliance de leur opposition*." Weber's translation is about as good as it gets. The phrase *noeud d'alliance* means something like the knot or bond of a union, covenant, or alliance; one speaks, for example, of *le noeud du mariage* to refer to the bonds of marriage or wedlock. As for the word *alliance*, it means not only alliance or covenant but *wedding ring*. Weber thus neatly ties all these significations together through the polyvalent English word *band*, the band—the wedding band—that binds into a covenant, pact, or alliance. But Derrida has also, notice, tied together in this one sentence two words formed from the verb *lier* (*partie liée* and *alliance*) in order to emphasize the pact, covenant, bond, bind, or band between knowledge and faith or science and *re-ligion*, a word, as we saw in the previous chapter, that is of Latin origin and that, according to one etymology, at least, has the same root as the French *lier*, namely, the Latin *ligare*. Everything in this sentence is, precisely, *linked* in a place where what is at issue is the link, bond, or band between knowledge and faith, science and a certain trustworthiness or *fiabilité*.

As for the term *fiabilité*, it is the word used by Derrida in *The Truth in Painting* to translate Heidegger's *Verlässlichkeit*, a notion that is prominent in "The Origin of the Work of Art" to describe, in Derrida's interpretation, a kind of reliability, engagement, or faith before use and utility, the kind of reliance, confidence, or faith that the peasant woman in Van Gogh's famous painting has in her shoes as she walks slowly home from the fields, the shoes she does not simply use like a tool, but, precisely, relies upon, has faith in, leans on, and gives herself over to. Derrida writes in 1978 in "Restitutions" of this adjective *verlässig*:

> The word is difficult to translate. I have laboriously specified "thanks to which," "by the force of which," "in virtue of which" because the relation (*Kraft*) is not that of a formal condition of possibility to its conditioned object or of a more profound foundation to what it founds, but of a sort of experience. An experience, let us say for the moment, of *reliability*: you can count on the product. The product is reliable. It is useful only if we can trust in its reliability. (*TP* 348)

Though one may come to rely on a product, on the shoes one wears to tread the earth, this reliability is first of all an experience, not a relationship to a particular object but an experience of openness, trust, faith, or confidence. (Derrida speaks in §34 of the "*experience* of belief" through trust or "trustworthiness [*fiabilité*].") Derrida continues, pushing this reliability further in the direction of what will be characterized in "Faith and Knowledge" as a kind of originary faith or, better, an elementary faith: "That which is *verlässig* deserves confidence, faith, or credit. In this case, the credit is anterior to any symbolic contract forming the object of an agreement signed (explicitly or not) by a nameable subject. It is not cultural any more than it is natural" (*TP* 349). We see here, in the *noeud d'alliance*, if you will, of this passage, so many of the themes we have been following throughout "Faith and Knowledge" woven together into a knot or band. *Fiabilité* would have to do with an experience that is prior to any nameable subject or community, prior to any contract some subject might enter into; it would be what we might call a threshold relationship, a relationship of the threshold, *before* any symbolic relationship with another subject or with a community. Recall Derrida's phrase from §3 where he spoke of the participants at the Capri conference, the members of their little "community," having a kind of "*minimal trustworthiness*" or minimal reliability—*une fiabilité minimale*—in this word *religion*. If, in the end, Derrida will question this reliability or *fiabilité*, if he will question their assurance or trust in some shared meaning of the word *religion*, some shared horizon that will give the word a single meaning or at least a controllable, countable, and accountable multiplicity of meanings, what will make this questioning and this conversation possible, what will make their very gathering possible, will be another kind of *fiabilité*, a trust or faith not in this or that meaning, this or that community or horizon, but in "*a certain absence of horizon*" (§9), in the coming of the other in the form of a response that is unforeseeable and is thus always beyond my expectations. This *fiabilité* or reliability would thus be something like the speech act that engages one in a profession of faith, or, as we shall see, something like the speech act that engages one to engage in such a profession. To cite "Restitutions" one more time and bring things full circle back to the *alliance* and the band we have been following from §2 of "Faith and Knowledge": "This notion of reliability is here anterior to the opposition between the useful and the sacred. Without reliability there would be no usable product, but nor would there be any symbolic object. . . . This elementary reliability [*fiabilité élémentaire*], this fidelity that predates everything, is a sort of ring (*Ring*, in the German), a sort of originary wedding ring [*alliance originaire*]" (*TP* 351).

Already back in "Restitutions" in *The Truth in Painting*, then, Derrida had linked the notion of an elementary fidelity or an originary trustworthiness to the covenant and the *alliance*, to the bond and the wedding band. The link is hardly fortuitous, for as Austin has taught us, the marriage bond or alliance is always brought about through nothing other than a promise or profession of fidelity, that is, through nothing other than a speech act that requires a certain faith. While this profession might appear to be a very specific and limited form of speech, Derrida seems to be suggesting that all speech—that all relations with the other—require it. For in speaking of the bond or alliance between "*technoscience ("capitalist" and fiduciary*) and *belief, credit, trustworthiness, the act of faith,*" Derrida is drawing attention to the way in which technoscience too—along with all our systems of monetary exchange—is dependent on belief, credit, trustworthiness, that is, on this performative dimension of language.[3]

We will return to this reliance of science upon faith or credit in a moment, but let us note first Derrida's emphasis once again on the performativity of language. In talking about religion—and recall that Derrida's very first sentence spoke not just of understanding religion but of talking about religion or simply "*talking religion*"—one must consider not only the significations, connotations, and valences of the terms and words we use but the way in which, to cite J. L. Austin, we "do things with words" whenever we promise, give oaths, or profess our faith.[4] As we saw earlier with regard to the irreducible French idiom *salut*, this emphasis on faith, trust, promises, oaths, and so on introduces two essential dimensions of language, the constative and the performative, the dogmas or tenets of belief and the performative faith that will be at the origin of all such beliefs—in religion but also, and this will be essential, in science.

If the first source of religion is a certain experience of the safe and sound, of what must be protected or restituted to an original state of purity, the second source would be even more original than this original state since it would mark the threshold of a relationship to the other, more original, then, as the promise to tell the truth, and so more original than all truth. Derrida writes once again of this originary alliance:

> No *religio* without *sacramentum*, without alliance and promise of testifying truthfully to the truth, which is to say, to speak the truth: that is to say, to begin with, no religion without the promise of keeping one's promise to tell the truth—and to have already told it!—in the very act of promising. To have already told it, *veritas*, in Latin, and thus to consider it told. The event to come has already taken place. The promise promises *itself*, it is *already* promised, that is the sworn faith, the given word, and hence the response. *Religio* would begin there. (§30)[5]

This second source of religion—of *religio*—is thus prior to any particular religion, any particular credo or profession of faith; it is, we might say, the opening to any such religion and the quasi-transcendental condition for any profession of faith. It is thus "minimal" in the sense that it is fundamental without being a foundation, essential without being a shared essence, a kind of threshold condition that cannot be a straightforwardly transcendental condition.

We thus have sacralization, indemnification, immunization, self-protection, salvation, health, the safe and sound, on the one hand, and reliability, faith, and credit, an originary "alliance" or engagement toward the other, on the other. These are, Derrida argues throughout "Faith and Knowledge," the two sources or *foyers* of religion, the two sources or source points that either form the two foci of the ellipsis of religion or—because the word *ellipsis* also means to leave out or to silence, to eclipse—the two foci that conflict with and can elide or eclipse one another. For it can always happen that one source elides the other, with religion as salvation and health, as the experience of the safe and sound, eclipsing or concealing the source of religion as credit or confidence or reliability, or vice versa. In order to understand religion, Derrida is arguing, we must understand this originary duplicity of origins *and* this originary conflict. To think religion itself, then, the essence of religion itself, we must think this originary duplicity. While these two sources of religion presuppose and reflect each other, as Derrida argues in §47, there remains an irreducible difference between them, a gap between the *possibility* (as a universal structure) of religion and the *determined necessity* of some religion or another. It is thanks to this gap or difference that one can always criticize the latter in the name of the former or locate the former within the latter.

The fact that there are not one but two sources of religion, one related to the sacred or the holy and one to belief or faith, suggests that belief and faith are not coextensive with religion and so must be distinguished from it. A certain faith or belief is required to engage another even before or, we might say, regardless of their religion, a kind of faith that would perhaps be compatible with what Derrida will call—and we will look at this in more detail in Chapter 6—"another tolerance." In *Islam & the West*, Derrida affirms this kind of belief or faith that goes beyond any particular culture, language, or, indeed, religion:

> I always distinguish between faith and religion. . . . If we limit ourselves to what we have customarily called religion in the Abrahamic universe of the religions of the Book, I will then distinguish between the religious adherences to Judaism, Christianity, and Islam and faith without which no social relationship is possible. I cannot address the other, whoever he or she might be, regardless of his or her religion, language, culture, without asking that other to believe me and to trust me [*me faire crédit*]. One's relationship to the other, addressing the other, presupposes faith. (*IW* 57–58)

The address to the other (the second source of religion) must thus be distinguished from every experience of the sacred (the first source). While the first always presupposes the second, even if this can be forgotten, elided or eclipsed, the second is what makes possible the first, even when this possibility is not realized.

> These two veins (or two strata or two sources) of the religious should be distinguished from one another. . . . In principle, it is possible to sanctify, to sacralize the unscathed or to maintain oneself *in the presence* of the sacrosanct in various ways without bringing into play an act of belief, if at least belief, faith or fidelity signifies here acquiescing to the testimony of the other—of the *utterly other* who is inaccessible in its absolute source. (§32)

If religion and faith are not coextensive with one another and can even be opposed to one another, then not all religion follows "the movement of **faith**" and not all faith "rushes towards faith in God" (§32; §13). As an identifiable institution, religion may be related much more to health, safety, or salvation than to faith or to God. Conversely, "not every sworn faith, given word, trustworthiness, trust or confidence in general is necessarily inscribed in a 'religion'" (§32), that is, not every *fiabilité* or act of faith is to be found in what is called religion. Not all faith, then, is religious, even if religion tends to bring together or to cross these two experiences or sources in a particularly revealing way—the experience of the *indemnified*, the *sacred*, the health and salvation of the self or the community, on the one hand, and the experience of belief or of an elementary faith, on the other.

Derrida will spend a good deal of time in "Faith and Knowledge" trying to define this notion of an elementary faith that is one of the sources of religion but is not coextensive with religion. He will identify it with testimony or witnessing and even, as we will see, with the social bond itself, that is, not only with the wedding bond or band but with *every* bond in the *socius*. But it is important to note here that Derrida does not—could not—develop this notion of elementary faith out of thin air (or ether). Just as he uses a few pointed references to the machine in Bergson to develop a new sense of the mechanical, so he uses Kant's notion of "*reflecting* (reflektierende) *faith*" as a way of thinking this elementary faith, a reflecting faith "*whose possibility might well open the space of our discussion*" (§15). In Observation 1, I try to explain just what Kant himself means by reflecting faith and why it is to be found only in a moral religion such as Christianity (I say "such as" even though there is no other), where the emphasis is on good conduct and not on knowing or thinking one can know what God will do for our salvation. In many ways, Kant's notion of reflecting faith anticipates Derrida's distinction between faith and religion. Because reflecting faith *"does not depend essentially upon any historical revelation and thus agrees with the rationality of purely practical reason,"* because—or at least this is Kant's claim—*"it breaks with this 'dogmatic faith'*... *insofar as the latter claims to know and thereby ignores the difference between faith and knowledge"* (§15), we can understand why Derrida might claim that such faith opens the space of his discussion. Hence Derrida can say *"even today, albeit provisionally, [the opposition between reflecting faith and dogmatic faith] could help us structure a problematic"* (§15). But while Derrida's notion of elementary faith "breaks" in some sense, just like Kant's, with dogmatic faith and all determinate religions, it is not exactly in opposition to these insofar as it is, precisely, one of its two sources, as well as the common source, as we will see, of all knowledge and all science. It is thus only in part on the basis of Kant's *Religion* that Derrida will develop throughout "Faith and Knowledge" what he will call, reinscribing Kant's terminology, *"a radically fiduciary form of the 'reflecting faith'"* (§16).

Religion has, again, two sources, one related to the safeguarding of the religious experience of the sacred and the protection and indemnification of the self and the community, to what Derrida in *Rogues* and elsewhere identifies as *ipseity*, and one related to a faith or trustworthiness in an absolutely other who, at the limit, compromises all identity and interrupts all indemnification. These are the two sources of religion that must not be conflated, the two sources that must "mingle their waters" (§32), as Derrida puts it, without becoming the same. In the beginning, then, there will have been two, always already two sources of religion, one of which, as we will see in what follows, is the common source of both religion and science.

It is this internal tension or even aporia—this ellipsis—between the two sources of religion that leads Derrida to his second thesis in "Faith and Knowledge": in order for religion or a religious community to protect and promote the first of its two sources, namely, the experience of *salut* as health, security, salvation, and indemnification, it must rely upon and enlist the resources of technoscience and telecommunications. An analysis of what is happening in religion today, says Derrida in 1994–95, makes very clear what has always been the case: while religion often rejects and tries to get beyond or before science, it can do so only by appropriating the very means of science—from the most elementary technologies of communication such as writing or, already, language and the voice, to satellite telecommunication networks and the Internet. As Derrida formulates this thesis already in the second section of the essay: *"In order to think religion today* abstractly, *we will take these powers of abstraction as our* point of departure, in order to risk, eventually, *the following hypothesis: with respect to all these forces of abstraction and of dissociation (deracination, delocalization, disincarnation, formalization, universalizing schematization, objectification, telecommunication etc.), "religion" is* at the same time *involved in reacting antagonistically and reaffirmatively outbidding itself*" (§2). In order to protect, purify, or indemnify the first of its two sources, religion must solicit the abstracting, delocalizing, and deracinating powers of teletechnology; in order to return to some supposed nature, idiom, family, or filiation that would remain immune from abstraction, translation, universalization, globalization, and so on, religion must appropriate the very things it opposes and court that which compromises and contaminates it. It does this today through the most sophisticated forms of teletechnology but also, and already, through the mechanical, repetitive, universalizable nature of the most rudimentary forms of ritual, sacrifice, and prayer. For Derrida, even the most heartfelt and seemingly spontaneous language— even the most rudimentary prayer—involves the possibility of abstraction, deracination, and thus, a movement that tends already toward repetition, translation, and universalization.[6]

Using language from Kant's *Religion* but already inscribing it within his own lexicon, Derrida says that there are "at least *two* families, two strata or sources that overlap, mingle, contaminate each another without ever merging; . . . one of the two is precisely the drive to remain unscathed, on the part of that which is allergic to contamination, *save by itself, auto-immunely*" (§28). There is, thus, an *autoimmune* relationship between religion and science. The "drive to remain unscathed" is autoimmune precisely to the extent that it enlists the powers of the teletechnological machine, that is, all those things that we might write off as inessential or external to religion in its indemnified essence but that today's "wars of religion" rely upon to an unprecedented degree.[7] For as we know better than ever today, the participants in these new wars of religion fight not only over how one is to imagine, represent, or speak about the celestial, about the nature of the heavens or the starry skies above, but over who is going to control those skies. In other words, today's wars of religion are *cyberspatialized* like never before, not simply played out or fought out and then reported and broadcast across the world but waged through and by means of teletechnoscience and its media. Digital culture is thus not simply the means of reporting on these wars but the battleground itself.

Like others before, the new "wars of religion" are unleashed over the human earth (which is not the world) and struggle even today to control the sky *with finger and eye*: digital systems and virtually immediate panoptical visualization, "air space," telecommunications satellites, information highways, concentration of capitalistic-mediatic-power—in three words, *digital culture, jet* and *TV* without which there could be no religious manifestation today, for example no voyage or discourse of the Pope, no organized emanation of Jewish, Christian or Muslim cults, whether "fundamentalist" or not. (§27)[8]

Digital culture, jet, and *TV,* that is, the encryption of information, the movements of people and materials across the globe, and televisual communication: all these are attempts at overcoming the constraints, the "limits," precisely, of time and space, attempts, as we will see in Chapter 5, at effacing themselves as media in order to give access to "the Thing itself." Derrida thus speaks of both the finger and the eye, the digital and the visual, in order to suggest that today's media and teletechnologies attempt to overcome the limits of time and space by means of a vision that touches us, that purports to provide immediate access to what comes before the machine, that is, access to the sacred and the sacrosanct, the first of the two sources of religion.

In "Faith and Knowledge," Derrida gives several examples of this fundamental complicity between media and cyberculture and today's religious "manifestations," from the worldwide travels of a pope "versed in televisional rhetoric" and the worldwide distribution of his encyclicals to the Rushdie Affair and the increasing use of cyberspace by fundamentalist groups (§27n17).[9] These examples could be supplemented by an endless series of our own, from the powers (political and otherwise) of televangelist churches in the United States and elsewhere to, for instance, the worldwide debates propagated through the media and the Internet over the publication in Denmark of what were taken to be offensive cartoons of Muhammad. So central is this theme of technology in "Faith and Knowledge" that Derrida, in §2, says he imagined the following possible titles for his essay, " '*Religion and mechane,*' '*religion and cyberspace,*' '*religion and the numeric,*' '*religion and digitality,*' '*religion and virtual space-time,*'" and so on.

In a particularly apt figure, Derrida speaks of the way in which "a heavenly glance, monstrous, bestial or divine, something like an eye of CNN, watches permanently" over us (§27n17), as if God's cyclopean eye in the sky, his celestial and synoptic vision, had been replaced by a global network of satellites that ensures not simply that "the whole world will be watching" every battle in these new wars of religion but that this technological network will actually *be* the front line for these new wars. This celestial eye, synchronized with all the Google maps in the world, would thus watch over everything all at once, "over Jerusalem and its three monotheisms, . . . over airborne pilgrimages to Mecca; over so many miracles transmitted live (most frequently, healings, which is to say, returns to the unscathed, *heilig*, holy, indemnifications) followed by commercials, before thousands in an American television studio; over the international and televisual diplomacy of the Dalai Lama, etc." (§27n17). These references to the media and to cyberculture as the place of religion's—let me now emphasize the terms—*manifestation* or even *revelation* point out both the novelty of the contemporary relationship between religion and technology *and* the continuity between these contemporary manifestations and more traditional or even archaic forms of religion. For while such manifestation has never been so worldwide, while teletechnoscience has never allowed religious manifestations to be disseminated to such an extent, such manifestation or spectrality has always been the lifeblood of religion. The figures religion now takes (tele-techno-media-scientific, capitalistic, politico-economic) are thus not original and without precedent. While cyberculture has amplified the virtual powers of religious manifestation to an unprecedented degree, while such powers today appear "remarkably adapted to the scale and the evolutions of global democracy" (§27n17), this virtuality and these powers are in fact the very element of religion from time immemorial. As Derrida puts it in a philosophical sound bite that would merit pages of explication, "the ether of religion will always have been hospitable to a certain spectral virtuality" (§27n17).

Hence the "return" to religion that was the object of so much media attention during the early to mid 1990s was not a simple return at all, Derrida argues, insofar as religion will have always made common cause with the virtuality facilitated by science and insofar as science, as we will soon see, will have always encrypted an originary source that it shares with religion. If there was, then, a "return" to or of religion, it was a becoming visible or manifest of what was always already there, a resurgence in religion's powers of manifestation through today's teletechnological machine. In what is, in many ways, the central argument of "Faith and Knowledge," the second of the three theses, Derrida claims that religion must court the delocalizing and deracinating techniques and processes of technoscience in order to protect, purify, and indemnify the first of its two sources. Teletechnoscience is thus put in the service of a return to what would claim to come *before* science, namely, the original community, an authentic and original relation to the divine, autochthony, blood, earth, language, sometimes even the nation—all those things that the intrinsically universalizable movement of teletechnoscience tends to disturb or dislocate. In order, then, to immunize itself against what is considered to be outside it, foreign to it, and threatening for it (science, the Enlightenment, modernity, the West in general), the religious community uses—often with extraordinary skill and intelligence—the very instruments of teletechnoscience and cyberculture it eschews and resists.[10]

Borrowing again Kant's language from *Religion Within the Limits of Reason Alone*, Derrida relates the deracination of technoscience to radical evil, that is, to *"forms of evil that are traditionally tied to* radical extirpation *and therefore to the deracination of abstraction, passing by way . . . of those sites of* abstraction *that are the machine, technics, technoscience and above all the transcendence of tele-technology"* (§2). Radical evil in Derrida's lexicon would thus have to do with religion's attempt to reject the deracinating movement of teletechnoscience by means of the very teletechnoscience it rejects. In §37, Derrida characterizes this rejection/appropriation as a machinal, automatic, unreflective movement. Precisely like a reflex, it repeats a double movement of abstraction and attraction, a movement that at once abstracts or uproots, that deracinates and attempts to universalize, *and* that attracts or is attracted to the literal and the idiom in an attempt to return to that from which it had been abstracted in the first place. But this second moment of attraction or rerooting can take place only through a repetition and intensification of the initial movement of abstraction and deracination.[11] Hence Derrida will characterize this as an *auto-immune auto-indemnification*, that is, as a self-indemnification, self-affirmation, or self-protection that, through the very gesture of self-affirmation and self-protection, opens the *autos* or the self up to an outside that goes beyond the self and penetrates or compromises the self-protection that was supposed to be reinforced.

> The same movement that renders indissociable religion and tele-technoscientific reason in its most critical aspect reacts inevitably *to itself*. It secretes its own antidote but also its own power of auto-immunity. We are here in a space where all self-protection of the unscathed, of the safe and sound, of the sacred (*heilig*, holy) must protect itself against its own protection, its own police, its own power of rejection, in short, against its own, which is to say, against its own immunity. It is this terrifying but fatal logic of the *auto-immunity of the unscathed* that will always associate Science and Religion. (§37)

Religion must thus reject the machine by means of the machine; it must go out of itself in order to return to and restore itself. This rejection/ appropriation of the machine can take, says Derrida in §46, at least two possible paths—yet another form of duplicity: it can result in either a fervent return to nationalism or patriotism, often linked to the church, or a new universalism, cosmopolitanism, or ecumenicalism—a new International of anti-tele-technologism or a new worldwide ecologism.[12] In either case, however, one can reject the technoscientific machine only by appropriating it, only by working through it in order to return to the proper or the safe and sound in the guise of ethnic identity, filiation, family, nation, culture, memory, tradition, nature, language, and so on, or in order to forge a new internationalism and humanism based on a common rejection of the supposed dehumanization brought on by the machine.

In addition to these two possibilities of rejecting technoscience through the inevitable reappropriation of it, there is also the possibility of a hyper-appropriation of technoscience whose underlying aim is its rejection, that is, a "counter-fetishism of the same desire inverted, the animist relation to the tele-technoscientific machine, which then becomes a machine of evil, and of radical evil, but a machine to be manipulated as much as to be exorcised" (§45). Derrida is here evoking the possibility of a more and more animistic, magical, mystical relation to the tele-techno-scientific machine, one that condemns the "evil machine," uses it, and comes to have a more and more "**primitive and archaic**" relation to it. According to this hypothesis, our growing fascination with the tele-technoscientific machine and its unprecedented powers of spectrality would be in direct relation to our growing incompetence with regard to it. As Derrida justly remarks, there has never been such a gap between our technical know-how in everyday life and our own technical knowledge, whence the mystical relation we can have to cell phones or the Internet or any number of machines we use on a daily basis. Indeed it would be difficult to deny Derrida's claim that "never in the history of humanity . . . has the disproportion between scientific incompetence and manipulatory competence been as serious" (§45).[13]

When Derrida thus refers in §15 to the "*absolute anachrony of our time,*" he is speaking in part of this mystical relation to technoscience that can combine the most archaic and primitive violence with the most sophisticated forms of weaponry and technology. There is no essential contradiction—only a thoroughgoing autoimmunity—between capitalistic techno-science and all forms of religious fundamentalism. Faced with an "**expropriative and delocalizing** tele-technoscience" (§45), reaction to the tele-technoscientific machine can appeal either to an "obscurantist dogmatism" or to "hypercritical vigilance," if not to both at once (§46). Fundamentalisms or extremisms of various kinds can thus combine brutal, reactive forms of violence with the most refined and elaborated forms of modern technoscience and critique. The simple denunciation of what appears to be obscurantism or irrationality thus misses what is most important in religion's reaction to technoscience. More sophisticated analyses are necessary.

> As for the phenomena of ignorance, of irrationality or of "obscurantism" that are so often emphasized and denounced, so easily and with good reason, they are often residues, surface effects, the reactive slag of immunitary, indemnificatory or auto-immunitary reactivity. They mask a deep structure or rather (but also at the same time) a fear of self, a reaction against that with which it is partially linked: the dislocation, expropriation, delocalization, deracination, disidiomatization and dispossession . . . that the tele-techno-scientific machine does not fail to produce. (§37)

What we have here, then, is a double movement of rejection *and* assimilation, impossible indemnification *and* mourning, the desperate, *autoimmune* attempt by religion to protect itself by means of what always threatens to destroy it (see §47). Derrida makes this even clearer in "Above All, No Journalists!"

> The apparent contradiction between faith and knowledge, between religion and enlightenment, thus repeats itself. It does so because in order to reach the light, in order to phenomenalize itself, to utter itself, to manifest itself, the sacralizing movement, the experience of the sacred, must cede to what I call "autoimmunity." In it, the living organism destroys the conditions of its own protection. Such auto-immunization is a terrifying biological possibility: a body destroys its proper defenses or organizes in itself . . . the destructive forces that will attack its immunitary reactions. When religion shows itself on television, wherever it manifests and deploys itself in the "world," in the "public space," it at the same time increases its power and its power to self-destroy; it increases both the one and the other, the one *as* the other, to the same degree. ("AANJ" 67)

Every auto-protection of the indemnified, the safe and sound, must thus protect itself against its own protection; religion must protect itself against the technoscience that promotes, projects, and protects it. It is, says Derrida in "Faith and Knowledge," "this terrifying but fatal [*fatale*] logic of the *auto-immunity of the unscathed* that will always associate Science and Religion" (§37). This autoimmune indemnification of religion through science is not something religion can simply refrain from doing or avoid falling victim to. It is, Derrida writes, *fatale*, that is, as Sam

Weber has translated it, "fatal," potentially destructive, disastrous, deadly, though also, since this is the other sense of *fatale*, fated or fateful, ineluctable or unavoidable. It is at once potentially deadly and the only chance religion has for living on.

It is important to note that this notion of autoimmunity, which had been used by Derrida in earlier texts such as *Specters of Marx* and *Politics of Friendship*, is really given its first full treatment only here in "Faith and Knowledge."[14] Much of this work is done in a long footnote to §37, where Derrida first recalls the ecclesiastical context of the term *immunity*, the notion of offering someone safe haven or asylum in a church, temple, or synagogue. Before diplomatic immunity or biological immunity, there would have been the immunity offered by religion or by religious communities to those being pursued or persecuted. As for *autoimmunity*, this is obviously a much more recent term of the biological sciences. As Derrida will go on to develop in even greater detail in *Rogues* and elsewhere in relationship to democracy (and we will see in Chapter 6 that this example is not fortuitous), autoimmunity has to do with the way a living organism protects itself by attacking its own self-protection and destroying its own immune defenses, thereby making it vulnerable to what it might have otherwise resisted. This attack on or protection against one's own mechanisms of self-protection is thus *fatale*—inevitable and always potentially deadly—though also, as in the case of immuno-depressants, essential to the organism's survival, essential to its acceptance of a graft or transplanted organ that will allow it to survive or live on. Indeed, without autoimmunity, without this breach in the immunitary and self-protective systems of the organism, there would be no possibility of a supplement that might destroy *or* save it, bring it to an end *or* allow it to live on. Without autoimmunity, the organism would have, in short, no future before it. Autoimmunity is thus another name for the aporia of the *salut* we saw earlier. Without the *salut!* as greeting and reception, without the welcoming of the supplement or graft of the other, the self would remain within itself, absolutely protected, which is to say, absolutely safe and sound and thus absolutely dead. Though the *phantasm* of absolute immunity remains—indeed this is, in the end, the only phantasm—absolute immunity is nothing short of absolute death.

Starting, then, from the strictly ecclesiastical notion of immunity and then the biological notion of autoimmunity, Derrida argues that a "sort of general logic of autoimmunization" seems "indispensable to us today for thinking the relations between faith and knowledge, religion and science, as well as the duplicity of sources in general" (§37n27). For there are always, it seems, two sources or two tendencies—a move toward indemnifying self-protection and another toward autoimmune self-destruction, or, put otherwise, a move toward complete self-indemnification that, if successful, would put an end to the life of the self or the community that is being protected, and an autoimmune movement—a kind of death drive—that at once threatens any organism or community and allows it to live on. This means that the self or the community is never itself without its self-expropriation into the other and the incorporation of the other into itself. In every attempt to purify, protect, and indemnify itself, the self or the community lives off what it is not, projecting a phantasm of life protected from all death, and yet living on only by means of all the supplements of death or, really, of *life-death*: writing, science, telecommunications, the graft, iterability, abstraction, the machine, and so on.

By "allying itself with the enemy, hospitable to the antigens, bearing away the other with itself, this resurgence [*déferlement*] grows and *swells* [se gonfle]," writes Derrida, "with the power of the adversary" (§37). Religion's power grows to the extent that it appropriates the very technoscience that threatens it. In order to indemnify itself, religion must take on even more of what it opposes. Only this immune/autoimmune double reactivity can account for the resurgence of religion today, that is, to use Derrida's word, this *déferlement*, a word often used to describe the breaking of waves or the spread of violence or a troop surge or insurgency (see Derrida's comments on this word at *MO* 31). Hence Derrida will speak in his own name throughout "Faith and Knowledge" not of a *return* to religion but of a *resurgence* of it, a new wave or surge in what has been an ever-present force or movement in European culture that has varied over time in intensity or visibility but that has never gone away in order, one day, to return. Religion is thus allied today as it has always been with technoscience, but because of the growth and intensification of the latter, the former has had to react against it with even greater force, upping the ante in order to match and go beyond a movement that will have already gone beyond it—fatefully.

Let me cite at length a passage from §37—just before "*et grenades*"—where this second thesis of "Faith and Knowledge" is laid out in its clearest and most explicit form.

> Religion today allies itself with tele-technoscience, to which it reacts with all its forces. It is, *on the one hand*, globalization; it produces, weds, exploits the capital and knowledge of tele-mediatization; neither the trips and global spectacularizing of the Pope, nor the inter-state dimensions of the "Rushdie affair," nor planetary terrorism

would otherwise be possible . . . But, *on the other hand,* it reacts immediately, *simultaneously,* declaring war against that which gives it this new power only at the cost of dislodging it from all its proper places, *in truth from place itself,* form the *taking place* of its truth. It conducts a terrible war against that which protects it only by threatening it, according to this double and contradictory structure: immunitary and auto-immunitary. The relation between these two motions or these two sources is ineluctable, and therefore automatic and mechanical, between one which has the form of the machine (mechanization, automatization, machination or *mechane*), and the other, that of a living spontaneity, of the *unscathed* property of life, that is to say, of another (claimed) self-determination. But the auto-immunity haunts the community and its system of immunitary survival like the hyperbole of its own possibility. Nothing in *common,* nothing immune, safe and sound, *heilig* and holy, nothing unscathed in the most autonomous living present without a risk of auto-immunity. As always, the risk charges itself twice, the same finite risk. (§37)

Religion is thus involved in two movements at once; it is involved, first, in a reactive movement that tries to return to the safe and sound, to earth and ethnicity, to the nation and the national idiom. But it is also involved in what Derrida calls *mondialatinisation,* in a globalizing or, better, a "worldwide" process that is first linked, as we saw in the previous chapter, to the language in which Christianity first spread across the globe, namely, Latin, though also, in a second moment, to religion's new lingua franca, namely, Anglo-American. Religion is thus attracted to, animated by, this globalatinization and embroiled in a reaction against it, engaged in a war that has been declared against that which gives religion this new power only by dislodging it from its proper place, disrupting the relationship between truth and place. In "Above All, No Journalists!" Derrida relates this disruption from place, this uncanny uprooting from house and home, to the *unheimlich,* which today takes on "a particularly striking form . . . in the irreducible bond between religion and media" ("AANJ" 68). As we will see later, the attachment to all those things that might appear most natural and without need of mediatization, attachments to idiom or the home—or to their phantasms—might be read as a reactive formation to this *unheimlich* or uncanny relationship to the tele-technoscientific machine.

As Derrida writes above in one rather dense and difficult sentence, "autoimmunity haunts the community and its system of immunitary survival like the hyperbole of its own possibility" (§37). To try to parse this out: autoimmunity is not a risk that the community may or may not run but the necessity to which it must yield, the necessity that haunts all of its immune structures and strategies, a necessity that haunts it from within, from the place where its very survival is secured. This risk of autoimmunity is thus the threat of radical evil, the threat of a deracination that threatens the community and its survival and yet makes that survival possible in the first place. Whence the hyperbole involved in raising the stakes of technoscience, multiplying and augmenting all the forces of delocalization and deracination in order to assure the presence and life of the putatively prescientific, original, or natural community.

What is truly "proper" to religion—its ineradicable allegiance and incurable allergy to science—is what makes it fundamentally improper. If autoimmune auto-indemnification is indeed, as Derrida suggests, inevitable, unavoidable, in a word, *fatale*, then what is "proper" to religion is both its attempt to indemnify the first of its two sources and the unavoidable expropriation of religion into what it is not. It is this expropriating movement, this improper propriety—this autoimmunity—that leads to various attempts on the part of religion to indemnify all those things that are traditionally considered proper to the self or the community: property, language, family, nature, blood, and soil, and, finally and most importantly for Derrida, *life*. If the French word *salut* appeared earlier to be the best way to identify one of the two sources of religion, it is in the name of life that this *salut* is always sought, life as what is restored in health or life as what is redeemed or saved. Religion attempts to protect, indemnify, and augment life by means of the technological supplement against which religion then reacts with the automaticity of a machine. Derrida writes, "The reactivity of resentment . . . *indemnifies* itself thus in a movement that is at once immunitary and auto-immune. The reaction to the machine is as automatic (and thus machinal) as life itself" (§37).

If this reaction cannot but happen, if it happens with the regularity of a machine, then such a reaction would appear to be part of religion itself, religion in its essence. Which means that the essence of religion, the "proper" of religion, is to be from the beginning improper, fundamentally duplicitous.

> Such an internal splitting, which opens distance, is also peculiar or "proper" to religion, appropriating religion for the "proper" (inasmuch as it is also the *unscathed*: *heilig*, holy, sacred, saved, immune and so on), appropriating religious indemnification to all forms of property, from the linguistic idiom in its "letter," to blood and soil,

to the family and to the nation. This internal and immediate reactivity, at once immunitary and auto-immune, can alone account for what will be called the religious resurgence in its double and contradictory phenomenon. (§37)

But the autoimmune logic by which Derrida tries to think the relationship between the two sources of religion and between religion and science would seem to apply to more than just religion "itself." As we saw Derrida arguing above, "the reaction to the machine is as automatic (and thus machinal) as life itself" (§37). In the end, it is not only religion but life itself that is autoimmune, life itself that reacts in an automatic, machinal way, life itself that must now be thought in relation to the machine. That is why Derrida places so much emphasis in "Faith and Knowledge" on autoimmunity. As a biological process, it is one of those places where life and the machine seem to intersect in a particularly palpable way, where a biological reaction seems to happen with the regularity and automaticity of a machine, that is, with a regularity or automaticity that is *fatale*, inevitable, predictable like a machine, and deadly, as a result, to any concept of a life *before* the machine, of a self or a community that might remain safe and sound before or without the other.

We will see in the following chapter how this machinelike and automatic movement contaminates everything from the beginning, from Genesis on, including the genesis of "Faith and Knowledge." But before that we must look at the third thesis, the third and final principal thesis, of "Faith and Knowledge." If religion turns to science in order to indemnify itself, if it turns, in an autoimmune fashion, to the very thing that will compromise what it is trying to protect, then that is because there is an even more intimate relationship between religion and science or faith and knowledge. Religion at once needs science and is in open antagonism against it in spite of the fact—because of the fact—that the two actually share a *common source*.[15] In addition to having a source in a kind of reason, rationality, or technological thinking, science too has *another* source, a second source, it, too, in the promise or performative faith that makes science itself *performative*. Indeed science, like religion, requires faith, trust, credit, reliability, and so on, an originary or elementary faith that is anterior to every science and is the quasi-transcendental condition of all knowledge.

Already back in §8 Derrida gives a first indication that religion and science perhaps share a common source when he points out that religion is always related to light, to appearance, and, thus, to phenomena, in a word, to a certain "phenomenology" and a certain "enlightenment."

I had insisted on the light, the relation of all religion to fire and to light. There is the light of revelation and the light of the Enlightenment. Light, *phos*, revelation, orient and origin of *our* religions, photographic instantaneity. Question, demand: in view of the Enlightenment of today and of tomorrow, in the light of other Enlightenments (*Aufklärung, Lumières, illuminismo*) how **to think religion** in the daylight of today without breaking with the philosophical tradition? (§36)

One is reminded here of Levinas's claim in *Totality and Infinity*, as reformulated by Derrida in 1964 in "Violence and Metaphysics," that philosophy, and particularly "*phenomenology*, in the wake of Plato, was to be struck with light" (*WD* 85). But it is not only phenomenology and philosophy that have been struck by light but also religion, science, and, clearly, a certain Enlightenment. In "Above All, No Journalists!" Derrida extends this centrality of light by suggesting a relationship between all of these and the media, particularly television, a thesis we will explore more fully in Chapter 5: "It would be easy, but not arbitrary, to think the motif of light—the figure of light in the *Illuminismo*, the *Aufklärung*, the *Lumières*—with that visibility, that phenomenality from which public space, and hence television, are constructed. From phenomenality in general, whether from the Greek or the Evangelical light, up to the lights that manifest themselves in television 'news,' there is a common element" ("AANJ" 66).

The trope of light is thus central to both faith and knowledge, philosophy and science, religion and the media. While it is thus tempting to want to see light, a certain revealability, a certain search for the "truth" as what is unconcealed, made manifest, or revealed, to be the common source of both religion and science, religion and the media, I think Derrida would ask us to be critical and vigilant at precisely this point in order to expose the assumptions behind this trope of light as well. The second source of both religion and science is thus not a common or shared light, an even more original light of revelation or manifestation, but the *nocturnal source* of light, a source that must be thought in relationship to faith or trustworthiness—to *fiabilité*—as we saw earlier. It will be related not to light or illumination, to some shared quality of truth or manifestation that would reside in the nature of things, but to a nocturnal source that is based in the inaccessibility of the other.

We will look at this second source in relation to science in particular in a moment, but let us simply note that it will be in part on the basis of this shared source that Derrida will go on to argue that the Enlightenment not only did not completely break with religion, as some have been led to believe, but that the very origins of the Enlightenment are to be found in religion. Indeed only by not drawing a single and indivisible line between religion and science, or religion and the secular, can we really begin to understand the so-called "return of religion." Derrida asks:

> *Why is this phenomenon, so hastily called the "return of religions," so difficult to think? Why is it so surprising? Why does it particularly astonish those who believed naïvely that an alternative opposed Religion, on the one side, and on the other, Reason, Enlightenment, Science, Criticism (Marxist Criticism, Nietzschean Genealogy, Freudian Psychoanalysis and their heritage), as though the one could not but put an end to the other? On the contrary, it is an entirely different schema that would have to be taken as one's point of departure in order to try to think the "return of the religious."*(§6)

Rather than simply assume he knows what is meant by the so-called return of the religious, rather than simply explain away or write off this return by resorting *"to what the* doxa *confusedly calls 'fundamentalism,' 'fanaticism' or, in French, 'integrism,'"* Derrida looks for another point of departure by identifying a common source of both religion and science (§6).[16] As Derrida argues, we will fail to understand religion today if we continue to believe in the strict opposition between religion and science or between religion and reason, critique, and technoscientific modernity. In other words, we will fail to understand religion so long as we remain in a certain Enlightenment tradition, in that secularizing, anti-religious Judeo-Christian filiation that would run, say, from Voltaire to Marx, Nietzsche, Freud, and even, though this is more ambiguous, as Derrida shows, to Heidegger (see Observation 4). We must thus question, Derrida claims, all those who, in a certain Enlightenment tradition, believed in the independence of reason, knowledge, technicity, philosophy and thought with regard to religion and faith (see §48).[17]

Instead of opposing religion and science, then, we must ask how technoscience supports religion even as religion attacks it and show that religion and technoscience have the same source, a common source—the testimonial engagement (*gage*) of every performative, which commits or engages one to respond *before* the other and *for* the performativity of technoscience. Hence religion wages a war on technoscience through technoscience and through our faith in technoscience. Religion has two sources, and one of these is the common source of both religion and science. Beyond a simple opposition between religion and science or faith and reason, it would be necessary to demonstrate that "religion and reason develop in tandem, drawing from this common resource: the testimonial pledge of every performative, committing it to respond as much *before* the other as *for* the high-performance performativity of technoscience" (§29). "Whence," writes Derrida, "the two sources in one," as the "same source" divides itself from itself from the very beginning—mechanically, automatically, like the autoimmunity of life itself (§29).

It is thus not only religion but science or teletechnoscience that requires and presupposes a certain reliability or trustworthiness or *fiabilité*, a kind of elementary faith. At the root of every institution, constitution, law, sovereign state, and even science, there is, Derrida argues, "an irreducible 'faith,'" a "sworn faith," the faith of a "social bond," a *promise* to tell the truth "beyond all proof and all theoretical demonstration" (§37). Because there is "no responsibility without a *given word*, a sworn faith [*foi jurée*], without a pledge, without an oath, without some *sacrament* or its *ius iurandum*" (§29), no scientific community is possible without this elementary faith: "Without the performative experience of this elementary act of faith, there would neither be 'social bond' nor address of the other, nor any performativity in general: neither convention, nor institution, nor constitution, nor sovereign state, nor law, nor above all, here, that structural performativity of the productive performance that binds from its inception the knowledge of the scientific community to doing, and science to technics" (§37). Derrida makes the connection between faith and science even more explicit in "Above All, No Journalists!":

> Even in the most theoretical act of any scientific community (there is no science without public space and without scientific community), every organization of the social bond appeals to an act of faith, beyond or this side of every species of proof. The "I believe you" or the "believe me," "sworn faith," is at once the social bond, the economic bond, and credit, just as truthfulness is the condition of truth. ("AANJ" 63)

What we discover at the "source" of both religion and science is thus not a more originary light that reveals the truth of things but, again, an aspect of language of a different order, one that does not reveal things in the light but, rather, *makes* the light without itself being light or even the possibility of light, in other words, a *performative* aspect of language. What we identified earlier as one of the two sources of religion in a performative faith, credit, or trust that is anterior to any contract of language or exchange within language is now seen to be operative in science as well. Though Derrida in "Signature Event Context" and elsewhere ended up questioning the pertinence of Austin's distinction between constative and performative, questioning whether the concept of the performative is not still too determined by the notion of a subject endowed with the ability or capacity to speak and thus bring something about, Derrida nonetheless always maintains the usefulness of the distinction. He will thus follow quite faithfully a distinction between, for example, credos, oaths, pledges of fidelity, or professions of faith, on the one hand, and observations, claims, or statements of knowledge on the other, in short, between performatives and constatives. But Derrida will then go on, in a second moment, to argue that there is a kind of "performative" at the origin of *both* the constative and the performative, and, thus, at the origin of both science and religion, both knowledge and faith—a source that might be called a kind of originary or elementary trust or confidence or an originary engagement or commitment, an originary faith or pledge.

The origin thus doubles or divides—automatically. The event of the origin divides into two sources; in the realm of language, the event, what Jean-François Lyotard would have called the *Arrive-t-il?*—his translation of *Ereignis*—automatically, spontaneously, divides into the constative and the performative, into the scientific utterance that is connoted and the religious utterance that is performed.[18] But as Austin himself came to see and Derrida develops, the constative is always a veiled performative. When a scientist says, for example, that tellurium is a metallic element whose atomic number is 52, he or she is not simply noting what is the fact but affirming and vouching for this "fact," asking us to believe him or her, to trust in his or her experience, to rely upon his or her good faith in declaring it. It is this faith, belief, or credit that thus opens up in a performative fashion not only the dimension of religion but the performativity of our science, our trust in teletechnoscience and in the fiduciary in general, our confidence not only in the other "right there" before us but in every anonymous monetary exchange or transaction of cybercapital. There is a testimonial performative required of all knowledge and all capital (§37).

It is no doubt this emphasis on performativity that leads Derrida in "Faith and Knowledge" to talk less about science than about technology or technoscience. He writes: "We associate here reason with philosophy and with science as technoscience, as critical history of the production of knowledge, of knowledge *as* production, know-how and intervention at a distance, teletechnoscience that is always high-performance and performative by essence, etc." (§29). Derrida argues in a similar fashion in "Above All, No Journalists!" that his use of the term *technoscience* indicates that "there is no science without technical apparatus, no separation possible between science and technology, which is to say, without a profound and essential 'performativity' of knowledge" ("AANJ" 63). The term *perform-ativity* seems to be the link in Derrida's discourse between the two sources of science: it would refer, on the one hand, to the way in which science—or, better, technology—performs and advances, the way it *works*, and, on the other, to the performative act of faith or the promise that brings one into a scientific community in the first place. Derrida thus uses the term *technoscience* (and not just science) in order to recall that "the scientific act is, through and through, a practical intervention and a technical per-formativity in the very energy of its essence" and that "this elementary act of faith also underlies the essentially economic and capitalistic rationality of the tele-technoscientific" (§37). When we understand this double per-formativity, the performativity of the machine and the act of faith upon which it depends, we can see "why, in principle, today, there is no incom-patibility, in the said 'return of the religious,' between the 'fundamen-talisms,' the 'integrisms' or their 'politics' and, on the other hand, rationality, which is to say, the tele-techno-capitalistico-scientific fiduci-arity, in all of its mediatic and globalizing dimensions" (§37).

Everywhere technoscience is at work, delocalizing, uprooting, distanc-ing, or bringing near, it confirms this elementary faith, which is "reli-gious" in vocation insofar as it is what makes religion possible. Every act of language, then, from the most ceremonial profession of faith to the most straightforward or seemingly transparent observation in science, pre-supposes an "I promise the truth." Every time I address another, "some sort of 'I promise the truth' is always at work, and some sort of 'I make this commitment before the other from the moment that I address him, even and perhaps above all to commit perjury'" (§29). Every time one bears witness, therefore, and even in science, the truth is promised beyond all proof, all perception, all imitative monstration. Even when I lie, Der-rida argues, I ask the other to *believe* this other who I am. This per-formativity or promise to tell the truth thus "conditions" like a quasi-transcendental all sincere declarations and all lies, every profession of faith within religion and every empirical claim in science. In *Rogues*, written seven years after "Faith and Knowledge," Derrida again speaks of "the irreducible spacing of the very faith, credit, or belief without which there would be no social bond, no address to the other, no uprightness or honesty, no promise to be honored, and so no honor, no faith to be sworn or pledge to be given" (*R* 153).[19] Derrida echoes and expands upon this notion of a social bond in relationship to science in "Above All, No Journalists!":

How can we link up again with the old form of the question, "faith and knowledge"? The "return of the religious" reintroduces a new sort of transcendental condition of the fiduciary. The social bond reveals itself increasingly, in particular through new capitalist structures, to be a phenomenon of faith. No social bond without the promise of truth, without an "I believe you," without an "I believe." The development of the sciences or of the techno-scientific community itself supposes a layer of credit, of faith, of credibility—which is not to be confused with Good News or a *determinate* religious revelation, nor with a dogmatism or religious orthodoxy, but simply reintroduces the necessity of faith in its most rudimentary [*nu*: naked, bare] condition. ("AANJ" 63)

This reference to a *rudimentary* or a *bare* faith expresses well the elemental character of this faith. Rather than a faith clothed in some religion or religious dogma, rather than a faith in some object or other, this faith would be the condition, milieu, or medium for any determinate faith or belief. Derrida thus speaks of this "element of faith" (§48) as a "bare belief [*cette croyance nue*]" ("AANJ" 65), as the very "air that we breathe" (*IW* 58) insofar as an "act of faith is implied in the social relationship, in the social bond itself" (*IW* 59). Like a latter-day Pre-Socratic, Derrida is, as it were, adding a fifth "element" to the traditional four (earth, fire, water, and air): the ether of faith that makes possible every testimony and every social bond.

Insofar as every community, every social bond, is based upon an originary act of faith that eludes all proof or monstration, an originary "I believe" or "I believe you" that is absolutely blind, this common source of both religion and science is compared by Derrida to a kind of *miracle*. The most developed account of this originary act of faith as a miracle can be found in §49—just three sections before the end—as Derrida draws together the various strands of his argument and offers what is to my ears the most striking formulation of this elementary faith: it amounts to saying, he writes, "Believe what I say as one believes in a miracle" (§49). I would like to follow this passage in some detail in order to see just how Derrida relates here the secret to publicity, the singular to iterability, and the miracle to the machine.

Derrida begins by claiming that "the experience of **witnessing** situates a convergence" of what we have already seen to be the two sources of religion: "the *unscathed* (the safe, the sacred or the saintly) and the *fiduciary* (trustworthiness, fidelity, credit, belief or faith, 'good faith' implied in the worst 'bad faith')" (§49). Witnessing or testimony would thus be the place where the unscathed, where a singular and unshareable experience, where the secret, becomes public by means of an appeal to trustworthiness, fidelity, credit, and faith. It is the place where an appeal is made to the other beyond all demonstration and proof, an appeal to the other to believe not necessarily that I have the truth but that I am giving voice to what I believe to be the truth—a belief that is completely beyond the knowledge or perception of the other.

> In testimony, truth is promised beyond all proof, all perception, all intuitive demonstration. Even if I lie or perjure myself (and always and especially when I do), I promise truth and ask the other to believe the other that I am, there where I am the only one able to bear witness and where the order of proof or of intuition will never be reducible to or homogeneous with the elementary trust [*fiduciarité*], the "good faith" that is promised or demanded. (§49)

Derrida argues next that this appeal to an experience beyond all demonstration and thus beyond all repetition is nevertheless "never pure of all iterability nor of all technics, and hence of all **calculability**. For it also promises its repetition from the very first instant." Whenever one swears to tell the truth, the whole truth, and nothing but the truth, one promises already to be willing and able to repeat this truth, to vouch for and thus promise to tell again this singular truth as the irreplaceable witness one is. As such, this irreplaceable witness must promise to repeatedly replace himself or herself, and he or she must give voice to a testimony that anyone who had been in his or her shoes, who had seen with his or her eyes, would have given.[20] The irreplaceable witness thus promises to replace him or herself in the future and promises to be virtually replaceable by anyone who would have witnessed what he or she did. Despite my use here of the codes and rhetoric of the court of law, this structural relation is to be found in every relation with the other— including those in science: "It is involved [*engagé*] in every address of the other. From the first instant it is co-extensive with this other and thus conditions every 'social bond,' every questioning, all knowledge, performativity and every tele-technoscientific performance, including those of its forms that are the most synthetic, artificial, prosthetic, calculable" (§49). It is at this point that Derrida says that this testimonial faith, "the promise of this axiomatic (quasi-transcendental) performative," which "conditions and foreshadows 'sincere' declarations no less than lies and perjuries, and thus all address of the other," "amounts to saying: 'Believe what I say as one believes in a miracle.'" But if this notion of the miracle is, as Derrida here suggests, coextensive with elementary faith, then we would have to speak of miracles in relation not only to religion but to science, and in relation not only to the most extraordinary or sacred experience but to the most secular and banal.

Even the slightest testimony concerning the most plausible, ordinary or everyday thing cannot do otherwise: it must still appeal to faith as would a miracle. It offers itself like the miracle itself in a space that leaves no room for disenchantment. . . . That one should be called upon to believe in testimony as in a miracle or an "extraordinary story"—this is what inscribes itself without hesitation in the very concept of bearing witness. (§49)

"*Pure* attestation, if there is such a thing," thus belongs "to the experience of faith and of the miracle," and it is implied in *every* "social bond"; it is thus as "indispensable to Science no less than to Philosophy and to Religion" (§49).

After suggesting various possibilities for this experience of faith and of the miracle, from a "sacredness without belief (index of this algebra: 'Heidegger')" to "faith in a holiness without sacredness" that would make "of a certain disenchantment the condition of authentic holiness (index: 'Levinas'—notably the author of *From the Sacred to the Holy*)," Derrida makes it clear that this testimonial faith that conditions every social bond is not some shared relation, some adhesive sentiment, some *common bond*, precisely, between members of a *same* community or a *same* humanity, but a kind of "interruption." The "social bond [*lien*]" of this originary faith or *fiabilité* is thus related not to a common relation with the other but to a certain inaccessibility of the other. If, as Derrida put it in his conversation in 2003 with Mustapha Chérif, "there is no social bond without faith" (*IW* 58), faith makes of this social bond a place not of communion but of interruption, a place not of shared ideals or a common community but of a "shared" secret.

> There is no opposition, fundamentally, between "social bond" and "social unraveling." A certain interruptive unraveling is the condition of the "social bond," the very respiration of all "community." This is not even the knot of a reciprocal condition, but rather the possibility that every knot can come undone, be cut or interrupted. This is where the *socius* or the relation to the other would disclose itself to be the secret of testimonial experience—and hence, of a certain faith. If belief is the ether of the address and relation to the utterly other, it is [to be found] in the experience itself of non-relationship or of absolute *interruption* (indices: "Blanchot," "Levinas" . . .). (§49)[21]

This undoing or this interruption, this caesura, is the very respiration of every "community," its perpetual opening to difference and surprise, in a word, to the future. Belief may thus be the ether of the address and of the relation to the other, but this ether is a medium of separation and not communion, an experience of "non-relationship or of absolute interruption."[22] Derrida's profound suspicion of community or at least of all communitarianism, which we saw in Chapter 1, here finds its theoretical confirmation. Such a testimonial faith could thus never be the basis of a new religion or a new communitarianism; indeed, even concepts such as secularism and laicization are, it seems, too "religious" for Derrida, "too Christian" in their origins to describe this interruption in the social bond and this experience of the miracle. Derrida speaks instead of a "hypersanctification" or "desacralization" of this "non-relation or of this transcendence," which would come about by way of a certain "atheism" or else—using a distinction made by Levinas—a "holiness" decoupled from the "sacred" (§49).[23] Derrida thus concludes §49 by suggesting that this testimonial faith, this experience of the miracle, the condition of every social bond, is—"as the *very resource of the religious*"—that which dis-joins in both space and time by introducing incommensurability and non-contemporaneity: "This interruptive dis-junction enjoins a sort of incommensurable equality within absolute dissymmetry. The law of this untimeliness interrupts and makes history, it undoes all contemporaneity and opens the very space of faith. It designates disenchantment as the *very resource of the religious*. The first and the last" (§49).

Derrida is quite clear about the disruptive nature of this faith. And yet it has to be said that, in speaking of *faith* at all, Derrida opens himself up to misunderstanding on several counts. There is, first, the possibility that one will confuse this elementary faith with a faith in some particular religion or religious dogma. But it might also look as if Derrida is sugarcoating an experience of the other that is anything but reassuring. Indeed it might appear as if he is willing, we might say, to "drop the F-bomb" here in order to appear more amenable to those of various religious faiths, and perhaps even to gain good conscience for himself. In "Above All, No Journalists!" Derrida himself worries about just this, that is, about what might appear to be a rather comforting or reassuring use of this term *faith*:

> I should "avow," without Christian confession, that I often find myself in a situation where, accused of diabolical, inhuman, and monstrous discourse, I pretend to beat a hasty retreat in saying that "for my part, I believe in faith." And, of course, this sounds reassuring. It reassures those who don't want to listen. . . . Blushing invisibly, I ask myself, "What am I doing? Am I not in the process of reassuring them? In view of what?" But as soon as one pronounces the word

"faith," the equivocation is there, disastrous and deserted. When, for my part, I yield to it, it is not simply out of opportunism, to please those listeners I would otherwise want to shock and to trouble. It is because I believe that the equivocation is undeniably there. . . . The religious, in its equivocal relation to faith (it is and it isn't faith, and faith supposes, in its purity, that nothing is assured, probable, or believable), is the equivocation in which we are. ("AANJ" 69)

Well, if the word *faith* poses potential problems for Derrida, the name *God* would seem to pose even graver ones. And yet Derrida does not shy away from this word either. In "Faith and Knowledge," he will go so far as to declare with regard to the elementary faith we have been following here that even in a secular oath God is called upon as a witness, called upon as the nameable-unnameable, *present-absent* witness of every oath.[24] It is thus not simply the truth that is made through testimony but, curiously, "God himself," God himself who is engendered in every oath and in every attestation:

Presupposed at the origin of all address, coming from the other to *whom it is also addressed*, the wager [*gageure*] of a sworn promise, taking immediately God as its witness, cannot not but have already, if one can put it this way, engendered God quasi-mechanically. *A priori* ineluctable, a descent of God *ex machina* would stage a transcendental addressing machine. . . . For in taking God as witness, even when he is not named in the most "secular" [*laïque*] pledge of commitment, the oath cannot *not* produce, invoke or convoke him as already there, and therefore as unengendered and unengenderable, prior to being itself. . . . God: the witness as "nameable-unnameable," present-absent-witness of every oath or of every possible pledge. As long as one supposes, *concesso non dato*, that religion has the slightest relation to what we thus call God. (§29)

Derrida thus does not shy away from speaking of either *faith* or *God*, but he does so only by reinscribing these names into his own idiom. Before rushing to conclude, therefore, that this is some starry- or weepy-eyed return to religious faith on Derrida's part, one must recall that these terms cannot be thought without all the references we have seen throughout this chapter to the machine, automaticity, autoimmunity, the death drive, and so on. Even before the beginning, then, as we will see in the following chapter, there is the promise to respond, and this promise is from the beginning compromised by the machine. In the beginning, before the beginning, there is the quasi-mechanical engendering of God in the promise to tell the truth and bring to light.

Derrida thus uses the words *faith*, *God*, and, as we shall see later, *messianicity* in ways that court misunderstanding, even though a closer and, I believe, more "faithful" reading would demonstrate where Derrida is taking his distance from traditional uses and understandings of these terms. But, then, what about the term *miracle*, which Derrida uses in this passage and which I have even used in the title of this book? This is the last term we need to look at in this chapter in order to draw this analysis of the three theses of "Faith and Knowledge" to a close.

Derrida says that we are called upon to believe every testimony—every claim to the truth, every claim that one is telling the truth about what one knows, believes, or sees—as an "extraordinary story" or a miracle. How are we to understand the word *miracle* here and throughout this work? As is always the case with Derrida's terminology, it must be read both in relationship to its traditional meaning and as a radical interruption of that meaning. If the very notion of a miracle entails just such a radical interruption of our habitual or predictable ways of interpreting events, then the reinscription of this term would perhaps be something like a miracle of meaning itself . . .

From the Latin *miraculum*, the term *miracle* typically refers, of course, to a marvelous event or an event that causes wonder, an extraordinary event that remains inexplicable in terms of ordinary natural forces, an event that violates natural law and so is usually attributed to some superhuman or divine cause or else is used as evidence for the superhumanity or divinity of that cause. One thinks immediately of the miracles of the Bible, those that took place, for example, during the Exodus—the burning bush, the ten plagues of Egypt, the parting of the Red Sea and the crossing of the Jordan, the fall of Jericho—or those that occurred in the time of Elijah and Elisha. Or else one thinks of all the miracles performed by Christ in the New Testament, his healing of the blind or the lame, his multiplication of the fish and bread, the miracle of the "languages" on the day of Pentecost that marks the beginning of the ministry of the apostles, and so on. The Gospels record close to forty so-called miracles performed by Christ, miracles that are supposed to act as signs to believers and nonbelievers alike of God's divinity or divine plan (John 10:37, 38; 20:31).

For Derrida too the miracle must break with all expectations, all horizons of preunderstanding, all "laws of nature," though it would be difficult to say that, for him, miracles are "performed" in the way they are in the Gospels. Miracles happen, and—miraculously—happen every day: nothing more ordinary, more extraordinary, than the miracle. If the miracle is thus to be read as a sign, it signals not some supernatural or superhuman presence or power but the extraordinary relationship to an *absolute other*, not some miraculous event within the world but the miracle by which a world first opens up. The miracle is thus not an event within history but the condition of history itself. As opposed to all those things we can see coming on the horizon, the miracle—what Derrida also calls the *event*—is what falls upon us from above, what befalls us without expectation or warning. Derrida says in an interview from 2001, "An event worthy of the name, the arrival of what or who arrives [*l'arrivée de l'arrivant(e)*] is as extraordinary as a miracle" (*AA* 62).

As we have seen, elementary faith is related to a belief in the other and to a kind of testimony to which I have no access, a belief in the other as belief in a miracle. In an essay in *Sovereignties in Question* entitled "Poetics and Politics of Witnessing," Derrida writes:

> "I bear witness"—that means: "I affirm (rightly or wrongly, but in all good faith, sincerely) that that was or is present to me, in space and time (thus, sense-perceptible), and although you do not have access to it, not the same access, you, my addressee, *you have to believe me*, because I engage myself to tell you the truth, I am already engaged in it, I tell you that I am telling you the truth. Believe me. You have to believe me." (*SQ* 76)

But what is it, exactly, in the testimony of the other that remains inaccessible to me? In one sense, it is the "consciousness" or "intentionality" of the other, the relationship of the other to the objects of his or her experience, that to which, as Husserl argued in his fifth *Cartesian Meditation*, I can have no direct access but can relate to only through "appresentation" or "analogical apperception."[25] Even if I can and do, on one level, "know," "perceive," and "understand" what the other says, does, and thinks, the intentionality or consciousness of the other—this opening of the world in the other—remains absolutely secret and beyond all measure. "No calculation, no assurance will ever be able to reduce its ultimate necessity, that of the testimonial signature (whose theory is not necessarily a theory of the subject, of the person or of the ego, conscious or unconscious)" (§37). In "Above All, No Journalists!" therefore, Derrida will speak of this relation to the other as nothing less than a miracle, as a "relation" to that with which I can have no relation insofar as it takes place on "the other side."

The primary miracle, the most ordinary of miracles, is precisely "believe me!" When one says to someone, "believe me!," the appeal to proof is itself not provable. What I think in my head, in my inner sanctum, will, for infinite structural reasons, never be accessible to you; you will never know what's going on on the other side [*de l'autre côté*]. You can simply "believe." Well, to tell someone "believe me!" is to appeal to the experience of a miracle. ("AANJ" 76)

The miracle is thus a relation to *the other side*, to *l'autre côté*—yet another phrase that Derrida is borrowing from the tradition and remarking within the context of his own idiom. For this *autre côté* refers not to some "other world" or some "afterlife," as it sometimes does in French—and as we will see in the final chapter of this work. Invisible or imperceptible to me in this world or in this life, the *other side* is that which takes place on *the side of the other*. What appears from out of this other side thus appears to me without any common horizon or foundation and so is, as such, nothing short of a miracle. Derrida continues:

Everything that exceeds the order of originary perception or of proof presents itself as miraculous: the alterity of the other, what the other has in his head, in his intention or in his consciousness, is inaccessible to an intuition or to a proof; the "believe me" is permanently inhabited by the miracle. To believe—what is called believing— what I tell you, to relate to what I say in the mode of belief, having faith in my good faith, as in something that surpasses the order of knowledge, of the ordinary or of the probable, is as if you were to believe in a miracle. It is always as extraordinary to *believe* someone who tells you "believe me" (to believe him unconditionally, with one's eyes closed, without any means of verification, without guarantee of probability, without index of confirmation, etc.) as to be present at a miracle. ("AANJ" 76)

Derrida's use of the term *miracle* is thus no mere figure or metaphor: insofar as I have no access to the testimony of the other, no shared horizon to assess it, no common world in which to access it, it is *as if* that testimony comes from a source beyond the natural world or beyond my world. "Believe what I say as one believes in a miracle," says Derrida, because, for you, *I* am the nocturnal source to which you have no access beyond my attestation, beyond what I bring to light.

"The pure 'relation to the other,' there where the alterity of the alter ego deprives me forever of proof and originary intuition," is thus, for Derrida, nothing other than an elementary "faith," and this faith is the element or the milieu of the miracle not only in religion but in science

("AANJ" 64). Whereas Derrida in his second thesis located technoscience at the very heart of religion, and so made the machine central to any thinking of religion today, he has now, by means of this third thesis, put the miracle and an elementary faith into the very heart of science. In the end, he has placed both the miracle and the machine at the origin of both religion and science. By opening the future through an elementary faith in the other, the miracle begins already from the origin to repeat itself, to promise to repeat itself—yet another miracle—like a machine.

To put the entire argument of "Faith and Knowledge"—or at least to put its three principal theses—into a single breath: from a single common source or element comes two, at least two, the two sources of religion but then also the duplicity of religion and science and the autoimmune relationship between them. As with America's favorite pastime, then, it is absolutely essential, when it comes to religion, to know where you are in the count.

PART II

The Religion(s) of the World

He is the divided, the one who—it took me so long to fathom this mystery—strikes the mountain *twice* yes, yes, twice, the one who makes the heart of belief tremble, the philosophical divider, the one who knows that one cannot say I believe without doubting, without crossing out *I* and *believe* and *doubt*.

—Hélène Cixous, *Portrait of Jacques Derrida as a Young Jewish Saint*

Interlude I

Waste, Weapons, and Religion (Underworld II)

Technology is our fate, our truth. It is what we mean when we call ourselves the only superpower on the planet. The materials and methods we
devise make it possible for us to claim our future. We don't have to depend
on God or the prophets or other astonishments. We are the astonishment.
The miracle is what we ourselves produce, the systems and networks that
change the way we live and think.

But whatever great skeins of technology lie ahead, ever more complex,
connective, precise, micro-fractional, the future has yielded, for now, to
medieval experience, to the old slow furies of cut-throat religion. Maybe
this is a grim subtext of their enterprise. They see something innately destructive in the nature of technology.

—Don DeLillo, "In the Ruins of the Future"

As we have seen, Derrida demonstrates throughout "Faith and Knowledge" the irreducible relationship between religion and science, that is,
between the miracle and the machine. I would like to begin this second
part of *Miracle and Machine* with just a few words about Don DeLillo's
Underworld, since it is precisely this relationship that motivates, inspires,
or moves DeLillo's novel from beginning to end. The novel in effect
mushrooms out of its ground-zero setting in New York City's Polo
Grounds, that miracle moment immortalized by Giants announcer Russell Hodges (a name with thirteen letters) when Bobby Thompson (also
thirteen letters) of the New York Giants hits a baseball off #13, Ralph
Branca, of the Brooklyn Dodgers, into the stands on October 3—that is

10/3—1951 (four thirteens that, for anyone who is counting, do indeed add up to fifty-two) (see *U* 678).[1] We then follow the unlikely voyage of that infamous memorabilia ball as it passes from one hand to another, finally coming to be owned by Nick Shay, the main protagonist of *Underworld*, who as a kid listened to the legendary baseball game on his portable radio in Brooklyn.[2] By the mid-1990s, Shay has moved out west—just like the Dodgers and the Giants—and is living in Phoenix, in the desert, working as a dealer for a waste containment and disposal company. From the magic of baseball and that miracle year of the Giants, we seem to have come—or fallen—a mighty long way, from the sacred to the very profane, from heroism and belief to waste and trash.

But if this really is a fall, the profane will not be without its own religion. It all depends on how you look at it, for in *Underworld* one man's trash is another man's religion. As Nick Shay says, "Waste is a religious thing" (*U* 88): "We were the Church Fathers of waste in all its transmutations" (*U* 102). For Nick Shay, for Don DeLillo, it seems, we misunderstand our relationship to waste, our growing preoccupation, even obsession with it—that is, with our garbage, our recyclables, our sewage, our landfills, our nuclear materials, and so on—so long as we consider them a mere nuisance to be jettisoned, disposed of, recycled, or transformed. As Nick later speculates, deep down "maybe we feel a reverence for waste, for the redemptive qualities of the things we use and discard" (*U* 809). That's because waste is, in some sense, just the underside of our inventions and teletechnology, not just the by-product but in many ways the main product of entire industries that do not just result in waste but aim at creating it through consumption, conspicuous and otherwise, and sophisticated machines of death and destruction. I am speaking, of course, among other things, of our contemporary arms industry, which produces everything from grenades and laser-guided missiles to nuclear weapons.

It is no coincidence, then, that Nick Shay's younger brother, Matt, works in weapons research and that one of his worksites is an isolated research lab in the desert, one of the privileged sites of religion and revelation (*U* 211), as Derrida recalls in "Faith and Knowledge," but also, as we know, of nuclear technology. The first nuclear-bomb test site in New Mexico was thus called "Trinity" (*U* 529), and the desert around that area is still, we read in *Underworld*, a place of "awe and terror" (*U* 71). "This was the supernatural underside of the arms race. Miracles and visions," says the narrator (*U* 452). As Matt's wife, Janet, says to her husband one day when he is describing his work, "You make it sound like God" (*U* 458).

Waste, weapons, and the godhead, the mushrooming landfill, the mushroom cloud, and the cloud of unknowing: this is the sacred-profane trilogy of *Underworld*, three emanations that haunt one another or are co- or trans-substantial with one another. As we ourselves thus consider not only how to dispose of our own nuclear waste, how we will not just disarm our nuclear stockpiles but dispose of the fissionable materials within them, we would do well to consider the secret connection between waste and weapons: "waste is the secret history, the underhistory" (*U* 791), says the narrator of *Underworld*, for "what we excrete comes back to consume us" (*U* 791). This sounds already like a first definition of what Derrida will refer to as the terrifying law of autoimmunity; the by-products of our consumption, which we believe we can simply discard or slough off, become the very things that consume us. What both DeLillo and Derrida seem to signal is the end of the dream already dreamed in Plato's *Timaeus* of a universe that could effectively manage or even live off its own waste, that could consume its own excrement as its only food or fuel, the dream of a perfectly autonomous, self-enclosed system with nothing outside it, a self-sufficient cosmos rather than that absolutely open, autoimmune receptacle in the same Plato dialogue that goes by the name of *khōra*. From Nick's visit to the desert cemetery of corroding B-52s (that number again!), which used to carry nuclear weapons around the globe 24–7 (*U* 70), to his inspections of gigantic landfills, from stories of freighters containing unspeakable toxins drifting aimlessly across our oceans to the dream or fantasy of vaporizing nuclear waste through nuclear detonations in a remote site in Kazakhstan (*U* 788), the connection between waste and weapons is central to *Underworld*—waste, weapons, and religion, in other words, the impending environmental crisis, weapons technology, and the faith that animates and makes these possible.

If one of the main characters of an early DeLillo novel can say that "weapons have lost their religion," I think it is fair to say that in *Underworld* they get it back, and with a vengeance.[3] There are guns, the gun with which Nick, in a strange kind of underworld ritual or initiation, unwittingly kills George Manza; there are the B-52s; there's agent orange— linked to the color orange, to the baseball about the size of an orange, and to Minute Maid orange juice, as we will see later;[4] there's the Cuban missile crisis and Lenny Bruce's paranoid but so paranoid rants about it in October 1962; and then there is the bomb itself, as we already saw in the prologue, where J. Edgar Hoover receives word of a nuclear blast right around the same time Bobby Thompson is hitting his miracle home run at the Polo Grounds. If "all technology refers to the bomb" (*U* 467), as the narrator says, then the apotheosis of technology is the mushroom cloud, an "almighty piss-all vision" (*U* 614), "the godhead of Annihilation and Ruin," the ultimate way—or at least that is the illusion—for the state to control not only the means of production but the "means of apocalypse" (*U* 563).

The mushroom cloud thus gathers into itself religion and science, faith and knowledge—"an underworld of images known only to tribal priests" (*U* 466): the atomic bomb, the hallucinogenic mushroom, and *The Cloud of Unknowing*—this important fourteenth century, anonymously authored text of a certain negative theology, which Nick Shay studied as an adolescent. If the story of *Underworld* is essentially Nick's attempt to understand himself and what happened in that underworld basement where a gun went off in his hands when he was a kid, what happened to his father who one day disappeared, killed, Nick thinks, by the mob or the underworld, then what Nick is ultimately after is not knowledge but *faith*. He thus moves according to the movement sketched out in *The Cloud of Unknowing* from the Cloud of Forgetting (from the self, from identity) to the Cloud of Unknowing, from the forces of forgetting that define the self to God as an unknowable force.[5]

At the origin, then, there is duplicity, a sort of splitting or fission, a single stroke that divides in two, into a game-winning home run and a nuclear blast, into faith and knowledge, religion and science, a baseball and a uranium core, an orange that sustains life and the agent orange that incinerates it, a miracle and a machine, and, as we will see much later, into two very different Edgars, one male and one female, one who wishes to protect himself from all contamination by being buried in a lead-lined coffin and one who exposes herself in the end not only to contamination and infection but to a miraculous event.

DeLillo seems to believe that in order to learn about ourselves we need only look at the weapons we build and the waste we leave behind. For "weapons reflect the soul of the maker" (*U* 790).[6] And the same goes for learning about the future—*our* future, we might add, as we think today about everything from climate change to the prospects of nuclear disarmament to the Yucca Mountain project for storing nuclear waste, *our* nuclear waste, *our* excretion and excrescence, and perhaps our own impending Vesuvius.[7]

La religion soufflée

The Genesis of "Faith and Knowledge"

As I argued in the Introduction, one must always try to understand how the form, style, and even the format of Derrida's texts reflect the theses within them. "Faith and Knowledge" would be a truly exemplary text in this regard. The three theses developed in the previous chapter concerning the nature of religion and the unprecedented forms it is taking today will thus have played, as we have already seen, a determining role in the form and writing of Derrida's essay. The many textual and graphic doublings and divisions noted earlier can all be read as reflecting the fundamental complicity between religion and science, as well as the duplicity at the heart of religion itself. Apart from the title "Faith and Knowledge," which is in effect a translation or double or mere repetition of a 1802–3 essay by Hegel, not to mention a work of Franz Rosenzweig with exactly the same title, and apart from the fact that the subtitle, which speaks of two sources of religion, is little more than a condensation of two canonical sources on the question of religion, almost every other source divides in two—at least two—from the very beginning: hence Derrida marks the essay with two places, one European and one American, the Italian island of Capri where an early version of "Faith and Knowledge" was first delivered and Laguna Beach in California where the essay was completed and signed; and these two seaside places correspond to two times, 28 February 1994, in Capri, and 26 April 1995, in Laguna Beach. As for the form of the essay itself, it has fifty-two sections that are themselves divided into two sets of twenty-six, the first set entitled "Italics" and printed in italics and the second, entitled "Post-scriptum," printed in roman font and divided into two un-equal sections, with two distinct though seemingly related headings, "Crypts . . . et grenades," the latter evoking, as we will see later, either a fruit that plays a major role in religion, and particularly in Judaism, a translation of *grenades* that inscribes it on the side of life, or a little, hand-held war machine, a translation that inscribes it on the side of a certain knowledge and a certain science, though also on the side of death.

That is just a small sampling of the many repetitions, doublings, and moments of duplicity in this at once improvised and highly constructed and organized text. But just as important as all these formal or structural duplicities, which underscore the fundamental duplicity within religion itself and the irreducible complicity between religion and science, is the way in which this duplicity influences Derrida's method or approach to the question of religion "itself." Note, for example, how Derrida begins both the essay itself (§1) and the first section of the second set of twenty-six sections (§27): in both places Derrida asks about the possibility of talk-ing *"of religion," "Singularly of religion, today"* (§1), the possibility of speaking "here and now, this very day," of religion, of the "essence" of religion and "with a sort of *religio*-sity" that tries "not to introduce any-thing alien, leaving it thus intact, safe, *unscathed*" (§27). Derrida's empha-sis in both places on the day, on what is happening to religion today, already suggests that the "essence" of religion, the seemingly ahistorical essence of religion, must be broached by means of the way religion mani-fests itself today, which is to say, by means of the question of the relation-ship between religion and science. Indeed, Derrida will assert in the passage from §35 where he recounts the origin of the conference at Capri:

> Of course, it would have been madness itself to have proposed to treat religion *itself*, in general or in its essence; rather the troubled question, the common concern is: "What is going on today with it, with what is designated thus? What is going on there? What is hap-pening and so badly? What is happening under this old name? What in the world is suddenly emerging or re-emerging under this appel-lation?" (§35)

Even if, as he will go on to say, "this form of question cannot be separated from the more fundamental one (on the essence, the concept and the his-tory of religion *itself*, and of what is called 'religion')," his approach, he says, would have to be "more direct, global, massive and immediate, spon-taneous, without defense, almost in the style of a philosopher obliged to issue a brief press release" (§35)—yet another way of explaining the tele-graphic and sometimes almost breathless pace of "Faith and Knowledge," yet another way of demonstrating that one cannot write about the nature or essence of religion at the end of the twentieth century as one could in 1793 (like Kant), or 1802 (like Hegel), or even 1932 (like Bergson).

In his claim that there are two sources of religion, Derrida already seems to be suggesting that any analysis that attributes to a religion a single source will miss what has always or from the beginning been the case about religion and what is most striking about it today. Here too, then, we see that two times (*from the beginning* and *today*), the archaic and the contemporary, are necessary to think religion "itself," that is, religion as it has been from the beginning, divided from itself because of its two distinct sources and because of its complicity with what might appear to oppose it—reason, science, technology, telecommunications, and so on.[1] In a word, in two words, religion must be understood today in relation to both faith *and* knowledge. For it just may be that the technoscientific forms religion is taking today will help us to define—in seeming violation of the very essence of essences—the nature of religion itself.

> "What is religion?" "What is . . .?" which is to say, *on the one hand,* what is it in its *essence?* And *on the other,* what *is* it (present indicative) at present? What is it doing, what is being done with it at present, today, today in the world? So many ways of insinuating, in each of these words—*being, essence, present, world*—a response into the question. So many ways of imposing the answer. Of pre-imposing it or of prescribing it *as* religion. (§33)

It might have been thought that to speak of religion one would have to speak with respect, with scruple (*religio*), with a kind of *religiosity* that would leave religion, in accordance with one of its two sources, intact, safe and sound, *indemnified* or unscathed. But in "Faith and Knowledge" Derrida will precisely not leave religion intact but will introduce all kinds of things into the discussion that might seem to be foreign, even antithetical, to it, beginning with science and technology and today's unprecedented use of these. Derrida seems to be suggesting that, in order to speak of religion today, it is necessary to *interrupt* the religiosity (though always in the right way), to introduce what may seem foreign to religion in order to understand everything that is happening to religion and in the name of religion today. He does this by thinking together the two themes or two sources we have identified, the indemnified presence of religion or of the religious community, an emphasis on the sacrosanct, the safe and sound, on the one hand, and faith or belief, reliability and credit, the promise or the *gage* that is at the origin of science as well as religion, on the other.

How is one to speak of religion in the singular? Of religion itself? Religion in its essence? In posing such questions, it is as if Derrida wished, as was his wont, to question or modify the themes of the conference or the terms in which it was couched, themes and terms that Derrida typically did not himself choose but on which he agreed to speak. But "Faith and Knowledge" is a rather particular case, because Derrida himself, it seems, chose the theme—religion in the singular—for the conference in Capri, and so he himself was the origin of this conference on the origins or the sources of religion. Derrida tells us as much in §35 of the "Post-scriptum" of "Faith and Knowledge," where he relates the origins, indeed the genesis, of this conference of February 1994 on the isle of Capri. Though it has the appearance of being a mere anecdote, a playful biographical gesture, I would like to demonstrate in this chapter that it is necessary to read this apparently simple and banal little passage in light of the three theses of "Faith and Knowledge" we have just developed.

As we will see, when asked by Maurizio Ferraris for a topic for the conference in Capri, Derrida seems to have blurted out, almost without hesitation, without taking a breath, a single word—"religion." But to hear Derrida speak in the same breath of religion and the breath should cause us to pause for a moment in order to consider not only the question of religion in this passage but the question of the breath. For Derridean deconstruction will have been, among a thousand other things, and already from the beginning, a story of breath. In early texts such as "Plato's Pharmacy," Derrida demonstrates the centrality of the breath in Plato's privileging of speech or *logos* over writing, or, in *Speech and Phenomena*, he shows the importance of breath in Husserl's privileging of meaning or meaning-to-say, of the living present and thus of life, over the repetitive processes of signification. In each case, breath is shown to be related to life, presence, and spontaneity, as opposed to mere mechanical reproduction and automaticity and the loss, absence, and death that results. For more than forty years, then, Derrida will have followed the destiny of this breath in the history of philosophy from Plato to Heidegger and beyond. For more than four decades he will have shown, in effect, how and why the breath is most often on the side of the miracle, and breathlessness, the loss of breath, artificial breathing, on the side of the machine.

As one of the privileged themes of Derridean deconstruction, the theme of breath cannot be avoided in a work that treats Derrida's analysis of the origins or sources of religion in "Faith and Knowledge." For it could well be said of the one who once wrote in "Circumfession" "I posthume as I breathe" (periphrasis 5, "C" 28) that *il déconstruisait comme il respirait*, that is, "he deconstructed as easily as he breathed," he deconstructed as if by second nature, effortlessly, spontaneously, almost miraculously. But in order to make such a claim we would first need to come to an agreement about what nature is and, of course, what the breath is. Unable to reconstitute here even the general lines of this extraordinary trajectory in Derrida's work, I will content myself with analyzing here a single breath in this entire story, a breath that will have had the merit of actually taken place one fine day in Paris in 1993, a real, genuine breath, a simple, single breath, that then became, as I will try to argue, a real *event*. It has the appearance, I realize, of a simple anecdote, but the anecdote is his, and it is published, in "Faith and Knowledge." It is thus a matter of a real breath, just one, but of a breath that divides in two—at least two—from the very beginning, that is, already at its genesis. If I thus restrict my analysis in this chapter to this single breath, to a single, seemingly nonphilosophical moment within what I have tried to argue throughout this work is a great philosophical text on religion, it is in order to show how Derrida deconstructed more or less as he breathed, deconstructed even when he was not deconstructing.

The passage in question recounts a meeting in Paris between Derrida and Maurizio Ferraris to discuss the theme of the upcoming conference in Capri, where Derrida would deliver a first version of "Faith and Knowledge." The meeting took place, we are told, at the Hotel Lutétia in Paris, right across the street from Derrida's office at the École des Hautes Études en Sciences Sociales on the Boulevard Raspail. Here are the crucial—though at first seemingly pedestrian—lines, first in French and then in the English translation of Sam Weber:

> Or **il faut bien répondre.** Et sans attendre. Sans trop attendre. **Au commencement,** Maurizio Ferraris au *Lutétia.* "Il faut, me dit-il, il nous faut un thème pour cette rencontre de Capri." Je souffle, sans souffler, presque sans hésiter, machinalement: "La religion." Pourquoi? D'où cela m'est il venu, et oui, machinalement? . . . Il me faudrait donc après coup justifier une réponse à la question: pourquoi ai-je nommé d'un seul coup, machinalement, "la religion"? Et cette justification serait alors, aujourd'hui, ma réponse à la question *de la religion.* De la religion aujourd'hui.

> But, **one still must respond.** And without waiting. Without waiting too long. **In the beginning,** Maurizio Ferraris at the Hotel Lutétia. "I need," he tells me, "we need a theme for this meeting in Capri." In a whisper, yet without whispering, almost without hesitating, machine-like, I respond, "Religion." Why? From where did

this come to me, and yes, mechanically? . . . I had thus subsequently to justify an answer to the question, why I had named, all of a sudden, machine-like, "religion"? And this justification would have become, today, my response to the question of *religion*. Of religion today. (§35)[2]

Almost everything about this seemingly simple, deceptively simple passage is double—at least double—and duplicitous. Notice, first, that, even before the beginning there is *response*—the *re-* of *response* coming even before the *re-* of *religion*, as we saw in Chapter 2. Before the beginning there is an obligation to respond, an obligation that is itself already divided in two by means of the double valence of the word *bien*—*il faut bien répondre*: on the one hand, one must respond, one has well (*bien*) to respond, and on the other hand, one has to respond well (*bien*).[3] One must respond, and one must respond well, respond, for example, to the invitation to go to the Capri conference and respond well to the request—which always comes from another—for a theme. Because the response is always an affirmation, the freedom it entails originates not in the self but in the other to whom one is responding. As Derrida writes elsewhere, "When you say yes, it's a free gesture, it is an absolute initiative, but it is already a response. When I say yes, the structure of the yes is the structure of a response" (*IW* 60).

But then *how* is one to respond in such a situation? Derrida argues that there are a least two possible responses, one of which can always contaminate the other, so that one is never able to prove in a theoretical way which is which. Either one's response will be an address to the absolute other as such, "with an address that is understood, heard, respected faithfully and responsibly," or else it will be a response that ripostes or retaliates, that "compensates and *indemnifies itself* in the war of resentment and of reactivity" (§29). Derrida's own response to the invitation to go to the Island of Capri cannot avoid this aporia of the response. In the beginning is the response, but since, as we will see, the beginning is already double, the response to or for the other can always turn into a response only to ourselves. Derrida writes in §33:

however little may be known of religion *in the singular*, we do know that it is always a response and responsibility that is prescribed, not chosen freely in an act of pure and abstractly autonomous will. There is no doubt that it implies freedom, will and responsibility, but let us try to think this: will and freedom *without autonomy*. Whether it is a question of sacredness, sacrificiality or of faith, the other makes the law, the law is other: to give ourselves back, and up, to the other. To every other and to the utterly other. (§33)

The beginning is thus preceded by a response, by an affirmation, by a certain responsibility to respond, a certain *engagement* or promise even before the beginning. As Derrida succinctly puts it in "Ulysses Gramophone," "In the beginning was the telephone" ("UG" 270). Hence the beginning is itself already a response to what will have come before it, a response to or a call for a response that *will thus have been* the "real beginning"—a beginning not in oneself but in the other, to whom I can only respond. In the beginning, then, was the response. As Derrida put it earlier, "The promise promises *itself*, it is *already* promised, that is the sworn faith, the given word, and hence the response. *Religio* would begin there" (§30).

Now, because of this irreducible delay in the beginning, because the beginning is always already a response to itself, just about everything in this passage is doubled—repeated, iterated, but in each case with a difference: one must respond, says Derrida, "without waiting / without waiting *too long* [trop]"; Ferraris says, "I need [*il faut*]/we need [*il nous faut*] a theme for this meeting in Capri," and Derrida responds, "in a whisper/ yet without whispering," "almost without hesitating, machine-like [*machinalement*]," "Religion." And Derrida then asks himself, or responds to himself, after what seems to be a brief time of reflection, "Why? From where did this come to me, and yes, mechanically [*machinalement*]?" More or less everything is thus doubled here save the response itself, "Religion," which, as we have seen, will be defined by Derrida in the conference to come in terms of two sources and an irreducible relationship to the machine. Six sections earlier Derrida writes: "Religion, in the *singular*? Response: 'Religion is **the response**.' Is it not there, perhaps, that we must seek the beginning of a response? Assuming, that is, that one knows what *responding* means, also *responsibility*. Assuming, that is, that one knows it—and believes in it. No response, indeed, without a principle of responsibility: one must respond to the other, before the other and for oneself" (§29).[4]

But how are we to understand the one phrase that is not simply repeated and qualified but seemingly negated—"in a whisper, yet without whispering [*je souffle, sans souffler*]"? Everything revolves, everything pivots, around what appears to be a way of qualifying the response and then negating that qualification. Since we are talking about a certain genesis of religion, it might appear that Derrida is repeating here—in an almost machine-like way—the language of negative theology, the language he analyzes so closely in "How to Avoid Speaking" and "*Sauf le nom (Post-Scriptum)*."[5] One might also be tempted to hear in this "in a whisper but without whispering" the kind of logic Derrida finds in Blanchot's narratives, where, as he writes elsewhere, the syntax of the *without* "comes to neutralize (without positing, without negating) a word, a concept, a term (X *without* X)" ("LO" 87).[6] *Je souffle, sans souffler* might thus indeed be heard as a way of qualifying Derrida's response in one breath and then negating that qualification in the next, or else as a way of neutralizing this notion of *souffler* as breathing or whispering: I breathe without breathing, or, indeed, I whisper without whispering. For when used with the preposition *à* and a direct and an indirect object, as in "*je souffle un mot à quelqu'un*," "*je lui souffle un mot*," *souffler* does indeed mean not so much to breathe but to whisper, to whisper, for example, a secret or word of confidence to someone, as when we sometimes say in English, "Don't breathe a word of this to anyone."

But between these two breaths, between *souffle* and *souffler*, in the silent but graphically visible scansion of this phrase in the form of "X without X," one might also hear not only negation or neutralization but displacement and dissemination. For the second *souffle* or *souffler* perhaps means something other than the first one, in which case there would be neither the negation nor the neutralization of meaning but a displacement of it. Hence one might want to translate this phrase in two different breaths, with two different words, as "I whisper without breathing," that is, I whisper without taking the time to breathe, or "I breathe without whispering," that is, I breathe but without whispering anything to anyone.

But there is another, even more likely meaning of *sans souffler* in this context: in its most common, idiomatic meaning this phrase might simply be translated as "without pause," "immediately, "right away," "without taking a breather," if you will. In other words, *sans souffler* is more or less synonymous with what follows it, namely, "without hesitation" or "machine-like." One would thus translate the phrase: "I breathe (or I whisper) without hesitation—religion." But if we are to read *sans souffler* as meaning not "without breathing" or "without whispering" but more simply and idiomatically "without pause," "immediately," "without hesitation," then we might well want to translate the first *souffle*, the *je souffle*, more simply or more naturally as "I answered, I responded," that is, "I answered or responded without pausing or without hesitating—religion." But were we to translate the phrase in this way, notice, we would be taking the "breath" right out of it. Derrida would have thus whispered without whispering, or whispered without pausing, or confided without hesitation, "religion." But then what will have happened to the *souffle*—

this irreducible French word that does indeed mean to whisper, to confide, even to blow into and animate, though also simply "to breathe"? What does *je souffle, sans souffler* mean exactly? How is one to translate this phrase? Is it a coincidence that we have such difficulty translating, and first of all understanding, this text in the precise place where Derrida speaks of a *souffle*, of a breath, that is in the philosophical tradition linked to meaning, to a *vouloir dire*, to life, and not to dissemination or undecidability, to the machinelike or the machine? How is one to determine Derrida's animating intention here, that is, his meaning, what he wanted to say, his *vouloir dire*—the animating breath behind this phrase now that Derrida is no longer around to answer for it?

This would obviously be the place—had we time and breath enough—to undertake a rereading of Derrida's entire corpus on this theme of breath and respiration in his work. As I suggested earlier, a text such as *Speech and Phenomena* would be central to this rereading, since Derrida there demonstrates how, in the work of Husserl, meaning or intention, the *vouloir dire*, is always attached to a concept of life linked to breath, to the *souffle*.[7] But let me cite instead a few lines on the question of breath and writing from another text written right around the same time as *Speech and Phenomena*, Derrida's 1968 essay "Plato's Pharmacy," a text I choose among so many others because of what Derrida says a bit later in the same section of "Faith and Knowledge" we are reading: "The response that I gave almost without hesitation to Ferraris must have come back to me from afar, resonating from an alchemist's cavern, in whose depths the word was a precipitate. 'Religion,' a word dictated by who knows what or whom: by everyone perhaps" (§35). Without wanting to claim that this "alchemist's cavern" is the same as the back room of "Plato's Pharmacy" where, says Derrida, Plato is "searching for gold . . . and the philosopher's stone" ("PP" 170), and without wanting to argue for a strict relation between the way Derrida reads the breath in Plato in 1968 and the way the breath is mise-en-scène in 1995 in "Faith and Knowledge," this earlier text can nonetheless help us to understand how the breath—the *souffle*—marks almost everything in Derrida's essay, from the syntax, the letter, even the punctuation of his text to the largest stakes of this work on the subject of religion.[8]

Let us consider, then, for a moment some of the things Derrida says about writing in his 1968 essay "Plato's Pharmacy," that is, some of the accusations made against writing by Plato and others following him. Each time, we see, the accusation against writing is made in the name of life, an accusation against what is mechanical and deadly in the name of what is living, animated, and full of breath, an accusation against what is automatic and mechanical in the name of what is living and spontaneous. If one of the essential attributes of life and particularly human life is the living breath of speech, we will want to see how Plato opposes this speech and this life, the spontaneity of speech and life, not simply to death but to the automaticity of the machine. Let me emphasize again that what I am looking for here is not some strict comparison between Plato's notions of speech and writing, on the one hand, and religion and science, on the other, but a *structural analogy* in *Derrida's reading*. In both cases what we see is a *contamination* of something that would claim to be "proper," safe and sound or unscathed, that is, in the end, an ineluctable contamination of *life* by means of a technoscientific supplement that comes to inscribe repetition, duplicity, and death into the heart of life or the living present.

In "Plato's Pharmacy," Derrida makes a case that writing is condemned in the Platonic corpus because it threatens the living present of speech, because what is proper to living speech is contaminated, exposed, and expropriated, uprooted or deracinated, we could say, by means of the lifeless signs of writing. Writing would thus be the name of the technical supplement that sucks the breath—and thus the life—right out of the spoken word. Whereas, on Derrida's reading of Plato, *logos* or speech is "a living, animate creature" ("PP" 79), writing "substitutes the breathless sign [*le signe essoufflé*] for the living voice" ("PP" 92), "the passive, mechanical 'by heart' for the active reanimation of knowledge, for its reproduction in the present" ("PP" 108). Writing is thus condemned for its "breathless impotence [*impuissance essoufflée*]" ("PP" 115), for its substitution of the dead letter for the living voice. It is dangerous and should be avoided because it contaminates speech with thoughtless and impotent repetition, with breathlessness—in a word, with death, though also, and perhaps especially, because it is a simulacrum that gives the *appearance* or the *image* of life and thus of breath. Though it is but a "breathless impotence," a "weakened speech," writing is "something not completely dead"; it is, writes Derrida, "a living-dead, a reprieved corpse, a deferred life, a semblance of breath [*un semblant de souffle*]" ("PP" 143), a technical supplement that looks like a living being but that has had all the wind, all the breath, and all the life knocked out of it. Though breathless and lifeless, writing gives the impression of being alive; though dead, it is a living, breathing simulacrum.

As Derrida will go on to argue in "Plato's Pharmacy," Plato condemns writing in order to protect and, so to speak, *indemnify* speech, the living breath of speech. In order to do so, however, Plato must borrow the resources of the technology called writing, namely, a system of differential and nonunivocal signs that can never be controlled by the living speech that Plato is trying to protect or indemnify. Just as life can be protected and indemnified in religion only through the autoimmune appropriation of the technoscientific supplement, so the life and spontaneity of *logos* can be safeguarded only through the lifeless, mechanical supplement of writing. In this text, which predates "Faith and Knowledge" by almost three decades, speech is thus related not only to breath and fertility but to life and spontaneity, while writing is related not only to breathlessness and impotence but to death and the automaticity of the machine: "Writing would be pure repetition, dead repetition that might always be repeating nothing, or be unable *spontaneously* [spontanément] to repeat itself, which also means unable to repeat anything *but* itself: a hollow, cast-off repetition" ("PP" 135). And elsewhere, he writes, using a word that is at the center of the passage from "Faith and Knowledge" that we have been commenting on throughout this chapter: "Writing would indeed be the signifier's capacity to repeat itself by itself, mechanically [*machinalement*], without a living soul to sustain or attend it in its repetition, that is to say, without truth's *presenting itself* anywhere" ("PP" 111).

But since, as Derrida will go on to show, living speech *needs* writing and, in the end, is but a species of writing or of archē-writing, it is as if Derrida were saying back in 1968 in "Plato's Pharmacy" that live speech, inner speech, the living breath, is *autoimmune*, a source that has need always of another source, of the other, in order to expropriate itself but also to express itself in the first place. In order for speech to express itself, in order for it, in the end, to be itself, that is, in order for a signifier to be understood as the same, it must court the powers of repetition and technique, in short, the powers of writing and the machine. Hence the only way for speech to live on, the only way for it to grow, swell, or multiply beyond itself, is for it to graft itself onto what is outside it, welcome and greet what is foreign to it and thus threatening for it, namely, the powers of death that go by the general name of "writing." In order for speech to respond spontaneously, then, it must answer without reflection, without hesitation, in short, without breath. The only chance for living, organic speech is thus to be contaminated by the expropriating powers of writing; the only chance for the living organism, the powers of the machine.

Derrida would thus seem to be suggesting in "Faith and Knowledge" that the source of religion, the "living" source of religion, cannot be thought without automaticity, repetition, and the machine, that is, without an immediate, automatic duplicity. Though it might seem that the one topic that should *not* be treated without hesitation or scruple, without deliberation and thoughtful reflection, would be religion, Derrida tells us that the topic of religion suggested itself to him in precisely this kind of automatic or mechanical way. Should we call it a revelation? Suffice it to say that a topic that would have to concern itself with *life*, with the salvation and preservation of life, imposed itself upon him in an automatic or *machinelike* way, and that just after these lines in which Derrida speaks of the automaticity of his response he makes his first allusion to Jensen's Gradiva, who seems to come to him, like the word *religion* itself, he will go on to say, "from an alchemist's cavern." At the heart of religion, at its source, Derrida has thus identified not unity but duplicity, and not life or purposeful creation, not living spontaneity and the indemnification of life, but repetition and reaction, an autoimmunity that turns every indemnifying movement against itself automatically or mechanically—like a machine.

This is perhaps the moment, in a work entitled *Miracle and Machine*, to specify exactly what a machine is for Derrida. Having seen in the previous chapter what Derrida understands the *miracle* to be, we need to look now at its counterpart, the *machine*. In *For What Tomorrow* . . . Derrida says that the machine is simply another way of speaking about calculation and repetition, but about a calculation and repetition in relationship always to the incalculable and the unforeseeable. In other words, in order to think the machine one must always consider what exceeds the machine, call it the event, the incalculable, or the other.

> There is *some* machine everywhere, and notably in language. . . . I would define the machine as a system [*dispositif*] of calculation and repetition. As soon as there is any calculation, calculability, and repetition, there is something of a machine. . . . But in the machine there is an excess in relation to the machine itself: at once the effect of a machination and something that eludes machinelike calculation. . . . The event—which in essence should remain unforeseeable and therefore not programmable—would be that which exceeds the machine. What it would be necessary to try to think, and this is extremely difficult, is the event *with* the machine. (*FWT* 49)

But how, then, are we to think or have access to the event that exceeds the machine and thus exceeds every system of calculation or repetition, beginning with language? Derrida appeals here not to some mystical experience in an abandonment of reason or calculation but precisely to calculation and the machine. In order to have access to the miracle, one must work through the machine:

> To accede, if this is possible, to the event beyond all calculation, and therefore also beyond all technics and all economy, it is necessary

to take programming, the machine, repetition, and calculation into account—as far as possible, and in places where we are not prepared or disposed to expect it.

It is necessary to track the effects of economic calculation everywhere, if only in order to know where we are affected by *the other*, that is, by the unforeseeable, by the event that, for its part, is incalculable: *the other* always responds, by definition, to the name and the figure of the *incalculable*. No brain, no neurological analysis, however exhaustive it's supposed to be, can render the encounter with the other. (*FWT* 49)[9]

These passages should help us understand Derrida's comments in §38 about the relationship between the machine, repetition, and iterability, on the one hand, and an unforeseeable future, on the other. Notice in what follows the way in which Derrida links elementary faith—or an "elementary promise"—to the confirmation and, thus, repetition of the promise, and thus to some machine.

> Of a discourse to come—on the to-come and repetition. Axiom: no to-come without heritage and the possibility of *repeating*. No to-come without some sort of *iterability*, at least in the form of a covenant with oneself and *confirmation* of the originary *yes*. No to-come without some sort of messianic memory and promise, of a messianicity older than all religion, more originary than all messianism. No discourse or address of the other without the possibility of an elementary promise. Perjury and broken promises require the *same* possibility. No promise, therefore, without the promise of a confirmation of the *yes*. This *yes* will have implied and will always imply the trustworthiness and fidelity of a faith. No faith, therefore, nor future without everything technical, automatic, machine-like supposed by iterability. (§38)

In an interview entitled "Nietzsche and the Machine," Derrida speaks quite explicitly of the relationship between the repetition and contamination of an originary "yes":

> There is a time and a spacing of the "yes" as "yes-yes": it takes time to say "yes." A single "yes" is, therefore, immediately double, it immediately announces a "yes" to come and already recalls that the "yes" implies another "yes." So, the "yes" is immediately double, immediately "yes-yes." . . . With this duplicity we are at the heart of the "logic" of contamination. One should not simply consider contamination as a threat, however. . . . Without contamination we

would have no opening or chance. Contamination . . . is the very possibility of affirmation in the first place. For affirmation to be possible, there must always be at least two "yes's." If the contamination of the first "yes" by the second is refused—for whatever reasons—one is denying the possibility of the first "yes." . . . Threat is chance, chance is threat—this law is absolutely undeniable and irreducible. If one does not accept it, there is no risk, and, if there is no risk, there is only death. ("NM" 247–48)

This is the "origin" of the duplicity we have been speaking about from the very beginning of this book, the duplicity we have seen at the origin, at the genesis, of any discourse about religion and of religion.

As we have seen, the machine makes possible not only the perfectibility of a sworn faith and promise to the other, a responsibility to and for the other, but the possibility of radical evil in a reactive denial of the other. The machine must thus be thought in terms of both repetition *and* difference, iterability *and* unpredictability. It makes possible the faith that opens up a future but it does not determine that future in one way or another.

In this sense, the technical is the possibility of faith, indeed its very chance. A chance that entails the greatest risk, even the menace of **radical evil**. Otherwise, that of which it is the chance would not be faith but rather program or proof, predictability or providence, pure knowledge and pure know-how, which is to say annulment of the future. Instead of opposing them, as is almost always done, they ought to be thought together, as *one and the same possibility*: the machine-like and faith. (§38)

While the comparison between "Faith and Knowledge" and Derrida's other works on the machine (including "Plato's Pharmacy") should be read, as I suggested a moment ago, less for what it says about the relationship between speech and writing, on the one hand, and religion and science, on the other, and much more for what is tells us about Derrida's approach to both, it is hard not to be impressed by a common matrix of terms and hierarchies. In both cases there is a contamination of what one claims to be proper, natural, and without artifice. In the end, both the Platonic discourse against writing and religious discourse against technoscientific modernity oppose life and the living breath to the machine. In both cases there is an inevitable—or *fatale*—contamination of life by the technoscientific supplement that inscribes repetition, duplicity, and even death at the very heart of life and the living present. Just as Derrida in

"Plato's Pharmacy" thus ended up figuring a notion of archē-writing at the origin of both speech and writing, so, as we will now see, he locates in "Faith and Knowledge" a kind of mechanical repetition at the origin—at the *genesis*—of both science and religion.

If the word *religion* welled up or resonated from some alchemist's cavern, from the backroom, perhaps, of Plato's Pharmacy or elsewhere, if the word came to Derrida's lips almost mechanically, without hesitation, it did so, perhaps, thanks to other resources or other echoes outside the Western philosophical tradition from, say, Plato to Husserl. "In the beginning," says Derrida, and then *Je souffle, sans souffler*: this *souffle* might well be that of live speech, of the entrusted secret, of the whisper or the breath, an inhaling or an exhaling, an affirmation or a negation, in short, the live speech of *philosophy*. But this *souffle* might also be, according to another tradition, that of a creative breath or the breath of a creator God, a breath that, in effect, infuses or breathes life into mankind. As we read in the second chapter of Genesis and as everyone could more or less mechanically recite, God "created man from the dust of the ground and breathed into his nostrils the *souffle* [the breath] of life" (Genesis 2:7). Given that Derrida begins his account of the genesis of the Capri conference with "In the beginning," the reference to Genesis seems umistakable.[10] Derrida's response to Ferraris, or at least his narration of his response after the fact, indeed seems to be nothing other than a retransmission or replay of Genesis, but—and the difference is essential, the greatest sign of *life*—one that puts the *machine* in the place of the living or animating breath, technique in the place of live speech, a machinelike reaction in the place of a spontaneous and purposeful response, automaticity in the place of a well-intentioned creation. If Derrida positions himself in this passage at the origin or as the author of the theme of religion at the Capri conference, he will refuse the role of a creator, for he will have provided the theme *without* creating it, without his breathing it, and even without reflecting before providing it, without willing it, without being the animating force behind it. One might thus parse Derrida's response: "I whisper (or I breathe), but without breathing, that is, without breathing life into anything"—"Religion." That helps explain Derrida's use—indeed his double use—of the word *machinalement*. It is as if the breath exhausted itself in an autoimmune process, as if the breath itself, each time it wanted to take a breath in order to say or express something, found itself drawn out, aspirated out of itself by writing, that is, as we just saw, by some machine. Because, for Derrida, there is no such thing as live speech, an animating intention, or a spontaneous response that is not already from the beginning contaminated by repetition and technique, by reactivity and the machine, there is no response and no beginning, no genesis even, that is not in some way machinelike—and thus double.

Hence Derrida repeats Genesis, this book at the origin of all three of the West's monotheisms, and he repeats it not once but, it seems, twice, giving us what would appear to be both versions of the creation of mankind, the one that speaks of man's creation by means of the breath and the one that speaks of it without breath.[11] For if, in Genesis 2, God "formed man from the dust of the ground, and breathed into his nostrils the breath of life" so that "man became a living being" (Genesis 2:7), in Genesis 1, "God created humankind in his image" (Genesis 1:27) without breath, it seems, or at least without any explicit reference to an animating breath.[12] One might thus say of the God of Genesis that He breathes without breathing, *il souffle, sans souffler*, or, rather, He creates man without breath before creating him with it; He creates man almost immediately, that is, *sans souffler*, after creating him without breath, that is, *sans souffler*, with His breath.

Je souffle, sans souffler would thus be an elliptical condensation of both versions of Genesis, a telegraphic retelling of this original retelling of the creation of man. And if an otherwise sympathetic reader were tempted to reproach me here for pushing my reading just a bit too far, that is, if such a reader were willing to grant me a reference to breath in the history of philosophy, maybe even a reference to the Book of Genesis in general, but not necessarily a discreet reference to the two versions of Genesis, one with breath and one without, well, I would be willing to grant such an objection but not before making one connection and asking one question. First, in *The Animal That Therefore I Am*, Derrida himself compares and contrasts the two versions of the creation of man and the animals in Genesis, the one where God commands man to have dominion over the animals and the one where man is charged with naming them. Derrida thus writes—and notice the way the notion of doubling is explicitly mentioned here, as well as, not coincidentally, the notion of breath: "That is the first narrative. God commands man-woman to command the animals, but not yet to name them. What happens next, in the second narrative? There occurs something, a single and double thing, twice at the same time, something that, it seems to me, gets little notice in most readings of this Genesis that is infinite in its second breath" (*ATT* 16). But, second, before conceding that this interpretation of the two versions of Genesis in §35 may be a bit too active, isn't this exactly what *souffler, sans souffler* means in this context? *Je souffle, sans souffler*: this means, it seems, to speak or, really, to write and to read without being fully able to control one's context or one's speech and meaning, to respond automatically, in a quasi-machinelike way, by letting oneself be invested, haunted, by voices or specters of all kinds, and to do so even when one believes oneself to be the master of one's speech and one's meaning. Because this *je souffle, sans souffler* is not under the control of a single, univocal meaning, it can never be translated, or first of all read and understood, all at once, that is, as Derrida put it, *d'un seul coup*, "all of a sudden" or "at one go." The phrase thus does not annul time but, on the contrary, *opens it up* (as any Genesis should); it opens up the time and space between two breathes, between two meanings of *souffler*, between *souffler* and *sans souffler*. And all this in excess of any *vouloir dire* or meaning to say.

Though Derrida seems to be recounting a more or less spontaneous, unrehearsed, quasi-anecdotal conversation one day with Maurizio Ferraris in the lobby of the Hotel Lutétia in anticipation of the Capri conference, I think we can see that this passage has also been carefully crafted or staged, and calculated even if Derrida did not calculate it all, around the two versions of creation in Genesis, the one with breath and the other without, the one with *souffle* and the other *sans souffler*. Derrida imitates Genesis, he repeats it, restages it, and perhaps—like the title "Faith and Knowledge" itself, which, as we saw, comes from Hegel—he makes off with it, takes it as his own, doubles and plagiarizes it; as one says in French, *il le souffle*. For as Derrida reminded us long ago in his 1965 essay "La parole soufflée," the word *souffler* means not only to confide, whisper, blow, or breathe, but to steal, swipe, or run off with, repeat, double, or spirit away. Writing in the context of a reading of the theatre of Antonin Artaud—and especially *The Theater and its Double*—Derrida brings to-gether several of these meanings of *souffler* in just a couple of sentences:

> This derivation of force within the sign divides the theatrical act, exiles the actor far from any responsibility for meaning, makes of him an interpreter who lets his life be breathed into [*insuffler*] him, and lets his words be whispered [*souffler*] to him, receiving his deliv-ery as if he were taking orders . . . To let one's speech be spirited away [*souffler*] is, like writing itself, the ur-phenomenon of the *re-serve*. ("LPS" 189; see also *TP* 96)[13]

One can begin to see the abyssal semantic resources of the word *souffler* that Derrida is staging in this little scene of "Faith and Knowledge." It is as if one word or one meaning comes without waiting, *sans souffler*, to supplement, augment, infuse, and make off with—that is, *souffler*—all the others. What presents itself as a mere repetition, a simple doubling, a word whispered on the stage of the Lutétia, comes to take away the breath of live speech and open up the uncontrollable dissemination of meaning that Derrida associates with writing and with living on. Though we might be tempted to ask what meaning Derrida, the author of these words, intended us to hear in this doubled and negated *souffler*, the "life" of this passage—like the entirety of "Faith and Knowledge"—is beyond the control of his intention or his meaning to say. It is impossible to say for certain what he meant; it has always been impossible to say for certain, and reading is at once condemned to this impossibility and freed for itself as a result. What thus can be said, and said without hesitation, *sans souffler*, is that the undecidability of *souffler* comes automatically, in a machinelike way, to contaminate the original intention at its very origin; it comes to infuse the animating breath with all these different possibilities, which are at once programmed and unforeseeable. Everything about this single passage thus speaks about the duplicity of religion and its necessary relationship to repetition and the technical supplement.

In the beginning, then, was the end of univocal meaning and the multiplication of tongues, the end of a single source and the beginning of repetition and dissemination. The task, then, Derrida seems to suggest, is to think religion in relationship not only to the elementary faith that is at the origin of every response but to the machine that always conditions that faith and repeats every response. Hence miracle *and* machine, elementary faith and its repetition, life and the survival or living on that conditions that life, the living on, for example, of a response that said *yes* to an invitation, that said *yes* to that *yes*, and the survival of that trace that repeats itself and, in repeating itself, engenders yet another response.[14]

In the beginning, then, was the machine, and the machine will have separated the author from the beginning from the beginning—all duplicity intended—that is, from the beginning from his words and, thus, from the beginning from himself. It is as if someone, perhaps everyone, a multiplicity of voices, perhaps an entire tradition, but a tradition that is already divided, had whispered from the alchemist's cavern, from the underworld of this text, or from backstage at the Hotel Lutétia, all these possibilities at once—possibilities within the French language but also in excess of that language. As Derrida reminds us again in "La parole soufflée," the one who whispers forgotten lines to an actor from the wings, what is called in English a "prompter," is in French a *souffleur*, that is, one who speaks, who breathes, who whispers, who simply reads or learns lines by heart and then repeats them in a mechanical way from off stage, from afar, the prompter being always a kind of *teleprompter*, giving us our cues, helping us to scan our breath, and giving us our lines, beginning with a line like "In the beginning . . ."

The Telegenic Voice

The Religion of the Media

As we have seen in previous chapters, religion must always—and especially today—be thought in relationship to the machine, to science and
technology, and, particularly, to the teletechnology that has overtaken our
world and transformed our very understanding of the world. Even when
we believe we have isolated a moment before the machine, a moment of
genesis before any repetition, there is already, as we have just seen, difference and duplicity. Even there where we believe we have found a speech
without writing, a response without reaction, a spontaneity without automaticity, the initiative of a miracle without any machine, there is, as we
have seen, already a *souffleur*, already a teleprompter, that is, already some
mediation or some media. In this chapter, I would like to concentrate not
on the relationship between religion and science in general but on the
relationship between religion and teletechnology, or religion and the
media. As Derrida argues both in "Faith and Knowledge" and in some
improvised comments from 1997 that expand on the principal theses of
that essay, religion is today inseparable from the media that have globala-
tinzed it, inseparable from the distribution and dissemination of the religious message via books, radio, the Internet, and especially, for Derrida,
for whom the medium is indeed always the meaning and the message,
television. Religion and the media, religion and television—that's what's
on the program for this chapter.

Let me begin, then, not with one of Derrida's many texts on the subject but with some improvised remarks made by Derrida in course of a

long interview with Bernard Stiegler conducted—and recorded and filmed—just weeks before he would deliver the first version of what would eventually be published as "Faith and Knowledge." In the midst of that interview of December 1993, Derrida is asked this seemingly mundane, journalistic question: "what kind of [TV] programs do you watch, aside from the news?" Derrida's response is initially equally mundane, indeed rather predictable, more or less what you would expect from a left-leaning, intellectually curious, widely read and well-traveled, secularly oriented French intellectual: "All kinds of things, the best and the worst. Sometimes I watch bad soap operas, French or American, or programs that give me a greater cultural awareness . . . [or] political debates . . . or else old movies. I could spend twenty-four hours a day watching good political archives. . . . And so I watch a little of everything." But then Derrida adds something a bit less predictable and a little more provocative: "What few people I know watch regularly, I suspect, and I watch very regularly Sunday morning, from 8:45 to 9:30, are the Muslim and Jewish religious programs, which I find very interesting—and if we had time to talk about them, I'd tell you why" (*ET* 138).

In this chapter I will argue that "Faith and Knowledge," along with a series of improvised remarks from December 1997, might be read as giving us precisely the explanation Derrida does not provide in the interview with Stiegler.[1] As we will see, Derrida's Sunday morning viewing ritual reveals much more than an ecumenical or multicultural interest in "the religions of the world"; more importantly and essentially, it reveals a long-standing interest in the very programming, mediatization, and dissemination of the religious message. In other words, what interested Derrida was not simply or even primarily the religious content of these programs but the relationship between religion and visibility, globalization and the media, including and especially the unique role played by television in the reproduction of the religious message, that is, the unique power of the simulacrum in television, the unique staging power of a putatively pure auto-affection and self-presence. What initially looks like a mundane and nonphilosophical answer to a journalistic question thus turns out to echo—and often in the very same terms—a critique of auto-affection, phonocentrism, and self-presence that goes back as far as Derrida's 1967 work *Speech and Phenomena* or, as it would be better translated for the argument that is to follow, *Voice and Phenomenon* (*La voix et le phéno-mène*). In the end, we will see how a critique of phonocentrism that dated back at least three decades—that is, a critique of the centrality of voice as opposed to writing—was fundamental to shaping Derrida's views about everything from the way in which the religions of the secret and of writing at once resist and rely upon the mediatization of their message to the way in which Christianity—via the televisual medium—performs miracles through the techno-scientific reproduction of the voice. But in order to make this case, we will need to slow down and return to the fundamental theses in "Faith and Knowledge" and elsewhere regarding religion and its relationship to technoscience and the media. Only then will we be able to understand why Derrida the philosopher, and not just the intellectual, citizen, or cultural critic, found himself everyday Sunday morning in front of the television in France, though also, as we will see, when he was visiting the United States, since it was perhaps there that Derrida came to see the real possibilities of televangelism and what I will call here, precisely in order to mix media, the *telegenic voice*.

Let me begin this time with what seems to be a certain invisible, indivisible, indisputable core of religion for Derrida, namely, the experience of the secret and a certain relationship to the absolute other (the second source of religion?), particularly as this is to be found in the alliance between YHWH and Abraham. According to Derrida, in *The Gift of Death* and elsewhere, the trial of Abraham would have consisted not only in the call to sacrifice Isaac (or perhaps Ishmael),[2] his beloved son, but the necessity to keep the secret imposed upon him by YHWH, the necessity not to report what was said or commanded of him by this absolute other in order to explain or justify himself, the necessity to keep it invisible or unspoken, secret, and secret even from himself. As Derrida parses YHWH's request that Abraham keep his secret, "all of this must remain absolutely secret: just between us. It must remain *unconditionally* private, our internal affair and inaccessible" ("AANJ" 56). In other words: "Above All, No Journalists!" YHWH would have said in effect to Abraham: Do not reveal, do not broadcast or publicize, do not evangelize or proclaim, what has happened between us; do not make our secret into some good news, or put it on the news, and especially do not televise it, or disseminate it via satellite or the Internet, and so don't even dream about putting it on your Face Book page, and as for Twitter, don't even get me started . . .[3]

This emphasis on the secret, indeed, this "taste for the secret," was at the center of many of Derrida's reflections during the 1990s. Derrida's seminar of 1991–92 was devoted entirely to the subject, as was his reading of Kierkegaard in *The Gift of Death*, where the secret is related to the absolute and to the absolute or total otherness of the other. Derrida says in *A Taste for the Secret*: "this is the absolute, and if there is something absolute it is secret. It is in this direction that I try to read Kierkegaard, the sacrifice of Isaac, the absolute as secret and as *tout autre* [wholly other]. . . . a resistance to the daylight of phenomenality that is radical, irreversible" (*TS* 57).

This understanding of the secret allows Derrida to begin sketching out some preliminary differences between the three monotheisms, casting doubt from the outset on whether there is a single essence, idea, or horizon of "religion itself." For if the secret of Abraham remains, as Derrida claims, "the major reference for Judaism and for Islam" ("AANJ" 57)—though probably even more for Judaism than for Islam—it obviously is not so for Christianity, an Abrahamic religion that is often understood to have replaced the centrality of the secret and the interrupted sacrifice of a son by the good news of the death and resurrection of a son who offered himself up to be sacrificed in order to become the mediator or intercessor between man and God. Derrida goes on to suggest that this relationship between the secret and the good news must be thought in relation to the general prohibition on the image as opposed to the mediatization of it. This would be analogous to the distinction in Levinas between the sacred and sanctity.

> When Levinas seeks to dissociate sacredness and sanctity, he associates the former with the cult, the image, and incarnation, whereas sanctity calls for the respect of distance, of separation, of the invisible, of the face as visible-invisible. Sacralization is on the side of idolatry, of the image, of the icon, and sanctity—even though I am well aware that Levinas would never have interpreted Abraham's sacrifice as I have proposed—would be on the side of the separation marked by the sacrifice of Isaac, above all, by its secretness. ("AANJ" 66–67)

For Derrida, then, the secret of Abraham has to be thought in relation to the "prohibition of the image" in Judaism and, especially, in Islam ("AANJ" 58). Christianity, by contrast, would have to be understood in relation to the possibility, even the necessity, of spreading the good news, of mediating or evangelizing it, in a word, of publicizing and mediatizing it. Hence differing relationships to the secret and the image imply differing relationships to communication, writing, and interpretation.

> What Judaism and Islam have in common is this experience of the imperceptible, of transcendence and hence of absence: they are religions of writing, of the experiences . . . of the infinite deciphering of traces. . . . This is where the experience of the secret is bound up with the experience of the infinite gloss. There where the Thing does not reveal itself, does not manifest itself directly, does not show its

face, there where the Cause remains secret, one has to gloss. This is why I began with Abraham and Isaac. We will never know what happened on Mount Moriah; we never saw anything and will never see it. ("AANJ" 84)[4]

As religions of the secret, both Judaism and Islam would call for an infinite commentary on the secret, while Christianity would emphasize instead the mediatization of its good news. Derrida thus draws a rather sharp distinction here between, on the one hand, Judaism and Islam as religions of the secret and of infinite commentary, and, on the other, Christianity as the religion of the word and of the good news. In *A Taste for the Secret*, Derrida not only reiterates this division within the three monotheisms but seems to come right out and admit his taste or his preference for the former.

> Between *this* secret and what is generally called secret, even if the two are heterogeneous, there is an analogy that makes me prefer the secret to the non-secret, the secret to the public expression, exhibition, phenomenality. I have a taste for the secret, it clearly has to do with not-belonging; I have an impulse of fear and terror in the face of a political space, for example, a public space that makes no room for the secret. . . . if a right to the secret is not maintained, we are in a totalitarian space. Belonging—the fact of avowing one's belonging, of putting in common—be it family, nation, tongue—spells the loss of the secret. (*TS* 59)

While Derrida here confesses a certain preference for the secret, and thus for religions of the secret, it would be a mistake to reduce this to a simple preference for Judaism or Islam over Christianity. For if the former seem to depend on the secret in a way the latter does not, they can also, Derrida will argue, close down the secret in their emphasis on family, nation, or language, on the idiom in general, just as Christianity can sometimes leave the secret intact—and leave it intact, perhaps, through the very mediatization and universalization that would seem to betray it. What Derrida is thus opposed to is any thinking within any religion that leaves no place for the secret. Right after suggesting, therefore, the distinction between religions of the secret and the religion of mediatization, Derrida begins taking this distinction back, or at least qualifying it, arguing that "no demanding and ambitious Christian theologian will accept this opposition. For the Christian gesture consists in internalizing this scene in the name of the infinite. The infinite secret remains, and (with it) virtualization. The Eucharist, real presence, is also a kind of virtualization. Between the secret and virtual manifestation what is the difference? No Christian would thus easily accept . . . the fracture that I am evoking" ("AANJ" 84–85). Derrida thus calls into question his own opposition between religions of the secret and Christianity as a religion of the good news, but he does so by putting other oppositions into play. Christianity would now be a religion of *internalization*, of the *virtualization* and *spectralization* of the body of Christ in the Eucharist. It would be a religion of spirit inasmuch as the Christian incarnation is "a spiritual incarnation" ("AANJ" 61). As a result, Derrida will go on to argue, Christianity would be a religion of mourning, a religion in mourning for the lost body and its virtualization in the Eucharist, a mourning for "the Man-God" that would have, says Derrida, "no place, in the strong sense of the term 'mourning,' either in Judaism or in Islam," which are instead "both thoughts of life and of living life in which mourning does not have the founding, originary place it has in Christianity" ("AANJ" 85).

Derrida covers quite a lot of ground and makes several very bold claims in the space of just a few pages in these improvised remarks published under the title "Above All No Journalists!" And while one should probably grant Derrida some leeway here, insofar as these are, after all, *improvised* remarks, one might also want to place even more emphasis on them because they are improvised, offered in a more unguarded fashion, less qualified and nuanced by the strategies of writing. Keeping Derrida's own caveats about these oppositions in mind, Judaism and Islam would be religions of the secret and of the infinite gloss or commentary, whereas Christianity would be a religion of the internalized secret and its virtualization, a religion of originary mourning that calls at once for internalization and mediatization. Whereas the Islamic and Jewish traditions thus favor a certain imperceptibility and incommunicability of the secret, Christianity favors a mediatization or publicity of the word and the image. It might thus be said that, for Derrida, mediatization is itself "fundamentally Christian and not Jewish, Islamic, Buddhist" ("AANJ" 58). There would be a fundamental or intrinsic mediatization in Christianity that lends itself to reproduction or to the simulacrum, to an intrinsic and not merely contingent relationship to the media and, thus, to the globalization of the media. As Derrida will say in another improvised discussion in 2002, "Christianity is the most plastic, the most open, religion, the most prepared, the best prepared, to face unpredictable transformations" ("EF" 33). While there are thus "phenomena of mediatization in all religions," there is "a trait that is absolutely singular in the power and structure of Christian mediatization" ("AANJ" 58). And while all religions, including Christianity, maintain a certain attachment to the proper and the idiom and so resist to a certain extent the deracinating powers of translation, mediatization, and universalization, while there is, as Derrida puts it, "a certain religion of the idiom in *all* religion," Christianity would be the religion that is least attached to its idiom and so the least resistant to these deracinating powers ("AANJ" 88).[5] On the other end of the spectrum would be Islam, the religion most attached, according to Derrida, to the untranslatable letter, and thus the most resistant to certain forms of mediatization and translation. While there is religion of the idiom even in Christianity, as when, for example, "French [Catholic] fundamentalism distinguished itself at a certain moment in time through its defense of Latin in the prayer service," "nowhere," says Derrida, "does the *fixed* literalness of language, the idiomatic form of the original message, in its very body, sanctify itself to the extent it does in the Muslim religion" ("AANJ" 88). Though there has been, to be sure, a long tradition of proselytizing in Islam, of spreading the word of the Koran, this has usually not been accompanied by a translation of the word into other languages or idioms. In Islam, as opposed to Christianity, what is most important is the body of the letter itself, the idiom itself: "the letter should be repeated, but this repetition *without alteration* should leave the letter intact and thus efface itself as repetition. . . . The body of the letter is what counts, above all else" ("AANJ" 88).

These reflections should give us an even better sense of what Derrida means in "Faith and Knowledge" by that rather unwieldy polysyllabic but essentially monotheistic neologism *globalatinization* (or *mondialatinisation*). If there is an intrinsic relationship between Christianity and globalization in the forms of teletechnology, mediatization, and translation, if the very name *religion* comes, as we saw in Chapter 2, from the language—namely, Latin—through which Christianity first spread and became a truly global religion, then globalatinization would not simply be a process that religion might or might not undergo but one that it cannot but undergo insofar as it defines the very nature of religion itself. Globalatinization would thus be *in its essence* Christian, even when Judaism or Islam engages in it or pursues its strategies and techniques, and the very category religion, related now both to its Latin roots and to the publicity and mediatization to which it has given rise and from which it has benefited, would be itself an intrinsically Christian notion.

From this perspective, Christianity would seem to be the only religion there is, the only set of practices or beliefs worthy of the name *religion*. Though one might be sorely tempted to object at this point that Derrida is unjustly excluding Judaism, Islam, and so on from the ennobling category of "religion," the opposite is perhaps more true. He is suggesting that we must be wary of calling other cults or belief systems or practices besides Christianity *religion*, because whenever we do—thinking, perhaps, that we are simply including them in a generous and ecumenical spirit into the world community of religions—we are perhaps already globalatinizing and thus unjustly Christianizing them.[6] The very term *globalatinization* would have thus been coined and used throughout "Faith and Knowledge" with the intention not just of showing the worldwide stakes of religion today or of distinguishing Christianity as a worldwide religion from all other religions but, in effect, of distinguishing Christianity as the *only* religion from all other practices or forms of belief.

> If I have allowed myself to resort to the rather clumsy term "globalatinization" [*mondialatinisation*], it is also in order to question what is going on when a non-Christian says, "Islam, or Judaism, or Buddhism is *my religion*." He begins by naming that in a Latin manner. I don't know if there is a word for "religion" in Arabic, but it is certainly not an adequate translation of "religion." Is Judaism a "religion"? Buddhism is certainly not a religion. ("AANJ" 74)

Derrida would hardly be alone, of course, in claiming that Buddhism is less a religion than a philosophy or a set of practices.[7] But instead of stopping there, he goes on much more controversially to question whether either of the other two monotheisms besides Christianity can rightly—or safely—be called *religion*: "I am not certain that the history of Abraham-Ibrahim should be counted as part of 'religion.' As soon as I call it a 'religious phenomenon' or 'the founding archive of religion *as such*,' the moment of Christianization has already begun" ("AANJ" 88).[8] As Derrida suggests in "Faith and Knowledge," "the history of the word 'religion' should in principle forbid every non-Christian from using the name 'religion,' in order to recognize in it what 'we' would designate, identify and isolate there" (§34).

At the same time as he looks, therefore, for a common source, origin, or essence of religion, of religion *as such*, Derrida multiplies the differences, first between the three monotheisms and other so-called religions, but then within monotheism itself, so that, in the end, one religion alone, Christianity, would seem to define the very essence of religion. For the essence of religion, that which all religions have in common, would be precisely the ability of a religion to represent or present itself in a global fashion *as a religion*—something Christianity does in an exemplary fashion. It would be the ability of a religion to represent itself *as* a religion that would make it a religion in the first place, that is, a religion like

Christianity. Perhaps we can now better understand Derrida's answer to his own question "What is a religion?" in "Above All, No Journalists!"

> To present oneself on the international stage, to claim the right to practice one's "religion," to construct mosques where there were churches and synagogues is to inscribe oneself in a political and ideological space dominated by Christianity, and therefore to engage in the obscure and equivocal struggle in which the putatively "universal" value of the concept of religion, even of religious tolerance, has in advance been appropriated into the space of a Christian semantics. ("AANJ" 74)

For a religion to call itself a religion on the world stage is thus for it to engage in a universal or globalatinizing process that is in its essence Christian. There are thus multiple religion*s* only to the extent that they can present themselves in a space that is essentially Christian. From differences between religions to a common essence of these religions to a singular religion that seems to define this essence, Derrida never stops in these improvised remarks going back and forth between the singular and the plural, the particular and the universal, determinate religions and the claim to universality.

> All these religions are doubtless religions with a universal vocation, but only Christianity has a concept of universality that has been elaborated into the form in which it today dominates both philosophy and international law. There is in St. Paul a concept of cosmopolitanism, a concept of world citizen, of human brotherhood as children of God, etc., which is closer to the concept of universalism as today it dominates the philosophy of international law than are other figures of universalism. . . . Thus one would have to distinguish very precisely the values of universality that are at the heart of the three religions called monotheistic. The universalism that dominates global political-juridical discourse is fundamentally Greco-Christian. . . . It is a Christianity speaking a bit of Greek. ("AANJ" 74)

All religions, Derrida is clear to point out here, have a "universal vocation," and, no doubt, a certain conception of universality, but it is Christianity's particular brand of universality that has gained such prominence and legitimacy on the world stage and that has marked international discourse, law, and institutions to such a degree.

Religion is thus in its essence as well as its etymological origins Christian, as are the movements of universalization and mediatization to which, especially today, it appears inextricably linked. We can perhaps now understand the enormous stakes of mediatization for Derrida: mediatization implies a rupture of the secret by a public message, the interruption of the incommunicable, of the singular, though also of the idiom and of the identification of meaning with a particular tongue. It implies a spectralization and even a spiritualization of the meaning or the message by means of the structures of visibility, communication, a certain conception of universalization, and translation.

Though all religions tend to resist the mediatization and universalization of their message by means of national networks that attempt to reroot the religious message in a particular culture and idiom, the religion that resists least and lends itself best to such universalization is Christianity. Derrida says straight out, "All the Christian churches are more mediatic than their Jewish, Muslim, Buddhist etc. equivalents" ("AANJ" 59). That is why Derrida will speak of "the televisual hegemony of the Christian religion (first of all Catholicism, but by emanation Christianity in general)"—a parenthetical qualification Derrida must add here because, as we will shortly see, the most widely disseminated, most dramatic, spectacular, and arguably the most successful televisual representations of religion in the United States and elsewhere are not Catholic but Protestant, Evangelical or Pentecostal ("AANJ" 59).

Conversely, then, it is the religions of the secret and of the infinite gloss, religions of the idiom—Judaism and Islam—that remain most resistant to certain globalatinized forms of universalization and mediatization, the most resistant, then, to a Christian hegemony that is at once "political, economic, and religious" ("AANJ" 62). Non-Christian religions or practices thus resist Christianity and yet, through the very globalization of their resistance, cannot help resembling it. Derrida testifies:

> I am struck by the muffled and almost desperate struggle of the non-Christian religions when they attempt *at the same time* to Christianize themselves *and* to defend themselves against Christianity. This holds no less for Islam than for Judaism. . . . But at the same time that they seek to resist the fascination to emulate [*fascination spéculaire*], these religions become ever more Christian in their form, in their discourse, in their manifestation. They seek to be different and to resemble, to acquire the global legitimacy of Christianity. ("AANJ" 73–74)

We thus see here a kind of *autoimmunity* of non-Christian religions as they adopt Christian forms of manifestation in their very resistance to

Christianity. This is precisely the autoimmunity of religion to techno-science that is at the core of Derrida's argument in "Faith and Knowledge." As Derrida phrases that argument in "Above All, No Journalists!" "technology is used to protest against technology," that is, "against the cosmopolitical tendencies of technology, against the dislocation, delocalization, uprooting associated with teletechnology" ("AANJ" 62).

In "Faith and Knowledge," Derrida characterizes this autoimmune reaction as a sort of hyperbolic outdoing or outbidding, an ever more intense appropriation of teletechnology in the name of what would claim to have come before teletechnology and so needs to be protected and indemnified all the more. In the improvised remarks of 1997 that we have been following in this chapter, Derrida thus speaks of "a religion that reacts and rebels against teletechnological knowledge, while at the same time outdoing itself [faisant de la surenchère]. This can be observed every day, not only for the Christian religion, but for the Islamic religion, perhaps even more than for the Jewish religion" ("AANJ" 68). The reaction against teletechnology is thus autoimmune, and it leads not only to a surreptitious Christianization but to a kind of Europeanization—and thus Americanization—of those who resist. Speaking elsewhere of globalization and of "a universal Europeanization through science and technology," Derrida argues that "even those who, through acts of terrorist violence, claim to oppose this violent Europeanization, this violent Americanization, do so most often using a certain technical, techno-scientific, sometimes techno-economic-scientific Europeanization" (IW 61). To follow this logic: if Islam reacts against the powers of teletechnological modernity by means of those very powers, and if those powers are allied not only with Europe but—and even more essentially—with the United States, then the autoimmunity of Islam consist in protecting itself from a certain Americanization by appropriating that very same Americanization.

While such resistance and autoimmunity can be found in Christianity as well, "*the most determined* protests against this hegemony . . . are going to come," argues Derrida, "from nationalities, from national-religious, phantasmatic complexes that are non-Christian" ("AANJ" 62). Hence "the appropriation of mediatic powers" on the part of Islam or Judaism "tends to be directed against Christian teletechnological hegemony" ("AANJ" 62). We thus witness a protest against the Christian hegemony of the media by means of the media itself, a national protest against globalization and universalization by means of a globalizing and internationalizing media network. Tied in their production and their organization to national phenomena, "to the national language and the nation-state" ("AANJ" 62), these protests are autoimmune in the precise sense Derrida gives to this notion in "Faith and Knowledge": religion attempts to indemnify and protect one of its two sources, to safeguard an originary experience of the sacred, only by enlisting the forces of a teletechnology that translates, mediatizes, and thus uproots the originary experience that religion wishes to protect.

We must thus give up thinking, in accordance with a certain Enlightenment tradition, that religion is opposed to science or faith to knowledge, for we are in fact "heir to religions that are designed precisely to *cooperate* with science and technology" ("AANJ" 62; my emphasis). In addition to the prevailing concept of "religion," then, which is essentially Christian in its roots, its history, and its dissemination, Derrida argues that our predominant understanding of the Enlightenment, as well as many of the notions associated with it, are Christian as well, from a certain conception—for there are others—of democracy or globalization or universality to a certain understanding of the world, cosmopolitanism, secularism, and so on. It is thus no coincidence that certain religions—or, to be clear, *certain tendencies* within them—have reacted in an autoimmune fashion against the very Enlightenment notions identified as Christian in their origins. (I underscore *certain tendencies* because, as Derrida makes clear elsewhere, "there are many Islams, there are many Wests" [*IW* 39], and the task remains to "deconstruct the European intellectual construct of Islam" [*IW* 38].)

Now, there are, to be sure, many similarities, in Derrida's account, between the three monotheisms, from the originary or elementary faith that underlies all three to a "fraternalist" and "implicitly phallocentric" privileging of "the brother (the father or the son) at the expense of the sister."[9] But what interests me here most are the differences Derrida sketches out between them, and especially between Christianity and the other two monotheisms with regard to the media. Christianity lends itself in a unique and essential way, Derrida argues, to translation, universalization, and mediatization, and, in a way that is absolutely unique, to *television*. From the empty tomb and the disappearance of the body to the spectralization of the body in the communal host, Christianity appears to have been, for Derrida, made for TV.[10] Derrida says, yet again in "Above All, No Journalists!": "The very process of incarnation, the *hoc est meum corpus*, the Eucharist is at the same time a spiritualization and a spectralization of the dead body of Christ, and thus an interiorization in the Host. Sent remotely via media, the message no less than the messenger (the angel or the evangelist) produces or implies this spectralization. Whence the relation between, the intimate complicity of the religious and the mediatic" ("AANJ" 61).[11]

We can thus understand better why Derrida would say in "Faith and Knowledge" not simply that the pope himself seems to accept the thesis of the death of God but that one "has the impression that he speaks only of that. . . . And that another death of God comes to haunt the Passion that animates him" (§37).[12] The death of God is an essentially Christian thesis, and the media is not simply the means by which this thesis or this claim is disseminated but the very milieu by or in which it is performed or produced. As Derrida claims again in "Above All, No Journalists!":

> This Christian hegemony in the world of televisualization is the hegemony of a religion founded on the ordeal of *kenosis* and of the death of God. Terrifying mystery. The Christian message remains tied to the incarnation, the death of God, under the form of Christ on the Cross giving his body, but also, *as a result*, through all the deaths of God that have followed in the history of European philosophy until Hegel and Company. What propagates itself as media, as Christian telemedia, is also a certain death of God. ("AANJ" 67)

The thesis of the death of God is thus essentially tied to Christianity, but to a kind of "Christianity *as the end of Christianity*" ("AANJ" 69), the end, perhaps even, of a Christianity that uses the media better than any other religion and the beginning of a religion of the media—at once Christian and yet already beyond Christianity. This is one of the theses Derrida seems to take away from Hegel, the author of both the *Phenomenology* and that other text entitled "Faith and Knowledge":

> At the end of the *Phenomenology of Spirit*, it is the figure of Absolute Knowledge, the structure of philosophy as the truth of revealed religion, which is to say of the Christian religion. The "Speculative Good Friday." In abusing these shortcuts, . . . I would venture to say that the *religion of the media* is a *phenomenology of spirit*. Today there is a *religion of the media*, and it is, for the moment, precisely *the religion of the media*: there is the religion *of the* media, which is to say, the religion that the media represent, incarnate, reveal. ("AANJ" 69)

One must thus follow the similarities and the differences, the continuities and the discontinuities, between the three so-called monotheisms, but then also the continuities and discontinuities within Christianity itself. While a certain spiritualization, spectralization, interiorization, and universalization have always been an essential part of Christianity, since they are, in Derrida's reading, implied in the incarnation itself, they have today been pushed to the very limits of the earth and have been given a hitherto unknown power. While "a certain 'analogous' structure has always been in place," "what is happening today in terms of the internationalization of television, the capitalist accumulation of televisual power, the digitization of images, etc., all develops a technical power of effective universalization that has never been attained before" ("AANJ" 68).[13]

The essential universalization and even televisualization of Christianity have today reached a new and unprecedented level, Derrida claims, giving Christianity a global presence that makes us rethink the very nature of Christianity and of presence. The globalization of the media would thus be the very means by which Christianity is today fulfilling its essence, an essence it will have had from the beginning but which is today being revealed and transformed by the unprecedented development and sophistication of teletechnology. "In Christian televisualization, global *because* Christian, we confront a phenomenon that is utterly singular, that ties the future of media, the history of the world development of media, from the religious point of view to the history of 'real presence,' of the time of the mass and of the religious act" ("AANJ" 58–59).

Now, this reference to "presence" or "real presence" echoes from afar some of the familiar themes of Derridean deconstruction, such as the critique of a metaphysics of presence, linked always to a critique of logocentrism and, especially, phonocentrism that goes back to the very beginning of Derrida's work. Indeed it is as if, in this place where Derrida is demonstrating the continuities and discontinuities in Christianity's relation to the media, we have an exemplary opportunity for exploring the continuities and discontinuities in Derrida's own work. In order to make this connection more manifest, however, a brief detour through Derrida's time in the United States will be necessary.

I began by referring to Derrida's habit of regularly—we might even say religiously—watching Jewish and Muslim TV programs every Sunday morning in France. There is good reason to believe, however, that Derrida kept up this habit when traveling abroad, and particularly in the United States, where his viewing attention would have naturally been drawn not to Jewish and Muslim programs but to the Christian ones that pervade our media.[14] Indeed, it is hard not to suspect that the very thesis concerning the fundamental relationship between Christianity and mediatization was actually first developed or at least found its most striking confirmation in the United States. As Derrida himself confesses in "Above All, No Journalists!" "the reference to America here is fundamental" ("AANJ" 58); "in France there is nothing comparable to what takes place in the United States" ("AANJ" 60).

But what is it exactly that takes place in the United States, or what is it that draws Derrida's attention to American TV? What fascinates, in short, would appear to be television's power of fascination, the power of a simulacrum that appears to give access to the thing itself—to the miraculous—without technical intervention or mediation, a power that persists even when one is vigilant and able to submit the televisual image to critique.[15] Capitalizing upon the original or elementary faith that Derrida claims to be the basis of all media, that is, capitalizing upon the "I believe" or the "I believe you" or the "Believe me as one believes in a miracle" at the origin of every form of communication and every social bond, Christianity attempts to combine the simulacrum of "real presence" via the televisual image with the production of miracles. The relationship between the media and religion thus "finds its space in this continuity, in this homogeneity between the ordinary miracle of the 'believe me' and the extraordinary miracles revealed by all the Holy Scriptures" ("AANJ" 76–77). The media exploit both the elemental faith of the social bond and our growing faith in teletechnology in order to produce miracles. It is "on the soil of this bare belief [cette croyance nue]," this originary or elementary or rudimentary belief, that "media construct themselves" ("AANJ" 65). "Television and media exploit this reduction of faith to the barest essentials," to "the barest foundation of the social bond"—the only foundation, Derrida would seem to believe, able to give rise to a universalizable culture of singularities:

> When one speaks of the end of ideologies, of the death of philosophy, of the end of systems, etc., one could conclude that all doctrines, all moral and ethical, legal and political systems have reached their limits, at least as historical constructions, and that we are experiencing their finitude as much as their precariousness, even their essential deconstructibility. Nothing will be left but the barest [nu] foundation of the social bond—on which everything will have to be reconstructed. What remains—the minimum, but it is "fundamental"—is faith. ("AANJ" 64)

For the moment, however, religion continues to exploit this bare or fundamental faith, which, as we saw earlier, is nothing other than the experience of the miracle. In other words, it is on the basis of this act of testimonial faith and this experience of the miracle that teletechnology is able to give the impression that miracles can actually be broadcast live. In "Faith and Knowledge" Derrida thus speaks of "so many miracles transmitted live (most frequently, healings, which is to say, returns to the unscathed, *heilig*, holy, indemnifications) followed by commercials, before thousands in an American television studio" (§27n17). In "Above All, No Journalists!" Derrida is even more explicit—and colorful:

> Even if masses are not generally celebrated, "miracles" are shown. Some of you will have seen in the United States such miracles on the screen: bodies falling backward on the order of the officiating thaumaturge or rising once cured, etc. One is truly in the Bible, seeing paralytics walk, the blind see—all of that, naturally, "live" before the eye of the camera, all organized by powerful industrial corporations, with formidable quantities of capital at their disposal. ("AANJ" 60)[16]

It is this capitalization upon the testimonial faith that is the condition of all teletechnology that leads to the production of miracles on the plasma screen. This can be pulled off, as Derrida notes, only through a high degree of technological knowledge, not to mention tremendous investments of capital, which thus provide a troubling continuity in American religious programs between preaching and promotion, prayer and product placement.[17] But the unique power of certain media, and of TV first among them, seems to reside in the way these media efface—or *seem* to efface—the means and modes of their production or, really, their reproduction.

This brings us to the very heart, to the living, beating heart, of Christianity's relationship to the media. According to Derrida, what is unique about the televisual mediatization of the religious message is precisely the way a *reproduction* passes itself off each time *as a production*, a reproduction of the *event itself*, the original event, be it the transubstantiation of the host, the performing of Biblical miracles or, more essentially, the reproduction of the live speech act of prayer. In other words, the televisual reproduction always effaces itself and tries to pass itself off as an original production.

> Television always involves a protest against television; television pretends to efface itself, to deny television. It is expected to show you the thing itself, "live," directly. Such "direct," "live" presentation, translated into the Christian code, is the "real presence," the "transubstantiation" or the "Eucharist," and, in a more general way, a phenomenon of incarnation: deictic and sensible *immediacy* of the mediator, here and now, in the *this*, the making present of mediation or of reconciliation. ("AANJ" 62)

While non-Christian religious programs of the kind Derrida watched on Sundays in France might, he says, "consist in filming a speech, pedagogy, or discussions," it is never an *event* that is filmed, whereas in a Christian mass, says Derrida:

the thing itself, the event takes place in front of the camera: commu- nion, the coming of real presence, the Eucharist in a certain sense, even the miracle (miracles are produced on American television)— the thing actually takes place "live" *as* a religious event, *as* a sacred event. In other religions religion is *spoken about*, but the sacred event itself does not take place in the very flesh of those who present them- selves before the camera. ("AANJ" 58)

If non-Christian programs might thus sometimes show Muslims or Jews praying on camera and may even accidentally capture their words, Chris- tian programs perform miracles *for* the camera and produce prayer *through* the microphone *for* transmission and reproduction via teletechnology. On these programs the audience actually bears witness to the event itself, the live event, the very moment of the production of prayer, via a medium that tends, as Derrida puts it, to efface—or at least that is the simula- crum—the technological apparatus and the structure of reproduction that made it possible.

Derrida himself does not go on to develop differences within Chris- tianity at this point, but we might wish to. While the mediatization of a Catholic mass does indeed attempt to represent "the coming of real pres- ence, the Eucharist" by means of the camera, there is still, it seems, an element of the spectacle about it, of the mass as an object of the viewer's gaze. Prayer is thus captured by the camera but not, it seems, produced for it. But in various forms of televangelism, prayer is actually produced *for* the camera, *through* the microphone. The voice performs the speech act of prayer not simply live before the camera but with, through, and for it, as if its mediatization or virtualization were its very element and breath, its very life.

We can perhaps now understand the centrality of television in Der- rida's analysis, the production of what I have called a *telegenic voice* that links the image to the voice and the voice to a live event—or at least that's the simulacrum. For television, more effectively than other media, Der- rida claims, presents the simulacrum of live presence and so lends itself to a unique kind of authority and credulity.[18] And it does this, curiously, crucially, not by means of the characteristic we would assume to be central to tele-vision, namely, the image, but by means of the voice, or the voice in conjunction with the image, a voice that presents itself as being as close as possible to the event itself:

What is most new, most powerful in what we are discussing here is not so much the production and transmission of images, but of the voice. If one holds the voice to be an auto-affective medium (a medium that presents itself as [*se donner pour*] being auto-affective, even if it isn't), an element of absolute presence, then the fact of being able to keep the voice of someone who is dead or radically absent, of being able to record, I mean reproduce and transmit, the voice of the dead or of the absent-living, is an unheard-of [*inouïe*] possibility, unique and without precedent. ("AANJ" 70)

The unheard-of power of radio and television—as opposed, for example, to painting or photography—comes from the reproduction of a voice that is heard, a voice that "presents itself as [*se donner pour:* that gives itself (out) as]" an auto-affective medium, even if it is not. In television the voice presents itself, precisely, as auto-affective, "an element of absolute presence," thereby giving the impression that we are witnessing the very production of signification, as close as possible to the living breath of the speaker. Though "one knows very well—and this is the most rudimentary knowledge concerning what television is in reality—that *there is never anything live*" ("AANJ" 63), the voice we hear on radio or television presents itself *as* live. That is the unique authority of the voice, especially, perhaps, when it is attached to the image of what we believe to be its source, the living source of life itself.

Hence "the power of television is vocal," Derrida argues, "at least as much as radio," and its unheard-of authority stems from the fact that "the artificial and synthetic recomposition of a voice is much less suspect than is that of an image" ("AANJ" 71). Whereas the image can always be questioned in its purity and its presence, its authenticity doubted, the voice presents itself to experience as much more natural, much more alive, and so much less suspect.

What Derrida argues here about television is repeated in an interview from 2001 with regard to cinema. He there argues that "the recording of the voice is one of the most important phenomena of the twentieth century" insofar "it gives to living presence a possibility of 'being there' anew that is without equal and without precedent" ("CF" 81). The integration of sound and, in particular, of the voice in cinema was thus not, for Derrida, some mere supplement to be celebrated or, for those advocates of a "pure cinema," lamented, but rather "a return to the origins of cinema" that allowed it to fulfill its original vocation. Hence Derrida can argue that "there is in cinema an absolutely singular modality of *belief*" ("CF" 78) that stems from the reproduction not of the image but of the voice. For "the genetic imprint [voice, speech] is more credible, better accredited, than the cinemagraphic imprint" ("CF" 80).

The power of television can thus be understood in one of two ways: either it stems, as in radio, from the mere reproduction of the voice, its extraordinary power simply the result of its worldwide dominance over the past few decades; or it stems from the voice's ability not only to neutralize or overcome the suspicion that is always cast on the image but actually to convert that suspicion into belief as the voice is reattached via the image to what seems to be the place of its production. Derrida seems to suggest the latter in a couple of places in "Above All, No Journalists!" He argues that television, as opposed now to radio and other media, gives access—through the voice or the voice in conjunction with the image—to "the thing itself," to the productive source of signification itself. "The presumption remains, and with it, the common prejudice, the structural credulity that television, by contrast with printed newspapers and radio, allows you to *see* the thing itself, *to see what touches*. . . . Like the ten thousand persons in the auditorium, one is confronted with the thing itself" ("AANJ" 64). To see what touches, says Derrida; we saw earlier in "Faith and Knowledge" this conjunction of the visual and the digital, of eye and finger, when Derrida spoke of "digital systems and virtually immediate panoptical visualization, 'air space,' telecommunications satellites, information highways, concentration of capitalistic-mediatic power—in three words, *digital culture, jet* and *TV*" (§27). It is this seeming kinaesthesia, this apparent conjunction of voice and image—one might even say voice and phenomenon—that seems to touch us in our very hearts and give us the impression that we are in proximity to the production of life itself:

> It is because phenomenal auto-affection refers us to a living proximity, to the emitting, *productive* source, something the camera that captures an image does not do. The recording of the voice reproduces a production. The vocal "image" is the image of a living production and not of an object as spectacle. In this sense it is not even an image any longer, but the re-production of the thing itself, of production itself. ("AANJ" 71)

And then Derrida adds to this claim in "Above All, No Journalists!" a couple of lines that recall the basic impulse of the deconstruction of phonocentrism from "Signature Event Context" right up through *Learning to Live Finally*.

> I am always overwhelmed when I hear the voice of someone who is dead, as I am not when I see a photograph or an image of the dead person. . . . I can also be touched, *presently*, by the recorded speech

of someone who is dead. I can, *here and now*, be affected by a voice from beyond the grave. All that is needed is to hear, *here and now*, what was, in the restored present of a self-affection, the listening-to-oneself-speaking . . . of the other dead: as another living present. ("AANJ" 71)[19]

It is as if the auto-affection of the voice effaces or presents itself as having effaced the distance of tele-vision, as if the spatiality of the visual image, a spatiality that always makes the image suspect, liable to reproduction and falsification, has given way to the pure temporality of the living voice, as if, in the reproduction of voices, we were watching the self-production and auto-archiving of life itself.[20] If Derridean deconstruction began by questioning the relationship in philosophy between speech and writing, if all of Derrida's questions seem to have been historically conditioned by advances in writing technology from the codex to the printing press—all those things decried by philosophers from Plato to Rousseau to Heidegger—it was, it seems, certain technologies developed for recording speech or the voice that affected Derrida most and helped demonstrate the "written" qualities of all speech—the phonograph, the gramophone, the tape recorder, the answering machine, and here radio and television. With the latter, there is thus "*re*production as re-*production* of life by itself, and the production is archived as the source, not as an image": "It is an image, but an image that effaces itself as image [*qui s'efface comme image*], a re-presentation that offers itself as pure presentation. Life itself can be archived and spectralized in its self-affection, whereas when someone presents himself to be seen he does not necessarily see himself. In the voice, self-affection itself is (supposedly) recorded and communicated" ("AANJ" 71). There is thus in television a claim of "transparency toward the thing itself, including the self-effacement of the media," a claim that the media "destroys itself or carries itself away, immunizes itself against itself," where progress "consists in claiming to efface oneself ever more effectively" ("AANJ" 75). We here see Derrida's earlier language of self-effacement and self- or auto-affection coming into contact with the language of autoimmunity, a conjunction that cannot but suggest a certain relationship—perhaps even auto-affection—between two rather distant parts of Derrida's corpus.[21]

We have seen Derrida speak in "Above All, No Journalists!" of "a medium that presents itself as [*se donner pour*] being auto-affective," of "an image that effaces itself as image [*qui s'efface comme image*]," and then of a medium that "immunizes itself against itself" by claiming a kind of "transparency toward the thing itself." It is this language of transparency or of a putative transparency, of self-effacement and the presumption of auto-affection, that brings us back to the very origins of deconstruction. If these analyses of religion and media from the 1990s are thus interesting, even fascinating, in their own right, they take on new relevance and interest when related to some of Derrida's earliest works. For the terms used to describe the mediatization of the voice on television—a medium that presents itself as a transparent or pure auto-affection, an image that effaces itself as image, and so on—are precisely those used by Derrida back in 1967 in *Speech and Phenomena* and elsewhere to develop a critique of phonocentrism in Husserl's theory of the sign.[22] He there writes, for example: "My words are 'alive' because they seem not to leave me: not to fall outside me, outside my breath, at a visible distance . . . the phenomenon of speech, the phenomenological voice, *gives itself out* [se donne] in this manner" (*SP* 76; for the same idiom, see *SP* 78, 80). The voice thus presents itself as, or gives itself out as, what is alive inasmuch as it seems not to leave or to fall outside the living speaker. It thus presents itself in a way that seems to efface its signifying body, that is, its dead, mechanical body, giving access to the thing itself. Again in *Speech and Phenomena*: "This immediate presence results from the fact that the phenomenological 'body' of the signifier seems to fade away [*s'effacer*] at the very moment it is produced" (*SP* 77). What Derrida says about the voice in his analysis of religion and media thus resonates rather uncannily with what he argued some three decades earlier in *Speech and Phenomena* about the auto-affection of the voice. And it is absolutely resonant with the way he goes on in *Speech and Phenomena* to contrast the phenomenological experience of the voice with other nonphonic forms of signification, including and especially the visual image:

> The objection will perhaps be raised that this interiority belongs to the phenomenological and ideal aspect of every signifier. . . . And yet every non-phonic signifier involves a spatial reference in its very "phenomenon," in the phenomenological (nonworldly) sphere of experience in which it is given. The sense of being "outside," "in the world," is an essential component of its phenomenon. Apparently there is nothing like this in the phenomenon of speech. In phenomenological interiority, hearing oneself and seeing oneself are two radically different orders of self-relation. (*SP* 76)

The voice gives itself in such a way as to efface itself, to make itself transparent, in a way the image does not. "When I see myself, either because I gaze upon a limited region of my body or because it is reflected in a mirror, what is outside the sphere of 'my own' has already entered the field of this auto-affection, with the result that it is no longer pure" (*SP* 78–79).[23] Hearing oneself and seeing oneself are indeed, as Derrida argued back in *Speech and Phenomena* and as his analyses of television lead one to believe he still believes, "two radically different orders of self-relation." For in hearing oneself speak "the signifier would become perfectly diaphanous due to the absolute proximity to the signified. This proximity is broken when, instead of hearing myself speak, I see myself write or gesture" (*SP* 80). What is reduced in this proximity of the self to itself in hearing oneself speak is thus nothing less than the body itself, or space in general, indeed, any notion of exteriority as that which is necessary for the sign's repetition. Pure auto-affection was thus understood by Derrida in *Speech and Phenomena* in the context of his reading of Husserl as nothing less than the temporal process of signification purified of all exteriority or spatiality. Though Derrida would go on to argue, of course, that this "pure inwardness of speech, or of the 'hearing oneself speak,' is radically contradicted by 'time' itself" (*SP* 86), that repetition, space, exteriority, and the other are also essential to the constitution of time, the lure or phantasm of this pure auto-affection remains. Moreover, it is the lure or phantasm of such an auto-affection that gives rises, through the reduction of all exteriority, to the very constitution of universality.

> As pure auto-affection, the operation of hearing oneself speak seems to reduce even the inward surface of one's own body. . . . This is why hearing oneself speak [*s'entendre parler*] is experienced as an absolutely pure auto-affection, occurring in a self-proximity that would in fact be the absolute reduction of space in general. It is this purity that makes it fit for universality. Requiring the intervention of no determinate surface in the world, *being produced in the world as pure auto-affection*, it is a signifying substance absolutely at our disposition. For the voice meets no obstacle to its emission in the world precisely because it is produced *as pure auto-affection*. (*SP* 79)

In *Of Grammatology*, written right around the same time as *Speech and Phenomena*, the voice is characterized yet again as a pure auto-affection that is able to efface—or at least that is the illusion—the exteriority and materiality of the signifier: "The voice *is heard* (understood)—that undoubtedly is what is called conscience—closest to the self as the absolute effacement of the signifier: pure auto-affection that necessarily has the form of time and which does not borrow from outside of itself, in the world or in 'reality,' any accessory signifier, any substance of expression foreign to its own spontaneity" (*OG* 20). The fact that this effacement of the signifier or this experience of effacement is but an illusion or a phantasm does little to dampen its effect. On the contrary, its effect comes precisely from the fact that it is an illusion or phantasm. As Derrida goes on to argue in *Of Grammatology*: "This experience of the effacement of the signifier in the voice is not merely one illusion [*illusion*] among many—since it is the condition of the very idea of truth . . . . This illusion [*leurre*] is the history of truth and it cannot be dissipated so quickly" (*OG* 20). In other words, it is the illusion of such an effacement of the signifier, the phantasm of total transparency and spontaneity, that makes possible the very constitution of truth as ideality. "It is the unique experience of the signified producing itself spontaneously, from within the self, and nevertheless, as signified concept, in the element of ideality or universality. The unworldly character of this substance of expression is constitutive of this ideality" (*OG* 20).

These references to "universality" in both *Speech and Phenomena* and *Of Grammatology* bring us back almost immediately, almost without detour, I'm tempted to say almost *sans souffler*, to the themes of mediatization and globalization that we have been following throughout this chapter. Television lends itself to universalization better than other media not simply because it can transmit images globally but because, in reproducing the voice, it can give the impression of reproducing the very moment of auto-affection; in filming what is "live," it can give the impression of presenting the very moment of the event and the very production of signification. The universality of signification is thus to be found not in the image but in a vocal sign that would *seem* to efface itself before the signified.

In his 1967 *Speech and Phenomena*, Derrida demonstrates how Husserl's description of the phenomenological experience of the voice in its seeming intimacy and proximity to self leads to an interpretation of the voice and of significance in general that conflicts with what is said elsewhere in Husserl about the very nature of signification, including the signification of speech. Husserl, like many thinkers before him, would have fallen prey to the temptation of thinking that the voice can, in short, archive itself, that it can signify in an interior space that has been purified of all space and all exteriority. But this temptation—this mistake, if you will—has its basis in a certain phenomenological experience of the voice. When we take such experience into account, it is hardly any wonder that Husserl or Saussure, or Rousseau or Plato, for that matter, would have understood the voice to be more natural than writing, closer to a pure auto-affection. The experience of the voice lends itself to just such an interpretation, even though, upon scrutiny, upon reflection and analysis,

such an interpretation is inconsistent with a general theory of signification. The problem thus arises not so much in experience but in the interpretation of that experience, as the seeming priority of the voice is
uncritically opposed to the secondariness and exteriority of writing so as
then to be adopted as the ideal of signification in general.

Derrida's interpretation of Husserl in *Speech and Phenomena*—a title
that, as I suggested at the outset of this chapter, would be better translated
as *Voice and Phenomenon*—would thus seem to be the basis, in part, of his
understanding some three decades later of the unique power of television
and, particularly, of the power of the voice in television. In both places it
is the seeming proximity and auto-affection of the voice that is emphasized. This seeming is essential here, the sign of a lure or phantasm that
endures even when the voice is mediated through teletechnology. Indeed
the seeming intimacy and auto-affectivity of the voice appear to remain
intact in teletechnology, perhaps even augmented through teletechnology,
and this is what allowed Derrida, around the time of "Faith and Knowledge," to compare the auto-affectivity of the voice to one of the most
widespread examples of today's teletechnology. In a session of his 1996
seminar on hospitality, Derrida contrasts in a striking way the deracinating, universalizing force of teletechnology with the (putatively) rooted and
resistant and yet absolutely mobile power of the voice or of speech—a sort
of cell phone or mobile phone avant la lettre. Whereas "the telephone,
the television, the fax or e-mail, the Internet as well, all . . . introduce
ubiquitous disruption, and the rootlessness of place, the dis-location of
the house, the infraction into the home," "speech, the mother tongue"
seems to resist this dislocation. "A force of resistance," speech is nonetheless the "portable condition of all mobilities: in order to use the fax or the
'cellular' phone, I have to be carrying on me, with me, in me, as me, the
most mobile of telephones, called a language, a mouth, and an ear, which
make it possible to hear yourself-speaking" (*OFH* 89–91). The voice is
thus at once absolutely rooted and resistant and absolutely mobile and
portable, a center or home that I carry along with me wherever I go. The
voice is my internal cell phone and I am its carrier, granting myself unlimited long-distance calls and absolutely no roaming charges. At once rooted
and portable, resistant and mobile, the self-presence and auto-affection of
the voice bear all the signs of what Derrida called from some of his very
earliest texts right up through his last a phantasm. Here, in *Of Hospitality*
in January 1996, less than a year after completing and signing "Faith and
Knowledge," Derrida calls this self-relation and auto-affection of the
voice the most enduring of phantasms: "What we are describing here,
which is not the same as endorsing it, is the most unbreakable of fantasies

[*le plus increvable des phantasmes*: the most un-deflatable or indefatigable of phantasms]. For that which doesn't leave me in this way, language, is also, *in reality, in necessity*, beyond the fantasy, that which never ceases to depart from me" (*OFH* 91).

If the experience of the voice gives us the fantasy or presents us with the phantasm of pure self-presence, auto-affection, and auto-appropriation, analysis and scrutiny of the form of speech, the reality, so to speak, of the voice, and of language in general, demonstrates precisely the opposite, namely, a constant distancing of the self from itself and an ex-appropriation of the self by itself. Indeed it demonstrates that the voice is never simply one's own but is from the outset taken up in structures of signification that lead it away from itself.

But even more, this phantasm of hearing oneself speak appears so powerful, so unbreakable, that is seems to operate even in my experience of another hearing him or herself speak. What we experience in ourselves, the apparent proximity of the voice to itself, appears to be the basis of our assumption—or perhaps even our experience—of the same or a similar self-proximity of the voice in another. The contrast Derrida drew from the 1960s right up through the 1990s between the phenomenological experience of seeing oneself and hearing oneself speak appears to be basis, in "Above All, No Journalists!" and elsewhere, of the contrast between the experience of seeing and hearing another speak on television, the experience, that is, of witnessing the auto-affection of another in speech or, in an exemplary fashion, in prayer.[24] It is as if everything Derrida argued in *Speech and Phenomena* about the self hearing itself speak were now being used to interpret or understand the other or the other's voice on television, which I seem to hear or experience as a self-production even though it is not my own.

This argument concerning one's experience of the other's voice has some precedent in Derrida's early work. Already back in *Of Grammatology* in 1967, Derrida argues something similar in a passage where he first parses Rousseau's claims about the relationship between seeing and hearing, before going on in his own voice, in his own name, it seems, to endorse Rousseau's insight and send the reader in a footnote back to *Speech and Phenomena*. Derrida writes in *Of Grammatology*:

> I can close my eyes, I can avoid being touched by that which I see and that which is perceptible at a distance. But my passivity and my passion are totally open [and then Derrida cites Rousseau] to "accents to which one may not conceal one's organ," which "penetrate through it to the bottom of one's heart, and carry there in spite of

us the movements which draw them forth." [And Derrida then adds to this quote from Rousseau just before sending us in a footnote back to *Speech and Phenomena*. . .] Voice penetrates into me violently, it is the privileged route for forced entry and interiorization, whose reciprocity produces itself in the "hearing-oneself-speak," in the structure of the voice and of interlocution. (*OG* 240)[25]

In the end, the distinction between hearing myself speak and hearing the voice of the other that touches and penetrates me is a false one, or, better, a deconstructible one. For my voice too always comes from outside me, like the voice of another, *as* the voice of another, before being interiorized and appearing to me as what is most fully mine and what is most truly *living* within me. Indeed what we seem to see or hear in the speech act, what we seem to bear witness to in a voice that is as close as possible to the living breath, is nothing other than the self-production of *life itself*—in oneself first of all but also, it seems, by analogy, in the other. As Derrida argued in *Speech and Phenomena*: "We ought to consider, on the one hand, that the element of signification—or the substance of expression—which best seems to preserve ideality and living presence in all its forms is living speech, the spirituality of the breath as *phōnē*; and, on the other hand, that phenomenology, the metaphysics of presence in the form of ideality, is also a philosophy of *life*" (*SP* 10). Derrida's analysis of phenomenology as a philosophy of *life* would have thus been at the origin, it seems, of his rethinking some thirty years later of the televisual image and of the telegenic voice associated with it. It was those early analyses of Husserl and others that would have allowed Derrida to watch TV with a different ear. When the spatiality of the image is thus attached to what presents itself as the purely auto-affective, purely temporal movement of the voice, when the image, which is always suspect, seems to give way to the seeming transparency of a voice that is as close as possible to the event and to the very self-production of life, then, well, it is hard not to believe—even at a distance.

To be clear—and "Above All, No Journalists!" is exceedingly clear on this point—Derrida is not opposing representation via the media to some putatively live, direct, and non-mediatic self-presence in perception. "The choice is not between media and presence," says Derrida, because "the presentation of presence itself supposes a mediatic structure" ("AANJ" 81). The media in its most general sense is the very condition of presence in perception and thus of desire in general.

As soon as I form a phrase there is already fragmentation, repetition, iterability, a mediatic machine is already at work. This only enflames the desire, the dream of the non-fragmented body. . . . Fortunately or not, auto-immunity resides within the living body, the living present, and fragmentation is itself the condition of this desire. Should one succeed, against all the media in the world, in reaching the body proper . . ., it would be the end of desire, the end of everything. ("AANJ" 81)

Fragmentation, mediation, repetition, and reproduction are the condition of both perception and desire, not the end or perversion of these. Recalling—and there is no coincidence in Derrida's choice of example—the common experience of having "on the phone an experience of desire, of presence that is much more intense than certain 'face-to-face' situations" ("AANJ" 81), Derrida argues that there is no desire before the media, no time and no life before the machine—even if the *phantasm* of a life before the machine is but the other side of this desire. And Derrida's point is that certain media, and chief among them television, are better able to efface themselves in order to produce such a phantasm, that is, in order to simulate a life before media and the machine.

As we have seen, religion is, for Derrida, an essentially Christian notion related to the movements of globalization, universalization, and mediatization. But because the essence of this universalization and mediatization is the putative self-effacement of the medium through the auto-affection attributed to the voice, to the self-production and life of the voice, then we might say not, as we did in the previous chapter, "in the beginning is the machine" but—so much closer to the animating breath of "our tradition"—"in the beginning is the miracle of the voice"—or at least that's the phantasm. In this genesis of the metaphysics of presence, which, though a phantasm, will have exercised such an authority over us, it will have always been the voice, not the image, that is telegenic.[26] The entire history of metaphysics, Derrida argues, is thus bound up with this project or projection of a voice that would seem to be coincident with itself, present to itself, able to speak and broadcast itself without exteriority or alterity, and thus without death—and thus without life. To cite Derrida's *Speech and Phenomena* one final time: "*The history of metaphysics therefore can be expressed as the unfolding of the structure or schema of an absolute will-to-hear-oneself-speak. . . . A voice without différance, a voice without writing, is at once absolutely alive and absolutely dead*" (SP 102). To present a voice at a distance, a voice that, despite the distance, would *seem* to be live and without difference, a voice that would be the simulacrum of a life without death, purely temporal and without exteriority—that is the miracle of the phantasm or, same difference, the phantasm of the miracle. And that is the secret of television, a far cry, to be sure, from the secret that took place but was never recorded, and was certainly never broadcast "live," from Mount Moriah.

6

"Jewgreek is greekjew"

Messianicity—Khōra—Democracy

In Chapter 3 we claimed that Derrida identifies two sources of religion, one of which is the common source of both religion and science, namely, a kind of originary or elementary faith, the "barest foundation" of every social bond. This reading of "Faith and Knowledge" is justified by just about everything Derrida says about these two sources in this essay and in the texts we have been reading around it. There are, however, a few places in "Faith and Knowledge" where Derrida's language lends itself to some ambiguity with regard to these sources. One such passage is found at the end of §20, where Derrida says he wishes to "*give two names to the duplicity of these origins*," to "*name these two sources, these two fountains or these two tracks that are still invisible in the desert*," to "*lend them two names that are still 'historical.'*"[1] Given everything said thus far about the "two sources" of religion, we might expect Derrida to go on to speak of an experience of the sacred that must remain indemnified, on the one hand, and a testimonial act of faith, on the other. Instead, Derrida goes on to write: "*To do this, let us refer—provisionally, I emphasize this, and for pedagogical or rhetorical reasons—first to the 'messianic,' and second to the* khōra, *as I have tried to do more minutely, more patiently and, I hope, more rigorously elsewhere*" (§20).

Though Derrida's language of "sources" and "fountains" at the beginning of this passage would lead the reader to believe that he is talking about the two sources of religion as I have identified them, we soon see that Derrida is instead gesturing in the direction of *khōra* and the messi-anic—both of which are to be identified, as I hope to demonstrate more clearly in what follows, with the second source of religion and not with the two sources. A more complete reading of this passage, which begins, "*Noctural light, therefore, more and more obscure*," and which goes on to speak of "*the ambiguity or the duplicity of the religious trait or retreat, of its abstraction or of its subtraction*," would confirm this suggestion.[2] The duplicity Derrida is speaking of here is thus not that of the two sources of religion but of two "historical" names for the second source, two names from two "historical" traditions, the Judeo-Christian and the Greek, as well as two different orientations or valences for this second source, one essentially temporal (*the messianic*) and the other essentially spatial (*khōra*), even if, of course, our notions of time and space will have to be rethought on the basis of these names. That these two names are indeed to be thought in temporal and spatial terms can be seen in a passage from "*Sauf le nom (Post-Scriptum),*" where Derrida speaks of two "abysses," one related to eschatology and historical revelation, terms linked through-out "Faith and Knowledge" to the messianic, and the other to "nontem-porality" and "an absolute impassibility . . . that gives rise to everything that it is not," terms related to *khōra*:

> This exemplarism joins and disjoins at once . . . .: *on one side*, on one way, a profound and abyssal eternity, fundamental but accessible to messianism in general, to the tele-eschatological narrative and to a certain experience or historical (or historial) revelation; *on the other side*, on the other way, the nontemporality of an abyss without bot-tom or surface, an absolute impassibility (neither life nor death) that gives rise to everything that it is not. In fact, two abysses. ("*SN*" 77)

Once again, it is as if Derrida is suggesting that in order to think reli-gion today and the "bare" foundation that makes it possible, one must rethink not only the Judeo-Christiano-Islamic messianic tradition by means of what Derrida will call a "messianicity without messianism," but the Greek philosophical tradition by means of something that will have resisted Greek thought from within and from the very beginning, namely, *khōra*. It is in this *chiasm* between the *messianic* and *khōra*, between a re-thinking of temporality and a reinscription of spatiality, between the reli-gions of the Book and Plato's *Timaeus*—this "Bible avant la lettre" ("*AV*" 12)—that Derrida might say again what he said in "Violence and Meta-physics" with a line from Joyce: "Jewgreek is greekjew. Extremes meet" (see *WD* 153).

In this chapter, I would like to look at these two "historical" names for the second source that can *"resemble a desertification"* but that must be thought in relationship to the *"fiduciary 'link' [that] would precede all determinate community, all positive religion, every onto-anthropo-theological horizon"* and that *"would link pure singularities prior to any social or political determination"* (§20). In both cases Derrida is trying to think a link that must be understood only in relationship to a kind of interruption, to a certain *without* (in the case of a messianicity without messianism) or a certain *withdrawal* (in the case of *khōra*) that opens up the possibility of religion without being reducible to any determinate form of religion. In each of these two "historical" names, one from a religious tradition and one from philosophy, Derrida will locate a promise of universality that will allow him to criticize—to deconstruct, if you will—all determinate religious traditions.

But before turning to the messianic and to *khōra*, another possible ambiguity needs to be clarified, a distinction or relation in "Faith and Knowledge" that seems to run parallel to that between *khōra* and everything that appears within it, or, indeed, between the messianic and all determinate messianisms, namely, the relationship between revealability and revelation. I addressed this question briefly in Chapter 3 when I spoke of light as a possible source of both religion and science, the common source of all revelation and all truth. I would like to argue here again that, despite the appearances, the language of revelation and revealability is ultimately more problematic for Derrida than that of either messianicity or *khōra*. Though all three might be taken as expressing the exact same aporia, dilemma, or oscillation between a universal experience of revealability, or messianism, or appearing and determinate or concrete revelations, messianisms, and appearances, there are good reasons for Derrida to want to displace these more traditional terms of revealability and revelation and speak instead of messianism and of *khōra*. Derrida will seem to find better resources within these two "historical" names for thinking the relationship between the universal and the singular than he will in the seemingly ahistorical language of revealability and revelation. While Derrida will thus never completely abandon the language of revelation and revealability, we see in "Faith and Knowledge" a marked preference for these two "historical" names that will allow him both to critique the underlying trope of light in revelation and to displace the problematic into a rethinking of time (in the form of a messianicity that opens the future beyond all time as presence), space (in the form of *khōra* as the groundless ground that lets things take place without or before being situated in space), and the name (in the form of "historical" names that do not try to pass themselves off as universal or ahistorical conditions but as promises that are at once conditioning and conditioned). It will thus be no coincidence that, after having raised this question of what is conditioning and what conditioned, of the transcendental and the empirical, in its more traditional terms, that is, in terms of a general structure of revealability (*Offenbarkeit*) and determinate revelations (*Offenbarung*), Derrida will go on to develop the question not in these terms but, rather, in terms of messianicity and *khōra*—placing equal emphasis, at least at first, on both but ultimately devoting more time and space in the essay "Faith and Knowledge" and in subsequent texts to the second.

If the question of the relationship between revealability and revelation, between a general structure of religion or religiosity and the revealed religions of the Book, the question, that is, of the relative priority or originarity of the one with regard to the other, is not Derrida's primary question in "Faith and Knowledge," it is not surprising that it has been treated as such in the secondary literature.[3] For it is in this form and in these terms that Derrida's essay can be read alongside Kant's, Hegel's, or Heidegger's treatment of the same question.[4] While it will be impossible to do justice here to the nuances of this debate in the secondary literature, it is essential to indicate one possible path through it. As many of his critics have argued, Derrida does indeed find himself caught on the horns of a traditional dilemma regarding the priority of revelation versus revealability. Rather than try to resolve or dissolve the dilemma, Derrida attempts to displace it into other contexts and other lexica so as to develop another (deconstructive) logic of the *name*. In the end, we will see why Derrida would write so much in the years just before and after "Faith and Knowledge" of these two "historical" names, the messianic and *khōra*, and why the question of revealability is almost always developed not in its own terms but in relationship to these names.

Having argued in §8 that religion in the West is always related to light, to the trope of light, to appearances and phenomena, to a certain revelation or coming to light, Derrida invokes the (Heideggerian) distinction between revelation (*Offenbarung*) and revealability (*Offenbarkeit*). Since *offenbar* suggests what is clear, evident, manifest, obvious, even public, the distinction here is between everything that appears in the light, everything that becomes manifest and so can be relied on or trusted, looked at or believed in, everything that is revealed or can be revealed, and the originary opening or manifesting of such revelations.

Light (phos), *wherever this* archē *commands or begins discourse and takes the initiative in general* (phos, phainesthai, phantasma, *hence*

specter, etc.), as much in the discourse of philosophy as in the discourses
of a revelation (Offenbarung) *or of a revealability* (Offenbarkeit), *of*
a possibility more originary than manifestation. More originary, which
is to say, closer to the source, to the sole and same source. Everywhere
light dictates that which even yesterday was naïvely construed to be pure
of all religion or even opposed to it and whose future must today be
rethought (Aufklärung, Lumières, *Enlightenment,* Illuminismo). (§8)

This relationship between revelation and revealability looks, to be sure,
a lot like the two sources of religion we have seen in "Faith and Knowledge," the one related to specific, historically conditioned revelations, and
the other to revealability as what precedes, exceeds, or conditions all revelation or all coming to appearance in general, whether in religion or in
science. It also looks a lot like Derrida's distinction between religion and
faith, or law and justice, or even, as Hent de Vries has argued, the Levinasian distinction between *le Dit* (or *Offenbarung*) and *le Dire* (or *Offenbarkeit*).[5] And yet the emphasis on light, on what is obvious, clear, or
manifest, on the one hand, and the condition of that clarity, on the other,
should give us some pause in this identification of revelation with one
of the two sources of religion, with the safe and sound, the indemnified,
and revealability with the other, that is, with faith and testimony. For this
trope of light, of coming to light or coming to appear, seems to determine
both revelation and revealability in a way that would seem to trouble or ill
serve what Derrida suggested earlier regarding the second source of both
religion and science, namely, that it is beyond all proof or demonstration,
all monstration, all coming or bringing to light. While the very notion of
revealability might, of course, be thought otherwise, that is, in terms of a
transcendental or quasi-transcendental structure that withdraws from that
which it conditions, it seems that Derrida wants to resist posing the
question in exactly these terms even as he recognizes their historical
importance.

Derrida thus calls the relationship between revealability and revelation
an aporia, and while it bears a striking resemblance to the aporia between
messianicity and messianism, it is this emphasis on light that should distinguish them from one another. Derrida writes in §19, in a passage that
ends with a reference to Heidegger—or, rather, to a certain Heidegger—
which should put us on guard against thinking that this is really *Derrida's*
formulation of the question, even if, at the outset of this passage, Derrida
seems to suggest precisely that:

*In its most abstract form, then, the aporia within which we are strug-
gling would perhaps be the following: is revealability* (Offenbarkeit)

more originary than revelation (Offenbarung), *and hence independent of all religion? Independent in the structures of its experience and in the analytics relating to them? Is this not the place in which "reflecting faith" at least originates, if not this faith itself? Or rather, inversely, would the event of revelation have consisted in revealing revealability itself, and the origin of light, the originary light, the very invisibility of visibility? This is perhaps what the believer or the theologian might say here, in particular the Christian of originary Christendom, of that* Ur-christentum *in the Lutheran tradition to which Heidegger acknowledges owing so much.* (§19)

Derrida is thus asking here whether revelation is conditioned by revealability or whether revealability is conditioned by an event of revelation. Though clearly engaged by this aporia, which has its origins in Kant and Heidegger, and clearly tempted to grant a certain priority to a universal structure of revealability over determinate revelations, Derrida will not go on to affirm the priority of either revelation or revealability but will instead mark what de Vries calls an "oscillation" between the two, before going on to displace or reinscribe the problematic in terms of messianicity and *khōra.*[6]

The problematic is thus first displaced by reinscribing the relationship between revealability and revelation in terms of the two sources of religion distinguished throughout "Faith and Knowledge." What we have identified as the second source of religion will thus make possible but not necessary any particular, determinate religion, while any particular, determinate religion will presuppose and reflect the source that made it possible. Derrida begins his argument here by repeating his "hypothesis" regarding the two sources: "Let us remember the hypothesis of these two sources: on the one hand, the fiduciary-*ity* of confidence, trustworthiness [*fiabilité*] or of trust [*fiance*] (belief, faith, credit and so on), and on the other, the unscathed-*ness* of the unscathed (the safe and sound, the immune, the holy, the sacred, *heilig*)" (§47). He then goes on to describe the relationship between these two sources, or what he also calls these "axioms," in language that resembles that used to describe the relationship between *Offenbarung* and *Offenbarkeit*, revelation and revealability.

Perhaps what in the first place ought to be stressed is this: each of these axioms, as such, already reflects and presupposes the other. . . .[7] Secondly, both of these two axioms render possible, but not necessary, something like a religion, which is to say, an instituted apparatus consisting of dogmas or of articles of faith that are both determinate and inseparable from a given historical *socius*

(Church, clergy, socially legitimated authority, people, shared idiom, community of the faithful committed to the same faith and sanctioning the same history). (§47)

In saying that each axiom "reflects and presupposes the other," Derrida would seem to be suggesting that every determinate religion reflects and presupposes an elementary faith and that this elementary faith opens up the possibility at least of a determinate religion without determining any particular religion. Indeed one could even say that this elementary faith continues to open up the possibility of determinate religions even when no religion is in fact determined, that is, even when what is determined is some "secular" relationship or even scientific community. As such, a gap—an *écart*, which might then become a trace—remains irreducible between this possibility as a universal structure and the determinate necessity of any given religion.

> But the gap [*écart*] between the opening of this *possibility* (*as a universal structure*) and the *determinate necessity* of this or that religion will always remain irreducible; and sometimes [it operates] within each religion, between on the one hand that which keeps it closest to its "pure" and proper possibility, and on the other, its own historically determined necessities or authorities. Thus, one can always criticize, reject or combat this or that form of sacredness or of belief, even of religious authority, in the name of the most original possibility. The latter can be *universal* (faith or trustworthiness, "good faith" as the condition of testimony, of the social bond and even of the most radical questioning) or already *particular*, for example belief in a specific originary event of revelation, of promise or of injunction, as in the reference to the Tables of the Law, to early Christianity, to some fundamental word or scripture, more archaic and more pure than all clerical or theological discourse. But it seems impossible to deny the *possibility* in whose name—thanks to which—the derived *necessity* (the authority or determinate belief) would be put in question, suspended, rejected or criticized, even deconstructed. (§47)

Notice the relationship here between possibility and universality in what has been identified as the second source of religion, the common source of both religion and science. While it might have looked as if respect or reticence before the sacred was the best candidate for such a universal structure for religion, we see here once again why elementary faith, the social bond, is an even better one. Such an elementary faith is better at questioning not only determinate forms of the sacred but the very distinction between the sacred and the secular, religion and science. It is only in the name of this "most originary possibility," in the name of the second source of religion, the elementary faith that is at the origin of both science and religion, that Derrida believes we are able to "put in question, suspend, criticize or deconstruct" "*Roman Occidentality*" and "*the bond it has contracted with the Abrahamic revelations.*" Only by means of a universality that is not determined and thus limited by some determinate religion, a universality related to a testimonial faith as a general structure of experience, will Derrida be able to show not only that a determinate (Abrahamic) revelation may indeed have been the condition for thinking revealability itself (as light or as coming to light) but that both revelation and revealability need to be thought in relationship to the elementary faith or testimonial engagement that opens up history in the first place. In other words, only a notion of elementary faith as the second source of religion (and science) can help demonstrate the limitations of structuring the question around the relationship between revealability and revelation. If, as Derrida argues, "*the Testamentary and Koranic revelations are inseparable from a* historicity *of revelation itself*" (§13), then it would seem that the one cannot be thought without the other and that this historicity is itself already somewhat determined and not at all the universal structure that it would seem to be or, more importantly, that it would present itself to be.

Derrida's first attempt to reformulate the relation between the singular and universal, revelation and revealability, can thus be seen in this attempt to map the two sources of religion onto these distinctions. The distinction between singular beliefs and determinate religions, on the one hand, and a universal faith, on the other, will allow Derrida to argue that faith opens up the possibility of religion without determining any religion in particular. It will also allow him to show that the faith that opens up the possibility of religion opens up at the same time the possibility of science as well as the *socius*. But because such Kantian distinctions between faith and belief or reflecting faith and dogmatic religion have their own limitations and quickly lead to the aporia, identified above, between a general structure of revealability (or faith) and determinate revelations (or beliefs), Derrida will risk two other "historical" names—messianicity and *khōra*—in order to reinscribe and displace the aporia.

We will look at Derrida's treatment of these two "historical" names in a moment. But since I have been granting some priority to texts written around the same time as "Faith and Knowledge," let us look briefly at how Derrida, in *Archive Fever*, a lecture first presented in London on 5

June 1994, that is, just months after the conference in Capri, rephrases the question of revealability in terms of the archive. As we will see, this rephrasing is, once again, a *reinscription* and *displacement* of the question of revelation and revealability in its traditional form. The question for Derrida in this rewriting of "Faith and Knowledge" is whether it is some event within the archive that makes the archivability of events possible or whether it is an originary archivability that makes possible the archive.

> With respect to this presupposition or this preunderstanding, we find ourselves here before an aporia. I have attempted to struggle with this elsewhere, and I shall say only a word about it, from the point of view of the archive: does one base one's thinking of the future on an archived event—with or without substrate, with or without actuality—for example on a divine injunction or on a messianic covenant? Or else, on the contrary, can an *experience*, an *existence*, in general, only receive and record, only archive such an event to the extent that the structure of this existence and of its temporalization makes this archivization possible? In other words, does one need a first archive in order to conceive of originary archivability? Or vice versa? This is the whole question of the relation between the event of the religious revelation (*Offenbarung*) and a revealability (*Offenbarkeit*), a possibility of manifestation, the prior thought of what opens toward the arrival or toward the coming of such an event. Is it not true that the logic of the after-the-fact (*Nachträglichkeit*), which is not only at the heart of psychoanalysis, but even, literally, the sinews of all "deferred" (*nachträglich*) obedience, turns out to disrupt, disturb, entangle forever the reassuring distinction between the two terms of this alternative, as between the past and the future, that is to say, between the three actual presents, which would be the past present, the present present, and the future present? In any case, there would be no future without repetition. (*AF* 80)

This displacement of the problematic into the question of the archive does more than just repeat the aporia in other terms. In posing the question of priority or originarity in terms of the archive and archivability rather than revelation and revealability, Derrida is able to address questions about the role of the substrate of the archive, the technical supplement that is required by an archive, and thus the possibility of even thinking an event before its inscription and repetition in an archive. Moreover, the displacement leads to the insight that perhaps the two horns of the dilemma need to be thought not in terms of what conditions (revealability) and what is conditioned (revelation), or in terms of a transcendental structure and an empirical one, universality and singularity, but in terms that might trouble the simple temporality involved in saying that revealability is more originary than revelation or that a revelation in history is what determines a historicity of revelation. Derrida suggests that the psychoanalytic concept of *Nachträglichkeit* can "entangle forever the reassuring distinction between the two terms of this alternative," making it difficult if not impossible to determine which comes first insofar as the things we are talking about—events being archived, the archivization of the event—are perhaps not simply present and chronologically or logically prior in the way we have been led to believe. Perhaps that is why the two names we must now turn to in Derrida are precisely—and the quotation marks are Derrida's—"historical," that is, names that appear in history and are marked by history but that themselves name the opening *of* history itself and *resist* that history from within.

Derrida speaks of the messianic, or of a messianicity without messianism, in several texts of the early 1990s, but most prominently in "Force of Law" (first presented in 1989–90) and *Specters of Marx* (1993). In these texts, the messianic names, to cite "Faith and Knowledge," "*the opening to the future or to the coming of the other as the advent of justice, but without horizon of expectation and without prophetic prefiguration*" (§21). The messianic, or messianicity without messianism, is thus that which opens the possibility for every concrete messianism and yet exceeds such messianisms. It is the name of a time or of an awaiting where that which is always beyond our horizon of expectations, where the other or where death, where the radically unexpected and indeterminate, can come at any moment, at any moment "in" history but also, insofar as the unexpected cannot be understood from within the horizon *of* history, as an interruption of history.[8] Derrida continues, "*The coming of the other can only emerge as a singular event when no anticipation sees it coming, when the other and death—and radical evil—can come as a surprise at any moment. Possibilities that both open and can always interrupt history, or at least the ordinary course of history*" (§21).

Messianicity without messianism is thus the name of an opening to what is radically other, an awaiting of that which cannot be closed off or determined by any particular revelation or messianism. This exceptional openness to the future must not be understood, however, as some exceptional moment within history that would have to be set apart from all other more banal, more ordinary, or more secular moments. This exceptional openness to an event that interrupts ordinary history is what makes ordinary history possible in the first place.[9] As that which exposes us to *absolute surprise*—to the best as well as the worst, to the miraculous as well as the traumatic—messianicity is for Derrida "a general structure of experience":

> The messianic exposes itself to absolute surprise and, even if it always takes the phenomenal form of peace or of justice, it ought, exposing itself so abstractly, be prepared (waiting without awaiting itself) for the best as for the worst, the one never coming without opening the possibility of the other. At issue there is a "general structure of experience." This messianic dimension does not depend upon any messianism, it follows no determinate revelation, it belongs properly to no Abrahamic religion (even if I am obliged here, "among ourselves," for essential reasons of language and of place, of culture, of a provisional rhetoric and a historical strategy of which I will speak later, to continue giving it names marked by the Abrahamic religions). (§21)

Derrida thus makes it clear that this messianicity does not belong to *any* religion, not even to Abrahamic religions in general, and, indeed, it is not even restricted to religion: there is no experience in general without messianicity. Derrida also emphasizes yet again that this name is "provisional," part of a "provisional rhetoric and historical strategy," the strategy, I think we could say, of deconstruction. That is why the name *messianicity* is not just another way of saying *revealability*. As a "historical" name that has itself been conditioned by what exceeds it, this name at once repeats a certain Judeo-Christiano-Islamic tradition of messianism and opens this tradition to the promise or the coming of what exceeds it.[10] In "*Sauf le nom (Post-Scriptum)*" Derrida speaks of a "singular exemplarism that at once roots and uproots the idiom," at once repeats the tradition from which the idiom has been drawn and opens it up to what is beyond it through displacement and translation: "Each idiom (for example, Greek onto-theology or Christian revelation) can testify for itself and for what it is not (not yet or forever), without this value of testimony (martyrdom) being itself totally determined by the inside of the idiom (Christian martyrdom, for example)" ("*SN*" 77).[11]

It is no doubt for this reason that Derrida put "historical" in scare quotes when speaking of *khōra* and messianicity as "*two names that are still 'historical'*" (§20): these two names are "historical" at the same time as they open up and resist history from within, like a "desert in the desert." They are not ahistorical abstractions but, precisely, "historical" *names* to the extent that they name within a particular idiom, language, culture, tradition, and so on, an opening to what exceeds that language, culture, and tradition. Though *revealability* too, like *messianicity* and *khōra*, is also a "historical" name—indeed, what name is not?—it passes itself off much more readily than these other two as a kind of universal, nonhistorical structure, as an ahistorical condition for all historical revelations. It is for this reason that Derrida displaces the problematic in "Faith and Knowledge" and elsewhere from the question of revealability to that of a messianicity without messianism and, ultimately, to *khōra*.

In the passage cited above from "Faith and Knowledge," Derrida links messianicity not only to absolute surprise—to the possibility of the best as well as the worst—but to a "phenomenal form" of peace or of justice. Though the messianic cannot be reduced to any of these forms, it nonetheless "*always takes the phenomenal form of peace or of justice.*" But let's now look closely at §22 to see how Derrida relates this messianicity without messianism to justice understood in what appears to be a "nonphenomenal" sense, that is, to justice understood as the elementary faith or the act of faith that "inhabits" all religion and even all science. We will then see how Derrida begins to link the first of the two "historical" names, messianicity without messianism, to the second, that is, to *khōra*.

After having spoken of how this "*messianic dimension does not depend upon any messianism,*" that is, how this opening to the future is not itself determined by any determinate messianism, Derrida writes:

> An invincible desire for justice is linked to this expectation. By definition, the latter is not and ought not to be certain of anything, either through knowledge, consciousness, conscience, foreseeability or any kind of program as such. This abstract messianicity belongs from the very beginning to the experience of faith, of believing, of a credit that is irreducible to knowledge and of a trust that "founds" all relation to the other in testimony. This justice, which I distinguish from right [droit], alone allows the hope, beyond all "messianisms," of a universalizable culture of singularities, a culture in which the abstract possibility of the impossible translation could nevertheless be announced. This justice inscribes itself in advance in the promise, in the act of faith or in the appeal to faith that inhabits every act of language and every address to the other. The universalizable culture of this faith, and not of another or before all others, alone permits a "rational" and universal discourse on the subject of "religion." (§22)

What motivates the law and motivates law to go beyond the law is thus not some vision, idea, or ideal but rather the *desire* for justice, or rather, a desire that essentially *is* justice, a messianicity that has to do with a faith that cannot be justified by any knowledge. Recall that, in the introduction to this work, I cited a brief passage from an interview from *Paper Machine* where Derrida says that, just as he makes "a distinction between justice and law," so he would "distinguish between faith and religion" (*PM* 117). It is this reference to justice, now linked to messianicity, that makes this more than a mere analogy. Just as justice would be, as Derrida calls it, an excess of law linked to "*an invincible desire*," the very motivation, inspiration, or aspiration of law, so faith would be the very opening and motivation of religion, never reducible to religion and yet always in some sense traced or figured within it. As Derrida says in his conversation with Mustapha Chérif:

> I always distinguish between faith and religion. . . . If we limit ourselves to what we have customarily called religion in the Abrahamic universe of the religions of the Book, I will then distinguish between the religious adherences to Judaism, Christianity, and Islam and faith, without which no social relationship is possible. I cannot address the other, whoever he or she might be, regardless of his or her religion, language, culture, without asking that other to believe me and to trust me. (*IW* 57)

It is this distinction between faith and religion, on the one hand, and justice—or messianicity—and law, on the other, that will lead, as we will see in what follows, to a rethinking of *khōra* and of democracy, and through this notion of democracy to a renewed understanding of the universal and universality.

Messianicity without messianism is thus the only thing that allows one to "hope," says Derrida—and *hope* would have to be heard as an almost technical (quasi-Kantian) term here—for what Derrida calls a "universalizable culture of singularities" (§22), that is, a culture of singularities that promotes and projects no determined and thus limited messianism, whether "religious" or "secular" (for example, Marxist). This is what motivates the law and what, as an act of faith or as a promise, inhabits every act of language and every address to the other. We would not address one another without this promise, says Derrida, which is a promise not for this or that conception of justice but a promise that is justice itself, a promise that then marks every determination or conception of justice in the law. The origin of the law is thus not some insight into what is the case, some recognition of what is objectively true—for example, that all human beings are created equal—but an event rooted in the absolute alterity of the other, which would exceed every determination it helps found. To use terms that Derrida had occasion to question but that we have found helpful throughout this work, the messianic belongs to the performative regimen of language, while all messianisms belong, in some sense, to the constative. All determinate messianisms thus rely upon the messianic through every affirmation and every address to the other, but the messianic *as* this address or *as* this affirmation remains radically heterogeneous to these messianisms—just as the *salut!* as the promise of every determination of *salut* as health or as redemption remains radically heterogeneous to such determinations.

Derrida will go on in the passage we are reading to speak of an "absolute night," setting up the transition to *khōra*, which will be the subject of the next three sections. He will thus begin crossing or mingling in this passage the two "historical" names he spoke of earlier, as if the one had to be thought in the light—or night—of the other. But before turning to *khōra*, Derrida again evokes the distinction between justice and law made most forcefully in "Force of Law":

This messianicity, stripped of everything, as it should, this faith without dogma which makes its way through the risks of absolute night, cannot be contained in any traditional opposition, for example that between reason and mysticism. It is announced wherever, reflecting without flinching, a purely rational analysis brings the following paradox to light: that the foundation of law—law of the law, institution of the institution, origin of the constitution—is a "performative" event that cannot belong to the set that it founds, inaugurates or justifies. Such an event is unjustifiable within the logic of what it will have opened. It is the decision of the other in the undecidable. Henceforth reason ought to recognize there what Montaigne and Pascal call an undeniable "mystical foundation of authority." The mystical thus understood allies belief or credit, the fiduciary or the trustworthy, the secret (which here signifies "mystical") to foundation, to knowledge, we will later say also, to science as "doing," as theory, practice and theoretical practice—which is to say, to a faith, to performativity and to technoscientific or tele-technological performance. (§22)

By evoking Montaigne and Pascal, Derrida is recalling his analysis of messianicity, performativity, and law in "Force of Law." It is there that Derrida demonstrates most clearly that the law is founded upon nothing other than an originary performative and the elementary faith that we have been following here. Derrida writes, for example, in this important text first delivered in 1989: "The very emergence of justice and law, the instituting, founding, and justifying moment of law implies a performative force, that is to say always an interpretative force and a call to faith" ("FL" 241). And again: "The authority of laws rests only on the credit that is granted them. One believes in it; that is their only foundation. This act of faith is not an ontological or rational foundation. Still one has yet to think what *believing* means" ("FL" 140)—a task that is left to "Faith and Knowledge" and other texts.[12]

There is thus more than a structural analogy between religion and faith or messianism and messianicity, on the one hand, and law and justice, on the one hand. Or, rather, such an analogy presupposes—as always—more than it says. Law would be turned always toward a past that must be remembered and protected, just as determinate religions or messianisms would be turned toward an original experience of the holy or the sacred that must be must safeguarded and indemnified. Justice, then, would motivate and "exceed" every determinate law much as faith would inspire but also go beyond every determinate religion and just as messianicity would open up a future for every determinate messianism. Messianicity is thus the place in Derrida's discourse where the registers of religion and law intersect, in the form of a faith that inspires and exceeds all religion *and* of a justice that motivates and goes beyond all law. It is the place where memory and the promise come together.

As we have seen, every act of language presupposes an "I promise the truth," an "I make this commitment before the other from the moment that I address him" (see §29). It is this faith in the form of a desire or promise that is the common source of both science and religion, a source that opens up the future for good or ill, as an endless perfectibility/pervertibility. As Derrida puts it (in §38), there is no *à-venir*, no future, no to come, without heritage and the possibility of repetition and iterability, without the confirmation of the originary "yes" and an originary affirmation in that confirmation, that is, without memory and promise. Technics is thus the possibility or the chance of faith—and this chance cannot be separated from the possibility of *radical evil*. Without this possibility, the future would be foreseeable, masterable, knowable—in other words, a kind of knowledge. Hence faith and knowledge, religion and science, the miracle and the machine, must be thought together as a single possibility, a single possibility that divides or fissures already at the origin. They are not the same thing, but they cannot be thought separately. Both are possible only on the basis of a "*testimonial deus ex machina*" (§29), which always already betrays and displays the duplicity of origins, a *deus* that from the beginning becomes *deux*, at once miracle and machine.

As we have seen, it is this same mystical foundation as belief or credit that founds both our techno-scientific knowledge and our faith in tele-technological performativity. But because this "foundation" is lost as soon as it arrives, religion can only begin again with the automaticity of a machine or the spontaneity of a source—for better or for worse, with no assurances:

Wherever this foundation founds in foundering, wherever it steals away under the ground of what it founds, at the very instant when, losing itself thus in the desert, it loses the very trace of itself and the memory of a secret, "religion" can only begin and begin again: quasi-automatically, mechanically, machine-like, spontaneously. Spontaneously, *which is to say, as the word indicates, both as the origin of what flows from the source,* sponte sua, *and with the automaticity of the machine. For the best and for the worst, without the slightest assurance or anthropo-theological horizon.* (§22)

If religion can do nothing but "return," then the so-called "return of religion" is but a pernicious pleonasm. Religion does nothing but return in the form of the first source of religion but always already thanks to the second, the one that founds by withdrawing at the origin. Without what Derrida calls this withdrawal of the origin, this desert in the desert, this origin that is immediately lost or this desert that is deserted even of the trope of the desert, there would be no promise and no future.[13]

The language of messianicity and messianism, as opposed to revealability and revelation, allows Derrida to rethink the relationship between the conditioning and the conditioned, the universal and the singular, in terms better suited to the complications of time (through the futurity or deferral of messianism) and language (through the distinction between the performative and the constative, or through a "historical" name or idiom that at once roots and uproots). Before turning to the other "historical" name cited by Derrida in "Faith and Knowledge," namely, *khōra*, I would like to conclude this brief look at the first historical name by turning once again to *Archive Fever*, a text written right around the same time as "Faith and Knowledge," and then to some improvised remarks made not long after the Capri conference where Derrida recapitulates much of the argument regarding messianicity that we have been following here.

Completed, I recall, in May 1994 in Naples, that is, just three months after the Capri conference, *Archive Fever* attempts to relate messianicity to the questions of the future, the archive, and the performative, questions that are central to any consideration of the possibility of religion, though not necessarily to the consideration of any particular, determinate religion. In other words, Derrida attempts at once to use the traditional resources of the "messianic"—an awaiting and an openness to the future—in order to find or await or invent another, unexpected, and barely receivable sense of the "messianic" (messianicity in its most universal sense).

Using the terms and logic of "Faith and Knowledge" in what initially appears to be a very different context, Derrida approaches the question of the archive through what seems to be a rather trivial example, his attempt to *save*—or indemnify—a text on his computer, that is, a text that has for the moment only "appeared" on his computer screen but has not yet been archived and saved. What we thus catch a glimpse of through this somewhat odd and surprising example is an insight not only into the way Derrida thinks or writes, but, better, into the way Derrida's former work—his archive, precisely—comes always and of necessity to mark what initially appears to be a completely new and unrelated theme, in this case, the archive.

> I asked myself what is the moment *proper* to the archive, if there is such a thing, the instant of archivization strictly speaking, which is not, and I will come back to this, so-called live or spontaneous memory (*mnēmē or anamnēsis*), but rather a certain hypomnesis and prosthetic experience of the technical substrate. Was it not at this very instant that, having written something or other on the screen, the letters remaining as if suspended and floating yet at the surface of a liquid element, I pushed a certain key to "save" a text undamaged, in a hard and lasting way, to protect marks from being erased, so as to ensure in this way salvation and *indemnity*, to stock, to accumulate, and, in what is at once the same thing and something else, to make the sentence available in this way for printing and for reprinting, for reproduction? (*AF* 25–26)

Though I cannot give this passage the attention it deserves, we can already begin parsing it in terms familiar to us from "Faith and Knowledge": there are, in effect, two sources of the archive, one turned toward safeguarding or indemnifying the past and one turned toward an affirmation of this past, an affirmation that opens this past to future possibilities of reinscription, transformation, deformation, living on, and so forth. But the two sources of the archive are not just analogous to the two sources of religion; the second of religion's two sources is actually the same as the second source of the archive. Derrida writes later in *Archive Fever*: "The affirmation of the future *to come*: this is not a positive thesis. It is nothing other than the affirmation itself, the 'yes,' insofar as it is the condition of all promises or of all hope, of all awaiting, of all performativity, of all opening toward the future, whatever it may be, for science or for religion" (*AF* 68). The first source of the archive, we might speculate, would thus be oriented toward the protection and indemnification of a unique past or experience of the past, while the second would have to do with an affirmation of that past in the form of a promise or performative that, we can already suspect, must enlist the deracinating powers of the technos-cientific supplement. It is thus hardly a leap to want to claim that the archive is autoimmune and that this autoimmunity is both what threatens the archive and allows it to live on.

The question of the archive concerns the future just as much as the past, and it is this concern with the future in the form of a promise that links it not only to science but to religion and to messiancity. Hence Derrida can write in *Archive Fever*: "A spectral messianicity is at work in the concept of the archive and ties it, like religion, like history, like science itself, to a very singular experience of the promise. And we are never far from Freud in saying this. Messianicity does not mean messianism" (*AF* 36). The archive is thus founded upon a promise—Derrida could have said a faith, an elementary or elemental faith—that must be thought before all knowledge:

> The condition on which the future remains to come is not only that it not be known, but that it not be *knowable as such*. . . . It is a question of this performative to come whose archive no longer has any relation to the record of what is, to the record of the presence of what is or will have been *actually* present. I call this the *messianic*, and I distinguish it radically from all messianism. (*AF* 72)

But if the messianic is to be radically distinguished from all determinate messianisms, then one might ask why Derrida uses a name for the former that risks conflation with the latter, that is, why he uses a name that would seem to be marked and thus determined by a particular (messianic) tradition. To begin to approach this enormous question—I have no pretensions of being able to answer it—I would like to turn to some of Derrida's improvised remarks at a roundtable at Villanova University in October 1994, that is, only about seven months after the Capri conference and six months before Derrida signs the essay from Laguna. In these comments we see Derrida following quite closely the itinerary of "Faith and Knowledge" but expressing much more openly his "hesitation" with regard to this "historical" name *messianicity* and explaining even more clearly its provisional nature and strategic necessity.

Asked by John Caputo during the roundtable discussion what "Judaism, the biblical tradition generally, and in particular the prophetic tradition of justice" have to do with the work of deconstruction, Derrida—still in the process of writing "Faith and Knowledge," it would seem, or in any case not yet having signed it—rolls out a series of arguments and claims that should be familiar to us by now (*DN* 20). After noting that within "what one calls religions—Judaism, Christianity, Islam or other religions—there are . . . tensions, heterogeneity, disruptive volcanoes" that call for new ways of reading, Derrida goes on to say that he would first of all "distinguish between religion and faith" (*DN* 21), a distinction that should be very familiar to us by now. If religion is understood to be "a set of beliefs, dogmas, or institutions," then "religion as such can be deconstructed, and not only can be but should be deconstructed, sometimes in the name of faith" (*DN* 21). This is precisely what we have seen in "Faith and Knowledge," "Above All, No Journalists!" and elsewhere. A universal faith—the second of religion's two sources—would be that by means of which or in the name of which determinate religions might be questioned, contested, submitted to critique, or deconstructed (see §47), in a word, exposed to the promise they harbor and opened to a faith that is not "conditioned by any given religion." This faith, Derrida then goes on to say, must be understood in relation to a testimony before or an address to the other that says, "Believe me . . . trust me, I am speaking to you," and so on, language that all comes right out of "Faith and Knowledge" (*DN* 22).

Derrida says next that he would wish to speak of messianicity in the same way he has just spoken of faith, namely, as that which must be opposed to all determinate religions and messianisms, as a universal or general structure of experience in its openness to what is to come, as a promise that cannot be reduced to or limited by any "determinate figures and forms of the Messiah." He then adds, bringing in concerns that are at the center of several of Derrida's seminars from the 1980s on "Philosophical Nationality and Nationalism," "As soon as you reduce the messianic structure to messianism, then you are reducing the universality, and this has important political consequences," for one then begins "accrediting one tradition among others and a notion of an elected people, of a given literal language, a given fundamentalism," and so on (*DN* 22–23). The deconstruction of determinate messianisms by means of messianicity, of religions by means of faith, is thus not only a theoretical exercise but a political intervention. The deconstruction of religion, of law, of all phenomenal forms of justice, would always be carried out *in the name* of what motivated them in the first place, that is, in the name of a messianicity *as* justice.[14]

Derrida might well have ended his discussion there, with this radical distinction between faith and religion, justice and law, or messianicity and messianism. But worried, it seems, that such a thinking of the future as radically open has itself been determined by a certain messianic tradition and feeling the need to justify his choice of the term *messianicity*, Derrida presses forward to clarify what remains for him a problem and an enigma and to explain his provisional solution. First, then, the problem:

> The problem remains—and this is really a problem for me, an enigma—whether the religions, say, for instance, the religions of the Book, are but specific examples of this general structure, of messianicity. There is the general structure of messianicity, as the structure of experience, and on this groundless ground there have been revelations, a history which one calls Judaism or Christianity and so on. That is a possibility, and then you would have a Heideggerian gesture, in style. . . . That is one hypothesis. The other hypothesis— and I confess that I hesitate between these two possibilities—is that the events of revelation, the biblical traditions, the Jewish, Christian, and Islamic traditions, have been absolute events, irreducible events which have unveiled this messianicity. We would not know what messianicity is without messianism, without these events which were Abraham, Moses, and Jesus Christ, and so on. In that case singular events would have unveiled or revealed these universal possibilities, and it is only on that condition that we can describe messianicity. Between the two possibilities I must confess I oscillate and I think some other scheme has to be constructed to understand the two at the same time, to do justice to the two possibilities. (*DN* 23–24)

In what follows, I will suggest that Derrida's reinscription of the Platonic *khōra* was an attempt to construct just such an "other scheme"—or, perhaps better, an "other *schema*" (at once name and schematism)—for doing "justice to the two possibilities." In some sense, *khōra* will appear even more promising than the messianic as a "historical" name. While it too will have been marked by a culture and an idiom, by the language of Greek philosophy, while it too, then, must be only provisional, it, unlike the messianic, will never have been appropriated by religion or theology. Nonetheless, Derrida is not yet prepared to give up on the strategic and pedagogical resources of this provisional notion of the messianic. He continues:

> That is why—and perhaps this is not a good reason, perhaps one day I will give up this—for the time being I keep the word "messianic." Even if it is different from messianism, messianic refers to the word Messiah; it does not simply belong to a certain culture, a Jewish or Christian culture. I think that for the time being I need this word, not to teach, but to let people understand what I am trying to say when I speak of messianicity. But in doing so I still keep the

singularity of a single revelation, that is Jewish, Christian revelation, with its reference to Messiah. It is a reinterpretation of this tradition of the Messiah. (*DN* 23–24)[15]

Because the messianic allows Derrida to reinscribe a thinking of the future in terms of the promise, awaiting, and justice, he is not willing *for the moment* to give it up. Even though it might always be heard as just another messianism, he is willing to take that risk in order "to let people understand what I am trying to say when I speak of messianicity." And in order to mitigate the risk of the messianic being heard as a master name or concept, in order to keep it open to reinscription and reinvention, Derrida speaks of not one but two "historical" names. It is time now to look at this second name, which will allow Derrida to rethink not just time but space, and not just justice but democracy. For if Derrida in "Faith and Knowledge" relates the messianic to a justice that exceeds the law, he will relate *khōra* to a democracy to come that exceeds all determinate forms of democracy. Derrida thus concludes §22, which is devoted for the most part to messianicity, by first distinguishing *khōra*, the desert in the desert, from a certain negative theology and then relating it to democracy.

> *Without this desert in the desert, there would be neither act of faith, nor promise, nor future, nor expectancy without expectation of death and of the other, nor relation to the singularity of the other. The chance of this desert in the desert (as of that which* resembles *to a fault, but without reducing itself to, that* via negativa *which makes its way from a Graeco-Judeo-Christian tradition) is that in uprooting the tradition that bears it, in atheologizing it, this abstraction, without denying faith, liberates a universal rationality and the political democracy that cannot be dissociated from it.* (§22)

Though Derrida does not name *khōra* in this passage, the reference to the desert in the desert makes it clear that he is gesturing toward the analysis of *khōra* that will take up the following three sections.

Recall that back in §9 Derrida names "three aporetical places," three places of aporia where a path or issue (*poros*) is unforeseeable or incalculable, three places "*with no way out or any assured path, without itinerary or point of arrival*"—the island, the Promised Land, the desert. "*These three places,*" says Derrida, referring, it would seem, to their discussion of the topic of religion on the quasi-deserted island of Capri, "*shape our horizon, here and now*" (§9). But because any truly aporetic place, that is, any "place" without itinerary or destination, would disrupt or puncture every horizon, Derrida goes on in this passage not to elaborate the shape of this *horizon* but to speak instead of "*a certain absence of horizon*," one that, in accordance with the notion of messianicity we have just seen, "*conditions the future itself*" (§9). What is thus initially presented as three places of aporia that form a shared horizon thus becomes by the end of this short passage the "*apprehension of an abyss*": "*The emergence of the event ought to puncture every horizon of expectation. Whence the apprehension of an abyss in these places, for example a desert in the desert, there where one neither can nor should see coming what ought or could*—perhaps—*be yet to come. What is still left to come*" (§9).[16] Derrida seems to be suggesting here that in order to think the event, we need to consider not so much the figure or aporia of the Promised Land, which might still be thought within the horizon of eschatology or historicity,[17] not so much the island, which might still be related to some revelation and apocalypse,[18] not so much even the desert, which still might be thought within the horizon of temptation, sacrifice, and redemption, but "a desert in the desert"—that is, *khōra*. If these places or *topoi* so common to religious thought in the West are indeed to remain unforeseeable or incalculable, they must be thought precisely without horizon, without preformed images or revelations.[19] Of these three places, then, one will seem to mark the place of an ultimate, unforeseeable, unfigurable event, a desert that is deserted or bereft even of the religious trope of the desert, bereft of the island as a place of revelation, whether Patmos or Capri, bereft of the Promised Land as a place of safety or salvation.

Having spoken in §20 of a "*nocturnal light*" as the origin of light itself, Derrida says we must hasten toward a third place "*that could well have been* more than *archi-originary, the most anarchic and anarchivable place possible*," namely, "*a certain desert, that which makes possible, opens, hollows or infinitizes the other.*"[20] This third place, this desert within the desert, would be *khōra*, which must be thought, as we saw in the very first section of "Faith and Knowledge," in accordance with an ultimate uprooting or deracination and the most extreme "abstraction." Derrida continues in §20:

> *That which would orient here "in" this desert, without pathway and without interior, would still be the possibility of a* religio *and of a* relegere, *to be sure, but before the "link" of* religare. . . . *The abstraction of the desert can thereby open the way to everything from which it withdraws. Whence the ambiguity or the duplicity of the religious trait or retreat, of its abstraction or of its subtraction. The deserted re-treat thus makes way for the repetition of that which will have* given way *precisely for that in whose name one would protest against it, against that which*

only resembles the void and the indeterminacy of mere abstraction.
(§20)

It is precisely here, at the end of §20, that Derrida explicitly gives the two "historical" names for the duplicity of origins in relationship to religion—the messianic and *khōra*. After devoting, then, as we just saw, two sections (§§21–22) to the messianic, Derrida devotes three to *khōra* (§§23–25). He begins the first of these three:

> *The* second name *(or first name prior to all naming), would be* khōra, *such as Plato designates it in the* Timaeus, *without being able to reappropriate it in a consistent self-interpretation. From the open interior of a corpus, of a system, of a language or a culture,* khōra *would situate the abstract spacing,* place itself, *the place of absolute exteriority, but also the place of a bifurcation between two approaches to the desert. Bifurcation between a tradition of the* "via negativa" *which, in spite of or within its Christian act of birth, accords its possibility to a Greek— Platonic or Plotinian—tradition that persists until Heidegger and beyond: the thought of that which is beyond being* (epekeina tēs ousias). *This Greco-Abrahamic hybridization remains anthropo-theological. In the figures of it known to us, in its culture and in its history, its "idiom" is not universalizable. It speaks solely at the borders or in view of the Middle-Eastern desert, at the source of monotheistic revelations and of Greece. It is there that we can try to determine the place where, on this island today, "we" persist and insist.* (§23)

Referring here to this central "figure" in Plato's *Timaeus* that came to play a critical role in his work from the late 1980s onward, and particularly in *"Khōra"* (from 1987; see *ON*), Derrida identifies yet again a dual role for *khōra*.[21] As this "third kind" or "third place," *khōra* disrupts not only a certain Platonic thinking of oppositions (between Being and becoming, the intelligible and the sensible, and so on) but, as the most extreme form of abstraction or desertification, a neo-Platonic and Christian tradition of negative theology that attributes a certain excess and fecundity to the Good beyond Being. *Khōra* would thus situate "abstract spacing," the place of absolute exteriority, but also, says Derrida, the place of a bifurcation of two approaches to the desert, *his* approach, it would seem, that is, the one found in Plato's *Timaeus* or in Derrida's reinscription of it, and a "desertification" of the kind one finds in negative theology— which is Christian but also Greek—from the *epekeina tēs ousias* (the Good beyond Being) of Plato to Pseudo-Dionysius and beyond.[22] Derrida will thus claim, both here and elsewhere, that this Greco-Abrahamic negative theology remains in the end anthropo-theological and that its idiom, as a result, is not "universalizable," as another thought of *khōra* would be. The fact that negative theology has made much more ample use of Plato's Good beyond Being from the *Republic* than Plato's *khōra* from the *Timaeus* would be but one indication of the suitability of the latter for a discourse that aims for justice in the form of a "universalizable culture of singularities."[23]

Before going on to develop this thought of *khōra*, Derrida again justifies his use, his provisional use, of these "historical" names—including, it seems, *khōra*: "*If we insist, and we must for some time still, upon the names that are given us as our heritage, it is because, in respect of this borderline place, a new war of religions is redeploying as never before to this day, in an event that is* at the same time both interior and exterior" (§23).

At the beginning of §24, Derrida argues that we will not be able to think what is happening today with regard to religion so long as we have not thought this "borderline place," this *lieu limitrophe*, this outside residing and resisting within. Because today's "wars of religion" are at once archaic and absolutely new, a return to religion and the emergence of the unprecedented, we must rethink such terms as *war* and *religion*, though also, and especially, for Derrida, *faith*, *messianicity*, and *khōra* in its relation to the *democracy to come*.

> *The surge* [déferlement] *of "Islam" will be neither understood nor answered as long as the exterior and interior of this borderline place* [lieu limitrophe] *have not been called into question; as long as one settles for an internal explanation (interior to the history of faith, of religion, of languages or cultures as such), as long as one does not define the passageway between this interior and all the apparently exterior dimensions (technoscientific, tele-biotechnological, which is to say also political and socioeconomic, etc.).* (§24)

We here see Derrida pointing to one of the resources or strategies of deconstruction. While it may take a particular intervention or reading from what one may characterize as the outside in order to make this apparent, certain quasi-concepts within the history of religion or philosophy will have in fact always resisted from within or from this borderline place. Just as it took a text—a textual supplement—such as "Plato's Pharmacy" to demonstrate the way in which the *pharmakon* will have resisted philosophical appropriation from within Plato's text from the very beginning, so it takes a text such as "*Khōra*" to demonstrate the way in which *khōra*, in perhaps an even more explicit way, has resisted philosophical mastery and domination from the very beginning. As a kind of third *genos*, it cannot be captured by any of the Platonic categories or identified through any of its dualisms; it is neither Being nor becoming, neither intelligible nor sensible, neither invisible model nor visible creation. As such, *khōra* will have been from the beginning a kind of "outside" within the Platonic text. Here is one of Derrida's most succinct and powerful accounts of *khōra*:

> *In addition to investigating the ontotheologico-political tradition that links Greek philosophy to the Abrahamic revelations, perhaps we must also submit to the ordeal of that which resists such interrogation, which will have always resisted, from within or as though from an exteriority that works and resists inside. Khōra, the "ordeal of khōra" would be, at least according to the interpretation I believed myself justified in attempting, the name for place, a place name, and a rather singular one at that, for that spacing which, not allowing itself to be dominated by any theological, ontological or anthropological instance, without age, without history and more "ancient" than all oppositions (for example, that of sensible/intelligible), does not even announce itself as "beyond being" in accordance with a path of negation, a* via negativa. *As a result,* khōra *remains absolutely impassible and heterogeneous to all the processes of historical revelation or of anthropo-theological experience, which at the very least suppose its abstraction. It will never have entered religion and will never permit itself to be sacralized, sanctified, humanized, theologized, cultivated, historicized. Radically heterogeneous to the safe and sound, to the holy and the sacred, it never admits of any indemnification. This cannot even be formulated in the present, for* khōra *never presents itself as such. It is neither Being, nor the Good, nor God, nor Man, nor History. It will always resist them, will have always been (and no future anterior, even, will have been able to reappropriate, inflect or reflect a* khōra *without faith or law) the very place of an infinite resistance, of an infinitely impassible persistence* [restance]: *an utterly faceless other.* (§24)

As that which comes before all determinate revelations without itself being revealed, or all appearances in general without itself appearing, *khōra* does indeed look like a desertification, an abandonment, a place of abstraction. It is not the opposite, exactly, of that other form of abstraction in the *Timaeus* that corresponds to the intelligible forms but the "event" or "taking place" whereby or within which these intelligible forms imprint themselves in the sensible realm. It is thus an abstraction that gives rise to that from which it then withdraws. In "*Sauf le nom (Post-Scriptum)*," it is characterized not only as "a figure of the pure place" ("*SN*" 57) but as the place of "an endless desertification of language" ("*SN*" 55–56). Though *khōra* would "itself" resist identification, anthropomorphization, relation in general, it would nonetheless be the place of relation, or, rather, the place or condition of the link that has been identified throughout "Faith and Knowledge" with an elementary faith.

Khōra is thus the name, for Derrida, of what has resisted all appropriation, the name of what has not let itself be dominated by any theological, ontological, or anthropological authority. Without age, without history, "older" than all oppositions, says Derrida, *khōra* does not announce itself or herself in the *epekeina tēs ousias* or the Beyond of Being of negative theology.[24] Unlike the latter, then, it has never entered into religion and has never allowed itself to be humanized or theologized as the Good beyond Being. In a word, it has never lent itself to indemnification and has never even presented itself as such. Derrida ends his long description of *khōra* in §24: "*the very place of an infinite resistance, of an infinitely impossible persistence* [restance]: *an utterly faceless other* [un tout autre sans visage]."[25] As a unique event rather than an identifiable being, a proper name without property, oscillating between a "what" and a "who," *khōra* has no face and cannot be identified with the face (we are no doubt invited to hear a reservation with regard to Levinas). It is an "*utterly faceless other*" not because its or her face or truth is hidden by a veil but because she—or it—is nothing but veil, a place where the face or anything else may come to imprint itself and leave its trace for a time while it "itself" remains without a face. It thus gives rise or place to all faces and all forms, to all figures, but then "itself" immediately withdraws, faceless and figureless. Despite the temptation, then, and despite Plato's own analogies in the *Timaeus*, *khōra* cannot even be thought as a mother, nurse, or womb, even though it—or she—gives rise to all these figures. As Derrida says in a late text on Jean Genet to which I will turn in Chapter 9:

> That is why the word "mother" and the determination of maternity bother me here. . . . it's a matter of going beyond the mother or womb, towards what in other texts I termed *Khōra*, trying to save the interpretation of *Khōra* in Plato's *Timaeus* from interpretations that precisely made a womb, a mother, of it. *Khōra*, the receptacle, the space that receives the impressions of the copies of paradigms, has often, and by Plato himself, been compared metaphorically to a womb. I tried to show how *Khōra* isn't one, how it doesn't even correspond to a maternal figure. ("CS" 34)

It is here that the relationship between *khōra* and all the figures that appear within her or thanks to her seems most like the relationship between revealability and all determinate revelations. In §25 Derrida asks in effect—in terms with which we are familiar by now—whether *khōra* (like revealability) can be thought only on the basis of figures or revelations we already know, or whether these figures can be thought only on the basis of *khōra*. While Derrida seems to suggest that he wants to maintain "*two originarities*"—the order of the revealed and the order of the revealable—the language of *khōra* will have displaced rather radically the terms in which any "originarity" is to be thought.

> Khōra *is nothing (no being, nothing present), but not the Nothing which in the anxiety of* Dasein *would still open the question of being. This Greek noun says in our memory that which is not reappropriable, even by our memory, even by our "Greek" memory; it says the immemoriality of a desert in the desert of which it is neither a threshold nor a mourning. The question remains open, and with it that of knowing whether this desert can be thought and left to announce itself "before" the desert that we know (that of the revelations and the retreats, of the lives and deaths of God, of all the figures of kenosis or of transcendence, of* religio *or of historical "religions"); or whether, "on the contrary," it is "from" this last desert that we can glimpse that which precedes the first* [l'avant-premier], *what I call the desert in the desert. The indecisive oscillation, that reticence* (epochē *or* Verhaltenheit) *already alluded to above (between revelation and revealability,* Offenbarung *and* Offenbarkeit, *between event and possibility or virtuality of the event), must it not be respected for itself? Respect for this singular indecision or for this hyperbolic outbidding between two originarities, the order of the "revealed" and the order of the "revealable," is this not at once the chance of every responsible decision and of another "reflecting faith," of a new "tolerance"?* (§25)

The enigma or oscillation that Derrida sketched out in the Villanova roundtable with respect to messianicity is here repeated with regard to *khōra*. As a "historical" name, *khōra* too is marked by a language and a culture, by everyday notions of place, country, and earth, on the one hand, as well as philosophical—and, through Derrida at least, theological—notions of space, abstraction, kenosis, and the desert, on the other. The question thus remains whether *khōra* can truly be thought as a desert within the desert before all the deserts of religion, or all the abstractions of philosophy, or whether it is itself already marked by religion and/or philosophy. The question, says Derrida, *"remains open"* and the oscillation must be *"respected,"* an oscillation that can be thought, we now see, on the basis of the aporia between revealability and revelation or, more promising still, on the basis of messianicity or *khōra*.

Yet again the lexicon of *khōra*—like that of messianicity—provides Derrida with resources that the language of revealability and revelation does not, even if the former is often contaminated by the latter. Hence *khōra*, which is neither Nothingness nor Being nor the Good beyond Being, will not be identified as a kind of quasi-transcendental revealability. It will instead be positioned as the nocturnal source of light, the source not only of particular revelations but of the very light of revealability, a source that would not be a fecund or life-giving source but simply the giving rise or the taking place of all phenomena. Already back in §8, in anticipation of the arrival of *khōra*, Derrida suggests that there may be a common source of both science and religion, of both knowledge and faith, both *savoir* and *foi*, by saying not "'Let there be light,' and there *was* light ['*Que la lumière soit!' Et la lumière fut*]" but "Light takes place [*La lumière a lieu*]" (§8). However difficult this difference may be to maintain, Derrida wishes to contrast the light of revelation and revealability and the giving place of *khōra*. Instead of a genesis, then, what we get is a *chorology*, to cite John Sallis;[26] instead of a story of creation or else the story of the Good beyond Being, a story of a Father and his life-giving fecundity and sovereignty, what we are given is an account of the *taking place of light*, of that which gives place to light and to the phenomena that come to appear in the light. Instead of the sovereign Father of the *Republic* who assures all analogies based on likenesses, instead of a Good that is in the intelligible realm what the sun is in the visible realm, what we are given is the *khōra* of the *Timaeus* as the "third *genos*," a sort of "mother" or "nurse" who makes possible all analogy and yet is so absolutely unique that it—or she—withdraws from all analogies and resemblances. Desert within the desert, *khōra* is thus "itself" no more *technē* than *physis*, no more a father who gives life than a mother who protects or shelters it. As this *third genos*, this third kind, species, genre, or gender, *khōra* is not a kind like the others; undialectizable, it resists a thinking that remains caught between two dialectically related alternatives.

Though *khōra* is compared by Plato to a receptacle, to that which would *receive* all phenomena within it or within her, she is in the end neither that which encompasses or holds everything within herself nor something to be located within the encyclopedic tradition of ontotheology, in which she has nonetheless left a trace. *Khōra* neither invests in that to which she gives rise nor is she invested in it; she neither gives life nor indemnifies it. She is barren, disinterested, withdrawn from every possible predicate. As Derrida once put it in a particularly idiomatic and colorful phrasing, "*khōra s'en fout complètement*"—that is, *khōra* couldn't care less, couldn't give a damn.

Derrida thus wishes to read *khōra* in Plato's *Timaeus* as a unique event, as unique and irreplaceable as an untranslatable idiom or a proper name. Though *khōra* is, of course, also a common name, a Greek name meaning place or location or country, so that the distinction between the proper and the improper is never assured, Derrida wants to see in Plato's development of *khōra* in *Timaeus* something so unique that it deserves to be called by a name so proper that it—or something within it, a desert within its desert—would have nothing common or comparable about it. As a common name, *khōra* is at once linked to the Greek language and idiom and yet opens itself to universalization and translation (as land or country or space), while as a proper name it at once resists translation and yet, as the name of a promise, remains absolutely open to replacement and substitution—*like a witness*. The name *khōra* thus testifies, in a sense, as a replaceable-irreplaceable witness to the universality marked in its idiom.

Khōra would thus be, for Derrida, more radical—because more withdrawn, more universal in some sense, more strategically and pedagogically useful—than the category of revealability or *Offenbarkeit*.[27] Neither Being nor a being, neither a being in space nor the substratum of space, *khōra* is the unique event that resists from within both Greek thought and Greco-Christian negative theology. Neither intelligible nor sensible, requiring, therefore, a third kind of discourse, *khōra* has remained—unlike the Good beyond Being of the *Republic*—heterogeneous to all anthropomorphism and all theologisms. Derrida suggests in "Abraham, the Other" that this "Greek" place or thinking of place might even have "a deep affinity with a certain nomination of the God of the Jews. He is also The Place" ("AO" 33). It is for all these reasons, it seems, that Derrida neither simply accepted nor abandoned the language of revelation and revealability but displaced it into registers that would allow him to rethink this traditional problematic and the assumptions on which it relies. And this is precisely what Derrida himself says in yet another set of improvised remarks from November 2002, where he addresses one more time—perhaps for the last time—the question of the relationship between revelation and revealability.[28] Asked by Kevin Hart to elaborate on the "relative priority of revelation and revealability," on what Derrida has sometimes called the "aporia" between these terms, Derrida begins by agreeing that this "distinction is an aporia" but that aporia does not mean for him simple "paralysis." "On the contrary, it's the condition of proceeding, of making a decision, of going forward" ("EF" 43). He then goes on to explain the distinction as it is found in Heidegger before expressing his reservations with regard to it.

> Heidegger says the *Offenbarung*, that is revelation, implies—*implies*, it's not logical, it's not chronological—implies that some revealability, some *Offenbarkeit*, was already there: the "already" has no chronological meaning. For some revelation to take place *Dasein*, the human existence, must be able to open itself to revelation, and this revealability is, let's say, ontologically—not chronologically, not logically—prior to *Offenbarung*, to revelation. If you want to think religious revelation, you have to first go backwards, so to speak, to the possibility of religion, to the possibility of revelation. The question is: Is this the proper order, first in the non-chronological, nonlogical sense, first revealability and the revelation? Or is it more complicated than that?
>
> My difficulty with Heidegger's very strong, very rigorous argument has to do with the possibility that revelation is not simply something that comes to confirm and to fulfill a revealability. Revelation is something that reveals revealability. It is something, an event. Revelation is always an event: an event that, in fact, breaks something, so that revealability, *Offenbarkeit* is open. Revealability is opened by revelation: that's putting it the other way round. But I was not satisfied by this other order, either. I would try to think the relation between the two in a different way. And I don't know which way. I must confess that the logical order, the chronological order, even the ontological order, is not appropriate. So I'm trying to think something that removes the event that one calls revelation from the scheme of veil, revelation, revealability. I'm trying to think the event as something other than an unveiling of a truth or the revelation of a truth, as something that has effects but makes no reference to light, no reference to vision, no reference to unveiling. ("EF" 43–44)

Derrida could not be clearer: it is the reference to light, to truth as unveiling, that needs to be rethought, and, along with it, the logic, chronology, and ontology of the alternative between revelation and revealability. Only then will we be able to think the *event* of revelation in a more radical way. Derrida thus concludes his answer to Kevin Hart's question in November 2002 by contrasting a phenomenological thought of the horizon with a rethinking of the event as what cannot be anticipated or predicted, what cannot appear on any horizon but comes to us—indeed what comes to all living beings (animal and God as well as human) always from above, unpredictably and blindly.

> Usually one thinks that there is phenomenologically or ontologically a background, a horizon, against which one sees the event coming. If so, there is no event: if you see it coming, it is not an event. The revelation or revealability is the neutralization of the event. One has to think of an event that affects every living being—human, animal, and God—without any essential revelation or essential revealability.[29] And to that extent the pair of concepts, *Offenbarung* and *Offenbarkeit*, is not useless but it remains secondary by way of thinking what an event is. ("EF" 43–44)

Hence the terms of the alternative or aporia will be reinscribed into other registers, first of all into the two sources of religion and then into the two "historical" names *messianicity* and, perhaps above all, *khōra*.

All this helps explain, I believe, why the figure of *khōra* came to play such a privileged role during the last two decades of Derrida's work.[30] Indeed were we to hear Derrida actually privileging this figure of *khōra* or the desert over others, perhaps even over the notion of the messianic, we would be in good company. In *"Sauf le nom (Post-Scriptum)"*—a text written in multiple voices—we read: "—In listening to you, one has more and more the feeling that *desert* is the other name, if not the proper place, of *desire*" ("*SN*" 80). As a desert within the desert, a desert that now testifies to a promise that goes well beyond the desert, *khōra* would be the place or the name of a *"link to the other in general,"* a *"fiduciary 'link'[that] would precede all determinate community, all positive religion, every onto-anthropo-theological horizon."* Hence, Derrida argues, *khōra* would *"link pure singularities prior to any social or political determination, prior to all intersubjectivity, prior even to the opposition between the sacred (or the holy) and the profane"* (§20). Before any social or political space, it would join or link singularities by saying simply, in an infinitely low voice, and in the name, as we will see in a moment, of *another tolerance*, "Space Available."

The relationship we saw earlier between messianicity, the performative, faith, and a justice that would exceed all determinate laws helps set up what initially appears to be a rather surprising evocation of democracy in relationship to *khōra*. Derrida claims in the midst of a passage on *khōra* as the desert in the desert: *"in uprooting the tradition that bears it, in atheologizing it, this abstraction, without denying faith, liberates a universal rationality and the political democracy that cannot be dissociated from it"* (§22). The arrival of democracy at the end of this sentence is, at least initially, almost as surprising and unexpected as Derrida's claim in *Rogues* in the middle of a discussion of democracy that "the democracy to come would be like the *khōra* of the political" (*R* 82). But these two sentences have more than these jarring and unexpected formulations in common. Insofar as *khōra*, like messianicity, is related to the promise and the future, insofar as it—or she—is neither an idea nor an ideal, neither a concrete existence nor a phenomenal form, it is the only thing capable of acting as a critique of all ideals and phenomena, opening up the horizon formed by these to the future—*just like the democracy to come.* That is why the democracy to come would be *like* the *khōra* of the political. As that which opens up a relationship to the future through a series of autoimmune gestures (elections in the form of the "by turns," freedom of expression and critique, "another tolerance"), democracy would be the only quasi-regime that is open in principle to the future, that is, to a perfectibility/pervertibility that remains at once its fragility and its only chance.

In Chapter 1, I cited Derrida recalling that all of them present at Capri shared "*an unreserved taste, if not an unconditional preference, for what, in politics, is called republican democracy as a universalizable model*" (§11). He goes on to explain in that passage that it is this commitment to republican democracy and universality that

> *bind[s] philosophy to the public "cause," to the* res publica, *to "public-ness," once again to the light of day, once again to the "lights" of the Enlightenment* [aux Lumières], *once again to the enlightened virtue of public space, emancipating it from all external power (non-lay, non-secular), for example from religious dogmatism, orthodoxy or authority (that is, from a certain rule of the* doxa *or of belief, which, however, does not mean from all faith). In a less analogical manner (but I shall return to this later) and at least as long and in so far as we continue speaking here together, we shall doubtless attempt to transpose, here and now, the circumspect and suspensive attitude, a certain* epochē *that consists—rightly or wrongly, for the issue is serious—in thinking religion or making it appear "within the limits of reason alone."* (§11)

The question, as we have seen, is whether "religion within the limits of reason alone" can be divorced from the elementary faith—or the reflecting faith—that opens the possibility of religion without determining any religion as such. This question of the universality of faith has, as we have seen, an explicitly political dimension. In the following section Derrida writes somewhat elliptically of these political implications but then appends two footnotes that send us to places in his work where we can follow out what is only suggested in "Faith and Knowledge":

Related question: what of this 'Kantian' gesture today? What would a book be like today which, like Kant's, is entitled, Religion Within the Limits of Reason Alone? *This* epochē *also gives its chance to a political event, as I have tried to suggest elsewhere.*(3) *It even belongs to the history of democracy, notably when theological discourse was obliged to assume the forms of the* via negativa *and even there, where it seems to have prescribed reclusive communities, initiatic teachings, hierarchy, esoteric insularity or the desert.*(4) (§12)

These two footnotes refer us to two of Derrida's most explicit attempts to address the question of negative theology, "How to Avoid Speaking: Denials" and "*Sauf le nom (Post-Scriptum)*," a text written just a couple of years before "Faith and Knowledge" and one that has, as we have already seen, much in common with it. This reference also seems to indicate, among so much else, a place of intersection in Derrida's thinking between the themes of friendship in *Politics of Friendship* (much of which was written in the late 1980s), law in "Force of Law" (first delivered in 1989–90), and the democracy to come, which is referred to in these earlier texts but is only fully developed in *Rogues* (2003). Derrida thus says in "*Sauf le nom (Post-Scriptum)*" that he would like to speak of "another 'community'" ("*SN*" 46), a reference that might seem rather surprising, given what we saw in Chapter 1 to be Derrida's professed and pronounced skepticism regarding the entire theme and lexicon of community. But if the scare quotes around the word suggest that Derrida's skepticism has not disappeared, the parenthesis that follows confirms that: "I would like to speak of another 'community' (a word I never much liked, because of its connotation of participation, indeed fusion, identification: I see in it as many threats as promises), of another being-together than this one here, of another gathering-together of singularities, of another friendship" ("*SN*" 46). Derrida thus goes on to suggest that in order to rethink community we would need to question certain inherited notions of friendship by emphasizing not communion and sharing but interruption and singularity, by suspending a certain "human" or "anthropocentric" community and withdrawing friendship "from all its dominant determinations in the Greek or Christian world, from the fraternal (fraternalist) and phallocentric schema of *philia* or charity" ("*SN*" 81).[31] Only such a rethinking of community and friendship will allow one to open up "a certain arrested form of democracy" ("*SN*" 47)—one that is Greek or Christian, or Greco-Christian—to what Derrida will call the democracy to come, a democracy that is related to that "universalizable culture of singularities" he speaks of in "Faith and Knowledge."

It is this promise of a messianicity without messianism and of a universalizable culture of singularities that allows one to criticize or question every determined messianism and every nonuniversalizable culture, this promise of a universal rationality (linked always, as we have seen, to an elementary faith) that allows one to contest or "deconstruct" all beliefs and all determinate notions of universality (such as *globalatinization*). It is this same promise that marks "historical" names as untranslatable idioms that nonetheless call out for reinscription and translation in other idioms and other contexts. As Derrida confirms in "*Sauf le nom (Post-Scriptum)*": "the movement toward the universal tongue oscillates between formalism, or the poorest, most arid, in effect the most desertlike techno-scientificity, and a sort of universal hive of inviolable secrets, of idioms that are never translated except as untranslatable seals" ("*SN*" 80). What Derrida calls the democracy to come would thus be the place of "translation" between these untranslatable idioms and a certain universality, in short, the place of a "universalizable culture of singularities" or, shifting idioms, a "universal hive of inviolable secrets." Later in the same essay, Derrida will thus speak of "two concurrent desires" and "a double injunction," "the desire to be inclusive of all, thus understood by all," "and the desire to keep or entrust the secret within the very strict limits of those who hear/understand it *right*" ("*SN*" 83).[32]

Rather than turn here to Derrida's 2003 *Rogues*, where the history of the concept of democracy is traced and analyzed from Plato and Aristotle up through Rousseau and Nancy, I would prefer to look briefly at some improvised remarks made by Derrida about democracy not long after *Rogues* and in the spirit of much that is said in "Faith and Knowledge." In a public discussion with the Algerian intellectual Mustapha Chérif in the spring of 2003, Derrida clarifies even further the relationship between democracy and universality. Because democracy must always in principle if not always in fact question its own presuppositions and historical limitations, because it must criticize whatever is being called democracy at any time and in any place, it is open to a universal application in a way that no other political regime is.

> What distinguishes the idea of democracy from all other ideas of political regimes—monarchy, aristocracy, oligarchy, and so on—is that democracy is the only political system, a model without a model, that accepts its own historicity, that is, its own future, which accepts its self-criticism, which accepts its perfectibility. . . . To exist in a democracy is to agree to challenge, to be challenged, to challenge the status quo, which is called democratic, in the name of a

democracy to come. This is why I always speak of a democracy to come. Democracy is always to come, it is a promise, and it is in the name of that promise that one can always criticize, question that which is proposed as de facto democracy. (*IW* 42–43)

Derrida speaks here of democracy in a way that should remind us of our earlier discussion of messianicity as opposed to determinate messianisms, or faith as opposed to religion. It is the historical origins and nonuniversalizable aspects of every democracy, of every determinate democracy, we might say, that lend themselves to being criticized or "deconstructed" *in the name* of the democracy to come. Hence the association of democracy with autochthony, blood, birth, a particular territory or nation-state— values we see attached throughout "Faith and Knowledge" to the first of the two origins of religion—are to be criticized in the name of the promise of a democracy to come, a promise that is related to the second of the two origins.

From the beginning, Greek culture associated the concept of democracy with concepts from which, today, the democracy to come is attempting to free itself: the concept of autochthony, that is, the concept of being born on a land and belonging to it through birth, the concept of territory, the very concept of State. I have nothing against the State, I have nothing against citizenship, but I dare to dream of a democracy that is not simply tied to a nation-state and to citizenship. And it is under these conditions that one can speak of a universal democracy, a democracy that is not only cosmopolitical but universal. (*IW* 43–44)

Derrida distinguishes here between the cosmopolitical and the universal because, as he has argued elsewhere, our inherited concept of the cosmopolitical is itself too heavily marked by its Christian origins (e.g., Paul) and so is hardly *universal enough*. Derrida is seeking a universality "which is not connected to a nation-state, which is not connected to citizenship, to territoriality" (*IW* 44). But because nothing would be less effective and potentially more dangerous than a purely empty, merely formal universality, Derrida attempts to think at once the universality of a democracy to come disconnected from every determinate culture and nation-state *and* a respect for the idiom. That is why he argues that "plurality is the very *essence* of civilization" and that "the principle of differences and the respect for alterity" are the "principles of civilization" (*IW* 80). These are not, notice, the *ideals* of every civilization but the essence and principles of civilization. Hence Derrida can go on not only to decry the "horrible linguistic hegemony [that] is taking over the earth" but to declare that the "homogeneous universal civilization" that seems foreshadowed by this hegemony would be "the opposite of a civilization" (*IW* 80). In short and by definition, "a civilization must be plural; it must ensure a respect for the multiplicity of languages, cultures, beliefs, ways of life. And it is in this plurality, in this alterity, that a chance . . . for the future is possible" (*IW* 81). The idiom must thus be respected for itself, for what is untranslatable within it, at the same time as it must be translated. The very discourse of deconstruction that we have been following here would thus already be the putting into practice of this translation of unique idioms. Rather than inventing some new language, it reinscribes already given "historical" names in the name of the promise they bear, not only messianicity and *khōra*, as we have seen, but the democracy to come, friendship, respect, and, as we will see shortly, tolerance.

What Derrida calls the democracy to come will thus borrow from the philosophical and political heritage of democracy in the West *and* submit this heritage to critique, that is, question, suspend, or deconstruct what is already too Christian about it. Derrida makes this thesis clear in *Rogues* when he follows various conceptions of democracy in relationship to certain theological notions of sovereignty. In "Above All, No Journalists!"—the series of improvised remarks we put such emphasis on in Chapter 5—Derrida says quite straightforwardly that "the concept of democracy, at least in the dominant form familiar to us, is itself marked by traits that are strongly Christian, indeed Pauline, etc." ("AANJ" 78),[33] and not only democracy but the related notions of freedom ("liberation movements are often also Christian movements"; "AANJ" 78), the world as *mundus* ("the concept of world remains a Christian concept"; "AANJ" 66), even secularization ("the concept of secularization has no meaning outside of Christianity"; "AANJ" 66). All this suggests that "what the Enlightenment claimed to oppose to Christianity is still Christian in its formation" ("AANJ" 66) and so needs to be submitted to critique—including the belief on the part of some that we have entered into a purely secular age. This explains why Derrida writes not far from the end of "Faith and Knowledge": "Nothing seems therefore more uncertain, more difficult to sustain, nothing seems here or there more imprudent than a self-assured discourse on the age of disenchantment, the era of secularization, the time of laicization, etc." (§49)[34] The democracy to come would thus be universal and "secular" in a way that existing democracies are not, for it would attempt to disengage or "liberate" even more this notion of secularism from its Christian origins so as to give an even greater chance to the universal rationality or elementary faith that is at the origin of every social bond.

I believe that the democracy to come . . . assumes secularism, that is, both the detachment of the political from the theocratic and the theological, thus entailing a certain secularism of the political, while at the same time, encompassing freedom of worship in a completely consistent, coherent way, and absolute religious freedom guaranteed by the State, on the condition, obviously, that the secular space of the political and the religious space are not confused. (*IW* 50)

In addition to this secularism within the state, Derrida argues that "a truly international law" is needed, one whose concepts and institutions are not linked to the interests and control of powerful nation states (*IW* 45). This secularism was thus often coupled in Derrida's later work with a more and more trenchant critique of American sovereignty and the international institutions largely under its influence and with a more and more marked hope for the future of a certain Europe.[35] This critique became more and more emphatic after the Gulf War and, especially, after the American invasion of Iraq in 2003, and it included a stinging critique of the United Nations and its Security Council, which, Derrida rarely failed to point out, remains under the tutelage of the United States (*IW* 71). Hence Derrida argued that new forms of shared sovereignty must be invented, though also, since "the concept of sovereignty that comes to us with a theological heritage presupposes indivisibility," a new concept of sovereignty (*IW* 71–72).

In these works, Derrida demonstrates quite clearly that he is not simply "against the state" or its sovereignty, since state sovereignty is often the best means we have of combating or limiting other kinds of international or transnational powers and of ensuring secularity and religious freedom. He thus calls for a rethinking or reinvention of state sovereignty, a reform of certain international institutions (such as the United Nations) and the development of others (e.g., the World Criminal Court). Already in *Specters of Marx*, Derrida speaks of a "new international" or a "new international alliance" beyond nation-state citizenship, and in *Islam & the West* he sees some of today's antiglobalization movements that aim to combat "imperial and imperialist hegemonies" as "the sign of a new alliance that is forming" (*IW* 74). Though one cannot be certain—though one cannot *know*—that this is what is happening, there are reasons, Derrida believed, to be hopeful and reasons, it seems, to take responsibility and to decide to commit oneself in this direction, that is, commit oneself on the basis of a faith that can and should insist on all the questioning and analysis in the world but that will in the end have to proceed beyond all knowledge. Notice in the passage I am about to cite the way in which the two terms we have been following throughout this work, *faith* and *knowledge*, are woven together to form the knot of a decision and the sign of an alliance that requires all the light in the world but that must proceed by means of a leap that is blind. For if the moment of decision must always be prepared by knowledge, analysis, argument, and calculation, the moment proper to it is one of faith.

> Responsibility, decisions, are taken in the darkness that is the lack of knowledge, which doesn't mean we must cultivate ignorance, lack of knowledge, obscurantism. . . . One must accumulate the most knowledge and critical awareness possible. One must be for scientific knowledge, science, as far as possible. . . . But we must also know that the moment of decision, the moment of responsibility, the moment of opening up, does not come out of knowledge. It is a leap that must be made by each person wherever he or she is and in the unique situation in which he or she happens to be. Between knowledge and responsibility there is an abyss. . . . Thus we must have knowledge, one must reject neither knowledge nor critical awareness, but there are also moments of faith, in which a leap is made, the leap of opening up, toward that new alliance that I mentioned earlier. (*IW* 75–76) [36]

If the notion of democracy emerges, as we saw, somewhat abruptly and unexpectedly in "Faith and Knowledge," many of the stakes of democracy and of the debates surrounding it are there from the outset. In the debate surrounding the "return" to religion, for example, Islam has had a certain privilege not only because of a few spectacular acts of violence carried out, Derrida is clear to specify, "*in the name* of Islam," but because of the declared opposition on the part of a certain Islam to Western notions of democracy and international law. Instead of simply focusing on the best-known and most-mediatized characterizations of this Islamic reaction to the West—"fanaticism, obscurantism, lethal violence, terrorism, oppression of women"—one must begin by admitting that this " 'Islamism' also develops a radical critique of what ties democracy *today, in its limits, in its concept and its effective power,* to the market and to the tele-technoscientific reason that dominates it" (§37n28). In other words, before writing off such Islamism as fanatical and obscurantist, one must recognize everything within it that—in autoimmune fashion—uses a certain nonfanatical and nonobscurantist power of critique to denounce Western democracy and the power of critique that is supposedly enshrined in it.

This does not mean, however, that such Islamism is to be endorsed or seen as a violable alternative for the future. On the contrary, as Derrida makes clear in *Rogues* and in the interview he gave after 9–11, it is ultimately a certain denial of the future that is most objectionable in this Islamic opposition to Western democracy—a denial, as we have seen, not just of democracy but of messianism. Because this future is also related, as we will see again in Chapter 9, not only to democracy but to literature, to the right to say everything, we can perhaps understand why Derrida would draw particular attention in "Faith and Knowledge," in 1994–95, to the fatwa against Salman Rushdie. The reaction to Rushdie is a reaction to literature and to democracy, the only political regime that, in principle at least, does not try to indemnify its future. In the wake of 9–11 Derrida draws all these arguments together with particular clarity and with an emphasis on religion, particularly on a dogmatic expression of it that elides or eclipses the source of religion that would leave it open to critique, universality, and, especially, the future. Asked in October 2001 whether he thinks al-Qaeda and bin Laden harbor international political ambitions, Derrida responds:

> What appears to me unacceptable in the "strategy" (in terms of weapons, practices, ideology, rhetoric, discourse, and so on) of the "Bin Laden effect" is not only the cruelty, the disregard for human life, the disrespect for law, for women, the use of what is worst in technocapitalist modernity for the purposes of religious fanaticism. No, it is, above all the fact that such actions and such discourse *open onto no future and, in my view, have no future.* If we are to put any faith in the perfectibility of public space and of the world juridico-political scene, of the "world" itself, then there is, it seems to me, *nothing good* to be hoped for from that quarter. What is being proposed, at least implicitly, is that all capitalist and modern techno-scientific forces be put in the service of an interpretation, itself dogmatic, of the Islamic revelation of the One. Nothing of what has been so laboriously secularized in the forms of the "political," of "democracy," of "international law," and even in the nontheological form of sovereignty (assuming, again, that the value of sovereignty can be completely secularized or de-theologized, a hypothesis about which I have my doubts), none of this seems to have any place whatsoever in the discourse "Bin Laden." ("AI" 113)

"Faith and Knowledge" thus needs to be read in conjunction with several of Derrida's subsequent texts, beginning perhaps with *Rogues*. Not only are both texts concerned with what we might call the *fictions*—or, better, the *phantasms*—of sovereignty, that is, the phantasms of the sovereignty of the self, the state, and God, but both are concerned with the nature of sovereignty itself, indeed with the autoimmune essence of sovereignty.[37] Though *Rogues* is somewhat more explicit than "Faith and Knowledge" on this point, it is in "Faith and Knowledge," interestingly, that we find a long footnote on Benveniste's analysis of the Indo-European origins of this concept. (We will look at this footnote more closely in the next chapter.) Moreover, both texts, as we saw a moment ago, bring a thinking of *khōra* to bear on their subject, and both, the one in relation to religion and the other in relation to democracy, speak about the performative engagement before all knowledge, of messianicity without messianism, of virtuality, media, globalization, and so on. Written some eight years apart, these two texts, the one written before 9–11 and the other after, call out to one another today and deserve to be read side by side.

Rogues and the interview after 9–11 help make explicit much that is only implicit in "Faith and Knowledge" and so can easily be misunderstood. If Derrida in "Faith and Knowledge" and elsewhere locates a kind of elementary faith at the origin of both science and religion, this obviously does not mean that Derrida now wants to locate religion *within* the political. On the contrary, throughout the 1980s and 1990s and right up to his death, Derrida relentlessly pursued a kind of radical or originary secularism or secularity that constantly questions and criticizes the imposition of any particular religion or religious doctrine upon political concepts. Motivated in part by the analyses of Carl Schmitt, Derrida takes up the project of demonstrating the ontotheological origins of what at first appear to be modern secular concepts such as popular sovereignty, democracy, and religious tolerance. Hence Derrida in §28 argues that "the fundamental concepts that often permit us to isolate or to *pretend* to isolate the *political*—restricting ourselves to this particular circumscription—remain religious or in any case theologico-political" (§28). After commenting, then, on how "in one of the most rigorous attempts to isolate in its purity the sphere of the political . . . Carl Schmitt was obliged to acknowledge that the ostensibly purely political categories to which he resorted were the product of a theologico-political secularization or heritage," Derrida claims that so many of our concepts associated with democracy—the sovereign state, the citizen-subject, public space and private space, and so on—have been "inherited in truth from a determinate religious stratum [*souche religieuse*]" (§28). Because these inherited concepts are themselves being "incarnated" and transformed in new and unprecedented ways by the developments in media and teletechnoscience that we have seen, the project of distinguishing religion and science, or religion and the political, is even more difficult in today's so-called secular age.

What is required is thus a thoroughgoing deconstruction of the theological origins of our concepts not only of sovereignty but, and this is just a partial list, of labor, the world, literature, even concepts such as secularism or religious tolerance, which we might mistakenly have assumed the Enlightenment severed forever from religion.[38] To return one more time to the interview given by Derrida in New York City just after 9–11:

> The word "tolerance" is first of all marked by a religious war between Christians, or between Christians and non-Christians. Tolerance is a *Christian* virtue, or for that matter a *Catholic* virtue. . . . Though I clearly prefer shows of tolerance to shows of intolerance, I nonetheless still have certain reservations about the word "tolerance" and the discourse it organizes. It is a discourse with religious roots; it is most often used on the side of those with power, always as a kind of condescending concession. ("AI" 126–27)

It is with these remarks in mind that we must read the question Derrida poses in §26 as to whether it is possible to think "tolerance" outside or beyond its Christian provenance. Derrida argues that Voltaire, for example, author of the *Philosophical Dictionary*, with its article on "Tolerance," believed that the Christian alone was able to provide an example of tolerance. While Voltaire opposes with great vehemence the latinization of Christianity and the hegemony of the Roman Church, he nonetheless believes that Christianity, a more originary, uncorrupted Christianity, is the only "moral" religion and the only one capable of an exemplary tolerance. Hence Voltaire is not so much against Christianity as for an originary or proto-Christianity that has been forgotten (§26n13).

Derrida is suggesting that we at once criticize different ideologies of secularism that are never quite secular enough *and* help support various forms of secularism in which the political and the religious risk being conflated. The theological origins of political concepts must thus be questioned not only in the Muslim world but in America and the European West. As for the Muslim world, which is already fractured and multiple, Derrida argues in *Rogues* that one must do everything possible to help movements *within* that world that are already advocating for this separation. The task, he argues,

> would consist in doing everything possible to join forces with all those who, and first of all in the Islamic world, fight not only for the secularization of the political (however ambiguous this secularization remains), for the emergence of a laic subjectivity, but also for an interpretation of the Koranic heritage that privileges, from the

inside as it were, the democratic virtualities that are probably not any more apparent and readable at first glance, and readable under this name, than they were in the Old and New Testaments. (*R* 33)[39]

Just a year later, in the improvised remarks we have been following here from the spring of 2003, Derrida makes a similar claim, this time emphasizing the separation of the political and the theological as a way of achieving a new form of religious tolerance. He there argues that we must

> *ally* ourselves to that in the Arab and Muslim world which is trying to advance the idea of a secularization of the political, the idea of a separation between the theocratic and the political—this both out of respect for the political and for democratization and out of respect for faith and religion. On both sides we have much to win from the dissociation between the theocratic and the political. (*IW* 53–54)

While Derrida questions "the religious origins of the idea of sovereignty" and even of "the idea of the State" (*IW* 52), he is the enemy of neither religion nor the state. Indeed it is only through a radical separation of religion and the state that a genuine freedom of religion within the state can be guaranteed, a freedom of religion that would be grounded not in any particular faith but in the elementary faith that is at the origin of the social bond. As a result, one can "become committed to the secularization of the political without the need to renounce faith or religion" (*IW* 72), that is, "one can radicalize the secularization of the political while maintaining this necessity for faith in the general sense" (*IW* 58). It is "on the foundation of this universal faith, this shared faith, this faith without which there is no social bond," that one can then "respect strictly defined religious affiliations" (*IW* 58).[40]

Just as Derrida in "Faith and Knowledge" demonstrates the necessity of thinking religion in relationship to science and technology, so he argues that religion in its "essence" or in its "indemnified purify" cannot be thought apart from questions of the political. While Derrida will always have been vigilant—and especially during the last two decades—in rooting out the theological origins of so many of our putatively secular concepts, he would have been the last to believe that the essence of religion can or even should be thought completely independently of the political.[41] In other words, he would have been the last to think that religion—or the possibility of religion—could be treated in isolation from its supposed others (civil society, science, the Enlightenment, etc.). He would have been the last to think that one can protect religion from these others or banish religion in the form of a universal or elementary faith from these others.

The universality of democracy would entail *both* the separation of the political from the theological *and* a form of religious freedom or religious tolerance that goes well beyond its Christian incarnation. Indeed, Derrida suggests in his conversation with Chérif that the latter can be truly achieved only through the former.

> This speech addressed to the other presupposes the freedom to say anything, on the horizon of a democracy to come that is not connected to the nation, the State, religion, which is not even connected to language. Naturally, the religion of the other must be recognized and respected, as well as his mother tongue, of course. But one must translate, that is, at the same time respect the language of the other and, through that respect, get his meaning across, and this presupposes what you have called a universal democracy. (*IW* 45)

The democracy to come thus requires at once respect for the idiom and the other *and* translation, at once religious freedom *and* a relation to a future that is disconnected from any particular religious tradition.

Returning to the relationship between revelation and revealability with which we began this chapter, it is notable that Derrida speaks of a "*respect for this singular indecision or for this hyperbolic outbidding between two originarities, the order of the 'revealed' and the order of the* 'revealable'" as being perhaps "*the chance of every responsible decision and of another 'reflecting faith,' of a new 'tolerance'*" (§25). Derrida appears to be calling for a "tolerance" not for this or that dogmatic faith as such, this or that revelation as such, but for the revealability of that revelation, or perhaps better, for the elementary faith that is one of its two origins. A new concept of tolerance is thus required that would break with its Judeo-Christian heritage:

> We would be here to try to think what "tolerance" could henceforth be. I immediately place quotation marks around this word in order to abstract and extract it from its origins. And thereby to announce, through it, through the destiny of its history, a possibility that would not be solely Christian. For the concept of tolerance, stricto sensu, belongs first of all to a sort of Christian domesticity. . . . It was printed, emitted, transmitted and circulated in the name of the Christian faith and would hardly be without relation to the rise, it too Christian, of what Kant calls "reflecting faith"—and of pure morality as that which is distinctively Christian. (§26)

Notice how the quotation marks in the above passage around "tolerance" are used to indicate the *abstraction* or *extraction* of this word from its original context (e.g., in Voltaire) and its grafting or reinscription into a new—call it a deconstructive—context. What is needed is a new tolerance or another tolerance that would at first be located in but then also abstracted from its Judeo-Christian origins. What is needed, says Derrida in the final lines of §26, the final words, presumably, of Derrida's more or less improvised remarks at the Capri conference in February 1994, those that thus conclude "Italics" and precede "Post-scriptum":

> another 'tolerance' [that] would be in accord with the experience of the "desert in the desert," it would respect the distance of infinite alterity as singularity. And this respect would still be religio, religio as scruple or reticence, distance, dissociation, disjunction, coming from the threshold of all religion in the link of repetition to itself, the threshold of every social or communitarian link.
>
> Before and after the logos which was in the beginning, before and after the Holy Sacrament, before and after the Holy Scriptures [les Saintes Écritures]. (§26)

By speaking here in the same breath of both the experience of the desert in the desert as a respect for "*the distance of infinite alterity as singularity*" and of *religio*, now, as distance, dissociation, and disjunction, Derrida is rethinking "religion" itself on the basis of another kind of social bond. Neither the experience of respect or modesty before what must remain safe and sound (*re-legere*) nor the gathering or recollection into a community (*re-ligare*) that then puts up "a resistance or a reaction to disjunction" and "ab-solute alterity" (§34), this *religio* would entail, it seems, a respect for disjunction, for the distance of alterity, or for the inviolable secret. In contrast to what we saw in Chapter 2 to be the two etymologies of religion, Derrida is trying to rethink—to reinscribe, perhaps even to "abstract" and "extract"—a *re-ligio* that would be related to the "link" to the singular other, on the threshold of every community, a "link" or "social bond" that is to be thought in relation not to the repeatable bond that allows for the identification of community members and the indemnification of the community but to the originary greeting—at once relation and interruption of relation—that first opens up, and interrupts in opening up, every community. In short, he is trying to think another "tolerance" in relationship not to some shared idea or ideal but to the testimonial faith that is at the origin of the social bond.

The future of the community is thus secured not by a repetition of the same, by an attempt to keep safe and sound, by an indemnification that would react against the machine in order to return to the original community, to the lived body, to an authentic religious experience, and so on, but by the repetition, which is never without risk, of a threshold gesture, the respect for an infinite alterity, that is, for a nonrepeatable and nongatherable singularity. The very life of the community is thus preserved not by a violence that would protect and indemnify the community from death but by the repetition that opens it to the future—that is, to death as well as living on. The life of the community—or, rather, its living on—is secured only through the machine, secured, I say, but never assured, and never without the risk or possibility of death or of a radical evil rooted in this very openness to the future. As Derrida put it way back in "Freud and the Scene of Writing" (1966), life can "defend itself against death only through an *economy* of death, through deferment, repetition, reserve" ("FSW" 202).

As we will see in what follows, it is precisely those discourses of life that believe they can exclude death, those that believe they can return to a life protected from corruption, that often lead to the worst possible violence, the most nightmarish scenes of death and destruction—all fed by the phantasm of a life greater than life, the dream, in short, of a miracle that can do without the machine.[42]

PART III

Underworlds and Afterlives

He plucks the ripe pomegranate
Looking to make sure
That some pure
Sunshine is left upon it,
Offers it to Persephone,
Who marvels, astonished
To find here in her night
A reminder of earth's light,
The lovely color of delight.
Now with more confidence
She smiles,
Gives way to her appetite,
Seizes the pomegranate,
Takes a bite. . . .
At once
Mercury flies off and
Pluto smiles.
　　—André Gide, "Persephone"

Interlude II

Cyberspace and the Unconscious (Underworld III)

I suggested at the outset of Part II that Don DeLillo's *Underworld* is a great contemporary novel about the relationship between waste, weapons, and faith, the environmental crisis, the weapons industry, and religion. This network of associations or connections is sometimes explicit, conscious and aboveground, and sometimes just below the threshold, in the underworld or unconscious of memory and history. DeLillo's use of the word or image of the *underworld* is itself a perfect example of this: it refers in the novel to the vast landfills that today pockmark our planet, to underground nuclear test sites, but also to the underworld of gangsters, where Nick's father Jimmy is thought to have lived and died; it refers to catacombs, to the New York City subway system, and to the underground basement where Nick's life changes forever as a loaded shotgun discharges in his hands, killing George Manza, a heroine addict who had aroused his interest, his anxiety, and his horror. These are the shades of Nick Shay's underworld, "the underground of memory and collection" (*U* 321), the shades of a past that is seemingly long gone but that can nonetheless rise out of the ashes of memory and of mourning. Living now in Phoenix, descending into the underworld for him means not just going "back East" but back in time (*U* 333), breathing onto the embers of the past in order to revive what remains living within them. For Nick, then, the underworld is both his present and his past, his past as it seeps into the present—and that is, of course, the point: for how does one keep one's underworlds separate, how does one dispose of one's waste or one's past without fear of return? How can one draw a line between one's desires and one's fears, one's dreams and one's nightmares?

"Underworld" thus names Nick's past but also our own; it has been part of our cultural imagination ever since Odysseus recounted his travels to the land of the dead in book 11 of the *Odyssey*. It is also the name, as DeLillo reminds us, of both a 1927 gangster film and Sergei Eisenstein's 1930s classic *Unterwelt*, a film that is described in detail at the center of the novel during a screening at Radio City Music Hall, a film that seems eerily prescient in its depiction of underground prisons, lasers, and nuclear weaponry.[1] By the very end of the novel, *underworld* seems to be the best name for what we now call cyberspace, a vast network of interconnections that can bring together in just a couple of keystrokes the miracle and the machine, faith and weapons, one website devoted to miracles and another to the war machine that is the nuclear bomb. DeLillo thus ends *Underworld* with two sections entitled "Keystroke 1" (*U* 817–24) and "Keystroke 2" (*U* 824–27), the first revolving around a miracle in the Bronx and the second around the bomb and the interconnections made possible by the Internet, by the web that—or at least this is the phantasm—is capable of bringing the entire twentieth century into relationship with itself. "Is cyberspace a thing within the world," the narrator asks, "or is it the other way around? Which contains the other, and how can you tell for sure?" On the Internet—and this will be the last reference to the title of the novel in the novel—you can "follow a word through the tunneled underworld of its ancestral roots" (*U* 826), a word, for example, like the last word of the novel, at once a noun and a greeting, a word that can be used in a constative or as a performative, as an idea or as a prayer—"Peace"—a word the narrator seems to utter, to whisper, whispering without whispering, breathing without breathing, perhaps, as he looks away from the screen, away from the underworld for a moment, to the everyday objects of the room around him.

The underworld of *Underworld* is thus all of this and more—the unconscious, the past, a scene of crime, waste, and weapons, a place of nightmares and, of course, of the triumph of death, the realm ruled over by Hades or Pluto. As Nick Shay, waste management expert, reminds us early in the novel: "We built pyramids of waste above and below the earth. The more hazardous the waste, the deeper we tried to sink it. The word plutonium comes from Pluto, god of the dead and ruler of the underworld. They took him out to the marshes and wasted him as we say today, or used to say until it got changed to something else" (*U* 106). We here see Nick Shay bringing together, tossing together, as if in a landfill, ancient Egyptian history, Greek mythology, contemporary waste and weapons technology, and speculation about his own father's death at the hands of the underworld or the mob, the story of his father being not just simply *whacked*—for that's one of the words it changed to—but, precisely, *wasted* out in the marshes. What waste, what a waste, we might say, but then what is one to do when everything is destined in the end to get wasted? While we would like to treat our waste as something apart, something we remove and keep at a remove, what is to be done when there are, strictly speaking, no limits to waste, when every limit you draw between inside and outside, the world and its waste, gets trashed?

Waste, weapons, and the underworld or the mob—in DeLillo's *Underworld* these are our common lot. And yet, at least initially, most of these seem to designate an essentially *man's* world, like the world of baseball with which we began and the world of gang violence with which we will end, a world with its heroes and its heroine but rarely its heroines, a world with four jacks or four kings, as we saw in the prologue, but not four queens, a world where women often figure but usually only as objects of violence or else as the idealization or phantasms of men. The mere mention of the name *Pluto* or *Hades* in the passage cited above is perhaps enough to recall one of our founding myths of sexual aggression, of violence against women and of death, though also, as we will see, of life and affirmation—the story of Hades and Persephone.

In "Faith and Knowledge," sexual violence and male phantasms of women are related, it would seem, to all the attempts to use the machine in order to return to a supposed nature that would remain intact, safe and sound, indemnified or undefiled. We should not be surprised, then, to see rise up before us the silhouettes of at least three feminine figures, to which we will add at the very end an unexpected and supplemental fourth. After *Khōra*, then, whom we have already seen, will come Gradiva and Persephone, both of whom are evoked by Derrida in "Faith and Knowledge," summoned from their underworld into his text, and then finally, beyond Derrida's essay, elsewhere, the specter of Esmeralda, not the heroine/victim of Victor Hugo's *The Hunchback of Notre Dame* but the runaway of DeLillo's *Underworld*. Like Persephone's, her story will be one of rape and violence; like Gradiva's, it will be a story of phantasms or delusions; and, like *Khōra*, it will be a story of space or of giving space, of giving rise, a story of what might emerge from the underworld whenever there is "Space Available"—the story, in short, of a miracle made manifest by the machine.

7

Mary and the Marionettes

Life, Sacrifice, and the Sexual Thing

As we saw back in Chapter 3, when we were developing the three principal theses of "Faith and Knowledge," religion attempts to indemnify the
first of its two sources by appropriating in an autoimmune fashion the
powers of technoscience. While it has done this from time immemorial,
insofar as "the ether of religion will always have been hospitable to a certain spectral virtuality" (§27n17), religion will have never been quite
as "hospitable" to the spectral as it is today, through all the cable networks and Internet sites and telecommunications satellites that form this
"ether." This autoimmune appropriation of teletechnoscience by religion,
this simultaneous appropriation and rejection of teletechnoscience is, as
we saw, *fatale*—potentially deadly and absolutely unavoidable, ineluctable, a "reaction to the machine [that] is as automatic (and thus machinal)
as life itself" (§37). It is thus not only religion that is autoimmune but,
Derrida suggests, life itself, life in its supposedly indemnified presence and
purity. In order for life itself to continue to be vital, to live on, it must at
once appropriate the machine (in the forms of repetition, the prosthesis,
supplementarity, and so on) and reject it.

But there is, it would seem, an even more essential relationship between
religion and life than this common reaction to the teletechnological machine. In §37, Derrida describes in some detail both the unprecedented
forms religion is taking today in its appropriation of technoscience and the
emphasis that is placed on the value and dignity of life, and particularly
human life, the attempt, in short, through a kind of "anthropological

re-immanentization," to found a new humanism whose origins would be located in religion, to be sure, but which would entail a displacement of absolute value and dignity from the divine order to man. This displacement, which would also seem to spell the end of certain forms of religion, would never be, however, as simple or straightforward as it might at first seem. For life can attain its absolute value and dignity, Derrida argues, only if it is worth more than life, and so only if it is sacrificed in the name of what is always worth more than it, that is, only if it sacrificed in its own name. We thus need to look more closely at this relationship between religion and life, for only then will we be able to understand not only religion's attempt to protect and indemnify life at all costs, indeed, even at the cost of life itself, but the inevitable phantasms of life that emerge from out of this sacrifice.

Derrida develops this emphasis on the human and on human life in a long passage in §37, where several possibilities or forms for today's "return of religion" are sketched out. One form of this "return," he says, can be seen in the "self-destructive affirmation of religion" in its globalatin form, that is, in the "auto-immune" reaction that is found in every "pacifist" appeal within the three Abrahamic monotheisms to a "universal fraternalization" that would seek to go beyond and so destroy all determinate religions in the name of a kind of "ecumenical reconciliation" (§37). These "pacifist," "fraternalistic," and "ecumenical" attempts to go beyond religion would thus be carried out, in conformity with a certain Kantianism, within "the *kenotic* horizon of the death of God" and a concomitant "anthropological re-immanentization (the rights of man and of *human* life)." Derrida describes this as a "self-destructive affirmation of religion" insofar as all obligation with regard to a divine order would seem to have been replaced or sacrificed in the name of the infinite dignity of man.[1]

Derrida thus interprets the "return of religion" not simply, as we saw him say in the interview from *Paper Machine* cited at the outset, in terms of church attendance but in relationship to movements that on their surface appear to be secular or nonreligious, whether national, cosmopolitan, ecumenical, or humanitarian. In §46, Derrida suggests that this appropriation and rejection of technoscience, this autoimmune rejection of technoscience by means of technoscience, can follow—as one might have already guessed—"two avenues that compete with each other and are apparently antithetical," even if both can "as easily oppose or support a 'democratic' tradition" (§46): "*either* the fervent return to national citizenship (patriotism of the home in all its forms, affection for the nation-state, awakening of nationalism or of ethnocentrism, most often allied with Churches or religious authorities), *or*, on the contrary, a protest that is universal, cosmopolitan or ecumenical: 'Ecologists, humanists, believers of all countries, unite in an International of anti-tele-technologism!' " (§46). Derrida follows up this mock call for a new International with one of the most succinct definitions as well as "concrete" examples of the thesis of autoimmunity in "Faith and Knowledge":

> What is involved here, moreover, is an International that—and it is the singularity of our time—can only develop through the networks it combats, using the means of the adversary. At the same speed against an adversary that in truth is the same. . . . Auto-immune indemnification. This is why these "contemporary" movements are obliged to search for their salvation (the safe and sound as the sacrosanct), as well as their health in the paradox of a new alliance between the tele-technoscientific and the **two** sources of religion (the unscathed, *heilig*, holy, on the one hand, and faith or belief, the fiduciary on the other). The "humanitarian" would provide a good example of this. "Peacekeeping forces" as well. (§46)

Derrida's emphasis here on cosmopolitanism and humanitarian in their appropriation of and reaction to the teletechnological machine underscores well the centrality of life and, particularly, human life in so many contemporary religious discourses. Religion makes use in an autoimmune fashion of that which it must resist—the deracinating, abstracting powers of technoscience, teletechnology, and the media—in order to re-root what has been uprooted and return to its origins, in a word, to life, and especially human life. It becomes more and more evident in "Faith and Knowledge" that what is at stake in religion—the beating heart, so to speak, of the first of its two sources, and particularly in the forms religion is taking today—is life, the value, worth, or dignity of life and the necessity of indemnifying that life.

> The *declared* stakes already appear to be without limit: what is the "world," the "day," the "present" (hence, all of history, the earth, the humanity of man, the rights of man, the rights of man and of woman, the political and cultural organization of society, the difference between man, god and animal, the phenomenality of the day, the value or "indemnity" of life, the right to life, the treatment of death, etc.)? (§27)

Life is what must be held in absolute respect, treated with dignity, with retenue or inhibition, protected at all costs. Derrida goes on in this passage to speak of the papal encyclical "*Evangelium vitae*" and its stances "against abortion and euthanasia" and "for the sacredness or holiness of a life that is safe and sound—unscathed, *heilig*, holy—for its reproduction in conjugal love—sole immunity admitted, with priestly celibacy, against human immuno-deficiency virus (HIV)" (§27n17). As we have seen in Derrida's emphasis on *salut*, the sacred or divine promises always to restore, to make intact, to restitute and make whole. All religion thus seems to require saving the living, keeping life intact, indemnified, safe and sound. In §40, it becomes clear that everything we have identified throughout as religion's first source, its drive toward health and salvation, all revolves around the question or the values of life.

> The religion of the living—is this not a tautology? Absolute imperative, holy law, law of salvation: saving the living intact, the unscathed, the safe and sound (*heilig*) that has the right to absolute respect, restraint, modesty. . . . that which is, should remain or should be allowed to be what it is (*heilig*, living, strong and fertile, erect and fecund: safe, whole, unscathed, immune, sacred, holy and so on). Salvation and health. Such an intentional attitude bears several names of the same family: respect, modesty, restraint, inhibition, *Achtung* (Kant), *Scheu, Verhaltenheit, Gelassenheit* (Heidegger), restraint or *holding-back* [*halte*] in general. (§40)

This respect for the living, this modesty or restraint before what must remain unscathed, before what has been identified as the first source of religion, is so central, says Derrida, that it might be seen as "a sort of universal, not 'religion' as such, but a universal structure of religiosity," that which "open[s] the possibility of the religious without ever being able to limit or restrain it." This universal structure might look at first glance like the elementary faith that opens religion without being limited to any determinate form of religion. But Derrida stops short of identifying this reserve or respect for life with the second source of religion for a couple of reasons. First, this second source is the source, as we have seen, not just of religion but of science, indeed it is the source of every social bond. But second, and more importantly, this respect or reticence can already be taken in two directions, toward the best as well as the worst: "On the one hand . . . it is respectful or inhibited abstention before what remains sacred mystery, and what ought to remain intact or inaccessible, like the mystical immunity of a secret. But in thus holding back, the same halting also opens an access without mediation or representation, hence not without an intuitive violence, to that which remains unscathed. That is another dimension of the mystical" (§40). A respect for life can thus lead not only to a reticence before the secret but to the assumption of an immediate access to it, a possibility, Derrida seems to suggest, that can lead to what we might call the "violence" of mystical union. It is at this point that Derrida suggests that this return to life, this indemnification of life, can take, yes, two forms, an absolute respect for life and a sacrifice of the living. Whereas the former would respect and protect life through an absolute prohibition against killing, through an interdiction against abortion, artificial insemination, gene manipulation, through certain forms of vegetarianism, and so on, the second would seek not only the protection of life but the hyperbolization of it through a sacrifice of life. Though very different, indeed as different as the vegetarian and the carnivore, these two movements nonetheless spring from a single source.[2] There is thus, on the one hand, "the absolute respect of **life**, the 'Thou shalt not kill' (at least thy neighbor, if not the living in general)," and, on the other, "the no less universal sacrificial vocation" seen in contemporary practices of animal breeding, slaughtering, and experimentation, practices of using animals or putting them to death, *sacrificing* them, precisely, in the name of a human life that would be worth more than life.[3]

> This mechanical principle is apparently very simple: life has absolute value only if it is worth *more than* life. And hence only in so far as it mourns, becoming itself in the labor of infinite mourning, in the indemnification of a spectrality without limit. It is sacred, holy, infinitely respectable only in the name of what is worth more than it and what is not restricted to the naturalness of the bio-zoological (sacrificeable)—although true sacrifice ought to sacrifice not only "natural" life, called "animal" or "biological," but also that which is worth more than so-called natural life. Thus, respect of life in the discourses of religion as such concerns "human life" only in so far as it bears witness, in some manner, to the infinite transcendence of that which is worth more than it (divinity, the sacrosanctness of the law). (§40)

Because life must ultimately be worth more than life, it is what must be sacrificed in the name of a hyperbolization of life, a life greater than life. Life is sacred, holy, infinitely respectable only in or as the name of what within it is worth more than it. Such a notion of life obviously cannot be limited to the naturalness of biological life, insofar as life, according to this hypothesis or this hyperbole, must go beyond the merely natural; it is thus related to "human life" only insofar as it bears witness to the infinite transcendence of what is worth more than it (divinity, the sacred-holiness of the law, and so on). It is empirical life, then, that must be sacrificed in the name of the law or in the name of life itself, sacrificed as the price to be paid for what is itself priceless, for what must then remain safe, immune, absolute, and so worthy of reserve and respect.[4] Such life would thus resemble what Kant called the "dignity [*Würdigkeit*]" of an end in itself—a value beyond the market and beyond all measurable values.[5]

This theme of sacrifice, so prominent in Derrida's work in texts from *Glas* to "'Eating Well,' or the Calculation of the Subject," to *The Gift of Death*, is complicated in the following section as Derrida speaks of an "ellipsis of **sacrifice**" (§41). The word *ellipsis* is used here in at least two different registers. It is used first to evoke the ellipsis formed around the two foci or sources of religion, one of which involves the indemnification of the safe and sound through sacrifice. As Derrida writes, "This reactivity is a process of *sacrificial indemnification*, it strives to restore the unscathed (*heilig*) that it itself threatens" (§29). The second sense of ellipsis has to do with the exclusion or elision of sacrifice, the ellipsis or—for this is a related meaning—the silencing of sacrifice, the silent respect within it.[6] Derrida thus calls this ellipsis of sacrifice a "*double bind*," a sacrifice of sacrifice that at once does away with sacrifice and transforms or interiorizes it. On the one hand, says Derrida, it seems difficult to imagine a religion "without sacrifice and without prayer" (§41).[7] On the other hand,

> the law of the unscathed, the salvation of the safe, the humble respect of that which is sacrosanct (*heilig*, holy) *both requires and excludes* sacrifice, which is to say, the indemnification of the unscathed, the price of immunity. Hence: auto-immunization and the sacrifice of sacrifice. The latter always represents the same movement, the price to pay for not injuring or wronging the absolute other. **Violence** of sacrifice in the name of non-violence. Absolute respect enjoins first and foremost sacrifice of self, of one's most precious interest. (§41)

A sacrifice of sacrifice, therefore. On the one hand, the violence of sacrifice is carried out in the name of nonviolence. Absolute respect requires *self-sacrifice*, sacrifice of the most proper in the service of the most proper. On the other hand, sacrificing sacrifice is the price to be paid for not damaging what is absolutely other. But, of course, as Derrida writes in an essay entitled simply "Sacrifice," "putting an end to sacrifice is not so easy," for "by sacrificing sacrifice" one simply makes it "undergo a mutation or a supplementary interiorization" ("S" 146; my translation). Sacrifice of sacrifice, therefore, or the replacement of sacrifice by prayer. In "A Silkworm of One's Own," a text written not long after "Faith and Knowledge," Derrida notes precisely this, namely, that "prayer tends to replace, in 'coming together,' the bloody sacrifice and the putting to death of the living creature," a "sacrifice of sacrifice, the end of sacrifice in coming together, its unterminated and perhaps interminable sublimation, the coming together of the infinite coming together in the orison of prayer" ("SW" 70).[8]

So, a respect for life and sacrifice—a double postulation that, says Derrida, happens with the regularity of a technique or a machine, death and repetition being situated, yet again, at the heart of processes that are supposed to protect and even augment life. As Derrida put it in the passage above, "This mechanic principle is apparently very simple: life has absolute value only if it is worth *more than* life" (§40). This is a *mechanics* because the autoimmune indemnification of life through either the absolute respect for life or through sacrifice "reproduces, with the regularity of a technique, the instance of the non-living or, if you prefer, of the dead in the living" (§40). As we will see in a moment, this mechanical and nonliving element or aspect within the living makes possible both life— what Derrida sometimes calls life-death—and what is worth more than life, an abundance of life, or at least the phantasm of such a life.

Derrida sets up this argument by first relating the dignity of life to fetishism and spectrality, which, as we have seen, have been associated with religion from the very beginning but which are playing new and unprecedented roles in the tele-technoscientific religions of today.

> This dignity of life can only subsist beyond the present living being. Whence, transcendence, fetishism and spectrality; whence, the religiosity of religion. This excess above and beyond the living, whose life only has absolute value by being worth more than life, more than itself—this, in short, is what opens the space of death that is linked to the automaton (exemplarily "phallic"), to technics, the machine, the prosthesis: in a word, to the dimensions of auto-immune and self-sacrificial supplementarity, to this death-drive that is silently at work in every community, every *auto-co-immunity*, constituting it as such in its iterability, its heritage, its spectral tradition. (§40)

While life is worth more than life, worth more than itself, in excess of itself, it can only be protected through those very things we have seen to be related to death—technicity, the machine, virtuality, the prosthesis, and, here, the phallus or the phallus effect. Life as what is always worth more than life—the first source of religion—can be indemnified only through an auto-immunitary and auto-sacrificial supplementarity. This excess of life over life is thus related, writes Derrida, to a "death-drive that is silently at work in every community, every *auto-co-immunity*, constituting it as such in its iterability, its heritage, its spectral tradition" (§40).

> Community as *com-mon auto-immunity*: no community [is possible] that would not cultivate its own auto-immunity, a principle of sacrificial self-destruction ruining the principle of self-protection (that of maintaining its self-integrity intact), and this in view of some sort of invisible and spectral sur-vival. This self-contesting attestation keeps the auto-immune community alive, which is to say, open to something other and more than itself: the other, the future, death, freedom, the coming or the love of the other, the space and time of a spectralizing messianicity beyond all messianism. It is there that the possibility of religion persists: the *religious* bond (scrupulous, respectful, modest, reticent, inhibited) between the value of life, its absolute "dignity," and the theological machine, the "machine for making gods." (§40)

The community thus tries to indemnify itself by positing a value greater than life, and so sacrifices the life it holds sacred. It thus opens itself up to all the supplements of life—the machine, the technological, the phallic, and so on—through a principle of sacrificial auto-destruction or a sort of death drive that ruins the principle of self-protection (immunity, life, the sovereignty drive), in view of some invisible and spectral *sur-vie* or survival. There is no community, Derrida argues, that does not entertain or support its own auto-immunity, that is, its own openness to what it cannot indemnify—the other, the future, death, freedom, messianicity.

There is thus violence and aggression in the name of life, a sacrifice of life in order to save life, a use of technoscience in order to indemnify a proper body that would purport to be foreign to and originally protected from all technoscience. This indemnification would be related to a ritual sacrifice that protects or compensates, that reconstitutes or attempts to reconstitute some intact purity, and that does so, oftentimes, upon the body itself, by marking or doing violence to the body itself, or else by replacing it with a kind of phantasm, namely, the phantasm of a body with *total immunity*. Though such a body might then seem to be most living, most protected from death, it would be in the end, as a body closed up within itself, closed off not only from what can harm it but from what can save it or allow it to live on, a body at once completely alive and completely dead. And the same holds for religion more generally: a religion of pure and total immunity would be a religion of death, a religion that would have to sacrifice its very lifeblood in order to live on.

Before turning to some of the phantasms that haunt "Faith and Knowledge," the phantasms, let me say in anticipation, of women, that is, the phantasms of women entertained by men, let us look briefly at how this thinking of the phantasm emerges (in §27 and §39) in relationship to a thinking of the fetish and the phallus. For it is the logic of the phallus that produces the phantasm of a life beyond life, a life to be protected from all exposure to death and thus protected from all life—a life that can be won only by being sacrificed.

To understand the phallus, or what Derrida calls the "phallus effect," in "Faith and Knowledge," it is useful to keep in mind the second of the three theses outlined in Chapter 3. Because the phallus, or the phallus effect, must always be understood in terms of its "double value," it is in the end the best illustration of the way the teletechnological supplement attempts in an autoimmune fashion to indemnify a source that must remain safe and sound (life, the value or dignity of life or of a life beyond life). In the *Beast and the Sovereign*, Volume I, Derrida defines the phallus in the following way: "The *phallus*, which is not the penis, first designated in Greece and Rome for certain ceremonies, that simulacrum, that figured representation of an erect penis, hard, stiff, rigid, precisely like a gigantic and artificially made-up puppet, made of tensed springs and exhibited during rituals and processions. The *phallus is*, itself, like the thing itself that it is, a sort of marionette" (*BS I* 222). I will return in a moment to this equation of the phallus with "a sort of marionette," an association we also see in "Faith and Knowledge" where Derrida speaks of a "marionette, the dead machine yet more than living, the spectral fantasy of the dead as the principle of life and of sur-vival [*sur-vie*]" (§40). For the moment, let me underscore the conjunction of fecundity and the simulacrum in the phallus. Derrida speaks of "this culture or this fetishistic cult of the phallic simulacrum, which honored fecundity or the generative potency in the Dionysiac mysteries," this culture or this cult, then, not of "the organic penis" but of "a prosthetic representation of the penis in permanent erection, a penis that is hard, stiff, and rigid but detached from the body proper, just like a prosthesis, a prosthetic and automatic machine, . . . a rigid automat," an erection that thus "seems to be automatic, independent of will and even of desire" (*BS I* 222). Derrida goes on in *The Beast and the Sovereign*, Volume I, to demonstrate that this simulacrum of sovereign power, now detached from man, now automatic and no longer under the control of an autonomous human being, "is not an attribute of man, of something proper to man, nor indeed proper to anyone, not to the animal and not to God" (*BS I* 222). It is this simulacrum of sovereignty, this figure of automatic movement by means of the technical or mechanical prosthesis, that gives rise to the phantasm of a spontaneous life that is immune from death, a nature before all culture and all technē. It is thus the automaton, the marionette, the prosthesis—all names for "the dead machine"—that produce the spontaneity or superabundance of life, or the fantasy or phantasm thereof.

In its phenomenal appearance, in its *phainesthai*, the phallus retains the values of both "pure and proper presence" and, "by virtue of the law of iterability or of duplication that can *detach* it from its pure and proper presence," "its *phantasma*, in Greek, its ghost, its specter, its double or its fetish" (§39). The phallus effect is thus at once "the *colossal automaticity* of the erection (the maximum of life to be kept unscathed, indemnified, immune and safe, sacrosanct), but also and precisely by virtue of its reflex character, that which is most mechanical, most separable from the life it represents." The phallus effect brings together at once the spontaneity of life, life in its purest form, safe and sound, immune, untouched by the machine, a life that promises what is even greater than life, and the automaticity of the machine, a hyperbolic life in the form of a machine that introduces repetition and duplicity, an automaticity without autonomy that nonetheless looks more living than life itself.

As a mechanical supplement, the phallus, "as distinct from the penis and once detached from the body," is thus nothing other than "the marionette that is erected, exhibited, fetishized,[9] and paraded in processions" (§39). The phallus is indeed to be thought as a marionette, a connection that is initially rather unexpected in "Faith and Knowledge." Though it comes on the scene in what appears to be a somewhat arbitrary and un-motivated manner, in a way that might seem to point back a bit too much to an author pulling the strings from behind the curtain, the logic and necessity of this reference becomes clear when we look at what Derrida says about the marionette in the seminar *The Beast and the Sovereign*, Volume I, and when we understand the crucial role it plays in the transition between a thinking of spontaneity in the male erection and the spontane-ous "swelling" of female pregnancy.

Let me briefly return, then, to the passage from *The Beast and the Sovereign*, Volume I, cited above. Derrida identifies the phallus with a mario-nette in his penultimate seminar of 2001–2 in order to introduce a reading of the marionette in Celan's "The Meridian" and so draw to-gether the themes of sovereignty and teletechnology that he will have been following throughout the seminar. He begins: "Even before holding the marionette to be a phallic figure, a simple figural representation of the phallus, one should remember to the contrary that the phallus is itself originally a marionette" (*BS I* 222).[10] What is significant here about the phallus as a marionette is that it appears more than living, more living than life itself; though a machine, its automatic movement or growth appears nonetheless spontaneous. What is at stake is thus nothing less than

> the equivocality of the living being, precisely, where the living being concentrates, as though into a single value, spontaneity (the "what goes of itself" and flows from the source, what moves by itself, spontaneously, *sponte sua*—this is how the living being in general is defined: the living is spontaneous and moves of itself, it is automotive), . . . automotive spontaneity that gives itself its law . . . [and] its opposite, namely automaticity, or in other words the automat's mechanics of action and reaction—without spontaneity, precisely, and with no autonomous liberty. (*BS I* 220–21)

We can thus see how the spontaneity of life becomes in the marionette or in the phallus indistinguishable from the automaticity of the machine. One might even suspect that it is precisely the automaticity of the machine that gives rise to the phantasm of spontaneity and life in the machine. In any case, it is precisely this concentration of opposing things "as though into a single value," "a single ambiguous value," that makes the phallus such a fecund place for the phantasm, for a phantasm that, as we are about to see, can always go both ways. For if this automatic swelling of the phallus appears to be simply a thing of man, of the male, Derrida warns us that "things are not so simple. In truth they are less simple than ever. As always when sexual differences are in play" (*BS I* 220). As he goes on to argue, "in our typical representation of the marionette, what insistently came to the fore was the feminine figure of the small and the young, the little girl, the touching young girl, even the virgin, the Virgin Mary (*mariole, mariolette*). With the grace, innocence, and spontaneity that usually go with that" (*BS I* 220). Derrida is suggesting here, it seems, that the phallus effect, the spontaneous growth of the phallus, must be thought in relation not only to male erection but to the spontaneous movement and life of the marionette and, thus, of the virgin, who too swells up in a seemingly spontaneous if not miraculous way: "The living being is automotive, autonomous, absolutely spontaneous, sovereignly automotive and at the same time perfectly programmed like an automatic reflex. I insist on this paradox to put back on stage the eminently phallic figure of the marionette, the phallic erection that comes to inhabit, haunt, and double that of the virgin girl. The virgin girl is inhabited by motion, movement, the essentially phallic law of the marionette" (*BS I* 221). It is in the phallic figure of the marionette, then, that spontaneity and automaticity, masculine and feminine, the miracle and the machine, the living and the dead, come together in a most striking way. That is why the question of marionettes keeps coming back, undecidably "whats" and "whos," feminine and masculine, taking on all forms, from marionette as virgin girl, little Mary, to phallic erection, the prosthesis of the phallus *as* marionette and the priapism of the erection without detumescence, erection unto death, the cadaverized erection, tragic and comic: all of which sketched out the *unheimlich*, worrying, and undecidable figure of the marionette as life *and* death, life-death, life death, both the spontaneous and graceful autonomy of the living and the rigid automatism of machine and death. (*BS I* 256)

If the phallus allows for the dream, the phantasm, of an erection without interruption or detumescence, a permanent erection as the source of life itself, the detachability and multiplicity of the phallus figure deflate this phantasm in the name of living on. After all, the permanent erection, what we call Priapism—the phantasm of eternal tumescence—is not just an object of ridicule and comedy but a symbol of tragedy and death.[11] Life, erection, spontaneous growth *without* interruption, life without what the French call *la petite mort*, leads straight to death. As in "Faith and Knowledge," Derrida will thus go on in *The Beast and the Sovereign* to relate this automatic or, rather, spontaneous growth to sovereignty.

This is not a figure, but an essential feature of sovereign power, an essential attribute of sovereignty, its absolute erection, without weakness or without detumescence, its unique, stiff, rigid, solitary, absolute, singular erection. And concretely, this translates, in the political effectivity of the thing, not only as an all-power of the state over life-death, the right of pardon, generation, birth, sexual potency as generative and demographic power, but also the height from which the state has the power to see everything, to see the whole, having literally, potentially, a right of inspection over everything. (*BS I* 215)

Having associated the phallus with the marionette and then both of these with the spontaneity of sovereign power, Derrida goes on to identify contemporary teletechnology as the most striking and visible site for the deployment of this sovereign power.

And today, the sovereign power, the international power of a national sovereignty is also proportionate to its power to see, power to have under surveillance, to observe, take in, archive from a superterrestial height, by satellite, the whole globalized surface of the earth, to the centimeter, and this in the service of the economic strategy of the market as well as of military strategy. This erection towards height is always the sign of the sovereignty of the sovereign, of the head of state or simply the Head, the Dictator, *Il Duce*, the *Führer* or quite simply the political leader, his "leadership." . . . Translated into the theatrical space of the politics of our time, namely the public space called televisual media, all political leaders, heads of state, or heads of parties, all the supposedly decisive and deciding actors of the political field are consecrated as such by the election of their erection to the status of marionette in the puppet show. (*BS I* 215–16)

The phallus thus brings together the calculable and the incalculable, tele-techno-science and the absolute value of life, "faith in the most living as dead and automatically *sur-viving*, resuscitated in its spectral *phantasma*, the holy, safe and sound, unscathed, immune, sacred—in a word, everything that translates *heilig*" (§39). A life, then, that protects itself by means of the technological supplement that sacrifices what it is supposed to protect: it is this logic of autoimmunity and of sacrifice that leads to the phantasm—to a cult or culture of the generalized fetish (of the Thing itself). Unlike Kant, then, who distinguishes between Christianity as the only truly moral religion and all other fetish-worshipping religions (see Observation 1), Derrida seems to be suggesting that we consider the irreducible traces of fetishism even in Christianity. Without putting it in exactly these terms, it is as if Derrida were tracing the spectral presence of fertility cults beneath or within contemporary monotheisms. Again, the contemporary is divided, doubled, at once contemporary and archaic, hyper-sophisticated and primitive.

All three monotheisms, Derrida claims, are thus founded upon a covenant or promise in a trial of the indemnified or an ordeal of the unscathed—that is, in "a circumcision, be it 'exterior or interior,' literal or, as was said before Saint Paul, in Judaism itself, 'circumcision of the heart'" (§39).[12] An originarily indemnified state can thus be brought about only retrospectively by means of a supplementary cut that turns the penis into the phallus, the fecundity of the phallus being assured then only through the fetish, life reaffirmed only through a supplementary violence or sacrifice. Through the circumcisional cut, the penis is transformed, resuscitated, erected into the phallus, so to speak, the undetachable organ transformed into the detachable fetish, a source of life beyond life, a sur-life, a *sur-vie*, that is, a survival but also a surplus life. To the values that have been identified from the beginning of this work with the first source of religion (the indemnified, the safe and sound, the intact, *heilig*) are now attached a new series (life, fertility, spontaneity, growth, and so on). In §38, Derrida puts them in a single line: "*heilig*, holy, safe and sound, unscathed, intact, immune, free, vital, fecund, fertile, strong, and above all, as we will soon see, 'swollen [*gonflé*].'"

Swollen, engorged, puffed up—gonflé: it is at this critical juncture, in the midst of this discourse on the fecundity of the phallus and the automaticity of the phallus effect, that Derrida says that this life force, this erection or swelling of life, can be related to the spontaneity of either erection or pregnancy, that is, to a spontaneity on the side of either the erect male or the bearing female: "One could, without being arbitrary, read, select, connect everything in the semantic genealogy of the unscathed—'saintly, sacred, safe and sound, *heilig, holy*'—that speaks of force, **life**-force, fertility, growth, augmentation, and above all *swelling* [gonflement], in the spontaneity of erection or of pregnancy" (§39).[13]

Vitality, fecundity, and fertility, the spontaneous "swelling" of life in either erection or pregnancy—these are, again, the values of that first source of religion, the one that must be protected, safeguarded, indemnified. But it does not take long for this first source of religion to become contaminated with the machine, as if it were the machine that produced these values in the first place, or at least the phantasm of their purity and indemnified presence. "The tele-technoscientific machine" is thus "this enemy of life in the service of life," and it leads, to cite this crucial passage one more time, to a "faith in the most living as dead and automatically *sur-viving*, resuscitated in its spectral *phantasma*, the holy, safe and sound, unscathed, immune, sacred . . . *heilig*. Matrix, once again, of a cult or of a culture of the generalized fetish, of an unlimited fetishism, of a fetishizing adoration of the Thing itself" (§39). With this reference to a "matrix" (from the Latin *matrix*, "womb"), Derrida is again suggesting that this fetishizing adoration can be found not simply in the putatively "natural" growth and fecundity of the phallus but in the spontaneous and putatively "natural" swelling of the matrix. Indeed, it just may be that it is the desperate attempt to indemnify the latter that needs to be thought in our new wars of religion, wars in which, as Derrida emphasizes, women are so often the primary victims: "And this would perhaps be the place to enquire why, in the most lethal explosions of a violence that is inevitably ethnico-religious—why, on all sides, women in particular are singled out as victims (not 'only' of murders, but also of the rapes and mutilations that precede and accompany them)" (§39). This is a crucial moment in the essay, the moment when Derrida draws attention to a kind of matriarchal and no longer simply patriarchal fertility (or to the phantasm thereof) that seems to operate below the surface, in the underworld, of the three monotheisms. Derrida here appends a long footnote in which he cites Benveniste at length on the common relationship in Indo-European languages between sovereignty, power, and a growth or swelling of strength or power that is related to pregnancy or carrying in the womb. To cite Derrida citing Benveniste, "The holy and sacred character is thus defined through a notion of exuberant and fecund force, capable of bringing to life, of causing the productions of nature to burst forth" (pp. 448–49) (§39n30). Derrida goes on to cite Benveniste on the origins of the Greek verb *kuein* and the adjective *kurios*, commonly translated as "sovereign," a word that was originally related to the sacred through a kind of automatic or spontaneous "swelling." The sacred or holy is related to an exuberant, fecund force capable of bringing to life and increasing the production of nature. It is this exuberant force that feeds religion's attempt to bring about health and salvation, restoration and redemption, indemnification and a maximization of fertility and life. It is also here that the values of spontaneity (life, originality, fecundity, nature, etc.) seem to become confounded with those of automaticity (death, repetition, sterility, technicity, etc.).

That this spontaneous swelling and automatic growth should be attached here not only to the male erection but also to the female womb should come as some surprise (like all pregnancy, perhaps) in this account of the origins of sovereignty.[14] Are there queens as well as kings in this sovereign genealogy? Can we—must we—think them together? As we have seen, the phallus is a fetish or a marionette, a technical supplement that gives the uncanny appearance of life, indeed, that promises to supplement life and give rise to a life more fecund and perhaps more holy and sacred than life itself. The phallus is a technical supplement that would seem to augment and indemnify male sovereign power. And yet it is also the place where the spontaneity and life of this power would seem to cross a female power of spontaneous growth. As Derrida recalls in *The Beast and the Sovereign*, Volume I, the phallus is a marionette and the marionette is a virgin, "even the virgin, the Virgin Mary (*mariole, mariolette*). With the grace, innocence, and spontaneity that usually go with that" (*BS I* 220). Hence the fecund exuberance Derrida speaks of here can be considered either on the side of the king's sovereign power or on the side of the queen's Immaculate Conception—which is, no doubt, why Derrida's *Glas* traces throughout Hegel the values of both Absolute Knowledge (abbreviated through *Glas* as *SA* [*Savoir Absolu*]) and the Immaculate Conception (abbreviated as *IC* [*Immaculé Conception*]).

It is starting from this reference to the phantasm of either the phallus or the womb, either erection or pregnancy, the phantasm of a life that is safe and sound, sacred and sacrosanct, spontaneous and fully alive, immune from aggression, that we should go back and pull together the many references Derrida makes throughout "Faith and Knowledge" to sexual difference. For it is at this point that Derrida recalls or asks why the victims of ethno-religious violence are so often women—and often by rape and mutilation (§39). The answer to this question should begin to become clear: violence against women *and* the sacralization and protection, the indemnification, of them are not opposed but can actually go hand in hand. When "real" women are forgotten, suppressed or repressed, we might even say, the phantasms of them are likely to emerge, their purity made into the object of fetishized desire. When life or life-death is forgotten, when the relationship between life and the technical supplement is denied or repressed, life or life-death is replaced by a hyperbolization of life, the colossal phallus or the spontaneously swollen womb. In an autoimmune reaction against the uprooting or deracination of the phallus effect, against the move beyond life into living on through media and technology, one turns against the living body—though always in the name of this living body and in the name of life. In a reaction against the radical evil of teletechnology, one turns against the living bodies of both men and women through what appear to be pretechnological gestures. Hence roadside bombs detonated by remote control are replaced by more direct, "hands-on" forms of degradation, humiliation, or mutilation, while guns and rocket-launchers give way to decapitations with a single blade stroke—oftentimes, of course, before a video camera.

Derrida thus argues (in §42 and elsewhere) that in today's "wars of religion" "**violence** has two ages" and, in effect, two faces—a *contemporary* violence that makes use of hyper-sophisticated military teletechnology, digital culture, cyberspace, and so on, and a *new archaic* violence that "counters the first and everything it represents" (§42).[15] We see here how the first two theses of "Faith and Knowledge" can help explain the phantasm: in order to indemnify the first of its two sources, religion resorts to the powers of the teletechnoscientific machine, indemnifying but also attacking in an autoimmune fashion its own powers of indemnification and producing the phantasm of a life before the machine: "Revenge. Resorting, in fact, to the same resources of mediatic power, it *reverts* (according to the return, the resource, the repristination and the law of internal and autoimmune reactivity we are trying to formalize here) as closely as possible to the body proper and to the premachinal living being. In any case, to its desire and to its phantasm" (§42).

By turning against the expropriating, decorporealizing machine, one turns to the bare hand—to decapitation and castration, mutilation and rape, to an exposure of bodies—and all this in order to return to the phantasm of the living body. "What is involved is always avowed vengeance, often declared as **sexual** revenge: rapes, mutilated genitals or severed hands, corpses exhibited, heads paraded, as not so long ago in France, impaled on the end of stakes (phallic processions of 'natural religions')" (§42). These are, as Derrida reads them, "symptoms" of a vengeance of the body proper against tele-technoscience, against the globalization or *mondialisation* of the European democratic model, which, as we have seen, is at once secular and religious (§42). It is this autoimmune reaction of the body against the deracinating forms of teletechnology that can explain in today's new "wars of religion" the seemingly paradoxical combination of "irrationalist obscurantism" and "hypercritical acumen and incisive analysis of the hegemonies and the models of the adversary" (§42).

This archaic reradicalization, at once "*modern and archaic*" (§6), thus claims, in the name of "religion," to re-root the living community, to relocate its place, body, and idiom, to leave it or to make it safe and sound, intact. We are back to some of the claims made by Derrida in the interview from *Paper Machine* cited in Chapter 1. But now we should be a bit better prepared to understand the motivations for this return to the proper body or the intact idiom and the reasons why such a return is doomed to its own autoimmune undoing.

> This archaic and ostensibly more savage radicalization of 'religious' violence claims, in the name of "religion," to allow the living community to rediscover its roots, its places, its body and its idiom intact (unscathed, safe, pure, proper). It spreads death and unleashes self-destruction in a desperate (auto-immune) gesture that attacks the blood of its own body: as though thereby to eradicate uprootedness and reappropriate the sacredness of life safe and sound. (§42)

Such violence in the name of religion tries to uproot the uprooting, to reappropriate the safe and sound, to save life by turning on the blood of its own body and on the bodies of its own members, men and, perhaps especially, women. What must thus be recognized is not only, as Joyce says and Derrida loves to cite, that paternity is a legal fiction, that the phallus effect is the effect of a phantasm, but that the Immaculate Conception too is a royal phantasm. As Derrida argues, in an essay entitled "The Night Watch," recent technological advances such as surrogate motherhood and in vitro fertilization have helped demonstrate today what has always and everywhere been the case, namely, that maternity too is a legal fiction, not something we can simply see with our own two eyes in the spontaneous swelling of the womb but something that must be defined, determined, and declared. By recognizing this fiction, we begin to deflate the phantasm of a maternity that would be absolutely pure and natural, and thus the one thing that would need to be protected and indemnified at all costs—even if it means mutilating or sacrificing women in order to protect or purify it. For the phantasm is always a phantasm of purity, the effect of a veiled or elided performative, a speech act that tries to pass itself off as a constative or statement of fact, an elision or an ellipsis of *is* and *ought*. It is always a phantasm of purity and of sovereignty, whence the sovereignty of the phantasm.[16]

Recall that Derrida spoke in the beginning of "Faith and Knowledge" of what is happening to religion today, what is happening that is unique to religion in our time. We now see that not even this *today* is a simple present or a simple unity; it is itself already divided, already duplicitous, inasmuch as today's wars of religion and violence are at once modern *and* archaic, unprecedented *and* already iterations of the origin(s) of religion. Today's wars of religion are thus turned at once toward a certain future and the past, toward the three monotheisms and toward the religions of Greece and Rome, toward hypersophisticated technoscience as well as the sexual thing.

Speaking of the "return of the religious," Derrida argues in "Above All, No Journalists!" that "this return follows the collapse of so many things: empires, totalitarian regimes, philosophemes, ideologemes, etc." He then goes on to emphasize both the *theatrical* dimension of this return and its *psychoanalytic* value, the way in which this "return" is not a rebirth but a return to the stage or a return of the repressed, a return from out of the underworld or the unconscious into the light of day.

> The return does not signify therefore that religion *comes back*, but that it comes back *onto the stage*, and onto one that is global and public. . . . Its return is its *reapparition* on the stage and in no way its rebirth: religion is not born again. . . . All of a sudden it returns to the stage, intact, more alive than ever before. Between *awakening* and *return* there is the outbreak of visibility: religion can finally be practiced in a *manifest* manner, in the force of phenomenality, the alleviation of repression (repression as much in the sense of the unconscious as of politics). There is, because of the repression, an accumulation of force, a heightening of potential, an explosion [*déferlement*] of conviction, an overflowing of extraordinary power. ("AANJ" 72–73)

One thus cannot speak today of religion and its relationship to science, Derrida argues, without psychoanalysis, which is today "receding in the

West," that is, on the decline, having never made it out of a part of "'old Europe.'" For the "return of religion" cannot be thought without "a logic of the unconscious," without some understanding of the repetition compulsion or the death drive, or without a thinking of the reaction to "radical evil," which, says Derrida, is at the center of Freudian thought.

> A *new cruelty* would thus ally, in wars that are also wars of religion, the most advanced technoscientific calculability with a reactive savagery that would like to attack the body proper directly, the **sexual** thing, that can be raped, mutilated or simply denied, desexualized— yet another form of the same violence. Is it possible to speak today of this double rape, to speak of it in a way that wouldn't be too foolish, uninformed or inane, while "ignoring" "psychoanalysis"? (§43)

Psychoanalysis would be necessary to rethink not only "the most powerful discourses today on right, morality, politics, but also on science, philosophy, theology, etc." (§43). It would also be essential to elaborating "a new space of testimoniality" or "a new experience of the symptom and of truth." In short, it would be essential to understanding this "*new cruelty*" that today links the technoscientific machine to a reactive savagery that attacks the body proper—and so raises the question of sexual difference and what Derrida calls the *sexual* thing.[17]

And so it was bound to happen, there on the Island of Capri, during that little retreatlike gathering of European philosophers. Gathered there, we recall, were philosophers from Germany, Spain, France, and Italy, from at least four European nation states speaking four European languages, philosophers from Catholic, Protestant, and Jewish backgrounds, but, we recall, no Muslims, no non-Europeans, and, of course, "*not a single woman!*" Derrida writes early on in the essay: "*We ought to take this into account: speaking on behalf of these mute witnesses without speaking for them, in place of them, and drawing from this all sorts of consequences*" (§5).[18] One must thus speak, says Derrida, "*on behalf of* [pour]" these silent victims and witnesses without speaking "*in place of them* [à leur place]." As Paul Celan wrote and Derrida cites in several places, "Niemand zeugt für den Zeugen," no one speaks for the witness, since the witness is, by definition, irreplaceable, the only one able to bear witness for what has happened uniquely to him or to her.[19] How, then, is one to speak not in place of these witnesses but for them or on their behalf? How is one to give them a place without taking their place?

Derrida recalls in a few places in "Faith and Knowledge" the violence perpetrated in the name of religion against these silent witnesses, the fact that in these contemporary "wars of religion" women are often the primary victims of a new archaic violence, "singled out as victims (not 'only' of murders, but also of the rapes and mutilations that precede and accompany them)" (§39). He explicitly recalls these nameless victims, but he also marks in his text in a more discreet fashion the presence, the spectral presence, not of these women but of certain figures of women, two of which I will follow here. The first of these two figures is, not coincidentally, the archetypal figure of the male phantasm in Freud, namely, Gradiva, while the second is the figure of a woman who, as the victim of rape by Hades, has become the figure of both death and ever-returning life, a figure of sexual violence and fertility or fecundity, namely, Persephone. Though I certainly do not wish to equate or conflate the "real" or historical victims of sexual violence with these figures, I do wish to argue that it is through the latter that we can see most clearly how a thinking of sexual difference in terms of simple opposition lends itself at once to the protection and indemnification of one side of the opposition and to an ever-increasing violence against what is supposedly being protected. In other words, it is only by understanding these *phantasmatic* projections of women by men that we can begin to understand the origins of the violence perpetrated against women and, as a result, begin to speak on their behalf.

Recall that, in the passage from §35 analyzed in detail in Chapter 4, Derrida, after recounting the origins, the genesis, of the conference at Capri, automatically thinks of Gradiva. Just after asking himself, "From where did this come to me, and yes, mechanically?" and after adding, "Once the theme was agreed upon, discussions were improvised— between two walks at night towards Faraglione, which can be seen in the distance, between Vesuvius and Capri," Derrida opens a parenthesis for the ghost of Gradiva to appear: "(Jensen refers to it, Faraglione, and Gradiva returns perhaps, the ghost of light, the shadowless shadow of noon, *das Mittagsgespenst*, more beautiful than all the great ghosts of the island, better 'habituated' than they, as she puts it, 'to being dead,' and for a long time)" (§35). But who exactly is Gradiva, and why does she make such an appearance in "Faith and Knowledge"?

Perhaps the best way to introduce the phantasmatic figure of Gradiva is to recall the way in which this figure so frequently returned to Derrida. In *Archive Fever*, a text written just months after the Capri conference, Derrida says: "For more than twenty years, each time I've returned to Naples, I've thought of her. Who better than Gradiva, I said to myself this time, the *Gradiva* of Jensen and of Freud, could illustrate this outbidding in the *mal d'archive*?" (*AF* 97).

But even when Derrida was not in Naples, Gradiva had a tendency to return or reappear. In an interview with Bernard Stiegler on 22 December 1993, just a couple of months, therefore, before the meeting in Capri, Gradiva returns yet again in the course of a discussion on film, specters, and the nature of the trace. To understand her reappearance on this stage, a bit of context and staging is necessary: Derrida is recounting for Stiegler the experience of making the 1983 film *Ghost Dance*, with the French actress Pascale Ogier, and of having to repeat the line, suggested by the filmmaker Ken McMullen, "And what about you, do you believe in ghosts?" to which Pascale Ogier was to respond, "Yes, now I do, yes" (*ET* 119). He then goes on to recall the strange experience he had some years later of watching and discussing the film with students at a university in Texas, the truly uncanny experience of seeing Pascale Ogier on the screen a couple of years after her unexpected death.

> Imagine the experience I had when, two or three years later, after Pascale Ogier had died, I watched the film again in the United States, at the request of students who wanted to discuss it with me. Suddenly I saw Pascale's face, which I knew was a dead woman's face, come onto the screen. She answered my question: "Do you believe in ghosts?" Practically looking me in the eye, she said to me again, on the big screen: "Yes, now I do, yes." Which now? Years later in Texas. I had the unnerving sense of the return of her specter, the specter of her specter coming back to say to me—to me here, now: "Now . . . now . . . now, that is to say, in this dark room on another continent, in another world, here, now, yes, believe me, I believe in ghosts." (*ET* 120)[20]

This anecdote about Pascale Ogier leads Derrida in this interview with Stiegler—this filmed and recorded interview—to reiterate a thinking of the trace, of the survival of the trace in the absence of the author or the speaker, a thesis Derrida had developed in texts as early as "Signature Event Context" in 1971 and that he would go on to develop in works right up to *Learning to Live Finally*, Derrida's interview with *Le Monde* in the summer of 2004. Relating this thinking of the trace as that which always, in principle, survives the living speaker, Derrida suggests that the uncanny experience of watching in Texas the screened image of Pascale Ogier speaking of ghosts after her death was a possibility inscribed already at the beginning, a possibility of repetition in her absence that already haunted the supposedly live presence of the original utterance. Derrida continues:

But at the same time, I know that the first time Pascale said this, already, when she repeated this in my office, already, this spectrality was at work. It was already there, she was already saying this, and she knew, just as we know, that even if she hadn't died in the interval, one day, it would be a dead woman who said, "I am dead," or "I am dead, I know what I'm talking about from where I am, and I'm watching you [*Je suis morte, je sais de quoi je parle, d'où je suis, et je te regarde*]," and this gaze remained dissymmetrical, exchanged beyond all possible exchange, eye-line without eye-line, the eye-line of a gaze that fixes and looks for the other, its other, its counterpart [*vis-à-vis*], the other gaze met, in an infinite night. (*ET* 120)[21]

It is just after recounting this experience that Derrida in effect turns to Stiegler, with the camera rolling, and says—as if he had just been haunted by the memory of another ghost—"You will remember what Gradiva said: 'For a long time now, I have been used to being dead'" (*ET* 120).

So, just a little more than two months before the gathering on Capri, Derrida thinks of an experience of spectrality that is made all the more poignant through teletechnology, through film, and as he recounts his experience of looking into the eyes of the then-deceased Pascale Ogier, he thinks of Gradiva. Then, in "Faith and Knowledge," at a conference organized on the topic of religion on the island of Capri, not far from Pompeii, Gradiva reemerges, not once but twice. She returns for the first time in §35, as Derrida recounts his meeting with Ferraris in the Hotel Lutétia in Paris: "Once the theme was agreed upon, discussions were improvised—between two walks at night towards Faraglione . . . (Jensen refers to it, Faraglione, and Gradiva returns perhaps)." Speaking, then, of not one but two walks towards Faraglione, and both at night—as if what was excluded by day were destined to return at night—Gradiva returns, briefly, parenthetically, only to return again, and again this can hardly be a coincidence, in the final, parenthetical paragraph of "Faith and Knowledge," which begins: "(*This, perhaps, is what I would have liked to say of a certain Mount Moriah—while going to Capri, last year, close by the Vesuvius of Gradiva.*)"

Twice within parentheses Gradiva returns, precisely like a specter, a specter, moreover—and Gradiva will not be the last of this kind—who comes to us from out of a literary text. For the figure of Gradiva comes from the 1903 novella of Wilhelm Jensen, which Freud reads in *Delusion and Dream*.[22] With a name that means "she of the graceful walk," the graceful marionette, we might even say, or the mariole full of grace, "Gradiva" is a delusional figure for the main character in Jensen's story, the German archeologist Norbert Hanold. Prompted by the vision of a bas-relief from Pompei of a young woman with a particularly graceful gait, a young woman buried in ash by the eruption of Vesuvius in 79 A.D., this figure comes to life in Norbert's delusions as he is visiting Pompei.

We eventually come to learn, in the course of Jensen's story, that Norbert's delusion is the result of his repressed desire for the daughter of a famous German professor who lives across the street in the German city where Norbert lives. When Norbert goes to Pompeii on the pretext of doing archaeological work, he ends up encountering the real-life version of Gradiva that led to his delusion, Zoë Bertgang, his neighbor's daughter, who is accompanying her father on his own research trip. There in Pompeii, Zoë Bertgang, feeling the same affection for Norbert that Norbert feels for her and understanding the nature of his delusion, helps cure Norbert of his delusional vision by trying, in effect, to substitute her own living and breathing existence for the dead Gradiva. Because Gradiva had come to replace her in the eyes of Norbert, she must remove the veil from Norbert's eyes and show him that she is the living woman behind the veil of the dead Gradiva. She does this, in the art of Jensen analyzed by Freud, through a series of equivocal statements that can be understood both from within Norbert's delusional state and from outside it. When Gradiva, a.k.a. Zoë Bertgang, thus says, for example, to Norbert, "For a long time I have been accustomed to being dead," Norbert, in his delusional state, can hear this as meaning, "For a long time now I, Gradiva, buried alive in Pompeii in 79 A.D. but now come to life, have been accustomed to being dead," while the reader, who begins to understand the repressed cause of the delusion and who, like Zoë Bertgang, occupies a place similar to that of the analyst, can hear it as meaning, "For a long time now I, Zoë Bertgang, have been accustomed to being dead in your eyes, accustomed to being ignored, neglected, repressed, as if I did not exist or as if I had been replaced by Gradiva."

It is hard to resist speculating upon the relationship here between the exclusion of women from the meeting on Capri and the double appearance of Gradiva, along with Derrida's reminders that women, unnamed women, have often been the principal victims of religious violence. There on the island of Capri, not far from Vesuvius, a number of European men had gathered to discuss religion. With no women in the room, no women at the table, it is as if this apparition were there to remind us that when women are forgotten they tend to return—like Gradiva—as delusions or phantasms to replace the living. In the story of Gradiva written by Jensen and interpreted by Freud, Zoë Bertgang is forgotten, abandoned, repressed by the protagonist archaeologist, and what takes her place in this repression, through this repression, is the dangerous delusion of a woman who would seem to go beyond mere life, beyond *Zoë*, precisely, in the figure of the once ashen and dead but now ivory-cheeked and living, resurrected and resuscitated, Gradiva, a walking talking marionette.[23] When living desire is repressed or goes underground, it is replaced by a symptom, in this case, by the delusion of a life beyond life or of a life that has overcome death some nineteen hundred years after the fact. Let me go beyond Freud's language in this text but not beyond Derrida's: when "real" life, life itself, which is to say life-death, life insofar as it is always compromised—*entamé*—by death, is repressed, what takes its place is a delusion or a phantasm of a proper body that goes beyond life, the phantasm of a body that has been resuscitated or resurrected from the ashes of Pompeii, a phantasm, then, that transcends life, death, language, and alterity. In other words, when the specter of life-death is repressed, what takes its place is the phantasm of pure life. Life without technique or without the machine, life that has not yet been compromised by death or repetition—*that*, in the end, is the phantasm.[24]

In addition, then, to the spectral presence of the unnamed women who are the victims of sexual violence, what appears in "Faith and Knowledge" are not, so to speak, "real" women for whom one might pretend or presume to speak, but a delusional or phantasmatic figure of women *for men*, or else, in the case of *khōra*, the figure of what resists and yet makes possible all figuration (and what, let me note parenthetically, made possible in Heidegger's "The Origin of the Work of Art" the projection or even the phantasm of a peasant woman into Van Gogh's famous "still life" with shoes).[25] In each case, it seems, women are mentioned in the context of the phantasms of men, as the delusions of men—and the woman most clearly evoked by Derrida himself, Gradiva, the phantasm of Jensen's archaeologist, makes this clear.

But it did not take an explicit reference to Gradiva for the notion of the phantasm to appear in "Faith and Knowledge." It is, we recall, introduced earlier in the essay in order to describe the "spectral virtuality" of today's "wars of religion," where, as we have seen, all kinds of teletechnology are appropriated in the name of the immunity, indemnity, and sacrality of *life*. Hence the pope uses the machine in order to protect life, a life, Derrida ultimately argues, that attempts to go beyond life, that hyperbolizes life, that tries to restore its health and secure its salvation, in a word, that makes life into the object of a phantasm.

Given this, the cyberspatialized or cyberspaced wars of religion have no stakes other than this determination of the "world," of "history," of the "day" and of the "present." The stakes certainly can remain implicit, insufficiently thematized, poorly articulated. By repressing them, on the other hand, many others can also be dissimulated or displaced. Which is to say, as is always the case with the topics of repression, inscribed in other places or other systems; this never occurs without symptoms and fantasies, without specters (*phantasmata*) to be investigated. (§27)

This would appear to be the first clue about how we should interpret the appearance of Gradiva in Derrida's text, Gradiva, who is not only explicitly called a fantasy or phantasm and a symptom in Freud's text but whose name, in psychoanalysis, is almost a synecdoche for repressed desire, Gradiva, whom Derrida will follow with much greater attention just a couple of months later when, in Rome and then Naples, he will write the final sections of *Archive Fever*.[26]

As Freud argues in *Delusion and Dream* and elsewhere, repression leads not to effacement but to displacement, to the transformation of desire into dreams, into art, into religion, and into delusions that can be read as the symptoms of desire. What is repressed, pushed into the unconscious or into the underworld, returns and returns again—as phantom, as delusion, or as symptom. That is perhaps why Derrida refers in not just one but two places to Gradiva, though perhaps also, even if her name is not spoken, to Persephone.

8

Pomegranate Seeds and Scattered Ashes

From n + 1 to the One + n

Though the name *Persephone* is never pronounced in "Faith and Knowledge," her story might nonetheless be heard, or her figure seen, lurking in the background of the essay, from the various references to rape and sexual assault to, perhaps, Jensen's story of Gradiva, where we read of "a winged messenger [who] had come up from the asphodel meadows of Hades to admonish the departed one to return."[1] But it is really an image or an emblem that most clearly brings the specter of Persephone onto the stage of the essay. Derrida concludes the next to the last section of "Faith and Knowledge" with this striking image, in a fragment without a verb: "Emblem of a still life: an opened pomegranate, one Passover evening, on a tray [*emblème d'une nature morte: la grenade entamée, un soir de Pâques, sur un plateau*]" (§51).[2] Emblem of a still life—of what is called in French *une nature morte* (literally "a dead nature"): a cut or opened pomegranate on a tray during a religious celebration. Everything about this phrase, as well as the lines preceding it, sounds like a memory (Sam Weber calls it a "screen memory"[3]), the memory of an actual painting, perhaps, or even more likely a childhood memory of Passover in a Sephardic Jewish family in Algeria, a memory that resurfaces from its underworld to haunt Derrida and invade his text on religion on its closing page, a memory whose central image is itself haunted by a long history of religion or religions.

In the Old Testament or Hebrew Bible, the pomegranate is an important religious symbol. It adorns, for example, priestly garments and the Palace of King Solomon.[4] As Sam Weber reminds us, it is also a fruit that, in the wake of the exile after the "Passover," came "to signify the pleasures left behind but also those they hoped one day to recover."[5] It is thus no surprise that this fruit would become associated with religious celebrations, particularly Jewish ones, and particularly Sephardic Jewish ones, in the Mediterranean and the Middle East, a fruit commonly eaten during celebrations of Rosh Hashanah or the Jewish New Year. But since, as we saw in Chapter 6, "Jewgreek" is always, for Derrida, "greekjew" (see "VM" 153), we must recall that the pomegranate is also an image out of Greek mythology, one that is almost a synecdoche for the underworld and, especially, for the goddesses of the underworld. Indeed it is difficult not to associate this image of the pomegranate with the figure of Persephone—or, more to the point, it would have been difficult for the one who wrote of Persephone, of the phonē of Persephone, in "Tympan" and elsewhere, not to associate the pomegranate with this goddess of the underworld, who spends half the year below the earth, in the land of the dead, and half the year above it.

In the context of "Faith and Knowledge" and of the figures of the phantasm that we have been following, it is also hard not to recall that Persephone (also named Korē, not exactly Khōra, but close), daughter of Demeter and Zeus, was abducted and sexually assaulted by Hades while picking flowers in a meadow and forced to live in the underworld with him. Inconsolable over the loss of her daughter, Demeter abandoned her role as fertility goddess, causing crop failure and famine and threatening the human race with extinction. To remedy these ills, Zeus sent Hermes to the underworld to persuade Hades to release Persephone, though Zeus tricked Persephone before her release into eating six (or in some accounts three) seeds of a pomegranate, making her unable to leave the underworld permanently and obliging her to return to Hades for six (or in some accounts three) months of the year. Hence Persephone was allowed to live part of the year with her mother Demeter above the earth and forced to live part with Hades in the underworld. Persephone thus came to symbolize the violence of men against women, and particularly the violence of rape, and young girls and women would offer sacrifice to her as the patroness and protectress of marriage and childbirth.[6] The pomegranate itself thus became, in Greek mythology and religion, an image of all these polarized and conflicting values. It is perhaps not a coincidence, then, that in a text on the duplicity of sources, a text first conceived on an island in the absence of women, Derrida would end—or almost—with this image, this still life, this *nature morte*, of the pomegranate and with this allusion to Persephone, who appears more than once in Derrida's corpus, from as early as "Tympan" in 1972, a text written from within the ear canals of

Amsterdam, so to speak, and whose right column begins with a quote from Michel Leiris's essay "Perséphone": "And I have chosen, as the sign beneath which to place them, the entirely floral and subterranean name of *Persephone*, which is thus extracted from its dark terrestrial depths and lifted to the heavens of a chapter heading" (*MP* x).[7]

"Emblem of a still life: an opened pomegranate [*grenade entamée*], one Passover evening, on a tray." The context leaves little room for doubt that the French word *grenade* should indeed be translated here as *pomegranate*. To translate it in any other way would be unwise if not downright perverse. But one will recall that, back in the opening chapter, when we tried to account for the rather baroque, even florid, layout of "Faith and Knowledge" we noted that the phrase . . . *et grenades* is used earlier by Derrida, between §37 and §38, to designate the final fifteen sections and to complete, it seems, the section title for the second half of the essay, "*Crypts . . . et grenades*." After recalling at the end of §37 the two sources of religion and the two notions of source, one taking the form of a machine (the form of mechanization, automatization, machination, etc.) and the other the form of living spontaneity (the indemnified propriety of life, the putative self-determination and spontaneity of the living community, etc.), Derrida places an ellipsis and two little words between the end of this section and the beginning of the following one: " . . . *et grenades*." He then opens a parenthesis and writes—once again in italics: "(*Having posed these premises or general definitions, and given the diminishing* space *available, we shall cast the fifteen final propositions in a form that is even more granulated, grainy, disseminated, aphoristic, discontinuous, juxtapositional, dogmatic, indicative or virtual, economic; in a word, more than ever telegraphic*.)" (My emphasis on "space available.") The allusion here to casting "granulated, grainy, disseminated" sections certainly helps justify the translation of *et grenades* in this case too as "and pomegranates," a word, a fruit, that immediately calls to mind the granulated seeds within it. But can we really assure ourselves of this translation and exclude from consideration the other meaning of *grenades*—namely, grenades?[8] Might not the title of what Derrida calls an ever more "disseminated," "discontinuous," and "telegraphic" presentation of propositions be translated—as Sam Weber, the translator of "Faith and Knowledge" has himself suggested—not only as "*and pomegranates*" but as "*and grenades*"?[9] If so, then Derrida could have hardly found a better word to express the duplicity of sources—the possibility of good or ill, chance or threat—than the French word *grenades*: a word that splits in two at the origin, that becomes immediately opened, *entamé*, divided, disseminated, exploded into all kinds of oppositions—an image of religion and science, of mythology and technoscience, of faith and knowledge, Greek mythology and Jewish religion, religious celebration and war, life and death. This word divides already from the beginning, automatically, spontaneously, mechanically, into two sources, the pomegranate as an image of fruitful dissemination, with its red seeds that can be eaten or scattered to bring new life—an image, then, that gathers and symbolizes, that inseminates and deseminates—*and* the grenade as an explosive machine that scatters and destroys, that tears into pulpy flesh with shrapnel, drawing blood and bringing death.[10]

Et grenades—and pomegranates, and grenades: we must not choose, it seems to me, at this crucial juncture in "Faith and Knowledge," even if the second use of the word *grenade* at the end of the essay would seem to argue for one meaning rather than another. Like the word *pharmakon*, already a kind of grenade thrown into Plato's critique of writing in the *Phaedrus*, the word *grenade* would itself be a *pharmakon*. It contains two opposing, conflicting, almost contradictory values that make it dangerous to grab hold of and turn in one direction or another without blowing one's hand off. Just like *pharmakon*, it means, in effect, both remedy and poison and so defies all our attempts to read, interpret, or even understand it all at once.

Et grenades—the phrase is itself a grenade that explodes on contact, a pomegranate that is already from the origin in dispersion, already opened or breached, already *entamé*.[11] Without a clear context, this two word phrase—inserted into the text like an oblique offering, lobbed into its midst like a little word bomb—defies any kind of univocal translation, any attempt to protect, safeguard, or indemnify one meaning from the other, the pomegranate from the grenade, the natural miracle from the technoscientific machine. It is in just these terms that Derrida, in "A Silkworm of One's Own," another important text on religion, speaks of a certain theory of translation: "In its received truth, translation bets on a received truth, a truth that is stabilized, firm and reliable (*bebaios*), the truth of a meaning that, unscathed and immune, would be transmitted from one so-called language to another in general, with no veil interposed, without anything essential sticking or being erased, and resisting the passage" ("SW" 55). What Derrida says here about translation pertains to all writing, and first of all to his own essay in *Veils* (that is, in *Voiles*, which means at once veils and sails), an essay entitled "Un ver à soie"—yet another title that divides and multiplies, since it can be heard to mean either "a silkworm [*un ver à soie*]" or "a worm [*un ver*: though perhaps also a verse, a line of poetry: *un vers*] of one's own [*à soi*]," hence the suitably rendered English title by Geoffrey Bennington, which brings with it an air of literature à la Virginia Woolf, "A Silkworm of One's Own." Written in November and December 1995, that is, just months after "Faith and Knowledge" was completed, Derrida's warnings about wanting to keep a meaning unscathed and immune should cause us to hesitate before a phrase like *et grenades* and to follow out all of its disseminal or explosive implications and consequences.

Yes, *all of them*, which probably cannot be counted or calculated—or else, why not, counted as a very large number, like 613, the number of commandments in the Torah but also the number of seeds often attributed to the pomegranate, one for each of these commandments, which is why the pomegranate is a particularly appropriate fruit for Jewish religious celebrations. Between *physis* and *nomos*, one might say, the number 613 would thus be both the natural number of seeds of the pomegranate and, as Derrida himself reminds us in "A Silkworm of One's Own," the lawful number of the positive (248) and negative (365) precepts of the Torah. It would also be the number that governs the weaving of the tallith or prayer shawl, "the numerical value of the word designating the fringes of the tallith, the tzitziths, is 600, plus 8 threads and 5 knots, making 613" ("SW" 64). In a later section of "A Silkworm of One's Own," Derrida speaks yet again of his tallith and inscribes or weaves into this passage, which dates from 24 November to 8 December 1995, the title of the essay that we have been reading throughout this work:

> I love it and bless it with a strange indifference, my tallith, in a familiarity without name or age. As if faith and knowledge, another faith and another knowledge, a knowledge without truth and without revelation, were woven together in the memory of an event to come, the absolute delay of the verdict, of a verdict to be rendered and which is, was, or will make itself arrive without the glory of a luminous vision. My white tallith belongs to the night, the absolute night. You will never know anything about it, and no doubt neither will I. ("SW" 84–85)

We have seen these terms and these themes before, but not woven together in precisely this way: "without age" is how *khōra* was described in §24; "a knowledge without truth and without revelation" is more or less how Derrida distinguishes *khōra* from the knowledge and revelation of a sovereign Good or a sovereign God; a verdict or decision "without the glory of a luminous vision" is how Derrida understands the place of *khōra*, or the place of a messianicity without messianism, "the memory of an event to come"; and, finally, the tallith, the white tallith, as what belongs to the "night, the absolute night" also resembles *khōra* as "the place of absolute exteriority," the "nocturnal source" of both religion and science. The tallith is thus, in some sense, another name for *khōra*, the place that gives place and has no name that is absolutely proper to it.

In "A Silkworm of One's Own," Derrida seems to oppose sight and touch, the veil and the prayer shawl, the unveiling of a truth that would be independent of our designation of it and the making of truth through the performative of prayer. For the tallith is not, after all, a veil that might be lifted to reveal the truth, the truth of being or the truth of religion, but a shawl of benediction or of prayer through which or thanks to which the truth is made.[12] "Like benediction," writes Derrida in the penultimate section of "Faith and Knowledge," "prayer pertains to the originary regime of testimonial faith or of martyrdom that we are trying to think here in its most 'critical' force" (§51). To return to the terms developed earlier, prayer does not belong to the regime of dogmatic belief or knowledge, the regime of truth as unveiling or as revelation, the regime of the constative, but to that of an originary, elementary, or testimonial faith, to the regime of the performative that is itself an event, beyond the possibilities and the power of the subject. As we read in "Faith and Knowledge," the truth of prayer "maintains itself . . . beyond the true and the false" (§51), that is, in a word, beyond ontotheology.[13]

It is here that Derrida in "Faith and Knowledge" invokes the figure of the Marrano that is so important to many of his texts on religion. He thus writes near the end of the fifty-first of the fifty-two sections of the essay: "ontotheology en**crypts** faith and destines it to the condition of a sort of Spanish Marrano who would have lost—in truth, dispersed, multiplied— everything up to and including the memory of his unique secret." And then Derrida adds the line we looked at above: "Emblem of a still life: an opened pomegranate, one Passover evening, on a tray" (§51). Faith would thus be encrypted like a Marrano within religion, given a chance to circulate within a religion only on the condition of hiding or being concealed within it. As Derrida recalls in several places, a Marrano was a Spanish or Portuguese Jew who was forced during the Inquisition to convert to Catholicism. The Marrano thus had to renounce or else conceal his or her Jewish identity to avoid persecution and so became a sort of secret Jew, a Jew who must keep his or her identity secret or maintain a secret identity.[14] Faith, Derrida suggests, would be encrypted in ontotheology in this way, sublimated, one might say, forced underground, forced to go by other names or go about in other guises, able to reveal its true identity only to other members of the same secret community.[15] If ontotheology is, as Sam Weber nicely summarizes it, "a tradition that seeks to subordinate the thinking of both being (*ontos*) and god (*theos*) to a certain *logos* and to its logic of self-presence and indivisible identity," then faith would be a Marrano that eludes this putative self-presence (like a crypt within ontotheology) and opens this seemingly indivisible identity (like a cut pomegranate).[16]

But the Marrano Derrida is evoking here would be a Marrano even to this secret community, a Marrano of Marranos, then, a secret even for or to those in on the secret, not unlike the desert within the desert that is *khōra*. It is in this sense that we must understand why Derrida refers to himself not only as "a sort of Marrano of French Catholic culture" but, in an untranslatable French phrase, as *le dernier des juifs*, that is, as the "last of the Jews," "the least of the Jews," but also "the most Jewish of Jews," the most because the least, the least became the most, the first because the last, and so on ("C" 154).[17]

We have thus seen how, in "Faith and Knowledge," a single source automatically, spontaneously, mechanically fissures or, through fission, splits in two, making possible the differences between science and religion, between religion as revealability and religion as revelation, between rootedness or enracination and tele-technological abstraction, between reactive aggression toward science and affirmative reappropriation of it, and, finally, between two sorts of *grenades*, the pomegranate and the grenade, Persephone and all the unnamed victims of religious violence. What we are left with, then, are the traces of this originary splitting or duplicity, the ashes of what cannot be revived or resuscitated like Gradiva in its indemnified purity but must be left to mark the place of an incineration—like a signature.

Derrida, in §51, begins to draw "Faith and Knowledge" to a close with what appears to be an autobiographical flourish, the childhood memory, we have speculated, of a pomegranate opened on a tray during a religious feast. This image of a pomegranate can lead us toward either myth and memory, toward a certain incalculability, or toward calculation and calculability, the number of seeds of the pomegranate or the number of precepts of the law. Perhaps this is the place, then, to consider a bit further the whole question of numbers and calculation, which haunts the entirety of Derrida's text and takes on a certain supplementary force at its end. It is a question that has been at the center of my book as well, and from the very beginning. Even in our brief look at DeLillo's *Underworld*, this great novel on religion in America, there have been innumerable references to number and calculability, from the number 13, so prominent on that miracle day (10/3) in '51 to the rusting B-52s of the following chapter, to the relationship between a certain calculability in science, in weapons technology and so on, and the incalculability of waste and of the weapons of war and religion. As for "Faith and Knowledge," pretty much everything in this essay will have been determined by a kind of numbers game that combines chance and calculation, from the 52 numbered sections of the essay to the two sets of 26 into which they are divided, one of these being further divided into 11 and 15. From the three theses about two sources and their one common element to the question of what legitimates putting all three monotheisms into the single category named "religion," at issue always and everywhere has been the question of the possibility of counting, the question of what counts and of what can be counted. As Gil Anidjar succinctly puts it in his introduction to "Faith and Knowledge," "religion counts" (*AR* 40).

In the crucial passage we looked at in Chapter 4, where Derrida at once recounts the origin of the theme of the conference at Capri and then proceeds to explain that his own contribution would be to write some 52 sections distributed over some 25 or so pages, Derrida asks, "But why, always the question of number, were there ten commandments, subsequently multiplied by so and so many?" (§35). We thus see Derrida, throughout "Faith and Knowledge," "constantly trying to think the interconnectedness . . . of knowledge *and* faith, technoscience *and* religious belief, calculation *and* the sacrosanct," as well as "the alliance, holy or not, of the calculable and the incalculable" (§44). In any number of ways, therefore, the question of number, of the machine and the counting machine, is at the center of Derrida's thinking about the nature of religion today.[18]

What are we to make, then, of the fact that the passage that speaks of the Marrano, of prayer, of the encryption of faith in ontotheology, and of an opened pomegranate on a tray (§51), is surrounded by two passages on calculation that offer two seemingly similar and yet very different formulations for thinking religion today: "*n* + One" (§50) and "the One + *n*" (§52)? As we will see, these two formulations are neither the same—they are not two different ways of saying the same one thing—nor opposites, since both will prove to be at once expressions and products of a process of supplementarity (or autoimmunity) that Derrida will have been developing with regard to religion from the very beginning of "Faith and Knowledge." Before turning to these passages, however, it will be worth looking briefly at other places in the essay where the question of numbers and calculation is raised.

In §44 Derrida addresses the question of numbers in a very explicit and direct way: "The question of number concerns as much the quantity of 'populations' as the living indemnity of 'peoples.' . . . When they feel themselves threatened by an **expropriative delocalizing** tele-technoscience, 'peoples' also fear new forms of invasion. They are terrified by alien 'populations,' whose growth as well as presence, indirect or virtual—but as such, all the more oppressive—becomes incalculable" (§44). Among the many questions of number that return quite regularly in "Faith and Knowledge" is thus the question of demographics, from the question of how to count peoples or the faithful when it comes to religion to the real or imagined problems that stem from demographic shifts in religious affiliations or practices. Recall that, in our analysis of §37 in the previous chapter, we saw Derrida referring, in the context of a passage on the value of the human and of human life, to a certain "demographic disproportion" that must be taken into account today. Derrida was, in essence, raising what might be called the biopolitical stakes of today's new "wars of religion," at the intersection, as always, of *bios* and *tekhnē*, life and technology. From "Islamism" (not to be confused with Islam), which, says Derrida, "represents today the most powerful example of such fundamentalisms as measured by the scale of global demography" (§37n28; see §6), to the survival of the State of Israel or of the Jewish people, the unique source of the three monotheisms, the question of numbers in relation to life is absolutely crucial.[19] At issue is always the safety and security, the indemnity, even the salvation of peoples and the reactive responses of populations when they are threatened. The question of numbers, of demographics, but also of calculation thus continues to haunt the three monotheisms, that is, the three great religions of One God or of the One God, of a God who, as Derrida often phrases it, "is One."

In §50—the section just before the reference to the pomegranate—Derrida again poses the question of number and asks why it is necessary for there to be always more than one source.

> **Calculability**: question, apparently arithmetic, of two, or rather of $n + $ One, through and beyond the demography of which we spoke above. Why should there always have to be *more than one* source? . . . Because there are, for the best and for the worst, division and iterability of the source. This supplement introduces the incalculable at the heart of the calculable. . . . But the more than One [*plus d'Un*][20] is at once more than two. There is no alliance of two, unless it is to signify in effect the pure madness of pure faith. The worst violence. The more than One is this $n + $ One which introduces the order of faith or of trust in the address of the other, but also the

mechanical, machine-like division (testimonial affirmation and reactivity, "yes, yes," etc., answering machine and the possibility of **radical evil**: perjury, lies, remote-control murder, ordered at a distance even when it rapes and kills with bare hands). (§50)

Already from the beginning there is division and iterability, a supplementarity that introduces incalculability into the heart of the calculable. There is thus immediately more than one, and, in fact, already more than two (see §29), since if there were in the end just two sources these might, says Derrida, enter into an alliance or covenant with one another and so produce the worst. Such an alliance would be, as he puts it, the pure folly of pure faith—the worst violence—since faith, originary faith, would then be bound to some singular expression or idiom, some singular religion, a religion absolutely coextensive with faith.[21] Neither 1 nor 2, then, but n + One, which introduces the necessity of the supplement (always one more, + One) to any set or number, the necessity, therefore, of incalculability and the order of faith or *fiabilité* in the address to the other, the opening of every set to what exceeds it, to a future that is incalculable from within it.[22]

The formula "n + One"—which Derrida speaks of earlier in relation to the testimonial deus ex machina (§29)—suggests that for any n there is already one more, already a supplement that would make for a new n and thus the addition of another one, that is, (n + One) + One, and so on to the nth degree. But, we might ask, what would happen to this formula if n were to have the value not of One or some other number but "the One"—which is not one number among others? It would suggest, it seems, that even the One is open to the addition of One, to the supplement of 1, that even "the One" is open to difference and iteration, in short, that even with "the One" there is more to be said and done. That is what Derrida would seem to be suggesting in §52 when he speaks not of "n + One" but of "the One + n." If every n is open to the supplement of One in an indefinite series of iterations (n + One), then even the One would be open to just such an indefinite series to the nth degree (the One + n). What this then means is that the One of ontotheology is never one with itself, that it begins already from the beginning to breach or broach itself (*s'entamer*), or indeed, as Derrida will say, to do violence to itself. It means, in a word, that even the One is autoimmune.[23]

Derrida begins the final section of "Faith and Knowledge": "At the bottom without bottom of this **crypt**, the One + n incalculably engenders all these supplements [*l'Un + n engendre incalculablement tous ses suppléments*]" (§52). The "crypt" referred to here is, it seems, the crypt of ontotheology mentioned in the preceding section, the one that encrypts faith and destines it to being a sort of Spanish Marrano.[24] Rather than repeating the formula $n + 1$, which can be found in so many places, from "Restitutions" onward, Derrida reverses the terms without completely reversing the meaning, suggesting that the One of ontotheology always engenders—spontaneously, automatically, mechanically—an incalculable number (n) of supplements, *its* supplements: the One + n.[25] This n would be like a Marrano that circulates within ontotheology, opening the One to what is other than it, to this incalculable other that cannot be identified without becoming part of the One, that at once threatens the One of ontotheology and keeps it alive. Derrida continues, and I will cite here without interruption the remainder of the section and, thus, the end of the essay:

> At the bottom without bottom of this **crypt**, the One + n incalculably engenders all these supplements. *It makes violence of itself, does violence to itself and keeps itself from the other* [Il se fait violence et se garde de l'autre]. The auto-immunity of religion can only indemnify itself without assignable end. On the bottom without bottom of an always virgin impassibility, *khōra* of tomorrow in languages we no longer know or do not yet speak. This place is unique, it is the One without name. It *makes way, perhaps*, but without the slightest generosity, neither human nor divine. The dispersion of ashes is not even promised there, nor death given. (§52)

The passage is compact, even cryptic, and it calls out to be unpacked and decrypted. Because of the autoimmune relation between its two sources, religion's attempt to indemnify itself remains interminable. The number of supplements to the One, to what would remain safe and sound, intact and unscathed, is incalculable. And all this takes place against the backdrop of *khōra*, at the bottom without bottom, within the desert in the desert, that is *khōra*, which is of "an always virgin impassibility," never marked and never named, or perpetually marked and named only to the extent that it—or she—withdraws from these marks and names. "*Khōra* of tomorrow," says Derrida, bringing together, it seems, the quasi-spatiality of *khōra* with the quasi-temporality of messianicity. *Khōra* would be that unique place that is not a place, a One that is not a one and surely not the One, having been named with names that are never proper, giving place or making way, perhaps, but nothing more, without, therefore, the generosity of a sovereign Good or an engendering father, without theology or humanism, promising nothing and yet already open to the future—*entamé*. Open and therefore *not* indemnified, *not* original and protected, *not* safe and sound, *khōra* would thus be open to languages we do not yet speak or no longer speak, open, therefore, to a supplement, in whatever language and from whatever time or place. Hence *khōra* would not—could not—be, despite the appearances, Derrida's final word in "Faith and Knowledge" or anywhere else, even if it is granted a certain privilege here and elsewhere; it is the name of this opening to other languages and other names, the proper name of what can have no proper name. To follow Derrida's thinking with regard to *khōra* is to understand that there can never be a final word—only the phantasm of one, and the worst possible violence—but always, so long as there is time, another supplement and another opening, another text or another iteration, another ending.

First, then, the other text. In *Archive Fever*, a text written in Naples in late May 1994 in preparation for a talk he would give just days later, in London on June 5, Derrida uses the same formulations as in "Faith and Knowledge" to speak of the relation of the one to itself, two French phrases that can each be divided in two—*l'un se fait violence*, that is, "the one does violence to itself" or "the one makes violence of itself," and *l'un se garde de l'autre*, "the one keeps itself from the other" or "the one keeps some of the other for itself."[26] There are thus two formulations, both of which are doubled—each one doing violence to itself by opening itself up to the other, to iteration and duplicity, each one keeping a little of its other for itself even as it tries to express itself and so ward off the other. Two expressions of the one, then, that turn on themselves, as if what Derrida suspected most were a one that is not divided in this way, a one that—in not doing violence to itself—would make itself into pure violence. We read in *Archive Fever*:

> The words that make (me) tremble are only those that say the One, the difference of the One in the form of uniqueness . . . and the One in the figure of totalizing assemblage. . . . The gathering into itself of the One is never without violence [*Le rassemblement sur soi de l'Un ne va jamais sans violence*], nor is the self-affirmation of the Unique, the law of the archontic, the law of *consignation* which orders the archive. (*AF* 77–78)

But if the One gathers itself, affirms itself, attempts always to return to itself in a moment of totalization, that is, if the One tries always to archive itself *once and for all*, it can do so only by repeating itself in and through what is other. In other words, again, the One is autoimmune. In order to protect and indemnify itself it must enlist the supplement that does it violence and begins to undo its self-protection. And that, as we have seen throughout this work, is the law of autoimmunity. Derrida writes, using the same phrase as in "Faith and Knowledge":

> *L'un se garde de l'autre.* The One guards against/keeps some of the other. It protects *itself* from the other, but, in the movement of this jealous violence, it compromises in itself, thus guarding it, the self-otherness or self-difference (the difference from within itself) which makes it One. The "One differing, deferring from itself." The One as the Other. At once, at the same time, but in a same time that is out of joint. . . . *L'Un se fait violence.* The One makes itself violence. It violates and does violence to itself but it also institutes itself as violence. It becomes what it is, the very violence—that it does to itself. Self-determination as violence. (*AF* 78)

This allusion to the One differing from or deferring itself should make us think of Heraclitus or again, since this has been the point of this study throughout, it should make us think that Derrida would here be thinking of Heraclitus. Indeed, in a text from 1990 in which Derrida reflects on his long engagement with Greek thought from as early as "Plato's Pharmacy" and "Ousia and Grammē" right up through "*Khōra*" and beyond, Derrida relates the self-violence of the One to Heraclitus, to différance, and—once again—to a certain interpretation of *khōra*. Derrida writes in parentheses in "We Other Greeks": "(The 'one differing from itself,' the *hen diapheron heautōi* of Heraclitus—that, perhaps, is the Greek heritage to which I am the most faithfully amenable and the one that I try to 'think' in its affinity—which is surprising, I concede, and at first glance so improbable—with a certain interpretation of the uninterpretable *khōra*)" ("WOG" 36).[27] Derrida thus returns to a certain "Greek heritage" in order to find what differs, what has always differed, within it. He repeats this heritage, repeats it as the same but as a same that is not the same with itself. That is what puts this repetition of a past tradition—here a Greek one—into relationship with the future. Insofar as "there would be no future without repetition" (*AF* 80), the One must repeat itself and, in repeating itself, do violence to itself, make itself into violence even—a bit like the *polemos* that Heraclitus calls the "father of all things."

> The One, as self-repetition, can only repeat and recall this instituting violence. It can only affirm itself and engage itself in this repetition. This is even what ties in depth the injunction of memory with the anticipation of the future to come. The injunction, even when it summons memory or the safeguard of the archive, turns incontestably toward the future to come. It orders to promise, but it orders repetition, and first of all self-repetition, self-confirmation in a *yes, yes.* (*AF* 79)

Derrida thus ends "Faith and Knowledge" by repeating what he would write or would already have written in *Archive Fever*, letting all these other texts emerge or well up within it, right down to the dispersion of ashes— not seeds—with which it seems to conclude: "The dispersion of ashes [*dispersion des cendres*] is not even promised there, nor death given."[28] This line has all the marks, as I suggested earlier, of a signature, of a parting gesture, a sort of benediction, a phrase that not only summarizes what precedes it but seems to certify and sign it, like a testament. One hears it as a final line, just as one hears the reference at the end of §51 to the opened pomegranate as a memory and a crypt. In the first published English-language version of the final fifteen sections of "Faith and Knowledge," which appeared under the title "and pomegranates," this *was* in fact the concluding line of the work.[29] It has the gravity and tonality, the compact singularity of a final phrase, and it even borrows some of the language of the infamous final line of *Dissemination*, a formulation so singular that the translator Barbara Johnson did not dare translate it: *il y a là cendre*. After concluding that book too with a reference to calculation— "$(1 + 2 + 3 + 4)^2$ times. At least."—Derrida attaches a note that also speaks of dispersion and of ashes:

> Moving off of itself, forming itself wholly therein, almost without remainder, writing denies and recognizes its debt in a single dash. The utmost disintegration of the signature, far from the center, indeed from the secrets that are shared there, divided up so as to scatter even their ashes [*pour disperser jusqu'à leur cendre*].
>
> Though the letter gains strength solely from this indirection, and granted that it can always not arrive at the other side, I will not use this as a pretext to absent myself from the punctuality of a dedication: R. Gasché, J. J. Goux, J. C. Lebensztejn, J. H. Miller, others, *il y a là cendre*, will recognize, perhaps, what their reading has contributed here. (*DIS* 366)

More than two decades before "Faith and Knowledge," then, at the end of *Dissemination*, in a footnote that is also dated—"December 1971"—Derrida seems to sign with a phrase of ashes. And much closer in time to "Faith and Knowledge," *Archive Fever* also ends with a reference to ashes, indeed, to "ash" (in the singular—as if there could be a single ash): "With no possible response, be it spectral or not, short of or beyond a suppression, on the other edge of repression, originary or secondary, without a name, without the least symptom, and without even an ash [*une cendre*]" (*AF* 101). In three different texts, then, Derrida ends— signs—with a reference to ashes, though in the last two cases ("without even an ash" [*AF* 101], where "the dispersion of ashes is not even promised" [§52]) the testament questions even the testament of ash, as if the promise of ashes already promised too much.[30]

Hence Derrida ends the fifty-second of the fifty-two sections of "Faith and Knowledge" with a reference to ashes and to crypts, an association that recalls the passage from *The Post Card* cited back in Chapter 1 as we were trying to understand why Derrida divided the essay into fifty-two numbered sections. For there too it is a question of number, of a crypt, of memory, and of ashes. After pointing out that a blank of some fifty-two spaces has sometimes been inserted to replace certain letters, words, or phrases, a blank inserted "at the very place of their incineration," Derrida explains the "52 signs, the 52 mute spaces," in this way: "in question is a cipher that I had wanted to be symbolic and secret—in a word a clever cryptogram, that is, a very naïve one, that had cost me long calculations." Derrida then goes on to say—to swear, even—that he has "totally forgotten the rule as well as the elements of such a calculation, as if I had thrown them into the fire." That's what it means, it would seem, to be in on the secret of a secret Marrano, in on a secret that would remain secret even to the one in on it because it has already been incinerated, a knowledge, we might say, without truth or revelation, without certainty, a knowledge that would thus be inseparable from a kind of faith.

Far be it for me or anyone else, then, to expose here what was and will forever remain for all of us a secret. But that should not prevent us from calculating and from counting, from speculating that if the number 7 was dear to Derrida because of the 2 x 7 letters of his name, then the number 52 might have been dear to him for a similarly personal reason, one that might have gone right back to his birth on July 15, 1930, a date Derrida would have probably repeated with the automaticity of a machine in any number of bureaucratic or institutional settings by saying, "date of birth: 7.15.30" (or as he would have said in French, in France or in Algeria, putting the day before the month: "*date de naissance*: 15.7.30"), numbers that just happen to add up to 52.[31] Derrida's own recounting of the origin of the number 613 (600 + 8 + 15) already leads us in this direction, as does the fact that the second division of "Faith and Knowledge"—after the division of the essay into two sets of twenty-six—separates off the final fifteen sections within the latter twenty-six as if to draw attention to an encrypted date.

Though it's amusing to speculate about such a secret number, we can never be certain that we are in on the secret, since it is not a secret that can be revealed. As Derrida says of the secret of his tallith, the secret of the absolute night, "You will never know anything about it, and no doubt neither will I" ("SW" 85). Beginning, we might say, with its proper name. Which is why Derrida uses many of the same terms to describe the tallith as he does to characterize *khōra*. Neither of these is the proper name of this absolute night, no more than the "absolute night" is. The proper name immediately multiplies and divides, producing all the oppositions between nature and culture, life and death, pomegranate and grenade, pomegranate and tallith, tallith and *khōra*, *khōra* and messianicity, perhaps even Greek and Jew, the two sources of religion, the calculable and— because the list could go on interminably—the incalculable. And that is why "deconstruction" itself has no proper name, and why it is open to an endless series of nonsynonymous replacements or substitutions; it is why it engages historicity at the same time as it questions the assurances of that history, and it is why it engages an essentially open series of quasi-concepts or nonsynonymous substitutes such as *différance, spacing, hospitality, autoimmunity*, and so on. It is true that the One of ontotheology is also always open to the play of the supplement, but the best formulation for this open series of quasi-concepts is not so much "the One + *n*" as "*n* + 1," where there is always one more, always another, always a "one differing from itself," always another supplement, so long, that is, as there is time and space available.

9

The Passion of Literature

Genet in Laguna, Gide in Algiers

Derrida thus ends "Faith and Knowledge" with a reference to the "dispersion of ashes" and to "death given." He concludes with what sounds like a testimony or a testament or, better, a signature that would come to punctuate, endorse, or sign a text that is now complete. As noted earlier, in the very first appearance of any part of "Faith and Knowledge" in any language, namely, in the fifteen sections first published in English translation under the title "and pomegranates," this was indeed the final line—a signature event to sign and punctuate the "Post-scriptum" and the essay as a whole.

But something must have happened in the end, or at the end; with time and space available, a supplement seemed called for, the supplement, once again, of memory, of a dedication, and the paying of another kind of debt. And so after the final line, after the essay properly speaking, Derrida adds one final paragraph ($n + 1$), unnumbered this time, in parentheses, and—as if we were returning to the opening sections—in italics:

(*This, perhaps, is what I would have liked to say of a certain Mount Moriah—while going to Capri, last year, close by the Vesuvius of Gradiva. Today I remember what I had just finished reading in* Genet at Chatila, *of which so many of the premises deserve to be remembered here, in so many languages, the actors and the victims, and the eves and the consequence, all the landscapes and all the specters: "One of the questions I will not avoid is that of religion."* Laguna, 26 April 1995.)

Derrida speaks here, notice, not of what he said, or even of what he wanted to say but did not, but of what, "*perhaps*," he "*would have liked to say*" of a certain Mount Moriah, the place of Abraham or Ibrahim's near-sacrifice of Isaac or Ishmael, a name, Moriah, that means "ordained by YHWH."[1] Derrida is here recalling from Laguna Beach in California, not far from the University of California at Irvine, where he was teaching at the time, what he would have perhaps liked to say of Moriah when he went, some fourteen months earlier, to Capri, not far from the Vesuvius of Gradiva. Writing from Laguna, not far from LA, in a post-scriptum to his "Post-scriptum" to "Faith and Knowledge," Derrida brings Laguna Beach into proximity with not only Capri but Mount Moriah, not far, some would say, from Jerusalem. Capri, Vesuvius, and Moriah: places of memory, sacrifice, and death. *Voir Capri et mourir*, as one says in French: "You have to see Capri before you die"; "Once you've seen Capri, you can die."

For Derrida, however, there could be no such acceptance of death after a trip to Capri or anywhere else.[2] So long as there is more time or more space available, another response is always called for, another trace and another name—up until the end. Hence Derrida goes on after this reference to Capri to recall yet another place and yet another proper name, another text that brings the two together, *Genet at Chatila*, a text, says Derrida, "*of which so many of the premises deserve to be remembered here, in so many languages, the actors and the victims, and the eves and the consequence, all the landscapes and all the specters.*" This is, as far as I can tell, the only reference in "Faith and Knowledge" to Jean Genet, certainly the only reference to *Genet at Chatila*, which, says Derrida, he "*today*" remembers having "*just finished reading*," that is, it seems, just finished reading in or before Capri. The temporality of this sentence is vertiginous, at the very least doubled, duplicitous: there in Laguna Beach, at the moment of signing and sending off the essay "Faith and Knowledge," Derrida recalls what he had just read in Capri, or at some point just before, a line from *Genet at Chatila* that would not be included in any obvious or explicit way in "Faith and Knowledge" but that would, at the moment of signing, find a place on its border—a line, moreover, that would be about nothing other than inclusion and exclusion, confrontation and avoidance: "*One of the questions I will not avoid is that of religion.*"

If "Faith and Knowledge"—the *title* "Faith and Knowledge"— gestures in the direction of the eponymous essay of Hegel, is it a coincidence that the essay would conclude with a discreet reference to Genet? It is as if Derrida wished to recall that other great text of his on religion, namely, *Glas*, which brought together in its left and right columns not only Hegel and Genet but philosophy and literature, along with two very different conceptions of the sacred.

And yet *Genet at Chatila* is not just any Genet. It is, as we will see, the name of a singular testimony that will lead us back to all the questions we have been addressing throughout this work about the relationship between the three monotheisms, language and land, the sexual thing and violence, religion and literature. Before turning to this singular text, then, a few words about these relationships, and especially the relationship between religion and literature, are necessary.

With a prologue, two interludes, and, soon, an epilogue on Don De-Lillo's *Underworld*, the question of literature has been at issue throughout in this book, even if the question of the status or role of literature in relation to religion has not been explicitly posed. In "Faith and Knowledge," this question is raised in several places, at once explicitly and implicitly, through references to the fatwa against Rushdie and the *"right to litera-ture"* (§§6–7, see §37), through the appearances of Gradiva, through lines and images in these final sections (the pomegranate, ashes) that suggest a desire on Derrida's part to sign this essay on religion with something like a poem, and, finally, through this final, parting reference to Genet.

Just as religion cannot, for Derrida, be considered completely apart from science, so it cannot be considered apart from literature. It is perhaps no coincidence that so many of Derrida's texts on religion revolve around literature, from "Shibboleth" and other texts on the poetry of Paul Celan to "Abraham, the Other," which looks at a short parable by Kafka, to *The Gift of Death*, which, in its second edition, includes the essay "Literature in Secret." In this essay, Derrida, returning again to the story of Abraham and Isaac in Genesis as well as to Kierkegaard's retelling of it, suggests that "literature descend[s] from Abraham," that it "inherits from a holy history within which the Abrahamic moment remains the essential secret," that it "remains a religious remainder, a link to and relay for what is sacrosanct in a society without God" (*GD 2* 157). It is thus essential to consider not only the relationship between science and religion but, in a work entitled *Miracle and Machine* on DeLillo and Derrida, that between literature and religion. For if this title is meant to bring together the two sources of religion as well as religion and science, it is worth recalling that, as a rewriting of the deus ex machina for a "secular age," the *god (or mira-cle) from the machine* was originally a literary device, a theatrical invention, a plot device and a staging mechanism, in short, a thing of literature or of what would become literature.

Derrida wrote so much on literature—on Joyce and Ponge, on Celan and Kafka, on Melville and Cixous—that it is obviously impossible to do any real justice to the subject here. But because I have been privileging throughout this work texts written around the same time as "Faith and Knowledge," I would like to turn briefly to "*Demeure*," an important text on the relationship between literature and religion in general but especially between literature and testimony, a testimony that, even in the most secular setting, cannot but invoke the elementary faith we have been following throughout "Faith and Knowledge."

As we have already seen, testimony is always a speech act, a sworn faith. It is also a place where the miracle and the machine intersect, where a deus ex machina comes to produce an unforeseeable event, a miracle from within the machine of language. Derrida will thus argue in "*Demeure*" that there is in essence a common source not simply to religion and science but now to testimony and literature. That common source is the *miraculous*, the miracle of an originary faith that is at the origin of both truth and falsity, attestation and fabrication, reality and fiction, autobiography and testimony, a miracle, as we will soon see, that is at the center of both Derrida's "Faith and Knowledge" and DeLillo's *Underworld*.

An extended commentary on Maurice Blanchot's short narrative "The Instant of My Death," "*Demeure*" appears to have been written not just around the same time as "Faith and Knowledge" but, in some sense, *within it*, that is, sometime between the Capri conference in February 1994 and the final lines of "Faith and Knowledge" written from Laguna Beach in April 1995. We should not be surprised, then, to find many points of intersection between these two otherwise very different texts.

"*Demeure*" is a line-by-line, often word-by-word analysis of Blanchot's 1994 narrative "The Instant of My Death," in which the narrator (who bears a striking resemblance to the author himself but can never simply be identified as such) recounts his near-execution and eventual escape from a German-Russian firing squad in 1944 during the waning days of the Second World War. Interested in the strange relationship in Blanchot's work between literature, autobiography, and testimony, Derrida entitles his extended commentary "*Demeure*: Fiction and Testimony," a transformation or rewriting of Goethe's *Dichtung und Wahrheit*. At once fiction and testimony, literature and, perhaps, autobiographical truth, the one trying to pass itself off for the other and vice versa, Blanchot's "The Instant of My Death" is for Derrida the perfect vehicle for exploring the questions of bearing witness, offering testimony, and taking responsibility that have been at the center of "Faith and Knowledge." It will also help Derrida demonstrate in an exemplary fashion the way in which every testimony is haunted by the possibility of fiction or of literature. Derrida writes, for example: "If the testimonial is by law irreducible to the fictional, there is no testimony that does not structurally imply in itself the possibility of fiction, simulacra, dissimulation, lie, and perjury—that is to say, the possibility of literature, of the innocent or perverse literature that innocently plays at perverting all of these distinctions" ("*D*" 29).

It is important to note here Derrida's emphasis on *structure*. Derrida is not saying that every testimony is false or a fiction but that every testimony *structurally implies* fiction or that falsehood we call perjury. Just as every letter in its structure may not reach its destination, so every testimony in its structure implies the possibility of fiction and, thus, the possibility of literature. Because testimony entails not simply explaining, showing, or demonstrating what is or was objectively the case but *bearing witness* to a singular experience to which only the witness has access, it involves not the unveiling or uncovering of the truth for all to see but the very making of truth. Inasmuch as every testimony must rely upon an elementary faith in the other, upon an elementary confidence that the other is telling us what he or she believes to be the truth, beyond all possibility of proof or demonstration, the price of this faith or this confidence is the irreducible possibility of fiction or falsehood. Hence testimony requires first of all, and in an exemplary fashion, the kind of originary belief or sworn oath that Derrida claims to be at the origin of both religion and science: "all testimony essentially appeals to a certain system of belief, to faith without proof, to the act of faith summoned by a kind of transcendental oath" ("*D*" 49).

In a passage where Derrida is clearly alluding to what he has already written or is in the process of writing in "Faith and Knowledge," testimony appeals to an act of faith that is nothing short of an appeal to the miracle. We thus read in "*Demeure*":

It is by the Russians that the French writer was almost executed and thanks to whom miraculously but without grace he escapes death.

(I intentionally say "miraculously" to suggest something I will not have the time to develop further, namely, that any testimony testifies in essence to the miraculous and the extraordinary from the moment it must, by definition, appeal to an act of faith beyond any proof. When one testifies, even on the subject of the most ordinary and the most "normal" event, one asks the other to believe one at one's word as if it were a matter of a miracle. Where it shares its condition with literary fiction, testimoniality belongs a priori to the order of the miraculous. This is why reflection on testimony has always historically privileged the example of miracles. The miracle is the essential line of union between testimony and fiction. And the passion we are discussing goes hand in hand with the miraculous, the fantastic, the phantasmatic, the spectral, vision, apparition, the touch of the untouchable, the experience of the extraordinary, history without nature, the anomalous. This is also why it is a canonical passion, canonizable, in the European-Christian-Roman sense.) ("*D*" 75)

Every testimony requires or appeals to faith, and yet this does not exclude the possibility of fiction, even of false testimony. On the contrary, the possibility of false testimony must be there from the beginning, and there would be no originary faith without it. Because testimony as the making of truth is thus always haunted by fiction, the truth to which one bears witness can never be completely separated from the possibility of falsehood, perjury, or lying. That is why testimony—why oaths and pledges of trust and faith—are necessary to begin with; and it is why testimony is not the process or activity by which some subject simply points out or uncovers the truth of what he or she has seen but a *passion* and a bearing witness to what the subject *believes* he or she has seen.

> In memory of its Christian-Roman meaning, "passion" always implies martyrdom, that is—as its name indicates—testimony. A passion always testifies. But if the testimony always claims to testify in truth to the truth for the truth, it does not consist, for the most part, in sharing a knowledge, in making known, in informing, in speaking true. As a promise to *make truth*, according to Augustine's expression, where the witness must be irreplaceably alone, where the witness alone is capable of dying his own death, testimony always goes hand in hand with at least the *possibility* of fiction, perjury, and lie. Were this possibility to be eliminated, no testimony would be possible any longer; it could no longer have the meaning of testimony. If testimony is passion, that is because it will always *suffer* both having, undecidably, a connection to fiction, perjury, or lie and never being able or obligated—without ceasing to testify—to become a proof. ("*D*" 27–28)

Just as there is an ineluctable relationship between the making of truth and the possibility of fiction or perjury, so there is a necessary relationship—a necessary contamination—between the singularity of that making, the singularity of a unique, unrepeatable experience or passion, the singularity, in short, of a secret, and the repetition and making public of that secret. On the one hand, Derrida argues, no one can bear witness for me or in my place. As Celan says, no one bears witness for the witness.[3]

Hence "I can only testify, in the strict sense of the word, from the instant when no one can testify in my place, testify to what I do. What I testify to is, at that very instant, my secret" ("*D*" 30). One thus testifies always in an instant to a secret, to a present to which only the witness was or is present in the indivisibility of an instant. And yet, in order actually to bear witness to this indivisible instant, to this passion, one must begin to divide and multiply it, to archive the testimony in a testament. To bear witness in the present to what has *already* happened, one must promise in the present to bear witness in the future to that to which one has already borne witness, even if this means just a moment later during some cross-examination. In other words, the secret must be put into words, made public, and the so-called present instant must from the outset entail a reference to both the past and the future: this is what I would have said yesterday about what I witnessed, and it is what I promise to continue to say tomorrow.

In this way, the living present opens itself up to repetition and the technical supplement. When linked to the production of signification, the instant of testimony becomes compromised by repetition and technological reproduction. But then there is a further complication, another form of repetition, as the unique, irreplaceable witness becomes in principle replaceable, indeed universalizable, not only by him or herself in the past or future but virtually by others who *would have said* the same thing had they been in the witness's place. No testimony would be reliable or convincing if those hearing it were not able to think that they would have given the same testimony had they themselves been witness to what took place. This leads Derrida, in "*Demeure*," to give us one of the clearest expositions in his work of the essential replaceability/irreplaceability of the witness, and thus, to borrow a term from "Faith and Knowledge," of the essential autoimmunity of all witnessing.

> The irreplaceable must allow itself to be replaced on the spot. In saying: I swear to tell the truth, where I have been the only one to see or hear and where I am the only one who can attest to it, this is true to the extent that anyone who *in my place*, at that instant, would have seen or heard or touched the same thing and could re-peat exemplarily, universally, the truth of my testimony. The exem-plarity of the "instant," that which makes it an "instance," if you like, is that it is singular, like any exemplarity, singular *and* univer-sal, singular *and* universalizable. The singular must be universaliza-ble; this is the testimonial condition. ("*D*" 41)

In yet another phrase that might have come right out of "Faith and Knowledge," Derrida argues that the "I swear, you must believe me" is at once "infinitely secret and infinitely public," absolutely live and yet already repeatable through the technological machine:

> What I say for the first time, if it is a testimony, is already a repetition, at least a repeatability. . . . To the extent that it is repeatable, the singular instant becomes an ideal instant. The root of the testimonial problem of *technē* is to be found here. The technical reproducibility is excluded from testimony, which always calls for the presence of the live voice in the first person. But from the moment that a testimony must be able to be repeated, *technē* is admitted; it is introduced where it is excluded. For this, one need not wait for cameras, videos, typewriters, and computers. As soon as the sentence is repeatable, that is, from its origin, the instant it is pronounced and becomes intelligible, thus idealizable, it is already instrumentalizable and affected by technology. And virtuality. ("*D*" 41–42)

In a word, in the words of my title, testimony always entails a relationship between the miracle and the machine.

If Derrida, in "*Demeure*," uses many of the same terms to describe the aporia of testimony as he does to describe the aporia of religion and science in "Faith and Knowledge," then that is perhaps because there is an even more intimate relationship between testimony and literature, on the one hand, and religion, on the other. In other words, the similarities may not only be structural but may stem from a common history and a shared origin. For it turns out that the word *literature*, like *religion*, is a Latin word that, according to Derrida, must be understood on the basis of its "Latin root," its "*souche latine*" ("*D*" 21). "*Literature* is a Latin word," he writes in "*Demeure*," even if "this belonging has never been simple," and even if this Latin filiation has been "exported and bastardized beyond its boundaries and affinities" ("*D*" 20). Derrida thus goes on to speak in "*Demeure*" of a certain universalization or, indeed, a certain *mondialatinization* of literature, and he refers the reader in a footnote to "Faith and Knowledge" ("*D*" 25n8).[4] Literature, it would seem, participates in the very same processes of *mondialatinization* as religion, that is, it participates in a worldwide movement that is essentially linked to Christianity. Speaking of Blanchot's narrative as a *passion* that recounts in the first person the narrow escape of the narrator/protagonist from a German-Russian firing squad during the Second World War, Derrida relates this passion first to literature, to testimony or bearing witness, and then to Christianity.

> "Passion" first implies a history in literature that displays itself *as such* in Christian culture. Literature forced upon the land of Christian passion—more precisely, in its Roman period—linked to the

history of rights, of the State, of property, then of modern democracy in its Roman model as well as its Greek one, linked to the history of secularization which takes over from sacrality, before and through the Enlightenment, linked to the history of the novel and of Romanticism. ("*D*" 26)

Derrida's last comment here is perhaps the most telling of all. Literature would be part of the globalatinizing movement of Christianity insofar as it takes over or acts as a kind of relay for various forms of sacrality during the Enlightenment. Literature would be a secularization of these sacred elements or, rather, a relay for the sacred in a so-called secular age. In *The Animal That Therefore I Am*, Derrida asks in a similar vein whether the unique form of bearing witness we call autobiography is perhaps not Christian as well insofar as it is always linked to confession. He asks—and notice here how autobiography, and thus confession, gets linked to the themes of immunity, redemption, and salvation that we have been following throughout this work:

> Is there . . . an ancient form of autobiography immune to confession, an account of the self free from any sense of confession? And thus from all redemptive language, within the horizon of salvation [*salut*] as a requiting? . . . Autobiography and memoir before Christianity, especially before the Christian institutions of confession? That has been in doubt for so long now, and a reading of the prodigious *Confessions* of European history, which have formed our culture of subjectivity from Augustine to Rousseau, would not suffice to dispel that doubt. (*ATT* 21–22; see also "*SN*" 38–40)

In *Archive Fever*, another text that can be read as something like a crypt within the borders of "Faith and Knowledge," Derrida again underscores this relationship between literature and Scripture, calling literature "a singular testimony," "an inheritor escaped—or emancipated—from the Scriptures" (*AF* 100). Literature would have thus both broken with sacred Scripture and inherited from it; it would have at once left it behind and taken from it a certain conception, for example, of the inviolability of the literary object as the work of an author-creator. Like the political concept of modernity, indeed, like democracy, literature would thus have a theological origin. Like democracy, it would be a form of ontotheology pursued otherwise. As Derrida writes in "Passions: 'An Oblique Offering,'" "No democracy without literature; no literature without democracy" ("P" 28). In the wake of the Enlightenment, both are universal or universalizable, even as both carry along with them an irreducibly Christian or globalatinizing element. We can thus now understand a bit better why Derrida would argue, in "Faith and Knowledge," "*directly or not, the theologico-political, like all the concepts plastered over these questions, beginning with that of democracy or of secularization, even of the right to literature, is not merely European, but Greco-Christian, Greco-Roman*" (§7).

It is on the basis of this relationship between religion and literature that we can read in "*Demeure*" another series of themes common to it and "Faith and Knowledge." Derrida evokes, for example, the resistance of certain nationalist movements or literary nationalisms to new types of technoscientific and capitalist internationalization ("*D*" 22, 24).[5] Such resistance to certain forms of technoscientific modernity often goes hand in hand, he argues, with a reaction against not only secularism, international law, and democracy but the "right to literature." The development of this theme in "*Demeure*" helps explain similar allusions in "Faith and Knowledge":

> *Everything that is hastily grouped under the reference to "Islam" seems today to retain some sort of geopolitical or global prerogative, as a result of the nature of its physical violences, of certain of its declared violations of the democratic model and of international law (the "Rushdie case" and many others—and the "right to literature"), as a result of both the archaic and modern form of its crimes "in the name of religion," as a result of its demographic dimensions, of its phallocentric and theologico-political figures.* (§6)

For Derrida, then, literature is the place where a singular testimony comes to cross the experience of democracy and the "right to literature" or the "right to say everything." "Islam"—that is, as always for Derrida, "a certain Islam"—would appear to have some "global prerogative" in this debate or this struggle over the future of democracy and over this right to say everything. It is surely appropriate, then, that Derrida ends "Faith and Knowledge" with a reference not simply to literature but to the very writer he contrasted with Hegel in *Glas* in 1974, a writer who, in the years after the publication of *Glas*, would become known, even infamous, for his engaged and powerful testimony on behalf of a certain Islam and for his very vocal support of the Palestinian people and their cause—including, and perhaps especially, the central role that women must play in that cause.

I recalled in Chapter 1 that, just weeks before the Capri conference, Derrida spoke in Paris at a meeting of the International Committee in Support of Algerian Intellectuals in order to call for the "effective dissociation of the political and the theological" in Algeria and elsewhere. In his remarks, Derrida spoke rather emphatically of the important role that women must play in this new dissociation of theology and politics and in Algerian politics. He declared—or professed: "I believe more than ever in the enlightened role, in the enlightening role which women can have, I believe in the clarity of their strength (which I hope tomorrow will be like a wave, crashing peacefully and irresistibly), I believe in the space which the women of Algeria can and must occupy in the future we call for" (*AR* 307). Derrida's double invocation of the Enlightenment and of women and his triple invocation of belief are significant. They bring together the question of religion and women, particularly in North Africa but no doubt also in the Middle East, a topic about which Jean Genet wrote a great deal in the final years of his life. This conjunction of religion, violence, and the repression of women became central to both Genet and Derrida, and it will provide us with yet another way to explain Derrida's final invocation of Genet at the very end of "Faith and Knowledge." Let it also be noted that this connection between Algerians and Palestinians, between Derrida's support of the former and Genet's support of the latter, is not being arbitrarily imposed upon Derrida. Indeed, Derrida himself makes just this connection in a letter of *Counterpath* dated 11 January 1998, written from "Jerusalem, Tel Aviv, Ramallah," where he evokes his "alliance with the Palestinian cause, *and* [his] affection and limitless compassion for so many Palestinians—and Algerians" (*CP* 263).[6]

We thus need to say a few words about Genet and Chatila, the figure and place Derrida is asking us to recall after our sojourn in Capri. What are we to make of this parting gesture toward Genet? Since Genet is the other central figure besides Hegel in *Glas*, it is as if *Glas* had opened up the space of "Faith and Knowledge" without, however, programming it, providing it with its title (from Hegel) and its final gesture (toward Genet) but leaving everything between these two borders radically undetermined. But because so much will have happened to both Genet and Derrida in the two decades separating *Glas* in 1974 and "Faith and Knowledge" in 1994, this reference to Genet comes with other associations and expectations. The reference is also all the more curious in light of the fact that, after *Glas*, Derrida would refer to Genet rather rarely and, to my knowledge, would devote no major text to him from the time of *Glas* to "Faith and Knowledge" some two decades later, though he would, as we will see, devote an essay to him some years after "Faith and Knowledge."[7]

Derrida thus begins "Faith and Knowledge" with Hegel, the same Hegel, and ends with Genet, but not the same Genet. For Derrida does not cite the texts of Genet that are at the center of *Glas*, texts such as *Notre Dame of the Flowers* or *The Miracle of the Rose*, but *Genet at Chatila*, a collection devoted to Genet's various writings on the Palestinian question and his controversial support of the PLO (the Palestinian Liberation Organization).[8] These texts are gathered under the name *Chatila* because of Genet's well-known account in "Four Hours in Chatila" of what he himself *witnessed* the day after the notorious massacre in September 1982 of Palestinians in the refugee camp in Chatila, Lebanon. Genet speaks in graphic detail in this text of the mutilated corpses he saw on that day in the camp and of the tortures the victims had undergone.

From 1970 to his death in 1986, Genet actively supported the Palestinian cause, finding a sort of solidarity and sympathy between himself and this people in exile, this strong, beautiful, and independent people whom he so much admired—and particularly its women. Genet thus notes in several places the refusal of Palestinian women to wear the veil, their refusal, as Genet puts it rather colorfully, to submit to the "mustaches," and their desire to take part in the struggle for a Palestinian homeland alongside men. It is this Genet that Derrida is referring to by making reference to *Genet at Chatila* in the unnumbered paragraph with which "Faith and Knowledge" concludes. To cite that passage one last time:

> (*This, perhaps, is what I would have liked to say of a certain Mount Moriah—while going to Capri, last year, close by the Vesuvius of Gradiva. Today I remember what I had just finished reading in* Genet at Chatila, *of which so many of the premises deserve to be remembered here, in so many languages, the actors and the victims, and the eves and the consequence, all the landscapes and all the specters: "One of the questions I will not avoid is that of religion."* Laguna, 26 April 1995.)

There can be little doubt: this final, supplementary mention of Genet is there to remind us yet again of what Derrida already reminded us of in §5:

> *No Muslim is among us, alas, even for this preliminary discussion, just at the moment when it is towards Islam, perhaps, that we ought to begin by turning our attention. No representative of other cults either. Not a single woman! We ought to take this into account: speaking on behalf of these mute witnesses without speaking for them, in place of them, and drawing from this all sorts of consequences.*

Indeed, just above these lines in §5 there is an earlier reference to Abraham or Ibrahim and to Mount Moriah, a reference to languages, names, and witnesses, and in the lines cited above, a call to take into account the consequences of all of this—the very words Derrida uses in the final passage of "Faith and Knowledge." And then there is the reminder, once again in §5, of yet another massacre from just "yesterday":

Difficult to say "Europe" without connoting: Athens—Jerusalem—
Rome—Byzantium, wars of Religion, open war over the appropriation
of Jerusalem and of Mount Moriah, over the "here I am" of Abraham or
of Ibrahim before the extreme "sacrifice" demanded of him, the absolute
offering of the beloved son, the demanded putting-to-death or death
given to the unique descendant, repetition suspended on the eve of all
Passion. Yesterday (yes, yesterday, truly, just a few days ago), there was
the massacre of Hebron at the Tomb of the Patriarchs, a place held in
common and symbolic trench of the religions called Abrahamic. (§5)

Derrida's *"yesterday . . . just a few days ago"* is no exaggeration. On 25 February 1994, just three days before the Capri meeting, there was a massacre of Muslim Arabs in the West Bank city of Hebron in the mosque located at the Tomb (or what is sometimes called the Cave) of the Patriarchs. The attack was carried out by Baruch Goldstein, an Israeli-American settler and member of an extremist group, who opened fire in the mosque, killing between thirty-nine and fifty-two Muslim worshippers, depending on the source. Goldstein was himself killed during the attack, which was strongly denounced by the Israeli government.[9]

Derrida thus recalls this massacre at the beginning of the Capri conference, but at the end of "Faith and Knowledge" he recalls another, much more organized massacre. The name *Chatila* at the very conclusion of "Faith and Knowledge" is enough to return us to this other yesterday, which is, of course, still our today. For if the name *Gradiva* has become almost a synecdoche for the phantasms men have of women, the name *Chatila* has become, in the wake of the massacre in 1982, almost synonymous with the Palestinian struggle and, perhaps, though these are clearly not the same thing—for there are, of course, many Christian Palestinians—the plight and place of Muslims in the Middle East. In Genet's account of the massacre, as in almost all his writings on the Palestinians, the question of religion is inseparable from the question of women in religion and, as we have seen, from the violence that is so often perpetrated against them.

The question of women and the question of Islam, along with the question of women in Islam, will thus have remained in the shadows in "Faith and Knowledge" but now comes to the surface, steps over the threshold, in this oblique reference to *Genet at Chatila*. "In the shadows," I say, because that is how Genet himself puts it in a 1983 interview on the subject of Chatila and the Palestinians: "when I went to school, that is, from the age of 6 to 12 or 13, the Orient, and thus Islam, was always presented in French schools . . . as the shadow of Christianity. I myself, a little French boy, lived in the light. Everything that was Muslim was in the shadows."[10] It is from within these shadows, it seems, that specters, living and dead, some identifiable and some not, jostle and crowd about the gate to gain our attention.[11] But to whom is one to respond when there are always $n + 1$ of them, incalculable and uncontrollable, always one more specter stepping for an instant into the penumbra, gesturing to us from the threshold?

In "Four Hours in Chatila," Genet answers this question for himself by bearing witness to what he saw in Chatila and to the plight of the Palestinians more generally, and in "Faith and Knowledge" Derrida answers it for himself by referring to and then citing *Genet at Chatila*. The line Derrida pulls from this book to end "Faith and Knowledge" is from Genet's reconstitution of a conversation he had one evening in Paris in September 1972 with seven young Palestinians: "*One of the questions I will not avoid* [je n'éviterai pas] *is that of religion*."[12] But when cited in this way, by itself and out of context, this line raises more questions than it puts to rest. For if Genet was a writer who did not in fact "avoid" religion, his treatment of it was rather singular, sometimes admiring and respectful but often rather dismissive or even blasphemous. It is thus hard not to want to ask Derrida—or to ask Derrida to ask Genet—what Derrida himself in essence asked Heidegger some eight years earlier in the opening line of a text, *Of Spirit*, that also brought together ghosts, ash, and the question of "avoidance": "What is avoiding [*éviter*]?"[13] What does it mean for Derrida to cite Genet as he is *claiming* that one of the questions he will not avoid is that of religion?

Genet at Chatila is a collection of short texts and interviews with Genet and others about Genet's involvement with the Palestinians. In "The Palestinians," the text that provides "Faith and Knowledge" with its closing line, Genet does not exactly avoid the question of religion but treats it by more or less dismissing it. Written in September 1972 after his stay with the Fedayin in Jordan, this text treats together the question of the Palestinian revolution with the question of the relationship between men and women, and particularly Muslim men and women. Genet begins by speaking of the way in which a "national conscience" of "Palestine" really took hold only after the great migration of Jews to the region. Jews bought the land right out from under the feet of the Palestinians, as Genet says, and forced them into becoming revolutionaries in exile. The question of religion thus really plays a subordinate role, in Genet's account, in the development of this national conscience of Palestine. Indeed Genet declares outright, "If my observations and memory are good, Palestinians are not as religious as all that."[14] Genet goes on to argue that religion can even be a hindrance to revolution, in conflict with the principle and project of revolution inasmuch as it supports, first of all, the hierarchy of men over women.[15] The revolution of this people in exile thus requires, Genet believes, the participation of women; "it is unthinkable," he says, "that the Palestinian revolution not be accompanied by the liberation of Palestinian women."[16] Genet makes it clear that his own dream for the Palestinians is a "socialist" revolution, not a religious one, a cultural and artistic revolution just as much as a political one[17]—a revolution that would require the liberation of women and a redefinition and revitalization of language.[18] In the end, what attracted Genet to the Palestinians was perhaps less their cause than their beauty and their sense of beauty, the fact that "their ethic was indissociable from their aesthetic."[19] As for the idea of a homeland, "the most intelligent among them have already understood that the mark of modernity is not putting down roots—trees, houses, rocks—but a greater and greater mobility."[20] For Genet, the beauty of the Palestinians comes from their exile and their nomadism, their deracination, to use the term at the center of "Faith and Knowledge." Genet in fact wonders aloud whether he would admire them as much as he does if they were to achieve their objective of gaining a homeland. Hence Genet's claim that one of the questions he will not avoid is that of religion is surely not false, but this question is, as we can see, just one question—and one interest—among others for Genet.

While the collection *Genet at Chatila* does not include, as its name would lead one to believe, the text "Four Hours in Chatila," originally published in *La revue d'études palestiniennes*, it does include a fascinating interview with Leila Shahid, a Palestinian scholar and activist who accompanied Genet to Chatila in 1982 and the person to whom Genet gave "Fours Hours in Chatila" upon its completion. In this interview, conducted some time after Genet's death, Shahid recalls Genet's longstanding desire to write a novel about the Palestinians. *Prisoner of Love* would be that novel, a work written when Genet was weakened by throat cancer and radiation treatment and published just after his death in 1986. This book, says Shahid, is "the summary of everything Genet was."[21] At the center of this work is thus not really the question of religion, not even the friendships between the men fighting for Palestine, but the relationship between the Palestinian combatant Hamza and his mother. For there was, says Shahid, "between Genet and Palestinian women a great love story."[22] Shahid goes on to explain Genet's great love of Palestinian women and his admiration for the part they played along with the men in the revolution. Shahid even speaks of Genet's interest in the unique form of *embroidery* for which these women were known and which they transformed into a kind of resistance.[23] According to Shahid, Genet would actually take this embroidery as a model for his own writing, "weaving his life" into the fabric of the text,[24] taking great care even over the spacing of his text—as we will see in a moment—and thus making his own work at once an exercise in resistance and a "revitalization of language." It is at this point that Shahid says to the interviewer:

> It is for this reason that I hope that Derrida will speak again of Genet. I think he is the one best able to speak about the structure and meaning of *Prisoner of Love*. Jean considered *Glas* to be the only critical work that added something to his work; and, in return, it's the only one he defended and accepted, the only one. Derrida would perhaps be able, in a certain way, to relocate Jean's position with regard to the Palestinians. . . . There is a proximity between Genet's thinking and Derrida's, a proximity in their modernity and in the disorder they were able to introduce, one in the literary domain, and one in philosophy.[25]

There are in fact so many places where the language of Genet in *Prisoner of Love* and Derrida in "Faith and Knowledge" and elsewhere intersect, from one of Genet's final sentences, scribbled in the margins of the manuscript of *Prisoner of Love* just hours before his death and now the epigraph to the novel, "Place all the images in language in a place of safety and make use of them, for they are in the desert, and it's in the desert we must go and look for them,"[26] to its unique opening, which weaves together reflections about language, writing, the Palestinian Revolution, and the role of women in it:

> The page that was blank to begin with is now crossed from top to bottom with tiny black characters—letters, words, commas, exclamation marks—and it's because of them the page is said to be legible. But a kind of uneasiness, a feeling close to nausea, an irresolution that stays my hand—these make me wonder: do these black marks add up to reality? . . . .
>
> Was the Palestinian revolution really written on the void, an artifice superimposed on nothingness, and is the white page, and every little blank space between the words, more real than the black characters themselves? . . .
>
> In Palestine, even more than anywhere else, the women struck me as having a quality the men lacked. Every man, though just as decent, brave and considerate, was limited by his own virtues. The women—they weren't allowed on the bases but they did all the

work in the camps—added to all their virtues a dimension that seemed to subtend a great peal of laughter.[27]

And then Genet writes this, some 370 pages later—after having affirmed that "this is *my* Palestinian revolution, told in my own chosen order":

> When a drawing has too many mistakes in it an artist rubs it out. Two or three rubs with the eraser and the paper's blank again. With France and Europe rubbed out I was faced with a blank space of liberty that was to be filled with Palestine as I experienced it, but with touchings-up that worry me. Like Algeria and other countries that forgot the revolution in the Arab world, my Palestine thought only of the territory out of which a twenty-second state might be born, bringing with it the law and order expected of a newcomer. . . .
>
> Perhaps the massacres at Chatila in September 1982 were not a turning-point. They happened. I was affected by them. I talked about them. But while the act of writing came later, after a period of incubation, nevertheless in a moment like that or those when a single cell departs from its usual metabolism and the original link is created of a future, unsuspected cancer, or of a piece of lace, so I decided to write this book.[28]

We here see Genet embroidering so much onto this piece of lace, everything from Palestine, the Revolution, Chatila, even the cancer that made it difficult for him to speak during those final days and that forced him to write after a long period of silence.

In *Prisoner of Love* as much as in "Four Hours in Chatila," Genet, the narrator, is a witness. For both Derrida and Genet, then, the autobiographical elements are always a kind of witnessing, a testimony. Derrida writes in *The Animal That Therefore I Am*—a work first presented at a conference that went under the title "The Autobiographical Animal": "All autobiography presents itself as a testimony: I say or write what I am, saw, see, feel, hear, touch, think; and vice versa, every testimony presents itself as autobiographical truth: I promise the truth concerning what I, myself, have perceived, seen, heard, felt, lived, thought, etc." (*ATT* 77) And near the end of *Prisoner of Love* Genet writes:

> After giving his name and age, a witness is supposed to say something like, "I swear to tell the whole truth . . ." Before I started to write it I'd sworn to myself to tell the truth in this book, not in any ceremony but every time a Palestinian asked me to read the beginning or other passages from it or wanted me to publish parts of it in some magazine. . . .

Any reality is bound to be outside me, existing in and for itself. The Palestinian revolution lives and will live only of itself. A Palestinian family, made up essentially of mother and son, were among the first people I met in Irbid. But it was somewhere else that I really found them.

Perhaps inside myself. The pair made up by mother and son is to be found in France and everywhere else. . . .

All I've said and written happened. But why is it that this couple is the only really profound memory I have of the Palestinian revolution?

I did the best I could to understand how different this revolution was from others, and in a way I did understand it. But what will remain with me is the little house in Irbid where I slept for one night, and fourteen years during which I tried to find out if that night ever happened.

This last page of my book is transparent.[29]

By ending "Faith and Knowledge" as he has, by signing it, in effect, with a reference to *Genet at Chatila* and thus to the long series of texts I have only begun to recall, Derrida is not only drawing our attention to Genet and the Palestinian question but *countersigning* Genet's text and commitments, as well as bearing witness to his friendship with him. As I mentioned earlier, Derrida would go on to write at least one more text on Genet after "Faith and Knowledge." In August 2000 he would participate in a colloquium at Cerisy-la-Salle devoted to Genet and would deliver a talk entitled, precisely, "Countersignature." In this essay Derrida returns to his own earlier reading of Genet in *Glas*, as well as to Genet's work published after *Glas*, in particular *Prisoner of Love*. But "Countersignature" is also a text of friendship, one that testifies to Derrida's unique relationship with Genet, a friendship that finds a striking confirmation if not a countersignature in Derrida's parting gesture toward Genet in "Faith and Knowledge."

But what does it mean to *countersign* a text?[30] It certainly does not mean simply and unambiguously to agree with everything Genet said and did. It is not a simple endorsement of the positions Genet took with regard to the Palestinians, to Israel, or to anything else. It is, rather, the mark of a response, the acknowledgment of a certain affinity or intersection between two moments or two signatures that echo but do not necessarily repeat one another. Derrida thus notes, for example, the way Genet "distinguishes his faith from theology and religion, in a way from all Churches," even if, in the end, he "liberates himself more easily from

Protestantism than from Catholicism" ("CS" 25). But it is really the theme of the countersignature itself that most interests Derrida in this 2000 text on Genet, a theme developed out of a reading of Genet's final book, his final testimony. After looking back toward his own reading of Genet in 1974 in *Glas*, at his juxtaposition in that text of "these two great Christians, Hegel and Genet" ("CS" 25), Derrida turns to Genet's final novel, *Prisoner of Love*,

> a great book that was not yet published when I was writing *Glas*, a book I love and admire, in spite of some questions that leave a kind of wound in me, in a disconcerted, divided "me," proving Genet both wrong and right, today more than ever. The book is *Prisoner of Love*. Countersigning without countersigning what is said there— for example about an occasionally undecidable frontier between a "Jewish question" and an "Israeli question." ("CS" 7)

Derrida goes on to try to think the countersignature in relationship to what Genet calls "the ecstasy of betrayal" ("CS" 15), particularly the betrayal of friends. For if a countersignature requires a kind of obedience to the other or faithfulness to the other's idiom, it is also the case that "to obey, to be faithful, it must be *possible* to betray. Someone who *couldn't* betray *couldn't* be faithful" ("CS" 29). Just as the possibility of fiction is central to testimony, so the possibility of betrayal is essential to faithfulness—which does not mean, of course, that to be faithful to the other one must betray him or that the best form of faithfulness is betrayal. Betrayal—the possibility of betrayal—is thus part of the countersignature, that is, the possibility of a signature that not only seconds, repeats, endorses, or affirms but appropriates and absconds (that *souffle*), or else counters and contradicts. Indeed "the word '*contre*,' counter or against, can equally and at the same time mark both opposition, contrariety, contradiction and proximity, near-contact. . . . The word '*contre*' possesses these two inseparable meanings of proximity and vis-à-vis, on the one hand, and opposition, on the other" ("CS" 17–18). One can thus understand why Derrida would write that "'Countersign' is a word I love, a word I have much loved. There is a sort of love story—the story of a love that holds me 'prisoner'—between that word and me" ("CS" 15–16).

In the countersignature there is at once respect for the absolute singularity of the other and the possibility of betrayal, the singularity of a response to the other and already the repetition or iteration of that response. As with the structure of testimony we looked at earlier, the countersignature promises already to sign again, promises to sign and endorse the same thing in the same way even if the very possibility of this repetition opens up the possibility of betrayal. "As soon as I sign, I promise that I can do so again, that I can confirm that it was I who signed" ("CS" 18). This then means that "iterability . . . is already haunting the proto-signature, or archi-signature, which is therefore from the outset its own countersignature," so that "all future countersignatures come to countersign what was originally a countersignature, an archi-countersignature" ("CS" 18). As we saw back in Chapter 4 and are now prepared to write or to countersign otherwise, "in the beginning was the countersignature," not an originary inscription withdrawn from all possible repetition or duplicity, all possible falsification or betrayal, but, already from the beginning, a counter-inscription of that beginning, a post-scriptum even. As Derrida writes in *"Sauf le nom (Post-Scriptum),"* "The *post-scriptum* remains a *countersignature,* even if it denies this" (*"SN"* 68). The countersignature endorses what comes before it—says "yes" to it, and promises to say "yes" again—as a kind of response that resembles the elementary faith we have been following throughout this work, the kind that is compared in Chapter 2, in reference to Heidegger, to a kind of alliance or wedding bond, a yes that says yes already to itself.

> the signature is constituted by a "yes"—as in a wedding. . . . "yes, yes": the doubling of the yes is irreducible. That begins by a "yes yes" as the promise to say "yes" to the "yes," that is to confirm, authenticate, countersign the first "yes" that already carries iterability, thus the countersignature, within it. In other words, the first "yes" inscribes the second "yes" in itself. ("CS" 22)

This *yes*, this affirmation or elementary faith in the coming of the other, is the "law" that motivates all responses, as we saw in Chapter 4, all responses to all questions and invitations, and thus, for Derrida, all writing.

> What I here call, with a word that leaves me a little dissatisfied because it is ambiguous, the ethics of my writing, the law it is out of the question I should infringe, is to say "yes" to the work that comes before me and that will have been without me, a work that was already affirmed and signed with the other's "yes," so that my own "yes" is a "yes" to the other's "yes," a sort of blessing and (ring of) alliance. ("CS" 28–29)

It is the law of a countersignature that affirms the idiom of the other without simply leaving it intact, without simply repeating or imitating it. One must at once "respect the absolute, absolutely irreducible, untranslatable idiom of the other" and "countersign the other's text without counterfeit" ("CS" 29). And that is what philosophy, in its desire to erase the signature and the proper name, has traditionally attempted *not* to do ("CS" 30). The "'philosophical' ambition" of *Glas* was thus to think, through a reading of Genet, "a remaining or a surviving that doesn't fall into the philosophical category of ontology, substance, being, existence, essence" ("CS" 31).[31] Everything from the encrypted proper names to the glottal *gl*—a remains of meaning, a phoneme that is not yet signification, not yet a concept—attests to this. In the end, then, it is this countersignature and not some explicit agreement, some shared principle, meaning, or cause, that seals a friendship for Derrida, a testimony that is not simply the recognition of some kinship between members of the same community but, as we saw in Chapter 6, the seal of "another friendship." Derrida writes in "Countersignature": "I would like to bear witness and counterwitness to a certain friendship between Genet and me, a friendship, however enigmatic it was and stays for me, that remains a chance for which I am grateful and that I will consider a blessing until the end" ("CS" 16).

That is where Derrida ends "Faith and Knowledge," rather unpredictably, I think most would agree, not with a reference to Capri but with Chatila, not with Hegel on the question of "Faith and Knowledge" but with Genet on the Palestinians. The ending is unpredictable and unique, inimitable, like a signature—or, as always, like a "countersignature."

Precisely because the supplement cannot be programmed or predicted, because it is the very law of the future and the possibility of the event, I would like to turn now to one more literary figure and text, one that was very familiar to Derrida but that Derrida makes no apparent allusions to whatsoever in "Faith and Knowledge," a text from an even more distant time in Derrida's life that will allow us to speculate about what lies beyond his life or beyond life in general. Before the apparition of Esmeralda from out of the underworld, we need to invoke or convoke, through another kind of *coup du calendrier*,[32] yet another specter in Derrida's work. Having come to the end of "Faith and Knowledge," we are now compelled to go beyond the end. Just as the origin will have arrived even before it arrived, as we saw in Chapter 4 on "*La religion soufflée*," so the end comes always after the end, which means that the end is always to come.

For Derrida, as for the tradition he is reading, the end is never quite the end—though there are, of course, many different ways to think what comes after the end. For both Derrida and the tradition he is reading, there is always something that comes after the end, whether this be a form of survival or a living-on that is, for Derrida, an intensification of life but certainly not an eternal life, a form of finite survival that is the most one can hope for and the origin of all hope—or else, for the tradition he is reading, something like an afterlife or an afterworld, some kind of life ever-lasting. It all depends, as we will see, on how we read or interpret the signs or, really, the sign, and on the value one places on the trace or on "The Fruits of the Earth."

In a letter written to Catherine Malabou in *Counterpath*, Derrida encounters a name, entertains a memory, and then reveals the work that was—and this is his word—the "Bible" of his adolescence.

> This name, Sidi-Bou-Saïd . . . bears Gide's signature, I must have read and dreamed of it. After decades of separation, I again open what was the Bible of my adolescence, and again find my Jardin d'Essai. *Les Nourritures terrestres* [*Fruits of the Earth*]: "In Tunis, the only garden is the cemetery. In Algiers, in the Botanical Gardens [*Jardin d'Essai*] (palm-trees of every species), I ate fruits that I had never seen before." (*CP* 267–69)[33]

Despite the somewhat light and wistful tone of this passage, the claim that Gide's *Fruits of the Earth* was the "Bible" of Derrida's adolescence merits some attention. For if André Gide (1869–1951) would have been a major figure in French letters when Derrida was an adolescent, he seems at first blush to be a somewhat unlikely model for Derrida. But this expression of admiration for Gide is not a hapax in Derrida's work. In one of the very last texts published during his lifetime, Derrida says that at the age of fourteen he believed he could see his own image—and thus, perhaps, his own future—in Gide: "I believed I could see myself (whence my admiration for him!) in the Gide who called himself 'Protean [*protéiforme*]' (it's from him that I learned who Proteus was)" ("SSS" 15; my translation).[34] If Derrida confesses to seeing himself in Gide, to having one day "confided in my adolescent diary in the mirror of Gide who said he was deprived of any nonproteiform identity" ("C" 198), then it is perhaps worth looking for a moment at the work of Gide that Derrida says he so admired.

First published in 1897, when Gide was twenty-eight, and republished in 1935, along with the *New Fruits of the Earth*, Gide's *Fruits of the Earth*—an *œuvre de jeunesse*—was, as Gide himself says in his preface to the second edition, an utter failure, selling only five hundred copies in its first ten years.[35] By the time Derrida would have read it in the mid-1940s, it would have enjoyed a good bit more success, though it would have probably not been the reading of choice of most Algerian adolescents. What is it, then, about *The Fruits of the Earth* that would have appealed to Derrida? One answer leaps to the fore: its unconditional embracing of life in the here and now, on earth and in this world, rather than sacrificing this world and this life to some beyond. Like Derrida, Gide also suspects all idols, communities, and families, indeed, every institution that would create solidarity and preference through some communal belonging.[36] Gide advises us, in effect, to seize the moment, to love life, to become what we are, and to reject all authority, particularly religious authority.

> Comrade, believe in nothing—accept nothing without proof. Never anything was proved by the blood of martyrs. No religion, however mad, that has not had its own, none that has failed to rouse passionate convictions. It is in the name of faith that men die; and it is in the name of faith that they kill. The desire for knowledge springs from doubt. Stop believing and begin learning. It is only when proofs are lacking that people try to impose their opinions. De not let yourself be imposed on.[37]

The book draws its title from a line in the Koran, "Here are the fruits of the earth, on which we are nourished,"[38] and it presents itself as a celebration of these fruits through a mixture of poetry, prose, song, and anecdote. Addressed to a young man named Nathaniel, *The Fruits of the Earth*—not unlike Derrida's *The Post Card*—is thus a hybrid work that combines autobiography, fiction, travel log, and a series of brief addresses or, why not, post cards to Nathaniel and, through him, the reader.[39] Through this artifice, the reader feels him or herself to be addressed in *The Fruits of the Earth* like the young Nathaniel, and it does not take much to imagine that the young Derrida would have felt himself similarly addressed—right down to the advice to read the book and then throw it away in order to embrace life itself. One can thus imagine how this book of travels might have made a deep impression on an adolescent who had scarcely left Algiers, let alone Algeria.

Without having to appeal to some vague notion like the "influence"—whether direct or indirect, with or without anxiety—of Gide on Derrida, there are several other important points of intersection between the lives of these two thinker-writers and many echoes between *The Fruits of the Earth* and Derrida's work on religion, which is what interests us here. In *The Fruits of the Earth*, Gide writes of his travels in North Africa and, particularly in Algeria, where he lived for a time, and he even evokes, as we have heard, the Jardin d'Essai in Algiers, the one Hélène Cixous makes so much of in her *Portrait of Jacques Derrida as a Young Jewish Saint* and elsewhere.[40] In the context of our reading of "Faith and Knowledge," there are numerous references in *The Fruits of the Earth* to faith, to the desert, and there is even a poem entitled "The Lay of the Pomegranate" ("Ronde de la grenade"), which begins: "Truly, three pomegranate seeds sufficed to make Proserina remember."[41]

There is thus much in *The Fruits of the Earth* that finds some echo in Derrida's work, though Gide's idiom is much different from Derrida's. *The Fruits of the Earth* is a hymn, a paean to life, an exhortation to embrace life—one's own life, to be sure, but also, and most importantly, the life of the other. It is an exhortation to develop a passionate interest in life, in all life, to cultivate the joys and emotions of the moment (and to cultivate these emotions "like a religion!" says Gide), to look for the beauty of creation (Gide will say God's creation) everywhere, in nature, light, plants, and fruit. Gide's work is thus a "benediction of joy" and an eschewal of melancholy, a celebration of the "voluptuousness" of nature through the identification of nature and God ("if then I call nature God"). And, finally, it is a call to break away from all teachers and all tradition, to "put the longest possible distance between you and the past."[42] Though all this sounds, at least in these terms, rather unlike Derrida, there is something in each of these notions that we can imagine Derrida "admiring"—that is, seeing himself in—particularly as a youth. One might thus imagine, for example, the attraction of the following lines from near the end of *The Fruits of the Earth* for a young man trying to find *his own* way, perhaps even his own voice, with the help of but also independently of all teachers.

> And now, Nathaniel, throw away my book. Shake yourself free of it. Leave me. . . . Nathaniel, throw away my book; do not let it satisfy you. Do not think *your* truth can be found by anyone else. . . . Throw away my book; say to yourself that it is *only one* of the thousand possible postures in life. Look for your own. Do not do what someone else could do as well as you. Do not say, do not write, what someone else could say, could write, as well as you. Care for nothing in yourself but what you feel exists nowhere else, and out of yourself create, impatiently or patiently, ah, Nathaniel, the most irreplaceable of beings.[43]

In their emphasis on this world, this finite world, there is in both Gide and Derrida, though in the former no doubt more explicitly than the latter, a plea not to sacrifice this world and not to forsake the obligations of this world for the promise of another. We thus read in *The Fruits of the Earth*: "Death is dreadful to those who have not filled their lives. In their case it is only too easy for religion to say: 'Never mind! It's in the other world [*de l'autre côté*] that things begin; you'll get your reward there.' It is *now* and in *this* world that we must live."[44] One could find many places where this sentiment is echoed by Derrida in another idiom or register, for example, in Derrida's many attempts to rethink, as we have seen, the discourse and logic of sacrifice. But instead of going in this direction, I would prefer to focus for a moment on Gide's use of the very common phrase *de l'autre côté* in the passage cited above. The same phrase is used by Derrida, as we saw in Chapter 5, in a somewhat different though not completely unrelated context to speak of what we have been tracing throughout this work, namely, the *miracle*. While the phrase *de l'autre côté* usually means simply "on the other side," on the other side of something that has two identifiable and distinct sides, the phrase is quite appropriately translated in the passage just cited as "in the other world." Like Nietzsche, Gide is here eschewing an otherworldly religion or ethics that asks us to sacrifice this world, this side, for that other world, for what is promised on the other side of life. Such a belief in the rewards—in the "fruits"—of some other world leads us, Gide believes, to renounce the richness, joy, and voluptuousness of this world and this life. But such a belief can also lead, for Derrida, to the neglect—to the ellipsis—of the "other side" that is to be found on *this side*, that is, of the other world *within this world*. That is because, for Derrida, there is already another side to this "other side," not some other world beyond this world but an "other side" or an "other world" within this world. Indeed it is from that other side—or from "the other" tout court—that an appeal to an originary or elementary faith is made, and it is out of an experience of that appeal that Derrida speaks in "Faith and Knowledge" and elsewhere of a *miracle*, the most extraordinary in the most ordinary. Let's listen one more time to a passage cited earlier from "Above All, No Journalists!" in which Derrida speaks of the miracle:

> the primary miracle, the most ordinary of miracles, is precisely "believe me!" When one says to someone, "believe me!" the appeal to proof is itself not provable. What I think in my head, in my inner sanctum, will, for infinite structural reasons, never be accessible to you; you will never know what's going on on the other side [*de l'autre côté*]. You can simply "believe." . . . Everything that exceeds the order of originary perception or of proof presents itself as miraculous: the alterity of the other, what the other has in his head, in his intention or in his consciousness, is inaccessible to an intuition or to a proof; the "believe me" is permanently inhabited by the miracle. ("AANJ" 76)

The "other side" is thus not some other world to which I might gain entrance after death but the inner sanctum of the other, to which I can have no access and in which I can only *believe*. Even more, because the other to whose consciousness or experience I have no immediate access opens up the world in a unique and unrepeatable way, because the other is the opening of *the* world, the "other side" is also another *other world*, not another world above or beyond this one but another world "within" the world, an infinitely other, nondialectizable, nonsynthesizable world "within" this one. It is thus hardly surprising that this thought of the "other side," of the other as what is on "the other side," becomes most poignant at the death of the other, whether this death has already taken place or is still to come. Derrida writes in April 1990, again from Laguna Beach, after having heard his mother on the telephone say a few words from her hospital bed in Nice: "I am as deprived of understanding what is going on on the other side [*de l'autre côté*], her side [*de son côté*], as I am of understanding Hebrew" ("C" 286).

Let me thus conclude this all-too-brief reading of the "Bible" of Derrida's adolescence by citing some of its concluding words and then Derrida's own "final words." Despite the enormous differences between them, we might hear in their juxtaposition something that would explain Derrida's avid reading of Gide as a youth and his professed "admiration" for him near the very end of his life. Here, then, are just a few lines from the final hymn—or final "Envoi"—that concludes *The Fruits of the Earth* and sends it off into the world:

> Look up, eyes bent down toward the grave! Look up! Not to the empty heavens, but to the earth's horizons. . . . Comrade, do not accept the life that is offered you by men. Never cease to be convinced that life might be better—your own and others'; not a future life that might console us for the present one and help us to accept its misery, but this one of our ours.[45]

This is the same sentiment, the same admonition, we heard earlier in *The Fruits of the Earth*, the same sort of discourse we might imagine having an influence on the young Derrida in Algiers as he was reading the "Bible" of his youth. But in these parting words from *The Fruits of the Earth* I am tempted this time to situate Derrida not in the place of Nathaniel receiving the advice of Gide or the narrator of *The Fruits of the Earth* but in the place of the narrator himself, no longer being spoken to by another but speaking now *to* another, to his reader, to his friends, to those who will remain after him, on the threshold of a departure—as if Derrida's life might be measured in some way by this transition from one side to the other, one side to *the other side*, from the side of the addressee to that of the addressor.[46] For here are Jacques Derrida's "final words"—words written, scribbled, on an envelope near the very end of his life, we are to presume, and read by his son Pierre at his graveside in Ris-Orangis on 12

October 2004, words that might be heard to echo from afar the "Bible of his adolescence" in its imperative but hardly imperious tone, at once celebratory and melancholic, thankful for the fruits of the earth and mindful of the need to advise others to embrace life in their turn:

> He asks me to thank you for coming and to bless you. He beseeches you not to be sad, to think only of the many happy moments you gave him the chance to share with him.
> Smile for me, he says, as I will have smiled for you until the end. Always prefer life and constantly affirm survival . . .
> I love you and am smiling at you from wherever I am [*Je vous aime et vous souris d'où que je sois*]. ("FW" 244)[47]

At once melancholic and affirmative, Derrida speaks in these words from "beyond the grave," for he knew—or at least he wagered on the possibility—that these words would survive him, that a trace would remain as a testament and a testimony. He wagered on the possibility, beyond all speech act theory, of a performative—a blessing or a prayer—that might be "successful" well beyond the so-called living present in which it was uttered or written, a performative that might be "successful" even in death, indeed, even through the proxy of another: "He asked me to thank you for coming and to bless you." As Derrida says in "Faith and Knowledge," the blessing or the benediction "pertains to the originary regime of testimonial faith or of martyrdom that we are trying to think here in its most 'critical' force" (§51). Though Derrida wrote these "final words" with his own "imminent" death in mind, though he seems to have seen death coming, seen it without seeing it, expecting it without expecting it, the performative is "successful" only in the absence of the one who had the power to perform it, "successful" only to the extent that it is open to the possibility of failure as well as to the possibility, which is always tenuous, always fragile and threatened, of an affirmation and a countersignature. These words thus remain an *event* far beyond anything Jacques Derrida himself could have ever endorsed. As he wrote in "Countersignature": "Waiting for death—a waiting that moreover waits for nothing, expects nothing—is the experience of something like an event exceeding every performative, and thus every signature and every countersignature. That is why I cannot sign my death, even if I sign my death sentence" ("CS" 40).

There is thus one final reason for concluding this work on Derrida's "Faith and Knowledge" with a look at Gide's affirmation of life and his admonition not to turn our attention away from this world in the pursuit of something "on the other side." Quite beyond my admittedly speculative mise-en-scène of voices or of specters from beyond the grave, it is difficult not to want to ask at the end of a book on religion whether Derrida himself believed in another world or in an afterlife. If not, then what exactly did Derrida mean when he wrote in words that he knew would be read only after his death, "I love you and am smiling at you from wherever I am [d'où que je sois]"? When faced with questions of this kind, I tend to answer as Derrida often answered, with a double postulation such as "on the one hand, on the other hand," "yes and no," and so on. This time, however, it is perhaps best to answer straightforwardly so as not to risk any misunderstanding. *No*, I do not believe that Jacques Derrida believed in an afterlife—and that is no doubt why he was so preoccupied by death, by the absolute limit that death imposes. In an interview conducted in January 1995, that is, just weeks before signing "Faith and Knowledge," Derrida makes this quite clear:

> I think about nothing but death, I think about it all the time, ten seconds don't go by without the imminence of the thing being there. I never stop analyzing the phenomenon of "survival" as the structure of surviving, it's really the only thing that interests me, but precisely insofar as I do not believe that one lives on post mortem. And at bottom it is what commands everything—what I do, what I am, what I write, what I say. (*TS* 88)[48]

So, no, Derrida did not believe that we live on elsewhere or that we live again; he did not believe in another world, in a world "on the other side" of this one. What Derrida did believe and would have been able to affirm every day through a thousand different signs is that, while we do not live after death in another world, while we are not resurrected for another life or in another life, "we" do sur-vive or live on for a time after death through the traces we produce and the marks that make us visible to others. And because we begin to produce these traces or signs as soon as we are born, "we" begin sur-viving or living on from the moment we are born, sur-viving through traces that, as we have seen, are readable and attributable to us only insofar as they are repeatable in our absence, that is, insofar as they repeatable at all. This surviving is thus an excess of life over itself. As Derrida writes in *Archive Fever*: "The afterlife [*survivance*] no longer means death and the return of the specter, but the surviving of an excess of life which resists annihilation" (*AF* 60).

Though Derrida argued for and demonstrated this logic of survival or of living on in a powerful and poignant way in some of his last writings, he had in effect argued from the very beginning that all "writing" is related to death and survival, that as soon as it comes to supplement life it can be iterated in the absence of the author and so can come to stand in or take the place of the author. Derrida argued from the very beginning that this possibility of iteration in the spoken or written word, in the recorded or recordable word, in the archivable word, is not some accident that supervenes at some point upon speech or writing but an essential possibility of these. This is the thought of the trace that Derrida developed from as early as *Of Grammatology* in 1967 and "Signature Event Context" in 1971, right up through his final interview, *Learning to Live Finally*, in the summer of 2004. In "Signature Event Context," he thus argued, for example, that writing—by which he means the trace in general—"must continue to 'act' and to be legible even if what is called the author of the writing no longer answers for what he has written, for what he seems to have signed, whether he is provisionally absent, or if he is dead" ("SEC" 316). And then, in *Learning to Live Finally*, more than three decades later, he leaves us with this, more prosaic in its formulation but also more powerful as an account of the general structure of the trace: "I leave a piece of paper behind, I go away, I die: it is impossible to escape this structure, it is the unchanging form of my life. Each time I let something go, each time some trace leaves me, 'proceeds' from me, unable to be reappropriated, I live my death in writing" (*LLF* 32–33).

Derrida thus never believed in an afterlife, but he developed throughout his work a singular thinking of survival or living on, a notion of the trace as what, in principal if not in fact, always survives the one who produced it or received it. As soon as I utter or even read a trace, as soon as I make a mark, my death and my survival are implied therein, my death and the trace or mark that can always survive me for a time. While there is no guarantee that the archivable, survivable trace will indeed survive, while every trace—as finite—is threatened by forgetting, erasure, indeed, by catastrophe or apocalypse, the trace in principle survives me. However powerful this thought of survival or living on may be, it is a far cry from any kind of belief in an afterlife or in the immortality of the soul. We begin living on already from the beginning, and "we" continue to live on in these signs after our deaths, living on, says Derrida not in the indicative but in the subjunctive, "from wherever I may be [*d'où que je sois*]," and so living on, I think we are to understand, only "in" these words as they are repeated or as they remain repeatable in others, for others—and only *for a time*.

But there is yet another dimension of death that must be taken into account here, one touched on above in relationship to *the other side*. Because Derrida did not believe in an afterlife or in an eternal or immortal life after death but always only in a finite and very mortal survival, it might be thought that this living on is something of a consolation in the face of death, solace in the recognition that, although we are not immortal, the traces we leave live on within the world in the memories of others, in the works available for others to read, hear, or experience, and so on. And yet any consolation to be found in this acknowledgment must compete with two other irrecusable truths. First, the survival or living on whose logic Derrida has developed is anything but a "personal" survival, for the trace I leave behind is precisely not "my own," and the desperate attempt to multiply traces in order to leave more of myself behind does little more than distance me even more from "myself" (which means, in effect, that the self is autoimmune). The second truth with which any consolation in the trace must complete is that with every death, including my own, there comes the end not of some individual within the world but the end of the world as such. If the birth of the other signifies nothing less than the birth or origin of the world, then the death of the other signifies not just a death within the world but the death of the world "within" the world, that is, nothing less than the end of the world itself—without recuperation or redemption, indeed, without the consolation of philosophy.[49] As Derrida writes at the very end of a long book dedicated to his friend Jean-Luc Nancy: "Just *salut*, greeting without salvation; just a *salut* on the way" (*OT* 310).

In the *Phaedo*, Socrates says he would be "wrong in not grieving at death" if he did not believe he was "going to other good gods, and, moreover, to men who have died, better men than those here" (63b).[50] Since Derrida did not believe that he would be going to other gods and other men, to another world, he could not but grieve at death. In Derrida's account, there might be living on for a time, but certainly no afterlife. To accept death would thus be to accept nothing less than "the end of the world," a thought that seemed to Jacques Derrida to be quite literally—and absolutely structurally—*unacceptable*. In an interview given to *Le Monde* in August 2004, just months before his death, Derrida rejects every economy of self-sacrifice and redemption, every thought that my death can be understood and dialectized within the horizon of other deaths; he rejects, in short, the idea of a common horizon of death and so persists in believing that death truly is "the end of the world." Though learning to accept death is commonly thought to be one of the achievements of a life well lived—and particularly for a philosopher—Derrida simply could not accept it. As he put it in the summer of 2004:

> Learning to live should mean learning to die, learning to take into account, so as to accept, absolute mortality (that is, without salvation, resurrection, or redemption—neither for oneself nor for the

other). That's been the old philosophical injunction since Plato: to philosophize is to learn to die. I believe in this truth without being able to resign myself to it. And less and less so. I have never learned to accept it, to accept death, that is. We are all survivors who have been granted a temporary reprieve. (*LLF* 24)

Accepting death, "absolute mortality . . . without salvation, resurrection, or redemption," is something Derrida could never do because it would be equivalent to accepting the end of the world. Just about a year before this final interview, in his preface to *Chaque fois unique, la fin du monde*, the French version of *The Work of Mourning*, a collection of Derrida's funeral orations for friends and colleagues, Derrida makes it very clear that death—in this case, the death of the other—must be understood not as an event within the world, not even as the end of *a* world, *a* world to be followed by other worlds, but as the end of the world itself. He thus wrote in the spring of 2003: "Death declares each time *the end of the world entirely*, the end of every possible world, and *each time the end of the world as a unique, and thus singular, and thus infinite, totality*" (*CFU* 9).

This thought of death as the end of the world is not something that came to Derrida only near the end of his own life, in his final interview or in the preface to this collection of funeral orations from the spring of 2003, when the diagnosis of the pancreatic cancer that would ultimately take his life was being confirmed. Already back in 1984, in "No Apocalypse, Not Now," Derrida relates the death of the individual to nothing less than the end of the world as such: "I live this anticipation [of my own death] in anguish, terror, despair, as a catastrophe that I have no reason not to equate with the annihilation of humanity as a whole: this catastrophe takes place with each individual death. There is no common measure able to persuade me that a personal mourning is less grave than a nuclear war" (*PSY I* 403). Derrida's argument in *Chaque fois unique, la fin du monde* helps explain what, in 1984, might have looked like an unjustified hyperbole. Derrida simply could not accept death because to do so would be to accept nothing less than the end of the world. He could not accept death and so could not accept the long philosophical tradition that begins already in the *Phaedo*, where philosophy itself is understood as a preparing for death and an acceptance of it. He could not accept death because he—like all of us—had a certain *preference* for life, and because all life and all preference tacitly and structurally reject such an end of the world.[51] He could not accept it because he could not think or assimilate it, because it, like birth, like every end or origin of the world, is beyond every horizon. And he could not accept it because he wished to question and thus rethink right up until the end the concepts he will have inherited from both Greek philosophy and the Abrahamic lineage, concepts such as death, sacrifice, salvation, and, so close to the end, with the end in some sense in view, redemption or resurrection. For Derrida there is living on but there would be no resurrection, and this living on is not even *my* living on at all, that is, the living on of a sovereign or self-same self.

In the fifth of the fifty-nine periods or periphrases of "Circumfession" (and Derrida reminds us here that $59 = 52 + 7$), in the fifth of what we might call its fifty-nine breaths, Derrida writes, "I posthume as I breathe." Playing on the French expression *il ment comme il respire*, "he lies as easily as he breathes," Derrida suggests that with every breath he takes he is already living on beyond himself, surviving, not at all immortal but living on as absolutely mortal in these marks emptied of all living breath. That is why Derrida's thinking of the trace was always tied to a reflection on death and on mourning, a mourning that begins, therefore, not with death but already at the beginning of life, indeed, as soon as one is first marked by a name or as soon as one leaves a first impression.[52] As we have seen from the very beginning of this work, life, for Derrida, is autoimmune, open to its own undoing, open to what will destroy it, but also to its own surplus, to what will allow it to live on elsewhere or to live tout court.[53]

Only insofar as a work allows itself to be—to use words that have been central to this work from the very beginning—uprooted, displaced and translated, transplanted elsewhere, can it live on for a time.[54] Derrida would no doubt have wagered, he would no doubt have had faith—a faith without, of course, any knowledge—that the work of deconstruction, that his own work, his own legacy, was destined to live on after his death much as it did before, that is, always elsewhere and otherwise. It would continue to be declared dead and over and it would continue to live on long after all these declarations, whether under this name or others, in this guise or others, the specter, as always, of itself.

As we have seen throughout this work, there is always one more specter ready to step forward into the light, always one more supplement, always $n + 1$, ready to vie for our attention, elicit our response, and call for translation. After this reading of Derrida on the afterlife and on survival, after the specters of Gradiva and Persephone have emerged from the underworld of "Faith and Knowledge" to haunt its pages, after the "appearance" of *Khōra*, yet another figure of the feminine, this one completely unexpected and well beyond Derrida's text, beckons to us and calls to be put on the scene, the very last of the queens in our deck, the specter of

Esmeralda Lopez from the closing scene of *Underworld*, yet another victim of sexual violence, yet another figure, though this time in America, for thinking the relationship between "faith" and "knowledge." When it comes to understanding her appearance in *Underworld*, it will all come down, as we will see, to how one reads the signs, or, really, the *sign* where the miracle takes place. It will all come down to whether one reads it as a resurrection or return of the living body, as the spontaneous return of a life more living than life itself, or as a hoax or mass delusion made possible by the machine or by the machinations of some ad agency, or else—a third option and the one I will tend to endorse or countersign here—as an affirmation that, for the moment, there is still time, and in the words of the sign itself, which can be read as the translation of either a messianicity without messianism or *khōra*, still SPACE AVAILABLE.

Epilogue

Miracle and Mass Delusion (Underworld IV)

As we have seen, Derrida's "Faith and Knowledge" ends and then ends again. The first twenty-six sections, presumably presented by Derrida at the conference in Capri, seem to have called for a long post-scriptum, and that post-scriptum, at the moment of the signature, seems to have called for the concluding paragraph we have just looked at in such detail. But, like every text that demands to be read, "Faith and Knowledge" requires not just faithful imitation and repetition but displacement and translation. It calls for a countersignature, for a testimony that runs the risk not of verifying or elucidating the text but of leading it astray or leading it to be forgotten. Such is the risk this book has run by introducing, twice interrupting, and now concluding a reading of Derrida's "Faith and Knowledge" by means of a few reflections on Don DeLillo's *Underworld*.

Like all literature, as we saw in the previous chapter, *Underworld* is related to the experience of the miracle, to the experience of a testimony that is equivalent to asking someone to believe in you as they would believe in a miracle. But *Underworld* is a novel not only *of* but *about* the miracle. It is a novel whose very theme is the miraculous and the everyday, the miracle of the everyday and the miracle that suddenly disrupts the everyday. The penultimate section of the novel, "Part 6: Arrangement in Gray and Black (*U* 657–782)," returns us to the time frame of the opening sequence, that is, to the days immediately following that famous baseball game between the New York Giants and the Brooklyn Dodgers spoken of in the Prologue. Set in Brooklyn from fall 1951 to summer

1952, this part of the novel features a high school science teacher, Albert Bronzini, who finds the miraculous in the streets of Brooklyn but believes God to be "a mass delusion"(*U* 683); it features Nick Shay, the main character, accidentally discharging a shotgun in a Brooklyn basement, in a kind of underworld, causing him to be sent to a reformatory for teenagers and then a Jesuit halfway house; finally, it features many stories of faith and belief, including several around the figure of Nick's mother, Rosemary, so close to Rosary, who works for a lawyer by day and beads sweaters at night (*U* 755, 757).[1] It's enough for Rosemary to get by, materially and spiritually, but it seems that she, like everyone else, is looking for something more. As the narrator puts it, "sometimes faith needs a sign. There are times when you want to stop working at faith and just be washed in a blowing wind that tells you everything" (*U* 757).

Well, in the following section of the novel, an Epilogue entitled *Das Kapital* (783–827), that sign comes, and it comes—as in the Prologue—to someone named Edgar. Recall that in the prologue to *Underworld*, a reproduction of the Pieter Bruegel painting *The Triumph of Death* drifts down from the upper decks of the Polo Grounds into the hands of J. Edgar Hoover, who is at once fascinated and repelled by its scenes of horror, death, and decay. Hoover, we learn later in the novel, is obsessed with purity and driven in both his professional and private life by a fear of infiltration and contamination (*U* 560). Familiar with the details of modern weapons technology, he knows that pathogenic bacteria are "every bit as destructive as megaton bombs. Worse, in a way, because the sense of infiltration was itself a form of death" (*U* 557). And so he dreams of being interred in "a lead-lined coffin of one thousands pounds plus. To protect his body from worms, germs, moles, voles and vandals. . . . Lead-lined, yes, to keep him safe from nuclear war, from the Ravage and Decay of radiation fallout" (*U* 577–78). In the terms of "Faith and Knowledge," Hoover dreams of a body that would remain safe and sound, indemnified and invulnerable, protected from every outside contaminant, fortified by the phantasm—for it is a phantasm—that the body is not already and from the beginning parasited from within by all kinds of germs and bacteria. He's a real case, this J. Edgar, a limit case for a law of purity and contamination. As Dominique Laporte succinctly put it in his infamous *History of Shit*, "The incapacity of this system to manage its own filth is lucidly betrayed by its intrepid fantasy of an elimination so complete it leaves no trace of waste."[2]

Hoover's obsessions are a limit case, to be sure, but they are not unique in *Underworld*. Also living in Brooklyn from around the time of the "shot heard 'round the world" in 1951 to the closing scene, which takes place sometime in the 1990s, is Sister Alma Edgar, a nun obsessed, like her homologue J. Edgar, with infection, infiltration, and germs. Though her ministry consists in tending to the poor, the drug addicted, and the AIDS infected of the Bronx, she does so with disgust and revulsion—and often with latex gloves (*U* 238–39).[3] But something happens that will change all that, an apparition that will go by the name *Esmeralda*.

Throughout the novel, Sister Edgar and her associate Sister Gracie attempt to track down an elusive, fleet-footed twelve-year-old runaway named Esmeralda Lopez (*U* 810). They hear about her long before they see her and then spend much of the novel trying to find her, protect her, and save her from the dangers of the neighborhood. Before they are able to catch up with her, however, Sisters Edgar and Gracie learn that the young girl has been raped and thrown off a building, her body found in a vacant lot. Soon thereafter, the short life of Esmeralda Lopez is "memorialized on a graffiti wall nearby" (*U* 808) by a well-known graffiti artist, who depicts her as a pink angel on a mural that already has several other blue and pink angels, all victims of an all-too-common violence and aggression in America (*U* 813–14).[4] The combination of the mural and the violence—and no doubt also the sexual nature of the violence—causes the story to be covered by CNN: the headline reads "tragic life and death of homeless child" (*U* 816). We have seen it all before, and so has Sister Edgar, but this time seems different, and it sends Sister Edgar into a tailspin, a new kind of trial or test of faith. She had had premonitions earlier of such a test of faith or change of faith, intimations of "the faith of suspicion and unreality," of "the faith that replaces God with radioactivity, the power of alpha particles and the all-knowing systems that shape them, the endless fitted links" (*U* 251). But until the death of Esmeralda she had always been able to protect herself from faithlessness, to cleanse herself of the scourge of doubt. This time, however, her faith is not just shaken but perverted, deformed, turned into "another kind of belief, a second force, insecure, untrusting, a faith that is spring-fed by the things we fear in the night, and she thinks she is succumbing" (*U* 817). Who knows what to call this second faith, this faith that feels like terror, abandonment, and hopelessness?

But then it happens, something totally unique and unexpected that breaks the walls of common experience, the horizon of the everyday, something that penetrates the protective coating of Sister Edgar and transforms her, turns her inside out. We learn about the event not through direct narration but, curiously, through what we might call the place of revelation and testimony for the latter days of the twentieth century, a website on miracles that Nick Shay's son has been monitoring from Phoenix, a name that evokes all by itself not only the desert but resurrection from fire and ash (*U* 806). DeLillo writes, in "In the Ruins of the Future," an essay published just weeks after 9–11, "the internet is a counternarrative, shaped in part by rumor, fantasy and mystical reverberation."[5] It is Nick Shay's son who first tells his parents about the miracle in the Bronx, at a place near where his father grew up but to which he, the son, now has a relation only through his Internet provider. It seems like a shallow substitute for the real thing, but, as we all now know, "the real miracle is the web, the net, where everybody is everywhere at once, and he [the son] is there among them, unseen" (*U* 808).

In a section entitled "Keystroke 1," the first of two keystroke sections—as if that stroke heard 'round the world in the prologue had divided in two, gone digital—we learn through Nick's son just what happened in the wake of Esmeralda's horrific death. Soon after her death and after what might be called Sister Edgar's dark night of the soul, "the stories began, word passing block to block, moving through churches and superettes, maybe garbled slightly, mistranslated here and there, but not deeply distorted—it is clear enough that people are talking about the same uncanny occurrence. And some of them go and look and tell others, stirring the hope that grows when things surpass their limit" (*U* 818). The focus of their attention and awe is not the mural where Esmeralda lives on as a pink angel but a billboard display for Minute Maid orange juice—yes, an ad for a juice that comes from a fruit a bit smaller than a pomegranate, indeed, just about the size of a baseball.[6] The billboard depicts a "vast cascade of orange juice pouring diagonally from top right into a goblet that is handheld at lower left—the perfectly formed hand of a female Caucasian of the middle suburbs" (*U* 820). Nothing miraculous yet about this appearance in the kingdom of *Das Kapital*, this advertisement for one of its commodities and its promise of life, health, and vitamin C. But as night falls this billboard becomes the place of a visitation, a miraculous, unique apparition, the commercial goblet for a well-known orange juice becoming something like the Holy Grail of faith and hope. Hearing the rumors, which Sister Gracie writes off as the worst kind of "tabloid superstition," Sister Edgar convinces Gracie to go and see for themselves why all these "people go there to weep, to believe" (*U* 819). Here, then, is what happens to them, which I cite at some length and without interruption so as not to take anything away from the event, or from the rhythm of DeLillo's pen or machine as it relates the event, which is, of course, a miracle:

They stand and watch the billboard. They stare stupidly at the juice. After twenty minutes there is a rustle, a sort of perceptual wind, and people look north, children point north, and Edgar strains to catch what they are seeing.

The train.

She feels the words before she sees the object. She feels the words although no one has spoken them. This is how a crowd brings things to single consciousness. Then she sees it, an ordinary commuter train, silver and blue, ungraffiti'd, moving smoothly toward the drawbridge. The headlights sweep the billboard and she hears a sound from the crowd, a gasp that shoots into sobs and moans and the cry of some unnameable painful elation. A blurted sort of whoop, the holler of unstoppered belief. Because when the train lights hit the dimmest part of the billboard a face appears above the misty lake and it belongs to the murdered girl. A dozen women clutch their heads, they whoop and sob, a spirit, a godsbreath passing through the crowd.

Esmeralda.

Esmeralda. (*U* 821)

It happens in an instant, and then it is gone. The light of the train sweeps the billboard and the face of Esmeralda is revealed, an instantaneous revelation in the light, through the light, and then the light and the revelation are gone. But everyone is certain of what they see, and Edgar first among them. "She sees Esmeralda's face take shape under the rainbow of bounteous juice and above the little suburban lake and there is a sense of someone living in the image, an animating spirit—less than a tender second of life, less than half a second and the spot is dark again" (*U* 822).

The crowd is awestruck, enthralled, positively rapt before this fleeting appearance, humbled before the miraculous appearance of what we might want to call Our Lady of the O.J., Esmeralda Lopez—E.L., for short—the Minute Maid Madonna. Had the crowd been asked at that moment "Do you believe in ghosts?" it would have surely answered with a single voice, "Yes, now we do, yes." Everyone is awed, dumbstruck, save Sister Gracie, who sees no miracle here, no moment of grace, no revelation, because she has quite literally seen through it all, seen through to the other side of the miraculous billboard with a knowledge that is able to cut through and deflate all faith and phantasms. "It's just the undersheet," she says, "A technical flaw that causes the image underneath, the image from the papered-over ad to show through the current ad" (*U* 822).[7]

So it's not a miracle at all, just an optical illusion, an easy case for a good skeptic or miracle debunker. For Sister Edgar, however, the event remains nonetheless miraculous, not Esmeralda's apparition, exactly, but the contact and contagion this supposed apparition brings her, the end of her fears of infection, infiltration, and contamination by foreign bodies.[8] Unlike Sister Gracie, Sister Edgar is taken up by the crowd, by the throng of believers that "see her and embrace her and she lets them. Her presence is a verifying force—a figure from a universal church with sacraments and secret bank accounts and a fabulous art collection" (*U* 822). Edgar is jubilant, even ecstatic, ready to shed her skin and mingle with those she had devoted her life to helping but never allowed herself to touch; she takes off her gloves and embraces those around her, even the HIV-infected graffiti artist responsible for the painted angels. Caught up in the moment, Sister Edgar gains a brief reprieve from herself:

> Edgar thumps a man's chest with her fists. She finds Ismael and embraces him. She looks into his face and breathes the air he breathes and enfolds him in her laundered cloth. Everything feels near at hand, breaking upon her, sadness and loss and glory and an old mother's bleak pity and a force at some deep level of lament that makes her feel inseparable from the shakers and mourners, the awestruck who stand in tidal traffic—she is nameless for a moment, lost to the details of personal history, a disembodied fact in liquid form, pouring into the crowd. (*U* 823)

This, it seems, is the miracle, the transformation of Edgar into liquid, into O.J. of a sort, no longer separate from others, allowing herself to be contaminated, to pour into others but also to distinguish herself, in effect, from the other Edgar who not only lived his life afraid of contamination and corruption but tried to protect himself even in death from these others by being buried in an armored coffin. *This*, it seems, is the miracle of everyday contact, a contact and contagion that does not promise some final fusion but, precisely, loss and lament, pity and force.[9] We can sense that the end is near.

The night after this first apparition of Esmeralda to Edgar and Gracie, word spreads even further, and the crowd swells to a thousand people, with vendors selling soft drinks, pinwheels, and "laminated images of Esmeralda." The following night "the mother shows up, Esmeralda's lost junkie mother, and she collapses with flung arms when the girl's face appears on the billboard" (*U* 823). What began as a rumor and then grew to be a local phenomenon has now become headline news. "Helicopter cameras record the scene and the police trail orange caution tape through the area—the very orange of the living juice" (*U* 824). The phenomenon has gone global, gone viral, and shots of the apparition are now seen 'round the world, from the Bronx to Phoenix, by means of the telecommunications networks that today form the very ether of religion.

And then the next night—well, the next night there is nothing, no revelation at all, except perhaps, for those who have read "Faith and Knowledge," the space of revealability itself, the space for phantasms to appear, it is true, but also, perhaps, for a faith before or beyond any revelation or phantasm, the place, perhaps, for "the most barren and desert-like . . . of all abstractions":

> The next evening the sign is blank. What a hole it makes in space. People come and don't know what to say or think, where to look or what to believe. The sign is a white sheet with two lonely words, *Space Available*, followed by a phone number in tasteful type.
>
> When the first train comes, at dusk, the lights show nothing. (*U* 824)

It is at this point that someone—is it the narrator? is it DeLillo?—turns to those who have witnessed the miracle and are now left abandoned, to ask them, to ask the reader, to ask us:

> And what do you remember, finally, when everyone has gone home and the streets are empty of devotion and hope, swept by river wind? Is the memory thin and bitter and does it shame you with its fundamental untruth—all nuance and wishful silhouette? Or does the power of transcendence linger, the sense of an event that violates natural forces, something holy that throbs on the hot horizon, the vision you crave because you need a sign to stand against your doubt? (*U* 824)[10]

One answer, it seems, is that it all comes down to the kind of signs we need or think we need, the kind of signs we are still looking for, or the kind of faith we still need as our search engine "searches." It would thus all come down in the end to the way we read the signs, to the space that is or is not open and available for those signs, to whether we read them as true signs of a miracle, signs of the resurrection or return of the living body, of what is more living than life itself, a return of the source of life itself, or as signs of a mass hoax or delusion made possible by the machine, a trick of light and motion, or else, third possibility, the one in which I would tend to put my faith, as an affirmation that, for a moment, for a time, there is still time left, still life, and, in the words of the sign itself, still "space available." It would thus be a question of faith, not a faith in our indemnity, salvation, or essential goodness, faith in our ultimate victory, but faith in the knowledge, which is always fragile and in need of verification, indeed in need of faith, that with an 0 and 1 count in the bottom of the ninth there is still time for another stroke, there at the plate or on the keyboard, still time to give it a shot, still time and space available, up until the moment, which is always divided and repeatable, when *it's going! it's going!*, when *it's out of here!* Still time, then, to hear the evangelist say *Holy cow!*[11]

Chicago, 11 February 2011

Observations

Derrida begins §36: "**In the beginning**, the title will have been my first aphorism. It condenses two traditional titles, entering into a contract with them. We are committed to deforming them, dragging them elsewhere while developing if not their negative or their unconscious, at least the logic of what they might have let speak about religion independently of the meanings they wanted to say." Derrida goes on in this section to speak of the theme of light and of Enlightenment, and he cites in relation to these themes Kant's *Religion Within the Limits of Reason Alone* and Bergson's *The Two Sources of Morality and Religion*. These are the two titles Derrida would appear to be referring to in the passage cited above, the two traditional titles condensed in the subtitle of "Faith and Knowledge: The Two Sources of 'Religion' at the Limits of Reason Alone." What Derrida passes over in silence, as we saw in Chapter 1, is the fact that the title is itself borrowed without any deformation (beyond translation) from Hegel. Hence Derrida's aphoristic title really brings together three traditional titles, three more or less canonical texts on the question of religion.

However one might wish to understand what Derrida calls here a *deformation* of these texts by means of the development of a logic or meaning beyond what the texts themselves consciously intend, it is pretty clear that Derrida does not intend to enter into an extended critical debate with any of these texts, whether considered on their own, in the context of the critical debate each has generated, or in relationship to one another (the way in which, for example, both Hegel and Bergson are responding in large part to Kant). That this is not Derrida's intention can be gleaned from the fact that almost all the comments on Kant, Hegel, and Bergson are confined to the "Italics," that is, to the portion of the text read or at least presented in some improvised form at the Capri conference. When we get to the "Post-scriptum," that is, to the twenty-six sections presumably added after the conference and written between the time of the conference (28 February 1994) and the date on which the text was signed (26 April 1995), little more than the two titles condensed in the subtitle really appear in the text, along with a citation of the final, "memorable" words of Bergson's text, about which Derrida will then ask: "What would happen if Bergson were made to say something entirely different from what he believed he wanted to say but what perhaps was surreptitiously dictated to him?" (§37). I will return to this question later, but for moment let me simply emphasize the relative absence of Kant and Bergson—and the total absence of Hegel—in these final twenty-six sections, along with, interestingly, the ever-growing presence of Heidegger.

If these four thinkers—Kant, Hegel, Bergson, Heidegger—provide Derrida with many of the themes he will treat and the majority of the terms he will use, from the title and subtitle onward, "Faith and Knowledge" is not a straightforward reading or commentary on any of them, with the possible exception of Heidegger, the only one of the four who is *not* alluded to in any obvious way in the title. These four figures form the border, so to speak, of the discussion of religion in "Faith and Knowledge," but they can in no way be construed to be at its center. Instead of treating these figures in any detail within the foregoing analysis of "Faith and Knowledge," I have opted to devote to each of them what might be considered—imitating Kant—a brief "Observation" or, better, a *parergon*, in order to provide some of the historical background for "Faith and Knowledge" that Derrida assumes and so does not himself spell out. Because subsequent figures sometimes refer to former ones, I will take the four in historical order: Observation 1, Kant (1724–1804); Observation 2, Hegel (1770–1831); Observation 3, Bergson (1859–1941); Observation 4, Heidegger (1889–1976).

Observation 1

Kant

Derrida focuses on the themes and terms of Kant's 1793 work *Religion Within the Limits of Reason Alone* in a few of the central sections of the "Italics" (§§11–17).[1] These comments on Kant can be organized around four basic themes: (1) the notion of radical evil;[2] (2) the two families of religion and the idea that Christianity is the only moral religion; (3) the four *parerga* for a religion within the limits of reason of alone; (4) the death of God and the relationship to universality and globalization. In what follows, I will try to develop each of these themes in a somewhat more comprehensive reading of Kant's *Religion* than Derrida gives us in "Faith and Knowledge." Of course, to get a more complete understanding of Kant's *Religion*, one would need to place it in the context of both Kant's earlier works on religion, including and especially those related to Kant's critical project, and contemporary debates over, for example, the relationship between pietism and deism or natural and revealed religion. But such considerations would take us too far afield of the central concerns of "Faith and Knowledge," which are, after all, what is happening to religion and in the name of religion today.

1. Radical Evil

The most prominent Kantian theme in "Faith and Knowledge," the one that runs from the second section right up through the next to last and is referred to more than a dozen times in between, is "radical evil"—in

French, *le mal radical*. This theme and this term can be found in many of Derrida's works before and after "Faith and Knowledge," always with a more or less explicit nod toward Kant. But in "Faith and Knowledge" the reference to Kant is absolutely explicit, even though, as we will see at the end of this Observation and as we saw in Chapter 3, Derrida's use of the term appears at first glance to deviate a good deal from Kant.

What, then, *is* radical evil—*das radikale Böse*—in Kant? Much of the first two books of Kant's *Religion* are taken up with this important notion, and Kant's entire argument hinges upon it. Kant defines it early on in *Religion* in this way: "We call a man evil . . . not because he performs actions that are evil (contrary to law) but because these actions are of such a nature that we may infer from them the presence in him of evil maxims" (16). Radical evil, then, has to do not with performing actions but with the nature of the maxims or motives on the basis of which our actions are performed. In short, it is evil to act out of any motive other than the moral law. Evil is thus an abuse or perversion of free will; it comes from "the propensity of the will to maxims which neglect the incentives springing from the moral law in favor of others which are not moral"—for example, "ambition, self-love in general, . . . even a kindly instinct such as sympathy" (25–26). Hence it is evil to act with a view to one's own advantage, either in this world or the next, or even to act in a way that one believes to be pleasing to God. The *only* motive for action must be the moral law, or what Kant calls in the *Critique of Practical Reason* the categorical imperative.

Kant calls this evil *radical* not because it is extreme or extraordinary but because it is a "propensity" "so deeply rooted in the will" (30) that it can never be completely extirpated or eradicated (from the Latin *radix*, meaning root). Radical evil is thus a deeply seated or rooted evil; it reaches down to the very roots of human freedom, into "the deeps of the heart" (46), into a ground of action that, Kant claims, is and must remain inscrutable to man.[3] It is because this evil runs so deep that Kant is able to say that man is "evil *by nature*" (27) or has a "natural propensity to evil," or that there is "a *radical* innate *evil* in human nature" (28).

Translating a certain biblical tradition of original sin into moral philosophy, Kant speaks of radical evil as a "debt which is original, or prior to all the good a man may do" (66). Of course, in order for the biblical parallel to hold and in order for there to be any real charge for moral philosophy, Kant must also argue that radical evil, no matter how deeply rooted and ineradicable, can be overcome. In other words, Kant will have to go on to argue—as he will do in the second and third books of *Religion*—that man is also capable of goodness, which is to say, capable despite the nature of radical evil of "incorporat[ing] the moral law into his maxim" (20). The terms *evil* and *goodness* can have meaning only insofar as there is human will and freedom, only insofar as our actions are not simply determined by natural causes. Radical evil is indeed inextirpable, but it does not determine all of man's actions. For in addition to a propensity to evil, man also has an "original predisposition to good" (21), an "original goodness" that consists in "the *holiness of maxims* in doing one's duty, merely for duty's sake" (42), that is, with no self-interest involved. Since there is, then, as Kant puts it, "a seed of goodness [that] still remains in its entire purity, incapable of being extirpated or corrupted" (41), one could say that there is a kind of *radical goodness* as well as radical evil in man. It is no doubt Kant's much greater experience of the latter, and the many more historical examples of the latter, that prevent him from actually putting it in these terms. But it is no doubt this notion of a "radical" or inextirpable goodness that motivates Kant's moral philosophy and, as we will see in section four of this observation, his hope for an ethical commonwealth.

There are, therefore, two originary principles in man—one good, one evil—and the moral drama that is played out between them becomes, as we will see next, the basis for the narrative of Christianity. While evil is radical, inextirpable, man's original predisposition is good; what determines whether man thus *becomes* good or evil are the maxims he adopts to guide his actions. As we will see in section 3, what is essential for the practical or moral use of reason is the determination of an action with a view *only* to its moral rightness and a use of reason that does not overstep the limits that have been set for it.

Though Kant's notion of radical evil is radically different from Derrida's, it is important to note Derrida's explicit borrowing of Kant's vocabulary. It is also important to note that Kant's own understanding of radical evil is itself already quite different from its traditional religious meaning, which might suggest that, in this regard at least, Derrida is following Kant in interpreting radical evil in a radically new way. Whereas evil in Kant is understood as the inversion or perversion of one's ethical "maxims," a substitution of self-interest for the categorical imperative as the fundamental principle of choice, Derrida's radical evil has to do with the abstracting, deracinating function of technoscience and telecommunication, which threatens always to lead the self or the community beyond itself, opening it up to the possibility of corruption and contamination but also to the possibility of health and "salvation," that is, to the possibility of *either* good *or* ill. In the second section of "Faith and Knowledge" Derrida asks:

And salvation, is it necessarily redemption, before or after evil, fault or sin? Now, where is evil [le mal]?²⁴ Where is evil today, at present? Suppose that there was an exemplary and unprecedented figure of evil, even of that radical evil which seems to mark our time as no other. Is it by identifying this evil that one will accede to what might be the figure or promise of salvation for our time, and thus the singularity of the religious whose return is proclaimed in every newspaper? (§2)

From this first introduction of the term, though without, as yet, any explicit reference to Kant, Derrida marks a clear distinction between his notion of radical evil and Kant's. It might even be said that Derrida uproots or extirpates the very notion of radical evil from the Kantian text in order to graft or transplant it elsewhere.⁵ Whereas in Kant radical evil would take on different figures and shapes in each individual and would no doubt vary in its figure or shape over time, it would in its essence or form be the same evil, an evil rooted in human will and freedom. Though the term *evil* obviously comes from the biblical tradition in which he is working, Kant appropriates the term and makes it more or less his own. What Kant calls radical evil is what he considers radical evil to be. He points out the evil and he names it as such.

As for Derrida, who is working within the same tradition as Kant, it is not so clear that the term *radical evil* is his own and that he is uttering it in his own name. Rather, *radical evil* would be what *others* call it, namely, the movements of deracination and expropriation that Derrida himself might simply term in a more neutral vocabulary *iterability* or *différance*. While iterability or différance is the condition for anything—good or evil—to happen, it is difficult to see Derrida appropriating these moral terms for his own discourse, at least not in the same way as Kant. Radical evil would thus be what others identify with these movements of deracination, expropriation, and abstraction—movements that, for Derrida, are ineluctable as soon as there is some machine, that is, as soon as there is repetition, which is already there from the beginning. Moreover, Derrida seems to suggest with all these references to time (*now*, is, today, *at present*, *our time*) that radical evil itself may be different from epoch to epoch, that it is not simply rooted in the nature of human freedom but is transformed over time and so needs to be reexamined at various historical epochs. How, Derrida asks, can one give an account of "*a history of radical evil, of its figures that are never simply figures and that—this is the whole evil—are always inventing a new evil?*" (§14).⁶ This will be related to Derrida's emphasis in "Faith and Knowledge" on the nature of religion today, on the forms our new wars of religion are taking today, on the so-called re-turn of religion that is not a return at all, and so forth. Hence both the meaning Derrida attributes to the term, and the uses he makes of it, are not at all symmetric with Kant's. Much the same could be said of Derrida's appropriation of the theme of the two families, sources, or stocks of religion in Kant and Bergson.

2. The Two Families of Religion

Well before Bergson spoke of "two sources of morality and religion," Kant argued that religion has, precisely, two families, two stocks, two sources or two genealogies. On the one hand, there is religion as simple cult, the religion of cult alone (*des blossen Cultus*) ("*teaching only prayer and desire*," writes Derrida), simple "*endeavors to win favor* (mere worship)," and, on the other, "*moral* [moralische] religions, *i.e.*, religions of *good life-conduct*" (47; see "FK" §15). Kant contrasts these two sources or families of religion on the basis of man's motivations for action, his will to become better—or not. In the first of these stocks or families, that is, in simple cult, "man flatters himself by believing . . . that God can make him eternally happy (through remission of his sins) without his having *to become a better man*," while in the latter, in moral religion, which is to say, in Christianity alone, "it is a basic principle that each must do as much as lies in his power to become a better man, and that only when he has not buried his inborn talent (Luke 19:12–16) but has made use of his original predisposition to good in order to become a better man, can he hope that what is not within his power will be supplied through cooperation from above" (47). This follows from what we saw above concerning radical evil. Because acting under any other motive than that of the moral law is evil, any expectation of compensation for one's good actions or for one's service to religion is evil as well. Man can "hope" for compensation from above, but he cannot expect it and he certainly cannot act in expectation of it.

If Christianity is the only moral religion "of all the public religions which have ever existed" (47), then it stands in contrast to all other public religions, which are thus all religions of mere cult or worship. Throughout *Religion*, however, Kant contrasts Christianity almost exclusively (I say *almost* because there are some references to Greek and Roman "religions") with the Jewish religion, which Kant characterizes as little more than "a collection of mere statutory laws upon which was established a political organization" (116). As such, "Judaism is really not a religion at all but merely a union of a number of people who, since they belonged to a particular stock, formed themselves into a commonwealth under purely political laws" (116). It is thus not only the case, as Derrida says in "Faith and Knowledge," that Christianity is, for Kant, the only *true* religion; in some sense it is the only religion at all. Because Judaism aims not at inner transformation but mere "outer observance" (e.g., the Ten Commandments; 116), because it presupposes revelation and so is merely contingent and nonbinding upon all men (95), it is unfit to become a "universal church" (117). Lacking such universality and thus falling short of the one true religion, it in some sense falls short of being a religion at all.

According to Kant, then, the Christian religion would be the only moral religion, the only true religion, if not the only real religion at all, the only religion charged with the mission of freeing "reflective faith." It is the only religion that favors good will over knowledge, the only one that subordinates knowing to doing and that aims for a "reflective faith" that depends upon no historical revelation and corresponds to the "rationality of pure practical reason." While dogmatic faith, that is, the belief of a cult, according to Kant, claims to *know* and so does not know the difference between faith and knowledge, Christianity does not claim to know but understands that knowledge must be subordinated to this "pure practical reason." Here is how Derrida characterizes Kant's argument concerning the singularity of Christianity as the only moral religion.

> *Are we ready to measure without flinching the implications and consequences of the Kantian thesis? The latter seems strong, simple and dizzying: the Christian religion would be the only truly "moral" religion; a mission would thus be reserved exclusively for it and for it alone: that of liberating a "reflecting faith." It necessarily follows therefore that pure morality and Christianity are indissociable in their essence and in their concept. If there is no Christianity without pure morality, it is because Christian revelation teaches us something essential about the very idea of morality. From this it follows that the idea of morality that is pure but non-Christian would be absurd; it would exceed both understanding and reason, it would be a contradiction in terms. The unconditional universality of the categorical imperative is evangelical. The moral law inscribes itself at the bottom of our hearts like a memory of the Passion. When it addresses us, it either speaks the idiom of the Christian—or is silent.* (§15)

Derrida's characterization of the moral law as ineluctably Christian finds further justification in the very language Kant uses to explain it. One will have noticed, for example, the way in which Kant, in his description of moral religion, slips in a reference to Scripture, in this case Luke 19:12–16, in order to help illustrate or make his philosophical point. In the Preface to the First Edition, Kant tries to justify this use of Scripture by arguing that what he proposes is a "philosophical theology [that] remains within the limits of reason alone" (8). Kant will thus use the history of religion, and even cite the Bible, but without, he says, carrying "these propositions into Biblical theology" (8). As he goes on to say in the Preface to the Second Edition, he wants to show how the religion of reason can coincide with the cult of Christianity, that is, how "reason can be found to be not only compatible with Scripture but also at one with it, so that he who follows one (under guidance of moral concepts) will not fail to conform to the other" (11). It is from this perspective that Kant reads Scripture as the visible narrative, so to speak, of the intelligible moral relationship. From the story of creation in Genesis to the fall and original sin (radical evil), to temptation by the devil and our resistance to that temptation (the moral law), Scripture represents in a visible and external form the invisible and internal drama of man's moral relationship. In its vivid depiction of the perpetual struggle between good and evil, Scripture is the visible narrative of the internal conflict between radical evil and radical goodness under the guidance of the moral law. Hence the genuine meaning of Scripture is "that there exists absolutely no salvation for man apart from the sincerest adoption of genuinely moral principles into his disposition" (78), the very same meaning as the one found in Kant's religion of reason.

In this narrative of Scripture, Christ thus becomes the personification of this moral disposition or this religion of reason. He is the "ideal of moral perfection," which we must imitate and to which we must thus "*elevate* ourselves" (54). There is no danger of idolatry here, Kant believes, so long as we imitate Christ not as the son of God or as a supernatural being but as the complete expression of moral virtue. In the end, therefore, the historical example of Christ is not absolutely necessary, inasmuch as the idea of moral perfection he represents is already furnished to us by our reason (56). As "the founder of the first *true* church" (147), Christ will have left behind him visible traces in the form of his teachings that can then be read "as indubitable evidence of religion in general" (147). Hence Kant is able to find in Scripture a Christian formulation—indeed two different formulations—of what he calls the categorical imperative: "Perform your duty for no motive other than unconditional esteem for duty itself, *i.e.*, love God (the Legislator of all duties) above all else," and "Love every one as yourself, *i.e.*, further his welfare from good-will that is immediate and not derived from motives of self-advantage" (148).

It is this compatibility or even convertibility between Christianity and moral religion that makes Christianity the first and only truly universal religion, available to all men insofar as they are able to obey the moral law. As Kant puts it, "Here then is a complete religion, which can be presented to all men comprehensibly and convincingly through their own reason" (150). Nothing, in Kant's view, could be further from this than Judaism, with its "statutory dogmas," which make it "almost entirely unfitted for the religion of reason" (150). We can thus see why Derrida would claim that, for Kant, morality and Christianity are unthinkable without one another. Inasmuch as the categorical imperative expresses unconditional universality in an irreducibly Christian idiom, it is already, says Derrida, "evangelical." Derrida thus asks (in §17) whether it is possible to think a "universal" religion that would not simply follow the Christian paradigm, that is, whether the very idea of writing a book entitled *Religion Within the Limits of Reason* is not already a Christian idea.

We will return to these questions in section 4, below. Before doing that, however, we need to say a word about Kant's treatment of Christianity, so that one does not get the impression that Kant is simply an apologist for some historical form of Christian faith. When Derrida notes in "Above All, No Journalists!" that "however little dogmatic he may have been in his Christianity, [Kant] considered the only morality to be Christian morality" ("AANJ" 69), he is acknowledging at once the Christian filiation of Kant's moral philosophy and, importantly, Kant's own nondogmatic relation to that filiation. For at the same time as Kant calls Christianity in the form we find it in Scripture a "complete religion," he reserves some of his most acerbic comments for various perversions within the history of Christianity, chief among them being what he calls in book 4 "clericalism," which is but a form of idolatry or "*fetish-worship*" (167–68). By imposing "not free homage, as that which *first and foremost* must be paid to the moral law, but submission to precepts as a compulsory service," such clericalism is but a pseudo-service to the Christian church. Through such clericalism "the masses are ruled and robbed of their moral freedom by subservience to a church (not to religion)" (168). Kant warns elsewhere in a similar vein against all kinds of "religious illusions," from anthropomorphizing God to offering sacrifices and self-sacrifices in the hopes of winning favor from this God. All this is but pseudo-service to God, and Kant is not only clear but radical on this point: "*Whatever, over and above good life-conduct, man fancies that he can do to become well-pleasing to God is mere religious illusion and pseudo-service to God*" (158). Organized religion thus becomes corrupted or perverted for the same reason that individuals do; by acting out of self-interest or self-serving motives, it goes against the ends of pure religion. Here is just one among many examples of Kant's clear distaste for all forms of organized religion that substitute ceremony and ritual as the means of obtaining grace for a genuine change of heart: "To this end man busies himself with every conceivable formality, designed to indicate how greatly he *respects* the divine commands, in order that it may not be necessary for him to *obey* them" (189).

We thus need to keep this critique of organized Christianity in mind at the same time as we note, along with Derrida, that Christianity for Kant is the only public religion that is a purely moral religion. Though there have been, as Kant spares no energy denouncing, a long litany of blind superstitions that have hindered the progress of Christianity, none of them ended up preventing "Christianity's first invention" from "shining forth," namely, "to introduce a pure religious faith" (122).

3. The Four *Parerga* for a Religion Within the Limits of Reason Alone

Throughout "Faith and Knowledge," Derrida evokes the notion of *limits*, beginning with the limits of his own discourse. This is, obviously, a nod toward Kant, who not only proposes in *Religion* treating the subjects of radical evil and goodness in terms of a "philosophical theology [that] remains within the limits of reason alone" (8) but who places at the end of each of the work's four "books" what he refers to as an observation or a "parergon" that treats something that does not properly belong to the work of which it nonetheless forms a part. Derrida explains the placement of these *parerga* at the beginning of §16.

> *This definition of* reflecting faith *appears in the first of the four* Parerga *added at the end of each section of* Religion Within the Limits of Reason Alone. *These* Parerga *are not integral parts of the book; they "do not belong within" religion in the limits of pure reason," they "border upon" it. I stress this for reasons that are in part theo-topological, even theo-architectonic: these* Parerga *situate perhaps the fringe where we might be able, today, to inscribe our reflections. All the more since the first* Parergon, *added in the second edition,[7]* thereby defines the secondary task (parergon) *which, concerning what is morally indisputable, would consist in surmounting all the difficulties connected to transcendent questions.* (§16; see TP 55–56, 64)

As their name suggests, the *par-erga*, the plural of *par-ergon*, are "beside" (*para*) or on the border of the work itself (the *ergon*).[8] As Kant will argue, consideration of such things as grace, miracles, illumination, and thaumaturgy cannot be located "within" the limits of reason alone because each makes claims about some transcendent reality, God and his actions, that is beyond the limits or bounds of reason. But Derrida is also suggesting here that his own reflections are in effect *parergonal* with regard to Kant's; that is, they can be read as being inscribed along the "frame" of Kant's reflections, along the four sides, so to speak, of this great book on religion by this great thinker of fours. He is also suggesting that, in order to consider the question of religion today, the question of what is happening in the name of religion, and thus what is happening through a name that perhaps cannot be radically separated from the thing it is supposed to name, we will need to take into account all these things that Kant thought to be parergonal to the question of religion, everything from belief in miracles to the fanaticism to which a belief in grace can lead. Derrida continues—and I cite him at length here, both because he provides a good summary of Kant's *parerga* and because he reveals several important elements of his own interests and agenda:

> *When translated into the element of religion, moral ideas pervert the purity of their transcendence. They can do this in two times two ways, and the resulting square could today frame, providing that the appropriate transpositions are respected, a programme of analysis of the forms of evil perpetrated at the four corners of the world "in the name of religion." We will have to limit ourselves to an indication of the titles of this programme and, first, of the criteria (nature/supernatural, internal/external, theoretical elucidation/practical action, constative performative): (a) the allegedly internal experience (of the effects of grace): the* fanaticism *or* enthusiasm *of the illuminated* (Schwärmerei);[9] *(b) the allegedly* external *experience (of the miraculous):* superstition *(Aberglaube); (c) the alleged elucidations of the* understanding *in the consideration of the supernatural (secrets,* Geheimnisse*): illuminatism, the frenzy of the initiates; (d) the risky attempt of acting upon the supernatural (means of obtaining grace): thaumaturgy.* (§16)

The program to which Derrida is referring here is not absolutely clear, though it would no doubt involve thinking what is meant by the expression, at once so common and so vague, *religious fanaticism*. Derrida begins "Faith and Knowledge," recall, by evoking the so-called "return to religion," a journalistic phrase that in the mid-1990s was linked to claims about religious fundamentalism and fanaticism. The program for thinking religion today would thus have to include an understanding of this "fanaticism" as not simply or not only what can be placed on the borders of reason—especially since, for Derrida, both reason and these seemingly irrational expressions of religious faith share a common source.

Another part of this program is suggested by Derrida in the following passage:

When Marx holds the critique of religion to be the premise of all ideology-critique, when he holds religion to be the ideology par excellence, even for the matrix of all ideology and of the very movement of fetishization, does his position not fall, whether he would have wanted it or not, within the parergonal framework of this kind of rational criticism? Or rather, more plausible but also more difficult to demonstrate, does he not already deconstruct the fundamentally Christian axiomatics of Kant? This could be one of our questions, the most obscure one no doubt, because it is not at all certain that the very principles of the Marxist critique do not still appeal to a heterogeneity between faith and knowledge, between practical justice and cognition. (§16)

What Derrida contests in the Marxist (as well as Kantian) critique of religion is precisely this "appeal to a heterogeneity between faith and knowledge." This will become the central element in Derrida's critique of an entire line of Enlightenment thought—one that is sometimes even represented as a line or "filiation," as in the one that runs, that dashes, "Voltaire-Feuerbach-Marx-Nietzsche-Freud-(and even)-Heidegger" (§29). Faith and knowledge are thus not, despite the title of Derrida's essay, two heterogeneous things that have to be conjoined with "and." As we have seen, faith lends itself almost immediately, *sans souffler*, to knowledge, while knowledge is always conditioned by the element of faith.

But let's return for a moment to Kant's own understanding of the four *parerga* and to their treatment in the four observations placed at the end of each of the four books of *Religion*. Each observation treats one of the following: (1) Works of Grace, (2) Miracles, (3) Mysteries, (4) Means of Grace. Each of these is, Kant argues, a "morally-transcendent idea," that is, an idea that exceeds the bounds of reason, and each therefore leads to a particular ill or injury when it is introduced into religion. For works of grace, that is, for the belief that grace is given by God, the danger or damage is fanaticism; for belief in miracles, it is superstition; for belief in the mysteries, illumination; and for belief that one has at one's disposal the means of grace, thaumaturgy. As Kant argues, these four things are "*parerga* to religion within the limits of pure reason; they do not belong within it but border upon it" (47). Reason can thus neither deny nor affirm the reality of any of these things and so must not incorporate any consideration of them into its maxims for action.

Reason does not dispute the possibility or the reality of the objects of these ideas; she simply cannot adopt them into her maxims of thought and action. She even holds that, if in the inscrutable realm of the supernatural there is something more than she can explain to herself, which may yet be necessary as a complement to her moral insufficiency, this will be, even though unknown, available to her good will. Reason believes this with a faith which (with respect to the possibility of this supernatural complement) might be called *reflective*; for *dogmatic* faith, which proclaims itself as a form of *knowledge*, appears to her dishonest or presumptuous. (48)

Hence Kant opposes a sort of reflective faith of reason, where reason remains within her limits, to the dogmatic faith that proclaims itself to be a form of knowledge and so exceeds the limits of reason. By making "assertions and pretensions to knowledge"—with regard, for example, to the possibility of an afterlife and the means for procuring a favored lot in that afterlife—"reason simply passes beyond the limits of its own insight" (63–64). It is thus possible to "admit a work of grace as something incomprehensible, but we cannot adopt it into our maxims either for theoretical or for practical use" (49). Grace may indeed be necessary, Kant claims, to supplement the incompleteness of our own virtue, but we can know nothing about it and, especially, we must not believe we can do anything to bring it about. Because it is a supersensible object, which resides wholly outside our experience, "we remain wholly in the dark as to when, what, or how much, *grace* will accomplish in us" (179).

As for miracles—a topic we must dwell on just a bit in a book entitled *Miracle and Machine*—these are, says Kant, "events in the world the *operating laws* of whose causes are, and must remain, absolutely unknown to us" (81). "In the affairs of life, therefore, it is impossible for us to count on miracles or to take them into consideration at all in our use of reason (and reason must be used in every incident of life)" (82). Belief in such things as miracles, mysteries, and various means of obtaining grace (including, interestingly, prayer) is thus an illegitimate extension of the bounds of reason into the workings of the supersensible. We must instead attempt to act as moral agents "within the limits of reason alone," since "to venture beyond these limits is rashness and immodesty" (84).

At their very best, miracles would be but the mere enticements of religion, the ornaments—the bells and whistles, as it were—that a historical religion may initially need in order to gain authority but that any true, moral religion must forego and understand to be superfluous. Kant will thus not claim or affirm that there are no miracles, that Christ, for example, did not perform miracles or that his life was not itself a miracle. To keep within the limits of pure reason, he can neither confirm nor deny the reality of miracles. What is essential is that "we do not make it a tenet of religion that the knowing, believing, and professing of [miracles] are themselves means whereby we can render ourselves well-pleasing to God" (80). A historical religion may indeed need to dress itself up in miracles in order at the outset to win converts, but the right use of reason ultimately dictates seeing beyond the dress and the dogma to the reasonable doctrine behind them.

This is perfectly in line with Kant's emphasis throughout *Religion* on using the visible (the visible Church, for example, or Scripture, the letter of the law or the letter of prayer) as the vehicle to the invisible (to the invisible Church, the moral law, the spirit of the law, etc.), his emphasis on the need to overcome the outer for the inner, to abandon the shell for what it contains. Speaking of prayer, for example, Kant argues that one may elevate one's moral disposition to the point where the "spirit of prayer alone [is] sufficiently quickened within us and that the letter of it (at least as directed to our own advantage) finally fall[s] away" (185). It is this movement away from the body of the letter, away from its body and toward its inner spirit, that propels Kant's thinking in the direction of universality, away from the visible church and toward the ethical commonwealth.

4. The Death of God, Universality, and the Ethical Commonwealth

Kant had the genius to encapsulate almost all of his argument in *Religion* in the very first sentence of the "Preface to the First Edition." Having seen Kant's emphasis on the moral law and his insistence that reason must not overstep its bounds in claiming anything about the supersensible or supernatural, we are now able to read this sentence in all its radicality: "So far as morality is based upon the conception of man as a free agent who, just because he is free, binds himself through his reason to unconditional laws, it stands in need neither of the idea of another Being over him, for him to apprehend his duty, nor of an incentive other than the law itself, for him to do his duty" (3). Kant thus makes it clear from the outset that, in effect, "morality does not need religion at all"; "by virtue of pure practical reason it is self-sufficient" and needs no other ends than itself in the form of the moral law (3). As Kant will go on to argue, not only does a free agent not need the idea of another Being over him, but he must act without any consideration of such a Being, disregarding all thought about whether this Being, if He exists, will or will not look favorably upon the agent's actions. Because one cannot *know* anything about such a supersensible Being, not even whether He exists, a free agent must thus act always *as if* such a Being did not exist. Hence Derrida is hardly overinterpreting when he says that Kant's moral philosophy implies a certain "death of God," insofar as the one who acts in accordance with the moral law must, says Derrida paraphrasing Kant, *"act as though God did not exist or no longer concerned himself with our salvation"* (§15). Christian morality can thus respond to its vocation only by means of a certain *epochē*, bracketing, or suspension of God's existence. Derrida can therefore conclude that, from this perspective, European Christianity must be a kind of paganism, a religion that will have been living the death of God since Kant and the Enlightenment, a thesis that would then make Judaism and Islam the only remaining "monotheisms" with faith in a single, *living* God.

> *That Christianity is the death of God thus announced and recalled by Kant to the modernity of the Enlightenment? Judaism and Islam would thus be perhaps the last two monotheisms to revolt against everything that, in the Christianizing of our world, signifies the death of God, death in God, two non-pagan monotheisms that do not accept death any more than multiplicity in God (the Passion, the Trinity, etc.), two monotheisms still alien enough at the heart of Greco-Christian, Pagano-Christian Europe, alienating themselves from a Europe that signifies the death of God, by recalling at all costs that "monotheism" signifies no less faith in the One, and in the living One, than belief in a single God.* (§15)

Well before Nietzsche, therefore, with whom this phrase is most often associated, the theme of the death of God will have been central to Kant, though also, as we will see in Observation 2, to Hegel. This "death of God" requires a mankind that has come of age and outgrown his need for God. It also suggests that the very locus of absolute value has shifted from God to man. Derrida thus refers in §40 to the Kantian theme of the dignity or absolute value of man (*Würdigkeit*) as an end in itself (and never a means), a value or dignity of human life that must go beyond life itself.

> The price of human life, which is to say, of anthropo-theological life, the price of what ought to remain safe (*heilig*, sacred, safe and sound, unscathed, immune), as the absolute price, the price of what ought to inspire respect, modesty, reticence, this price is priceless. It corresponds to what Kant calls the dignity (*Würdigkeit*) of the end

in itself, of the rational finite being, of absolute value beyond all comparative market price (*Marktpreis*). This dignity of life can only subsist beyond the present living being. (§40)

In Chapter 7 we looked at the way in which, for Derrida, this value of life always exceeds life itself and so often comes to be affirmed through self-sacrifice and the sacrifice of life.[10] The dignity of human life, the value of *all* human life, thus implies a movement beyond particular cults and nation states, beyond historically determined churches and commonwealths, toward various forms of universality that Kant will characterize in terms of either the invisible church or the ethical commonwealth. Derrida introduces this question of universality in §17.

> How then to think—within the limits of reason alone—a religion which, without again becoming "natural religion," would today be effectively universal? And which, for that matter, would no longer be restricted to a paradigm that was Christian or even Abrahamic? What would be the project of such a "book"? For with Religion Within the Limits of Reason Alone, *there is a World involved that is also an Old-New Book or Testament. Does this project retain a meaning or a chance? A geopolitical chance or meaning? Or does the idea itself remain, in its origin and in its end, Christian? And would this necessarily be a limit, a limit like any other?* (§17)

In book 3 of *Religion*, Kant envisions, to cite the title of that book, "The Victory of the Good over the Evil Principle, and the Founding of a Kingdom of God on Earth." But what is meant by a "Kingdom of God *on Earth*"? Having seen what Kant calls radical evil and the means for its overcoming, as well as Kant's understanding of Christianity as the only truly moral religion, we can already guess at the answer. A Kingdom of God on earth would be one in which all of mankind lives and acts—or at least strives to do so—according to no other maxim than that of the moral law, a mankind that no longer needs the letter of Christian Scripture because it has internalized its spirit. Kant calls this an "ethical commonwealth," that is, "a society whose task and duty it is rationally to impress these laws in all their scope upon the entire human race. For only thus can we hope for a victory of the good over the evil principle" (86). Unlike a political commonwealth, then, where membership is restricted to a particular group, "an ethical commonwealth is extended ideally to the whole of mankind" (88). Hence Kant envisions the one true moral religion becoming the one true religion, universal in its scope, a kingdom of ends in themselves where each treats the other as an end in itself in accordance with the absolute value or dignity that is due an individual endowed with freedom.

The great challenge for such an ethical commonwealth is, of course, trying to bring about what Kant calls the invisible church within the visible one, trying to make not only *universal* but *public* the invisible church that exists in the heart of every right-acting moral agent. As Kant puts it, "such a commonwealth, being a Kingdom of God, can be undertaken by men only through *religion*, and, finally, in order that this religion be public (and this is requisite to a commonwealth), that it must be represented in the visible form of a *church*" (139). There is thus a tension here between the historical determinations of every visible church, every public church, which, because of the particularities of language, culture, and understanding, will necessarily be limited and contingent, and the universality of the invisible church that is sought. As the only religion that is able to shed its historical determinations and so achieve such universality, Christianity is the only religion that *requires* that this be done.

As Kant argues, every church originates in some historical or revealed faith, what he goes on to call an ecclesiastical faith, and churches that have a scripture to pass on are the ones most likely to survive and spread. But as we have seen in Kant's critique of Judaism as a merely statutory religion, an emphasis on scripture alone can hinder the development of "an institution whose laws are purely inward" (91). By focusing on the letter of the law or on the letter of scripture rather than its spirit, a church becomes necessarily *limited* in its scope. Kant thus sees a certain necessity of scripture for most men for a certain period of time, though he dreams of a commonwealth that could ultimately do without it. As he says with the characteristic sarcasm we noted earlier, "A holy book arouses the greatest respect even among those (indeed, most of all among those) who do not read it" (98). Only a church founded not upon scripture but upon a religion *within the limits* of reason alone, then, can be *unlimited* in its scope and achieve true universality. The advent of monotheism, of belief in *one* God, was itself already a major step in this direction. But what was then needed was a monotheism founded upon a scripture that was in complete conformity with the moral law. Christian Scripture was the answer to that need. Kant writes: "How fortunate, when such a book, fallen into men's hands, contains, along with its statutes, or laws of faith, the purest moral doctrine of religion in its completeness—a doctrine which can be brought into perfect harmony with such statutes ([which serve] as vehicles for its introduction)" (98). In Christian Scripture, Kant argues, the various statutes or laws of faith presented there, though necessarily contingent and historically determined, can nonetheless serve as "vehicles" for the intro-duction of a pure religious faith that would not be historically determined and continent. Hence Kant will go on to argue that ecclesiastical faith, the faith of the visible church, can become the "historical vehicle" of pure religious faith, a vehicle that can in time be "dispensed with" (106). As he says later with a more naturalistic metaphor, historical or ecclesiastical faith would be but the "shell" from which "pure religion" might eventu-ally emerge (126). The goal of ecclesiastical faith is thus, in some sense, its own overcoming, that is, "setting up the religion of good life-conduct as the real end, in order, at some future time, to be able entirely to dis-pense with the statutory articles [of ecclesiastical faith]" (163).

Only when a religion has thus dispensed with its "statutory articles" of faith can it become truly universal. It is able to do this to the precise extent that pure religious faith becomes the "highest interpreter" of "ecclesiasti-cal faith" (100). Because "the predisposition to the moral religion lay hid-den in human reason" (102), pure religious faith—which *in principle* needs no historically revealed religion though *in fact* often does—can in-terpret that which within ecclesiastical faith does or does not belong to a religion within the limits of reason alone. Hence it is possible for Kant to say that "there is only *one* (true) *religion*; but there can be *faiths* of several kinds" (98). That is, there can be churches of various kinds but only one religion that acts as their "highest interpreter," one religion that would try to find that which is universal in each church and so conforms to the one truth of pure religious faith. As Kant argues, a "rightful claim to uni-versality" is a church's "most important mark of truth" (100). Kant thus opposes the universality of the "true church" or the one true religion, which is necessary and singular, to historical faiths, which are based upon revelation and so are contingent, have only partial validity, can reach only a portion of humanity, and so on. Though Derrida would reverse these terms and speak of many historical or determinate religions but only one true faith, this drive toward a certain conception of universality—even if it is not the same universality—is central in both thinkers.

Let me end this Observation with a passage from *Religion* that demon-strates Kant's reverence for a "pure religion of reason," whose universality is expressed so well by Christian Scripture (in this case Paul's First Letter to the Corinthians) but which, according to Kant, requires no faith in or knowledge of the Christian God referred to in this Scripture, not even whether such a Being exists. It is a universality that is related, for Kant, to a kind of coming of age for mankind, a "putting away of childish things"—a verse from the New Testament that Kant is willing to use to make his point, obviously, but that in the end would itself have to be one those "childish things" to be put away in mankind's final coming of age:

> in the end religion will gradually be freed from all empirical deter-mining grounds and from all statutes which rest on history and which through the agency of ecclesiastical faith provisionally unite men for the requirements of the good; and thus at last the pure reli-gion of reason will rule over all, "so that God may be all in all." The integuments within which the embryo first developed into a human being must be laid aside when he is to come into the light of day. . . . While he (the human race) "was a child he understood as a child" and managed to combine a certain amount of erudition, and even a philosophy ministering to the church, with the propositions which were bestowed on him without his cooperation: "but when he be-comes a man he puts away childish things." (112)

As Derrida puts it in a phrase that begins with the title of the essay we have been following throughout this work: "Faith and knowledge: be-tween believing one knows and knowing one believes, the alternative is not a game" (§35).

Observation 2

Hegel

If, as we have seen, Derrida in "Faith and Knowledge" makes frequent reference to the terms and themes of Kant's work on religion but gives no sustained reading or interpretation of that work, this is even more so for Hegel. Beyond the opening reference to Hegel's 1807 "Who thinks abstractly?" there are only two other explicit mentions of Hegel, one little more than a passing reference to the Christian or Greco-Christian concept of the world and of history "extending to Kant, Hegel, Husserl, and Heidegger" in §27, and the other a more extended reference in §18. The latter is the only section in "Faith and Knowledge" where Derrida speaks of Hegel's philosophy of religion in any detail and the only one that evokes, in the same breath as the *Phenomenology of Spirit*, the title of the text that Derrida's essay "doubles" or "reproduces," Hegel's 1802 *Faith and Knowledge*. While it might thus be tempting to want to claim that Hegel's text of the same title must play a significant if not determining or organizing role in Derrida's essay, neither the one section where Derrida refers to it nor the rest of the essay bears this out.

What, exactly, does Derrida say about Hegel in §18? Only this: after asking in the preceding section a series of questions about the meaning of religion today, the meaning of a "religion within the limits of reason alone," and the relationship between particular religions and a universal religion, Derrida begins §18:

Keeping these questions in mind, we might be able to gauge two tempta-
tions. In their schematic principle, one would be "Hegelian": ontotheol-
ogy which determines absolute knowledge as the truth of religion, in
the course of the final movement described in the conclusions of The
Phenomenology of Spirit *or of* Faith and Knowledge, *which an-*
nounces in effect a "religion of modern times" (Religion der neuen
Zeit) *founded on the sentiment that "God himself is dead." "Infinite*
pain" is still only a "moment" (rein als Moment), *and the moral sacri-*
fice of empirical existence only dates the absolute Passion or the specula-
tive Good Friday (spekulativer Karfreitag). *Dogmatic philosophies and*
natural religions should disappear and, out of the greatest "asperity,"
the harshest impiety, out of kenosis and the void of the most serious pri-
vation of God (Gottlosigkeit), *ought to resuscitate the most serene lib-*
erty in its highest totality. Distinct from faith, from prayer or from
sacrifice, ontotheology destroys religion, but, yet another paradox, it is
also perhaps what informs, on the contrary, the theological and ecclesias-
tical, even religious, development of faith. The other temptation (per-
haps there are still good reasons for keeping this word) would be
"Heideggerian." (§18)

Derrida's intentions with regard to Hegel here seem relatively clear.
Drawing on the relationship in Genesis between temptation and knowledge, Derrida calls the Hegelian determination of absolute knowledge as
the truth of religion one of the two temptations he will try to avoid. Derrida makes this connection between knowledge and temptation explicit
later in the essay:

As always, recourse to knowledge is temptation itself. Knowing is
temptation, albeit in a somewhat more singular sense than believed
when referring habitually (habitually, at least) to the Evil Genius or
to some original sin. The temptation of knowing, the temptation of
knowledge, is to believe not only that one knows what one knows
(which wouldn't be too serious), but also that one knows what
knowledge is, that is, free, structurally, of belief or of **faith**—of the
fiduciary or of trustworthiness. (§31)

Insofar as Derrida is attempting to "avoid" the Hegelian determination
of absolute knowledge as the truth of religion, it should come as no surprise that Derrida offers no real reading of *Faith and Knowledge* in "Faith
and Knowledge." Indeed Derrida gives us little more than a paraphrasing
of its final paragraph, where Hegel is laying out the project of his own
speculative philosophy ("the Idea of absolute freedom and along with it

the absolute Passion, the speculative Good Friday") in opposition to critical philosophy or to what Hegel calls the "reflective philosophy of subjectivity."[1] That is no doubt in large part because the vast majority of Hegel's *Faith and Knowledge* is not, as the title might suggest and as the conclusion cited by Derrida might lead one to believe, a development of Hegel's own speculative philosophy but a critique, often rather detailed and sometimes quite blistering and polemical, of Kant, Jacobi, and Fichte. This is evident from the subtitle of this text—for it too, like Derrida's essay, also has a subtitle, and a rather long one at that—"the *Reflective Philosophy of Subjectivity* in the complete range of its forms as Kantian, Jacobian, and Fichtean Philosophy." If the title *Faith and Knowledge* is meant to give us some idea of the ultimate ambition of Hegel's text, a radical rethinking of the relationship between religion and reason, the subtitle makes clear the immediate focus of his critique and, true to the methodology Hegel is in the process of developing, the material through which the greater ambitions of the speculative project will be clarified.

Published in 1802 in the *Journal of Critical Philosophy*, the journal Hegel co-edited with Schelling, *Faith and Knowledge* is an approximately hundred-page essay (in the original German) that consists of a nine-page introduction, a two-page conclusion (which is what Derrida cites), and three more or less independent chapters or essays devoted to criticisms of Kant, Jacobi, and Fichte from the perspective of Hegel's own thought. (Hegel's *Phenomenology of Spirit* would not be published until 1807, five years after *Faith and Knowledge*.) From its opening page, Hegel pulls no punches and hones in on the object of his critique:

> Enlightened Reason won a glorious victory over what it believed, in its limited conception of religion, to be faith as opposed to Reason. Yet seen in a clear light the victory comes to no more than this: the positive element with which Reason busied itself to do battle, is no longer religion, and victorious Reason is no longer Reason. The new born peace that hovers triumphantly over the corpse of Reason and faith, uniting them as the child of both, has as little of Reason in it as it has of authentic faith.
>
> Reason had already gone to seed in and for itself when it envisaged religion merely as something positive and not idealistically. And after its battle with religion the best that Reason could manage was to take a look at itself and come to self-awareness. Reason, having in this way become mere intellect, acknowledges its own nothingness by placing that which is better than it in a *faith outside and above* itself, as a *beyond* [to be believed in]. This is what has happened in the *philosophies of Kant, Jacobi, and Fichte*. (55–56)

And then Hegel adds this little line, which was surely meant to strike at the heart of the one who famously wrote in the Preface to the Second Edition of his *Critique of Pure Reason* that he "had to deny knowledge in order to make room for faith": "Philosophy has made itself the handmaid of a faith once more." This is, of course, exactly what Kant thought he was avoiding by limiting the claims both of reason and of a faith based on an illegitimate use of that reason. As Walter Cerf humorously muses in his preface to *Faith and Knowledge*, "if Kant had read the *Essays*, they might have shortened his life" (xxxv).

According to Hegel, then, critical or reflective philosophy gives us neither genuine faith nor genuine reason.[2] Hegel returns again and again, in *Faith and Knowledge*, to what he believes to be the false dichotomy between the infinite and the finite in these philosophies of subjectivity, a dichotomy that forever severs man from any cognition of God, thereby leading to an impoverished reason and a "pollution"—Hegel's word—of genuine faith. "The fundamental principle common to the philosophies of Kant, Jacobi and Fichte is, then, the absoluteness of finitude and, resulting from it, the absolute antithesis of finitude and infinity, reality and ideality, the sensuous and the supersensuous, and the beyondness of what is truly real and absolute" (62). Because of this absolute antithesis, "the sphere of the eternal is the incalculable, the inconceivable, the empty—an incognizable God beyond the boundary sakes of Reason" (60). This, argues Hegel, is the "fixed standpoint" and predicament of the times, the common ground of these otherwise quite different philosophies of subjectivity. "In this situation philosophy cannot aim at the cognition of God, but only at what is called the cognition of man," and man becomes, complains Hegel, "not a glowing spark of eternal beauty, or a spiritual focus of the universe, but an absolute sensibility," able only to employ his "faculty of faith" in order to "touch himself up here and there with a spot of alien supersensuousness" (65).

Hegel's critique of Kant is thus all-encompassing, taking aim at his ontology, epistemology, aesthetics, and, especially for our purposes here, his moral philosophy and philosophy of religion. Even in the parts of *Faith and Knowledge* seemingly devoted to a critique of Fichte or Jacobi, Kant is never very far from Hegel's thoughts. Here is just one example:

> This pollution of faith and this hallowing of subjectivity must lead
> us briefly into the practical philosophy of Jacobi. Kant's practical
> reason, being the empty concept in its unmoved opposition to na-
> ture, can produce nothing but a system of tyranny [of the Law of

Reason over human nature], a rending of ethical integrity [*Sittlich-keit*] and beauty, or else like Kantian morality cleave to so-called duties of a formalistic kind that determine nothing. (143)

This is not the place to enter into the long debate about this critique, especially since Derrida does not do so himself in "Faith and Knowledge." It should at least be noted, however—since the conclusion of Hegel's essay, which Derrida cites, really only makes sense when seen in this light—that Hegel's critical reading of Kant, and to a lesser extent Fichte and Jacobi, is tempered throughout by his attempt to find within these philosophies of subjectivity something positive from the viewpoint of speculative thought. Insofar as the philosophies of Kant, Fichte, and Jacobi brought certain aspects of reflective philosophy to their point of culmination and conclusion, they in some sense prepared the way for speculative philosophy. Reflective philosophy will have revealed and pushed to their extreme a series of dichotomies (between the finite and the infinite, subject and object, receptivity and spontaneity, the phenomenal or the sensuous and the noumenal or supersensuous) that speculative philosophy will now be called on to reconcile. Kant himself will thus often have glimpsed without fully recognizing the significance of many speculative ideas.[3] Hence Hegel will argue, for example, that the thought of an a priori synthesis through the "productive imagination is a truly speculative idea" (71; see 80) and, elsewhere, that it is in *"reflecting judgment* that Kant finds the middle term between the concept of nature and the concept of freedom" (86). Kant will thus have anticipated speculative philosophy but in each case will have fallen short of it by making subjectivity absolute and separating thought from being.

Hegel begins his conclusion to *Faith and Knowledge*: "In their totality, the philosophies we have considered have in this way recast the dogmatism of being into the dogmatism of thinking, the metaphysic of objectivity into the metaphysic of subjectivity" (189). But now that "this metaphysic of subjectivity has run through the complete cycle of its forms in the philosophies of Kant, Jacobi, and Fichte," "the external possibility directly arises that the true philosophy should emerge out of this [completed] culture" (189). Hegel can thus at once criticize these philosophies of subjectivity and argue that "they have their positive, genuine though subordinate, position within true philosophy," that is, within speculative philosophy, whose task, then, is to rethink or reexpress the philosophy of subjectivity in a way that does not oppose thought to being or the infinite to the finite.[4] H. S. Harris writes, in his introduction to *Faith and Knowledge*:

The Idea is the *true* infinity of life, an infinity that is not, like the concept (the moral law, or the "law of Nature" in the earlier tradition), essentially *opposed* to the finite. It does not exist simply as a thought or concept to be *reflected* on by the finite consciousness. It is an infinity that contains the finite, a concept that involves existence, an ideal that is the life of the real. (16)

This is the Speculative Good Friday of Hegel's conclusion, the one Derrida cites both here and in *Glas*, the one which he characterizes as a kind of onto-theological temptation.

Derrida's "Faith and Knowledge" thus refers to Hegel's text with the same title, it even cites its closing paragraph, and thus, implicitly at least, it evokes Hegel's critique of Kant and the debate between their various philosophies of religion, but it remains more or less silent or agnostic about this debate. The fact that Derrida ends up devoting much more of his attention to Kant's *Religion* than to Hegel's *Faith and Knowledge* may tell us something about where Derrida's sympathies or at least his interests lie, but it is important to underscore yet again that Derrida is doing something quite different from either Hegel or Kant in his exploration of the relationship between faith and knowledge or, rather, for these are not the same thing, faith and technoscience.

It will always be possible, of course, to argue that Derrida's relative silence with regard to Hegel as opposed to Kant—and Kant, as we shall see later, as opposed to Heidegger in the second half of the essay—is evidence for the determining role the former must be playing in his work. Perhaps, but a lot of interpretative work would need to be done to make this case, and even more would need to be done to show that Derrida was trying, in "Faith and Knowledge," to intervene in the debate between Kant and Hegel. In his attempt to understand the nature of religion today, Derrida had other things in view. For instead of ending his text with a reference to the speculative Good Friday, he concludes with an equally dramatic reference to violence, to ashes, to the massacre at Chatila, and to "an open pomegranate, one Passover evening, on a tray" (§51).

Observation 3

Bergson

Derrida's title and subtitle—"Faith and Knowledge: The Two Sources of 'Religion' at the Limits of Religion Alone"—combine, as we have seen, not just two but three classic texts on religion: Hegel's *Faith and Knowledge*, Kant's *Religion Within the Limits of Reason Alone*, and Henri Bergson's 1932 *The Two Sources of Morality and Religion*. Such a combination is striking insofar as Bergson is a far less common reference in Derrida's work as a whole than either Hegel or Kant. If Derrida devoted a significant amount of work to Hegel (especially early on, in "The Pit and the Pyramid," *Glas*, and elsewhere) and to Kant (in *The Truth in Painting* and his various works on hospitality, cosmopolitanism, and the university), there is really no comparable engagement or dialogue with Bergson anywhere else in Derrida's published works.[1] Given the significance of Bergson in twentieth-century French philosophy, this absence may come as something of a surprise, even if it is hardly unique. For reasons that would surely call for extended analysis, Derrida's twentieth century "sources" or "influences" tended to be much more German than French. Although Derrida does have punctual debates with Foucault, Ricoeur, and Lacan, among others, there is nothing to compare to his more sustained engagements with Husserl, Heidegger, and Freud. And while there are commentaries on important French philosopher-writers (Montaigne, Descartes, Rousseau, etc.) and readings of poets and novelists writing in French (Ponge, Jabès, Blanchot, Genet, Bataille, Leiris), as well as an extended engagement with the philosopher Emmanuel Levinas, writing in French but born in Lithuania, there is a noticeable lack of engagement with the major figures of twentieth-century French philosophy, such as Sartre, Merleau-Ponty, and Bergson.[2]

Given this history, it is hardly surprising that Derrida does not closely read or analyze Bergson's *The Two Sources of Morality and Religion* in "Faith and Knowledge." And yet Bergson's work remains nonetheless always in the background of the essay, from the very notion, alluded to in the title, that there are "two sources" of religion to Derrida's citing, in §37, Bergson's final sentence, which speaks of "the essential function of the universe" as "a machine for the making of gods," a line that appears to lend to the essay some of the vocabulary if not the very theme of mechanicity and of the automatic or machinelike splitting of sources. Though the two sources of religion are hardly the same in Derrida and Bergson, there are, as we will see, some similarities between them, and Bergson will leave us, in the end, with questions that will resemble those of not just Derrida but DeLillo. Written between the two world wars in 1932—just two years, then, after Derrida's birth and four years before DeLillo's—Bergson's book on religion poses questions about the future, about our future, that neither Kant nor Hegel really could. It will thus be important for us to look a bit more closely at this book, even if Derrida does not, in order to see the premises for Derrida's rethinking of the question of religion in relationship to science and, especially, the miracle in relation to the machine.

As Bergson announces clearly in the title of his book, there are indeed, for him, two sources of morality and religion. Arguing throughout against an intellectualist account or approach such as Kant's, which does not give sufficient weight to the *fact* of moral obligation in human society, Bergson identifies the first of these two sources of morality as *habit*. From our earliest childhood on, we are taught by parents, teachers, and society more generally to follow certain rules and to act in certain ways; in a word, we are taught or trained to obey, and this habituation to obedience can become so strong that it resembles what we call animal instinct. In this regard, human society is not unlike an ant colony—one of Bergson's favorite images—where each individual does his or her job and follows his or her quasi-instinct to obey society's conventions. It is thus under the pressure of habit, this first source of morality, that the individual obeys society and society, in return, gives security and well-being to the individual.

Bergson characterizes societies that tend to favor the first source of morality as *closed societies*, and he terms the religions they tend to foster *static religions.* The aim of such closed societies and static religions is, essentially, to meet society's needs and secure social cohesion, stability, and survival—in a word, they aim at society's *salut* as health and salvation. What the individual in such a society loves or is concerned with is thus not humanity as a whole but his or her own, his or her kin or community. Such societies are closed, for Bergson, because they reject what is beyond or outside them and thus always turn inward toward their own perpetuation and survival. The religions that correspond to such societies are static because they resist innovation and progress and quickly devolve into mere cult and ritual, that is, into mere observance or obedience. For many philosophers, first among them Kant, this is hardly a morality or a religion worthy of the name. For Bergson, however, it is important to recognize this first source of religion and morality, even if he too will be dissatisfied with it alone.

There is thus another source of morality and religion, one that, at its extreme, at its limit, is opposed to the first as a divine realm would be opposed to an ant colony. This second source is not another acquired habit that takes on the look of an animal instinct but a *natural emotion* that almost every individual, and certain individuals in an exemplary fashion, can experience. This emotion, characterized by Bergson in various ways as a kind of enthusiasm or joy, is what inspires in individuals a desire for freedom and a love of humanity in general. This embracing of humanity is an emotion or an impetus (an *élan*, as Bergson famously calls it) that goes beyond both animal instinct and human intelligence. If the first morality is more or less anonymous insofar as just about everyone—from parents and teachers to society in general—helps to inculcate it, a morality that extends throughout all of society and exercises a force or pressure from below, so to speak, this second morality is a morality of certain great individuals—Bergson calls them heroes, or, later, mystics—who have opened themselves up in an exemplary way to a love of humanity as a whole and who thereby become models for others in society to look up to and follow. While the first source of morality thus comes from below and is in its automaticity and inflexibility akin to animal obedience (or else the machine), the second comes from above and in its freedom and creativity is akin to the divine (or the miraculous).

Bergson calls societies that tend to favor the second source of morality *open societies*, and the religions they tend to encourage, *dynamic religions*. In such societies and religions, the goal is no longer mere self-preservation or social cohesion but creativity, progress, and love. While certain religions, as we will see, embody this dynamism better than others, the spirit of such religions can be seen in its purest form in the singularity of mystical experience. Rather than being turned inward toward particular communities, dynamic religions aim at universality and at a love of humanity as a whole, and they contribute to societies that resemble that of a people of gods. Insofar as closed societies and static religions aim at self-preservation, at what might be called the *indemnification* of society, they are perpetually concerned with war. Open societies and dynamic religions, on the other hand, are inherently *universalizable* and so aim always at peace.

Habit and emotion, obedience and love, these two sources of morality are thus at the basis of all religions, and they explain why religions can be used either to consolidate and reinforce a particular society's already-established habits, ideals, and institutions or else to elevate human beings above their particular society so as to embrace humanity as a whole. Though elements of dynamism exist in all static religions and all dynamic religions are always liable to become static, Bergson contrasts static, organized, doctrinal religions with dynamic, creative, mystical religions and, especially, with mystical experience that has not yet been appropriated by any religion at all. Not unlike Kant, he contrasts the religions of cult and mere observance, mere statutory religions, one might say, with the religions—or, really, the religion—that seeks to go beyond mere observance and ritual in order to embrace humanity as a whole.

But the real specificity of religion, as opposed to morality, is to be found in what Bergson calls the "myth-making function," a natural human ability derived from human intelligence that allows man to confront and overcome his fear of death and the uncertainties of life through the creation of religious stories and images. Whereas the stories and images of static religions thus aim to comfort, conserve, and reinforce a particular society's ideals, those of dynamic religions aim to give expression to a love of all humanity and all creation. Even when this love comes to be expressed in the images and words of a static religion, the original inspiration or *élan* of these images and words always exceeds the dogmatism of that religion. It is thus only through dynamic religion and open societies that there is the push or drive—and always by leaps—toward greater and greater universality and peace. Such leaps are made by individuals who exceed the limitations of their societies or static religions so as to become models for others to imitate and follow. Bergson finds forerunners of dynamic religion in other religious cultures, for example, in certain forms of Greek mysticism, but, as the emphasis on love might suggest, it is really only in Christian mysticism that dynamic religion finds its *élan* and its truest expression, as well as its highest point of evolution.

This reference to evolution by the author of *Creative Evolution* (1907) puts everything we have seen thus far in a somewhat different light. For it suggests that both kinds of religion, static and dynamic, and both kinds of morality, closed and open, along with both instinct and emotion, are in the end the products of a single, ongoing, "evolutionary" process. It suggests that all of these are, in the end, expressions of *life*. Life is the common source of both kinds of morality and religion, even if the development of one kind of religion, static religion, has been blocked and become predictable, simply turning in circles like a machine, while the development or progress of dynamic religion, inspired and drawn out of itself, is unpredictable and sudden, coming to humanity from above, so to speak, through an unexpected mutation, through a leap or an *élan*, a *tout d'un coup* (just one of the many connections, in addition to habit, to Proust) that might be compared to a kind of miracle.

As in Derrida, then, there is in the end really only one source that divides in two as human intelligence, in Bergson's account, tries to understand it. What Derrida thus retains from Bergson's account, or what Derrida's account has in common with Bergson's, is, among other things, this notion of a single source of religion that, already at the origin, divides in two, though also a thinking of religion in relationship to the machine (the last part of Bergson's work is entitled "Mechanics and Mysticism"), along with a certain a displacement of reason by that which comes before it or exceeds it, habit and inspiration, or obedience and love, for Bergson, faith for Derrida.

Those are just a few of the places of contact between Bergson and Derrida, even if a rigorous account of the differences between them would no doubt cast a good deal of doubt on the real pertinence of these comparisons. For, in addition to the enormous differences in style between these two thinkers, there is the obvious emphasis in Bergson, born to Jewish parents, on Christianity and Christian mysticism, leading Derrida to call Bergson in "Faith and Knowledge" "that great Judeo-Christian" (§36). Derrida would thus no doubt question the degree to which Bergson's thought draws on a particular culture and tradition, in this case, Christian culture and the Christian religious tradition (making it into what Derrida might have called, imitating Bergson, a kind *static philosophy*), with, precisely, little opening to what exceeds it. One can also imagine that Derrida would have rejected a good deal of the language associated with this tradition, beginning with the notion of the "call of the hero."

As for the relationship between Kant and Bergson, there is one clear place of intersection among their many differences. As we saw, Kant claims that the Christian religion would be the only true religion because it is the only one concerned with the good conduct of life and thus the only one that is universalizable. Though Bergson is always critical of Kant's intellectualist approach to religion, his conclusion is not totally incompatible with Kant's on this score. Christianity would be the highest expression of creative evolution, of the *élan vital*, insofar as it goes beyond the parochial concerns of static religion, beyond the tenets of a particular religion, to embrace humanity in general through love. Static religions could thus be considered those with a living God—Judaism and Islam, for example—while Christianity would be the only religion with a death of God that opens onto the *élan vital* itself. For Bergson as well as for Kant, there are two stocks or two families of religion, and while both thinkers are willing to give the name *religion* to both stocks, only one of the two stocks, moral religion for Kant, dynamic religion for Bergson, is really worthy of the name—worthy of a name that both thinkers would in the end be willing to give up as humanity progresses toward a universal ethical commonwealth or a people of gods.

Let me conclude this all-too-brief consideration of Bergson by citing a short passage from near the end of *The Two Sources of Morality and Religion* that will bring us back to both Derrida and DeLillo. The passage concerns humanity's capacity to take over what was given to it by nature in order to produce through science things of which nature itself is incapable. In it we will see Bergson's enthusiasm and hope for the progress of science in humanity's evolution toward greater and more complete forms of open morality and dynamic religion:

> But now intelligence, raising the construction of instruments to a degree of complexity and perfection which nature (so incapable of mechanical construction) had not even foreseen, pouring into these machines reserves of energy which nature (so heedless of economy) had never even thought of, has endowed us with powers beside which those of our body barely count: they will be altogether limitless when science is able to liberate the force which is enclosed, or rather condensed, in the slightest particle of ponderable matter. (312)

Bergson expresses his genuine admiration here for the invention of certain machines (such as the steam engine) that are able to extract from matter, such as coal or oil, the energy that had been stored up and kept in reserve for millions of years. He sees these machines being used to meet human needs in order to free human activity for the kinds of things favored by dynamic religions—love of humanity, charity, good works, and so on. Though Bergson clearly recognizes that such machines might also be used for the production of needless luxuries and expectations of a standard of living that can lead to conflicts between nations and thus war, he nevertheless celebrates man's intelligence and, here near the end of *The Two Sources of Morality and Religion*, glimpses something like an ideal limit and thus an optimal development for mankind.

These lines were written, let me recall, in 1932, nine years before Bergson's death, in what would turn out to be his last completed work. One can only imagine what he might have thought, had he lived just a few more years, of the prodigious, unimaginable, almost unlimited extractions of power yielded by atomic energy. One can only imagine how the images of Hiroshima or Nagasaki—or indeed of Trinity, New Mexico—would have dampened his admiration for the machine and its potential for freeing mankind for the activities of dynamic religion. One can only imagine what Bergson might have thought of these unimaginable attempts "to liberate the force which is enclosed, or rather condensed, in the slightest particle of ponderable matter."

But Bergson, who died in 1941, did not need to live into the nuclear age in order to have intimations of this sort, worries, in any case, about not just the enormous war machines he saw in use during the First World War but about the deadly uses to which the smallest particles of matter might be put. Indeed Bergson seems to have had an inkling already in 1932 that the threat today comes not just from these great machines of death but from something infinitely smaller within the machine, or from something within us, something more powerful than that in which it is contained, something, therefore, that is beyond all "containment." In the closing lines, therefore, of *The Two Sources of Religion and Morality*, Bergson's initial optimism in the passage cited above is more than tempered, as he asks whether humanity is still truly capable of living up to its own vocation in order to become what it is, or whether humanity's progress— the very progress Bergson had identified with open societies and dynamic religions—has not led to man's own undoing. In the final words of the book, Bergson seems to leave the issue undecided—or, rather, he leaves it up to us to determine which way we will go.

Mankind lies groaning, half crushed beneath the weight of its own progress. Men do not sufficiently realize that their future is in their own hands. Theirs is the task of determining first of all whether they want to go on living or not. Theirs the responsibility, then, for deciding if they want merely to live, or intend to make just the extra effort required for fulfilling, even on their refractory planet, the essential function of the universe, which is a machine for the making of gods. (317)

Bergson asks in these final, dramatic lines whether humanity wishes only to survive, to preserve itself by living in a closed society that aims only at social cohesion, or whether it should, whether it *must*, seek something beyond this. For even though closed societies and static religions all aim to preserve societies and sustain life, they are all organized around war, and war seems to have evolved in the twentieth century into something quite new or qualitatively different. True, war and peace will always have been in tension with one another, just as closed and open societies or static and dynamic religions have been, but "progress" in the sciences over the past few centuries seem to have changed this dynamic. For it has now become possible, Bergson seems to have understood in 1932, for humanity not only to do irreparable damage to the drive toward universal love that characterizes dynamic religion but to destroy itself completely. And the terrible hypothesis Bergson seems to entertain at the very end of *The Two Sources* is that humanity may not only be *able* to destroy itself in this way but may *want* to. In short, the hypothesis Bergson considers is that human life—perhaps even life itself—is autoimmune.

Faced with the possibility not just of humanity's stagnation but of its destruction, Bergson ends with the hope that humanity might instead pursue and accomplish what he famously characterizes as the essential function of the universe—the making of gods. What he means here, it seems, is not the creation of gods through a myth-making function that would calm humanity's fear of death but the appearance of individual human beings who have become, through the organization of open societies and through the impetus and inspiration of dynamic religions, divinities or gods in their own right, who have become, through their love of humanity, or their representation of the God of love, a people of gods *who are love*. Though matter remains recalcitrant or refractory to this ambition, though human society tends to resist it, though the myth-making function is often used to domesticate this vital force, Bergson seems to bank on the hope that humanity is still capable of achieving the highest point of its evolution, that it is still capable of advancing through science to the point where it can liberate itself from certain kinds of repetitive and oppressive labor in order to devote itself to the charitable works that make each human being into a quasi-god. In effect, he seems to be hoping that humanity is still capable of reading the final word of *Underworld*— "Peace"—without irony or cynicism.

Observation 4

Heidegger

Though "Faith and Knowledge" makes no explicit allusion to Heidegger in its title (which comes from Hegel) or its subtitle (which crosses texts of Kant and Bergson), Heidegger plays a significant role in the essay. Indeed it could be argued that Heidegger is, in the end, Derrida's principal interlocutor, especially in the latter sections of the essay, where Derrida, in both the main body of the text and the notes, multiplies references to him. If the majority of Derrida's comments on Kant and Hegel occur in the first half of the essay, in the "Italics," the second half of the essay is almost entirely dominated by references to Heidegger, as if a dialogue with Heidegger were not only developing but growing in intensity as Derrida was working on the "Post-scriptum" and drawing the essay to a conclusion. This dialogue would even include references to a few of Heidegger's most prominent contemporary commentators (e.g., Françoise Dastur and Jean-François Courtine), something we do not see at all in Derrida's readings of Kant, Hegel, or Bergson.[1] All this suggests an engagement with the Heideggerian text and with scholarship on Heidegger that is unique.[2] In the end, no other thinker, ancient or contemporary, is granted a similar privilege.

Because Heidegger comes to play a more and more prominent role in "Faith and Knowledge" and Derrida refers to more than one text by Heidegger, this Observation will be different from the preceding three. Whereas in the previous observations I attempted to give a fuller reading of Hegel's *Faith and Knowledge*, Kant's *Religion Within the Limits of Reason Alone*, and Bergson's *The Two Sources of Morality and Religion*, no analogous reading of Heidegger can be given here, since Derrida refers to a series of texts written over a period of decades. By looking at a large swath of Heidegger's work, Derrida wishes not just to pull a few themes from Heidegger's work but to demonstrate a coherence or consistency within Heidegger's thought about religion from his early to his late works, namely, a consistent and coherent ambivalence with regard to the role of faith or belief in philosophy and in thinking more generally. If Derrida thus uses Kant, Hegel, and Bergson to develop his own thesis regarding the relationship between religion and science, he actually develops something of a reading and a thesis with regard to Heidegger on this question of the relationship between religion and science and the role faith plays in both. In this observation, I will not try to reconstitute Heidegger's own thinking in this regard but, much more modestly, simply try to follow Derrida's itinerary in his reading of Heidegger.

Beyond a few passing references to what Heidegger calls, in *Being and Time*, Dasein's *"preunderstanding"* of Being (in §3) or Heidegger's relationship to negative theology (in §23) or his development of the notion of "world" (in §27) or his rethinking of the nature of justice or *Dikē*,[3] most of the references to Heidegger can be grouped into three related categories, which, when taken together, form something like an argument if not a brief essay within the essay "Faith and Knowledge." At issue throughout is what Derrida perceives to be Heidegger's insistence on the *originary*: his insistence, for example, on an originary determination of the concept of religion in Rome, on a more originary Christianity or proto-Christianity that would come before this Roman determination, and, finally, on an originary *gage* or *engagement*—an originary or elementary faith or belief—that would precede and condition even this proto-Christianity and would perhaps be the condition of thought in general.

If Heidegger comes to play a major role late in the essay, his importance can already be discerned in a few earlier sections (in §§15, 18, 19, 20). In §15 for example, Derrida follows up a discussion of Kant's notion of "reflecting faith" and an implied "death of God" by speaking of Heidegger's attempt to think a different possibility for thought in the wake of this death of God. According to Derrida, Heidegger, at once like and unlike Kant, looks for pre-religious possibilities, pre-Christian possibilities, at the same time as he seeks a more originary Christianity.

With regard to this logic, to its formal rigor and to its possibilities, does not Heidegger move in a different direction? He insists, indeed, in Sein und Zeit *upon the character of originary conscience* (Gewissen), *being-responsible-guilty-indebted* (Schuldigsein) *or attestation* (Bezeugung) *as both* pre-moral . . . *and* pre-religious. *He would thus appear to go back before and beyond that which joins morality to religion, meaning here, to Christianity. This would in principle allow for the repetition of the Nietzschean genealogy of morals, but dechristianizing it where necessary and extirpating whatever Christian vestiges it still might contain. A strategy all the more involuted and necessary for a Heidegger who seems unable to stop either settling accounts with Christianity or distancing himself from it—with all the more violence in so far as it is already too late, perhaps, for him to deny certain proto-Christian motifs in the ontological repetition and existential analytics.* (§15)

Derrida thus sees in Heidegger both an attempt to find pre-Christian (perhaps Greek) possibilities and an attempt to dechristianize a certain Christian tradition—a strategy that would be not completely unlike Derrida's. And yet Derrida also discerns a sort of proto-Christianity in the themes Heidegger develops and the rhetoric he deploys.

Having contrasted Heidegger with Kant in §15, Derrida goes on in §18 to contrast him with Hegel. We already saw in Observation 2 the way in which Derrida characterizes Hegel's understanding of *"absolute knowledge as the truth of religion"* as a first *temptation.* In §18, Derrida goes on to speak of a second temptation, which he labels "Heideggerian":

The other temptation *(perhaps there are still good reasons for keeping this word) would be "Heideggerian": beyond such ontotheology, where the latter ignores both prayer and sacrifice.*[4] *It would accordingly be necessary that a "revealability"* (Offenbarkeit) *be allowed to reveal itself, with a light that would manifest (itself) more originarily than all revelation* (Offenbarung). *Moreover, the distinction would have to be made between* theo-logy *(the discourse on God, faith or revelation) and* theiology *(discourse on being-divine, on the essence and the divinity of the divine). The experience of the sacred, the holy or the saved* (heilig) *would have to be reawakened* unscathed. (§18)

This relationship between revealability and revelation is, as we demonstrated in Chapter 6, a leitmotif throughout "Faith and Knowledge." It is first raised in §8, where Derrida speaks of *"discourses of a revelation* (Offenbarung) *or of a revealability* (Offenbarkeit), *of a possibility more originary than manifestation. More originary, which is to say, closer to the source, to the sole and same source"* (§8). More originary than all manifestation or revelation, this revealability would be the *"possibility or virtuality of the event"* (§25) rather than the event itself, and it would seem to be—or at least this is Derrida's question, his hesitation—*"independent of all religion? . . . Independent in the structures of its experience and in the analytics relating to them?"* (§19). It is this important distinction that will allow Heidegger—and perhaps Derrida in turn—to develop a notion of faith, testimony, or attestation that is independent of all religious faith. Derrida continues in §18, introducing the theme of the pre-Roman in Heidegger:

> *As for the "Roman," does not Heidegger proceed, from* Sein und Zeit *on, with an ontologico-existential repetition and rehearsal of Christian motifs that at the same time are hollowed out and reduced to their original possibility? A pre-Roman possibility, precisely? Did he not confide to Löwith, several years earlier, in 1921, that in order to assume the spiritual heritage that constitutes the facticity of his "I am," he ought to have said: "I am a 'Christian theologian'"? Which does not mean "Roman." To this we shall return. (§18)*

The reading of Heidegger we saw a moment ago in relation to Kant is here confirmed: Heidegger repeats but also attempts to "hollow out" (perhaps we could say *"dechristianize,"* the term used in §15) certain Christian themes in order to return to a more originary, pre-Roman Christianity.

In the accompanying footnote to this section, Derrida cites a passage from Heidegger's 1943 *Remembrance (Andenken)*, in which a contrast is drawn between the prophetic word of poets, who "restrict themselves to the anticipatory-founding word of the Sacred" and whose "poetic prediction only opens the time of an apparition of the gods," and the word of prophets in the "Judeo-Christian sense of the word," who, not being so restrained, "immediately announce the god upon whom one can subsequently count as upon the certain guarantee of salvation in superterrestrial beatitude." We see here something that resembles the contrast Derrida draws between faith and religion, or indeed between the two sources of religion, the one related to salvation and assurance and the other to a more "anticipatory" opening up of the future beyond all assurances or determinate horizon. Developing this contrast in terms we have already seen, Heidegger goes on to say that "the poetry of Hölderlin should not be disfigured with the 'religious' element of 'religion,' which remains the business of the Roman way of interpreting the relations between humans and gods" (§18n9). Again it is the Roman—we might even be tempted to say the *globalatin*—that Heidegger questions or critiques in the name of a more originary possibility, in this case, the possibility offered by Hölderlin's poetry.

The same contrast between the divine or the sacred and religion, and particularly Roman religion, can be seen, says Derrida, two decades later, in 1962, in a passage from Heidegger's *Sojourns: The Journey to Greece*, where Heidegger recounts his trip to Greece and his visit to the orthodox monastery of Kaisairani, near Athens. In this later text, Heidegger's "protest is renewed against Rome, against the essentially Roman figure of religion," but this time the indictment covers much more than Roman religion. "It brings together into a single configuration," writes Derrida, "modern humanism, technics, politics, and law"—a configuration that Derrida too, it seems, tries to rethink in "Faith and Knowledge" and elsewhere.[5] Through this critique of Rome, Heidegger would thus have tried to recover a more originary Christian possibility, one that is "in harmony with ancient Greece" and that does not "bow before" the Roman Church, its theology and its canon law (§18n9). By citing texts by Heidegger that are separated by almost two decades, Derrida wants to demonstrate a persistence or consistency in Heidegger's desire to return to a pre-religious notion of belief or the prophetic, or a pre-Roman possibility for religion.

Much later in "Faith and Knowledge," and once again in a footnote, Derrida returns to this argument regarding Heidegger's critique of religion. Referring to a study by Jean-François Courtine on Heidegger's *Contributions to Philosophy* Derrida underscores the way in which Heidegger's critique of religion is essentially related to his critique of technology.[6] He writes: "Heidegger directs suspicion at the same time against 'religion' (especially Christian-Roman), against belief, and against that in technics which menaces the safe and sound, the unscathed or the immune, the sacrosanct (*heilig*)" (§40n31). Derrida will thus want to argue that these two reactions of Heidegger—against religion and against technology—are part of the same immune/autoimmune attempt to indemnify and keep safe and sound a more original possibility for thinking. As Courtine speculates and Derrida cites with approval, Heidegger would have insisted on "modern nihilism as 'uprooting' (*Entwürzelung*)" in relationship always to the critique of "the *Gestell* and all 'technical-instrumental manipulation of beings' (*Machenschaft*), with which he even associates 'a critique of the idea of creation directed primarily against Christianity'" (§40n31). Derrida's thesis regarding the reaction against the deracinating powers of telecommunication here finds a striking confirmation in Heidegger. The deracination of teletechnology and the reaction against it in the name of something more originary that must be kept intact, protected, and indemnified, is explicitly related to this Heideggerian idiom of "uprooting" a few sections later. Derrida writes: "Violent sundering [*arrachement*], to be sure, from the radicality of roots (*Entwürzelung*, Heidegger would say; we cited him above) and from all forms of originary *physis*, from all the supposed resources of a force held to be authentically generative, sacred, unscathed, 'safe and sound' (*heilig*): ethnic identity, descent, family, nation, blood and soil, proper name, proper idiom, proper culture and memory" (§45).

In §19, Derrida returns to the contrast between revelation and revealability, to the question of the originarity of one with regard to the other, in order to offer a hypothesis on the subject with regard to Heidegger, namely, that Heidegger would have considered a certain Christian revelation to be what ultimately revealed a kind of revealability more originary than all revelation, a sort of "*originary Christendom*" or "Urchristentum." This originary Christian possibility would thus, like its Greek counterpart, precede and so escape the disfigurement brought about by Rome and Roman Christendom. Having posed the aporia between revelation and revealability, *Offenbarung* and *Offenbarkeit*, the latter being perhaps "*independent of all religion*," Derrida asks whether faith itself would be independent of all historical revelation or whether "*the event of revelation [would] have consisted in revealing revealability itself, and the origin of light, the originary light, the very invisibility of visibility?*" He then adds: "*This is perhaps what the believer or the theologian might say here, in particular the Christian of originary Christendom, of that* Urchristentum *in the Lutheran tradition to which Heidegger acknowledges owing so much*" (§19). Again, Derrida sees Heidegger as being tempted by a pre-Roman possibility for religion, a pre-Roman Catholic possibility that would recover not a pre-Christian possibility but a more original Christianity. It is this critique of Roman Catholicism, coupled with an emphasis on a more originary Christianity or a proto-Christianity, that licenses Derrida to compare Heidegger to Voltaire, however unlikely this conjunction might at first appear: "If one were not fearful of shocking too many people all at once, one could say that by their vehement anti-Christianity, by their opposition above all to the Roman Church, as much as by their declared preference, sometimes nostalgic, for primitive Christianity, Voltaire and Heidegger belong to the same tradition: proto-Catholic" (§26n13).[7]

Derrida thus emphasizes throughout "Faith and Knowledge" Heidegger's tendency to try to find a more original possibility than religion (e.g., poetry) or a more original religion (pre-Roman). But the question that will motivate Derrida most will be whether or not there is in Heidegger an originary *gage* or engagement—an originary or elementary faith—in thought itself, or whether thought must be considered independent of such faith. Already in §20, Derrida suggests this relation when he speaks of "*the holding-back* [halte] *of scruple* (religio), *the restraint of shame, a certain* Verhaltenheit *as well, of which Heidegger speaks in the* Beiträge zur Philosophie, *the respect, the responsibility of repetition in the wager* [gage] *of decision or of affirmation* (re-legere) *which links up with itself in order to link up with the other"* (§20). Though Derrida strings these various terms together as if they were more or less synonymous, everything we have seen in our reading of "Faith and Knowledge" would suggest a difference, in Derrida's account, between scruple, restraint, and respect (all related to the first source of religion) and the wager or *gage* of decision or affirmation (notions associated with the second source). It will be precisely an inability to keep these two sources separate, separate in general but particularly in Heidegger, that will come to preoccupy Derrida in §48, which is something of a summary of all the other references to Heidegger in "Faith and Knowledge" and a development of them in the direction of the question of originary faith.

In order to set up this question of originary faith, Derrida concludes §47:

> It seems impossible to deny the *possibility* in whose name—thanks to which—the derived *necessity* (the authority or determinate belief) would be put in question, suspended, rejected or criticized, even deconstructed. One can *not* deny it, which means that the most one can do is to deny it. Any discourse that would be opposed to it would, in effect, always succumb to the figure or the logic of denial [*denegation*]. Such would be the place where, before and after all the Enlightenments in the world, reason, critique, science, tele-technoscience, philosophy, **thought** in general, retain the *same* resource as religion in general. (§47)

Derrida thus ends this section by referring to a "logic of denial [*dénégation*]" with regard to the possibility of faith in relation to reason, science, philosophy, and thought. According to this logic, what is denied is affirmed in its denial. The logic of autoimmunity is thus a kind of denegation and vice versa. By denying the elementary faith at the origin of both religion and science, religion and philosophy or thought, one is doing nothing other than reaffirming it—hence the ambivalence Derrida will find in Heidegger with regard to this originary faith.[8] Derrida will thus try in this section to follow such a logic of denial or denegation in Heidegger. In relation, then, to this question of thought, thought in general but also the thought of religion, in relation to all those who, "before and after all the Enlightenments in the world, believed in the independence of critical reason, of knowledge, technics, philosophy, and thought with respect to religion and even to all faith," Derrida says he is going to "privilege the example of Heidegger" (§48).

Derrida begins his analysis of this Heideggerian example by citing once again, just as he did back in §18, the famous line of Heidegger's from a letter to Löwith in 1921: "I am a 'Christian theologian.'" Derrida then adds: "This declaration would merit extended interpretation and certainly does not amount to a simple declaration of faith. But it neither contradicts, annuls nor excludes this other certainty: Heidegger not only declared, very early and on several occasions, that philosophy was in its very principle 'atheistic' . . . and the idea of a Christian philosophy as absurd as a 'squared circle'" (§48). Heidegger would thus have not only "proposed a radical separation between philosophy and theology" and attempted "a 'destruction' of all forms of the ontotheological" but would even have written in 1953: "Belief [or faith] has no place in thought (*Der Glaube hat im Denken keinen Platz*)" (§48). Derrida will thus try to square this claim with everything in Heidegger that would seem to suggest precisely the opposite, namely, that a certain faith in the form of a *Zusage* is inseparable from thought itself. He will therefore seem to endorse Heidegger in his separation of thought from various forms of dogmatism and religious authority, but he will then question those places in Heidegger where thought is distinguished from faith in general. Hence Derrida contests Heidegger's claim of 1953 from within Heidegger's own thought when he writes:

> Heidegger still extends with force and radicality the assertion that belief *in general* has no place in the experience or the act of thinking *in general*. And there we would have difficulty following him. First along his own path. . . . [For] it still seems difficult to dissociate faith in general (*Glaube*) from what Heidegger himself, under the name of *Zusage* ("accord, acquiescing, trust or confidence"), designates as that which is most irreducible, indeed most originary in thought, prior even to that questioning said by him to constitute the piety (*Frömmigkeit*) of thinking. (§48)[9]

Derrida goes on to suggest—at once with and without Heidegger—that this notion of a *Zusage* "'before' all questioning, thus 'before' all knowledge, all philosophy," "accords with everything which, beginning with the existential analytics of the thought of being and of the truth of being, reaffirms continuously what we will call (in Latin, alas, and in a manner too Roman for Heidegger) a certain *testimonial sacredness* or, we would even go so far as to say, a sworn word [*foi jurée*]" (§48). These references to testimony and sworn faith, terms developed by Derrida at some length in "Faith and Knowledge" and identified with the common source of both religion and technology, both faith and knowledge, demonstrate just how close Heidegger, or at least a certain Heidegger, is to Derrida. What Derrida gives us in what follows is nothing less than an entire program for rereading Heidegger, beginning with *Being and Time*, on the basis of these terms. Derrida suggests returning to "the decisive and largely underestimated motif of attestation (*Bezeugung*) in *Sein und Zeit*," as well as to "all the other motifs that are inseparable from and dependent upon it, which is to say, *all* the existentials and, specifically, that of conscience (*Gewissen*), originary responsibility or guilt (*Schuldigsein*) and *Entschlossenheit* (resolute determination)" (§48). After then raising and setting aside "the immense question of the ontological repetition, in all these concepts, of a so markedly Christian tradition," that is, the question of how determining the Christian tradition was in the very formulation of these notions, Derrida makes a suggestion and lays down a principle.

> Let us therefore limit ourselves to situating a principle of reading. Like the experience of authentic attestation (*Bezeugung*) and like everything that depends upon it, the point of departure of *Sein und Zeit* resides in a situation that cannot be radically alien to what is called *faith*. Not religion, to be sure, nor theology, but that which in faith acquiesces before or beyond all questioning, in the already common experience of a language and of a "we." The reader of *Sein und Zeit* and the signatory who takes him as witness are already situated in this element of faith from the moment that Heidegger says "we" to justify the choice of the "exemplary" being that is *Dasein*, the questioning being that must be interrogated as an exemplary witness. (§48)

After recalling what Heidegger labeled in *Being and Time* the *Faktum* of a "vague and ordinary pre-comprehension of the meaning of being," a *Faktum* that allows a "we" to elaborate the question of Being, Derrida goes on to argue that the notion of the *Zusage*, of sworn faith, "communicates with" everything in Heidegger that has to do with restraint, modesty, and reserve in relationship to the sacred. Derrida thus seems to see in Heidegger a "communication" between, or perhaps even a conflation of, the two sources of religion identified and distinguished throughout "Faith and Knowledge." Heidegger's ambivalence—his denegation or denial—with regard to the place of faith or belief in thought seems to stem from this conflation.

> This zone is that of a faith incessantly reaffirmed throughout an open chain of concepts, beginning with those that we have already cited (*Bezeugung, Zusage*, etc.), but it also communicates with everything in Heidegger's way of thinking that marks the reversed holding-back of restraint (*Verhaltenheit*) or the sojourn (*Aufenthalt*)

in modesty (*Scheu*) in the vicinity of the unscathed, the sacred, the safe and sound (*das Heilige*), the passage or the coming of the last god that man is doubtless not yet ready to receive. (§48)

Having suggested the communication or conflation of these two sources in Heidegger, Derrida hones in on the relationship between faith or belief, on the one hand, and religion, on the other: "That the movement proper to this faith does not constitute a religion is all too evident. Is it, however, untouched [*indemne*] by all religiosity? Perhaps. But by all 'belief,' by that 'belief' that would have 'no place in thinking'? This seems less certain" (§48).

Derrida thus contests Heidegger's 1953 claim that "Belief [or faith] has no place in thought," but, even more importantly, he seems to provide an explanation for why Heidegger would make such claim: in order to protect or safeguard the indemnity of a pre-Christian or proto-Christian experience of the sacred or the holy (the first source of religion),[10] Heidegger would have reacted against an experience of belief or faith in general (the second source), reducing it to a dogmatic belief in authority or to a belief in accordance with the religions of the Book and onto-theology.[11] By reducing belief or faith to one of these forms, Heidegger would perhaps have foreclosed too quickly the question of the nature of belief in general, the very question that Derrida is intent on opening back up.

> Since the major question remains, in our eyes, albeit in a form that is still quite new: "What does it mean to believe?" we will ask (elsewhere) how and why Heidegger can at the same time affirm one of the possibilities of the "religious," of which we have just schematically recalled the signs (*Faktum, Bezeugung, Zusage, Verhaltenheit, Heilige*, etc.) and reject so energetically "belief" or "faith" (*Glaube*). Our hypothesis again refers back to the two sources or two strata of religion which we distinguished above: the experience of sacredness and the experience of belief. More receptive to the first (in its Greco-Hölderlinian or even archeo-Christian tradition), Heidegger was probably more resistant to the second, which he constantly reduced to figures he never ceased to put into question, not to say "destroy" or denounce: dogmatic or credulous belief in authority, to be sure, but also belief according to the religions of the Book and ontotheology, and above all, that which in the belief in the other could appear to him (wrongly, we would say) to appeal necessarily to the egological subjectivity of an *alter ego*. (§48)

This is where Derrida parts ways with Heidegger in a more definitive fashion. By contesting Heidegger's claim that philosophy is in principle "atheistic," a claim that takes both religion *and* faith (which are not, as we have seen, co-extensive with one another) out of philosophy, Derrida seems to be suggesting that another understanding of the alterity of the other might have led to another, more positive understanding of "faith." Referring to a faith that would come from the "wholly other," from the address to the other in general, a faith that would be the very condition of *Mitsein*, Derrida—in a gesture that seems to show once again the ambiguity in Heidegger with regard to such a faith—suggests that just such a faith can be found in the Heideggerian notion of the *gage*, or pledge.

> We are speaking here of the belief that is demanded, required, of the faithful belief in what, having come from the utterly other [*de l'autre tout autre*], there where its originary presentation in person would forever be impossible (**witnessing** or given word in the most elementary and irreducible sense, promise of truth up to and including perjury), would constitute the condition of *Mitsein*, of the relation to or address of the other in general. (§48)

We have here, then, both Derrida's critique of Heidegger in relation to what Derrida has shown to be the common source of both faith and knowledge, religion and science, religion and thought, and an entire program for rereading Heidegger based on this critique. Derrida is suggesting a reading of *Being and Time* that would take into account the testimonial or elementary faith that makes the very "we" of that work possible. By proposing that we read Heidegger through a different relation to the other, through this elementary relation to the other, through questions of testimony and witnessing, we end up seeing that Heidegger—either in spite of or in accordance with himself—situates a kind of elementary faith at the origin or source of all thought. In many ways, therefore, Heidegger's understanding of the *gage*, of the *Zusage*, at the origin of all thought would have been the closest and most explicit precursor to Derrida's own thinking of an originary faith at the origin of both religion and science. And yet, in order emphasize this aspect of Heidegger's thought, other passages from Heidegger's corpus, both early and late, will have to be explained away.

One final word, then, about Derrida's reading of Heidegger: Derrida suggests in a few places in his reading of Heidegger in "Faith and Knowledge" that he would like to return to these questions elsewhere, since all of them "require more time and space" (§48)—beyond the limits of time and space assigned to the participants of the Capri conference or to their published contributions.[12] This is yet another sign of a kind of engagement with Heidegger that we do not quite see with Kant, Hegel, or Bergson. As Derrida was completing from Laguna Beach in California his long

"Post-scriptum" to "Faith and Knowledge," he returned again and again to Heidegger, as if to an island he could not bring himself to leave behind definitively. One will notice, moreover, Derrida's interest throughout "Faith and Knowledge" in Heidegger's interest in islands, his reflections in his 1962 *Sojourns: The Journey to Greece* on, for example, Corfu, Sicily, and Delos—which Heidegger calls "the 'saintly' or 'sacred' island [*die heilige Insel*]" (§17n9). This engagement with Heidegger would last right up until the end, that is, right up until Derrida's final seminar in 2002–3, *The Beast and the Sovereign*, Volume 2, a seminar that revolves almost entirely around just two books, Heidegger's 1929–30 seminar, published as *The Fundamental Concepts of Metaphysics: World, Finitude, Solitude*, and, as its second source, the second of its two foci, Daniel Defoe's *Robinson Crusoe*—"two great texts," says Derrida, that he would like "to isolate like islands" so as to "read as closely as possible, as faithfully but, as always, as freely as possible" (*BS 2* 13). A reading that is at once faithful and free, faithful to the text and yet free to criticize it or to develop what is undeveloped in it—that is the principle Derrida will have followed in reading Heidegger from the late 1950s right up to 2004, leaving Heidegger behind from time to time only to return to him again, like an island he would forever sail away from only to find himself perpetually blown back, attracted from the beginning right up to the end to something on this island that goes beyond the island, beyond its isolation and ipseity, an island within this island, perhaps, that would have given Derrida the most to think.

Reference Matter

Timeline of Selected Derrida Publications, Conferences, and Interviews: 1993–95

1993

22–23 April: Conference at the University of California, Riverside, where much of what would become *Specters of Marx* is first presented.

16 July: Interview with Maurizio Ferraris in Paris (published in *TS* 3–18).

17 July: Interview with Maurizio Ferraris in Ris-Orangis (published in *TS* 19–34).

19 November: Derrida and Gadamer speak at a conference in Paris; Gadamer's presentation is subsequently published as "Hermeneutics and Deconstruction," while Derrida's remains unpublished.

22 December: Interview with Bernard Stiegler (published in *ET* 29–143).

"Stops" listed in *Counterpath*: Kassel; Lyon; Oslo; Warwick; University of California, Santa Barbara; University of California, Riverside; Pécs; Budapest; Reykyavik (see *CP* 20).

Seminar 1993–94: "Questions of Responsibility III: Testimony"

French Publications

Khōra. Paris: Éditions Galilée (see *ON*).

Passions. Éditions Galilée (see *ON*).

Sauf le nom (*Post-Scriptum*). Paris: Éditions Galilée (see *ON*).

Prégnances. With wash drawings by Colette Deblé. Paris: Brandes.

Spectres de Marx. Éditions Galilée (see *SM*).

First version of *Aporias* published in *Le passage des frontières, autour du travail de Jacques Derrida*. Paris: Éditions Galilée, 309–338 (see *AP*).

"Artefactualités," in *Passages,* no. 57 (September 1993); selections reprinted in *Echographies de la télévision,* 9–35 (see *ET*).

1994

18 January: Takes part in a discussion at the Sorbonne with Jean Poperen and Alain Minc on the topic of "thinking what comes" (published in *PCQ*).

25–26 January: Interview with Maurizio Ferraris in Paris (published in *TS* 35–59).

7 February: Address at the Sorbonne during a public meeting organized by the ICSAI (International Committee in Support of Algerian Intellectuals) and the League of Human Rights.

28 February–1 March: Conference in Capri with Vincenzo Vitiello, Hans-Georg Gadamer, Aldo Gargani, Maurizio Ferraris, Eugenio Trías, Gianni Vattimo (see photo at *CP* 145).

April: Roundtable at University of California, Irvine, around Derrida's "Of the Humanities and Philosophical Disciplines: The Right to Philosophy from the Cosmopolitical Point of View" (see *EIRP*).

22–28 May: *Archive Fever* completed in Naples.

25 May: Interview with Maurizio Ferraris in Naples (published in *TS* 60–71).

5 June: Presents a lecture in London at a conference on Freud that would be published in 1995 under the title *Mal d'Archive* (1995) (see *AF*).

9 November: Delivers much of what will be published as *Demeure* during his seminar in Paris (see *"D"*).

10 November: Interview with Maurizio Ferraris in Paris (published in *TS* 72–77).

"Stops" listed in *Counterpath*: Grenoble; Naples; Amsterdam; Capri; New York; Lisbon; SUNY Buffalo; Strasbourg; Turin; Berlin; Villanova, Philadelphia; George Mason University, Fairfax, Virginia; Chicago; London; Oslo; Moscow (see *CP* 94); St. Petersburg; Murcia; Madrid.

Seminar 1994–95: "Questions of Responsibility IV: Testimony"

French Publications

Politiques de l'amitié. Paris: Éditions Galilée (see *PF*).

Force de loi. Paris: Éditions Galilée (see *"FL"*).

"Faxitexture." In *Noise* 18/19, Paris: Maeght Éditeur.

1995

19 January: Interview with Gianni Vattimo in Turin (*TS* 78–92). Delivers a lecture on Blanchot at the University of Turin.

26 April: Date of the final paragraph of "Faith and Knowledge" from Laguna Beach. See *CP* 231 for a picture of Derrida from April 1995 and *CP* 115 for a picture of Derrida with Sam Weber in Los Angeles.

24 July: Conference in Louvain, where the first version of *Demeure* was presented.

1 August: Participates in a press conference at the United Nations Educational, Scientific, and Cultural Organization (UNESCO) under the auspices of the International Parliament of Writers. Derrida's remarks were published as "Pour Mumia Abu Jamal," in *Le Monde*, 9 August 1995, then reprinted as the Preface to Mumia Abu-Jamal, *En direct du couloir de la mort*, trans. Jim Cohen (Paris: Editions la Découverte, 1996), 7–13 (see *N* 125–29).

28–30 September: Conference "Futures of Jacques Derrida" at the University of Alabama, Tuscaloosa, organized by Richard Rand and Patrick Hermann.

6 November: Meeting of the International Parliament of Writers in Strasbourg.

24–29 November: Writes "Toward Buenos Aires," chap. 1 of "SW," 19–46.

29 November–4 December: Writes "Santiago and Valparaiso, Chile," chap. 2 of "SW," 47–71.

4–8 December: Writes "São Paulo, Brazil," chap. 3 of "SW," 73–92.

27 December: The first part of *Adieu* is read during a funeral ceremony for Emmanuel Levinas at the cemetery in Pantin (see *AEL*).

1995: Receives honorary doctorate at Queens University–Ontario, in Kingston.

"Stops" listed in *Counterpath*: Bordeaux; Athens; London; Madrid; Cosenza; Turin; Vienna; Trento; London; Luton; Louvain-la-Neuve; New York; Tuscaloosa, Alabama; Milan; Kingston, Ontario; Frieburg-im-Breisgau; Buenos Aires; São Paolo, Santiago.

Seminar 1995–96: "Questions of Responsibility V: Hostility/Hospitality." Seminar sessions from 10 January 1996 and 17 January 1996 published in *De l'hospitalité*. Paris: Calmann-Lévy, 1997 (see *OFH*).

French Publications

Mal d'Archive. Paris: Éditions Galilée (see *AF*).

"Parti pris pour l'Algérie," *Les Temps Modernes*, no. 580 (January-February 1995); subsequently published in *PM* 219–27 (*AR* 301–8/*N* 117–24).

"Sauver les Phénomènes," in *Contretemps* 1 (Winter 1995): 14–24.

Notes

Introduction: *Miraculum ex Machina*

1. "Faith and Knowledge: The Two Sources of 'Religion' at the Limits of Reason Alone," translated by Samuel Weber, can be found in two different places, in *Acts of Religion*, ed. and introd. Gil Anidjar (New York: Routledge, 2002), 42–101, and in *Religion*, ed. Jacques Derrida and Gianni Vattimo (Stanford, Calif.: Stanford University Press, 1998), 1–78. In order to facilitate reference to either edition, as well as to the original French, I will refer throughout to section numbers (e.g., §1) rather than page numbers.

2. The other participants were Eugenio Trías, Aldo Gargani, and Vincenzo Vitiello. A photograph of the meeting can be found in *CP* 145.

3. Hent de Vries argues similarly that " 'Faith and Knowledge,' [Derrida's] most explicit discussion of the theme of religion to date, allows Derrida to bring together different threads that run through his numerous earlier writings" (Hent de Vries, *Philosophy and the Turn to Religion* [Baltimore: Johns Hopkins University Press, 1999], 16).

4. It is perhaps closer to a kind of "Guide to Derrida for the Perplexed," since this title evokes one of the great works of philosophy and theology, Moses Maimonides' twelfth-century *The Guide for the Perplexed*, a book Derrida says in *Counterpath* he recalls having seen as a young boy on his grandfather's bookshelves in Algeria (*CP* 267). (See Julian Wolfreys's well-titled *Derrida: A Guide for the Perplexed* [New York: Continuum, 2007] and John D. Caputo's preface to *The Prayers and Tears of Jacques Derrida: Religion Without Religion*, "A Map for the Perplexed" [Bloomington: Indiana University Press, 1997], xxvii–xxix.) Maimonides' *Guide* attempts to reconcile Rabbinic Judaism with Aristotelian philosophy as it had been taken up and modified by Arabic interpreters. Derrida's

interest in Maimonides (1135–1204), and the association of this Jewish philosopher with the memory of his grandfather, was no doubt reinforced by the fact that Maimonides was born in Cordoba, Spain, the same region in which Derrida's family probably lived before migrating to North Africa. Maimonides is mentioned briefly at *AR* 163.

5. See, e.g., the four books reviewed in a December 2007 issue of the *Times Literary Supplement* (14 December 2007): Tina Beattie, *The New Atheists: The Twilight of Reason and the War on Religion* (Maryknoll, N.Y.: Orbis Books, 2008); John C. Lennox, *God's Undertaker: Has Science Buried God?* (Oxford: Lion Hudson, 2009); Hans Küng, *The Beginning of All Things: Science and Religion* (Grand Rapids, Mich.: William B. Eerdmans, 2007); John Polkinghorne, *From Physicist to Priest: An Autobiography* (London: SPCK Publishing, 2007). One might also point to films such as Ben Stein's *Expelled* and Bill Maher's *Religulous* as evidence of popular interest on both sides of the debate over the role religion should play in contemporary American society.

6. See, e.g.: Caputo, *The Prayers and Tears of Jacques Derrida*, and de Vries, *Philosophy and the Turn to Religion*, as well as Hent de Vries, *Religion and Violence: Philosophical Perspectives from Kant to Derrida* (Baltimore: Johns Hopkins University Press, 2002). See also Yvonne Sherwood and Kevin Hart, eds., *Derrida and Religion: Other Testaments* (New York: Routledge, 2005). Both Caputo's and de Vries's works are much more comprehensive than my own. While I concentrate on "Faith and Knowledge" and the texts written in the years just before and after it, Caputo looks at the question of religion across the span of Derrida's entire corpus. De Vries's work ranges even further, situating "Faith and Knowledge" in relationship not only to other texts by Derrida on religion but to a whole host of other thinkers, from Kant, Hegel, and Heidegger to Marion, Levinas, Dufrenne, Patočka, and Kripke, to name just a few. For a more comprehensive analysis of Derrida on some of the questions this work broaches but does not treat in detail—for example, Derrida's relationship to negative theology or his rethinking of apocalypse, circumcision, the gift, hospitality, prayer, sacrifice, death, and so on—the reader would be well advised to turn to the above-mentioned works by Caputo and de Vries. Other excellent works that treat Derrida's work on religion before the publication of "Faith and Knowledge" include: Kevin Hart, *The Trespass of the Sign: Deconstruction, Theology and Philosophy* (Cambridge: Cambridge University Press, 1989; rpt. New York: Fordham University Press, 2000), esp. 64–67; Mark C. Taylor, *Altarity* (Chicago: University of Chicago Press, 1987) and Taylor, *Erring: A Postmodern A/theology* (Chicago: University of Chicago Press, 1987).

7. As de Vries incisively asks in *Religion and Violence*: "Why is it that, *in this day and age*, pressing questions of ethics and politics, of multicultural citizenship and education, of institutions and the new media, of knowledge, science, and the technologies of life, appear through the prisms of 'religion' and 'faith'?" (395). This is in many ways the underlying question of *Miracle and Machine*.

8. "AANJ"; the conference was organized by Hent de Vries and Samuel Weber, and the contributions were subsequently published in Hent de Vries and

Samuel Weber, eds., *Religion and Media* (Stanford, Calif.: Stanford University Press, 2001).

9. Martial Guéroult (1891–1976) was a major figure in French philosophy in the mid twentieth century; he wrote important books on Spinoza, Leibniz, Malebranche, and Descartes, among others. But he was also a major influence on an entire generation of thinkers and professors as a pedagogue.

10. In a series of as yet unpublished remarks, Geoffrey Bennington has shed light on Derrida's frequent use of this curious idiom *un X digne de son nom*, that is, "an X worthy of the name" or "worthy of its name."

11. Derrida rightly notes that the "affinity" between philosophy and literature is really only taken advantage of, with just "a few exceptions," in what is called "continental philosophy" (*EIRP* 29; see 34–36).

12. A couple of DeLillo's recent novels employ the same device, interrupting the main narrative by embedding a second narrative in two parts, like an ellipsis, within it. See, e.g.: the two sections of *The Body Artist* (New York: Scribner, 2001): "Rey Robles, 64, Cinema's Poet of Lonely Places," 27–29; and "Body Art in Extremis: Slow, Spare and Painful"; 103–10. See also the two sections of DeLillo's even more recent *Omega Point* (New York: Scriber, 2010): "Anonymity," 3–15; "Anonymity 2," 101–17. In both cases, the interruption is, interestingly, related to art, the embedding of art within art, whether the obituary of a famous filmmaker, the review of an art performance, or the description of an art installation.

Prologue: Miracle and Mass Destruction (*Underworld* I)

1. Carson McCullers, *The Heart Is a Lonely Hunter* (New York: Houghton Mifflin Company, 2000), 286.

2. My thanks to Christopher Ruth of Villanova University for bringing to my attention a fascinating 2007 HBO documentary on the game, *Brooklyn Dodgers: The Ghosts of Flatbush*.

3. Toots Shor is today the least known of the four, but at the time Shor was a legendary restauranteur or, as he called himself, saloonkeeper, who entertained and rubbed elbows with American's elite. His restaurant—"Toots Shor"—was a mecca during the 1950s for celebrities from the worlds of sports, entertainment, and politics. To learn more about this wonderfully colorful character, see Kristi Jacobson's 2006 documentary *Toots*.

4. Much later in the novel, one of the main characters, Albert Bronzini, actually thinks that the newspaper headline "The Shot Heard 'Round the World" refers to the atomic test in Russia (*U* 668).

1. Context Event Signature

1. These are but a few of the many places we would have to look to find the premises for Derrida's "Faith and Knowledge." For a fuller list of Derrida's texts on religion and secondary sources on these texts, see the bibliography included in *AR* 421–26, as well as *DN* 205 and Caputo, *The Prayers and Tears of Jacques*

Derrida, 371–74; for bibliographies that include works on Derrida and others on religion, see the bibliographies at the end of de Vries, *Philosophy and the Turn to Religion* and *Religion and Violence*.

2. I am referring here, of course, to Dominique Janicaud et al., *Phenomenology and the "Theological Turn"* (New York: Fordham University Press, 2000).

3. Derrida himself uses the verb *décortiquer* in *"Des tours de Babel."* After citing Walter Benjamin's "The Task of the Translator" on the text as a kind of fruit, with skin and a "core [*noyau*]"—an "untouchable remainder"—that both calls for and resists translation, Derrida plays on the analogy between the text and a fruit by writing: *"Décortiquons un peu la rhétorique de cette séquence."* Since translation is what is at issue here, it is worth noting that the "original" English translation of Derrida's essay, which can still be found in *Acts of Religion*, has "Let us dissect a bit more the rhetoric of this sequence" (*AR* 125), thereby substituting an animal metaphor for a vegetal one. The revised translation in *Psyche 1*, however, has restored the vegetal analogy: "Let us peel away a bit more the rhetoric of this sequence" (*PSY 1* 215).

4. It is also significant that Laguna Beach is not far from Santa Monica, which Derrida always associated, for obvious reasons, with Augustine's mother, though also with his own mother (see "C" 260).

5. As Derrida writes in *"Sauf le nom (Post-Scriptum),"* "a colloquium is a place one goes to (as to a synagogue)" (*"SN"* 45). While Derrida's most comprehensive response to the question of the relationship between deconstruction and negative theology is to be found in "HAS," there are many more points of comparison on the level of both form and content between "Faith and Knowledge" and *"Sauf le nom (Post-Scriptum)."* Both texts were written for or in response to conference invitations, both were written in places of retreat, the former in Capri and Laguna, the latter in Nice, "a town of familial exile" (*"SN"* 41), and both contain a *"Post-Scriptum,"* the first corresponding to what was written after the conference Derrida attended and the second—the entire text, in effect—corresponding to what was written in response to a conference Derrida could not attend (see *"SN"* 45).

6. Though Capri is, of course, surrounded by water, it is also a kind of desert, having no fresh water source of its own, though this did not keep Roman emperors such as Tiberius from building luxurious villas there.

7. On the question of the inclusion/exclusion of women at the Capri conference, in Derrida, and in religion more generally, see Cleo McNelly Kearns's essay "Mary, Maternity, and Abrahamic Hospitality in Derrida's Reading of Massignon," in *Derrida and Religion: Other Testaments*, ed. Yvonne Sherwood and Kevin Hart (New York: Routledge, 2005), 73–94. See also Ellen T. Armour's *Deconstruction, Feminist Theology, and the Problem of Difference: Subverting the Race/Gender Divide* (Chicago: University of Chicago Press, 1999).

8. Derrida writes in "Force of Law": "There was a time, not long ago and not yet over, in which 'we, men' meant 'we adult white male Europeans, carnivorous and capable of sacrifice'" ("FL" 246).

9. "We met, thus, at Capri, **we Europeans**, assigned to languages (Italian, Spanish, German, French) in which the same word, *religion*, should mean, or so we thought, the same thing. As for the trustworthiness of this word, we shared our presupposition with Benveniste" (§33). Some of those in attendance spoke, of course, more than one of these languages, and at least one spoke practically all of them. In "Comme il avait raison! Mon Cicérone Hans-Georg Gadamer," a brief text written after the death of Gadamer in March 2002, Derrida recalls their meeting in Capri and the long "philosophical" walks during which they "listened with fascination [to Gadamer] in all the languages he spoke so well: French, Italian, and English" ("CIA"). Derrida does not even need to mention Gadamer's native German.

10. Hent de Vries makes the same connection in *Philosophy and the Turn to Religion*: " 'Faith and Knowledge' submits that the very concept and growing geopolitical role of what would seem—if only for the purposes of ideological justification—to be religious wars might well offer a key to understanding present-day reality in the Balkans, in the Middle East, and elsewhere" (16).

11. In the mid 1990s, the two movements most often identified with such a return or resurgence were Islamic fundamentalism and Christian Evangelicalism (particularly in the United States). Today, one might well point to Pentecostalism, not only in the United States but in South America, Africa, and Asia. As David Martin puts it in a review of four recent books on the rise of Pentecostalism throughout the world, "Pentecostalism is *the* contemporary religio-cultural phenomenon" (*Times Literary Supplement*, 19 September 2008, p. 3). As for the complex relationship between religion and the media, Martin cites an unnamed commentator who succinctly captures one of the central arguments of "Faith and Knowledge": "Pentecostals look for Eden with a satellite dish."

12. Derrida says they had *"to respond to a double proposition, at once philosophical and editorial"* (§4). The book containing the contributions to the Capri conference was thus published more or less simultaneously in these four languages and subsequently translated into English (among other languages) soon thereafter.

13. This is a fairly common argumentative strategy in Derrida's work. Derrida first contests the *fact* that there is a return to religion in the United States but not in Europe. But since a full refutation on these grounds would require facts and figures of a sociological or demographic nature that would be open to debate and possible refutation, Derrida moves on quickly to the *premise* of the argument. Is it really a return? In *The Animal That Therefore I Am* Derrida argues in a similar fashion. He begins by contesting the so-called fact that animals lack a certain capacity or quality commonly attributed to human beings—e.g., language, technology, mourning, a relationship to death, etc. But since a full refutation of this sort would require zoological or ethological evidence that might always be contested by experts in the field, Derrida moves on to question the more philosophical premise at the origin of the claim: are we really certain that the *human* animal has the capacities he so readily grants himself and denies the animal—e.g., the

capacity for a genuine response that is not contaminated by mechanical reaction, the capacity for a pure or authentic relationship to death?

14. In chap. 3 of my *Derrida From Now On* (New York: Fordham University Press, 2008), I trace Derrida's critique of the religious origins of not just our concept of sovereignty but our concepts of world, globalization, work, literature, tolerance, marriage, etc. See also *BS 1*, where, in a reading of Hobbes, Machiavelli, Foucault, and Agamben, among others, Derrida contests the claim that modernity breaks entirely with a theological notion of sovereignty.

15. Gil Anidjar's remarkable introduction to *AR* anticipates many of the themes of the present work, from the double meaning of *grenades* and the question of avoidance to the presence of Gradiva and the importance of *Genet at Chatila*.

16. For the most complete account of the traces of Derrida's religious background in his work, see Caputo's *The Prayers and Tears and Jacques Derrida*. For a good thumbnail sketch of these traces, see Yvonne Sherwood's introductory remarks at a conference in Toronto in November 2002 ("EF" 27–28).

17. Speaking in an interview from 1991 of his early interest in the poetry of Francis Ponge, Derrida says, "without too much faith or credulity I share with him the religion of the *Littré* [Dictionary], a playful and secular religion [*une religion laïque et ludique*]" (*DP* 15).

18. For the figure of the "Arab-Jew," see Gil Anidjar's *The Jew, the Arab: A History of the Enemy* (Stanford, Calif.: Stanford University Press, 2003) and "'Once More, Once More': Derrida, the Arab, the Jew," Anidjar's excellent introduction to *AR*, 1–39. On the "figure" of Judaism in Derrida's work, see the interview with Elisabeth Weber on the subject ("TG") and Dana Hollander's very helpful treatment of the subject in *Exemplarity and Chosenness: Rosenzweig and Derrida on the Nation of Philosophy* (Stanford, Calif.: Stanford University Press, 2008), 132–38.

19. A bit of context for this line might be helpful. "Leave tomorrow for New York, after a meeting on 'Postmodernism and Religion' (two things that are foreign to me, as you know, but they are always situating me between the two, as you also know, one has to get used to it, resist, it all goes too quickly. My atheism develops in the churches, all the churches. . . .) Here it's an Augustinian university. Feel better here than in certain other philosophy departments, my friend Caputo has something to do with that" (*CP* 95). Derrida participated fairly regularly in a series of conferences organized by John D. Caputo at Villanova University on the theme of religion.

20. As Derrida puts it in "*Sauf le nom (Post-Scriptum)*," "apophasis inclines almost toward atheism" ("*SN*" 36).

21. Derrida writes of his *bar-mitzvah* (which was also called "communion") in "Circumfession": "I pretended to learn Hebrew so as to read it without understanding it" ("C" 288).

22. "One could go on forever . . . recounting what we were told, indeed, about the history of France, meaning by that what was taught in school under

the name of the history of France, an unbelievable discipline, a fable and a bible, but a semipermanent indoctrination for the children of my generation: not a word about Algeria, not a single word about its history and its geography" (*IW* 34).

23. An exception to this would have been during the war, when Algiers became, "right after the landing of the Allies in North Africa in November 1942, a sort of French literary capital in exile" (*IW* 32).

24. Though Derrida suggests in *Islam & the West* that his philosophical resistance to religious communitarianism might be but a "personal idiosyncrasy," he would develop in many places, such as *Politics of Friendship*, a vigorous philosophical critique of such communitarianism. "Personally—but perhaps I am translating a personal idiosyncrasy here—I have always had the tendency to resist religious communitarianism, that is, any form of gregarious community that oppresses the individual, that prevents the individual from acting as a nonreligious citizen" (*IW* 51).

25. David Farrell Krell, *The Purest of Bastards* (University Park: Pennsylvania State University Press, 2000). For the phrase "the purest of bastards," see *PC* 84.

26. Benoît Peeters makes the very same point in the introduction to his own excellent biography *Derrida* (Paris: Flammarion, 2010), 9–16.

27. In *Paper Machine*, Derrida says he often dreams of "an absolute memory. . . . A multimedia band, with phrases, letters, sound, and images: it's everything, and it would keep an impression of everything" (*PM* 65). As Martin Hägglund notes in *Radical Atheism* (Stanford, Calif.: Stanford University Press, 2008), "Derrida's desire to keep traces of his life in his writing is not only evident in the way he signs and dates his texts, . . . but also in the way he lets autobiographical material invade his philosophical work" (156).

2. Duplicity, Definition, Deracination

1. Hegel's *Glauben und Wissen* can be found in *Gesammelte Werke*, Vol. 4, *Jenaer Kritische Schriften* (Frankfurt am Main: Suhrkamp, 1970), 287–433; *Faith and Knowledge*, trans. Walter Cerf and H. S. Harris (Albany: State University of New York Press, 1977). The entire final paragraph of this work is cited in *Glas* 96a [111a], and Derrida briefly summarizes it at §18. In *"Demeure,"* a text written to all appearances between the time of the Capri conference and the final lines of "Faith and Knowledge," Derrida again evokes the speculative Good Friday at the end of Hegel's *Faith and Knowledge*: "If one wanted to speak here of resurrection through the experience of a Christlike passion (the Germans would be the Romans, this time), there would be no Christology, no speculative Good Friday, no truth of religion in the absolute knowledge of Hegel" ("*D*" 63).

2. Immanuel Kant, *Religion Within the Limits of Reason Alone*, trans. and introd. Theodore M. Greene and Hoyt H. Hudson (New York: Harper & Row, 1950); Derrida cites this text in *Glas* at 207a [232a]. Henri Bergson, *The Two Sources of Morality and Religion*, trans. R. Ashley Audra and Cloudesley Brereton, with W. Horsfall Carter (Garden City, N.Y.: Doubleday & Company, Inc.,

1935). On the title and the two subtitles of "Faith and Knowledge," see de Vries, *Philosophy and the Turn to Religion*, 13.

3. Derrida speaks of his "desire to draw . . . the famous conclusion of the *Two Sources . . .* towards another place, another discourse, other argumentative stakes. . . . The book's concluding words are memorable: **'the effort required to accomplish, down to our refractory planet, the essential function of the universe, which is a machine for the making of gods.'** What would happen if Bergson were made to say something entirely different from what he believed he wanted to say but what perhaps was surreptitiously dictated to him?" (§37).

4. "Already in speaking of these notes as of a machine, I have once again been overcome by a desire for economy, for concision." Derrida's description in the same passage of contemporary technology could be heard as a comment on his own writing: "it plays with place, putting distances and speeds to work. It delocalizes, removes or brings close, actualizes or virtualizes, accelerates or decelerates" (§37).

5. There are, of course, serious limitations to this notion of limit. One of the crucial questions of "Faith and Knowledge" will be to determine whether one really can "delimit the religious" (§28), especially today when the "*declared* stakes [of the question] already appear to be without limit" (§27), when it is difficult to perceive the "limits" of globalatinization (§30), when we are talking about "a cult or of a culture of the generalized fetish, of an unlimited fetishism" (§39), of "the indemnification of a spectrality without limit" (§40), and, especially, when the religious, or at least a certain notion of faith, will be not only one of the two sources of science as well as religion but the very condition of the social bond.

6. Speaking of this agreement to restrict the essays to "25 pages or a few more," Francis Landy notes with humor: "Derrida characteristically confines himself to 78!" Francis Landy, "Smith, Derrida, and Amos," in *Introducing Religion: Essays in Honor of Jonathan Z. Smith*, ed. Willi Braun and Russell T. McCutcheon (London: Equinox, 2006), 211.

7. My thanks to Eileen Daily, Professor of Theology at Loyola University, for calling this to my attention. The encyclical can be found at www.vatican.va/holy_father/john_paul_1ii/encyclicals.

The basic claim of the encyclical "Fides et Ratio" of Pope John Paul II is that faith and reason, once joined through theology and philosophy in a common search for the truth, have become severed from one another and so need to be reunited. As the encyclical puts it in its opening line, "Faith and reason are like two wings on which the human spirit rises to the contemplation of truth." The pope goes on to argue that philosophy must once again play a central role in the search for this truth. Taking as the title of its introduction the words inscribed on the temple of Delphi, "Know Yourself," the encyclical argues that the search for self-knowledge—a search that sets human beings apart from the rest of creation—will be complete only when one has contemplated and understood the mystery of Christ's incarnation. Hence philosophy needs the revelations of faith in order to fulfill its vocation, and faith must be deepened through reason.

Philosophy's primary role must thus be to understand and then communicate to believers and nonbelievers alike the universality of Christian truth. For without reason, faith can become little more than personal feeling or experience and risks losing its universal dimension ("Fides et Ratio," §48). Because "Christianity proclaimed from the first the equality of all men and women before God" (ibid., §38) and because "the word of God is addressed to all people, in every age and in every part of the world" (ibid., §64), philosophy is necessary to understand and communicate the universality of Christian truths. There is, then, the pope emphasizes, "the duty to go beyond the particular and concrete, lest the prime task of demonstrating the universality of faith's content be abandoned" (ibid., §69). Philosophy is given the task of this demonstration. Indeed philosophy must play a leading role in what is called a "*new evangelization*" by communicating Christian truths across cultures, languages, and traditions (ibid., §103) .

The encyclical ends with a rather striking and somewhat unexpected appeal to the Virgin Mary, who is scarcely mentioned before the conclusion. Philosophy, it is argued, must play a role that is comparable to that of the Virgin Mary:

> I turn in the end to the woman whom the prayer of the Church invokes as *Seat of Wisdom*, and whose life itself is a true parable illuminating the reflection contained in these pages. For between the vocation of the Blessed Virgin and the vocation of true philosophy there is a deep harmony. Just as the Virgin was called to offer herself entirely as human being and as woman that God's Word might take flesh and come among us, so too philosophy is called to offer its rational and critical resources that theology, as the understanding of faith, maybe fruitful and creative. And just as in giving her assent to Gabriel's word, Mary lost nothing of her true humanity and freedom, so too when philosophy heeds the summons of the Gospel's truth its autonomy is in no way impaired. Indeed, it is then that philosophy sees all its enquiries rise to their highest expression. This was a truth which the holy monks of Christian antiquity understood well when they called Mary "the table at which faith sits in thought." In her they saw a lucid image of true philosophy and they were convinced of the need to *philosophari in Maria*. (Ibid., §108)

In the conclusion to this book, I too will turn to the relationship between philosophy, faith, and women—faith not in the Virgin Mary but, as we will see, in the miraculous appearance of Esmeralda Lopez at the end of *Underworld*.

8. Originally published in the *Frankfurter Allgemeine Zeitung*, the article was translated from the German by Jeffrey Craig Miller and is available online at http://www.logosjournal.com/issue_4.2/ratzinger.htm.

9. Derrida speaks of cards in many places, especially, as one might expect, in *The Post Card*. Even in "Faith and Knowledge," he speaks of "*play[ing] the card of abstraction*" (§3). It is perhaps worth noting that fifty-two, like every good deck of cards, can be divided up or dealt out into four suits of thirteen—the last a crucial number in DeLillo's *Underworld*.

10. More fancifully—for there is absolutely no suggestion that Derrida intends us to hear this reference—52 is the atomic number of tellurium, a naturally occurring silvery-white element with fifty-two protons and fifty-two electrons, named after the Earth, *tellus*, in Latin.

11. In "Circumfession" and elsewhere, Derrida talks about circumcision as a rite that typically takes place on the seventh day of life. In *AF* Derrida cites the beginning of a letter from Jakob Freud to his son, Sigmund, "Son who is dear to me, Shelomoh. In the *seventh in the days* of the years of your life the Spirit of the Lord began to move you and spoke within you" (*AF* 23). See also *PC* 254, where Derrida speaks of the number seven (*sept*) and of the importance of this *set theory* in his life. He recalls there that his first telephone number in El-Biar was 73047, with a 7 at the beginning, a 7 at the end, and 3 + 4 in the middle, all turning about a 0.

12. This passage from *The Post Card* might be read in relationship to the following from *Archive Fever*, where Derrida, not long after the Capri conference, is writing about Freud—and particularly his Gradiva—from Naples, within eyeshot, therefore, of Pompeii: "We will always wonder what, in this *mal d'archive*, he may have burned. We will always wonder, sharing with compassion in this archive fever, what may have burned of his secret passions, of his correspondence, or of his 'life.' Burned without him, without remains and without knowledge. With no possible response, be it spectral or not, short of or beyond a suppression, on the other edge of repression, originary or secondary, without a name, with the least symptom, and without even an ash" (*AF* 101). We will return to this passage in another context in Chapter 8.

13. So named after Aldus Manutius, 1450–1515, the Italian scholar, printer, publisher, and founder of the Aldine press. The first twenty-six sections are thus printed in the form of script first used in the early sixteenth century for an Italian edition of Virgil, a pre-Christian author who recounts the foundation of Rome.

14. At least two, I say, because the "writing" of "Faith and Knowledge" will have continued on long after the publication of the essay, in "Above All, No Journalists!" for example, and it will have started well in advance of the conference itself: "On the boat that brought us from Naples to Capri, I told myself that I would begin by recalling this sort of too luminous evidence, but I did not dare. I also told myself . . ." (§29).

15. Because the final section of the "Italics," that is, §26, actually ends with a reference to "Scripture," the "Post-Scriptum" is also post-Scripture: "*Before and after the* logos *which was in the beginning, before and after the Holy Sacrament, before and after the Holy Scriptures.*" Derrida again addresses the question or notion of the post-scriptum in "*Sauf le nom (Post-scriptum)*"; he writes, for example, "the theologico-negative maxim remains as a *post-scriptum*. It is originally a *post-scriptum*, it comes after the event" ("*SN*" 60). It is also worth noting that "Force of Law," too, contains a "*Post-Scriptum*" (*AR* 293–98).

16. Kierkegaard's *Fear and Trembling*, and particularly his reading of the story of Abraham's sacrifice of Isaac, is at the center of Derrida's *The Gift of Death* (see

GD 2 54–81) and "Literature in Secret" (*GD 2* 121–29). Derrida refers again to "fear and trembling" at the beginning of §13 and in §31. Philippians 2:12 reads, "continue to work out your salvation with fear and trembling." Kant refers to this passage from Philippians in *Religion* (62). Much later in *Religion*, Kant worries about how to determine the exact charge of the moral law and wonders how anyone could be without fear of mistake or error when obeying the injunction—or indeed interpreting the divine call—to "slaughter his own son like a sheep" (175).

17. In *Of Spirit*, Derrida questions the pertinence and limits not just of the "What is?" question but of the question in general in Heidegger, who at once privileges the question and yet speaks of a mode of engagement prior to it. Derrida anticipates this theme when he writes: "We shall see why and wherein the question of religion is first of all the question of the question. Of the origins and the borders of this question—as of the response. 'The thing' tends thus to drop out of sight as soon as one believes oneself able to master it under the title of a discipline, a knowledge or a philosophy" (§35). We will return to this theme in Observation 4 on Heidegger.

18. On the importance of the date 1807 in Hegel (the year after Napoleon rode past the Hegel's residence in Jena), and on Blanchot's reference to Hegel and this date in "The Instant of My Death," see *"D"* 83, 112–113n16.

19. The Salvation Army, e.g., is called in French *L'armée du Salut*.

20. Much later in the essay, Derrida will cite a passage from Benveniste that comes very close to making explicit this duplicity, that is, the double value of *salut* as health and a wish for health—"health" and "hail!" *salut* and *salut!* (§39n30).

21. On the *adieu* or *a-dieu*, see de Vries, *Philosophy and the Turn to Religion*, 25–28 and passim, and his *Religion and Violence*, 178–87.

22. Derrida recalls this yet again in the penultimate paragraph of the essay, where he speaks of "the truth of this prayer that maintains itself, recalling Aristotle one more time, beyond the true and the false, beyond their opposition, in any case, according to a certain concept of truth or of judgment" (§51).

23. Derrida comments in *"Sauf le nom (Post-Scriptum)"*: "In the course of the so-called Gulf War, the allied Western democracies often kept up a Christian discourse while speaking of international law" (*"SN"* 78).

24. Derrida will thus speak of "the concept of world or of history in its Western tradition (Christian or Greco-Christian, extending to Kant, Hegel, Husserl, Heidegger)" (§27; see §29) and he will argue that "the Christian history of this word, 'world,' already puts us on guard; the world is not the universe, nor the cosmos, nor the earth" (§35).

25. Caputo translates *mondialatinisation* as "world-Latinization" (*The Prayers and Tears of Jacques Derrida*, 154).

26. It is unclear whether Derrida is referring with this latter notion to a general theory of iterability that posits that repetition always reinscribes a past meaning *and* holds open the possibility of novelty or else to the necessary practice

of what he used to call *paleonomy* (see *POS* 71), that is, "the 'strategic' necessity that requires the occasional maintenance of an *old name* in order to launch a new concept," e.g., as we will see in more detail in Chapter 6, the "historical" names *messianicity* and *khōra*.

27. Emile Benveniste, *Indo-European Language and Society*, trans. Elizabeth Palmer (London: Farber and Farber, 1973).

28. While Derrida will often have recourse to the work of Benveniste, he will also often question and criticize it. Even in this passage, where Derrida is citing Benveniste's assertion that in the Indo-European language there is a notion of 'god' (*deiwos*) whose "*'proper meaning' is 'luminous' and 'celestial'*" (§8), Derrida goes on in a note to criticize Benveniste for having such confidence in a *proper* meaning. "We shall often cite Benveniste in order to leave him a responsibility— that of speaking for example with assurance of 'proper meaning,' precisely in the case of the sun or of light, but also with regard to everything else. This assurance seems greatly exaggerated and more than problematic" (§8n2). Derrida criticizes Benveniste once again (in §31 and following) for the confidence he shows in thinking he knows how to distinguish a proper or literal meaning of a word from an improper meaning, as if one could ever identify and circumscribe a properly religious vocabulary. He thus criticizes him, it seems, for not approaching the question of religion, the question, therefore, of scruple and reticence, with more scruple or reticence, more hesitation. Derrida cites Benveniste to point out the "chasms over which a great scholar walks with tranquil step, as though he knew what he was talking about, while at the same time acknowledging that at bottom he really doesn't know very much" (§31). Derrida thus argues, in effect, that we must be careful not to believe in the authority of someone who will have believed a bit too much in his own knowledge. In other words, Benveniste will have fallen prey to the temptation to *know*: Derrida cites Benveniste on the etymology of "responding" and then adds: "As always, recourse to knowledge is temptation itself" (§31). And the problem is less believing that we know what we think we do than believing that we know what knowledge *is*—for example, that it is distinct from faith. Derrida thus says that "the temptation to believe in knowledge, here for example in the precious authority of Benveniste, can hardly be separated from a certain fear and trembling" (§31). (Just before the example from Benveniste in question, Derrida remarks somewhat elliptically and enigmatically on the example from Plautus that Benveniste is about to give: "'I promise you that it happened.' What happened? Who, to be precise? A son, yours. How beautiful to have an example. Religion, nothing less"; §31.)

This double treatment of Benveniste—at once admiration and critique—runs throughout "Faith and Knowledge." Derrida speaks, for example, of "the premises here of a work to come" that would be drawn, "once again, from that rich chapter of Benveniste's *Indo-European Language and Society*, addressing the Sacred and the Holy" (§39n30). But in the same passage Derrida will refer to certain "methodological difficulties" (Benveniste's phrase) and accuse Benveniste, in effect, of "maintaining the cult of 'original meaning' (religion itself, and the 'sacred')" (§39n30).

29. Traces of this critique can be found even in "Faith and Knowledge." Derrida writes in a note: "As I have tried to do elsewhere (*Specters of Marx*, p. 23 ff.), I propose to think the condition of justice in relation to a certain sundering [*déliaison*], in relation to the always-safe, always-to-be-saved possibility of this secret of disassociation, rather than through the bringing-together (*Versammlung*) towards which Heidegger retraces it, in his concern, doubtless legitimate in part, to extract *Dike* from the authority of *Ius*, which is to say, from its more recent ethico-juridical representations" (§26n15).

30. Derrida will go on in §31 to cite Benveniste at length on the etymology of *re-spondeo*, a word that brings together—and this will be important for Derrida in what follows—notions of response, promise, offering, swearing, testimony, responsibility, etc.

31. This title for Chapter 3 bears an uncanny similarity—which I discovered only after the fact—to the three subtitles of John P. Manoussakis's excellent article on "Faith and Knowledge," "The Revelation According to Jacques Derrida," in *Derrida and Religion: Other Testaments*, ed. Yvonne Sherwood and Kevin Hart (New York: Routledge, 2005), 309–23. His three subtitles are "Three Readings," "Of the Two Sources," "Of the One Possibility."

3. Three Theses on the Two Sources and Their One Common Element

1. For one of the most lucid and perceptive analyses of the principal theses of "Faith and Knowledge," see Serge Margel's "Foi et savoir: L'essence du religieux, le mal radical et la question de la modernité," in *Derrida* (Paris: Éditions de l'Herne, 2004), 261–68.

2. Notice that "*Sauf le nom (Post-scriptum)*" also begins with an ellipsis, as if the voice(s) of Derrida in the text were responding to the "voices" of the conference he could not attend.

3. DeLillo frequently evokes an attack on world financial systems through an attack on the faith that supports those systems. In *The Players* (New York: Random House, 1977), a terrorist group attacks the stock market in an attempt to "Attack the idea of their money." When one character thus asks, "Do you believe in the value of that?" another responds, "I do, actually. The system. The secret currents. Make it appear a little less inviolable. It's their greatest strength, as you said, or your brother, and to incapacitate it, even briefly, would be to set loose every kind of demon" (183). Such an attack on the world financial market is also at the center of *Cosmopolis*.

4. See J. L. Austin, *How to Do Things with Words* (Cambridge: Harvard University Press, 1962), and Derrida's reading of Austin in "SEC."

5. Here is the second formulation of the question, followed up, once again, via Benveniste, by the theme of the promise or the oath: "**And if *religio* remained untranslatable?** . . . What does it mean to respond? It is to swear—the faith: *respondere, antworten, answer, swear (swaran)*: 'to be compared with the got. *swaran* [from which come *schwören, beschwören,* 'swear,' 'conjure,' 'adjure,' etc.], "to swear, to pronounce solemn formulas": this is almost literally *respondere*'" (§31, citing Benveniste, *Indo-European Language and Society*).

6. In *The Animal That Therefore I Am*, Derrida questions the traditional philosophical opposition between response and reaction, that is, between a capacity for response and language that is traditionally reserved for humans and a mere reaction, which is commonly attributed to animals.

7. As for the term *war of religion*, Derrida remarks in §28 that it is always possible that other interests (economic, politico-military) are behind these new "wars of religion" and that we may not always know what declaration or claim is hiding what. Moreover, to identify a "war of religion" we would have to know exactly what *religion* and *war* mean, something Derrida questions throughout. "To determine a war of religion *as such*, one would have to be certain that one can delimit the religious. One would have to be certain that one can distinguish all the predicates of the religious" (§28). The entirety of "Faith and Knowledge" is devoted, in effect, to showing the difficulty of such a project, and especially the folly of thinking that it has been accomplished. Derrida will thus continue to use both terms, but never without warning us about their semantic ambiguity or instability or about the interests that are often involved in using or manipulating them.

8. Caputo expresses in a particularly vivid way the reliance of certain fundamentalist groups on the science and teletechnology that they eschew: "Bible-thumping televangelists make use of a satellite technology that reduces to absurdity their geocentric, flat-earth fundamentalism. People who actually believe that the human race goes back to Adam and Eve use advanced digital systems to address a world in which the completion of the human genome project is foreseen" (*The Prayers and Tears of Jacques Derrida*, 153).

9. In "Above All, No Journalists!" Derrida underscores both the fact that "the Roman Catholic Church is today the sole global political institution that structurally possesses a head of state, even if the Vatican is, of course, no ordinary state" and that "John Paul II knew how to exploit the power of media technology" ("AANJ" 59). One might want to recall what John Paul II himself called, in "*Fides et ratio*," a "new evangelization" in relationship to this exploitation of the media. It is perhaps worth noting that the Vatican announced on 25 January 2009 that it has its own You Tube "Channel."

10. It has frequently been argued that one of the sources of contention between the Taliban and Bin Laden was the latter's understanding of and attraction to technology.

11. Derrida later calls this "double movement of abstraction and attraction" *mechanical*, though in a sense of the mechanical that needs to be developed. "'Mechanical' would have to be understood here in a meaning that is rather 'mystical.' Mystical or secret because contradictory and distracting, both inaccessible, disconcerting and familiar, *unheimlich*, uncanny to the very extent that this machinality, this ineluctable automatization produces and re-produces what *at the same time detaches from and reattaches to* the family (*heimisch*, homely), to the familiar, to the domestic, to the proper, to the *oikos* of the ecological and of the economic, to the *ethos*, to the place of dwelling. This quasi-spontaneous automaticity, as irreflective as a reflex, repeats again and again the double movement of

abstraction and attraction that *at the same time detaches and reattaches* to the country, the idiom, the literal or to everything confusedly collected today under the terms 'identity' or 'identitarian'; in two words, that which at the same time ex-propriates and re-appropriates, de-racinates and re-enracinates, *ex-appropriates* according to a logic that we will later have to formalize, that of auto-immune auto-indemnification" (§37).

12. Derrida argues something similar with regard to ecology in *The Animal That Therefore I Am*. After claiming that "Cartesianism belongs, beneath its mechanistic indifference, to the Judeo-Christiano-Islamic tradition of a war against the animal, of a sacrificial war that is as old as Genesis," he argues that "no ethical or sentimental nobility must be allowed to conceal from us that violence, and acknowledged forms of ecologism or vegetarianism are insufficient to bring it to an end, however more worthy they be than what they oppose" (*ATT* 101).

13. Derrida explains: "To be sure, in the recent past every soldier did not *know* how his firearm functioned although he *knew* very well how to use it. Yesterday, all the drivers of automobiles or travelers in a train did not always know very well how 'it works.' But their relative incompetence stands in no common (quantitative) measure nor in any (qualitative) analogy with that which today characterizes the relationship of the major part of humanity to the machines by which they live or with which they strive to live in daily familiarity. Who is capable of explaining scientifically to children how telephones function today (by undersea cables or by satellite), and the same is true of television, fax, computer, electronic mail, CD-ROMS, magnetic cards, jet planes, the distribution of nuclear energy, scanners, echography, etc.?" (§45).

14. For a fuller development of the notion of autoimmunity in Derrida, see chap. 7 of my *Derrida From Now On*.

15. Hent de Vries nicely summarizes these three theses in *Philosophy and the Return to Religion*: "If, as Derrida notes in 'Faith and Knowledge,' religion shares at least the same condition of possibility as the tele-techno-scientific world of the new media, it is produced by them as much as it in turn produces them. This is not to deny that religion must, in a sense, also deny this very 'mechanics' that *seems* to deny it its proper cause, its *sui generis* and its *causa sui*, that is to say, its exclusivity and irreducibility, as well as its originator, its God" (115).

16. Derrida suggests that this "return" is repeated out of confusion or haste. He asks, for example: "When we speak, **we Europeans**, so ordinarily and so confusedly today about a 'return of the religious,' what do we thereby name? To what do we refer?" (§32). Later, he writes: "Today once again, today finally, today otherwise, the great question would still be religion and what some hastily call its 'return'" (§35).

17. On this relationship between philosophy or reason and faith, C. E. Evink, in "Jacques Derrida and the Faith in Philosophy," *Southern Journal of Philosophy* 42, no. 3 (2004), rightly speaks of a certain "faith in philosophy" (321) and, later, of a "force of faith" (323). He concludes, following Derrida, that even "the

Enlightenment critique of all faith cannot but give a testimony of its own 'faith in reason'" (324). Caputo makes a similar point in *Deconstruction in a Nutshell*: "The whole point of a deconstructive, postcritical, postsecularizing analysis of what is called reason—that is, the point of a New Enlightenment—would be to show the extent to which reason is woven from the very fabric of faith" (*DNS* 164). I would agree with this claim, so long as the "postsecular" is meant to suggest here not a postsecular return to religion but a critique of the religious origins of our political concepts, as well as an acceptance of the universalizing faith at the origin of the social bond, that is, so long as postsecularism remains both a secularizing task to be accomplished and a recognition of the elementary faith that makes this task possible.

18. See Jean-François Lyotard, *The Differend*, trans. George Van Den Abbeele (Minneapolis: University of Minnesota Press, 1988).

19. Martin Hägglund analyzes this passage with great perspicuity in *Radical Atheism: Derrida and the Time of Life* (Stanford, Calif.: Stanford University Press, 2008). If, as Hägglund argues, "we can never know for sure what will happen because experience is predicated on the unpredictable coming of time" (126), then "whatever one has faith in is itself subjected to the undecidable future, which requires one to 'take in trust' what may be a menace" (127).

20. That is what Derrida means when he writes just a few lines later: "The act of faith demanded in bearing witness exceeds, through its structure, all institution and all proof, all knowledge ('I swear that I am telling the truth, not necessarily the 'objective truth,' but the truth of what I believe to be the truth, I am telling you this truth, believe me, believe what I believe, there, where you will never be able to see nor know the irreplaceable yet universalizable, exemplary place from which I speak to you; perhaps my testimony is false, but I am sincere and in good faith, it is not false [as] testimony')" (§49). For a lucid and insightful reading of this passage, see Geoffrey Bennington's *Other Analyses: Reading Philosophy* (Seattle: CreateSpace, 2004), 88–89. Bennington begins by reading this passage in light of Austinian speech act theory, and he draws special attention to the inherent performativity of even the constative, to the elementary faith, therefore, that is at the origin of not only all promises or professions of faith but all scientific observations. Bennington then goes on to anticipate much of what I will be arguing later in this chapter when he writes—to Derrida: "this seems to involve a memory of your earliest analyses of Husserl, where the inaccessibility to me of the other's lived experience, and the recourse to analogical appresentation of it, is a major consequence."

21. Derrida says something similar in *Islam & the West*: "I have never believed that it is possible to synthesize the existence of any individual, in any case not my own, and therefore I believe that dissociation is inescapable. The social relationship is made of interruption. To relate to the other, as other, is not simply to be linked to the other; it is also to respect the interruption. . . . To relate to the other presupposes faith" (*IW* 66).

22. See Maurice Blanchot's *The Unavowable Community*, trans. Pierre Joris (Barrytown, N.Y.: Station Hill Press, 1988).

23. Derrida speaks earlier of "*the rigorous dissociation that Levinas wishes to maintain between a natural sacredness that would be 'pagan,' even Greco-Christian, and the holiness* [sainteté] *of (Jewish) law, before or under the Roman religion*" (§18). In a footnote to §18 we are reminded that the "Latin (even Roman)" word used by Levinas in *Du sacré au saint* (Paris: Editions de Minuit, 1977) to designate holiness, *sainteté*, is "only the translation of a Hebrew word (*kidouch*)" (§18n8). On the Levinasian relationship between the sacred and the holy, see §32 and §40n33. See also "FL" 250.

24. Recall Derrida's reading of the Declaration of Independence, where it is God who ultimately secures the declaration through the rectitude of the intentions of the good people of the United States. See "Declarations of Independence," trans. Tom Keenan and Tom Pepper, in *N* 46–54.

25. Edmund Husserl, *Cartesian Meditations*, trans. Dorion Cairns (The Hague: Martinus Nijhoff, 1977), 108–111.

Interlude I: Waste, Weapons, and Religion (*Underworld* II)

1. Derrida himself was not indifferent to the number 13, having lived as a boy in El-Biar at 13, rue d'Aurelle-de-Paladines (see *JD* 247).

2. A good part of the narrative of *Underworld* consists in trying to trace the unlikely and uncertain trajectory of the baseball hit by Bobby Thompson into the stands of the Polo Grounds on 3 October 1951. But how does one *know* whether a ball being sold for an exorbitant price as a piece of baseball memorabilia really is the ball in question? It's all about belief—about believing it's the ball (see *U* 647–48).

3. Don DeLillo, *Running Dog* (New York: Alfred A. Knopf, Inc., 1978), 4. The relationship between religion and weaponry is a common theme in DeLillo's novels. *White Noise* is only the most famous of these works. Already in *End Zone* (New York: Penguin Books, 1972)—a novel, incidentally, about the religious dimensions of football—we read: "There's a kind of theology at work here. The bombs are a kind of god. As his power grows, our fear naturally increases. . . . There's a kind of theology of fear that comes out of this" (80). And in *The Names* (New York: Vintage Books, 1982), a novel that revolves almost completely around questions of faith and religion, revelation and language, one of the main characters asks, "Why is the language of destruction so beautiful?" (115).

4. After speaking of how the "drums [of Agent Orange] resembled cans of frozen Minute Maid enlarged by a crazed strain of DNA" (*U* 463), the narrator asks: "How can you tell the difference between orange juice and agent orange if the same massive system connects them at levels outside your comprehension?" (*U* 465). This reference to Minute Maid orange juice prefigures the appearance of Esmeralda in the billboard for Minute Maid at the end of the novel, the scene of a miracle that takes place under a "madder orange moon," not far from the scene of a brutal crime scene cordoned off by orange tape (*U* 820).

5. What attracts Nick to *The Cloud of Unknowing* is the understanding of God as a force whose power comes from his "unknowability," a God who "keeps his secret" (*U* 295).

6. While the Soviets make nukes to maximize their "throw-weight," Americans have the neutron bomb—the perfect capitalist weapon, a bomb that kills people but leaves property intact (*U* 790).

7. Eerily, we see throughout the novel the two World Trade Center Towers "under construction" (*U* 371, 377, 385): "I think of it as one, not two. Even though there are clearly two towers" (*U* 372). DeLillo's *Underworld* has been read as a sort of visionary, prophetic, or even "telepathic" novel about 9/11. See, e.g., Pamela Thurschwell's excellent essay, "Forecasting Falls: Icarus from Freud to Auden to 9/11" (*Oxford Literary Review* 30, no. 2 (2008): 201–33). Thurschwell draws attention, for example, to the cover of *Underworld*, which depicts the twin towers and a soaring bird that, in the wake of 9/11, looks like a plane about to crash into one of the towers. And she points out that DeLillo's descriptions of New York's Freshkills Landfill in *Underworld* takes on an uncanny new relevance in the wake of 9/11, since it was there that much of the debris from the World Trade Towers was disposed of.

4. *La religion soufflée*: The Genesis of "Faith and Knowledge"

1. In thinking of Derrida's keen eye for the out of joint and the noncontemporaneous, I am reminded of the final pages of Nicholas Royle's recent work *In Memory of Jacques Derrida* (Edinburgh: Edinburgh University Press, 2009), 187, an exquisite dream sequence in which Royle—telepathic, as ever—gives Derrida a chance to speak from what will be characterized in Chapter 9 below as "the other side": " *I asked him what year it was—he must have seen that I was asking this question as a visitor, or not in the same world as him, for he laughed (very beautifully) and replied in a reassuring simple fashion: 'Oh, it's no problem. I can jump around from one time to the other.'* "

2. Derrida tells us, in what appears to be an aside within this anecdote, that the meeting took place in the Hotel Lutétia—that is, I presume, in the lobby of the hotel, where Derrida often met friends, colleagues, and students because it was right across the street from his office at the École des Hautes Études on Boulevard Raspail. Considering Derrida's emphasis in "Faith and Knowledge" on *mondialatinisation* and the two possible Latin etymologies of the word *religio*, it is perhaps worth noting that Lutetia is actually the Latin name for Paris, which was once called "Lutetia Parisiorum," named after a people called the Parisii. As for the name *Lutétia* or *Lutèce*, it originally meant either "mud" or "wolf." The Hotel Lutétia also has the dubious distinction of having been requisitioned by the Nazis in World War II and converted into one of their headquarters. It was also used after the war as a hospital and relocation center for concentration-camp survivors.

3. Michel Lisse has reminded me of the duplicity of the word *Or* that begins this passage. As Derrida himself remarked in his reading of Mallarmé in "The Double Session," it can have either a temporal signification ("now") or a logical one ("so," "hence").

4. See Hélène Cixous's beautiful reading of this passage in *Judeities: Questions for Jacques Derrida*, ed. Bettina Bergo, Joseph Cohen, and Raphael Zagury-Orly (New York: Fordham University Press, 2007). 70–71.

5. On the "without" of negative theology, see, e.g., "*SN*" 76 and 81–83. In both "How to Avoid Speaking" (originally written for a conference in Jerusalem in 1986) and "*Post-Scriptum*"—later published as "*Sauf le nom (Post-Scriptum)*"—Derrida speaks of how the language of negative theology can so easily become mechanical. The formalization of language in the form of "X without X" would be but one example of this. "What we are identifying under these two words [i.e., *negative theology*], today, isn't it first of all a corpus, at once open and closed, given, well-ordered, a set of statements recognizable either by their family resemblance or because they come under a regular logicodiscursive type whose recurrence lends itself to a formalization? This formalization can become mechanical . . ." Hence the discourse of negative theology can always be thought—and we will recognize these terms from "Plato's Pharmacy" and other texts—to be "on the side of the empty and then of mechanical, indeed purely verbal, repetition of phrases without actual or full intentional meaning" ("*SN*" 50). In other words, the language of negative theology can be seen to oscillate between the miracle and the machine. Derrida himself speaks of "the genius or the machine of apophatic dialectics" in Pascal ("*SN*" 72). For two critiques of Derrida's reading of negative theology, see Eric D. Perl, "Signifying Nothing: Being as Sign in Neoplatonism and Derrida," in *Neoplatonism and Contemporary Thought*, ed. R. Baine Harris (Albany: State University of New York Press, 2002): 2:125–52, and Jeffrey Fischer, "The Theology of Dis/similarity: Negation in Pseudo-Dionysius," *The Journal of Religion* 81, no. 4 (October 2001): 529–48. For support of Derrida's interpretation, see Leo Sweeney, S.J., "Jacques Derrida and Dionysius the Areopagite," *Neoplatonism and Contemporary Thought*, ed. Harris, 2:93–119, and Shira Wolosky, "An 'Other' Negative Theology: On Derrida's 'How to Avoid Speaking: Denials,'" *Poetics Today*. 19, no. 2 (Summer 1998): 261–80.

6. Translation slightly modified. Commenting on Blanchot's "The Instant of My Death" in "*Demeure*," Derrida speaks of "the *stigma* of a verdict that condemned him to death without death . . . a death without death and thus a life without life. . . . a logic without logic of the 'X without X,' or of the 'not' or of the 'except,' of the 'being without being'" ("*D*" 89). Derrida then comments on the logic of this formula or formulation: "The 'without' in the 'X without X' signifies this spectral necessity, which overflows the opposition between reality and fiction. This spectral necessity . . . allows what does not arrive to arrive, what one believes does not arrive to succeed in arriving. Virtually, with a virtuality that can no longer be opposed to actual factuality. . . . This constituting structure is a destructuring fracture. It is the condition that is common to literature and non-literature" ("*D*" 92).

7. Breath is not always, of course, on the side of life or of the human. In *The Animal That Therefore I Am*, Derrida demonstrates the way in which breath in

Descartes is on the side of the animal-machine and so is opposed to the cogito as a thinking substance. We can thus deduce nothing about the essence of the cogito from a statement such as "I breathe," though one can determine its essence as a thinking substance from the statement "I think I breathe" (*ATT* 86).

8. Derrida himself encourages us from very early on to read him in precisely this way, displacing a configuration of terms from one text to another as a way of illuminating both. In an early interview from 1967, Derrida is asked about the relationship between his various books, and he answers: "what is first of all put in question is the unity of the book and the unity 'book' considered as a perfect totality." He goes on to argue that "it would be impossible to provide a linear, deductive representation of these works that would correspond to some 'logical order.'" He says, e.g., "One can take *Of Grammatology* as a long essay articulated in two parts (whose juncture is not empirical, but theoretical, systematic) *into the middle* of which one could staple *Writing and Difference*. . . . Inversely, one could insert *Of Grammatology into the middle* of *Writing and Difference*. . . . In any case, that two 'volumes' are to be inscribed one *in the middle of* the other is due . . . to a strange geometry, of which these texts are doubtless the contemporaries" (*POS* 3–4). In what follows, I will argue that the same could be argued for texts that are much further apart in time. By grafting, by "stapling," in effect, "Plato's Pharmacy" (1968) into the middle of "Faith and Knowledge" (1995), we will be better able to understand the way in which the technological supplement comes with the regularity of the machine to interrupt life and take its breath away.

9. Derrida says something similar in an interview with Richard Beardsworth on the question of "life" in Nietzsche (and Heidegger): "As a self-relation, as activity and reactivity, as differential force, and repetition, life is always already inhabited by technicization. The relation between *physis* and technics is not an opposition; from the very first [*dès l'origine*] there is instrumentalization. . . . a prosthetic strategy of repetition inhabits the very moment of life: life is a process of self-replacement, the handing-down of life is a *mechanike*, a form of technics. Not only, then, is technics not in opposition to life, it also haunts it from the very beginning" (*N* 244).

10. Derrida will often have played off this phrase from Genesis. In "Force of Law," e.g., he writes: "At the beginning of justice there will have been *logos*, speech or language, but this is not necessarily in contradiction with another *incipit*, which would say, 'In the beginning there will have been force'" ("FL" 238).

11. My thanks to Louis Ruprecht for drawing my attention to this doubling.

12. Here are the two versions of creation in Genesis in a popular French translation and an English one. Genesis 1:1–2, 27: "*Au commencement*, Dieu créa les cieux et la terre. La terre était informe et vide, les ténèbres couvraient l'abîme et *le souffle* de Dieu planait sur les eaux. . . Dieu créa l'homme à son image; à l'image de Dieu il le créa, homme et femme il les créa"; "*In the beginning* when God created the heavens and the earth, the earth was a formless void and darkness covered the face of the deep, while a *wind* from God [or the spirit or breath of

God] swept over the face of the waters. . . . So God created humankind in his image, in the image of God he created them; male and female he created them." Hence the *souffle*, the breath, wind, or spirit—all possible translations of the Hebrew *ruah*—is present in Genesis 1:2 but does not enter into the actual creation of the world, and particularly not into the creation of man. But at Genesis 2:7 this breath or *souffle* plays an essential role in man's creation: "Le Seigneur Dieu forma l'homme avec la poussière du sol, et il lui *insuffla* dans les narine un *souffle* de vie, et l'homme devient un être vivant"; "The Lord God formed man from the dust of the ground, and *breathed* into his nostrils the *breath* of life; and the man became a living being" (*La Sainte Bible* [Paris: Turnhout, 1973]; *New Revised Standard Version, The New Oxford Annotated Bible* [New York: Oxford University Press, 1991]). Already in 1963, in "Force and Signification" Derrida spoke of *ruah* and of pneumatology, "the science of *pneuma, spiritus,* or *logos*" ("FS" 9).

13. In an interview from 1978, Derrida himself talks about his own use of *souffler* and its derivatives in his early essay on Artaud. Derrida recalls that in "La parole soufflée" he spoke of God being, for Artaud, "the Great Thief" and that the phrase *parole soufflée* means, among other things, "stolen word." "So theft is something that has always interested me" ("PSI" 162).

14. The question of the possibility of thinking a response that is not contaminated by reaction is at the center of Derrida's *The Animal That Therefore I Am*: "Everything seems to hinge here on these two understandings of nonresponse, at the heart of the disturbing analogy between them. (What never even crosses the mind of any of the thinkers we are listening to or will listen to here on the subject of the response, from Descartes to Lacan, is the question of how an iterability that is essential to every response, and to the ideality of every response, can and cannot fail to introduce nonresponse, automatic reaction, mechanical reaction into the most alive, most 'authentic,' and most responsible response.)" (*ATT* 111–12).

5. The Telegenic Voice: The Religion of the Media

1. Though the full explanation is to be found only in "Faith and Knowledge" and "Above All, No Journalists!" Derrida does go on in *Echographies* to explain that what interests him about these Muslim programs is their dissemination of a message that is at once religious, social, and political: "I try to imagine what is going on with the producers of this program in France, their politics. . . . In general, it is extremely smart, but in the end it translates a politics, and I find this interesting. It's the same with the Jewish program, which occasionally (it is inconsistent) teaches me a lot about the texts and the religion, but also about the ideological strategy or the political 'positions' of those who are responsible for these programs, whether they are declared openly or not" (*ET* 139).

2. My thanks to Jaafar Aksikas of Columbia College in Chicago for reminding me of this crucial difference between the Hebrew Bible and the Koran.

3. Derrida's remarks in "Above All, No Journalists!" are among his boldest, most speculative and provocative, about religion in general and Christianity in

particular. Though Derrida says little that is not already implicit or adumbrated in texts on religion ranging from "How to Avoid Speaking" and "*Sauf le nom*" to "Faith and Knowledge," we encounter in "Above All, No Journalists!" a Derrida much more willing to spell out in the clearest of terms the relationship between religion and the media, religion and technology and globalization, and, most provocatively, the differences between the three monotheisms with regard to these. While we must acknowledge that the improvised nature of these remarks might account for some of the differences between them and previously published texts, the differences are, I think, too profound to be attributed only to this.

4. Derrida speaks in *Memoirs of the Blind* of "this God of Abraham, of Isaac, and of Jacob who is never seen face to face and whose ways are secret" (*MB* 98).

5. The universalizing message of Christianity as well as the globalizing technologies designed to deliver it are, as we have already seen, at the center of "*Fides et ratio.*" Pope John Paul II writes, for example, "The truth communicated in Christ's Revelation is therefore no longer confined to a particular place or culture, but is offered to every man and woman who would welcome it as the word which is the absolutely valid source of meaning for human life" ("*Fides et ratio*," §12). And later: "Christ's mandate to his disciples to go out everywhere, 'even to the ends of the earth' (Acts 1:8), in order to pass on the truth which he had revealed, led the Christian community to recognize from the first the universality of its message and the difficulties created by cultural differences" (ibid., §70). Even the incarnation must thus be thought in relationship to the expression of meaning through the *body* of a particular language, for "human language embodies the language of God, who communicates his own truth with that wonderful 'condescension' which mirrors the logic of the Incarnation" (ibid., §94). One of the tasks of what John Paul II calls a "new evangelization" is thus to "reconcile the absoluteness and the universality of truth with the unavoidable historical and cultural conditioning of the formulas which express that truth" (§95). John Paul II ends the encyclical by calling on philosophers to play a central role in this reconciliation.

6. Derrida is less categorical just a bit earlier in his remarks: "It is not certain that one can speak of a Buddhist 'religion' without globalatinizing it surreptitiously" ("AANJ" 61). For a fascinating debate over this question of whether or to what extent the concept of religion is Christian, see Gil Anidjar's essay on the work of Talal Asad, "The Idea of an Anthropology of Christianity,' *Interventions* 11, no. 3 (2009): 367–93, and Asad's response, "Response to Gil Anidjar," *Interventions* 11, no. 3 (2009): 394–99. Asad is the author of, among many other important works, *Formations of the Secular: Christianity, Islam, Modernity* (Stanford, Calif.: Stanford University Press, 2002).

7. Derrida argues in a similar vein in his conversation with Mustapha Chérif in *Islam & the West*: "I believe that there are many religions, positive religions, to which one can belong or not belong; there are religions that I call Abrahamic that are the Jewish religion, the Christian religion, the Muslim religion, with their

common foundation or 'trunk [*tronc*].' There are other cultures that one calls religions and that are not perhaps religions. The concept of religion is an obscure concept. In *Faith and Knowledge*, I attempted to write on this subject, on the obscurity of the very concept of religion. Is Buddhism a religion? Is Taoism a religion?" (*IW* 57).

8. Derrida says of negative theology in "*Sauf le nom*": "Whatever the translations, analogies, transpositions, transferences, metaphors, never has any discourse expressly given itself this title (negative theology, apophatic method, *via negativa*) in the thoughts of Jewish, Muslim, Buddhist culture" ("*SN*" 63). In other words, negative theology would be an "idiom of Greco-Latin Filiation" ("*SN*" 54).

9. "For this universalism, the sister is a subset of the brother, the sister is fraternal. On the other side, speaking the language of familial or national genealogy, sometimes of autochthony, this fraternalist model has a limit that is Judeo-Christian, and naturally also massively Islamic. The motif of the brother dominates the three religions. And in none of them is the essential bond to the nation, or to the people, called into question" ("AANJ" 91). In "Countersignature," a text written in 2000 on Jean Genet, Derrida speaks of his suspicion of the fraternal and its Christian genealogy, a "fraternalistic schema" he "tried to deconstruct in *Politics of Friendship* as a Christian schema, a phallocentric, macho schema and a genealogistic, familial schema. One's neighbor, in the Christian sense, being first of all a brother" ("CS" 24).

10. My thanks to John Kitchen of the University of Alberta, who pointed out to me that Saint Clare of Assisi (1194–1253) was named patron saint of television in 1958 because, when she was too ill to attend Mass, she is said to have seen and heard it on the wall of her room—a virtual, televisual Mass avant la lettre.

11. Derrida clarifies this relation later in his remarks: "Whether it is a question of the cenotaph, of the tomb without corpse, or of the void of the *kenosis*, that absence or emptiness, the disappearance of the body does not necessarily contradict the appeal to visibility or to the image. In a certain manner television itself would be the figure: the appeal to the media is the disappearance of the body, whether because there is no longer a corpse, and it is going to resuscitate, it's *imminent* . . . or because it has become wine and bread, wafer, spiritualized blood and body, spectralized, virtualized, sanctified and consumable" ("AANJ" 92). For an excellent analysis of contemporary media—and particularly television—in relation to Derrida's work, see Samuel Weber's *Mass Mediauras: Form, Technics, Media*, ed. Alan Cholodenko (Stanford, Calif.: Stanford University Press, 1996), esp. 108–51. This volume includes an interview with Weber fittingly titled "*Deus ex media*."

12. Derrida appears to be justifying this claim from "Faith and Knowledge" about Pope John Paul II when he says, in "Above All, No Journalists!": "It is without any irony that, in speaking of the mediatic authority of the Pope today, I said it was founded on the death of God. What he speaks of, what is essential in what his message *propagates*, is a certain death of God. . . . It can be sensed

almost immediately, without delay, like the air that one breathes, as soon as his Holiness appears on the screen. This popularity of the Pope is linked to that profound and shared certainty, in anguish, despair, or relief: God is dead; it's just been announced on television. And if you want proof, here it is in the *revenant*, here is revenant, returning" ("AANJ" 67–68).

13. Derrida goes on to suggest that in this universalization and globalization of images "the Christian concept of the world finds its adequation in the concept of *earth*" ("AANJ" 68), for we can today "reach the limits of the earth . . . by television and by satellites" to a degree we never could before ("AANJ" 68). The same technologies have allowed us not only to reach the limits of the earth but to leave it altogether, even though, says Derrida, "leaving the earth is also Christian. The relation between the terrestrial and the supraterrestrial, between the heavenly and the worldly, is also Christian (hi)story" ("AANJ" 69).

14. Peggy Kamuf affirms this speculation on my part; Derrida, she writes, was "fascinated . . . by the phenomenon of Christian evangelists on American television" ("The Affect of America," in *Derrida's Legacies*, ed. Simon Glendinning and Robert Eaglestone [New York: Routledge, 2008], 147).

15. I speak of fascination here because, as Derrida himself admits, television continues to fascinate even when one knows what is happening and even, perhaps, when one is trying to resist it: "This effect of presence cannot be erased by any critique. Even if *I know* what's going on, even if I am extremely vigilant, the simulacrum is part of the thing itself, if one can put it that way. No critique can penetrate or dissipate this structural 'illusion.' I know without a doubt that it isn't true; I don't believe in it. But another belief, another fascinated belief continues to operate, and its operation requires a different phenomenological analysis" ("AANJ" 85–86). In other words, and even more succinctly, "no critique of television will ever erase what I will call the transcendental illusion of the media" ("AANJ" 85).

16. On the notion of "live" video, see *CAS* 48–50.

17. As Derrida writes in "Faith and Knowledge," "everything down to the signs of presence in the mystery of the Eucharist is 'cederomized'; over airborne pilgrimages to Mecca; over so many miracles transmitted live (most frequently, healings, which is to say, returns to the unscathed, *heilig*, holy, indemnifications) followed by commercials, before thousands in an American television studio" (§27n17).

18. For a reading of "the thing" in Derrida's work, see Michael Marder's *The Event of the Thing* (Toronto: University of Toronto Press, 2009).

19. Everything after the words "I can be touched . . ." is labeled "Postscript" in the text, a written addendum, it seems, to Derrida's spoken remarks.

20. This theme is central to *Archive Fever*. As the inscription of a unique and singular event from the past, the archive must itself be absolutely unique and singular. And yet, in order to be read, in order to function precisely as origin and as archive, it must be open to repetition and reproduction. Derrida writes, "each time in its original uniqueness, an archive ought to be idiomatic, and thus at

once offered and unavailable for translation, open to and shielded from technical iteration and reproduction" (*AF* 90). Derrida's reading and critique of Freud in this work—written, let me recall, just weeks after the Capri conference and in view of Pompeii—is that, even though Freud has a concept of the archive as prosthetic, he nonetheless privileges live memory and still dreams of a hypomnesis where the archive *"comes to efface itself,"* where "it becomes transparent or unessential so as to let the *origin* present itself in person" (*AF* 93). In his reading of Jensen's *Gradiva*, Freud believes he can uncover an origin more originary than that of the specter and that he can get to the place where the stones themselves speak. In other words, Freud thinks he can return to a moment of auto-affection *before* the archive.

21. The language of autoimmunity thus comes to communicate with Derrida's rethinking elsewhere of the archive and the phantasm. We will look at this relationship in more detail in Chapter 7. For the moment, notice that it is the idea of a life that in its living presence would be able to *archive itself* that is at the origin of the phantasm. Derrida attempts to deflate this phantasm in *Archive Fever*, particularly with regard to Gradiva, by demonstrating that it is life itself that is autoimmune, life itself that, in archiving itself, is always already beyond and outside itself.

22. Though I will be looking here primarily at Derrida's analysis of Husserl, a similar analysis of Hegel can be found in "The Pit and the Pyramid: Introduction to Hegel's Semiology" (*MP* 69–108).

23. Derrida's work on photography, as well as his refusal up through 1979 to be photographed, might be considered from this perspective. Derrida writes in *A Taste for the Secret*: "There were several different reasons for my refusal to be photographed, which did last a long time. One of them, a profound one, unquestionably has to do with being ill at ease with my own image—the relation to death that one reads in every portrait, the dissimulation of the face in writing, the problem I always have, for that matter, with my own face. . . . I felt that the author should not appear, it was ridiculous, vulgar, and inconsistent with the very things I had written about authors" (*TS* 52–53). But Derrida goes on to say, in conformity with what I have been arguing in this chapter, that "since the early 1980s the question of photography has become relatively secondary—now we have the big question of television" (*TS* 53).

24. Derrida recalls in "Above All, No Journalists!" the story of a Brooklyn Jew who gave his cell phone to a friend visiting Israel so that he might, still in Brooklyn, call his own cell phone at the Wall of Lamentations and so "pray" at the wall ("AANJ" 72).

25. Derrida's claim in early texts such as *Of Grammatology* that phonocentrism is a quasi-universal phenomenon is echoed in later texts, such as *A Taste for the Secret*: "From this point of view, if you will, logocentrism is something very Western, while there is a phonocentrism in practically all writing and especially in the relation, in the interpretation of the relation between speech and writing. In all writing in general. The authority of speech can be found at a certain point within every culture in general, as an economic phase of humanization" (*TS* 77).

26. Derrida also recalls this priority of the voice in *Memoirs of the Blind*: "One must always remember that the word, the vocable, is heard and understood, the sonorous phenomenon remaining invisible as such" (*MB* 4). As Derrida will go on to argue, the artist does not see himself see but does not have the impression of doing so either, while a speaker *does* have the impression of hearing himself speak, the impression of hearing the act of speaking at its origin. It is because this "desire for self-presentation is never met" that "the simulacrum takes place" (*MB* 121). And that is why Christian drawing or painting ultimately subordinates the image to the voice, and why "a Christian drawing should be a hymn, a work of praise, a prayer, an imploring eye" (*MB* 121).

6. "Jewgreek is greekjew": Messianicity—*Khōra*—Democracy

1. Derrida uses very similar language in "*Sauf le nom (Post-Scriptum)*": "Isn't the desert a paradoxical figure of the *aporia*? No marked out or assured passage, no route in any case, at the very most trails that are not reliable ways, the paths are not yet cleared, unless the sand has already re-covered them" ("*SN*" 53–54).

2. It would interesting to try to think this "nocturnal light" in relation to the following from "Violence and Metaphysics": "If light is the element of violence, one must combat light with a certain other light, in order to avoid the worst violence, the violence of the night which precedes or represses discourses" (*WD* 117).

3. In an incisive essay entitled "At the Limits of Religion Without Religion: A Problem That Cannot Be Resolved," Jeffrey A. Hanson argues that this question of the priority or originarity of revealability or revelation is "the central question" of "Faith and Knowledge" and "arguably the central question of Derrida's entire engagement with the question of religion" (*Philosophy Today* 53, no. 2 [Summer 2009]: 136). If we read this question as just another name for the question of the relative priority of messianicity and messianism or *khōra* and determinate appearances, that is, if we understand Derrida to be treating the same question by means of three different sets of more or less interchangeable terms, then Hanson may well be right, even though other questions (e.g., the question of the relationship between religion and science) appear just as central to Derrida's engagement with religion. I will argue in what follows, however, that while the form of the question initially appears quite similar in all three cases, messianicity and *khōra* will allow for a more radical rethinking of time and space in terms other than presence or revelation. My argument will thus be that Derrida sees what Hanson sees, namely, the irresolvability of "the question of which comes first, the chicken of *Offenbarkeit* (revealability, conditions for the possibility of revelation) or the egg of *Offenbarung* (revelation)." Instead of simply opting for the chicken *or* the egg, Derrida expresses a preference in many places, Hanson is right, for the chicken (revealability, messianicity, *khōra*), but he uses names that comes from the egg ("*messianicity*," "*khōra*,"—the two "historical" names). This does not resolve the question, but it does complicate it, and it requires us to rethink otherwise the relationship between the singular name and the universal

structure, the singular name and the promise that is proffered by the name. By re-posing the question by means of other historical names and lexica, Derrida does not evacuate the problem but displaces it. One such displacement, Hanson argues, would involve Derrida's rethinking of the *without*, which would "hold in tension the messianic and the messianisms, the desert and the religions that blossom in it" (140). But since this is not the avenue Derrida pursues in "Faith and Knowledge," a rethinking of the name and the promise is required. Hence Derrida does indeed argue for the "impossibility of a neutral, metalinguistic site of translation" between determinate messianisms, but that does not mean, as Hanson argues, that this "seems to militate against a universal structure of messianicity" (141). On the contrary, it is the reinscription of the particular, determinate name *in the name* or *as the name* of a promise that marks the idiom and opens it to translation. While Hanson, who follows to a large extent the analyses of James K. A. Smith, believes that Derrida, "gripped by 'simple indecision,'" nonetheless "thinks the issue should be settled in one way or another" (142) and that, when Derrida does try to settle it, he comes down on the side of the messianic or the transcendental, on the side of the Enlightenment and a certain hyperbolization of Kant's strategy (143), I think Derrida's emphasis on the name, the promise, and the relationship between faith and reason complicates all these alternatives. (See James K. A. Smith, "Re-Kanting Postmodernism? Derrida's Religion Within the Limits of Reason Alone," *Faith and Philosophy* 17 [October 2000]: 558–71. See also Robert Gibbs's very helpful comments on this aporia between the messianic and messianisms in his essay "Messianic Epistemology," in *Derrida and Religion: Other Testaments*, ed. Yvonne Sherwood and Kevin Hart [New York: Routledge, 2005], 121–23.)

4. For the question of revelation and revealability and the necessity of a horizon for all phenomena, see §7 of Heidegger's *Being and Time*.

5. See "Force of Law," in particular, for this distinction. As Derrida says elsewhere: "I believe that the relationship to the other is the condition for justice. I always distinguish law from justice" (*IW* 67). For de Vries's comments on these distinctions, see *Philosophy and the Turn to Religion*, 138, and *Religion and Violence*, 317.

6. Whereas de Vries emphasizes the "mutual implication and oscillation" between the two terms of the aporia and not the displacement of the problematic into a rethinking of the Platonic *khōra*, his conclusions are not incompatible with my own. After phrasing the question as follows: "Should one base one's thinking of the open future—of the to-come—on the events and the names of particular, historically unique or positive religions? Or should one, conversely, situate these events and names in a structure or revealability that is the very possibility of their manifestation or occurrence?" de Vries concludes: "Derrida has made very clear what a careful reading of his recent writings should have stressed all along, namely, that one cannot simply choose here. More precisely, that here it is irresponsible to choose. . . . Messianicity and messianism thus stand in a relation of mutual implication and oscillation" (de Vries, *Philosophy and the Turn to Religion*,

333). And elsewhere: "A supposed revelation (*Offenbarung*), then, reveals as much as it is itself in turn revealed by a structure of revealability (*Offenbarkeit*), which is, properly speaking, nothing determinable outside or before or beyond—over and above—the said (concrete, positive, empirical ontic) revelation or account thereof" (ibid., 330–31). This "oscillation" is central to de Vries's entire reading of Derrida. What de Vries says about the *adieu* in the final paragraph of *Philosophy and the Turn to Religion* might thus be read as providing the schema not simply for the relationship between revealability and revelation but, for my purposes here, between *salut!* and *salut*, as we saw in Chapter 1, or between the two sources of religion sketched out in Chapter 3: "The term *adieu* conveys and economically summarizes this complicated and asymmetrical structure that any plausible or responsible turn to 'religion' seems—so far—to take upon itself. In the very ambiguity of its meaning—once again, a turning 'toward' (*à Dieu*) and 'away from' (*adieu*) the absolutely other, a turning, moreover, that is never without risk, because never simply reciprocal or returned—it expresses the secret alliance and, perhaps, the co-originarity, of revelation and profanation, of the sacred and the secular, of the infinite and the infinitely finite, of prayer and blasphemy, of theology and idolatry, of violence and nonviolence, of the self and the other, and, indeed, of religion and philosophy" (ibid., 435).

7. Referring to the Greek etymology of *axiom* (*axios* as "goodly, worthy, estimable"), Derrida says that "an *axiom* always affirms, as its name indicates, a value, a price; it confirms or promises an evaluation that should remain intact and entail, like every value, an act of faith" (§47).

8. In *Religion*, Kant explains Luke 17:21–22, "the kingdom of God is within you," by arguing that such "a kingdom of God is represented not according to a particular covenant (*i.e.*, not Messianic)" but through a *moral* relation that is "knowable through unassisted reason" (note on 127). One might want to compare this opposition to the one sketched out by Derrida between determinate messianisms and a messianicity without messianism, though the latter is not in Derrida, as it is in Kant, "knowable through unassisted reason."

9. Derrida thus relates this coming of the other to what he calls here and elsewhere a "passive decision," "*the apparently passive form of the* other's decision: *even there where it appears in itself, in me*" (§21).

10. As Dana Hollander suggests in her reading of this passage, Derrida's "strategy for detaching the 'messianic' from 'messianism'" is related to what he has argued elsewhere regarding "philosophy's simultaneous claim to universality and dependence on particular names" (*Exemplarity and Chosenness*, 198). By *not* trying to forge a new philosophical vocabulary, by reinscribing traditional names and concepts, and not only the messianic but the gift, hospitality, and, as we will see in a moment, democracy, Derrida is trying, according to Hollander, "to negotiate the interdependence between the particular idiom and philosophy as a universal democracy" (ibid., 201).

11. He continues in "*Sauf le nom (Post-Scriptum)*": "There, in this testimony offered not to oneself but to the other, is produced the horizon of translatability—then of friendship, of universal community, of European decentering,

beyond the values of *philia*, of charity, of everything that can be associated with them, even beyond the European interpretation of the name Europe" ("*SN*" 77).

12. "Force of Law" is perhaps Derrida's most strident and direct attempt to define the "engagements" of deconstruction. Derrida there writes, for example, that "the *task* of a historical and interpretative memory is at the heart of deconstruction. . . . Deconstruction is already pledged, engaged [*gagée, engagée*] by this demand for infinite justice" ("FL" 248). Or again: "Where would deconstruction find its force, its movement or its motivation if not in this always unsatisfied appeal, beyond the given determinations of what one names, in determined contexts, justice, the possibility of justice?" ("FL 249). And, most famously, "Justice in itself, if such a thing exists, outside or beyond law, is not deconstructible. No more than deconstruction itself, if such a thing exists. *Deconstruction is justice*" ("FL" 243).

13. This messianicity thus looks very much like a negative theology, so much so that it has often been mistaken for it. As Derrida says of negative theology in "*Sauf le nom (Post-Scriptum)*," "this would seem to be a literature for the desert or for exile" ("*SN*" 85). Though Derrida goes on in the essay—as well as in "How to Avoid Speaking: Denials"—to distinguish deconstruction from negative theology, he nonetheless asserts in favor of the latter, "I trust no text that is not in some way contaminated with negative theology" ("*SN*" 69).

14. Martin Hägglund, in his compelling work *Radical Atheism*, contests claims of this sort by arguing that the openness that goes by the name of justice is a general description or structure of experience. As such, one does not and cannot choose such a deconstruction in the name of justice or "carry out" any kind of deconstruction in its name. This is surely true, but by using the language of justice Derrida is trying to do more than provide a theoretical or constative description of experience in general. He is trying to give an account of the very motivation of deconstruction, its performative dimension, the way in which, for example, a certain conception of human rights or, better, a certain trust or faith in the other that exceeds these rights, has motivated the questioning or deconstruction of certain determinations or codifications of these rights. In other words, Derrida is trying not only to give a description of experience in general but to provide an account of the historicity of deconstruction and of the historical notions it comes to question, criticize, or deconstruct.

15. John Caputo has suggested quite helpfully that the aporia between revelation and revealability might have to remain irresolvable precisely because we are dealing here with two heterogeneous orders—in the terms of medieval philosophy, between an order of being and an order of knowing. After citing *Specters of Marx*, where Derrida says that "the two hypotheses do not exclude each other," that is, the hypotheses according to which either messiancity or determinate messianisms are more originary, Caputo writes: "I take this as follows. It may well be that, in the order of being (*ordo essendi*), the messianic is the formal condition of possibility of the concrete messianisms, even while, in the order of

knowing (*ordo cognoscendi*), of how we actually learn about it, the historical messianisms are the only way we have come to learn about the structure of the messianic in general. What is first in the order of being is last in the order of knowing" (*DN* 170). As intriguing as this suggestion is, it is not offered by Caputo as anything like a final solution to the dilemma or "conundrum" put forth by Derrida (*DN* 169). Caputo goes on in the same passage to argue that "there is something deeply unsatisfactory about the dilemma that Derrida has posed, and this is because it moves within the most classical distinctions between fact and essence, material and formal, particular and universal, example and originary exemplar, empirical and transcendental, ontic and ontological, that is, within distinctions that Derrida has spent his entire life troubling and destabilizing" (*DN* 170). This diagnosis is surely correct, and it is hard to imagine that Derrida did not share this dissatisfaction over the traditional terms in which the dilemma is couched. Following Derrida's suggestion from *Archive Fever*, we might want to think these two orders, in the wake of psychoanalysis, in terms of a delayed or deferred action whereby, for example, the order of knowing will reveal what only *will have been* prior in the order of being. This might then be thought in relationship to what Caputo says in a chapter title of the *Prayers and Tears of Jacques Derrida*, namely, "Messianic Time Is Out of Joint" (122–25).

Caputo will argue, in effect, that this dilemma needs to be thought in relationship to the situation of deconstruction itself, which cannot simply be just one more "universal, formal, transcendental ontological condition of possibility" or just "one more historically specific, let us say postmodern messianism." Hence Derrida's turn to messianicity must be read not simply from within the matrix of these philosophical distinctions but as part of "a certain reinvention of Judaism," "a reinvention of Judaism as deconstruction" (*DN* 171). While there is a certain truth to this claim, and it helps explain Derrida's reinscription of the messianic in texts ranging from "Force of Law" all the way up to *Rogues*, I will argue in what follows that this "reinvention of Judaism" is never carried out to the exclusion of what we might call a "reinvention of Greek philosophy." Derrida's emphasis not only on messianicity but on *khōra* in all these texts, and, as we will see shortly, in "Faith and Knowledge," makes this clear. Yet again Derrida is demonstrating the necessity of the duplicity of sources, the necessity of there being always *more than one* source.

In *The Prayers and Tears of Jacques Derrida*, Caputo rephrases the dilemma in this way: "*Either*: the messianic fits into a Heideggerian-Bultmanian schema of a demythologizing fundamental ontology in which one would strip away the existentiell particularities of the particular historical religions in order to unearth the universal, existential structures, the existentialia that represent the condition of possibility of ontico-existentiell messianisms. *Or*: the historical messianisms have a kind of absolute anteriority without which the messianic would be completely unknown" (137). Making reference yet again to the two orders of being and knowing, Caputo says that these "two possibilities are entirely compatible and complementary approaches." But Caputo goes on to argue that the problem with all of this is that "the whole discussion is framed within an assured set of distinctions—between fact and essence, example and exemplar, real and ideal, particular and universal—which it is the whole point of deconstruction to disturb," and that "Derrida can hardly put himself in the position of saying that the 'messianic' represents the over-arching, universal metalanguage into which the various concrete messianisms can be translated" (138). I agree with Caputo's conclusions here, but would add that it is for this reason that Derrida—seeing the dilemma—displaces the problematic into other registers. While such displacements do not banish or resolve the dilemma, they do provide Derrida with other resources for rethinking it. Derrida's rethinking of the promise to be found in the two "historical" names (messianicity and *khōra*) is an attempt to unsettle or displace the traditional relationship between the transcendental or quasi-transcendental structure of the messianic and determinate messianisms. This is in keeping, I think, with what Caputo argues throughout *The Prayers and Tears of Jacques Derrida* about deconstruction "repeat[ing] the passion for the messianic promise and messianic expectation, *sans* the concrete messianisms of the positive relations that wage endless war and spill the blood of the other" (xxi).

16. Just a few years earlier, in *Politics of Friendship*, Derrida justified at some length this use of "perhaps" (see *PF* 26–48).

17. The "Promised Land" would perhaps be a figure that brings together both time and space, both historicity and a determinate place: "*The figure of the Promised Land—is it not also the essential bond between the promise of place and historicity?*" (§13).

18. There are several islands evoked in "Faith and Knowledge," from Capri to Patmos (§12; see §36), and, in a footnote on Heidegger, Corfu, Sicily, and Delos (§18; see §36).

19. In "Force of Law," Derrida expresses his skepticism with regard to the notion of a "horizon": "One of the reasons I am keeping such a distance from all these horizons—from the Kantian regulative idea or from the messianic advent, for example, at least in their conventional interpretation—is that they are, precisely, *horizons*. As its Greek name suggests, a horizon is both the opening and the limit that defines either an infinite progress or a waiting and awaiting. Yet justice, however unpresentable it remains, does not wait. It is that which must not wait" ("FL" 255).

20. In *Archive Fever*, a text written in the months immediately following "Faith and Knowledge," Derrida says that "the death drive is above all *anarchivic*, one could say, or *archiviolithic*. It will always have been archive-destroying, by silent vocation" (*AF* 10). Since we have been following the work of Don DeLillo throughout this book, it might be worth thinking the death drive in relation to what DeLillo calls in a recent novel the "omega point," that is, the place of "a leap out of our biology," where "consciousness is exhausted," where we desire to return to "inorganic matter," to "stones in a field" (*Point Omega* [New York: Scribner, 2010], 52; see 72). This is, perhaps, what happens to Richard Elster's daughter Jessica in the novel.

21. See "*Khōra*," trans. Ian McLeod, in *ON* 89–127. The first version of the essay was published in 1987 in *Poikilia: Etudes offertes à Jean-Pierre Vernant* (École des Hautes Études en Sciences Sociales).

22. Caputo writes in *The Prayers and Tears of Jacques Derrida*, "Negative theology is always on the track of a 'hyperessentiality,' of something hyper-present, hyper-real or sur-real, so really real that we are never satisfied simply to say that it is merely real" (2–3). See also Caputo's note (at ibid., 344n13) on Kevin Hart's alternative reading of negative theology in light of Derrida's critique of it. For a lively debate over this "hyperessentialism" in negative theology, see Jean-Luc Marion's essay "In the Name: How to Avoid Speaking of 'Negative Theology,'" in *God, the Gift, and Postmodernism*, ed. John D. Caputo and Michael J. Scanlon (Bloomington: Indiana University Press, 1999), 20–42, and Derrida's response to Marion, ibid., 42–47. See also Derrida and Marion's discussion entitled "On the Gift" in the same volume, 54–78. On Derrida's relationship to negative theology and to a "hypertheology" of God or the Good, see chap. 2 of de Vries, *Philosophy and the Turn to Religion*, 96–157.

23. For Derrida's understanding of the hollowing out of discourse in negative theology, see chap. 5 of de Vries, *Philosophy and the Turn to Religion*, "The Kenosis of Discourse," 305–58. On the notion of *khōra* in Derrida, see *DN* 82–96, esp. 92–96, for the contrast between *khōra* and the Good. I have also tried to clarify this relationship in *Derrida From Now On*, 37–61.

24. See "How to Avoid Speaking: Denials," in *PSY II* 143–95.

25. This reference to the "face" is a discreet though unmistakable allusion to Levinas and to the humanism that Derrida, in *The Animal That Therefore I Am*, *The Beast and the Sovereign*, vol. 1, and elsewhere, diagnoses in his work.

26. See John Sallis, *Chorology: On Beginning in Plato's "Timaeus"* (Bloomington: Indiana University Press, 1999).

27. Hent de Vries comes to a similar conclusion in *Philosophy and the Return to Religion*: "By invoking the Platonic *khōra*, Derrida reminds us here of a 'possibility' that eludes both Meister Eckhart's *Vorbürge* or *parvis* and Heidegger's *dimension* of *Offenbarkeit*, as well as, it would seem, Derrida's own insistence on the preliminary and proleptic structure of messianicity. . . . *Khōra* therefore reminds us that with the exploration of messianicity and Christianity in their respective relations to the phenomena of so-called positive religion, not everything—and not even the 'essential'—has yet been said" (324).

28. There is, it should be noted, yet another public iteration of the question between the Villanova roundtable of October 1996 and the joint meeting of the American Academy of Religion and the Society of Biblical Literature in Toronto in November 2002. In September 1997, yet again at Villanova, Derrida returns to the distinction between *Offenbarung* and *Offenbarkeit* in a public discussion with Richard Kearney and Jean-Luc Marion. After laying out the two hypotheses in favor of one or the other of these Heideggerian alternatives, Derrida adds, in terms that echo but also add to what he said the year before at Villanova: "that is why I am constantly really hesitating. That is part of—what can I call this

here—let us say, my cross. Since it is impossible for me to choose between these two hypotheses, my last hypothesis is that the question is not well posed, that we should displace the question, not to have an answer, but to think otherwise the possibility of these possibilities" (*GGP* 73). It is this displacement of the question into the two sources of religion and then into an analysis of the two "historical" names, the messianic and, especially, *khōra*, that I have been arguing for here. It is thus no coincidence that, a few minutes later in the same discussion, Derrida returns to the distinction between *Offenbarung* and *Offenbarkeit* in order to suggest that there is yet another problem with this Heideggerian distinction, not simply the reference to light and revelation, to unveiling, but the implied reference to "historicity." It will be *khōra* that, in Derrida's view, offers the most hope for a discourse that is able to resist this historicity. We thus see very clearly in the long passage I am about to cite the importance Derrida placed on *khōra*—this place of an "absolute universality"—for developing the "universal politics" that we will look at later in this chapter: "When I referred a moment ago to *Offenbarkeit* and *Offenbarung*, I was sincere but at the same time I am also perplexed. I am also perplexed without a guide in this respect. The discourse of *Offenbarung* and *Offenbarkeit*, in Heidegger or anywhere else in this context, implies the historicity of *Dasein*, of man and God, the historicity of revelation, historicity in the Christian or European sense. My problem is that when I refer to *khōra*, I refer to some event, the possibility of taking place, which is not historical, to something non-historical that resists historicity. In other words, there might be something that is excluded by this problematic, however complex it may be, of revelation, of *Offenbarung* and *Offenbarkeit*, whether in Heidegger or out of Heidegger. That is why I refer to what I call the 'desert in the desert.' There is a biblical desert, there is an historical desert. But what I call a 'desert in the desert' is this place which resists historicization. . . . This place of resistance, this absolute heterogeneity to philosophy and the Judeo-Christian history of revelation, even to the concept of history, which is a Christian concept, is not simply at war with what it resists. It is also, if I may use this terrible word, a condition of possibility which makes history possible by resisting it. . . . I think that this reference to what I call *khōra*, the absolutely universal place, so to speak, is what is irreduceable to what we call revelation, revealability, history, religion, philosophy, Bible, Europe, and so forth. I think the reference to this place of resistance is also the condition for a universal politics, for the possibility of crossing the borders of our common context—European, Jewish, Christian, Muslim, and philosophical. I think this reference to this non-history and non-revelation, this negativity has heavy and serious political implications. I use the problematic of deconstruction and negative theology as a threshold to the definition of a new politics. . . . I am trying to find a place where a new discourse and a new politics could be possible" (*God, the Gift, and Postmodernism*, 76; see Robyn Horner's references to these passages in her chapter "Aporia or Excess? Two Strategies for Thinking r/Revelation," in *Derrida and Religion: Other Testaments*, ed. Yvonne Sherwood and Kevin Hart [New York: Routledge, 2005], 325–36). Though Derrida confesses at the beginning of this passage to being "perplexed without a guide," he furnishes us here with many clues as to how we should understood what is only suggested in "Faith and Knowledge" and then argued more explicitly and directly in "*Khōra*," "*Sauf le nom (Post-Scriptum)*," *Rogues*, and the other public discussions between 1996 and 2003 that we are considering in this chapter.

29. Derrida goes on to say, in these roundtable remarks before the American Academy of Religion and the Society of Biblical Literature: "to be true to science, knowledge, and to be true to faith, we have to find in our experience, each as a living being, the experience of faith far beyond any received religious tradition, any teaching. That is why I constantly refer to the experience of faith as simply a speech act, as simply the social experience; and this is true even for animals. Animals have faith, in a certain way. As soon as there is social bond there is faith, and there are social bonds in animals: they trust one another, they have to. . . . This trust, this bond, this covenant within life, is the resource to understand the heterogeneity between faith and knowledge. Both are absolutely indispensable, but they are indissociable and heterological. That's the ground of our experience of faith as living beings" ("EF" 45).

30. For an interesting reading of *khōra* in relationship to Derrida's early work, from *The Problem of Genesis in Husserl's Philosophy* to *Speech and Phenomena* and "Plato's Pharmacy," see Herman Rapaport's "Deregionalizing Ontology: Derrida's Khōra," *Derrida Today* 1, no. 1 (2008): 95–118.

31. Derrida is thus not opposed to all communities or gatherings but to all conceptions of community or gathering that do not entail interruption. He can thus say, during a public discussion in 2002 on the topic of religion: ""Even if I am in public, even if I am in a synagogue and praying with others, I know that my own prayer would be silent and secret, interrupting something in the community" ("EF" 30).

32. Derrida speaks similarly, in "Force of Law," of "respect for equity and universal right, but also for the always heterogeneous and unique singularity of the unsubsumable example" ("FL" 252).

33. On the importance of Paul in Derrida's work, see Theodore Jennings, *Reading Derrida/ Thinking Paul* (Stanford, Calif.: Stanford University Press, 2006). I would also like to thank Mark D. Given of Missouri State University for sharing with me an unpublished essay on Derrida and what he calls Paul's "apocalyptic logocentrism." Given cites a passage from *Of Spirit* in which Derrida speaks of a "pneumatology" of the Gospels and its "ineradicable relationship of translation with *ruah*" (*OS* 101). The term *pneumatology* was used by Derrida as early as *Of Grammatology* (*OG* 17).

34. Derrida will insist later on in "Faith and Knowledge," in part through Levinas, that we must distinguish the sacred, *le sacré* (the first source of religion), from the holy, *le saint* (understood in relation to the second source). Distinguishing the self-indemnifying experience of the sacred from the holy, from the opening that is the holy, disjoining them through a kind of atheism, all contemporaneity is undone, argues Derrida, in the experience of a faith in the holy. Derrida thus speaks of "faith in a holiness without sacredness, in a desacralizing

truth," "a certain disenchantment [as] the condition of authentic holiness (index: 'Levinas'—notably the author of *From the Sacred to the Holy*)," "disenchantment as the *very resource of the religious*" (§49). This disenchantment, a certain atheism, might thus open up an experience of the holy before or beyond all historical revelation, provided that this disenchantment is not confused, as we will see later, with some weak version of secularism—a concept Derrida believes to be indelibly marked by Christianity. In a series of improvised remarks from 1997, Derrida again traces this distinction between the sacred and the holy (or sanctity)—the two sources of religion—back to Levinas: "When Levinas seeks to dissociate sacredness and sanctity, he associates the former with the cult, the image, and incarnation, whereas sanctity calls for the respect of distance, of separation, of the invisible, of the face as visible-invisible" ("AANJ" 66–67). In some improvised remarks from 2002, Derrida relates secularization to autonomy, symmetry, and contract, as opposed to heteronomy, asymmetry, and a certain thinking of covenant; it is the moment when one tries to "transform an asymmetrical covenant into a somewhat symmetrical, autonomous contract" ("EF" 35).

35. During the last decade of his life, and particularly after 9–11 and the American invasion of Iraq, Derrida suggests that Europe, not the United States, is the place most welcoming to this secularism. See Chapters 3–5 of my *Derrida From Now On*. To supplement the many works I cite in those chapters with regard to this difference between the United States and Europe, let me cite here a few lines from the recently published *Islam & the West*, a public conversation between Derrida and Chérif Mustapha during the spring of 2003: "I believe that we are at a moment in history, we have been for some time and in particular within the last few months, when the division between a certain America—I'm not speaking of the United States in general, but of a certain American power, a certain American politics—the division between a certain American politics and a virtuality of European politics is increasingly possible" (*IW* 62). Derrida goes on to argue that it falls to Europe "both to differentiate itself, to break away from a certain hegemonic unilateralism of the United States, and to engage those forces in the world, in the Arab-Muslim world, that are in turn ready to open up to the democracy to come" (*IW* 62). He continues: "there is something common to all the European States, which is a certain principle of separation between the State and religion, without scorn for religion. By contrast, in the United States and in certain Arab-Muslim States, there is, on the contrary, in different forms on either side, very often merging or an alliance between politics and the theocratic, which, today, we must, in my opinion, question and transform" (*IW* 65).

36. Justice and decision thus have to be distinguished from the "automatism" by which one simply follows a pregiven law or determinable rule: "Wherever I have at my disposal a determinable rule, I know what must be done, and as soon as such knowledge dictates the law, action follows knowledge as a calculable consequence: one *knows* what path to take, one no longer hesitates. The decision then no longer decides anything but is made in advance and is thus in advance annulled. It is simply deployed, without delay, presently, with the automatism

attributed to machines. There is no longer any place for justice or responsibility (whether juridical, political, or ethical)" (*R* 84–85).

37. In a public discussion in November 2002, Derrida says, "when I speak of sovereignty as an onto-theological phantasm or heritage, I have the name of God in mind" ("EF" 37). It is for this reason that Derrida, in *Rogues* and elsewhere, will attempt "to dissociate God's sovereignty from God," "to think of unconditionality without sovereignty, and to deconstruct the political concept of sovereignty" ("EF" 42). On the constitution of the self and the phantasm that can result from this self-constitution, see *ATT* 56.

38. As will become clear with the publication of Derrida's seminars of 1999–2000 and 2000–1, the death penalty in the West would be yet another of these seemingly political concepts or practices that is linked essentially to Christianity. Derrida there says, for example, invoking along the way the question of avoidance that will be at center of my analysis of the final passage of "Faith and Knowledge": "But we must not avoid the question of the relations between religion and the death penalty, of course, or the question of the relations between Christianity, Christianities, and the other monotheisms in this regard" (*The Death Penalty I*, Seminar of 1999–2000, trans. Peggy Kamuf [Chicago: University of Chicago Press, forthcoming]).

39. Chérif could be one of the thinkers Derrida had in mind. In *Islam & the West*, Chérif claims, for example, that "the principle of *secularity* is, despite appearances, intrinsic to Islam, and this has been true since its origins" (*IW* 13). Hence Chérif calls on Muslims and non-Muslims alike to recall a common heritage. He asks Muslims to "recall that the Koran and the words (*hadiths*) of the Prophet prescribe an opening up, democracy, and the universal" (*IW* 23), and he asks those who have thoughtlessly and unjustly declared Islam to be the new enemy of the West to recall that "whereas the Classical-West was Judeo-Islamo-Christian and Greco-Arab, we have been led to believe that it was only Greco-Roman and Judeo-Christian" (*IW* 3). Chérif thus argues that "we must rediscover a common memory" (*IW* 22), "a faithfulness to the common memory of the two shores" (*IW* 25), that is, to the common memory of the northern and southern shores of the Mediterranean. Chérif says, in his concluding words about Derrida, written after Derrida's death, "He was of the two shores, he came from the edge of the world" (*IW* 103).

40. Derrida goes on to make a rather different claim, which would require a different kind of support, including some kind of understanding of just what an "authentic believer" is: "And I am persuaded that authentic believers, those who are truly Jewish, Christian, or Muslim, those who are truly living their religious beliefs and not simply endorsing the dogma of those religions, are more ready to understand the religion of the other and to accede to that faith, whose universal structure I have just described, than others" (*IW* 58). And just a bit later in the same conversation: "I am persuaded that authentic believers, those who are not what one calls fundamentalists, dogmatists ready to transform their belief into weapons of war, those who are not dogmatic and fundamentalists are more ready

to understand the religion of the other and universal faith. Consequently, I believe that far from there being a contradiction, there is a connection between the secularization of the political, the dissociation, in a sense, of the social bond, from the political bond, and what you call the relationship to the Mystery of life" (*IW* 59). These passages would seem to suggest that Derrida does not hold the position attributed to him by Eddo Evink, that "pure tolerance can only be reached if one distances oneself from any religious tradition and denies every religious testimony," "expect[ing] oneself and others to renounce any religious belief or conviction" (C. E. Evink, "Jacques Derrida and the Faith in Philosophy." *The Southern Journal of Philosophy*, vol. 42 [2004]: 325). To expect such a denial or renunciation would indeed be, as Evink argues, *intolerance*. But Derrida's position actually seems closer to Evink's own, namely, that "tolerance is dependent on the recognition of the finiteness and contextuality of one's convictions and beliefs" (325). In other words, "authentic" belief always includes a recognition of finitude and a certain skepticism, even atheism. In a series of public remarks in November 2002, Derrida explains this "authentic" belief—as well as his dissatisfaction with the word *authentic*—in this way: "There must be a critique of idolatry, of all sorts of images in prayer. . . . Negative theology, prophetic philosophical criticism, deconstruction: if you don't go through these in the direction of atheism, the belief in God is naïve, totally inauthentic. In order to be authentic—this is a word I almost never use—the belief in God must be exposed to absolute doubt. . . . However paradoxical it may sound, believing implies some atheism; and I am sure that true believers know this better than others, that they experience atheism all the time. It is a part of their belief. It is in the *epochē*, in the suspension of belief, the suspension of the position of God as a thesis, that faith appears" ("EF" 46–47).

41. Of course, this interest in uncovering the theological origins of seemingly nontheological concepts goes back to the very beginning of Derrida's work. Already in *Of Grammatology*, for example, he would write, "the age of the sign is essentially theological" (*OG* 14), and in *Positions* he would go on to affirm that "grammatology must deconstruct everything that ties the concept and norms of scientificity to ontotheology, logocentrism, phonologism" (*POS* 35). One would be able to find a thousand similar claims from writings of that period.

42. As Martin Hägglund rightly argues, the "necessary intertwinement of life and death spells out the autoimmunity of mortality as a general condition and undercuts the Idea of immortality" (*Radical Atheism*, 48). Though Hägglund does not use the term *phantasm* here, it is possible to hear behind Hägglund's idea of "the Idea of immortality" something like the phantasm of a life beyond every economy of death.

Interlude II: Cyberspace and the Unconscious (*Underworld* III)

1. We are reminded that the score for *Unterwelt* is "that Three Oranges thing, whatever it's called," by Prokofiev (*U* 442).

7. Mary and the Marionettes: Life, Sacrifice, and the Sexual Thing

1. A related form of this "*pacifying* gesture," of this "declaration of peace" that would in truth be "pursuing war by other means," would be the "European-colonial" gesture that consists in imposing "surreptitiously a discourse, a culture, a politics and a right . . . on all the other monotheist religions, including the non-Catholic Christian religions," imposing "the same juridico-theologico-political culture . . . in the name of peace." This imposition, this globalatinization, would be more and more imperative as a certain "demographic disproportion"—the growth of Islam, for example—threatens "external hegemony" and leaves no other strategic alternative besides "internalization," which, we might speculate, can take on the form of a more or less successful integration or incorporation within the body or else a phantasmatic projection of the enemy lodged within (§37).

2. Derrida writes: "Be it said in passing that certain ecologists and certain vegetarians—at least to the extent that they believe themselves to have remained pure of (unscathed by) all carnivorousness, even symbolic—would be the only 'religious' persons of the time to respect one of these two pure sources of religion and indeed to bear responsibility for what could well be the future of a religion" (§40). Derrida also points us in a footnote to his long interview with Jean-Luc Nancy entitled "'Eating Well,' or the Calculation of the Subject," where he addresses "what in Western cultures remains sacrificial, up to and including its industrial, sacrificial and 'carno-phallogo-centric' implementation" (§40n32).

3. In *The Animal That Therefore I Am*, Derrida points back to "the animal sacrifices of the Bible or of ancient Greece," to millennial traditions of hunting, domesticating, and exploiting animals, but he then goes on to claim that "in the course of the last two centuries these traditional forms of treatment of the animal have been turned upside down by the joint developments of zoological, ethological, biological, and genetic forms of *knowledge*," by means of everything from farming on a demographic scale that could not even be dreamed of in the past to genetic experimentation and artificial insemination to "the industrialization of what can be called the production for consumption of animal meat," and all of this, says Derrida, "in the service of a certain being and putative human well-being of man" (*ATT* 25; see *FWT* 57).

4. This sacrifice of life in the name of the law is one of the central themes of Derrida's seminars of 1999–2000 and 2000–1 on the death penalty. It is no coincidence that Kant, a proponent of the death penalty, plays such a central role in these seminars.

5. Back in 1984, in "No Apocalypse, Not Now," Derrida argued that those who contemplate the possibility of a nuclear war imagine—fantasize—a sacrifice of life in the name of something greater than life. "Today, in the perspective of a remainderless destruction, without symbolicity, without memory and without mourning, those who contemplate setting off such a catastrophe do so no doubt *in the name* of what is worth more in their eyes than life ('Better dead than

red'). . . . Nuclear war, at least as a hypothesis, a phantasm, of total self-destruction, can only be waged in the name of what is worth more than life. What gives life its worth is worth more than life" ("NA" 407–8).

6. Derrida relates the figure of the ellipsis throughout "Faith and Knowledge" to the mark of an omission of words, a keeping silent: "And what if the ellipsis, the silent figure and the 'keeping quiet' of reticence were precisely, we will come to that later, religion?" (§35). Derrida treats the figure of the ellipsis in his early text on Jabès entitled "Ellipsis," in *Writing and Difference* (*WD* 294–300).

7. Derrida adds: "The sign through which Heidegger believes ontotheology can be recognized is when the relation to the absolute Being or to the supreme Cause has freed itself of both, thereby losing access to sacrificial offering no less than to prayer" (§41). Several sections later Derrida repeats this claim, "Ontotheology does the same when it suspends sacrifice and prayer" (§51).

8. Derrida recalls in the following line that Maimonides, author of the *Guide for the Perplexed*, which we mentioned earlier, says that "God himself preferred mankind not to end in one go the murderous sacrifice" ("SW" 70). See Derrida's two interpretations of prayer at "HAS" 194–95.

9. The version of "Faith and Knowledge" found in *Acts of Religion* has here "festishized" rather than "fetishized." While such a neologism would be in keeping with the way in which the fetish is paraded during religious festivals, it is probably a typo, since neither of the other two versions of the essay (in *Religion* and in "of pomegranates") have it, and the French—*qu'on érige, exhibe, fétichise et promène en procession*—does not really signal that Derrida wishes us to hear this play.

10. See also *SQ* 108–34 for a reading of Celan's "Meridian."

11. Priapism is named, of course, after Priapus, a god who, according to myth, attempted to rape a goddess and so was punished by the other gods by being given a huge set of wooden genitals that would remain forever erect but absolutely useless.

12. Derrida speaks of how, for Nietzsche, Paul became one of "*his privileged targets*" insofar as "*a certain internalizing movement within Christianity . . . was his primary enemy and . . . bore for him the gravest responsibility. The Jews and European Judaism even constituted in his eyes a desperate attempt to resist, in so far as there was any reistance, a last-ditch protest from within, directed against a certain Christianity*" (§15).

13. An earlier, far less complete analysis of this passage is to be found in my *Derrida From Now On*, 202–9. It was in many ways this earlier analysis that motivated me to try to understand this passage in relationship to "Faith and Knowledge" as a whole.

14. Derrida explicitly relates this spontaneity to a certain thought of the future as unforeseeable and without horizon: "From the shores of whatever island, one doesn't know, here is the resurgence we believe we see coming, without doubt, in its spontaneous swelling, irresistibly automatic. But we believe we see it coming without any horizon. We are no longer certain that we see and that there is a future where we see it coming. The future tolerates neither foresight nor

providence. It is therefore in it, rather, caught and surprised by this resurgence, that 'we' in truth are carried away—and it is this that we would like to *think*, if this word can still be used here" (§37).

15. Concerning this combination of archaic passions and sophisticated technical weaponry, see "US." On the relationship between contemporary forms of violence and law, sovereignty, sacrifice, and political theology, see Paul W. Kahn, *Sacred Violence: Torture, Terror, and Sovereignty* (Ann Arbor: University of Michigan Press, 2008).

16. On the whole topic of the relationship between maternity and technology, see Elissa Marder's brilliant new book, *The Mother in the Age of Mechanical Reproduction: Psychoanalysis, Photography, Deconstruction* (New York: Fordham University Press, 2012).

17. Derrida investigates the notion of cruelty in "PSS."

18. Derrida later writes: "*Hence the even more pressing obligation: not to forget those [of either gender] whom this implicit contract or this 'being-together' is obliged to exclude. We should have, we ought to have, begun by allowing them to speak*" (§10).

19. See esp. "PPW."

20. Derrida also speaks of this scene with Pascale Ogier in *CAS* 39–40. See Kas Saghafi's excellent analysis of this passage in *Apparitions—Of Derrida's Other* (New York: Fordham University Press, 2010), 55–57, 65–66, 77–79. Sean Gaston writes of this scene in *The Impossible Mourning of Jacques Derrida* (London: Continuum, 2006), his poignant memoir written in the wake of Derrida's death: "Perhaps it is only now that I understand the specters that Derrida never stopped talking about, *à la vie à la mort, à paraître*" (75). *À la vie à la mort* was the first title Derrida proposed for what would eventually be published as *Chaque fois unique, la fin du monde*. The original title was dropped in part because French rock singer Johnny Hallyday released an album at the end of 2002 with the same title.

21. These words echo somewhat uncannily Derrida's final words, which I examine in Chapter 9: "Je vous aime et vous souris, d'où que je sois" ("FW").

22. Sigmund Freud, *Delusion and Dream*, trans. Helen M. Downey (New York: New Republic, Inc., 1927). See also Hélène Cixous's novel on Gradiva, *The Third Body*, trans. Keith Cohen (Evanston, Ill.: Hydra Books/Northwestern University Press, 1999).

23. Caputo writes of Hanold: "He dreams of touching Gradiva's living foot, of that singular, unrepeatable instant when imprinting and impression are one, when, with her peculiar gait, Gradiva must have left the unique 'imprint of her toes'—her trace—'in the ashes distinct from all the rest'" (*The Prayers and Tears of Jacques Derrida*, 276).

24. In an essay in *Paper Machine* entitled "Paper or Me, You Know . . .," Derrida speaks of two fantasies or phantasms, that of "an absolute memory," where everything would be archived "without delay, and *on paper*," and then the "dream of living paperless," a dream, Derrida confesses, that sometimes "sounds to my ears like a definition of 'real life,' of the living part of life" (*PM* 65).

25. See "Restitutions" (*TP* 255–382) and my analysis of the figure of *Khōra* in this text in chapter 2, "Given Time for a Detour: The Abyssal Gift of *Khōra*," in *Taking on the Tradition: Jacques Derrida and the Legacies of Deconstruction* (Stanford, Calif.: Stanford University Press, 2002).

26. In the "Postscript" (yet again the "Postscript"!) to *Archive Fever*, Derrida speaks of Gradiva as a postscript to the discussion of the archive and to the essentially masculine story of circumcision and of the gift of a Torah by Freud's father to Freud (*AF* 83–101).

8. Pomegranate Seeds and Scattered Ashes: From $n + 1$ to the One $+ n$

1. Freud, *Delusion and Dream*, 60–61. After one of the apparitions of Gradiva to Norbert, the narrator says: "He stood up, breathless, as if stunned; yet with heavy understanding he had grasped what had occurred before his eyes. The noonday ghost hour was over, and in the form of a butterfly, a winged messenger had come up from the asphodel meadows of Hades to admonish the departed one to return" (ibid.).

2. It was perhaps the context of this phrase and a knowledge of Derrida's Jewish origins that inspired Sam Weber to translate *Pâques* as Passover rather than Easter, though *Pâques*—with an *s*—*le Pâques*, in the masculine, is often translated as Easter, while the feminine *la Pâque* or *la Pâque juive*, without an *s*, usually means Passover. Between the two, of course, is nothing less than the whole story of religion in the West—*pesah*, Passover, sacrifice of the firstborn, sacrifice of a lamb in place of a son, exodus and exile, and then the sacrifice of an only son, the lamb of God as sacrifice and substitute, immaculately conceived, crucified, resurrected, and waiting to return from the dead. Sam Weber himself makes this contrast even sharper: "In the one case, the angel of death 'passes over' the houses of those whose doors have been marked for survival, but only at the cost of giving up their houses and affronting an even more uncertain future. In the other, it is the promise of a certain homecoming and overcoming of the border itself—the singular limit of finitude—that is commemorated and celebrated in and as the resurrection of Jesus." Weber makes this observation in a beautiful memorial essay on Derrida written not long after Derrida's death ("Once and for All," *Grey Room* 20 [Summer 2005]: 114). In a section of the essay entitled "The Plurality of the Singular: *A Pomegranate*," Weber looks at everything in this passage from the duplicity of the word *grenades* to the role of ontotheology as a Spanish Marrano in Derrida's work to the idioms of the still life (or *la nature morte*) and the possibility of translating *Pâques* as not only Passover but Easter. My reading of this passage follows Weber's on almost all these things, though it also tries to situate this passage a bit more within the general context and overall argument of "Faith and Knowledge."

3. Weber, "Once and for All," 113.

4. See 1 Kings 7:18, 20 and Exodus 28:31–34.

5. Weber, "Once and for All," 114. Weber cites Numbers 20:3–5: "And wherefore have ye made us to come up out of Egypt, to bring us in unto this evil

place? It is no place of seed, or of figs, or of vines, or of pomegranates; neither is there any water to drink."

6. The story of Korē/Persephone is told in Homer's *Hymn to Demeter*. The name Korē stresses her pedigree as Demeter's daughter, and Persephone her place as Hades' wife.

7. Derrida's "Tympan," in *Margins of Philosophy* (*MP* ix–xxix), speaks of Persephone and particularly of Michel Leiris's "Perséphone," in *Biffures* (Paris: Gallimard, 1975), 77–138. Derrida also writes of Persephone in *Athens, Still Remains* (New York: Fordham University Press, 2010). "At the center of one of the photographs, a spectacular street sign commemorates Korē. . . . Does not Persephone reign over this entire book, Persephone, wife of Hades, the goddess of death and of phantoms, of souls wandering in search of their memory?" (*ASR* 49). For the figure of Persephone in Derrida's work, see Thomas Dutoit's "Mythic Derrida," *Mosaic* 39, no. 3 (September 2006): 103–32, and "Unearthing the Field of English Studies: Discoursing *Pensées* in Jacques Derrida," in *European Journal of English Studies* 6, no. 3 (2002): 327–42.

8. J. M. Coetzee writes, in *Age of Iron* (New York: Penguin Books, 1990), 56: "Slowly, like a pomegranate, my heart bursts with gratitude; like a fruit splitting open to reveal the seeds of love. *Gratitude, pomegranate*: sister words."

9. I am hardly the first to underscore this ambivalence. John Caputo already identified these *grenades* as grenades in *The Prayers and Tears of Jacques Derrida*, 231; Gil Anidjar recalls it in his introduction to *Acts of Religion*, 21; and Sam Weber makes it the center of his reflections in his essay "Once and for All." We know, too, that between the Capri conference and the completion of "Faith and Knowledge" Derrida encountered the word *grenade* at least once, in Blanchot's *The Instant of My Death*, in a context in which it clearly and unambiguously means "grenade" (see "*D*" 60).

10. As Marco Katz, at the University of Alberta, reminded me, *Grenada* is also the name of the Spanish city famous for a time as a place of religious harmony and tolerance between Jews, Christians, and Muslims.

11. On the importance of the word *entamé* in *Of Grammatology*, see my brief essay in *Reading Derrida's* Of Grammatology, ed. Sean Gaston and Ian Maclachlan (New York: Continuum Press, 2011), 119–23.

12. As Mireille Calle-Gruber argues, "the operation of poetic writing consists in certain ways in making of the text signed 'Derrida' a tallith" (*Jacques Derrida, la distance généreuse* [Paris: Éditions de la Différence, 2009], 55; my translation).

13. As Derrida says again in "A Silkworm of One's Own," prayer "is neither true nor false, as a Greek philosopher [i.e., Aristotle] even said. Even a Greek knew that!" ("SW" 67). Derrida also said of prayer, during a public discussion in 2002: "On the one hand, a prayer has to be a mixture of something that is absolutely singular and secret—idiomatic, untranslatable—and, on the other, a ritual that involves the body in coded gestures and that uses a common, intelligible language" ("EF" 30). Derrida goes on in these remarks to explain the relationship between prayer and skepticism, even atheism, and the necessity of a

certain *epochē* in prayer, that is, "the suspension of certainty, not of belief" ("EF" 30–31). For a fuller explanation for these two aspects of prayer, see "HAS" 194–95.

14. Derrida writes, in "Circumfession": "I am one of those *marranes* who no longer say they are Jews even in the secret of their own hearts" ("C" 170). See Caputo, *The Prayers and Tears of Jacques Derrida*, 303–4: "The Marranos were Spanish or Portuguese Jews who were forcibly converted to Catholicism, under threat of death or exile, who practiced Judaism in secret. Deriving from the Spanish word for 'pigs,' from the Jewish prohibition against eating pork, the word carried a pejorative ring." Derrida speaks again, in *Archive Fever*, of "the Marranos, with whom I have always secretly identified (but don't tell anyone) and whose crypto-Judaic history greatly resembles that of psychoanalysis after all" (*AF* 69–70). And he concludes *Aporias* with the words: "Let us figuratively call Marrano anyone who remains faithful to a secret that he has not chosen" (*AP* 81); see also *CP* 13.

15. Derrida speaks again of the Marrano as "encrypted" in "Marx & Sons." He thus writes of the "sons" and "daughters" of Karl Marx: "And now the supreme twist, the abyssal upping of the ante, the absolute surplus-value: they would have been Marranos who were so well disguised, so perfectly encrypted, that they themselves never suspected that that's what they were!—or else had forgotten the fact that they were Marranos, repressed it, denied it, disavowed it. It is well known that this sometimes happens to 'real' Marranos as well, to those who, though they are really, presently, currently, effectively, *ontologically* Marranos, no longer even know it themselves" ("MS" 262).

16. Weber, "Once and for All," 112.

17. This last meaning has often been overlooked, even though it is perhaps the most audible in colloquial speech. One says in French, for example, usually in exasperation after having made an error or mistake, *je suis le dernier des imbéciles*, I am the biggest idiot, I am such an idiot, I am such a complete and utter idiot . . . Derrida's "claim" to being the least, last, though also the biggest of Jews, the most Jewish of Jews, is thus laced with a certain self-deprecatory humor when heard in relation to this idiom. Derrida explains this idiom in an interview with Elisabeth Weber entitled "A Testimony Given . . ." ("TG" 56–57).

18. In addition to the problem of counting in religion (e.g., counting the practicing versus the nonpracticing, the believers versus the nonbelievers), Derrida points out in "Faith and Knowledge," as he did in his interview on 9–11, that the victims of various forms of natural catastrophe or religious or political violence are not counted in the same way across the globe. One "never count[s] the dead of Rwanda, for instance, in the same manner as those of the United States of America or of Europe" (§42).

19. This question of demographics is "perhaps the most grave and most urgent for the state and the nations of Israel, but it concerns also all the Jews, and doubtless also, if less obviously, all the Christians in the world. Not at all Muslims today. And to this day, this is a fundamental difference between the

three original 'great monotheisms'" (§44). Derrida speaks of the various ways of interpreting the "unheard-of survival of the small 'Jewish people' and the global extension of its religion, single source of the two monotheisms which share in a certain domination of the world and of which, in dignity at least, it is the equal" (§44).

20. The translator here recalls that "'*Plus d'un*' can also mean 'one no more'" (§51n44).

21. Derrida argues something similar in *Archive Fever* when he demonstrates how Freud dreams of an archive that would give direct access to the past, an archive—language or idiom—that would be the unique expression of the past. This would be the pure folly of pure faith, the worst violence. Martin Hägglund writes, in *Radical Atheism*, with regard to this passage: "Deconstructive logic undermines the notion that it would be desirable to attain an absolute peace. . . . Such a peace would in fact abolish the very possibility of relations and thus be the equivalent of an absolute violence. For Derrida, then, Levinas's ideal ethical relation between two is not only untenable but undesirable; it would be 'the worst violence,' Derrida writes in 'Faith and Knowledge'" (99). On this phrase "the worst violence [*la pire violence*]," see de Vries, *Philosophy and the Turn to Religion*, 20.

22. A note in the essay "Restitutions" in *The Truth in Painting* says that it is a "'polylogue' (for *n* + 1—female—voices)" (*TP* 256).

23. As Caputo nicely puts it: "Deconstruction is never monism, never One-ism, but n + Oneism, at least two" (*The Prayers and Tears of Jacques Derrida*, 157).

24. Derrida speaks of the "crypt" in many places, from *Glas* to "Fors" to "*Demeure*," a text written around the same time—perhaps even *at* the same time—as "Faith and Knowledge." In his reading of Blanchot, Derrida speaks of "the crypt of a secret friendship" ("*D*" 70).

25. In *Of Hospitality*, Derrida opposes two different kinds of plurals in the laws of hospitality: the one, a mere "multiplicity, distribution, differentiation" of conditional laws of hospitality, represented by the formula n + n + n, etc., the other, "the antinomic addition . . . that adds conditional laws to the unique and singular and absolutely only great Law of hospitality, to *the* law of hospitality, to the categorical imperative of hospitality," a plural made up of "One + a multiplicity," represented by the formula "One + n" (*OFH* 81).

26. In "Abraham, the Other," Derrida uses the related idiom *se garder du Judaïsme*, that is, "to keep Judaism at bay" and "to keep some Judaism for oneself." See the translator's very helpful footnote on this phrase at "AO" 239n7.

27. Such references to the *hen diapheron heautōi* are numerous in Derrida, and from the very beginning. We read in "Différance," from 1968: "Perhaps this is why the Heraclitean play of the *hen diapheron heautōi*, of the one differing from itself, the one in difference with itself, already is lost like a trace in the determination of the *diapherein* as ontological difference" ("D" 22).

28. In *Archive Fever*, Derrida once again associates ash and signature. Hanold "dreams of bringing back to life. He dreams rather of reliving. But of reliving the

other. Of reliving the singular pressure or impression which Gradiva's step [*pas*], the step itself, the step of Gradiva herself, that very day, at that time, on that date, in what was inimitable about it, must have left in the ashes. He dreams this irreplaceable place, the very ash, where the singular imprint, like a signature, barely distinguishes itself from the impression. And this is the condition of singularity, the idiom, the secret, testimony" (*AF* 98–99).

29. ". . . and pomegranates," trans. Samuel Weber, in *Violence, Identity, and Self-Determination*, ed. Hent de Vries and Samuel Weber (Stanford, Calif.: Stanford University Press, 1997), 326–46.

30. The theme of ashes can be found in many texts by Derrida, and in an exemplary fashion in "Shibboleth" and other texts on Paul Celan; see *Sovereignties in Question*.

31. In addition to dating several texts July 15 (see, e.g., "The Night Watch," Derrida's introduction to Jacques Trilling's *James Joyce ou l'écriture matricide*), Derrida delivered three of his marathon conferences at Cerisy—and this was apparently his choice—on July 15: "Aporias" on 15 July 1992, "The Autobiographical Animal" on 15 July 1997, and the first part of *Rogues* on 15 July 2002.

9. The Passion of Literature: Genet in Laguna, Gide in Algiers

1. Gil Anidjar has an excellent reading of this line in his introduction to *Acts of Religion* (*AR* 20–31).

2. In *Monolingualism of the Other*, Derrida evokes the possibility of being able to "die in peace": "The obscure chance, my good fortune, a gift for which thanks should be given to goodness knows what archaic power, is that it was always easier for me to bless this destiny. Much easier, more often than not, and even now, to bless than to curse it. The day I would get to know to whom gratitude must be rendered for it, I would know everything, and I would be able to die in peace" (*MO* 64).

3. See, e.g., *SQ* 88–91.

4. Though Derrida looked at the origins of words—Greek, Latin, etc.—from the very beginning of his work, there seems to be a greater emphasis in the 1990s on *Latin* roots. See, e.g., Derrida's work on hospitality, or, in *Rogues* and elsewhere, his emphasis not on the Greek *autos* but on the Latin *ipse* of *ipseity*. One will notice that these Latin words and etymologies are often accompanied by a reference to Benveniste.

5. In "Interpretations at War: Kant, the Jew, the German," a lecture first delivered in Jerusalem in 1988, Derrida examines the question of nationalism in relationship to religion, and particularly the German-Jewish relationship, through a reading of Hermann Cohen's *Deutschtum und Judentum* (*AR* 137–88).

6. For Derrida on Palestine and the Palestinians, see Benoît Peeters, *Derrida* (Paris: Flammarion, 2010), 622–23.

7. In addition to *Glas*, there is also "Letter to Jean Genet (Fragments)" in *N* 41–45. Dated 20 August 1971, the letter bears the following note from the editors of the volume: "This unsent letter was written in response to Jean Genet's

appeal on behalf of George Jackson, whose letters from prison, *Soledad Brother*, had just been published (New York: Coward-McKann, 1970) with a preface by Genet. The project to publish a collection of texts on Jackson was never realized; Jackson was shot and killed in San Quentin Prison on 21 August 1971" (*N* 388). Genet speaks on the opening page of *Prisoner of Love* of the close relationship between his support of the Palestinians and the cause of "Blacks" in America. Derrida returns again to Genet in his 1999–2000 seminar on the death penalty.

8. Edited by Jérôme Hankins, *Genet à Chatila* (Paris: Éditions Solin, 1992) is a collection of essays by Tahar Ben Jelloun, Albert Dichy, Alain Milianti, Georges Banu, François Regnault, and Jérôme Hankins, along with an interview with Leila Shahid on Genet and the Palestinian question. The volume also includes a text by Genet from 1972, "Les Palestiniens," Genet's summary of a conversation he had with seven young Palestinians in September 1972. Because the original French version of this text has been lost, the summary in *Genet à Chatila* is a retranslation into French of the English translation that appeared in 1973 in *The Journal of Palestinian Studies*. The line Derrida quotes from *Genet à Chatila* thus comes from this retranslation of Genet's text.

9. In "Interpretations at War," Derrida insists on the institutional context of his lecture, and he evokes the Palestinian uprising that began in 1987 (*AR* 137–88; see esp. 137).

10. "Jean Genet et la Palestine," *La revue d'études palestiniennes*, 1997, 35.

11. DeLillo concludes "In the Ruins of the Future": "But the dead are their own nation and race, one identity, young or old, devout or unbelieving—a union of souls. During the hadj, the annual pilgrimage to Mecca, the faithful must eliminate every sign of status, income and nationality, the men wearing identical strips of seamless white cloth, the women with covered heads, all recalling in prayer their fellowship with the dead: Allahu akbar. God is great."

12. Hankins, ed., "Les Palestiniens," in *Genet à Chatila*, 103.

13. Here is how *Of Spirit*, from 1987 opens: "I shall speak of ghost [*revenant*], of flame, and of ashes. And of what, for Heidegger, *avoiding* means. What is avoiding [*éviter*]?" (*OS* 1). See also "To Speculate—On 'Freud'" where Derrida remarks on Freud's avoidance of Nietzsche: "The avoidance never avoids the inevitable in whose grasp it already is" (*PC* 263). The theme of avoidance—as well as the related themes of denial, denegation, forgetting, and repression—runs through all of Derrida's work, from the very beginning to the very end.

14. Hankins, ed., "Les Palestiniens," in *Genet à Chatila*, 104.

15. Ibid., 107.

16. Ibid., 101.

17. Ibid., 144.

18. The same could be said of Genet's support of the Black Panthers. Derrida writes in "Countersignature": "I do not know if the common expression 'political engagement' is appropriate for Genet, for his engagement was always that of a writer and poet who acted only at the margin, by speaking and writing, and who never separated the idea of revolution from that of poetic event, whether for May 68, the Black Panthers or the Palestinians" ("CS" 23).

19. Hankins, ed., "Les Palestiniens," in *Genet à Chatila*, 115.

20. Ibid.

21. Hankins, ed. "Entretien avec Leila Shahid," in *Genet à Chatila*, 47.

22. Ibid., 50.

23. Ibid., 52, 57. To the question: "Have you ever been interested in women?" Genet answered in an interview cited by Derrida in "Countersignature": "Yes, four women interested me: the Holy Virgin, Joan of Arc, Marie-Antoinette and Madame Curie" ("CS" 14).

24. Hankins, ed., *Genet à Chatila*, 60–61, 64–65.

25. Ibid., 62.

26. See ibid., 66.

27. Jean Genet, *Prisoner of Love*, trans. Barbara Bray (Middletown, Conn.: Wesleyan University Press, 1992), 3–4.

28. Ibid., 355, 373.

29. Ibid., 374–75.

30. The following analysis of the countersignature might be read as something of a supplement to the excellent analyses of Derek Attridge in *Acts of Literature* (New York: Routledge, 1992), 18–20, and of Timothy Clark in *Heidegger, Derrida, Blanchot* (Cambridge: Cambridge University Press, 1992), 150–80, works published well before the appearance of Derrida's essay on Genet.

31. If it appears to some that I am forcing a reading of the encryption of dates or references from Derrida's life in what otherwise might appear to be a straightforwardly philosophical text, one would do well to look at Derrida's own comments in "Countersignature" about how his own name (*déjà, derrière le rideau*) runs throughout *Glas*: "My proper name is thus like a countersignature constantly at work in my reading of Genet" ("CS" 33).

32. Derrida writes, in the Genet column of *Glas*: "*Glas* is written here—uniquely—to celebrate, in the depths of an absolute crypt, that *calendar trick* [coup de calendrier] whose chance will have marked an epoch" (*GL* 107bi).

33. A couple of pages later in the same letter, Derrida returns to Gide: "Since my return to Ris-Orangis, desire to reread Gide, to look for Sidi-Bou-Saïd there. Lo and behold, in the fourth book of *Les nouvelles nourritures*, final scene . . . on the same page, after he evokes a type of kenosis (an 'immense void' and a refusal of the 'mystical'), I stop short, falling upon the same pillar of salt, three times in one day, without counting the Bible, which I also wanted to reread" (*CP* 271). In *The Animal That Therefore I Am*, Derrida mentions Gide alongside other writers such as Proust, Woolf, Stein, Celan, Bataille, Genet, Duras, and Cixous who will have favored a more autobiographical form of writing (*ATT* 49). The famous Jardin d'Essai is evoked in, among other places, *H. C. for Life, That Is to Say . . .*; Cixous responds to these references at some length with a return to Algiers and a furtive visit to the Jardin in *Si près* (Paris: Editions Galilée, 2007), 179ff. Derrida cites as an exergue to *Moscou aller-retour* a line from Gide's *Retouches à mon Retour de l'URSS*, "J'avais . . . trop lu de récits de voyage," "I had read too many travel narratives," and he refers to him again at *MAR* 82. Like

Derrida in "*Demeure*," Gide refers in *The Fruits of the Earth* to Goethe's *Dichtung und Wahrheit*.

34. Published in August 2004, this text is dated 20 May of the same year. Derrida speaks again of this term of Gide in "Les voix d'Artaud (la force, la forme, la forge)," an interview with Évelyne Grossman in *Magazine littéraire*, no. 434 (September 2004), 35. Derrida thus seems to have returned to Gide with some insistence during the final year of his life. Speaking of Derrida's desire to give up neither philosophical nor literary writing, John Caputo invokes "the 'Protean' right to say everything" (*DN* 58). On Derrida's "admiration" for Gide, see Ginette Michaud's *Veilleuses* (Cap-Saint-Ignace, Quebec: Éditions Nota bene, 2009), 24.

35. André Gide, *The Fruits of the Earth*, trans. Dorothy Bussy (New York: Alfred A. Knopf, 1949).

36. "Do not sacrifice to idols" (ibid., 293). "A preference seemed to me an injustice; wishing to belong to all men, I would not give myself to any *one*" (ibid., 71).

37. Ibid., 282–83.

38. Ibid., 2.

39. As early as "Force and Signification" in 1963, Derrida refers to Gide's "melancholy" ("FS" 5).

40. "At Tunis the only garden is the cemetery. At Algiers, in the Botanical Gardens (palm trees of every species), I ate fruits I had never seen before" (Gide, *Fruits of the Earth*, 56). "Nathaniel, I will speak to you of towns. . . . Algiers trembles for love in the sun, and swoons for love at night" (ibid., 133). Many of Derrida's earliest trips, as we learn from *Jacques Derrida* and *Counterpath*, coincide with places Gide speaks of in *The Fruits of the Earth*, from Honfleur to Venice.

41. Gide, *Fruits of the Earth*, 79. To cite just a couple of lines from the poem: "Nathaniel, what of pomegranates? / They were sold for a few pence in that Eastern market . . . / Guarded treasure, honeycomb partitions . . . / Crimson seeds in azure bowls, / Or drops of gold in dishes of enameled bronze" (ibid., 83). In 1934, Gide also would publish a play entitled *Persephone* that would subsequently be set to music by Stravinsky (see André Gide, *My Theater*, trans. Jackson Mathews [New York: Alfred A. Knopf, 1952], 237–56.

42. Gide, *Fruits of the Earth*, 257, 287, 289. Consider also: "Comrade, you must refuse henceforth to seek your nourishment in the milk of tradition, man-distilled and man-filtered" (ibid., 288); "Stand up erect, naked and valiant; burst your wrappings, push aside your props; to grow straight you need nothing now but the urge of your sap and the sun's call" (ibid., 288).

43. Ibid., 179.

44. Ibid., 282.

45. Ibid., 290, 293.

46. I am supported in this hypothetical mise-en-scène of voices in Derrida by lines such as the following, from *Memoirs of the Blind*: "I had sent to myself, who did not yet exist, the undecipherable message of a convocation" (*MB* 37).

47. In addition to the passage from Gide, one might also hear some resonance between these words and the famous line of Diderot, cited in *Memoirs of the Blind,* where Diderot says, in a love letter he is writing in the dark, "Wherever there will be nothing, read that I love you" (*MB* 102).

48. In an article by Mitchell Stephens in the *New York Times Magazine* from 23 January 1994—that is, just a couple of weeks before the Capri conference—Derrida is quoted as saying, "All my writing is on death. . . . If I don't reach the place where I can be reconciled with death, then I will have failed. If I have one goal, it is to accept death and dying." Stephens comments: "Might that, for someone whose eyes see what Derrida's see, be impossible?" It is not easy to reconcile Derrida's expressed desire to be reconciled with death with his many statements over many years that death would be, in the end, that with which one cannot be reconciled.

49. As Derrida writes of both birth and death in an interview from *Negotiations*: "With the birth of a child—the first figure of the absolute arrivant—one can analyze the causalities, the genealogical, genetic, and symbolic premises, or the wedding preparations. But even if such an analysis could ever be completed, one could never reduce the element of chance [*aléa*], the place of the taking-place; there will be someone who speaks, someone irreplaceable, an absolute initiative, another origin of the world. . . . What is absolutely new is not this, rather than that; it is the fact that it arrives only once. It is what is marked by a date (a unique moment and place), and it is always a birth or death that a date dates. . . . What resists analysis is birth and death: always the origin and the end of a world" (*N* 104).

50. Plato, *Phaedo,* trans. Harold North Fowler (Cambridge: Harvard University Press, 1982).

51. In 1993, in *Specters of Marx,* Derrida writes, speaking of Marx and Stirner: "They both share, apparently like you and me, an unconditional preference for the living body" (*SM* 141).

52. What goes for the individual goes for deconstruction itself. Derrida was frequently amused by the way in which deconstruction had to be declared dead or dying every few years in America or in France. "I've heard this for at least twenty-five years: it is finished, it is dying. . . . I'm totally convinced that deconstruction started dying from the very first day" ("AID" 224–25).

53. The question of life, or life-death, is pervasive in Derrida's work, from *Speech and Phenomena* in 1967 to Derrida's 1975 seminar "La vie la mort" to his 1998 *H.C. for Life, That Is to Say . . .* See *JD,* 138–39.

54. Derrida says of translation, in an interview from 1985 entitled "Deconstruction in America": "And when these translations produce this augmentation, these new textual bodies, then I think that nothing better could happen to me. At that point it's not a matter of survival in the sense of posterity, but of another type of *survival,* of 'more living.' . . . Survival isn't simply life after death, but a strange dimension of 'plus de vie'—both 'more life' and 'no more life.' Or 'plus

que vie,' that's it, 'more than life.' . . . Really, I think that that's the best thing that happens to me in America, when it happens" ("DA" 25).

Epilogue: Miracle and Mass Delusion (*Underworld* IV)

1. Rosemary speaks of a woman living in a basement apartment at 607 (= 13!) who recited the rosary and claims to have seen St. Anthony (*U* 755).

2. Dominique Laporte, *History of Shit*, trans. Nadia Benabid and Rodolphe el-Khoury (Cambridge: MIT Press, 2000), 13.

3. As we see at the end of the novel, the Internet is capable of bringing these two Edgars together, the sacred and the profane, female and male. Through a kind of "fantasy in cyberspace" (*U* 826), a kind of Apocalypse (*U* 825), Edgar is "exposed to every connection you can make on the world wide web" (*U* 824).

4. Earlier in the novel, Janet describes the scenes she has witnessed as a nurse in a Boston hospital in terms that remind us of the opening scene with Bruegel: "She described scenes that were like paintings of the European masters, the ones who did miracles and war" (*U* 414).

5. First published in *Harper's Magazine* (December 2001) and then republished in *The Guardian* on 22 December 2001.

6. This connection is explicitly made in the novel as someone says: "You squeeze a baseball. You kind of juice it or milk it" (*U* 131).

7. The same might be said, and indeed was said, when the image of the Virgin Mary appeared on a cement wall of an underpass on Fullerton Avenue in Chicago in April 2005. "Our Lady of the Underpass," as she came to be known, became the subject of a play by Tanya Saracho, produced by the Teatro Vista. The announcement for the play began: "The same week that Rome announced a new Pope, a woman driving home from work spotted an image of the Virgin Mary on a discolored wall of the Fullerton Avenue underpass." Such an event puts to the test in an exemplary fashion the relationship between *Offenbarkeit* and *Offenbarung* discussed in detail in Chapter 6, that is, the relationship between revealability and revelations, messianicity and all particular, "concrete" messianisms.

8. This contact is reminiscent of the way Eric Packer, the protagonist of *Cosmopolis*, strips naked and joins a crowd of extras being filmed on a New York City street. Again the moment of contact occurs at night, in a crowd, near the end of the novel.

9. We see something similar in the opening scene of *Mao II*, as well as in a chapter of *The Names* (New York: Vintage Books, 1989) entitled, appropriately, "The Desert": "Was it a grace to be there, to lose oneself in the mortal crowd, surrendering, giving oneself over to mass awe, to disappearance in others" (285).

10. As for Edgar, she clings to this sign, this vision; she "holds the image tight in her mind, the fleeting face on the lighted board, her virgin twin who is also her daughter. And she recalls the smell of jet fuel. This is the incense of her experience, the burnt cedar and gum, a retaining medium that keeps the moment

whole, all the moments, the swaying soulclap raptures and the unspoken close-ness, a fellowship of deep belief. // There is nothing left to do but die and this is precisely what she does, sister Alma Edgar, bride of Christ" (*U* 824).

11. For those not familiar with the national idiom, this was the signature phrase of legendary Chicago Cubs broadcaster Harry Caray (1914–98).

Observation 1: Kant

1. Derrida broaches a reading of Kant's *Religion Within the Limits of Reason Alone* in a few different places in the *Right to Philosophy*. See, e.g., 1:51 and 2:53–54, 86, 174. This is almost always done within the context of a more detailed reading of Kant's *Critique of the Faculties*. For an excellent analysis of Derrida's reading of Kant, see chap. 1 of Hent de Vries, *Religion and Violence: Philosophical Perspectives from Kant to Derrida* (Baltimore: Johns Hopkins University Press, 2002), 18–122.

2. Derrida's summary in §36 indeed suggests that the question of "radical evil" is the first of his interests. After calling Kant's *Religion* "a book on radical evil," Derrida opens a parenthesis and asks: "What of reason and of radical evil today? And if the 'return of the religious' was not without relation to the return—modern or postmodern, for once—of certain phenomena, at least, of radical evil? Does radical evil destroy or institute the possibility of religion?"

3. Kant argues, e.g.: "The rational origin of this perversion of our will whereby it makes lower incentives supreme among its maxims, that is, of the propensity to evil, remains inscrutable to us" (38). Without getting into the details of this Kantian notion of a supersensible freedom, what is crucial here are the limits placed on reason. Both the ground of our actions, that is, our freedom, and the nature of God—as we will see in the next section of this Observation—are inscrutable to us.

4. Derrida's use of the idiomatic phrase *Où est le mal?*—"Where is (the) evil?" but also "Where is the problem?" or even "What's the harm?"—points out some of the difficulties of simply translating *mal* as "evil." It was no doubt to signal this problem that the translator left the French in brackets.

5. For an excellent analysis of Derrida's notion of radical evil, see Martin Hägglund, *Radical Atheism*, esp. 112–14. Hägglund argues that "Derrida's notion of radical evil undercuts the very Idea of something that would be good in itself" (113). Indeed, "the possibility of evil is intrinsic to the good that we desire" (113) insofar as "everything that is good must be open to becoming evil" (114). In this context, Hägglund cites Derrida's emphasis, in *Arguing with Derrida*, on the possibility of radical evil: "The thought of 'radical evil' here is not concerned with it as an eventuality. It is simply that the *possibility* of something evil, or of some corruption, the *possibility* of the non-accomplishment, or of some failure, is *ineradicable*. And it is so because it is the condition for every felicity, every positive value—the condition for ethics for instance. So, if you want to eradicate the *possibility* of this negative then you destroy what you want to save. Thus ethics could not be ethical without the ineradicable *possibility* of evil.

(That's why it is not simply Kantian—although it has something to do with Kant.)" (*AD* 54).

6. Derrida wants to take into account the history or historicity of this radical evil "*so as to permit the treatment today of* religion within the limits of reason alone." He goes on to ask: "*How can a history of political and technoscientific reason be inscribed there and thus* brought up to date, *but also a history of radical evil, of its figures that are never simply figures and that—this is the whole evil—are always inventing a new evil? The radical 'perversion of the human heart' of which Kant speaks, we now know is not one, nor given once and for all, as though it were capable of inaugurating figures or tropes of itself. Perhaps we could ask ourselves whether this agrees or not with Kant's intention when he recalls that Scripture does indeed 'represent' the historical and temporal character of radical evil*" (§14).

7. To be precise, the first Parergon was labeled section 5 in the first edition and then made into the first Parergon (or General Observation) in the second edition. A conclusion was then added to the first General Observation in order to explain the location of these *parerga* to religion within the limits of reason alone (47–49). In what follows, Derrida essentially cites from this conclusion.

8. Derrida treats the notion of the parergon in Kant's *Critique of Judgment* in an essay of *The Truth in Painting* entitled, precisely, "Parergon" (*TP* 15–147). In a chapter of *The Purest of Bastards* entitled "Broken Frames," David Farrell Krell offers what at first looks like little more than a play on the word *parergon* but soon reveals itself, as often happens with Krell, to be the key to an entire rereading of the text. In an analysis of Kant's *parerga* in the *Critique of Pure Reason*, though also in *Religion*, Krell suggests calling these *parerga* by the name *parurerga*, from the French *parure*, meaning "dress or ornament." As bordering on reason but not actually within its limits, the *parurerga* of *Religion* would be but the costume dressing of historical churches, adornments that are often wrongly adopted and adored for their own sake and so should ultimately be dispensed with in a purely moral religion. The *parerga* would be *parurerga*, mere embellishments or superfluities, the "trappings" of religion (79).

9. On this notion of *Schwärmerei* in Kant, see "NAAT."

10. Derrida writes: "If Kant speaks of the 'holiness' of the moral law, it is while explicitly holding a discourse on 'sacrifice,' which is to say, on another instantiation of religion 'within the limits of reason *alone*': the Christian religion as the only 'moral' religion. Self-sacrifice thus sacrifices the most proper in the service of the most proper. As though *pure* reason, in a process of auto-immune indemnification, could only oppose religion as such to *a* religion or *pure* faith to this or that belief" (§41).

Observation 2: Hegel

1. Here is the final paragraph of *Faith and Knowledge* in the translation of Walter Cerf and H. S. Harris (Albany: State University of New York Press, 1977): "But the pure concept or infinity as the abyss of nothingness in which all being is engulfed, must signify the infinite grief [of the finite] purely as a moment

of the supreme Idea, and no more than a moment. Formerly, the infinite grief only existed historically in the formative process of culture. It existed as the feeling that 'God Himself is dead,' upon which the religion of more recent times [*Religion der neuen Zeit*] rests; the same feeling that Pascal expressed in so to speak sheerly empirical form: 'la nature est telle qu'elle *marque* partout un Dieu *perdu* et dans l'homme et hors de l'homme.' [Nature is such that it *signifies* everywhere a *lost* God both within and outside man.] By marking this feeling as a moment [*rein als Moment*] of the supreme Idea, the pure concept must give philosophical existence to what used to be either the moral precept that we must sacrifice empirical being [*Wesen*], or the concept of formal abstraction [e.g., the categorical imperative]. Thereby it must re-establish for philosophy the Idea of absolute freedom and along with it the absolute Passion, the speculative Good Friday [*spekulativer Karfreitag*] in place of the historic Good Friday. Good Friday must be speculatively re-established in the whole truth and harshness of its God-forsakenness [*Gottlosigkeit*]. Since the [more] serene, less well grounded, and more individual style of the dogmatic philosophies and of the natural religions must vanish, the highest totality can and must achieve its resurrection solely from this harsh consciousness of loss, encompassing everything, and ascending in all its earnestness and out of its deepest ground to the most serene freedom of its shape" (190–91). This passage, which is summarized at §18, is cited in *Glas* 96a.

2. These philosophies of subjectivity are considered "reflective" because, as Harris puts it in his introduction to *Faith and Knowledge*, "consciousness, even at its furthest reach, its most 'objective' and rational limit, can only *reflect on* a reality that is independent of, and indifferent to, its presence or absence" (ibid., 7). Harris continues, "Knowledge, so far as it occurs, is an accident in the scheme of things. But it follows from this assumption that the understanding *of* the scheme of things claimed by the philosopher is itself not really a matter of knowledge but of *faith*. . . . What is *called* the 'theory of knowledge' is actually a matter of articulating and explicating rational *faith*" (ibid., 7).

3. As Walter Cerf argues in "Speculative Philosophy and Intellectual Intuition: An Introduction to Hegel's *Essays*," his introduction to *Faith and Knowledge*, "intellectual intuition became, in Schelling and Hegel, the vision of the whole, a vision in which God, nature, and self-consciousness (or reason) came into their truth" (ibid., xxv).

4. Here's a good example of Hegel—in the paragraph just before the final one Derrida cites—at once giving a critique of the philosophies of subjectivity and demonstrating their positive role within speculative philosophy: "In [truly philosophical] cognition, infinity as this negative significance of the Absolute is conditioned by the positive Idea that being is strictly nothing outside of the infinite, or apart from the Ego and thought. Both being and thought are one. But, *on the one hand*, these philosophies of reflection cannot be prevented from fixating infinity, the Ego, and turning it into subjectivity instead of letting it directly somersault into the positivity of the absolute Idea. By this route infinity fell once more into the old antithesis, and into the whole finitude of reflection which it

had itself previously nullified. But *on the other hand*, the philosophy of infinity is closer to the philosophy of the Absolute than the philosophy of the finite is; for although infinity or thought is rigidly conceived as Ego and subject, and must, *in this perspective*, share the same rank as the object or the finite which it holds over against itself, still there is the *other perspective* in which infinity is closer to the Absolute than the finite is, because the inner character of infinity is negation, or indifference" (190; my emphasis throughout).

Observation 3: Bergson

1. Derrida apparently did devote part of three early seminars to Bergson, his seminar of 1960–61 (on the "present") and that of 1961–62 and 1963–64 (on Bergson's "Introduction to Metaphysics" and the idea of the "nothing").

2. Derrida does treat Merleau-Ponty in *On Touching—Jean-Luc Nancy*, trans. Christine Irizarry (Stanford, Calif.: Stanford University Press, 2005) and Sartre in "'Dead Man Running': Salut, Salut" (in *N* 257–92), but it would be difficult to argue that either of these figures is as formative for Derrida's thought as Heidegger is.

Observation 4: Heidegger

1. In *Rogues*, Derrida makes a declaration regarding the famous line of Heidegger in *Der Spiegel*, "Only a god can save us now," that it is hard to imagine Derrida repeating in other contexts or with regard to other thinkers: "I think I know just about everything that has been said or could be said about this declaration, along with everything else in the *Der Spiegel* interview, everything about what is revealed there and what is kept silent. I think I know rather well the program, the irony, the politics, and the caustic responses to which such a provocation might give rise. Trust me on this. My intention is not for the moment to enter into the debate or take sides" (*R* 110).

2. A mere count of the number of times these four figures' names appear in the text is illuminating: Hegel, 3; Bergson, 3; Kant, 22; Heidegger, 58.

3. Derrida refers here (§26n15) to *Specters of Marx* (23ff), where "the condition of justice" is thought "in relation to a certain sundering [*déliaison*]" rather than to "the bringing-together (*Versammlung*) towards which Heidegger retraces it, in his concern, doubtless legitimate in part, to extract *Dikē* from the authority of *Ius*, which is to say, from its more recent ethico-juridical representations."

4. See §41, where Derrida returns to the question of ontotheology in Heidegger.

5. In §34n25, Derrida speculates that Heidegger would have understood the "return of the religious" to be "nothing but the persistence of a Roman determination of 'religion,'" one that "would go together with a dominant juridical system and concept of the state that themselves would be inseparable from the 'machine age.'"

6. This footnote begins by underscoring the importance for Heidegger of the verb *halten* (and all the words related to it, from *Aufenhalt*, "stopover, ethos," to

Verhaltenheit, "modesty, scruple, reserve, or silent discretion") in relation to religion and the "last god" (§40n31; see §44n36). Derrida had a penchant for following a term or matrix of terms through several texts, a corpus, or indeed a tradition. We have already seen this in his repetition of the litany of terms related to the first source of religion—the holy, the indemnified, the safe and sound, etc. This penchant is never more on display than in Derrida's many readings of Heidegger. Whether he is following the value of *Geist* (in *Of Spirit*) or *Geschlecht* (in the *Geschlecht* essays) or *walten* (in *The Beast and the Sovereign,* Volume 2), Derrida finds in Heidegger a configuration of terms that illuminates something essential about Heidegger's thought.

7. Later in §29, Derrida will put Heidegger at the end of a long Enlightenment tradition or filiation that would be not only anti-Christian but, writes Derrida, "anti-Judeo-Christiano-Islamic": "Voltaire-Feuerbach-Marx-Nietzsche-Freud-(and even)-Heidegger."

8. In *Artaud le Moma,* Derrida speaks of a Heideggerian ontology "marked by a denied Christianity" (*AM* 89).

9. In §48n40, Derrida recalls having taken up this theme in *Of Spirit,* 129–36, and he sends us to Françoise Dastur's "Heidegger et la théologie," *Revue Philosophique de Louvain 92,* no. 2 (1994): 233n21. He is referring to a long footnote in *Of Spirit,* inspired, it seems, by comments made by Dastur during a conference organized by David Krell in 1986 in Essex, England, where Derrida presented material related to that book. Dastur's comments about Heidegger's treatment in *On the Way to Language* of a *Zusage* that would precede even the question apparently provoked the long footnote added by Derrida, which concludes: "At the Essex conference . . . Françoise Dastur reminded me of this passage of *Unterwegs zur Sprache* which indeed passes a question. I dedicate this note to her as a pledge of gratitude" (*OS* 129–36n5). On the notion of the Heideggerian *Zusage* in relation to Derrida, see Caputo, *The Prayers and Tears of Jacques Derrida,* 31.

10. In §48n41, Derrida recalls that in *Contributions to Philosophy* it is the poet who says and *saves* the "unscathed, *das Heilige,*" while the Thinker awaits signs of god. Earlier, Derrida recalls that the French *indemne* "has often been chosen to translate *heilig* ('sacred, safe and sound, intact') in Heidegger" (§27n16).

11. This helps explain Derrida's final reference to Heidegger in "Faith and Knowledge," an elliptical reference to a "sacredness without belief (index of this algebra: 'Heidegger')" (§49).

12. A similar remark can be found in a later note to the same section; Derrida says he was reminded by Samuel Weber, the translator of "Faith and Knowledge," of "the very dense and difficult pages devoted by Heidegger to 'The Thought of the Eternal Return as Belief (*als ein Glaube*)' in his *Nietzsche,*" prompting Derrida again to promise a future reading of "belief" in Heidegger's *Nietzsche:* "In re-reading these passages it strikes me as impossible in a footnote to do justice to their richness, complexity, and strategy. I will try to return to this elsewhere" (§48n42). Derrida actually begins this reading here, in this footnote, but then interrupts it and defers a fuller development to elsewhere. I don't know whether Derrida was ever able to make good on this promise.

Index to Sections of "Faith and Knowledge"

Name and Subject Index

Austin, J. L., 71–72, 89–90, 349n4, 352n20

auto-affection, 126, 143–49, 151, 361n20

autobiography, 37–38, 233, 246, 251, 259, 265, 343n27, 383n33

autoimmunity, immunity, 3, 5, 10–11, 32, 50–54, 66–69, 73, 76, 79–86, 89, 96, 100, 105, 117–18, 121, 134–36, 144, 151, 157, 169, 183, 189, 191, 202–5, 207–10, 211, 214–15, 217–18, 225, 230–31, 234, 236–39, 242, 249, 251, 272, 274, 300, 318, 323, 325, 351n11, 14, 361n21, 373n42, 388n10

automaticity, 5, 17, 29, 79, 84–86, 89–90, 96, 110, 116–22, 124, 125, 166–67, 202, 210–16, 221, 230, 233, 237, 241, 312–13, 350n11, 357n14, 375–76n14

Banu, Georges, 382n8

baseball, 8, 13–18, 100, 103–6, 201, 277, 280, 353n2, 386n6

Bataille, Georges, 311, 383n33

Beardsworth, Richard, 356n9

Beattie, Tina, 338n5

benediction, blessing, 232, 240, 262–63, 266, 269

Benjamin, Walter, 50, 340n3

Ben Jelloun, Tahar, 382n8

Bennington, Geoffrey, 230, 339n10, 352n20

Benveniste, Emile, 61–63, 66, 191, 216, 341n9, 347n20, 348nn27–28, 349n30, 349n5, 381n4

Bergson, Henri, 5, 40–42, 69, 74, 109, 285–86, 291, 311–19, 320, 329, 343n2, 344n3, 390nn1–2

Bible, 10–11, 14, 97, 140, 153, 227, 264, 268–69, 293, 343, 350n8, 357n12, 357n2, 369n28, 374n3, 383n33. *See also* scripture

Bin Laden, Osama, 190, 350n10

biopower, 235

Black Panthers, 382n18

Blanchot, Maurice, 94, 114, 246, 250, 311, 334, 347n18, 352n22, 355n6, 378n9, 380n24

breath, 6, 10, 45, 60, 92, 100, 108, 110–11, 114–17, 120–24, 141–42, 145, 150–51, 195, 200, 224, 274, 282, 355–56n7, 8, 356–57n12, 360n12

Bruce, Lenny, 105

Bruegel, Pieter, 17, 277, 386n4

Buddhism, 130, 132, 134, 358–59nn6–8

Byzantium, 24, 255

calculation (number), 11, 40, 42–45, 90, 98, 105, 118–19, 189, 231, 233–37, 240–41, 243, 254, 345n9, 346nn10–11, 353n1

Calle-Gruber, Mireille, 378n12

Capri, 1, 5, 9–10, 12, 19, 22–25, 27–30, 34, 37, 40, 44, 46, 61, 65–66, 71, 107–8, 110–13, 121, 123, 160, 167, 169, 172–73, 183, 195, 220–24, 234, 243–44, 246, 252–55, 263, 277, 286, 329, 334, 340nn5–7, 341nn9&12, 343n1, 346n12, 361n20, 367n18, 378n9, 385n48

Caputo, John D., 169, 337n4, 338n6, 339n1, 342n16, 19, 347n25, 350n8, 351–52n17, 365–67n15, 368n22, 376n23, 378n9, 379n14, 380n23, 384n34, 391n9

Caray, Harry, 387n11

Catholicism, Catholic Church, 25, 34, 35, 43, 131, 134, 141, 192, 220, 232–33, 261, 324, 350n9, 374n1, 379n14

Celan, Paul, 211, 220, 245, 248, 375n10, 381n30, 383n33

Cerf, Walter, 308, 343n1, 388n1, 389n3

Cerisy la Salle, 260, 381n31

Chatila, Lebanon, 243–45, 253–57, 259–60, 263, 310, 342n15, 382nn8& 12, 382nn14–17, 383nn19–22, 383nn24–26

Chérif, Mustapha, 35–36, 94, 164, 185, 194, 358n7, 371n35, 372n39

Christianity, 10, 25–26, 28, 30, 34–35, 42, 49, 56, 58–60, 62–63, 73–74, 77, 84, 88, 95, 127–41, 151, 153, 157–58, 162, 164, 169, 171–72, 174, 180, 184, 186–87, 192, 194–95, 214, 248, 250–52, 255, 261, 287, 289, 291–95, 297, 300–304, 305, 314–16, 320–24, 326–28, 341n11, 344–45n7, 346n13, 347nn23–24, 351n12, 353n23, 357n3,

378n9, 380n24, 383–84n33; "DA,"
385–86n54; *DIS*, 240; "DMR,"
390n2; *DN*, 169–72, 339n1, 352n17,
365–66n15, 384n34; "DOI," 353n24;
DP, 342n17; "EF," 130, 180–82,
342n16, 370nn29&31, 371n34,
372n37, 373n40, 378–79n13; *EIRP*,
334, 339n11; "EL," 25; *ET*, 126,
222–23, 334, 357n1; "EW," 207,
374n2; *"FI,"* 50; "FL," 21, 33, 161,
165–66, 184, 334, 340n8, 346n15,
353n23, 356n10, 363n5, 365n12,
366n15, 367n19, 370n32; "FS,"
357n12, 384n39; "FSW," 196; "FTA,"
45; "FW," 268–69, 376n21; *FWT*,
118–19, 374n3; *GD 2*, 4, 67, 127, 207,
245, 346–47n16; *GGP*, 368n22,
368–69n28; *GL*, 4, 19, 21, 40, 207,
216, 244, 252–53, 258, 260–61, 263,
310–11, 343nn1–2, 380n24, 381n7,
383nn31–32, 389n1; "HAS," 4, 21,
114, 184, 340n5, 355n5, 358n3,
365n13, 368n24, 375n8, 379n13; *IW*,
35–37, 59, 73, 92, 94, 112, 135–36,
164, 185–89, 193–94, 343nn22–24,
352n21, 358n7, 359n7, 363n5,
371n35, 372n39, 372–73n40; "IW,"
381n5, 382n9; *JD*, 384n40, 385n53;
"K," 174–75, 368n21, 370n28; *LLF*,
143, 222, 271–73; "LO," 114; "LPS,"
123–24, 357n13; *MAR*, 383n33; *MB*,
21, 37, 358n4, 362n26, 384n46;
385n47; *MO*, 34–35, 37, 83, 381n2;
MP, 229, 361n22, 378n7; "MS,"
379n15; *N*, 253n24, 356n9, 382n7,
385n49, 390n2; "NA," 273,
374–75n5; "NAAT," 388n9; "NM,"
119–20; "NW," 218, 381n31; *OFH*,
21, 148–49, 380n25; *OG*, 48, 146–47,
149–50, 271, 356n8, 361n25, 370n33,
373n41, 378n11; *OH*, 35; *OS*, 256,
347n17, 370n33, 382n13, 391n6, 9;
OT, 272, 390n2; "P," 251; *PC*, 36–37,
45, 241, 265, 345n9, 346n12, 382n13;
"PCQ," 334; *PF*, 82, 184, 343n24,
359n9, 367n16; *PM*, 31–32, 50, 52,
163–64, 203, 218, 343n27, 376n24;
POS, 347–48n26, 356n8, 373n41;

"PP," 41, 110, 115–17, 120–21, 175,
239, 355n5, 356n8, 370n30; "PPW,"
98, 376n19; "PSI," 357n13; "PSS,"
376n17; *PSY 1*, 273, 340n3; *PSY 2*, 45;
R, 31, 51, 64, 75, 82, 91, 182–85, 187,
190–93, 368n24, 370n28, 371–72n36,
372n37, 381n31, 381n4, 390n1; "S,"
207; "SEC," 89, 143, 222, 271, 349n4;
"SH," 245, 381n30; *SM*, 82, 161, 188,
333, 349n29, 365n15, 385n51, 390n3;
"SN," 4, 21, 114, 153, 162, 177, 182,
184–85, 251, 262, 333, 340n5,
342n20, 346n15, 347n23, 349n2,
355n5, 358n3, 359n8, 362n1,
364–65n11, 365n13, 370n28; *SP*, 41,
110, 115, 126, 145–51, 370n30,
385n53; *SQ*, 98, 375n10, 381n30,
381n3; "SSS," 264; "SW," 4, 21,
207–8, 230–32, 242, 375n8, 378n13;
"TB," 21, 25, 340n3; "TG," 342n18,
379n17; *TP*, 69–71, 123, 295, 311,
377n25, 380n22, 388n8; *TS*, 5–7, 22,
34, 38, 127–29, 270, 334, 361n23, 25;
"TYM," 228, 378n7; "UG," 113;
"VA," 384n34; "VM," 87, 153,
362n2; *WD*, 87, 153, 356n8, 362n2,
375n6; *WM*, 273; "WOG," 239
Descartes, René, 311, 339n9, 357n14,
356n7, 357n14; Cartesianism, 351n12
desert, 16, 23–24, 43, 47, 49, 55, 104–5,
152, 162, 167, 172–74, 176–80, 182,
184, 185, 195, 233, 237, 258, 265,
280, 283, 340n6, 362n1, 363n3,
365n13, 369n28, 386n9
Dichy, Albert, 382n8
Diderot, Denis, 385n47
différance, 151, 239, 242, 290, 380n27
dignity (of human life), 202–4, 207–10,
300–302, 380
Dufrenne, Mikel, 338n6
Duras, Marguerite, 383n33
Dutoit, Thomas, 378n7
dynamic religions, 42, 313–18

Eckhart, Meister, 368n27
ecumenicalism, 80, 126, 132, 203–4
Eisenstein, Sergei, 200
élan vital, 314–16

Elijah, 97
encyclicals, 43–44, 77, *"Evangelium vitae,"* 43, 204, *"Fides et ratio,"* 44, 344–45n7, 350n9, 358n5
Enlightenment, 8, 27, 30, 41, 79, 81, 86–88, 136, 156, 183, 187, 192–93, 251, 253, 285, 297, 300, 325, 351–52n17, 363n3, 391n7, 364n7
etymology, 55, 61–64, 70, 133, 195, 348n28, 349n30, 354n2, 381n4
Eucharist, 129–30, 136, 140–41, 360n17
Europe, Europeans, 25–26, 27, 30–31, 35–37, 57, 59, 61, 63, 83, 107, 135, 136–37, 188, 191–92, 216, 218, 220, 224, 248, 251–52, 255, 259, 300, 340n8, 341nn9&13, 348n28, 351n16, 364–65n11, 369n28, 371n35, 374n7, 375n12, 379n18, 386n4
evangelists, evangelization, 14–15, 87, 127–28, 136, 284, 292, 294, 345n7, 350n9, 358n5; evangelicalism, 134, 341n11, televangelism, 77, 127, 141, 350n8, 360n14
event, 5, 7–8, 12, 14–17, 22, 24, 28, 34, 42, 72, 90, 97–98, 106, 111, 118–19, 140–41, 147, 150, 157–58, 160–61, 164–65, 171, 173, 175–78, 180–82, 184, 231–32, 243, 246–47, 263, 269, 273, 280, 282, 321, 324, 346n15, 360nn18&20, 363n6, 368n28, 382n18, 386n7
evil, radical evil, 42, 50–53, 79–80, 85, 120, 161, 166, 196, 217, 220, 236, 287–91, 293, 295–96, 301, 387nn2–5, 388n6
Evink, C. E., 351–52n17, 373n40

faith, 1, 3–6, 8, 12–18, 21, 26–28, 30, 32–33, 37, 40–44, 51, 54–56, 63, 67–75, 81–82, 86–96, 98–100, 105–6, 109, 112–13, 119, 120, 124, 136, 139–40, 152, 156–59, 163–66, 169–70, 172, 175–79, 182–83, 185–91, 193–95, 199–200, 204–5, 214–15, 230–37, 241, 246–48, 260, 262, 265, 267, 269, 274–75, 277–80, 283–84, 292, 294–95, 297–98, 300, 302–4, 306–8, 310, 315, 320–22,

324–29, 338n7, 342n17, 344n5, 344–45n7, 348n28, 349nn3&5, 351–52n17, 352nn19–21, 353n3, 362–63n3, 364n7, 365n14, 370nn29&34, 372–73n40, 380n21, 388n10, 389n2; elementary, 27, 37, 41, 51, 54, 63, 67, 70, 74–75, 86, 89–96, 98–100, 119, 124, 136, 139–40, 152, 158–59, 163, 165, 169, 177, 183, 185, 187, 191, 193–95, 205, 232, 236, 246–48, 262, 267, 269, 324–25, 329, 352nn20&21, 370nn29&34, 372–73n40; reflective/reflecting, 74–75, 157, 178, 183, 194, 292, 295, 298, 320
Ferraris, Maurizio, 1, 5, 22, 29, 110–11, 113, 115, 121, 123, 223, 333–34
fetish, fetishism, 80, 208, 210–11, 214–17, 294, 297, 344n5, 375n9
Feuerbach, Ludwig, 297, 391n7
Fichte, J. G., 307–9
Fischer, Jeffrey, 355n5
Foucault, Michel, 6, 311, 342n14
France, 33–35, 127, 138, 140, 218, 220, 241, 259–60, 342–43n22, 357n1, 385n52; Nice, 340n5; Paris, 5, 27, 29, 35–36, 111, 223, 252, 256, 333–34, 354n2. *See also* French language
fraternalism, 24, 27, 136, 184, 203, 359n9
French language, 1–3, 19, 22, 25, 30, 33–35, 40, 44–46, 50, 57–58, 61, 66, 68, 70, 72, 85, 88, 99, 111, 115, 123–24, 213, 227, 229, 233, 238, 241, 244, 273–74, 288, 337n1, 341n9, 347n19, 356n12, 375n9, 379n17, 382n8, 387n4, 388n8, 391n10
Freud, Sigmund, 11, 24, 88, 169, 220–21, 223–26, 297, 311, 334, 346nn11–12, 360–61n20, 376n22, 377n26, 377n1, 380n21, 382n13, 391n7
friendship, 184, 187, 257, 260, 263, 364–65n11, 380n24
fundamentalism, 4, 28–32, 77, 80, 88, 91, 131, 170, 235, 296, 341, 350n8, 372–73n40

Gadamer, Hans-Georg, 1, 25, 333–34, 341n9

Gargani, Aldo, 334, 337n2
Gasché, Rodolphe, 240
Gaston, Sean, 376n20
Genesis, 3, 10, 12, 29, 43, 86, 111, 113,
    120–23, 125, 179, 221, 293, 306,
    351n12, 356–57nn10–12
Genet, Jean, 11, 21, 40, 177, 243–45,
    253–61, 263, 311, 342n15, 359n9,
    381–82n7, 382nn8&10, 392nn12&
    14–18, 383n19–33
German language, 25, 30, 44, 50, 71, 220,
    224, 246, 250, 307, 311, 341n9,
    343n1, 345n8, 381n5
Gibbs, Robert, 363n3
Gide, André, *The Fruits of the Earth*,
    11–12, 197, 264–69, 383–84n33,
    384nn34–45, 385n47
gift, gift-giving, 21, 338, 364n10, 381n2
Given, Mark D., 370n33
Gleason, Jackie, 16–17
Globalization (*mondialisation*), 1, 3, 8, 10,
    32, 58–60, 63, 76, 83–84, 91, 126,
    130–31, 134–36, 138, 147, 151, 188,
    191, 213, 218, 287, 342n14, 358n3,
    358n5, 360n13. *See also* Latin,
    Globalatinization
God, 13, 40, 42, 44, 55, 60–62, 74, 77,
    96–97, 103–6, 121–22, 128, 130, 133,
    137, 176, 178, 180, 182, 190, 200,
    203–4, 209–10, 228, 231–32, 235,
    245, 266, 272, 278, 279, 287–88, 291,
    293–94, 296, 297, 299–304, 306, 308,
    312, 314, 316–18, 320–22, 328,
    338n5, 344n3, 345n7, 348n28,
    351n12, 353n24, 353n3, 5,
    356–57n12, 357n13, 358nn4–5,
    359–60n12, 364n8, 368n22, 369n28,
    372n37, 373n40, 375nn8&11, 377n2,
    378n7, 382n11, 387n3, 389nn1&3,
    390n1, 391nn6&10; death of, 40, 60,
    128, 137, 178, 203, 287, 299–304,
    316, 320, 359–60n12, 389n1
Goethe, J. W., 246, 383–84n33
Good beyond Being, 179, 237, 174–77,
    179–80, 231, 237, 368n22–23. *See also*
    Plato, *Republic*
Good Friday, 40, 137, 306–7, 310, 343n1,
    389n1

Gradiva, 11, 24, 29, 118, 201, 221–26,
    227, 233, 243–45, 254–55, 274,
    342n15, 346n12, 361nn20–21,
    376nn22–23, 377n26, 377n1,
    380–81n28
Greco-Christian, Greco-Abrahamic, 133,
    172, 174, 180, 184, 252, 300, 305,
    347n24, 353n23, 372n39
Greek, Greece, 2, 10, 19, 23, 44, 49, 60,
    62, 87, 133, 153, 162, 171, 174, 176,
    178, 180, 184, 186, 200, 210–11, 216,
    219, 228, 230, 239, 242, 251, 274,
    291, 314, 321, 323–24, 330, 364n7,
    366n15, 367n19, 374n3, 378n13,
    381n4
grenade ("pomegranate," "grenade"), 6,
    11, 38, 43, 46, 83, 104, 108, 197,
    227–35, 240, 242, 243, 245, 265, 280,
    310, 342n15, 375n9, 377n2,
    377–78n5, 378nn8–9, 381n29,
    384n41
Guéroult, Martial, 6–7, 339n9

Hades, 200–201, 221, 227–28, 377n1,
    378nn6–7
Hägglund, Martin, 343n27, 352n19,
    365n14, 373n42, 380n21, 387n5
Hallyday, Johnny, 376n20
Hankins, Jérôme, 382n8, 12, 14–17,
    383n19–26
Hanson, Jeffrey A., 362–63n3
Harris, H. S., 309, 343n1, 388–89nn1–2
Hart, Kevin, 180–81, 338n6, 340n7,
    349n31, 363n3, 368n22, 369n28
Hebrew, 227, 268, 342n21, 353n23,
    357n12, 357n2; Hebrew Bible (Old
    Testament), 227, 357n2
Hebron (massacre), 255
Hegel, G. W. F., 5, 21, 40–41, 48–50, 69,
    107, 109, 123, 137, 155, 216, 244–45,
    252–53, 261, 263, 285–86, 300,
    305–12, 319–21, 329, 338n6, 343n1,
    347nn18&24, 361n22, 388–89nn1–4,
    390n2
Heidegger, Martin, 5, 26, 41, 58, 62,
    69–70, 88, 94, 110, 144, 155–57, 171,
    174, 181, 205, 225, 256, 262, 286,
    297, 305–6, 310–11, 319–30, 338n6,

241, 245–46, 250, 275, 280, 283, 290,
312–13, 315–17, 344nn3–4, 351n13,
355n5, 355–56n7, 356n8, 371–72n36,
390n5
McMullen, Ken, *Ghost Dance*, 222
Maher, Bill, 338n5
Maimonides, Moses, 337–38n4, 375n8
Malabou, Catherine, 35, 264
Malebranche, Nicolas, 339n9
Mallarmé, Stéphane, 354n3
Manoussakis, John P., 349n31
Marder, Elissa, 376n16
Marder, Michael, 360n18
Margel, Serge, 349n1
Marion, Jean-Luc, 338n6, 368n22, 28
marionette, 7, 210–14, 216, 223, 225
Marrano, 11, 36, 232–34, 237, 241,
377n2, 379nn14–15
Martin, David, 341n11
Marx, Karl, Marxism, 88, 164, 297,
379n15, 385n51, 391n7
Mary, *see* Virgin Mary
Mecca, 78, 360n17, 382n11
media, mediatization, 1–2, 6, 8, 10, 12,
15, 21, 28, 76–78, 84, 87, 91, 125–45,
148, 150–51, 189, 191, 204–5, 214,
217, 296, 338n7, 341n11, 343n27,
350n9, 351n15, 358n3, 359n11,
359–60n12, 360n15
Melville, Herman, 245
Merleau-Ponty, Maurice, 312, 390n2
messianicity, messianism, 1, 10, 12, 21, 97,
119, 152–67, 169–75, 178–79,
182–83, 185–87, 190–91, 209, 231,
237, 242, 275, 347–48n26, 362–63n3,
363n6, 364nn8&10, 365n13,
365–67n15, 367n19, 368n27,
368–69n28, 386n7
Michaud, Ginette, 384n34
Milianti, Alain, 382n8
Miller, J, Hillis, 240
miracle, 8, 10, 12–18, 54, 78, 92–95,
97–100, 103–6, 110, 118, 124–25,
127, 139–41, 151, 166, 196, 200–201,
212, 230, 233, 245–47, 250, 267,
275–76, 280–83, 296–99, 312, 315,
353n4, 355n5, 360n17, 386n4
Monica (Saint), 340n4

monotheism, 2, 48, 78, 122, 128–29,
131–33, 136–37, 174, 203, 214, 216,
219, 234–36, 245, 300, 302, 358n3,
372n38, 374n1, 379–80n19
Montaigne, Michel de, 165, 311
Moriah, Mount, 129, 151, 223, 243–44,
254–55
Moses, 171
mourning, 21, 81, 130, 178, 199, 206,
273–74, 341n13, 374n5, 376n20
Muhammad, 77
Muslims, *see* Islam
mystics, mysticism, 18, 80, 118, 165–66,
205–6, 280, 313–15, 350, 383n33

Nancy, Jean-Luc, 185, 272, 374n2, 390n2
Naples, 23, 167, 221–22, 226, 238, 334,
346n12, 14
Napoleon, 347n18
Neoplatonism, 174, 355n5
New York City, 15–16, 103, 192, 199,
277, 334–35, 342n19, 354n7, 386n8
Nietzsche, Friedrich, 25, 61, 88, 267, 297,
300, 321, 356n9, 375n12, 382n13,
391nn7&12

Offenbarkeit, Offenbarung, 155–57, 160,
178, 180–82, 321, 324, 362–63n3,
363–64n6, 368n27, 368–69n28,
386n7
Ogier, Pascale, 222–23, 376n20

Palestine, Palestinians, 12, 28, 252–60,
263, 381n6, 382nn7–10, 12, 14–18,
383nn19–22&24–29
Parergon, parerga, 3, 286, 287, 295–304,
388nn7–8
Pascal, Blaise, 165, 355n5, 388–89n1
passion, 40, 137, 248–51, 255, 292, 300,
306–7, 343n1, 366–67n15, 388–89n1
Passover, 22–29, 232, 310, 377n2
Patočka, Jan, 388n6
Paul (saint), 133, 186–87, 214, 303–4,
370n33, 375n12
Peeters, Benoît, 343n26, 381n6
Pentecostalism, 134, 341n11
performatives (speech acts), performativity,
51, 54–56, 64, 68, 72, 86, 88, 89–91,

128, 136, 141, 152, 157–59, 166, 176, 182, 204–6, 209, 214–18, 245, 251, 300, 321–23, 326–28, 330, 348n28, 353n23, 364n6, 370–71n34, 376n15, 386n3, 391nn10–11

sacrifice, 1, 4, 6, 11, 66, 76, 127–28, 173, 203, 206–10, 214, 228, 244, 255, 266–67, 272, 274, 294, 301, 306, 321, 338n6, 340n8, 346n16, 374n3, 374nn4–5, 375nn7–8, 376n15, 377n2, 384n36, 388n10, 389n1

Saghafi, Kas, 376n20

Sallis, John, 179, 368n26

salut, salvation, 50–55, 64, 66–69, 72–75, 82, 85, 118, 165, 168, 173, 204–5, 207, 216, 225, 235, 251, 272–74, 284, 289–90, 293, 300, 313, 322, 347nn16&19–20, 363–64n6

Saracho, Tanya, 386n7

Sartre, Jean-Paul, 312, 390n2

Saussure, Ferdinand de, 147

Schelling, F. W. J., 307, 389n3

Schmitt, Carl, 191

science, 2–4, 6, 8, 10, 12, 15, 18, 21, 29–30, 32, 40, 42, 48, 52–55, 64–65, 69–72, 75–76, 78–83, 85–94, 99–100, 103, 106–9, 116, 120–21, 125, 127, 135–36, 152, 154, 156, 158–59, 163, 165–66, 168–69, 179, 189, 191, 193, 202–5, 209, 214, 218–20, 229–30, 232–35, 245–47, 250, 289, 310, 312, 316, 318, 320, 325, 329, 338n5, 7, 344n5, 350n8, 362n3, 370n29. *See also* technoscience, technology

Scripture, 139, 158, 195, 251, 293–94, 299–303, 346n15, 388n6; Exodus 28:31–34, 377n4; Kings 7:18, 20, 377n4; Numbers 20:3–5, 377n5; 1 Corinthians, 303; Luke 17:21–22, 364n8; Luke 19:12–16, 291, 293; Philippians 2:12, 48, 347n16. *See also* Genesis

secret, 45, 92, 94, 98, 105, 114, 121, 126–30, 134, 151, 165, 167, 185, 195, 205, 232–33, 240–41, 245, 248–50, 296, 346n12, 349n29, 349n3, 350n11, 353n5, 358n4, 364n6, 370n31, 378n13, 379n14, 380n24, 381n28

secularism, 1, 4, 10, 16, 27, 30–32, 57–58, 88, 93, 95–96, 126, 136, 158–59, 161, 164, 183, 187–88, 190–93, 203, 218, 245–46, 251–52, 342n17, 351–52n17, 358n6, 363–64n6, 370–71n34, 371n35, 372n39, 372–73n40

September 11 (9–11), 190–92, 280, 354n7, 371n35

sexuality, sexual difference, 1, 11, 28, 201, 212–13, 217–21, 225, 227–28, 245, 275, 279

Shahid, Leila, 257–58, 382n8, 383nn21–23

Sherwood, Yvonne, 338n6, 340n7, 342n16, 349n31, 363n3, 369n28

Shor, Toots, 16–17, 339n3

signature, countersignature, 5–6, 22, 98, 233, 240, 243, 260–64, 269, 277, 380–81n28, 383nn30–31, 387n11

Sinatra, Frank, 17

Smith, James K. A., 362–63n3

social bond, 37, 74, 89, 91–95, 139, 152, 158, 187, 193, 195, 205, 344n5, 351–52n17, 370n29, 372–73n40

sovereignty, 1, 6, 31, 51, 56–58, 62, 89, 98, 179, 187–88, 190–93, 209–14, 216, 219, 231, 237, 274, 342n14, 372n37, 376n15

Soviet Union, *see* Russia

specters, ghosts, 1, 8, 12, 123, 156, 201, 211, 221–23, 225–27, 243–44, 254, 256, 263, 270, 274, 281, 339n2, 360–61n20, 376n20, 378n7

Spinoza, Baruch, 339n9

spontaneity, 17, 29, 34, 76, 84, 90, 108, 110–11, 116–18, 121, 123, 125, 146–47, 166–68, 211–13, 215–17, 219, 229–30, 233, 237, 275, 309, 350–51n11, 375–76n14

static religions, 42, 312–16, 318

Stein, Ben, 338n5

Stein, Gertrude, 338n33

Stiegler, Bernard, 5, 126, 222–23, 333

Stirner, Max, 385n51

Stravinsky, Igor, 384n41

supplement, supplementarity, 3, 5, 8, 10, 18, 25, 82–83, 85, 116–17, 120, 123–24, 142, 160, 169, 175, 201–2,

207–11, 214, 216–17, 233–38, 242–43, 249, 254, 263, 271, 274, 298, 356n8

survival, 82, 84–85, 124, 209–10, 214–15, 222, 235, 263, 269–72, 274, 313, 377n2, 379–80n19, 385n54

Sweeney, Leo, S.J., 355n5

tallith, 231–32, 241–42, 378n12

Taoism, 359n7

Taylor, Mark C., 338n6

technology, teletechnology, technoscience, 1, 3–6, 10, 12–13, 30, 32, 42, 52–55, 60–61, 69, 71, 75–81, 83–86, 88–93, 100, 103–5, 109, 116–17, 120, 125, 127, 131, 135–36, 138–41, 144, 148, 165–66, 169, 175, 185, 189–91, 193, 201–4, 208–11, 213–15, 217–20, 223, 225, 230, 233–35, 249–50, 252, 278, 289, 310, 323, 325–26, 338n7, 341n13, 344n4, 350nn8–10, 351n15, 356n8, 357–58n3&5, 360n13, 388n6. *See also* science

television, 77–78, 81, 87, 125–27, 134, 136–51, 214, 351n13, 359n10–11, 359–60n12, 360nn13–17, 361n23. *See also* evangelism

temptation, 49, 147, 173, 293, 306, 310, 321, 348n28

testament, 14, 159, 240–41, 243, 249, 269, 301. *See also* Scripture

testimony (witnessing), 1, 4, 13–15, 25, 60–61, 67–68, 74, 88–99, 135, 139–42, 149–50, 152, 156, 158–59, 162–63, 166, 170, 180, 195, 206, 220, 232, 236, 243, 245–52, 254, 256, 259–61, 263, 269, 277, 279, 283, 322, 326–27, 329, 333–34, 349n30, 351–52n17, 352n20, 364–65n11, 372–73n40, 380–81n28, 386n4

theology, 22, 27, 31–33, 57, 63, 67, 129, 154, 157–58, 167, 171–72, 174–78, 180, 182, 184, 187–88, 190–94, 209, 220, 237, 251–53, 260, 293, 295, 300, 306, 322–24, 326–27, 337n4, 342n14, 344–45n7, 353n3, 364n6, 373n41, 374n1, 376n15; negative, 21, 35, 49, 106, 113, 172, 174–75, 177, 180, 184,

320, 338n6, 340n5, 346n15, 355n5, 359n8, 365n13, 368n22–24, 368–9n28, 372–3n40; onto-, 31, 58, 67, 162, 176, 179, 191, 232–34, 236–37, 242, 251, 306, 310, 321, 326, 328, 372n37, 373n41, 375n7, 377n2, 390n4

Thompson, Bobby, 14–17, 103, 105, 353n2

Thurschwell, Pamela, 354n7

Tiberius, 340n6

tolerance, religious tolerance, 10, 31, 58, 73, 133, 178, 182–83, 187, 191–95, 342n14, 372–73n40, 378n10

Tomb of the Patriarchs, 255

trace, 13–14, 19, 34, 37, 45, 124, 128, 158, 164, 167, 177, 179, 214, 222, 244, 264, 269–72, 274, 278, 293, 342n16, 343n27, 376n23, 380n27

Trías, Eugenio, 334, 337n2

Trilling, Jacques, 381n31

Trinity, New Mexico, 104, 317

underworld, 8–12, 17, 25, 29, 41, 105–6, 124, 199–201, 215, 219, 226–28, 263, 274, 278

United Nations, 188, 335

United States, 31, 57, 77, 127, 134–35, 138–40, 188, 222, 341nn11&13, 353n24, 354n6, 360n14, 371n35, 379n18. *See also* America

universality, 8, 27, 53, 55–60, 73, 76, 78–80, 129, 131, 133–39, 146–48, 151, 154–55,157–61, 163–64, 167, 170–72, 174–75, 180, 182–87, 190, 193–94, 203–6, 249–51, 282, 287, 292, 294, 299–305, 314, 316, 318, 344–45n7, 351–52n17, 352n20, 358n5, 359n9, 360n13, 361n25, 362–63n3, 364nn10–11, 365–67n15, 368–69n28, 370n32, 372n39, 372–73n40

Vattimo, Gianni, 1, 25, 46, 334, 337n1

Villanova University, 169, 178, 334, 339n2, 342n19, 368n28

violence, 11, 21, 28–29, 34, 80, 83, 135, 189, 196, 201, 205–7, 209, 214–15,

217–21, 224–25, 228, 233, 235–39,
245, 252–53, 255, 275, 279, 310, 321,
351n12, 362n2, 364n6, 376n15,
379n18, 380n21

Virgil, 9, 45, 346n13

Virgin Mary, 212–13, 216, 345n7,
383n23, 386n7

Vitiello, Vincenzo, 334, 337n2

voice, 6, 10, 15–16, 39, 75, 116, 122, 124,
126–27, 141–51, 182, 250, 266, 270,
281, 349n2, 362n26, 380n22, 384n46

Voltaire, 88, 192, 195, 297, 324, 391n7

Vries, Hent de, 156–57, 337n3,
338nn6–7, 338–39n8, 341n10,
343–44n2, 347n21, 351n15, 363n5,
363–64n6, 368nn22–23&27, 380n21,
381n29, 387n1

war, religious wars, 11, 12, 17, 19, 24, 28,
56–57, 76–77, 84, 88, 108, 112, 175,
192, 200, 215, 217–21, 225, 230,
234–35, 246, 250, 255, 273, 278, 291,
312, 314, 317–18, 341n10, 350n7,
351n12, 354n2, 367n15, 368–69n28,
372–73n40, 374n1, 374–75n5, 386n4;
First World War, 42, 317; Gulf War,
188, 347n23

Weber, Elisabeth, 342n18, 379n17

Weber, Samuel, 50, 58, 69–70, 82, 111,
227, 229, 232, 335, 337n1, 338–39n8,
359n11, 377nn2–3, 377–78n5, 378n9,
379n16, 381n29, 391n12

Wolfreys, Julian, 337n4

women, 11–12, 24–26, 29, 39, 189–90,
201, 210, 215, 217–19, 221, 224–25,
228, 252–58, 281, 340n7, 344–45n7,
382n11, 383n23

Woolf, Virginia, 231, 338n33

writing, 2–4, 10, 21, 25, 37, 46, 55, 75,
83, 110, 115–17, 120–21, 123,
125–26, 128, 130, 144, 147–48, 151,
230, 240, 258–59, 262, 271, 343n27,
344n4, 346n14, 361nn23&25,
378n12, 382n18, 383n33, 384n34

Yucca Mountain, 106